Making It in America

Making It in America

A Sourcebook on Eminent Ethnic Americans

Elliott Robert Barkan, Editor

A B C ⬛ C L I O

Santa Barbara, California   Denver, Colorado   Oxford, England

Library of Congress Cataloging-in-Publication Data

Making it in America: a sourcebook on eminent ethnic Americans/
Elliott Robert Barkan, editor.
    p. cm.
  ISBN 1-57607-098-0 (Hardcover one volume : alk. paper) —
ISBN 1-57607-529-X (e-Book)
    1. Minorities—United States—Biography—Dictionaries. 2. United
States—Biography—Dictionaries. 3. United States—Ethnic
relations—Dictionaries. I. Barkan, Elliott Robert.
  E184.A1 M263 2001
  920.073—dc21   2001001068

07 06 05 04 03 02 01 10 9 8 7 6 5 4 3 2 1

ABC–CLIO, Inc.
130 Cremona Drive, P.O. Box 1911
Santa Barbara, California 93116-1911

This book is printed on acid-free paper ⊗.

Manufactured in the United States of America

To the memory of my mother, Tessie Barkan (1913–1999),
a second-generation American who endured her own set of trials
and tribulations and did her best to overcome some real hurdles.

CONTENTS

Making It in America: A Sourcebook on Eminent Ethnic Americans

Contents

INDIVIDUALS BY ETHNICITY

Some smaller groups have been combined into regional aggregations, but all individual ethnicities are indicated. Ethnicities grouped separately in this list appear in all-capitalized format (e.g., AFRICAN). Ethnicities grouped by region rather than separately appear in cap/lower case style (e.g., Arab)

CATEGORIES

ACADIAN
AFRICAN
AFRICAN AMERICAN
Arab (See Middle Eastern)
Argentinean (See South American)
ARMENIAN/ARMENIAN-AMERICAN
Asian Indian (See South Asian)
AUSTRIAN
Bahamian (See West Indian)
BALTIC
Barbadian (See West Indian)
BASQUE/BASQUE-AMERICAN
BELGIAN
Bolivian (See South American)
Bosnian (See Yugoslavian [former])
Brazilian (See South American)
CANADIAN/CANADIAN-AMERICAN
CARPATHO-RUSYN-AMERICAN
CENTRAL AMERICAN
Chaldean (See Middle Eastern)
Chilean (See South American)
CHINESE/CHINESE-AMERICAN
Costa Rican (See Central American)
Croatian (See Yugoslavian [former])
CUBAN/CUBAN-AMERICAN
CYPRIOT/CYPRIOT-AMERICAN
CZECH
DANISH/DANISH-AMERICAN
Dominican (See West Indian)
DUTCH/DUTCH-AMERICAN
ENGLISH
Eritrean (See African)
Estonian (See Baltic)
Ethiopian (See African)
FILIPINO/FILIPINO-AMERICAN
FINNISH/FINNISH-AMERICAN
FRENCH/FRANCO-AMERICAN
FRENCH CANADIAN/FRANCO-AMERICAN
GERMAN/GERMAN-AMERICAN
GREEK/GREEK-AMERICAN
Guatemalan (See Central American)
Haitian (See West Indian)
HAWAIIAN
Hmong (See Southeast Asian)
Honduran (See Central American)
HUNGARIAN
Iranian (See Middle Eastern)
IRISH/IRISH-AMERICAN

Israeli (See Middle Eastern)
ITALIAN/ITALIAN-AMERICAN
Jamaican (See West Indian)
JAPANESE/JAPANESE-AMERICAN
JEWISH/JEWISH-AMERICAN
Kenyan (See African)
KOREAN/KOREAN-AMERICAN
Kurdish (See Middle Eastern)
Latvian (See Baltic)
Lebanese (See Middle Eastern)
Lithuanian (See Baltic)
Macedonian (See Yugoslavian [former])
Mayan (See Central American)
MEXICAN/MEXICAN-AMERICAN
MIDDLE EASTERN/SOUTHWEST ASIAN
NATIVE AMERICAN/ALASKA NATIVE
Nigerian (See African)
NORWEGIAN/NORWEGIAN-AMERICAN
Okinawan (See Japanese)
Pakistani (See South Asian)
Palestinian (See Middle Eastern)
Panamanian (See Central American)
POLISH-AMERICAN
PUERTO RICAN
ROMA
ROMANIAN
RUSSIAN/RUSSIAN-AMERICAN
Salvadoran (See Central American)
SCOTCH-IRISH/SCOTCH-IRISH-AMERICAN
SCOTTISH
Serb (See Yugoslavian [former])
Sierra Leonean (See African)
SLOVAK-AMERICAN
Slovene (See Yugoslavian [former])
SOUTH AMERICAN
SOUTH ASIAN
SOUTHEAST ASIAN
SPANISH/SPANISH-AMERICAN
Sudanese (See African)
SWEDISH/SWEDISH-AMERICAN
SWISS/SWISS-AMERICAN
Syrian (See Middle Eastern)
Thai (See Southeast Asian)
UKRAINIAN/UKRANIAN-AMERICAN
Vietnamese (See Southeast Asian)
WELSH/WELSH-AMERICAN
WEND
WEST INDIAN/CARIBBEAN
YUGOSLAVIAN (FORMER)

INDIVIDUALS BY OCCUPATION

Because many individuals have multiple areas of achievement and involvement, they can be found in more than one category.

CATEGORIES
ARTS/ENTERTAINMENT
BUSINESS/INDUSTRY
COMMUNITY, POLITICAL, AND LABOR
    ACTIVISM
LITERATURE/SCHOLARSHIP/JOURNALISM
MILITARY AND MISCELLANEOUS
PHILANTHROPY
POLITICAL OFFICE/POLITICS
PROFESSIONS
RELIGION
SCIENCE/INVENTIONS/ENGINEERING
SPORTS

ARTS/ENTERTAINMENT

Ahmed, Ismael N. (1947–); Community organization director, political activist, and musician; Arab-American, 5

Ahn, Philip (1911–1978); Actor and community activist; Korean-American, 6

Akiyoshi, Toshiko (1929–); Jazz musician and composer; Japanese, 8

Amara, Lucine (1926–); Opera star; Armenian-American, 12

Arce, Elia (1961–); Performance artist, director, and writer; Costa Rican–American, 19

Archipenko, Alexander (1887–1964); Sculptor; Ukrainian, 20

Arnaz, Desi (1917–1986); Television star and producer; Cuban, 21

Balanchine, George (1904–1983); Choreographer; Russian, 26

Bartók, Béla (1881–1945); Pianist, composer, teacher, and ethnomusicologist; Hungarian, 30

Bergman, Ingrid (1915–1982); Film and stage actress; Swedish, 38

Bierstadt, Albert (1830–1902); Painter; German-American, 40

Bikel, Theodore (1924–); Stage and screen actor and folksinger; Israeli, 41

Blades, Ruben (1948–); Singer, actor, and political activist; Panamanian, 43

Borge, Victor (1909–2000); Pianist, comedian, conductor, and philanthropist; Danish, 46

Borglum, Gutzon (1867–1941); Sculptor; Danish-American, 47

Burton, Richard Walter (1925–1984); Actor; Welsh, 51

Callas, Maria (1923–1977); Opera singer; Greek-American, 56

Chaplin, Charlie (1889–1977); Movie actor and director; English, 67

Chin, Frank (1940–); Playwright and author; Chinese-American, 69

Cohan, George M. (1878–1942); Actor, dancer, composer, and playwright; Irish-American, 74

Cronyn, Hume (1911–); Actor, director, and writer; Canadian, 80

Damrosch, Walter Johannes (1862–1950); Conductor and composer; German-American, 84

De Kooning, Willem (1904–1997); Artist; Dutch, 87

Delerue, Georges (1925–1992); Composer; French, 92

Delgado, Marcel (1898?–1976); Film special effects pioneer; Mexican, 93

Estefan, Gloria Fajardo (1957–); Singer; Cuban-American, 116

Forman, Miloš (1932–); Filmmaker; Czech, 128

Friml, Rudolf (1879–1972); Composer; Czech, 129

Garbo, Greta (1905–1990); Film actress; Swedish, 132

Gibran, Kahlil (1883–1931); Poet and artist; Syrian, 135

Hanson, Howard Harold (1896–1981); Composer, conductor, and music educator; Swedish-American, 149

Ivask, Ivar Vidrik (1927–1992); Artist, poet, and scholar; Estonian, 161

Jean, Nelust Wyclef (1970–); Musician; Haitian-American, 165

Kahanamoku, Duke (1890–1968); Champion Olympic swimmer, actor, and surfer; Hawaiian, 169

Kazan, Elia (1909–); Writer and director for stage and cinema; Greek-American, 172

Kuniyoshi, Yasuo (1889–1953); Artist and art teacher; Japanese, 185

Lee, Ang (1954–); Filmmaker; Chinese, 196

Lennon, John (1940–1980); Musician; English, 200

Luahine, Iolani (1915–1978); Dancer and dance teacher; Hawaiian, 210

Lugosi, Bela (1882–1956); Actor; Hungarian, 211

BUSINESS/INDUSTRY

COMMUNITY, POLITICAL, AND LABOR ACTIVISM

LITERATURE/SCHOLARSHIP/ JOURNALISM

PROFESSIONS

RELIGION

SCIENCE/INVENTIONS/ ENGINEERING

SPORTS

INTRODUCTION: ACHIEVING EMINENCE IN AMERICA'S CULTURE OF SUCCESS

Elliott Robert Barkan

Establishing a Framework

"Patrons are requested not to shoot at the piano player. He's doing his best." Thus did Cedric Larson quote a Nevada saloon keeper's sign in his 1958 history of *Who's Who in America* and the procedures its editors employed to select biographical subjects. Given the similar nature of the collection before you, the admonition may be applicable here, too.

This volume contains more than 400 brief biographies of eminent ethnic Americans, representing about ninety American ethnic groups and a broad array of their achievements in legitimate enterprises. In that one statement are a number of central challenges. Who and what is eminent? Why not prominent? distinguished? renowned? famous? Is that focus on eminence meant to imply that this collection is simply a panegyric to America? Why 400? Who selected them and how? Why only short biographies and how short? What is meant here by "ethnic" and does that imply that the book excludes "ordinary" ("real"? "authentic"?) Americans? What ninety groups are included and why that number? (Why not more? Why not fewer?) What does it mean that they encompass a broad spectrum of "legitimate enterprises"? Furthermore, with so many variables coming into play, can there be any unity or connectedness—commonalities—in the overall collection? In other words, are its contents more random than not?

In so far as this piano player can, he will do his best to address these questions and shed some light on the coherency that does weave together these many contributions by ninety-three scholars. In some respects the brief narratives in this book do represent a collective celebration of the United States. They do give testimony to the enduring power of the American Dream. They are the living proof that the myth of America has a reality, a reality that has generated an extraordinary magnetism for peoples around the world—and not merely millions but tens of millions. The United States has offered many kinds of opportunities to its peoples—opportunities quite often unavailable, even out of the question, perhaps even forbidden, in the lands from which many came, or simply opportunities previously out of reach of those already here. These are the stories of men and women, past and present, who seized those opportunities and distinguished themselves in the process of contributing to American society. They are the evidence that the promise of America has been embraced by immigrants and their children, by migrants brought here voluntarily and eventually by those transported against their will, as well as by many of those native to the land from time immemorial.

Yet the vignettes are not meant to imply that all groups have had equal access to those opportunities or that there have not been many failures and many who have chosen not to remain in the United States. Rather, my intent is to convey that the breadth of possibilities—from organizing a nascent community to winning the Nobel Prize—has broadened, deepened, extended to more and more groups and been recognized and enhanced by our oldest Americans and newest newcomers.

Moreover, the subjects of these biographies, by their singularity—by the qualities for which they have been set apart and by which they have set themselves apart—have been (to employ *Esquire* magazine's typology[1]) among the nation's "Trailblazers," "Builders," "Visionaries," "Legends," "Advocates," and "Champions": They have provided the guidance for all the others who have been either inspired by them or content to follow their lead.

Given that such an array of types of distinguished people is not meant to suggest that the United States is or ever has been a paradise for all of its peoples—or that those types are representative of all Americans—the qualification does not preclude an analysis of those who have been able to make the most of America's opportunities in order to learn more about the nature of the American experience; the ways some key figures have helped to shape it; and, in particular, the myriad roles the multicultural U.S. population has played in defining the composite nature of "American Civilization." This book is an ensemble of profiles of men and women who, if they "did not set out with courage in their luggage, [they] found it along the way"—along with an "unprecedented freedom and stimulus to develop their potential."[2] To apply the inimitable comment of that nineteenth-century New York City politician, George Washington Plunkitt: These eminent Americans "seen their opportunities and they took 'em."

In sum, there are many important reasons for a unique collection such as this, spanning all of American history; encompassing ninety American ethnic populations; concentrating on immigrants, the children of immigrants, and several indigenous and long-present racial populations;[3] focusing heavily on the achievements of men and women; and taking into account a very broad array of activities whereby these individuals have achieved not just success (and in numerous cases fame and wealth) but also renown, prestige, distinction—eminence. Collectively, this compendium of biographies supports five central themes:

1. America has become what it is because of the drive, determination, persistence, creativity, contributions, and sacrifices of men and women of all racial, religious, and national backgrounds—no one group can lay claim to a monopoly of American successes.

2. By virtue of their representativeness, the subjects of these biographies demonstrate how Americans of all generations have seized opportunities found here or created them precisely because the United States has provided an environment that has nurtured such openness (and certain malleable traditions)—there has been no one path to success and distinction.

3. Countless numbers of Americans of all backgrounds have been able to overcome obstacles of poverty, discrimination, gender biases, racial and religious biases, and cultural or normative prohibitions, in order to attain their goals, enriching the nation and opening doors for still others—no one generation and no one cultural heritage can claim all the credit for what America is.

4. Those who have enriched the United States with their contributions can be found in all groups, among all mixtures of peoples, and in all places—from Hawai'i to Maine and from Alaska to Florida and Puerto Rico—and implicitly those in this collection represent both persons who have achieved recognition and all those who have not but whose less visible labors are equally part of the American story.

5. Across the decades and across all groups, many, many Americans have understood, appreciated, and responded to the American ideal, the American value, that success is measured not only by what one wins or earns or acquires but also by the quality of what one returns to one's community and to the larger society that made such accomplishments possible—including those whose labors and sup-

port have often been the means to bringing those eminent achievements to fruition.

Determining Eminence

To establish the coherence of this set of biographies, the first task is to define what is meant by "eminent," the adjective in the title. Immediately, let me emphasize that one criterion was *not* implying any predictions in the choices, or suggesting that those selected were chosen because they would undoubtedly *remain* among the nation's most enduring individuals. Such modesty is especially called for after reading Cedric Larson's explanation (in 1958, you will recall) that the reason why the editors of *Who's Who in America* in the latter part of the 1950s chose to omit Elvis Presley was that "the editors doubt that he will be a permanent influence in America."[4]

Let me begin by noting the richness of the English language in its subtle degrees of separation between eminent, prominent, distinguished, renowned, notorious, and famous. Larson emphasized that "the eminent of any nation are clearly its greatest resource."[5] He started the exploration by pointing out that eminence is essentially relative and means more than being a celebrity, for being so well known as to be a celebrity "is often ephemeral and, far too frequently, a synthetic marketable commodity."[6] Moreover, it is rare that "two individuals agree as to what constitutes success, let alone eminence." Threading his way between celebrated, renowned, and famous, Larson cleverly suggested: "To be eminent is to be prominent rather than conspicuous. It connotes elements of being high in merit or esteem, if not necessarily of distinction." Francis Galton, the nineteenth-century eugenicist, defined eminence as "the awarding of a high mark in the test of life" to one who has *achieved* a position or place that few others attain.[7]

A key to eminence in the United States can be found in Theodore Greene's study of American models of success as depicted in popular magazines. Prior to the 1820s, the ideal of success was rooted in the Puritan be-

lief in the contract, or covenant, between the individual and God. Inseparably included was an obligation to one's community, a subordination of the individual to the needs of society: a "concern for the nation, for the society, rather than for the individual career," a "mutuality of obligation." What, it was asked, had the eminent individual contributed to society? This is akin to Cotton Mather's argument in the first third of the eighteenth century that one ought—of one's own accord—"to do good" for one's fellow human beings and that such actions were good (that is, pious) in and of themselves. Such behavior, he argued, was vital for preserving the fabric of the community where no established church existed to provide such guidance or monitor such behavior. That tradition-rooted perspective endured, Greene pointed out, for "the essential vision of the founding fathers was a public philosophy not a private one." By 1819, however, the "ambitious, industrious, persevering, inner-directed individual," who was pursuing *his* own interests, had begun to prevail, undergirded by the belief that "the individual is the world." This self-made individualist became the model of American success.[8]

Although by the late nineteenth century the measure of success was emphasizing business skills, achievement, and personal fame, the countervailing concerns for merit acquired by virtue of one's social actions above and beyond one's specific accomplishments had not entirely vanished. Abraham Lincoln had come to be revered precisely because he represented "a self-made man of the most humane instincts," noted Greene. Indeed, by the early 1900s, another profound shift had occurred, this time within the Progressive movement. It began to reemphasize the primacy of social contributions by otherwise successful men as a vital measure of their true worth. Merit, recognition, prestige, and respect—*the essence of eminence*—did not derive entirely from one's professional or entrepreneurial accomplishments. The individual's societal activities and the esteem derived from them had to be factored in too. Thus, in 1907, *Everybody* magazine posed the following questions for a panel discussion entitled "What Is a Good Man?" "Is goodness still a man's private attitude to his God and to some group bound to him by ties of blood, or does he owe a debt outside his home and his business? How much time and thought must he pay to his community if he would be a good man?"[9]

Greene, in his sample of magazine stories about successful men during the decade prior to World War I, found that three-fourths of the accounts stressed such involvement. However, the pressures of war then prompted the magazines to modify their focus and priorities—that is, their measure of success and merit—to include "results efficiently achieved through a large scale organization."[10] The pendulum of values would nevertheless continue its movements, marking the periodic swings in emphasis from less to more concern about the balance between success and social consciousness.

Thus, when President John F. Kennedy declared in his 1961 inaugural address, "Ask not what your country can do for you but what you can do for your country," his words resonated with enduring power precisely because they tapped into more than three centuries of American tradition. Richard Weiss pointed out in *The American Myth of Success* that real success was "always in the context of a larger framework of values"—"the general conduct of life." Acquiring wealth was alone insufficient, for what particular significance is attached to that achievement? The true rewards and recognition are "commensurate with merit." Men of wealth, the empire builders, the men of great power and influence, indeed had power—the power to awe and to instill fear. But their *eminence* came not with (or from) that power; it arose from the demonstrated sense of responsibility to the community, the acknowledgment of America's social expectations that with wealth and power comes the obligation to serve society. This value in American culture was eventually recognized and acted upon by many leading figures, for example, Andrew Carnegie, the

Rockefellers, the Guggenheims, the Fords, and, most recently, Bill Gates.[11] In fact, Bruce Coad noted that the original Horatio Alger stories—paralleling the late-nineteenth-century trend—actually stressed monetary gain as the principal measure of a successful man (more hustler than humanitarian). But, he emphasizes, "what is expected of the contemporary [1970s] 'typical Alger hero' is something more than a talent for piling up huge sums of money. . . . [It is] an acceptance of public responsibility far beyond making a profit."[12]

Phillip Moffitt, in his Foreword to *Esquire*'s collection of biographies, *Fifty Who Made the Difference,* noted that the individuals profiled in that book had "not been chosen because they were perfect models of human potential, or even because their actions were admirable in all respects, but because in the final analysis, they made a positive difference." For "some time each was able to humanize the institutions mankind uses to regulate twentieth century civilization. . . .Things can change for the better by the power of individual initiative." With great eloquence Moffitt went to the heart of eminence: "What gives our society its life and breath is the communal and often unspoken effort of certain members to make it a just and enlightened one. A successful society is built on individual effort that dares to go against convention, to think big, to believe that all is possible, to persevere without reinforcement, to create spontaneously."[13]

It is clear, then, that eminence arises from the esteem men and women receive for their accomplishments, not simply from their possession of power, wealth, and influence. It goes beyond awe, perhaps beyond admiration, for it reflects the respect (even awards) garnered for actions that merit distinction, actions that (in most instances) also link moral and communal deeds to one's professional or conventional attainments. Such personal distinction can lead to renown and greater prominence or recognition but not necessarily to fame, which usually entails a celebrity status and adulation among a broader spectrum of people than in one's particular community or profession.

Clive James, in *Fame in the Twentieth Century,* acknowledged that famous people do influence events, yet such fame is only "a rough guide to reality," for "[a]chievement without fame can be a good life[, whereas] [f]ame without achievement is no life at all." He added that twentieth-century media really "created" the phenomenon of fame, of celebrity status. Identifying people whose perceived impact was a product of the media led to the notion of attributing to them "charisma." A more extreme reality is that of people famous for merely being famous. On the one hand, fame thus "simplifies what was real so people could take it in." At the same time, the famous were being viewed as celebrities "for the lives they led" while being famous. However, James concluded, although the famous may help people live by providing symbols of certain essences of human behavior (e.g., goodness, evil, bravery, artistic talent, scientific genius), "[f]ame is [also] what we do to them. We turn them into characters and put them in a show."[14] That is not eminence.

Clearly, fame is *not* synonymous with eminence—or with the more modest representations of distinction, prominence, renown, or the recognition and respect that come within one's more narrow domain or specialization. In fact, questionable (namely, negative) behavior can move one from renown, or even fame, to notoriety and, ultimately, infamy.

The modern, pervasively intrusive, ubiquitous media have confounded the definitions and blurred the gradations along this spectrum of recognition. Jeffrey Louis Decker, in his 1997 book, *Made in America,* on "self-styled success" in the United States, contended that, historically, we focused on "character," the inner qualities that defined a person. By the 1920s that had been more and more overshadowed by references to "personality" (how one appeared) and depictions of "personal magnetism" (charisma) as the winning features in success rather than one's substantive personal traits. Although this type of self-esteeming and self-promotion was seen as morally bankrupt during the Great Depression of the 1930s, Decker maintained that it was revived and has now been advanced by media-generated celebrity images that go even further to obscure aspects of what is valued in eminent people.[15]

Still, others have continued to dissect the components that truly contribute to success, and, particularly for this work, the kind of success that leads to a degree of eminence. Success, after all, is certainly an important reality among those in this collection, for the eminent persons described herein have achieved some measure of success. Those accomplishments have been their stepping stones to recognition, prestige, and renown. Moreover, the fundamental premise of this collection is that such successes, and the prominence that has resulted from the successes, could have taken place within the individual's ethnic community, and/or within the more immediate general, state, or regional context, and/or within the larger U.S. society, or all three. Furthermore, it appears that many of the underlying character traits and circumstances behind these achievements are quite similar whether that success was accomplished in one or the other of those realms.

Any description of the components of success and the garnering of a reputation of eminence must therefore be broad enough to encompass various conditions or factors within those realms. For example, Christopher Jencks, in *Who Gets Ahead?,* focused on economic success and the relative statistical importance of family background, test scores, cognitive ability, noncognitive personality traits, and education. He and his coauthors concluded that such personality traits as industriousness, particularly as manifested during adolescence, along with the number of years of schooling, were important predictors of success.[16] But that particular approach can be no more applicable to all the people in this volume than J. A. Kiegel's description of eminent economists as those whose "fundamental importance to the discipline of economics" would readily be acknowledged and who, therefore, "have earned their renown" in their profession.[17] Nor would all the features of Mary Alice Kellogg's 1978 description of young superachievers apply—people whom she defined as those who have "attained a level of responsibility or achievement normally held by someone fifteen to twenty years their senior." However, she did find that they shared definite traits, some of which do have a relevance here: They were loners; they had stronger ties to adults than to peers; they knew how to use their youth constructively (and diplomatically); they possessed a restlessness, a drive, and a willingness to work hard; they had survived tragedies and hard knocks; and they were products of the 1960s but had worked behind the scenes rather than on the streets. Moreover, additional features that those in her study did share lift us beyond the narrow, occupation-oriented profile of a particular segment of unusually ambitious men and women. Such individuals who strove for success had an intense desire to excel; they had benefited from luck; and, perhaps related to that luck, they had the overriding characteristic of recognizing opportunities and not being afraid to grab them: They were risk takers,[18] often those willing to challenge existing norms or strive for objectives that others regarded as improbable.

Thus, although no one denies the role of heredity, there is a constellation of behaviors and traits that we see among successful people and notably among those who are both successful and eminent: Most often, they are strivers, possessing determination, zeal, motivation, courage, perseverance, and an ability to work hard and rise above obstacles that would deter ordinary people. They are goal oriented, willing to challenge conventions, take risks, be creative, exploit good fortune. They tend to be leaders rather than followers and are more likely to be concerned that they not only accomplish specific objectives but also make a difference in society; they therefore consider their contributions to society and their impact upon others. Even though that observation will not apply to all those included here, this overall array of traits does define the qualities

in the persons most likely to succeed and to earn respect and prestige and be held in high esteem—the components of eminence. Such persons do, indeed, often serve as role models and are frequently agents of change.[19]

And to all of this must be added one other ingredient: This particular volume principally focuses on people who are or were foreign born or second-generation Americans. The exceptions are Native Americans, Alaska Natives, most African Americans, Hawaiians, and Puerto Ricans. I also included a small number of third- and later-generation Americans of other ethnicities. Sixty years ago, Will Irwin, of the Common Council for American Unity, prefaced *Notable Americans of Foreign Birth* (drawn from *Who's Who in America*) by extolling the subjects' "venturesome spirit" that made them "half Americanized" even before their ships left for the United States (a theme Oscar Handlin would lyrically describe a decade later in *The Uprooted*). They—and their children, too—often had to overcome poverty, language difficulties, economic insecurity, and cultural clashes in order to succeed in the United States. They contributed their special mind-set, their skills, their courage to conquer many obstacles, and they were determined not to be "robot[s] who worked to live and lived to work." In the process, they gave the country "gifts of hand, heart and brain"— and for this the most successful among these foreign-born and second-generation Americans achieved a well-earned eminence.[20] I would, in addition, stress that such a description could be easily applied as well to distinguished persons among several peoples of color whom we do not in most instances classify as immigrants but who are included here as eminent ethnic Americans.

It is fitting, then, to return to *Esquire*'s eloquent portrayal of eminent people who made a difference, men and women who possessed the traits noted here. The editor, Lee Eisenberg, divided them into six categories, which are worth bearing in mind when reading the biographies in this volume: *Trailblazers* "led us to new and sometimes unthinkable realizations. They got there first. . . . We met up with them at the fork in the road. And . . . as most of us waited, they . . . figured things out—until it became fully clear that it was this way, not that, and off we went." *Legends* were "imbued with heroism. . . . [T]hey were intrinsically gifted. . . . [S]imply enough, we needed their greatness." *Builders* worked with ideas, ideals, and sometimes with money, mortaring them in ways "to withstand obsolescence," "intent on changing our destiny." *Visionaries* were set apart by "the conviction that a greater reality lay a number of years down the pike." They "were determined to seize the future . . . [, and] our destiny was defined by their vision." They believed and acted on those beliefs and, "[w]hen they had finished, the rest of us saw." *Advocates* surmounted oppression and were master politicians within their own domains. They led assaults that changed our ways of working, living, driving, reading, and more, ending "in universally accepted, utterly self-evident principles." *Champions* are "the measure by which others would be judged." They "establish bench marks." "They are the summit of our aspirations."[21]

Models of Eminent Americans

I do not doubt that most of the eminent Americans included in our work fall into these various categories, and there may be other classifications reflective of this particular cross-section of people, composed as it is largely of first- and second-generation Americans and Americans of color. They have all accomplished important objectives that set them apart.

My first model consists of people whose accomplishments are within their ethnic group and who have earned the respect and recognition of their communities for their contributions. Their eminence is more local but no less viable for that. In fact, particularly among newer groups, such people have generally not been in the United States long enough to have achieved recognition or prominence in the larger society but have made significant advancements within those

newly emerging communities (and, often, within the immediate city or region, too), and that can tell us much about the processes of ethnic community development. Marie Prisland, Alison Liam, Kim Tran, Meserak Ramsey, Dijana Groth, Sara Amir, Reza Jalali, Choua Eve Lee, Fenda Akiwumi, Josip Marohnić, and Elphège Daignault are a few who come to mind.

The second model includes those who have accomplishments in their fields of endeavor or professions that have set them apart, often earning them renown beyond those specialties and thus denoting them, too, as eminent Americans. Most of them retain their ethnic ties and identities and, along with the more general accolades, have been recognized and admired within their ethnic communities and beyond. Thurgood Marshall, A. Philip Randolph, Shardad Rohani, Ingrid Bergman, Senator Olympia Snowe, William Saroyan, Governor Ben Cayetano, Thomas L. Thomas, and Duke Kahanamoku illustrate this group.

The third scenario stands apart, for although our objective was to include those who clearly preserved their ethnic bonds, a number of people (particularly among the first generation) achieved distinction within the larger American society without explicitly retaining many of those community ties. They have been more representative among those newcomers who made the most of the opportunity structure in the United States and contributed more to the general society than to their ethnic societies (or had far less need of them in order to gain their foothold in American society). Naturally, among some groups that have come already speaking English and possibly familiar with U.S. culture, the number of such people has been greater, for example, among Canadians, Britons, and, more recently, Asian Indians. Consequently, their renown lay, by and large, within the nonethnic realm (or only limitedly within their ethnic community). Immigrant professionals, scientists, and artists are commonly found in this group. The pattern is clearly another feature of the American ethnic story and represents variations on the *immigrant* success story theme. As contributor Zdenek Salzmann pointed out regarding his Czech figures: "All these people were/are very successful professionals who have little time or inclination to engage with others simply because of a shared background. They are simply successful Americans, but I am sure they are proud of their Czech background, and that Czech-Americans are proud of what these people have accomplished."[22]

As noted, it is principally among the foreign born that we identify such distinguished (but not actively ethnic) persons, including George Papanicolaou, Georges Delerue, Othmar Ammann, Rudolf Friml, Willem de Kooning, Edward Teller, Willem Kolff, Jarmila Novotná, Martina Navratilova, Nikola Tesla, and Vladimir Zworykin. Because it is likely that the eminent individuals in this third model, who were reared in their homelands, retained cultural and social elements of their native societies after migrating to the United States, they are for us here "implicitly ethnic" and, therefore, belong in this collection.

Finally, in a fourth variation, a few of the subjects are or were third- or later-generation Americans, and among, for example, Native Americans, Hawaiians, Puerto Ricans, and African Americans, most are of a later generation and are included because, along with their achievements, they did retain clear ties with their ethnic groups. As I have noted, that was a principal consideration underlying as many of the choices made here as possible. These people represent accomplishments combined with ethnic persistence and many acquired their eminence within both the ethnic community and the broader American society. Frank Chin (a fifth-generation Chinese-American on his mother's side), Senator Barbara Mikulski (a fourth-generation Polish-American), Frank Lloyd Wright (a third-generation Welsh-American), Claire Quintal (a fourth-generation Franco-American), Suzanne Shea (a third-generation Polish-American), and George M. Cohan (a third-generation Irish-American) are splendid examples of such people.

In three of the four scenarios just described, ties to the ethnic group are an important variable. How, then, do I define that term; how wide am I casting the net? In other studies I have discussed at length my definition of ethnicity.[23] Here, let me briefly state that I apply the term to many "racial," religious, and nationality groups that meet the criteria that have long been associated with ethnicity, including shared identities, histories, cultures, values, foods, festivals, communities, organizations, sometimes religion and language, and patterns of endogamy. Such peoples, from indigenous Native Americans, colonial settlers, and formerly enslaved African Americans to more recently arrived Arabs, Hmong, Cambodians, and Salvadorans, obviously do not share the same historical experiences but in their group practices—in their patterns of identifying, relating, organizing, and preserving communities—they share, over and above their diverse histories, many similarities that can be denoted as ethnic. Hence, we have attempted to include men and women who would represent the broadest array of such American groups, past and present, subject to the limitations of the book's contractual length. Once it was determined that 500–530 words (plus references) was reasonable (and not unprecedented) as a length in which the life and achievements of men and women could be *succinctly* described, it was a matter of math to settle upon including approximately 400 entries.

The far more complex task was allocating these 400 slots to as many groups as possible. And here, this piano player had to establish the three fundamental premises of this volume. First, all groups could not be represented and all groups could not be treated equally. I used census reports, ancestry tables, immigration records, immigration histories, and my thirty-two years of teaching and researching comparative immigration and ethnic history to develop a rough tabulation of the relative size (contribution) of as many recognizable ethnic peoples as possible and then distributed the 400 so that the principal populations were appropriately represented at the same time that as many of the newer peoples as possible would have at least one or two representatives. It was imperative that this volume include not merely the classic, historic ethnic communities but also the very newest, for all are components of the portrait of the American "Nation of Peoples."

Second, it was obviously not at all feasible to include *all* eminent ethnic Americans, which is why, from the outset, nearly all of the third generation was omitted, for the potential pool would have jumped exponentially and hugely complicated the task of linking accomplishments with enduring ethnic affiliation or identification. Beyond that, the intent was not to offer an exhaustive set of individuals—clearly an impossibility—but *a representative array of mostly first- and second-generation Americans (along with native peoples and certain peoples of color,* as noted above), past and present, men and women, in a broad spectrum of endeavors and areas of accomplishment. These are people who illustrate the opportunities America has provided those able to overcome the obstacles (and motivated enough) to take advantage of those opportunities, people who could demonstrate how Americans of numerous ethnic backgrounds could provide leadership within those communities and/or provide models of achievement.

Third, it was essential to include as many women as possible and as many different occupations as possible, except crime (after all, the criterion was eminence rather than notoriety or infamy). Among many groups, women had not historically been permitted public roles—or had not previously had the opportunity to work outside the home and thereby garner the recognition and eminence men have (especially among more recently arrived groups). Women in the United States have, nonetheless, moved into virtually as broad an array of occupations as have men, and many have now managed to carve out active roles within their ethnic communities and within the larger society, often achieving distinction and eminence for accomplishments, innovations, leadership, and electoral

victories. This has been true among all the types of ethnic groups included here, with the developing roles particularly visible (and sometimes very contentiously so) among more recent newcomers still experiencing the earlier stages of cultural and normative adjustment. Among the more than 100 women included are Elizabeth Gurley Flynn and Marie "Mother Jones"; Emma Goldman; Anne Hutchinson; Harriet Tubman and Sojourner Truth; Ida Wells-Barnett and Oprah Winfrey; Mary Oakar, Olympia Snowe, and Donna Shalala; Maria Callas; Ilka Payán; Fatima Abu Eid and Azizah al-Hibri; Carmen Zapata and Isabel Allende; Emma Tenayuca and Luisa Moreno; Patricia Campos and Elizabeth Figueroa; Mary Beck; Angela Oh; and Susan LaFlesche Picotte.

With these points in mind, I asked contributors to use their expertise to assemble lists of men and women, encouraging them to diversify their selections as much as possible in an effort to portray the broadest representation by period, group, gender, and endeavor. Once we agreed on the names, the contributors proceeded, sometimes even offering additional persons whose backgrounds were too good to pass up. These 400 plus stories, therefore, reveal much about the U.S. immigrant and ethnic experience—indeed, a lot about the American experience in general and about achieving eminence and recognition in American society in particular.

In terms of the structure or content of each biography, I urged each contributor to provide—subject to the word limitation and the availability of information—background information (such as where and when the person was born and died, parents' names, where educated [if at all], when migrated and/or where lived, and types of occupation, where appropriate), followed by a description of the principal activities that the subject participated in and that were the reason(s) why he or she was successful and gained the prestige, esteem, recognition that warranted being viewed as an eminent ethnic American. Although many of these people distinguished themselves outside the United States and such information was noted, the primary concern here was to focus on achievements in the United States on the premise that these people are or were eminent Americans mainly because of their actions in the United States. However, some did also achieve renown for activities that bridge Old World and New, such as John Devoy, Hans Mattson, Rudolph Perpich, Ferenc Nagy, Syngman Rhee, Ian Hancock, Taraknath Das, Aleš Hrdlička, Bronius Kviklys, Paul Petrescu, and "Cher" Sarkisian.

Furthermore, to minimize confusion and simplify differences for readers, I emphasize a distinction between those born outside the United States and those born within it by identifying the former only by their ethnicity of origin, for example, Latvian, Polish, Chinese (unless they arrived with dual identities, such as Mayan-Guatemalan), and the latter by the combined phrase Italian-American, African American, Native American, and Japanese-American. There is one exception in the foreign-born category—Jews. Most foreign-born Jews are identified as Jewish and those born in the United States as Jewish American. There is also an exception among native born. Puerto Ricans and Hawaiians, who are all native-born Americans, are identified only in that manner—as Puerto Rican or Hawaiian—and not as Hawaiian American or Puerto Rican American.

Finally, the entry header for each person presents his/her name; birth and (obviously, where appropriate) death dates; principal areas or occupations or spheres wherein, or whereby, the eminence was achieved; and ethnicity. On that last item I made the editorial decision to view this label as an adjective—as it also appears within the text—rather than as a noun. That is why hyphens are used for combined ethnicities (e.g., Mayan-Guatemalan) and for second and later generation Americans (e.g., Italian-American). Hence, I am reading the header as, for example, "Frank Chin is Chinese-American" (adjective, with hyphen) rather than "Frank Chin is a Chinese American" (noun, no hyphen). I do not want readers to conclude erroneously that second-

and later-generation persons are being presented as "hyphenated Americans" but instead to be aware that gramatically word clusters that modify nouns in English are hyphenated: This is a book about many foreign-born persons—a study of the foreign born in America.

Yet there is one final caveat here, as well. Research has shown that children brought from their homeland to a new country prior to their teenage years (particularly to the United States) have usually experienced much of their socialization and cultural development in the new setting quite rapidly—notably with respect to learning the new language and adopting the new cultural practices. Therefore, the few such individuals have here been labeled with the joint terms (i.e., Polish-American rather than just Polish), such as Claire Cifuentes, who came from Guatemala at age three; Gloria Estefan, from Cuba, age two; Charles Lindbergh, Sr., age one from Sweden; Paweł Rhode from Poland, age nine; and Louis B. Mayer, a Jew born in Ukraine, brought to Canada as an infant and living in New Brunswick by the age of seven who then migrated south to Boston at age nineteen (making him Jewish-Canadian).

There are three ways that those written up in this volume can be located and identified.

1. The table of contents, and hence the entire book itself, is arranged alphabetically by last names.
2. The list of individuals by ethnicity arranges all the subjects by their principal ethnicity. However, because in several instances the number included from particular countries within a given region were few, it seemed more practical to group such persons together (although each one's nationality remains listed): Baltic States; Middle East/Southwest Asia; West Indies/Caribbean; South Asia; Southeast Asia; Central America; South America; and the former Yugoslavia. (Beginning on page xi, there is a list that indicates which nationality groups are presented separately and which by regions.)

Similarly, Native Americans and Alaska Natives are identified by tribe or nation but all are grouped as American Indian/Alaska Native.

3. The list of individuals by categories of occupation and activities has been organized by broad categories such as Arts/Entertainment; Business; Community/Labor/Political Activism; Science/Inventions/Engineering; and Sports. It was otherwise impractical to devise a great number of categories. Those prominent in more than one category are listed accordingly. Furthermore, because a significant number of individuals were eminent in large part because of their philanthropic activities, that category also appears separately in the list.

Finally, I must reemphasize that no attempt was made to include *all* those ethnic Americans who have achieved eminence past and present and who deserve to be included in such a collection. With the aim of assembling *a representative cross-section* of eminent ethnic Americans, the objective was to select from among those whose eminence is well known and well recognized as well as from among those not so generally prominent but who have also contributed significantly and meaningfully to the American experience and are eminent in their own right. In this way we can make it abundantly clear that what the United States has become is the product of the achievements of peoples of virtually all backgrounds who compose U.S. society. A larger sample would simply be this collection writ large, but the point would remain: The United States is more than the cumulative accomplishments of those of European origin; it is even more than the cumulative work of a nation of immigrants, and it is certainly more than the cumulative deeds of native-born people alone. It is most truly the collective achievement of a Nation of Peoples, the native and foreign born, those present a few generations and those here countless ones—men and women of all origins.

Themes from Eminent Lives

What have the contributors and I garnered from the collection of biographies in this volume, about 240 of which are on immigrants? Stephen Fischer-Galati, who emigrated from Romania, has written exceptional works on Romanian history; Nikola Tesla, from Serbia, made profound contributions to radio communications; Edward Teller, from Hungary, helped develop the H-bomb; Willem Kolff, from the Netherlands, developed the artificial heart; and George Papanicolaou, from Greece, devised the Pap Smear test, which has saved the lives of thousands of women. Louise Nevelson, from Russia, is regarded as one of the greatest sculptors of the twentieth century. Those newcomers—like Hilda Geiringer, the great Austrian mathematician, or Jarmila Novotná, the premier Czech opera star—represent people whose achievements and renown marked them as most eminent men and women. But they were not especially involved in the ethnic communities rooted in their homelands, particularly those whose organizations focused on local concerns and were preoccupied with providing assistance and social contacts for their members—even though it is clear in most cases that those illustrious individuals were attached to and proud of their national origins. In a way, they have been the harbingers of that supra-ethnic cohort that the sociologist Milton Gordon in the 1960s referred to as the emerging transnational ethnic group (meant differently than the way the term has come to be used today).[24]

By way of contrast, Meserak Ramsey, born in Ethiopia and subjected to female genital mutilation (FGM), has labored, sometimes at great risk, to educate women about FGM and to change state and federal laws. Ilka Payán, the Dominican-born actress, demonstrated great courage in fighting for her community's needs at the same time that she publicly disclosed her AIDS affliction, which killed her at age fifty-three. Choua Lee, a Laotian Hmong, showed her own courage, too, in defying Hmong traditions and norms, running for public office (the first Hmong to be elected in the United States), and then providing leadership for other Hmong women. Reza Jalali may not be well known outside of Portland, Maine, but this Kurdish refugee has accomplished remarkable things in helping his people and educating his larger community. Alison Liam, a young Thai businesswoman, has been similarly active helping immigrants adjust to life in her St. Louis community. Those five persons have all been close to their ethnic and immigrant roots but have not established broader, national reputations. Yet, they are no less eminent than the ones who have. Moreover, it is clear from many contributors that, as contributor Dennis R. Papazian wrote, "immigrant women rarely became leaders in the community." Therefore, if we are witnessing such women emerging as prominent figures in their communities (and we have at least twenty in this volume)—especially those from the Middle East and Central America—then their achievements all the more merit them recognition as eminent.

In contrast, there are those who are more problematic because they immigrated, achieved undoubted success—even enough fame in some cases to be regarded as cultural icons—but about whom we must ask, Are they "eminent" in terms of their larger contributions to their ethnic community or to the larger society. Have their achievements substantively affected society and/or have they "given back" to society from what they have received? The line between fame and eminence is often not a sharp one, and a judgment call is unavoidable. Consider Cary Grant (English), Claudette Colbert (French), and Norma Shearer (Canadian). Stars. Famous. Yet, little evidence for eminence. Some performers are included because their achievements were so highly regarded by fellow countrymen and women, in the United States and at home, and/or because their overall contributions were so substantial, such as Mary Pickford (Canadian), Hume Cronyn (Canadian), Ingrid Bergman (Swedish), Greta Garbo (Swedish), and Charlie Chaplin (English). But this issue is not limited to movie stars. Martina Navrati-

lova (Czech) was a great tennis player and John L. Sullivan (Irish) a great boxer. Were they eminent in terms of their larger impact and significance? I decided the recognition Navratilova has received merited her inclusion, whereas Sullivan's life was a far less illustrious one and he was not included.

Or consider others who lived in America for so short a time that their inclusion could likewise be problematic, notably the Marquis de Lafayette. But what about Robert Louis Stevenson, Tom Paine, or the French utopian Étienne Cabet. Was their impact substantive enough—even within the relatively short time frames—to warrant regarding them as eminent? Certainly, contemporaries so viewed Stevenson and Paine (in his initial years in America), whereas Lafayette fought for the new nation in the Revolution but never really immigrated to America with any intent to settle. Cabet's utopian scheme did not ultimately succeed in the nineteenth century, but he persuaded a large number of people to follow him to the United States, and his ideas persisted for a time beyond his life. In view of these points, Stevenson, Paine, and Cabet are included but Lafayette is omitted. Still another variation pitting success against eminence involves those who are rather well known in a more limited sense, such as the Iranian restaurateurs in Chicago, Reza and Joe Toulabi, or Hendrick Meijer, the Dutch barber who built a large-scale grocery–department store chain, beginning in Greenville, Michigan, during the depression. It is debatable if such successes—whatever the business reputations of these people—raise them to the level of eminence we have been exploring here.

However, we have included some people from the colonial period—when "ethnic" would have been a more questionable concept—because these settlers[25] from their homelands made important and lasting contributions: for example, Peter Stuyvesant (Dutch), John Winthrop (English), Anne Hutchinson (English), Rowland Ellis (Welsh), Conrad Weiser (German), John Treutlen (Austrian), and William Penn (English).

Thus, among immigrants we find those whose concerns focused their energies (with outstanding results) on their more specialized fields without strong regard to their ethnic communities to any significant degree (e.g., John Ericsson, Walter Damrosch, Jarmila Novotná, Eero Saarinen, Othmar Ammann, and Igor Sikorsky). Other newcomers did preserve various degrees of ties to those communities and/or homelands (Wyclef Jean, Taraknath Das, Howard Rock, Bronius Kviklys, Susan LaFlesche Picotte, William Aubuchon, Sr., Fatima Abu Eid, Omelian Pritsak, Philip Christopher, Josip Marohnić, Juan Romagoza, and Xavier Martin). Eminence has no *definitive* yardstick, but we see in all these instances a vast array of newcomers—past and present—who have made their mark on stages large and small and in many different ways. They represent, as I have suggested, immigrants seizing opportunities to accomplish what they could not have done—or done so easily—in their homelands.

Since members of the second-generation are presumed to have more substantially acculturated—from partially acculturated to almost fully assimilated—yet by definition have/had retained some measure of ethnic identity, we can identify many of them who qualify as both eminent and ethnic. Pinpointing such persons is not the problem: For example, Dijana Groth (Bosnian-American); Mary Beck (Ukrainian-American); Carl Sandberg (Swedish-American); Thomas Bell (Slovak-American); Emma Tenayuca, José Angel Gutiérrez, and Jovita Idar (Mexican-American); Geraldine Ferraro and Amadeo P. Giannini (Italian-American); Daniel Inouye and Fred Makino (Japanese-American); Alex Spanos, Michael Dukakis, and Olympia Snowe (Greek-American); Richard DeVos and Jay Van Andel (Dutch-American); Andy Warhol (Carpatho-Rusyn-American); and "Kirk" Kerkorian and William Saroyan (Armenian-American). With the exception of our few second-generation colonial subjects—notably the two Franco-Americans, Paul Revere and Henry Laurens—we determined that second-generation Americans needed to have components of achievement as well as ethnic ties to be included here.

More problematic of members of the second generation are those who have in fact integrated so extensively as to be far more eminent than ethnic, such as Charles Evans Hughes, whose Welsh father acquired an American wife and a respectable social position and assimilated easily, so that, said the younger Hughes, "despite my father's antecedents, he was so completely American and my upbringing so dominated by American thought that I never had any sense of being identified with his family abroad."[26] To which, added Douglas Caulkins (one of our two contributors on Welsh subjects), "This is true of many of the most accomplished Welsh Americans." Nona Balakian (of Armenian descent), former editor of the *New York Times Book Review,* falls into a similar category. Natalie Wood achieved fame as a movie star but for little more (in our terms) and hardly identified with her Russian origins. Thus both Balakian and Wood are not included.

On the other hand, Angela Oh is a much more connected Korean-American, both in political and legal affairs; even Jack Palance, the well-known movie actor, explicitly identifies with his Ukrainian roots and writes and speaks Ukrainian; "Cher" Sarkisian, who has likewise achieved stardom on stage and screen and been much honored by her peers, has rediscovered her Armenian roots and came to the aid of her family's homeland. Such second-generation writers as Jack Kerouac (a French Canadian Franco-American), James Farrell (Irish-American), Suzanne Shea (Polish-American), Maxine Hong Kingston (Chinese-American), Helen Barolini (Italian-American), and Fred and Dorothy Cordova (Filipino-American) provided voices for their ethnic communities, achieving high regard and eminence in the process. Other writers featured in this volume whose accomplishments are comparable are Ida Wells-Barnett, W. E. B. Du Bois, Frederick Douglass (African American); Bernardo Vega and Pura Belpré (Puerto Rican);

Mary Pukui (Hawaiian); and Vine Deloria, Jr., Mary TallMountain, and Howard Rock (American Indian/Alaska Native).

Although one can readily identify second-generation individuals active in politics or literature who retain ethnic ties while achieving distinction or success, sports figures pose a more complex problem because they are often so popular that they achieve iconic status among Americans in general and among those of similar ethnic origin. Joe Namath (Hungarian-American), Joe DiMaggio (Italian-American), and Martina Navratilova (Czech) are three classic cases of this, for none of them much acknowledged his/her ethnicity. However, the extent to which Italians and Czechs embraced the latter two heroes (respectively) was a major reason for keeping them in this volume but omitting Namath. Sammy Lee (Korean-American) remains active within the Korean community; Al Lopez returns to the Latin community in Tampa every year; Stan Musial embraced his Polish roots and has been involved in providing sports assistance in Poland; Chuck Bednarik forthrightly proclaims, "I'm primarily an American but I am Slovak, too"; and Tamio "Tommy" Kono (Japanese-American) went through the internment camp experience and was much admired in the Japanese-American community for his sports achievements. Moreover, noted Brian Niiya, who wrote the Kono entry, Kono was "a hero and role model, one of the world's best athletes in his chosen sport," a sport that was "hyper-masculine." With his success he not only helped alter the general stereotype of Japanese as nonathletic but also helped reshape Japanese-American men's self-image—and that surely has made him eminent.[27]

Beyond the second generation, we generally found that ethnic ties become far more tenuous and uneven, often limited to symbolic gestures of ethnicity, and the numbers of people too great to make possible meaningful selections. However, several individuals—third and later generations—did clearly preserve their ties or have been so embraced by their ethnic community as to justify (along with their accomplishments) their inclusion: George M. Cohan (Irish-American); Michael Novak (Slovak-American); Barbara Mikulski and Suzanne Shea (Polish-American); Claire Quintal (Franco-American); Emma Lazarus (Jewish-American); Frank Lloyd Wright (Welsh-American); Donna Shalala (Lebanese-American); and, fifth generation on his mother's side, Frank Chin (Chinese-American). Martha Stewart (Polish-American), who uses various Polish references and acknowledges her Polish roots, has been honored by the Polish Institute of Arts and Science in America for her extraordinary achievements. In contrast, we determined that third-generation Kareem Abdul-Jabbar (Trinidadian-American) might occasionally refer to his West Indian origins but has far more thoroughly integrated into American society as an African American, and his ethnic linkages are simply too negligible. Thus, he was not included.

Besides those examples are the multitude of people whose roots go much farther back and/or, having been identified by their race, have faced greater hurdles to achieving success or greater challenges in retaining their ethnic bonds. All the African Americans, Native Americans, Hawaiians, and Puerto Ricans included here fall into these categories, for one could not doubt the eminence and accomplishments of men and women such as Mary McLeod Bethune, Frederick Douglass, Mary Church Terrell, Oprah Winfrey, Malcolm X, Ada Deer, William Paul, Red Cloud, Susan LaFlesche Picotte, Vine Deloria, Jr., Iolani Luahine, Nainoa Thompson, Jesús Colón, Bernardo Vega, Antonia Pantoja, and Tito Puente.

Finally, when I grouped the contributions of eminent individuals, particularly in light of the discussions that took place early in the 1900s regarding the socially responsible successful people, I saw that philanthropy figured prominently. For that reason, those who followed up their achievements with substantive financial contributions to the ethnic and more general communities merit particular attention and a separate cross-listing (on page xxi).

At least eighteen persons from fifteen different ethnic groups are especially representative of this aspect of eminence. All of them have enriched U.S. society not only with their talents and energies but also with their largesse.

"I came here because here there was hope." So I have been told by many. The United States has offered hope and opportunity for individuals to achieve their goals in many areas of life or to feel they could have an impact—make a meaningful change—in their community and/or the larger society. This belief does not ignore the obstacles of race and gender biases, or the cultural constraints, or the differing effects of the cultural heritages brought to (or native to) the United States. In this volume these are not just stories of rags to riches, but you will find some of them here. These are not just tales of culture-bound individuals breaking free of restraints, but some of those also appear here. These are not only accounts of women repudiating gender-prescribed roles, but some of them, too, are included. These are not embellished, romanticized portrayals of the mythic American Dream, but many people actually had that experience, and some of their accounts are here as well.

What these 400 all-too-brief biographical profiles of eminent ethnic Americans show is that, from nearly A to Z—from African to (former) Yugoslavian and from Abdullah to Zworykin—so many people have come to America and they and/or their children have found opportunities, and where those opportunities did not exist they made them—not solely to achieve great wealth (though many did) but to make a difference. *Making It in America* is about people making a difference, about having and finding the chance to contribute their talents, their creativity, their drive, their idealism, their convictions. *Making It in America* suggests that for a vast array of newcomers and their children (and for people of color as "newcomers" to such opportunities) arcane and archaic restraints could be surmounted. This is not a novel idea, but here are more than 400 variations of that historic American theme.

Notes

1. Lee Eisenberg, ed., *Fifty Who Made the Difference,* with a foreword by Phillip Moffitt, an Esquire Press book (New York: Villard Books, 1984).

2. I expand on Elinor Richey, *Eminent Women of the West* (Berkeley, CA: Howell-North Books, 1975), 13–14.

3. I will here necessarily sidestep the anthropological debate over "race" and indicate that "race" is here being used in its contemporary, conventional, societal sense, e.g., referring particularly to African Americans, Native Americans/Alaska Natives, and Hawaiians.

4. Cedric Larson, *WHO: Sixty Years of American Eminence: The Story of Who's Who in America* (New York: McDowell, Obolensky, 1958), 261.

5. Larson, 18.

6. Larson, 2.

7. Quoted by Larson, 3.

8. Theodore P. Greene, *America's Heroes: The Changing Models of Success in American Magazines* (New York: Oxford University Press, 1970), 45, 11–12; and Richard Weiss, *The American Myth of Success: From Horatio Alger to Norman Vincent Peale* (New York: Basic Books, 1969), 5.

9. Quoted in Greene, 251.

10. Greene, 115–116, 129, 251–252, 320.

11. See, for example, Charles A. Madison, *Eminent American Jews, 1776 to the Present* (New York: Frederick Ungar, 1970), on the extent to which the Jewish community emphasizes philanthropy as central in Jewish tradition. It is especially expected from successful Jews and is seen as contributing to their eminence in the community. Such philanthropy is rooted in the long tradition of *tzedakah,* the *obligation* to help one's fellow human beings.

12. Bruce Coad, "The Alger Hero," in Ray B. Browne, Marshall Fishwick, and Michael Marsden, eds., *Heroes of Popular Culture* (Bowling Green, OH: Bowling Green University Press, 1972), 44. See also Weiss, 4, 6.

13. Eisenberg, x.

14. Clive James, *Fame in the Twentieth Century* (New York: Random House, 1993), 8–9, 12, 13–14, 29, 51, 252.

15. Jeffrey Louis Decker, *Made in America: Self-Styled Success from Horatio Alger to Oprah Winfrey* (Minneapolis: University of Minnesota Press, 1997), xxii–xxix.

16. Christopher Jencks et al., *Who Gets Ahead? The Determinants of Economic Success in America* (New York: Basic Books, 1979), Chap. 8.

17. J. A. Kiegel, ed. *Reflections of Eminent Economists* (New York: New York University Press, 1989), xix.

18. Mary Alice Kellogg, *Fast Track: The Superachievers and How They Make It to Early Success, Status and Power* (New York: McGraw-Hill, 1978), 7, 9, 51, 70–77.

19. Matt S. Meier, with Conchita Franco Serri and Richard A. Garcia, *Notable Latino Americans: A Biographical Dictionary* (Westport, CT: Greenwood Press, 1997), xii–xii. See also Madison, on Jews and community, note 11.

20. Will Irwin, quoted in Larson, 233–234. The entire essay is reprinted in Larson, 361–365. See too Cecyle Neidle, *Great Immigrants* (New York: Twayne Publishers, 1973), Preface. In his recently edited collection of *Distinguished Asian Americans,* Hyung-chan Kim outlined criteria governing the selection of the 166 persons included in his volume, criteria that resonate with concerns similar to those described here: He and his co-editors chose individuals whose lives are inspiring, especially to Asian Americans; whose stories could instruct Asian American youth "to become more giving and less self-serving"; who have made significant contributions to Asian Americans' collective memory, to their professional field, and to American society; and who represent positive role models for Asian American youth. Hyung-chan Kim, with Dorothy Codova, Stephen S. Fugita, Franklin Ng, and Jane Singh, *Distinguished Asian Americans: A Biographical Dictionary* (Westport, CT: Greenwood Press, 1999), xvii.

21. Eisenberg, 3, 73, 133, 235, 355, 459–460.

22. Letter to author, June 24, 2000.

23. See Elliott Barkan, "Reflections on the Roots of American Ethnicity," in *Norwegian-American Essays,* edited by Øyvind T. Gulliksen, David C. Mauk, and Dina Tolfsby, pp. 31–60 (Oslo: Norwegian American Historical Association, 1996); Barkan, "Race, Religion and Nationality in American Society: A Model of Ethnicity—From Contact to Assimilation," *Journal of American Ethnic History* 14.2 (Winter 1995): 38–75, 95–101; and Barkan, ed., *A Nation of Peoples: A Sourcebook on America's Multicultural Heritage* (Westport, CT: Greenwood Press, 1999), ix–xv, 1–18.

24. Milton M. Gordon, *Assimilation in American Life: The Role of Race, Religion, and National Origins* (New York: Oxford University Press, 1964).

25. By and large foreign-born "settlers" become "immigrants" when the colonies become a nation—although one speaks in general terms about people who "settled" the West.

26. Quoted by contributor Douglas Caulkins.

27. E-mail, Niiya to editor, 4 July 2000.

References

Adams, Jane. *Women on Top: Success Patterns and Personal Growth.* New York: Hawthorn Books, 1979.

Barkan, Elliott. "Race, Religion and Nationality in American Society: A Model of Ethnicity—From Contact to Assimilation," *Journal of American Ethnic History* 14.2 (Winter 1995): 38–75, 95–101.

———. "Reflections on the Roots of American Ethnicity." In *Norwegian-American Essays,* edited by Øyvind T. Gulliksen, David C. Mauk, and Dina Tolfsby, 31–60. Oslo: Norwegian American Historical Association, 1996.

Barkan, Elliott, ed. *A Nation of Peoples: A Sourcebook on America's Multicultural Heritage.* Westport, CT: Greenwood Press, 1999, ix–xv, 1–18.

Coad, Bruce. "The Alger Hero." In *Heroes of Popular Culture,* edited by Ray B. Browne, Marshall Fishwick, and Michael Marsden, 42–59. Bowling Green, OH: Bowling Green University Press, 1972.

Decker, Jeffrey Louis. *Made in America: Self-Styled Success from Horatio Alger to Oprah Winfrey.* Minneapolis: University of Minnesota Press, 1997.

Eisenberg, Lee, ed. *Fifty Who Made the Difference.* Foreword by Phillip Moffitt. An Esquire Press book. New York: Villard Books, 1984.

Gordon, Milton M. *Assimilation in American Life: The Role of Race, Religion, and National Origins.* New York: Oxford University Press, 1964.

Greene, Theodore P. *America's Heroes: The Changing Models of Success in American Magazines.* New York: Oxford University Press, 1970.

James, Clive. *Fame in the Twentieth Century.* New York: Random House, 1993.

Jencks, Christopher, et al. *Who Gets Ahead? The Determinants of Economic Success in America.* New York: Basic Books, 1979.

Kellogg, Mary Alice. *Fast Track: The Superachievers and How They Make It to Early Success, Status and Power.* New York: McGraw-Hill, 1978.

Kiegel, J. A., ed. *Reflections of Eminent Economists.* New York: New York University Press, 1989.

Kim, Hyung-chan, editor, et al. *Distinguished Asian Americans: A Biographical Dictionary.* Westport, CT: Greenwood Press, 1999.

Larson, Cedric A. *WHO: Sixty Years of American Eminence: The Story of Who's Who in America.* New York: McDowell, Obolensky, 1958.

Madison, Charles A. *Eminent American Jews, 1776 to the Present.* New York: Frederick Ungar, 1970.

Meier, Matt S., with Conchita Franco Serri and Richard A. Garcia. *Notable Latino Americans: A Biographical Dictionary.* Westport, CT: Greenwood Press, 1997.

Neidle, Cecyle S. *Great Immigrants.* New York: Twayne Publishers, 1973.

Richey, Elinor. *Eminent Women of the West.* Berkeley, CA: Howell-North Books, 1975.

Weiss, Richard. *The American Myth of Success: From Horatio Alger to Norman Vincent Peale.* New York: Basic Books, 1969.

ACKNOWLEDGMENTS

I owe an enormous debt of thanks to my more than four score contributors, who gave generously to meet the standards and guidelines I imposed upon them all. I am amazed at the effort they put forth in order to provide biographies that are as substantive as one could ever hope for under the limiting circumstances. In particular, my appreciation goes to William E. Van Vugt for doing twenty-five entries, as it extends to several persons who provided key contributions: Ernesto Sagás, John M. Shaw, Jeffrey P. Shepherd, Gillian Leitch, Nancy C. Lespérance, Zaragosa Vargas, James M. Bergquist, and Susanne Schick. I also owe a huge debt of gratitude to my assistant, Regina Williams, who had the mind-boggling task of organizing all 400-plus entries for the table of contents and lists of individuals by ethnicity and occupation. She took a substantial burden off my shoulders. Our departmental secretary, Stacey Topping, also provided some important help that enabled this complicated project to proceed smoothly. I am also most appreciative to California State University for providing Professional Development funds, including release time, so that I could complete this book; the university came through when I really needed it. A full measure of my gratitude goes, as well, to my acquisitions editor at ABC-CLIO Books, Alicia Merritt, and my production editor, Melanie Stafford, both of whom proved to be wonderfully responsive, flexible, and helpful. A special thanks goes to three colleagues/contributors who read and critiqued the Introduction. Their suggestions have been most appreciated, but, of course, the end product is my responsibility alone. Finally, spouses and partners must also endure lapses of sanity that take place in authors with whom they live during the final stages of such a project as this, and my thanks go beyond measure to my wife, Bryn Barkan.

—*Elliott Robert Barkan*

Abdullah, Mohammed Nur Ali
"Sheik Nur" (1946–)
Religious leader and teacher
Sudanese-Nubian

As the St. Louis area's Islamic leader, Mohammed Nur Ali Abdullah works closely with leaders of the Jewish and Christian communities to increase cultural and religious understanding, seeking to reduce potential tensions among people of different religions. A member of several interfaith organizations, Sheik Nur has become a cornerstone in the dynamic interfaith dialogue that is taking place in St. Louis and nationwide.

Raised in Port Sudan, a multiethnic and multireligious city, Sheik Nur learned a critical life lesson from his parents, Alhaj Ali Abdullah and Hajja Zeinab Hamad: Value and respect people, whatever their cultural or religious background. Although fervent Moslems, they sent him to Catholic schools, where his teachers and his fellow students came from a broad range of international backgrounds. In his first position after graduating from high school, teaching at Port Sudan Coptic School, he continued his multiethnic experiences.

Soon, however, his desire to continue learning led him to study Islamic law in Saudi Arabia. After he finished his studies, representatives from the World Community of Islam in the West (formerly the Nation of Islam) invited him to be an Islamic scholar for them in the United States and Canada. Sheik Nur moved to Chicago in 1978 with his wife, Zeinab G. Abdullah, who came from the same familial, ethnic, and religious background. He stayed in Chicago from 1978 to 1990, helping, teaching, guiding, and sharing religious doctrines and traditions as imam. During this time, he was also imam for an Arabic mosque on the South Side and a multiethnic mosque in downtown Chicago. In working with different mosques, his goal was to give the same religious instruction to each, while being aware of cultural variations. In the late 1980s the St. Louis, Missouri, Islamic community, seeking an imam trained in religious matters and certified in Islamic law, recruited Sheik Nur. In 1990 he and his family moved, and he again found himself the religious leader of a multiethnic Islamic community, with two multiethnic mosques.

Today, Sheik Nur has multiple roles in addition to his duties as imam and religious leader in the mosque. As principal of the Al Salam Day School, an Islamic institution, he oversees the religious and educational training of young Muslim students. As advocate and counselor, he protects members of his community from religious discrimination, assisting them in their legal rights, whether in employment, education, or personal matters. He continually works to forge a bridge between the growing multinational Islamic community and the surrounding Christian and Jewish communities. He does this by encouraging schoolchildren to visit the students at Al Salam and vice versa, and by organizing discussions on Islam for the general public. He participates in a number of interfaith organizations, such as the Interfaith Partnership of Metropolitan St. Louis, the Interfaith Clergy Council of Greater St. Louis, Muslim Christian Relations, the National Conference for Community and Justice, and the World Parliament of Religion.

As St. Louis becomes more cosmopolitan and strikingly multiethnic, it would be easy for dissension to spread. Sheik Nur's efforts at achieving interfaith understanding and tolerance have laid the groundwork for peaceful coexistence among potentially divisive and hostile groups.

Pamela A. DeVoe

REFERENCES

Abdullah, Sheik Mohammed Nur. Interviews by author, 17, 26 May 1999.

Pinsky, Mark I. "Do the Rite Thing." *St. Louis Post-Dispatch,* 9 November 1996, Religion, 27.

Rogers, Kathryn. "God Is . . . What? 3 Faiths Answer: Muslims, Christians and Jews of Area Meet to Share Their Stories." *St. Louis Post-Dispatch,* 17 October 1992, D5.

———. "Interfaith Partnership Broadens Its Outreach, Services." *St. Louis Post-Dispatch,* 16 October 1993, D5.

———. "Pilgrims Find That Religions Share Goal of Achieving Peace, Justice in the World." *St. Louis Post-Dispatch,* 22 May 1993, D6.

Shapiro, Mary. "Catholic, Islamic Students Learn from Each Other." *West County Journal,* 9 February 2000, 1.

"Where Pope Might Go, Whom He Might Meet." *St. Louis Post-Dispatch,* 26 April 1998, A11.

Abu Eid, Fatima (1956–)

Community activist
Palestinian

Fatima Abu Eid is the founder and executive director of Social Services Assisting Neighborhood Arab-American Development (SANAD). A culturally sensitive social service organization, SANAD is dedicated to helping Arab women on Chicago's South Side.

Abu Eid, born in Betunia (or Bituniya), Palestine, on 1 January 1956, and her brother joined their mother in the United States in the 1970s. As a member of a large Arab community on the South Side of Chicago, she followed the traditional path for Middle Eastern girls, getting married and having a family. After a series of marital problems, Abu Eid found herself on her own with four children but unprepared for the demands of the U.S. welfare system.

In the midst of her own struggles, she dreamed of finding a way to help others like herself so that "no one would be lost" because of her cultural or religious background. Gradually, she improved her situation, keeping her children in school and out of gangs and looking for ways to help the community. She learned English at Holy Cross Hospital, eventually earned a general equivalency diploma (GED) by attending night school, became president of the Marquette Elementary School Local School Committee, and began developing relationships with Arab and other local community groups. In 1991 she formed the Society for Arab Women's Welfare Aid (SAWA), now known as SANAD.

A deeply religious woman, Abu Eid feels that God has given her the ability to succeed and that it is her duty to help others. A woman begging for food for her children on the street will soon find Abu Eid instructing a local Arab merchant to put a few purchases on her account for them. A woman turned out of her home may find a space for a few days in SANAD's back room. With Abu Eid's focus on local needs, she has become a respected and trusted figure for neighborhood women with no place else to turn. Located in the old Arab neighborhood on Chicago's South Side, around Sixty-third Street and Kedzie—a community with increasing poverty and episodes of gang activity—SANAD provides services for many families that do not know where else to seek help. Abu Eid manages to generate just enough money to keep the organization going and pay herself a small salary, cobbling together a variety of social service programs from across the city. SANAD, which is open to anyone, Arab or not, offers a variety of services, including marital and family counseling, homemaker training, a food pantry, English classes, assistance filling out forms and applications, and low-income energy assistance.

Abu Eid has managed to build an organization where women and families of all backgrounds can seek help, knowing that their religion, customs, dignity, and privacy will be treated with the utmost respect. Those in need know that they will always be listened to and understood by someone who has suffered as they have. With SANAD a thriving success, Abu Eid continues to look for ways to help others and established a similar program in her hometown of Betunia, Palestine, in 1999.

Elizabeth Plantz

REFERENCES

Abu Eid, Fatima. Interview by author, 8 May 1999.

Arab American Institute. "About Arab Americans. National Partners" (2000): www.aaiusa.org/ arabamericans/census/partners.htm (accessed 17 July 2000).

"Arab Women to Host Multi-cultural Meeting." *Southwest News-Herald* (Chicago), 1 July 1993.

Hanania, Ray. "Chicagoland Arab American Organization Information Guide": www. hanania.com/araborg.htm (accessed 17 July 2000).

Adamic, Louis (1898–1951)

Journalist, writer, and community activist
Slovene

Louis Adamic, born in what is today the Republic of Slovenia, was an American writer, ethnic activist, and a Guggenheim fellowship winner in 1932. As a political organizer, he achieved wide recognition in Slovenia and the United States.

Adamic was born in 1898 in Blato, near Grosuplje, Province of Carniola, then part of Austria-Hungary. The son of a relatively rich farmer, he immigrated to the United States in 1913, not for economic reasons but for adventure, after being expelled from secondary school for his nationalist, pro-Yugoslav views. During his first years in the United States, he worked in New York City for the Slovene ethnic newspaper *Glas Naroda* (Voice of the people). He joined the U.S. Army in 1916, became a citizen in 1917, and served until 1923. He then lived in California and thereafter New York City, traveling extensively across the United States until 1937, when he bought a farm in Milford, New Jersey.

Adamic's early work as a translator of Slovene and other Yugoslav literature helped him master the English language. He continued his literary career with a romanticized history of the American labor movement, *Dynamite: The Story of Class Violence in America* (1931), and the autobiographical *Laughing in the Jungle* (1932). He received a Guggenheim fellowship, which enabled him to visit the then Kingdom of Yugoslavia in 1932. After he came back, he wrote *The Native's Return,* dealing with the problems of the dictatorship in Yugoslavia during that period.

Adamic is widely considered one of the founders of the movement for the right of American ethnic communities to retain their ethnic identities. In 1934, he became a member of the board of the Foreign Language Information Service and, in 1939, helped reorganize it as the Common Council for American Unity. He advanced his ideas between 1940 and 1942 as editor of its periodical *Common Ground* and in numerous books. Adamic's *A Nation of Nations* (1944) is the predecessor of the *Harvard Encyclopedia of American Ethnic Groups* (1980).

After Axis forces attacked Yugoslavia on 6 April 1941, Adamic and other Slovene-American leaders organized the Slovene American National Congress. It elected the Slovene American National Council, with Adamic its honorary president. Partly owing to their efforts, the U.S. government abandoned its support of the Serbian nationalists (Chetniks) and began backing the Communist Partisans under Tito. In June 1943, Adamic was elected president of the United Committee of South Slavic Americans, which supported the Partisans of Yugoslavia. He then wrote *My Native Land,* describing Yugoslavia during the war.

Adamic supported Henry Wallace's Progressive Party in 1948 and published articles by its members, along with his own, in his magazine *Trends and Tides.* He even helped write Wallace's platform. Adamic's final book, *The Eagle and the Roots,* was the product of his visit to Yugoslavia in 1949. It includes his comments on the situation in Yugoslavia and a relatively favorable view of Marshal Tito (Josip Broz), the Yugoslav president. While finishing this book, Adamic died under mysterious circumstances at his farm in Milford in 1951. The book was published posthumously.

Matjaž Klemenčič

REFERENCES

Christian, Henry. *Louis Adamic: A Checklist.* Kent, OH: Kent State University Press, 1973.

"Dve domovini, Razprave o izseljenstvu" *Two Homelands, Migration Studies* (Ljubljana: Inštitut za slovensko izseljenstvo) 9 (1998): 7–110.

Gantar-Godina, Irena, ed. *Intelektualci v diaspori: zbornik referatov simpozija ob 100. obletnici rojstva Louisa Adamiča—Intelektualci v diaspori, Portorož, Slovenija, 1.–5. septembra 1998* (Proceedings of the symposium on the occasion of the 100th anniversary of the birth of Louis Adamic—Intellectuals in Diaspora, Portorož, Slovenia, 1–5 September 1998). Ljubljana: Inštitut za slovensko izseljenstvo, 1999.

Klemenčič, Matjaž. *Ameriški Slovenci in NOB v Jugoslaviji* (American Slovenes and the national liberation struggle in Yugoslavia). Maribor: Založba obzorja, 1987.

Stanonik, Janez, ed. *Louis Adamič, Simpozij* (Louis Adamic Symposium). Ljubljana: Univerza Edvarda Kardelja v Ljubljani, 1981.

Aguirre, Valentin (1891–1953)
Sailor, entrepreneur, and community activist
Basque

Valentin Aguirre and his wife, Benita, who established a boardinghouse in New York City for Basque newcomers, played an instrumental role in aiding newly arrived compatriots. For the variety of services he provided them and for his involvement in establishing community institutions, Aguirre well deserved his place in the Basque Hall of Fame.

Born in 1891 in Monte Sollube, Bizkaia, Spain, Aguirre left at age ten, finding work aboard a merchant vessel that sailed to South America, Cuba, and New York. At twenty-six, he gave up that life for work as a tugboat stoker in New York harbor. Four years later he successfully completed the civil service exam in English and began working on New York City's boat and ferry system. During those New York years, he met and married Benita Orbe, also from the Basque region.

In 1917, the Aguirres opened a Basque boardinghouse on Cherry Street, in Manhattan, and named it the Casa Vizcaina. It became a jumping-off point for thousands of Basque sojourners, and thus the Aguirres were known throughout the American West. Their boardinghouse catered exclusively to Basques, helping them find their way to destinations in the United States. As their clientele expanded, the Aguirres relocated several times, finally settling in Greenwich Village. There, Valentin opened the Aguirre Travel Agency, switching from informally advising customers to actually handling every aspect of their travel arrangements to the West. When his three sons were old enough to drive, Aguirre sent them to the docks each afternoon to greet arrivals from Spain and France. They shouted greetings in Basque and usually returned to the boardinghouse with a carload of relieved travelers. This process of welcoming newcomers and sending them on their way lasted from 1917 through 1941, when the Vizcaina closed its doors and the Aguirres went into semiretirement.

Aguirre is also fondly remembered by New York's Basque community for his work with the Euzko Etxea of New York (Basque home, in Bizkaian Basque). The dream of building a Basque club in New York City began around 1905, when Aguirre and four others began promoting the idea. In 1913, fourteen Basques, including Aguirre, met and formalized their organization. The Central Vasco-Americano Sociedad de Beneficencia y Recreo (Central Basque American society for beneficence [assistance] and recreation, in Spanish) evolved into Euzko Etxea in the mid–twentieth century.

Aguirre served as club president for several years and oversaw its activities, which included regular meetings and social events, such as receiving dignitaries from the Basque region, hosting card and handball tournaments, dances, and other festivities. Etxea has also served as an aid society for New York Basques in need of assistance during illness or hard times. It continues today in its Brooklyn location, having served many New York Basques. Just as they have appreciated the assistance and hospitality of Euzko Etxea, thousands of Basque-Americans in the West are indebted to the Aguirres for the help they received at Casa Vizcaina during their first days in the United States.

Aguirre died in 1953. In 1982 he was inducted into the Basque Hall of Fame.

Jeronima Echeverria

REFERENCES
Douglass, William A., and Jon Bilbao. *Amerikanuak:*

A History of Basques in the New World. Reno: University of Nevada Press, 1975.

Doyaga, Emilia. "History of *Euzko Etxea* of New York." In *Proceedings of the First International Conference in North America,* 132–141. Society of Basque Studies. Bilbao, Spain: La Gran Enciclopedia Vasca, 1982.

Echeverria, Jeronima. *Home Away from Home: A History of Basque Boarding Houses.* Reno: University of Nevada Press, 2000.

Ahmed, Ismael N. (1947–)
Community organization director, political activist, and musician
Arab-American

Ismael Ahmed is the executive director of the Arab Community Center for Economic and Social Services (ACCESS), in Dearborn, Michigan. ACCESS, an organization that assists low-income and immigrant Arab-Americans, has become, under Ahmed's leadership, a nationally and internationally recognized model social service agency. Ahmed is also a major leader both in the Detroit region and in Arab-American communities nationwide.

Ahmed's mother, of Lebanese origin, was born in New York. His father had emigrated from Egypt, going to Brooklyn, where he met and married Ahmed's mother and where Ahmed was born. Five years later, the family moved to the Detroit-Dearborn area. In school, his teacher told him not to speak Arabic at home. His parents obliged, and he regrets that to this day. Nonetheless, although he grew up in an ethnically mixed, working-class community, he felt that his Arab background was a form of identification. He was also influenced by African-American music and culture, and his grandmother, Aliya Hassan, invited him to New York, where he met Ahmed Jamal, the jazz musician, and Malcolm X. His grandmother, a New York City detective and community activist, became Ahmed's mentor and relocated to Dearborn to become the first president of ACCESS.

After serving in Korea during the Vietnam War, Ahmed became an activist during the civil rights and anti–Vietnam War era. His involvement with the Arab community at this time was prompted by the 1967 Arab-Israeli War—which resulted in the occupation of additional Palestinian lands by Israel and the displacement of more Palestinian refugees—and by an effort of the City of Dearborn to raze his community under the guise of "urban renewal" and to re-zone it for heavy industry, in particular, for Ford Motor Company's expansion. The city failed, but this period of activity led to the establishment of ACCESS. At the same time, Ahmed completed a B.A. in sociology.

Since helping to establish ACCESS in 1972, Ahmed has served on twenty-eight local, state, and national task forces concerning matters ranging from health care and infant mortality to fair housing. He was vice-chair and served on the board of trustees of New Detroit, Inc. As executive director of ACCESS since 1982, Ahmed administers all mental health social services, along with physical health, employment and training, cultural arts, and advocacy programs. He is responsible for the direct supervision of 150 full- and part-time staff, who provide services to more than 40,000 people each year in forty-five programs. The annual dinner of ACCESS is attended by 2,500 and is the second-largest ethnic gathering in the Detroit area.

Many of his community efforts include interethnic activities. For example, with his continuing interest in music, he founded the "Earth Island Orchestra" and coproduced and cohosted "Radio Free Earth" in Detroit. He also started the annual Arab Village Street Fair, which is attended by 25,000 people each year. Most of all, however, Ahmed remains an advocate for low-income people and has been highly successful in alleviating many of their problems. Although he has received many honors, he has never forgotten his roots.

Barbara Aswad

REFERENCES
Ahmed, Ismael. Interviews by author throughout 1998.
"Arab Community Leader: He's at His Best When Tearing Down Ethnic Barriers in His Neighborhood." *Detroit News,* 15 March 1992 (Michiganian of the Year Award).

"Arab-American Leader Finds a Supportive Family Helps." *Detroit Free Press,* 18 March 1992, 4H.

Aswad, Barbara C., and Nancy Gray. "Challenges to the Arab American Family and the Arab Community Center for Economic and Social Services (ACCESS)." In *Family and Gender among American Muslims: Issues Facing Middle Eastern Immigrants and Their Descendants,* edited by Barbara C. Aswad and Barbara Bilgé, 223–240. Philadelphia: Temple University Press, 1996.

"Ismael Ahmed: Community Coalitions and Culture." *Metro Times* (Detroit), 10–16 November 1999.

"Ismael Ahmed, Executive Director of the Arab American Community Center for Economic and Social Services Named '1992 Executive of the Year' by the United Community Services of Metropolitan Detroit." *Detroit News,* 22 June 1992, 17F.

"Making a Difference: A Passion for Equality. Ismael Ahmed Serves as a Cultural Conscience." *Coalition* (Detroit), 10–16 November 1999.

Ahn, Philip (1911–1978)
Actor and community activist
Korean-American

Despite the barriers faced by Asian Americans in the arts, Philip Ahn, a native of Los Angeles, managed to forge a successful career in film and television. He was a pioneer in the field and both visually and symbolically helped to create space for Asian Americans within the artistic landscape. Perhaps best known for his role as a monk and teacher in the 1970s television series *Kung Fu,* the versatile and talented Ahn also appeared on many other shows and in more than 300 films throughout a career that began in the 1930s.

Ahn's success as a working actor was noteworthy because Hollywood has hardly been hospitable toward Asian American artists. Current actors still face considerable obstacles, but Ahn managed to find work during an era when roles for Asian Americans were few and far between. He appeared in such major productions as *The Good Earth* (1937) and *Love Is a Many Splendored Thing* (1955), but he also encountered the perennial dilemma of balancing dedication to craft with the need to survive in the face of limited and stereotypical roles.

His skills notwithstanding, Ahn occupied the position of an "ethnic" actor. Although European American actors did in fact take on roles in which they portrayed racial or ethnic minorities, actors like Ahn were hired only to play people of Asian ancestry. Moreover, use of Asian characters, like Hop Sing's uncle in *Bonanza,* portrayed by Ahn, often underscored the desires of the television industry to espouse a racially inclusive rhetoric that hardly reflected the state of race relations in the United States. Despite these conditions, Ahn sought to bring dignity and depth to the characters he played, even as the industry itself afforded little space to challenge racially scripted and dehumanized roles.

Although known nationally for his work in television and film, Ahn was also a prominent figure within the Korean-American community because he was the son of Ahn Chang-ho, a key immigrant leader of the Korean independence movement centered in the United States. Philip Ahn was influenced by his patriot-father's vision that the spiritual and moral regeneration of the Korean people was a key step to their liberation from Japanese colonial rule. While the elder Ahn participated in the work of the independence movement, Philip assumed responsibilities for his family, evident in his attempts to have his father released after he was arrested by the Japanese in China. After Ahn Chang-ho's death at the hands of the Japanese in Korea in 1938, Philip and the Ahn family continued to work for the cause of Korean liberation.

As an actor and an active member of the Korean-American community in California, Philip Ahn was clearly a pioneer in his generation. He was the first Asian American actor to be granted a "star" by the Hollywood Chamber of Commerce on the "Walk of Fame." As a member of the Ahn family, Philip also contributed to the Korean-immigrant community as it struggled to make a home in the United States and in its efforts on behalf of Korea.

David Yoo

REFERENCES
Hamamoto, Darrell. *Monitored Peril: Asian Americans*

and the Politics of TV Representation. Minneapolis: University of Minnesota Press, 1994.

Kim, Hyung-chan. *Tosan Ahn Chang-ho: A Profile of a Prophetic Patriot.* Seoul, Seattle, and Los Angeles: Tosan Memorial Foundation, Korean American Historical Society, and Academia Koreana, Kiemyung Baylo University, 1996.

Kim, Hyung-chan, ed. *Dictionary of Asian American History.* Westport, CT: Greenwood Press, 1986.

"Ahn, Phillip." In *The Asian American Encyclopedia,* edited by Franklin Ng, 410. New York: Marshall Cavendish, 1995.

Akiwumi, Fenda (Aminata Maund) (1955–)
Scientist and teacher
Sierra Leonean

Fenda Akiwumi is currently a geology and geography instructor at Hill College in Hillsboro, Texas, and the epitome of the multicultural person. She has dedicated herself not only to her teaching but also to educating her community about Africans and to participating actively in Sierra Leonean associations in Oklahoma and Texas.

Akiwumi was born in London to parents who were college professors. Her father also served as a leader in Sierra Leone's independence movement and was an ambassador. He is a Krio of West Indian, Liberian, and Sierra Leonean ancestry. Her mother is an American from Massachusetts. Fenda's earlier education was in England and Sierra Leone, but she is pursuing her Ph.D. at the University of Texas, Arlington. She and her husband, who is of mixed Nigerian, Ghanaian, and Sierra Leonean ancestry, have three children. She identifies herself and her family as "African–African American."

In her work and community activity, Akiwumi's dedication to science and multiculturalism are evident. After receiving her M.S. in hydrogeology from the University of London, she worked in Freetown, Sierra Leone, as a hydrogeologist for the Ministry of Agriculture. She also taught science courses at the high school and university level there. Much of her research is on water resources and development in the Third World, especially in Africa. More recently, she has become inter-

ested in gender issues and urban and community development.

In 1992 she moved with her family to Fort Worth, Texas. At Hill College, Akiwumi does more than teach science to her students, many of them first-generation college students with little exposure outside their small-town environment. Although there were few blacks in Hillsboro and only one other black faculty member when she was hired, her personal example and efforts to inform students and the community about Africa and African culture have made her many friends. She has given numerous talks at churches and civic organizations, is a sponsor for her campus International Club, and was awarded the National Institute for Staff and Organizational Development (NISOD) Excellence Award in Teaching and Leadership.

In the Dallas–Fort Worth area, Akiwumi has been very active in the Sierra Leonean community, working with such organizations as the Sisters of Sierra Leone, the Sierra Leone Association of Oklahoma and Texas, and Sa Lonas (a Sierra Leonean organization in Dallas–Fort Worth), which host events and raise funds for various causes in Sierra Leone. For example, the Sierra Leone community has adopted the Leonenet Street Children's Project in Freetown, which looks after refugee orphans of the nine-year civil war. For the past two years an annual fund-raiser has been held on Sierra Leone's independence anniversary, 27 April, which includes an exhibition on Sierra Leone, dinner, and a dance. Akiwumi organizes this event, specifically the exhibition.

Akiwumi and her siblings also developed an educational program for children called Voyage to Africa and a six-week summer program for United Way–sponsored youth centers in Fort Worth (primarily for the African American community). Such activities and groups as these provide a sense of community and an important connection for Akiwumi's family to their African culture and roots.

April Gordon

REFERENCES
Akiwumi, Fenda Aminata Maund. Curriculum vitae, March 2000.

————. E-mail to editor, 25 April 2000.

————. Personal correspondence with author, 26 March 2000.

Hasselstrom, Linda G. "Keep 'em on the Pavement." *Lakelander* (Whitney, TX), 5 March 1997.

"Hill College Spotlight." *Reporter* (Hillsboro, TX), 25 June 1998.

Akiyoshi, Toshiko (1929–)

Jazz musician and composer
Japanese

Jazz pianist Toshiko Akiyoshi has led perhaps the most critically acclaimed big band of the past twenty years. Many of her compositions reflect her bicultural heritage.

Akiyoshi was born in 1929 to Japanese parents who had settled in Manchuria. The youngest of four daughters, she began classical studies in piano at age six. After World War II, her family moved back to Beppu, Japan, which had become a resort city for Occupation soldiers. It was there that she took on her first job, as piano player in a dance hall, and it was there that she first became interested in jazz when a fan introduced her to the music of Teddy Wilson. She soon became a serious student of jazz and moved to Tokyo in the early 1950s, becoming part of an active jazz scene there.

In 1953, she was "discovered" by the legendary pianist Oscar Peterson, who introduced her to Verve Records head Norman Granz. Granz signed her to Verve, which also led to her coming to the United States after getting a scholarship to the Berklee School of Music in Boston in 1955. Over the next decade, she pursued her music through her own small groups and through work with such figures as Charles Mingus, Oscar Pettiford, and Charlie Mariano. Alto saxophonist Mariano also briefly became her husband.

In the mid-1960s, Akiyoshi became disillusioned with music during a period that saw her playing piano bars in the East and Midwest and she considered dropping out of music, even going to an employment agency to seek other work. But Lew Tabackin, whom she met in 1967 and would marry two years later, convinced her to stick with it, becoming her biggest fan and supporter.

Perhaps the turning point of Akiyoshi's life in jazz came with the death of Duke Ellington, one of her idols, in 1974. Reflecting on how Ellington drew on his ethnic heritage for inspiration, Akiyoshi began to do the same in her own work. She also realized that her love of composition and arrangement demanded a larger canvas and started the Toshiko Akiyoshi Jazz Orchestra in 1973. Featuring Tabackin as lead soloist on tenor saxophone and flute and Akiyoshi's Japanese-tinged compositions, her big band has gone on to record eighteen albums and has received fourteen Grammy Award nominations since 1976. Among the best known of her big band albums are *Kogun* (1974), *Notorious Tourist from the East* (1978), and *Carnegie Hall Concert* (1991). *Long Yellow Road* (1975), which was inspired by the travails of being a Japanese woman in the American jazz world, has become her theme.

Nonetheless, Akiyoshi has been somewhat representative of many of the more recent, post–World War II Japanese immigrants—the "shin-Issei"—who now constitute 30 percent of Japanese Americans: She identifies as Japanese but not as Japanese American, that is, not with those whose families arrived prior to 1924.

Akiyoshi and Lew Tabackin have made New York their home since 1982.

Brian Niiya

REFERENCES

Jazz Is My Native Language: A Portrait of Toshiko Akiyoshi. Directed by Renee Cho. Rhapsody Films, 1986.

Long Yellow Road, with the Toshiko Akiyoshi–Lew Tabackin Big Band. RCA Victor JPL1–1350, 1975.

Albright, Madeleine Korbel (née Marie Jana Körbelová) (1937–)

Professor, diplomat, and U.S. secretary of state
Czech

A major historical event took place on 23 January 1997, when Czech-born Madeleine Albright was sworn in as the first woman to hold the position of secretary of state of the United States. The Senate voted unanimously to confirm her, and the appointment was received with great enthusiasm. Her reputation was that of a no-nonsense woman who "tells it like it is."

Albright was born in Prague on 15 May 1937 as Marie Jana Körbelová, the oldest of three children of the Czechoslovak diplomat Josef Körbel. Drawing on his connections in Yugoslavia, where he had served two years as press attaché at the Czechoslovak embassy in Belgrade, Körbel and his family were able to leave for England soon after the Nazi invasion of what was left of Czechoslovakia on 15 March 1939. Since the Körbels were Jews, this move saved their lives; Albright's grandparents perished in concentration camps. The Körbels became Roman Catholics in 1941, when Madeleine was four years old, and changed their name to Korbel after returning to Prague in 1945. Soon after the Communist takeover of Czechoslovakia in 1948, the family left for the United States, where they formally requested political asylum in February 1949.

Madeleine Korbel graduated from Wellesley College with honors in 1959 and three days later married Joseph Albright. The Albrights had three daughters. Madeleine received her M.A. in political science in 1968 and eight years later her Ph.D., both from Columbia University. In 1972 Albright worked as a fund-raiser for Senator Edmund S. Muskie during his unsuccessful run for the Democratic nomination for president; later, she became his chief legislative assistant. In March 1978 she was invited by Zbigniew Brzezinski, national security adviser to President Jimmy Carter, to serve as the National Security Council's congressional liaison. For eleven years, beginning in 1982, she was research professor of international affairs and director of the Women in Foreign Service Program at Georgetown University. Her hard work, many skills, and good understanding of both domestic legislation and foreign policy issues soon came to be highly valued. In addition to teaching, she served as foreign policy coordi-

nator for presidential and vice presidential candidates Walter Mondale and Geraldine Ferraro, was senior policy adviser for presidential candidate Michael Dukakis, and was actively involved in matters relating to international affairs.

Although her marriage ended in divorce in 1983, her political career was rapidly advancing: Her Washington home became a foreign policy salon where members of the Democratic Party frequently met. As one of the advisers to President William J. Clinton, whom she had met in 1988, Albright was appointed in 1993 ambassador to the United Nations and four years later became secretary of state, one of the most powerful positions in the U.S. government. One of her accomplishments was to restore much of the bipartisanship in foreign policy that had characterized the Cold War period. She expressed her activism in the statement: "We have a responsibility in our time . . . not to be prisoners of history, but to shape history."

Zdenek Salzmann

REFERENCES

Blackman, Ann. *Seasons of Her Life: A Biography of Madeleine Korbel Albright.* New York: Simon & Schuster, 1998.

Dobbs, Michael. *Madeleine Albright: A Twentieth-Century Odyssey.* New York: Henry Holt, 1999.

"Madeleine Albright." In *Britannica Book of the Year 1998,* 65. Chicago: Encyclopaedia Britannica, 1998.

"Albright, Madeleine Korbel." In *Current Biography Yearbook 1995,* edited by Judith Graham,. New York: H. W. Wilson, 1995, 56.5 (May 1995): 6–11.

Alegría, Fernando (1918–)
Poet, literary scholar, and educator
Chilean

Fernando Alegría is a renowned novelist, essayist, poet, and one of the pioneers in the teaching of Spanish-language literature in the United States. He was also a distinguished professor at Stanford University for two decades.

Born in Santiago, Chile, on 26 September 1918, Alegría was educated at some of the best schools in Chile. His father, Santiago Alegría

Toro, was a businessman. His mother, Julia Alfaro, along with his grandmother, encouraged Fernando, already an avid reader, in his writing. In 1938, when he was twenty years old, he published his first novel, *Recabarren,* a fictionalized biography of a Chilean labor leader. He majored in Spanish and philosophy at the University of Chile, where he became a professor in 1939.

Alegría first came to the United States as the world teetered on the brink of World War II. He was attending an international gathering in New York City of the Youth for Peace movement. Thereafter, he divided his time between the United States and Chile, until the military dictatorship that overthrew Salvador Allende in 1973 forced Alegría to stay out of Chile.

Alegría attended both Bowling Green University, in Ohio, where he received his M.A. in literature in 1941, and the University of California at Berkeley, where he received his doctorate in Spanish. He became an instructor at Berkeley in 1947, the same year he completed his Ph.D. dissertation, and a professor in 1949. In 1967, Alegría accepted a full professorship with an endowed chair at Stanford University, where he remained until he retired, holding the title of professor emeritus since 1987.

A distinguished novelist, essayist, and poet, Alegría was one of the pioneers in the recognition and teaching of Spanish-language literature in the United States. His *Historia de la novela hispanoamericana* (History of the Spanish-American novel, 1965) has served as a standard text for Latin American literature classes. He also made use of translations to introduce American literature to Spanish-speaking countries, including *Walt Whitman en Hispanoamérica,* a collection of Walt Whitman's writings that he translated into Spanish.

Alegría's experiences as an expatriate and his deeply felt opinions about the course of Chilean politics have, especially in recent years, informed his writings and given voice to human rights abuses in the country of his birth. Among his works are *Chilean Spring,* a fictionalized account of a photographer's ordeal and death at the hands of the junta, and *Allende: A Novel,* a quasi-fictional biography of the socialist hero.

Alegría's honors include a Guggenheim fellowship (1947–1948), the Latin American Prize for Literature (1943, for *Lautaro: Joven libertador de Arauco* [Lautaro: Young liberator from Arauco]), and the Premio Atenea and Premio Municipal (both Chile), for *Caballo de copas* (Jack of Hearts). In 1977, he cofounded with a friend a literary magazine, *Literatura Chilena en el Exilio* (Chilean literature in exile). His memberships include Instituto Internacional de Literatura Iberoamericana, American Association of Teachers of Spanish, and Sociedad de Escritores (Chile).

Alegría married Carmen Letona Melendez in 1943, and they had four children. They reside in Berkeley.

Kathleen Paparchontis

REFERENCES

Epple, Juan A. *Para una Fundación Imaginaria de Chile. La Literatura de Fernando Alegría* (For an Imaginative Foundation of Chile: The Literature of Fernando Alegría). Lima: Latinoamericana Editores, 1987.

Gaicomán, Helmy F. *Homenaje a Fernando Alegría: Variaciones Interpretativas en Torno a su Obra* (Homage to Fernando Alegría: Various Interpretations of His Works). New York: Las Américas Publishing Co., 1972.

Ruiz, René. *Fernando Alegría: Vida y Obra*. Madrid: Playor, 1979.

Valenzuela, Victor. *Fernando Alegría: El Escritor y su Epoca*. Madrid: Artes Gráficas Belzal, 1985.

Allende, Isabel (1942–)
Writer
Chilean

Isabel Allende, journalist, author, feminist, world traveler. After surmounting obstacles that kept many women of her generation in Latin America from careers outside of marriage, she became the first Latin American woman novelist to achieve international prominence. Her books have been translated into thirty languages, and two of them have been made into films.

Allende was born on 2 August 1942 in

Lima, Peru, but identifies herself as Chilean. Her father, Tomás Allende, a Chilean diplomat, and her mother, Francisco Llona Barros Allende, were divorced when Isabel was three. Although her mother never explained why her father disappeared from her life, her mother's marriage to another diplomat allowed Allende to enjoy a varied education and extensive travel. She attended a Quaker school in Beirut, where English was spoken. She graduated from a private high school in Santiago when her family returned to Chile.

In 1962, at age nineteen, Allende married a young engineering student, Miguel Frías, and they had two children. After living in Europe, they returned to Chile in 1966, where Allende worked as a journalist and television personality. Her cousin, General Salvador Allende, president of Chile, was a victim of a military coup in 1973. Two years later, Isabel and her family escaped Augusto Pinochet's fascist rule by leaving Chile for Caracas, Venezuela.

A letter that Isabel wrote to her grandfather as he was dying inspired her first novel, *La Casa de los Espíritus* (The house of the spirits), published in 1982 with great success. In 1987, she divorced Frías and moved to the United States, where she married San Francisco attorney Willie Gordon in 1988. She settled in California. Her education, which had included English, enabled her to make the transition easily into North American life, although she writes all of her fiction in Spanish.

In 1991, Allende wrote *The Infinite Plan,* in which she deviates from her usual female protagonist. Her main character is fashioned after her American husband. She sees the blending of cultures in the United States as positive and views American life for women as having moved past the survival stage. Yet, she describes the American family as disconnected morally and spiritually disadvantaged. She also asserts that although immigrants in California are part of the culture, they do not benefit from it. Her recent novel, *Daughter of Fortune,* set in Gold Rush California, begins as romantic fiction and quickly develops into a young

woman's search for self-knowledge. In contrast, her first nonfiction book, *Paula,* an autobiographical memoir, began as a letter to her daughter, Paula, who was afflicted with porphyria, a hereditary blood disease, and died in 1992. Allende considers *Paula* her most important work because she shares the oldest sorrow of women, the death of a child.

Allende appears to have kept her distance from ethnic causes but does support many organizations. Her honors and awards have come from the international world of literature and arts; for example, she received the Hispanic Heritage Award in Literature in 1996. Allende toured with "Read About Me," a program promoting multiculturalism in the United States, and in 1996 the program honored her as "Author of the Year."

Kathleen Paparchontis

References
Allende, Isabel. *Daughter of Fortune: A Novel.* Translated by Margaret Sayers Peden. New York: HarperCollins, 1999.
———. *Hija de la fortuna* (Daughter of fortune). 2d ed. Barcelona: Plaza & Janés, 1999.
———. *The Infinite Plan.* Translated by Margaret Sayers Peden. New York: HarperCollins, 1993.
———. *Paula.* Barcelona: Plaza & Janés, 1994.
Rodden, John, ed. *Conversations with Isabel Allende.* Austin: University of Texas Press, 1999.

Alvarez, Julia (1950–)
Writer
Dominican-American

Julia Alvarez is the best-known Dominican-American writer in the United States. Two of her novels, *How the García Girls Lost Their Accents* (1991) and *In the Time of the Butterflies* (1994), became national best-sellers and have been translated into several languages.

A second-generation Dominican-American, Alvarez was born in New York City into a well-to-do family who lived in both the United States and the Dominican Republic. Shortly after her birth, the family moved back to the Dominican Republic, where she attended Carol Morgan, an (American) English-language school in Santo Domingo. In

1960, the Trujillo dictatorship forced the family to flee to the United States, where Alvarez finished her education. She earned a B.A. from Middlebury College (1971) and a M.F.A. from Syracuse University (1975) and embarked on a career as a writer and college professor. She is a professor of English and creative writing at Middlebury College in Vermont, where she has taught since 1988.

Although Alvarez attained wide recognition in literary circles for her poetry when *Homecoming* (1984)—her first book-length work—appeared in print, the publication of *How the García Girls Lost Their Accents* catapulted her into the national spotlight. It was selected a Notable Book in 1992 by the American Library Association and in 1991 it received the PEN Oakland/Josephine Miles Award. The novel is based on Alvarez's own family experience, as the García family has to leave the Dominican Republic to protect themselves from the dictator. Once in the United States, the family has to adapt to a new society with a different set of values. Thus, Alvarez's major themes are the pains and tribulations of the migratory experience, as well as family and generational conflict and the ubiquitous machismo of Latin American societies. *In the Time of the Butterflies* extends Alvarez's involvement with the topic of the Trujillo dictatorship. The novel is based on the real story of the Mirabal sisters, three young women who were brutally assassinated by Trujillo's henchmen for their (and their husbands') involvement in the resistance movement. This novel was selected a Notable Book and Book of the Month Club choice in 1994. She has also recently published *¡YO!* (1997) and *In the Name of Salomé* (2000). Alvarez has also published books of poems, including *Homecoming* (1984) and *The Other Side* (1995), and a collection of essays entitled *Something to Declare* (1999).

The literary contributions of Julia Alvarez have been recognized in both the United States and the Dominican Republic, where she is considered an accomplished writer. To the U.S. public, Alvarez writes about the im-migrant experience from the particular perspective of a Latina. Alvarez is also the first Dominican-origin writer to be widely publicized in the United States. As such, she is a groundbreaker in a new literary category: the English-language Dominican literature of the diaspora. To Dominicans, Alvarez writes about repressed memories, about a time that many would rather forget. Moreover, Alvarez represents those who left, the masses of Dominicans who ventured overseas, where many of them—like Julia Alvarez—have made it big.

Ernesto Sagás

REFERENCES

Alvarez, Julia. "Vita": www.middlebury.edu/
~english/facpub/JAlv-vita.html (accessed 13 June 2000).

Behar, Ruth. "Revolutions of the Heart." *Women's Review of Books* 12.8 (May 1995): 6–7.

Luis, William. "A Search for Identity in Julia Alvarez's *How the García Girls Lost Their Accents.*" *Latinos in the U.S. Review* 1 (1994): 52–57.

Molina Morillo, Rafael. *Personalidades dominicanas 1993.* Santo Domingo: Molina Morillo & Asociados, 1993.

Novas, Himilce. "Julia Alvarez." In *The Hispanic 100: A Ranking of the Latino Men and Women Who Have Most Influenced American Thought and Culture,* edited by Himilce Novas, 426–430. New York: Carol Publishing Group, 1995.

Stavans, Ilan. "Las Mariposas." *Nation,* 7 November 1994, 552–556.

Torres-Saillant, Silvio. "History and Heroines." In *Caribbean Poetics: Toward an Aesthetics of West Indian Literature,* 242–247. New York: Cambridge University Press, 1997.

Amara, Lucine (née Lucine Armaganian) (1926–)

Opera star
Armenian-American

Soprano Lucine Amara became an authentic "American Success Story" by starring in the New York Metropolitan Opera for over forty years. She also performed in twenty-one foreign countries.

Amara was born to Kevork and Adrina Armaganian in Hartford, Connecticut, in 1926 and raised in an Armenian family atmosphere, with all of its Armenian characteristics, including singing in the Armenian Apostolic Church choir. She received her musical education in the San Francisco Conservatory and trained with the famous voice teacher Stella Eisner-Eyn.

In 1948, at the All-American Atwater-Kent Competition, in which 1,500 singers participated, Amara won first prize. That was to be the golden key to her future, as she was sent on a concert tour for two years to major European cities. When she returned with great acclaim, she joined the Metropolitan Opera company in New York City in 1950 as the Celestial Voice in *Don Carlo.* She has since played the main roles in such operas as Puccini's *La Boheme,* Offenbach's *The Tales of Hoffmann,* Tchaikovsky's *Yevgeny Onegin,* and Verdi's *Aida.* In 1957, Amara was given the honor of appearing in the Metropolitan's season opener, *Yevgeny Onegin.* When the greatest artists in the United States were invited to perform in 1962 at the opening of New York's Lincoln Center, Amara was included.

Amara has had 780 on-stage performances, 5 opening nights, 9 new productions, 57 Texaco radio broadcasts, and 56 roles in her career at the Metropolitan Opera. She has performed throughout the United States, in 33 opera houses and 25 symphony orchestras and before royalty and other dignitaries in 21 foreign countries and commonwealths, and she has sung in hundreds of recitals and concerts. Amara's name appears in music dictionaries, encyclopedias, and opera-performance histories. She has also been instrumental in the development of new voices for the opera, giving concerts and conducting master's classes. She has always included Armenian songs in her repertoire.

Amara has also been active in the Armenian community, singing in many benefit concerts for Armenian organizations. In 1999 she performed for the Armenian International Women's Association of New Jersey/New York (AIWA-NJ/NY) and was awarded a statuette of a victory maiden in recognition of her successful career. *Ararat Quarterly* magazine referred to Amara as the first American-

born Armenian to sing in Yerevan, Armenia, more than three decades ago. That 1965 tour included performances in Moscow, Leningrad, and Tbilisi. When she returned to independent Armenia, on 23 September 1991, for a special performance sponsored by the Diocese of the Armenian Church of America—celebrating her forty-first anniversary with the Met—she received a five-minute standing ovation. The trips to Armenia fulfilled a lifelong dream of hers.

Most recently, Amara served as a committee member for the successful campaign to raise $1 million for the staging of the Armenian opera *King Arshak II* (composed by Dikran Tchoukhadjian) by the San Francisco Opera in September 2001.

For more than fifty years Amara's success in the opera has been a shining example to aspiring artists all over the world.

Barlow Der Mugrdechian

REFERENCES
"AIWA-NJ/NY Honors Met Opera Star Lucine Amara." *Armenian Reporter* 32.33 (15 May 1999).
"Amara Onstage: The Operatic Career of Lucine Amara." *Opera Quarterly,* Autumn 1992.
"Dramatic Soprano, Lucine Amara, to Headline Sumptuous Buffet/Extravaganza April 1st." *Armenian Reporter* 28.24 (18 March 1995).
"Lucine Amara, Opera Star, in Series of Concerts." *Armenian Reporter* 25.712 (December 1991).
Navarsagian, Alice. *Armenian Women of the Stage.* Translated by Barlow Der Mugrdechian. Glendale, CA.: n.p., 1999.

Amaya, Dionisia (1933–)
Teacher and community activist
Honduran

Dionisia Amaya overcame considerable obstacles to acquire an education. In the process, she became a recognized leader and community service provider for the Honduran Garifuna community in New York City.

Amaya was born in 1933 in La Ceiba, Honduras, and came to the United States in 1964. A decade later, she began a long career in community work, first in an organization that provided hurricane relief for the victims of the Fifi disaster in Honduras. Amaya helped organize the Committee for Development in Honduras (the acronym for its Spanish name is COPRODH). She worked with it for two years, providing support and resources for hurricane victims as well as for the Honduran community in the United States in general. Since then, she has dedicated herself to serving her community through education.

In 1976, Amaya was a secretary when a merger left her unemployed for six months. During that time she set her goals on her own education and went to school to earn her general equivalency diploma (GED). She then went on, earning a B.A. in education and an M.A. in counseling. She became a teacher for second and sixth grades in New York City and for a time also taught reading classes. Amaya worked as a teacher and counselor for sixteen years.

While she was teaching, Amaya continued her involvement with the Garifuna community. For her, it is crucial that recent immigrants learn English and obtain an education, so that manual labor is not their only employment option. Her education enabled her to contribute significantly to her community, and she has since dedicated herself to providing that community with the same opportunities, working to educate it in all possible avenues—via the schools, the church, and the public sector. For example, in January 1989, she came together with other Garifuna women leaders for the purpose of garnering international recognition for Garifuna women's accomplishments. This group of women organized a conference, and Garifuna Women Marching in Action (Mujeres Garinagu [plural of Garifuna] en Marcha)—(MUGAMA) was born. A year later it became a nonprofit organization, and it now offers English as a second language (ESL), GED, and citizenship classes for adults in New York City. Amaya served as secretary and president of MUGAMA before becoming its executive director. She provides resources to inform and empower the Honduran Garifuna population and also teaches classes for the organization.

In 1991, MUGAMA served as one of the sponsors of the First Intercontinental Garifuna Summit Meeting at Medgar Evers College in Brooklyn, New York. This historic event brought together Garinagu from all over the United States for a cultural and political exchange of accomplishments, goals, and resources. Amaya recounts that at the summit MUGAMA passed a resolution to begin a fund for a scholarship to be given every two years to help students in college.

In addition to these activities, for twenty-two years Amaya has been an active member of the Catholic church and, in 1996, was appointed a Eucharistic minister at Lady of Mercy Church in Brooklyn.

Leticia Hernández-Linares

REFERENCES
Amaya, Dionisia. Telephone interview by author, 12 January 2000.
Flores, Justin. *The Garifuna Story, Now and Then*. Los Angeles: J. Flores, 1979.
"The Garifuna Journey." *Cultural Survival Quarterly* 20.2 (July 1996).
Garifuna Web site: www.garifuna-world.com (accessed 14 June 2000).
Gonzalez, Nancie. *Sojourners of the Caribbean: Ethnogenesis and Ethnohistory of the Garifuna.* Urbana: University of Illinois Press, 1988.
Macklin, Catherine Lynn. "Crucibles of Identity: Ritual and Symbolic Dimensions of Garifuna Ethnicity." Ph.D. diss., University of California, Berkeley, 1986.

American, Sadie (1862–1944)
Social welfare activist and educator
Jewish-American

In 1893, Sadie American helped found the philanthropic, middle-class reform organization, the National Council of Jewish Women (NCJW), of which she later became executive secretary. In her thirties she held positions in dozens of social welfare, charitable, and educational institutions, among them the presidency of the New York Section of the NCJW and of the Consumers' League of New York State (1893–1894). She also directed the Woman's Municipal League in New York City and was chair of its Tenement House Committee (1893–1894).

American was born in Chicago in 1862, the daughter of Oscar L. American, a German-Jewish immigrant, and Amelia Smith. Little is known of her childhood, but she was educated in Chicago public schools. In 1896 she became president of the League for Religious Fellowship in Chicago, where she also served as a director of the Cook County League of Women's Clubs. She was interested in promoting general education as well as Jewish education and in 1897–1898 served on the executive committee of the Committee of One Hundred to revise laws regulating education in Illinois. Between 1899 and 1903 she was a member of the Public Education Association's Committee on Night School and Social Centers.

American's most important work, beginning in 1903, was to help protect immigrant women and girls arriving in the United States. She helped raise funds to establish a "complete chain of protection" for "our immigrant sisters," including the posting of women agents at the ports of entry. Her efforts enabled the NCJW to extend aid, advice, and vocational training to tens of thousands of immigrant women and children. The NCJW also established social clubs for these immigrants. American noticed a growing incidence of prostitution in the immigrant Jewish community and increasing claims about Jewish participation, as perpetrators and victims, in the "white slave trade." Worried about anti-Semitism, American tried to counter these exaggerated charges, while also striving to stamp out Jewish involvement. She was the U.S. delegate to both the Jewish International Conference on the Suppression of Traffic in Girls and Women in London in 1910 and the International White Slave Traffic Conference in Madrid, also held in 1910.

By various public means, American attacked the sexual double standard and advocated treating the "whole question of prostitution differently" by emphasizing the poverty of prostitutes and by holding their male patrons accountable. In 1913 she became a founder—and for a short time the president—of the Lakeview Home for Girls on Staten Island, which hoped to "reclaim" young female first offenders.

Most Jewish philanthropic organizations were controlled by men, but Sadie American, along with other women of the NCJW, took greater responsibility for the welfare of Jewish women immigrants and their children. In so doing, she not only helped the less fortunate but also found useful and rewarding work for herself and helped redefine acceptable behavior for women.

American never married, and after being forced out of the NCJW in 1914 for the "self-righteous defense" of her "controversial" opinions, she almost disappears from the historical record. She died alone in 1944.

Gerald Sorin

REFERENCES
Baum, Charlotte, Paula Hyman, and Sonya Michel. *The Jewish Woman in America.* New York: Dial Press, 1976.
Marcus, Jacob Rader. *The American Jewish Woman: A Documentary History.* New York: Ktav Publishing Co., 1981.
Rogow, Faith. *"Gone to Another Meeting": The National Council of Jewish Women, 1893–1993.* Tuscaloosa: University of Alabama Press, 1993.
Sochen, June. *Consecrate Every Day: The Public Lives of Jewish American Women, 1880–1980.* Albany, NY: State University of New York Press, 1981.

Amir, Sara (née Sarayeh Amir) (1949–)

Scientist and community and political activist
Iranian

An active resident of Los Angeles for nineteen years, Sara Amir was the first Iranian-American to run for statewide political office in California: as lieutenant governor on the Green Party ticket in 1998. She is a passionate advocate of environmental issues and women's rights.

Sarayeh (she adopted the name Sara Amir in 1992) and her twin sister were born in Tehran in 1949. As a girl and as an excellent student, she was from a very young age outspoken and committed to challenging sex role norms that limited her budding scientific mind.

Amir was passionate about her education and graduated with honors from Tehran University, earning a B.S. in biology in 1970. She worked for the Tehran Regional Water Board as a microbiologist before coming to the United States to continue her education. In 1976 she received her master's degree in environmental engineering from the University of Southern California. She returned to Iran to take part in the struggles against the Islamic Republic in 1979 and emerged as a leader among her female coworkers. As the political situation became more repressive, she says, "I ran for my life," having witnessed the "torture and killing of many people."

Arriving in Los Angeles, Amir began working as an environmental engineer at the California Air Resources Board and since May 1990 has been overseeing toxic cleanups. Becoming a U.S. citizen in 1987, she has continued her activism and commitment to "grassroots, common sense democracy," leading sexual harassment workshops at the University of California, Los Angeles (UCLA) as well as sponsoring events and lecturing in Iranian communities throughout California on such issues as campaign finance laws, electoral reform, affirmative action, and domestic violence in immigrant communities.

Amir became a Green Party candidate for lieutenant governor in 1998. As an immigrant and a woman, she has been very active in advocating issues related to strengthening bilingual education and the reinstatement of affirmative action in California. Her own experiences of discrimination and exclusion have made her very vocal and outspoken about injustices experienced by immigrants, minorities, and women. She also wants to see democratic electoral reforms, tougher enforcement of environmental laws, universal health care, equal pay for women, and more emphasis on math and science programs for girls in elementary and high school. In 2000 she ran for the California Forty-second Assembly District seat on the Green Party ticket but lost.

Particularly in the Iranian community in Los Angeles, Amir has been active on local Persian radio stations (such as IRTV), in Persian monthly magazines (notably *Rah-e-Zendegi*), addressing issues of women's rights and civic participation, and frequently on the British Broadcasting Corporation (BBC) and the Voice of America Farsi program—broadcast to Iran—on issues concerning Iranians abroad. She has organized women's support and consciousness-raising groups, focusing on such topics as sexual harassment and work conditions among immigrant women and family dynamics and domestic violence among Iranian-immigrant families, in addition to workshops directly focused on empowerment of women both in the family and in the public sphere. She remains painfully aware of the cultural displacement and isolation many immigrant women from the Middle East experience, particularly in relation to intergenerational conflict and changes in family dynamics that have adversely affected some Iranian women. In line with this concern, Amir is also very active in social service agencies, promoting more cultural sensitivity to the needs of different immigrant populations. Although viewed as threatening to some men and women because of her demands for change, she has been considered a role model for women and young Iranian-Americans, in both Iran and the United States.

Amir lives in Los Angeles with her husband.

Arlene Dallalfar

References
Amir, Sara. Candidate Statements—Lieutenant Governor. *California Voter Pamphlet,* 3 November 1998.
———. Interview by author, 21 January 2000.
———. "Lieutenant Governor." *San Francisco Bay Guardian,* 17–21 October 1998.
Amir, Sara, articles about. In *Rah-e-Zendegi,* 866 (6 March 1998), 882 (16 October 1998), and 918 (3 March 2000), and in *Tehran International Weekly Magazine,* no. 74 (17 April 1998) and no. 87 (17 July 1998).
Bozorghemr, Mehdi. "Diaspora in the Postrevolutionary Period." In *Encyclopedia Iranica* 7, edited by Ehsan Yarshater, 380–383. Costa Mesa, CA: Mazda Publishers, 1995.
———. "Iranians." In *American Immigrant Cultures: Builders of a Nation,* edited by David Levinson

and Melvin Ember, 442–448. New York: Macmillan, 1997.

Bozorghemr, Mehdi, Claudia Der-Martirosian, and Georges Sabagh. "Middle Easterners: A New Kind of Immigrant." In *Ethnic Los Angeles,* edited by Roger Waldinger and Mehdi Bozorgmehr, 345–378. New York: Russell Sage, 1996.

Dallalfar, Arlene. "The Iranian Ethnic Economy in Los Angeles: Gender and Entrepreneurship." In *Family and Gender among American Muslims: Issues Facing Middle Eastern Immigrants and Their Descendants,* edited by Barbara C. Aswad and Barbara Bilgé, 107–128. Philadelphia: Temple University Press, 1996.

Ammann, Othmar H. (1879–1965)
Civil engineer and bridge builder
Swiss

Othmar Ammann played an extraordinary role in the construction of the George Washington and Verrazano Bridges in New York City. He was also prominent in the building of the Golden Gate Bridge in San Francisco as well as several other well-known bridges.

Born in Feuerthalen, Schaffhausen Canton, Ammann grew up in Kilchberg, Zurich Canton, to which his middle-class family had moved in 1885. After basic schooling he completed his professional studies at the Swiss Federal Polytechnic Institute in Zurich (1902) and gained experience in steel building in Brugg, Switzerland, and Frankfurt, Germany. In 1904 he moved to the United States and worked in engineering offices in New York, Philadelphia, and Chicago. In 1912 he joined the office of Gustave Lindenthal, then engaged in building the Hell Gate Bridge in New York City. After working for others for a few years, he rejoined Lindenthal in the newly formed Hudson River Bridge Company in 1920, which was planning a twenty-lane car and railroad bridge crossing the Hudson into Manhattan at Fifty-seventh Street. When the project encountered opposition owing to cost and concerns about its feasibility, Ammann opened his own engineering office.

Teaming up with George Silzer, who was elected governor of New Jersey in 1922, Ammann developed plans for a 3,000-foot sus-pension span bridge over the Hudson River, from Fort Lee, New Jersey, into northern Manhattan at 179th Street. Between 1922 and 1924 Ammann tirelessly lobbied citizen groups and leaders of New Jersey, New York, and southern Connecticut for his project. It was approved by the federal government and state and local bodies in 1925 and entrusted to the newly created Port Authority, with Ammann as the project's engineer. Groundbreaking took place in 1927, and the George Washington Bridge was completed in October 1931, ahead of schedule and at a cost lower than had been projected. From 1930 to 1937, Ammann served as the Port Authority's chief engineer and, from 1937 to 1939, as its director of engineering. He served on the board of engineers reviewing plans for San Francisco's Golden Gate Bridge and was the principal investigator of the collapse of the Tacoma Narrows suspension bridge near Seattle, writing a highly praised report for the Federal Works Administration (comparable to one he had written in 1908 after examining the collapse of a cantilever bridge in Quebec). Among other bridge constructions his firm supervised in the New York region, in 1954 Ammann and Whitney planned and oversaw the building of the Verrazano Narrows Bridge. It opened in 1964 and, with its 4,200 feet length, has the world's longest suspension span.

Amman's works have been marked by technical excellence and functionality as well as esthetic beauty: The George Washington, Bronx-Whitestone, and Verrazano Bridges are monuments to his engineering as well as artistic genius. He was, in Robert Moses's words, "at once a mathematician, forerunner of the industrial revolution and a dreamer in steel." His internationally recognized structures shaped the possibilities for people's employment and recreation in two states. They also assured the triumph of the automobile in the region.

Leo Schelbert

REFERENCES
Doig, Jameson W. "Politics and the Engineering Mind: O. H. Ammann and the Hidden Story of the George Washington Bridge." In *Yearbook of*

German-American Studies 1990 25, 151–199. Lawrence, KS: Society for German-American Studies.

Durrer, Margot Ammann. "Memories of My Father." *Swiss-American Historical Society Newsletter* 15 (June 1979): 26–33.

Rastorfer, Darl. *Six Bridges: The Legacy of Othmar Ammann.* New Haven: Yale University Press, 2000.

Stüssi, Fritz. *Othmar Ammann. Sein Beitrag zur Entwicklung des Brückenbaues.* Basel, Switzerland: Birkhäuser, 1974 [contains some of O. Ammann's texts in English and a listing of his works].

Widmer, Urs C. "Othmar Hermann Ammann, 1879–1965. His Way to Great Bridges. With a Bibliography." *Swiss-American Historical Society Newsletter* 15 (June 1979): 4–24, 34–42.

Aratani, George (1917–)
Entrepreneur and philanthropist
Japanese-American

A bilingual entrepreneur, George Tetsuo Aratani started three extremely successful corporations after World War II. He also supports many Asian American community organizations.

Aratani was born in 1917, in Guadalupe, California. His father, Setsuo, a Japanese immigrant who came to the United States in 1905, had become one of the leading farmers of the central coast area and had expanded his business empire to include a multitude of side businesses, from packing sheds to hog farms.

Setsuo and Yoshiko Aratani's only son, George grew up in a relatively privileged setting, learning how to run various aspects of a business. He also learned about baseball, for his father, a big baseball fan, sponsored a local team. Young Aratani became a star player at Santa Maria High School. Upon graduation, he was sent to Keio University in Japan. In addition to starring on its baseball team, Aratani learned Japanese language and culture, one of the keys to his later success. But after his mother died and his father fell ill, Aratani returned and enrolled at Stanford University. His father died in 1940, leaving his entire business to his son.

World War II was a turning point in Aratani's life, for he and his stepmother, along with all other Japanese Americans on the West Coast, were sent to detention camps, in his case to dusty Gila River, Arizona. He also faced myriad legal and business problems arising from his father's death, the sudden internment, and his own limited knowledge of his father's businesses; much of the family enterprise was lost during the war. In 1944 Aratani married Sakaye Inouye, and they left the camp for Fort Snelling, Minnesota, where Aratani joined the faculty of the Military Intelligence Service Language School in order to teach Japanese to American soldiers.

Three years later, Aratani left Fort Snelling and, like a number of Nisei, saw postwar Japan as a great business opportunity. Using his Japanese-language skills and the contacts made during his time with the Military Intelligence Service, he began a trading company called American Commercial, Inc., eventually finding a niche selling Japanese-made chinaware with contemporary designs for the American market of suburban families looking for a less expensive alternative to fine china. Soon, the renamed Mikasa Corporation was multimillion-dollar company and a household name brand. Not content to stay in only one business, in the 1950s and 1960s Aratani started AMCO, a medical supply company that brought modern American equipment to Japan. Later, he started Kenwood, an electronics company that sold Japanese-made high-fidelity equipment in the United States. Both also became very successful enterprises.

His fortune secured, Aratani turned to philanthropy in the 1980s and 1990s. In 1994, he and his wife established the Aratani Foundation, which has provided major funding to myriad Japanese-American and Asian American organizations in Los Angeles and across the country, including East-West Players, the Japanese American National Museum, Keiro Homes, and the National Japanese American Memorial Foundation.

Brian Niiya

REFERENCES
Hirahara, Naomi. *The Road to Mikasa: The Life and Trials of Nisei Entrepreneur George Aratani.* Los Angeles: Japanese American National Museum,

forthcoming [based on the museum's collection of interviews, photographs, letters, and other documents].

Arce, Elia (1961–)

Performance artist, director, and writer
Costa Rican–American

Elia Arce has received prestigious grants from the Rockefeller Foundation, the National Endowment for the Arts, and the J. Paul Getty Foundation. She has been working since the mid-1980s on creative projects that incorporate and represent disempowered communities.

Arce was born in Los Angeles when her father was studying at the University of Southern California, but she was raised in Costa Rica. She studied theater arts and dance at the University of Costa Rica and was also involved with solidarity efforts for El Salvador and Nicaragua. Holding dual Costa Rican and U.S. citizenship, at eighteen Arce returned to the United States so that she could pursue a career in the arts. Costa Rica had become a difficult place to be a woman involved in art and politics.

Arce traveled to New York, where she became involved with the Latin American Workshop, an organization that housed a theater space and provided offices for Central American solidarity groups. While volunteering at the workshop, she became involved with Skylight Pictures. At first she worked on a volunteer basis for such films as *El Salvador: Another Vietnam;* then she was hired as a production coordinator on the feature film *Latino.* She began to learn how to make films and in 1983 participated in a film workshop at New York University. Later, she went back to school; she graduated from UCLA's Motion Picture and Television Fine Arts Program in 1994.

After working on numerous films and making three of her own cinematic shorts, Arce moved into performance art. Her aims are to portray the lives of actual people and to offer a voice to the disempowered. She has directed and performed pieces in theaters and conferences, such as the National Conference of Women and HIV/AIDS, and at nontraditional sites, including the Clinica del Pueblo in Washington, D.C. While in residency at Banff Center for the Performing Arts in Canada, she directed the housekeeping staff in performance works.

In 1989, Arce became part of the Los Angeles Poverty Department (LAPD), a group that raises awareness about social issues and does performances about them with the people whom the issues affect. For example, the group worked on Skid Row in Los Angeles for several years with homeless people and sex workers. Arce has also worked with Latina women living with HIV in her show *Don't Tell Anybody/No Le Digas a Nadie.* The relationship of humans to power structures is the underlying concern in much of her work: She sees her community in a larger context as those struggling with power structures. Yet Arce has also focused on what identity and culture mean to her as a Central American immigrant woman. In a seminal piece, "Mom," she redefines the ideal of motherhood in Latina/o culture.

Arce has performed internationally and throughout the United States. She is an important voice in performance art and film and has maintained her dedication to her various communities through being a voice for them as well as providing them a voice.

Leticia Hernández-Linares

REFERENCES

Arce, Elia. *I Just Hope That My Body Rots at the Sound of a Stretch,* 16mm, color, 10 min.

———. Interview by author, February 24, 2000.

———. "Leche Que Nutre—Leche Venenosa" (Milk that nourishes—Poisonous milk). In *Out of Character: Rants, Raves and Monologues from Today's Top Performance Artists,* edited by Mark Russell, 23–31. New York: Bantam Books, 1997.

———. "Mom." *Heresies: A Journal of Ideas,* no. 27 (1993): 28.

———. "My Grandmother Never Passed Away." In *Let's Get It On: The Politics of Black Performance,* edited by Catherine Ugwu, 109–111. Seattle: Bay Press, 1995.

———. *Unas Cuantas Punzaditas* (A few little sharp pains), 16mm, black & white, 5 min.

———. *Unpack it!* video 8, color, 15 min.

Gutierrez, Eric. "Healing Stages." *Latina,* November 1999, 84.

Archipenko, Alexander (1887–1964)

Sculptor
Ukrainian

Alexander Archipenko was an artist who revolutionized modern sculpture, achieving great renown in Europe and the United States. The diversity of his work, including that based on Ukrainian themes, represented a major contribution to twentieth-century art.

Archipenko was born on 30 May 1887 in Kyiv, Ukraine. His grandfather, Antony, was an icon painter, and his father, Porfyry, an inventor and professor of mechanical engineering at the Kyiv University. Creativity and innovation became a trademark of Archipenko's life. His peripatetic art education started in 1902 at the Kiev Institute of Fine Arts, but he was expelled after three years and went to Moscow and Paris. In 1910, he opened his studio at the Beehive (La Ruche), an avant-garde artists' quarter near Montparnasse. He was impressed by the new style of painting by Picasso and Braque, known as cubism. His *Cirque Medrano* series of works in 1912 embodied the tenets of cubism, carving Archipenko's mark in the history of modern art. *The Juggler* of that group was the first multimedia construction in modern sculpture—wood, glass, metal wire, including a movable arm, a precursor of the kinetic art. *Woman Combing Her Hair* (1915) became his "signature," exemplifying the elemental characteristics of his sculptures—including empty space as part of the visual reality—which revolutionized modern sculpture. Some consider the years 1910 to 1921 his most creative period.

Archipenko's first individual exhibit, in Hagen, Germany, in 1910, brought him international recognition. He then exhibited in Berlin and Paris, and six of his sculptures were at the famous 1913 Armory Show in New York City. During World War I, he lived in France but afterward moved to Berlin and there married a fellow sculptor, Angelica Bruno-Schmitz (she died in 1957; in 1960 he married Frances Grey). In 1923, the thirty-six-year-old artist immigrated with his wife to the United States, becoming an American citizen in 1928 and living chiefly in New York City. Around twenty of his works that remained in Germany were later destroyed by the Nazis as decadent creations.

In the United States, Archipenko continued his sculpture work largely in the abstract and surrealist genre, although from time to time he produced other types of art, including a series of lithographs. He had about 150 exhibits throughout the United States and many in other countries. Besides his artistic creative work, he lectured widely throughout the United States. He had a studio in Woodstock, New York, where he also taught.

In his art Archipenko was universal, but privately he never forgot his ethnic roots, although he was not a community activist. Nevertheless, he always reached for some contacts with Ukrainians wherever he was, and when the Ukrainian-American community sponsored a Ukrainian Pavilion at the World Exhibition in Chicago in 1933, he sent his works to be displayed, making it one of the best attended places at the exhibition. Although his works are in numerous museums and collections around the world, only a few are in Ukraine.

Archipenko died in New York City in February 1964. In 1969–1971, the Smithsonian Institution organized a retrospective exhibition of his works, which also toured a number of European countries.

Daria Markus

REFERENCES

Archipenko, Alexander, et al. *Fifty Creative Years, 1908–1958.* New York: TEKHNE, 1960.

Karshan, Donald, ed. *Archipenko: International Visionary.* Washington, DC: Smithsonian Institution Press, National Collection of Fine Arts, 1968.

———. *Archipenko: Themes and Variations.* Daytona, FL: Museum of Arts and Science, 1989.

Michaelsen, Katherine Jánsky, and Nehama Gruink. *Alexander Archipenko: A Centennial Tribute.* New York: Universe Books, 1986.

Arnaz, Desi (né Desiderio Alberto Arnaz y de Archa III) (1917–1986)
Television star and producer
Cuban

Desi Arnaz, performer, musician, and comedian, made television history with *I Love Lucy,* innovating production techniques and legitimizing the Cuban male image for millions of viewers. The show remains in syndication in more than eighty countries.

Desiderio Alberto Arnaz y de Archa III was born in 1917 to a wealthy Cuban landowner. The political turmoil of the early 1930s on the island encouraged his mother to immigrate with her young son to the United States. Hardship did not make Arnaz, then sixteen, abandon his goal of becoming a musician. He joined Xavier Cugat's band in 1937 and even put together his own rumba band. Three years later, he appeared in the stage and movie versions of *Too Many Girls* and met a red-headed, vivacious actress, Lucille Ball. They eloped.

For a decade, Ball stayed in Hollywood making movies and Arnaz toured with his band. The couple wanted to work together in a TV series, but the Columbia Broadcasting System (CBS) thought that because Desi was Cuban it would not work. Lucy and Desi set out to prove them wrong, going on tour, performing before live audiences, and pouring their total savings—$5,000—into producing a pilot. When *I Love Lucy* premiered on 15 October 1951, it immediately became one of the most popular shows on television. In its six-year run, it was number one for four years, never ranking lower than third, and won more than 200 awards, including 5 Emmys. The couple had turned their $5,000 investment into millions.

Arnaz built the character of Ricky Ricardo precisely on the one characteristic CBS had seen as his worst flaw: being Cuban. He cultivated his accent, played the macho, jealous, cigar-smoking, music-loving, soft-hearted husband with gusto. He was a pioneer, convincing the show's sponsor that Lucy should have their baby on the show. The episode drew a then-record 44 million viewers. Arnaz changed for-

ever the way TV comedies were made, shooting each episode on film, with three cameras, in front of live audiences, so that it could be rebroadcast many times.

Nonetheless, in 1960 they ended their twenty-year marriage. Arnaz remarried in 1963, but after his second wife, Edith, died of cancer in 1985, he spent the rest of his life struggling with alcoholism. With the help of his son, he finally stopped drinking. He died on 2 December 1986, at age sixty-nine.

In his last years, Arnaz rekindled his links with the Cuban community and was featured as the king of the traditional Calle Ocho Carnival in Miami. His contribution to the Cuban community in the United States is invaluable. Years before the mass exodus of Cubans began in 1959, Arnaz had become a household word in U.S. homes. He refused to mask his ethnic attributes and succeeded by playing himself, indeed stressing his Cubanness. It is no small tribute to his country of origin.

Arnaz, having come with nothing and achieved so much, was an inspiration to successful Cuban-American stars, such as Gloria Estefan and Andy García, and to ordinary Cubans as well. He legitimized their cultural heritage and the belief that it was acceptable to preserve it along with their new U.S. identity.

Uva de Aragón

REFERENCES
Arnaz, Desi. *A Book.* New York: Warner Books, 1976.
"Ball, Lucille." *Encarta Online Encyclopedia 2000:* encarta.msn.com/find/Concise.asp?ti= 06E3C000 (accessed 21 June 2000).
"Desi Arnaz Tribute Page" (1997): members.aol.com/CHICKA2/desi.html (accessed 21 June 2000).
"Desi Arnaz, TV Pioneer, Is Dead at Sixty-nine." *New York Times,* 3 December 1986, D26.

Asbury, Francis (1745–1816)
Preacher and founder of the Methodist Episcopal Church
English

Francis Asbury was more responsible than any other person for bringing Methodism to

America. He founded the Methodist Episcopal Church and helped it grow into a major American religious denomination.

Francis Asbury was born in Staffordshire, England, the son of farmer Joseph Asbury and his wife, Elizabeth Rogers. His mother was deeply religious, taught her son to read the Bible at an early age, and took him to Methodist prayer meetings. He quit school at the age of twelve because of his brutal schoolmaster, but his lack of formal education did not prevent him from becoming one of the most influential religious leaders in early America.

At a prayer meeting in 1760, the fifteen-year-old Asbury felt overwhelmed by his own sinfulness and dedicated his life to God and the cause of Methodism. Soon, he was leading prayer meetings himself. By eighteen he was a local preacher, and by twenty-one he was traveling throughout the county as a minister. Then, for five years, he was appointed as an itinerant minister throughout southern England. At a meeting in Bristol in 1771, John Wesley himself called for volunteers to preach in the American colonies, and Francis Asbury eagerly accepted, arriving later that year.

Asbury's early years in America were dominated by the growing tension between Britain and the colonies and the Revolutionary War itself. He attempted to stay out of politics and cared little about people's own earthly allegiances, though he remained loyal to his family and friends in England. Thus, Asbury and the growing number of Methodists in America were often suspected of being Tory spies or sympathizers. When he refused to take a loyalty oath in Maryland, he had to flee to Delaware for his safety. Such hostility convinced Asbury, as well as Methodists in England, that the movement would have to split along national lines, which happened officially in 1784. He was already recognized as the leader of American Methodism and became Bishop Asbury, superintendent of the Methodist Episcopal Church.

In this capacity Asbury extended his preaching circuit and, quite literally, "lived in the saddle," as he traveled continually to preach, as much as 6,000 miles per year. By the end of his life he had traveled over 250,000 miles and had preached an estimated 17,000 sermons. Owing in large part to these efforts, the church grew to include more than 2,500 preachers and 140,000 parishioners in the United States by the time of his death. Although the continual travel in all weather conditions wore down his health, he never let up on his demanding preaching schedule. Consequently, he never married or had a real home, for he did not stay in one place more than a few days. And he never became a U.S. citizen—nor did he ever return to England—because he considered himself a citizen of heaven.

Asbury died in Spotsylvania, Virginia, in 1816. Asbury College and Asbury Theological Seminary, in Wilmore, Kentucky, and Asbury Park, New Jersey, are named in his honor.

William E. Van Vugt

REFERENCES

Ludwig, Charles. *Francis Asbury: God's Circuit Rider.* Milford, MI: Mott Media, 1984.

Rudolph, L. C. *Francis Asbury.* Nashville: Abingdon Press, 1966.

Strickland, William Peter. *The Pioneer Bishop, or the Life and Times of Francis Asbury.* New York: Carlton and Porter, 1858.

Aubuchon, William E. (1885–1971), and Aubuchon, William E., Jr. (1916–)

Entrepreneur and business executive, respectively
French Canadian and
Franco-American, respectively

William Aubuchon and his son of the same name both achieved prominence in the retail hardware business. The father, born in the Province of Quebec, Canada, was the oldest child of a widowed mother who immigrated to the United States, desperate to eke out a living for her four fatherless children. William E., Sr., had been barely seven when his father died of pneumonia in 1892. In 1908, after working in various mills in both Fitchburg and Leominster, Massachusetts, he became a partner in a hardware store in Fitchburg's "Little Canada." By the time of his death in 1971, the father had bequeathed a retail empire that was to grow to 147 stores throughout the Northeast under the leadership of his son William E., Jr.

From destitute adolescent, William E. Aubuchon, Sr., rose to ownership of a retail empire focused on serving the individual homeowner. Service to community, church, and fellowman has been the creed of both father and son. This philosophy has guided them not only to success in business but also to prominence at both the local and state levels. The immigrant father who saw the United States as a land of opportunity was emulated by his son, who has remained firmly grounded in his New England community.

Although widowed at the age of thirty-two, Georgianna L'Abbée Aubuchon had managed, against all odds, to squirrel away the $2,000 received from the sale of the family farm in Canada. Even though her eldest son, William, inherited only one-fourth of that sum—the rest going to his three siblings—it was the mother's foresight that enabled him, early on, to become a business partner in a small hardware store in the Cleghorn section of Fitchburg. When his partner retired, William took over the ownership of the store. He quickly enlarged his operation by investing in those of his employees who gave evidence of managerial ability. By supplying some of the capital and inventory to these promising men, he became the owner of nine stores by 1932, incorporating the Aubuchon Hardware Company in 1934, during the depths of the Great Depression; the firm would own ninety-five hardware stores by the time he died in 1971. Following his death he was referred to as a "giant" in the field. And during his lifetime, he had also been active in neighborhood affairs, served on Fitchburg's Planning and Public Welfare Boards, in addition to having been a director of four financial institutions.

Aubuchon's first clients were immigrants like himself. As his customer base grew, he never lost sight of his reliance on them and al-

ways remained close to his people, his parish, and his city. His son followed in his footsteps—taking over as president of the company in 1950, a few years after his wartime service in the Army Signal Intelligence Corps. Aubuchon, Jr., was closely linked to the Credit Union Movement—patterned on the Quebec model instituted by Alphonse Desjardins in the early twentieth century—and he became director of three countywide banking institutions. Moving beyond the local level, he became one of the founders of the Massachusetts State College board of trustees, serving as its chairman in 1973–1974. He also chaired the first lay-cleric board of trustees of his alma mater, Assumption College, from 1972 to 1980. Fitchburg State College conferred upon him an honorary doctorate in the humanities in 1974, and Worcester State College did the same in 1978, praising his "unparalleled initiative and foresight" as a founding trustee of the Massachusetts State College System and founder of the Massachusetts State College Building Authority.

Like his father, Aubuchon, Jr., has been a faithful member of his church. In 1983, he was invested as a knight of Malta, an order that is known for its charitable works worldwide on behalf of the sick and the poor. He is also a knight grand cross of the Holy Sepulchre. In addition, service to community in his case also includes his ethnic community. Founder of the Administrative Council of Assumption College's French Institute, he guided it with a sure hand, all the while donating generously to establish it on a solid financial footing. In recognition of his benefactions, an award was instituted in his name in 1995. The text lauded him for "his personal integrity, his interest in the history of the French in North America, and his ability to communicate his own belief in the validity and importance of the existence of such an institute." The Harmony Club of Worcester granted him its highly prized Lafayette Award in 1975 on the occasion of the club's fiftieth anniversary "as a perfect symbol of what the Harmony Club stands for—service."

Aubuchon, Jr., who inherited his father's flair for business, built a retail empire upon the rock-solid foundation bequeathed by his father, for their success was based upon an innate sense of retail marketing. When the son retired in 1993, after being its president for forty-three years, the W. E. Aubuchon Company, the largest privately owned retail hardware corporation in the United States, was celebrating its eighty-fifth year of success and operating 136 stores. Father and son had proven themselves to be a winning combination. And the Aubuchon story continues apace in the capable hands of the next generation, which has acquired new stores while remaining true to the Aubuchon formula for success in the retail hardware business: Know your customer base, position yourself with an eye to the future, and provide the best wares at the lowest possible price.

Claire Quintal

REFERENCES

"Aubuchon Strengthens Northeast Base." *National Home Center News,* 1 January 1997.

Aubuchon, William E., Jr. Interviews by author, periodically, the latest in October 1999.

"The Biggest 'Little Giant.'" *Hardware Retailer,* January 1972.

"Franco-Americans—We Remember." Documentary program produced by New Hampshire Public Television, Summer and Fall 1999.

"Hardware Store Chains." *Home Improvement Market,* August 1997.

"Life Isn't All Hardware." *Worcester Telegram and Evening Gazette,* 9 July 1967.

"So You Want More Stores?" *Hardware Age,* 7 July 1966.

Badovinac, John (1907–1981)
President, Croatian Fraternal Union
Croatian-American

John Badovinac achieved recognition within the Croatian community in the United States and in Croatia as a major leader of the Croatian fraternal movement in the United States. He also actively promoted Croatian culture in the United States.

Badovinac was born of Croatian parentage in Calumet, Michigan. His father died before his birth, and he was raised by his mother and stepfather, a miner. After the big 1914 copper strike, the family left Michigan, eventually settling in Cleveland in 1923. Badovinac studied business administration and accounting in night schools. He joined Lodge 21 of the Croatian Fraternal Union (CFU) in 1924 and became one of the organizers and secretary of "Pioneers" English-speaking Lodge 663, one of the CFU's first lodges organized for the children of Croatian immigrants. He served as lodge officer for fifty years, editing the Pioneers' *Monthly Bulletin* for twelve.

After he lost his job as an accountant in 1931 because of the Great Depression, he joined the clerical staff in the CFU home office in Pittsburgh. Soon, he became director of the Junior Order, an organization that served the needs of immigrants' children within the CFU. He held that post until elected national secretary of the CFU in 1947; he was elected president of the CFU High Trial Board in 1955 and, twelve years later, president of the CFU. As director of the Junior Order, he had launched the CFU's *Ju-*

nior Magazine and had organized the first CFU junior convention. He also cochaired the 1939 CFU membership campaign, which brought in 10,000 new members, and in 1951, as national secretary, he initiated convention reforms that saved the CFU thousands of dollars.

When Badovinac became national president of the CFU, its 100,000 members were mostly Americans of Croatian descent. (There were also lodges in Canada.) During his presidency, a most difficult period in the CFU's history, political differences within the society as a result of the situation in Croatia and Yugoslavia reached the violent stage, resulting in attacks and threats to CFU officers, including Badovinac. Right-wing political-émigré groups opposed even cultural contacts with Croatia, then part of Communist Yugoslavia. Moreover, Badovinac, as CFU functionary and president, visited Yugoslavia many times, which did not please those groups.

Nonetheless, Badovinac actively promoted Croatian culture in the United States. In the late 1920s, he had organized the *Croatian Radio Hour* in Cleveland and subsequently hosted his own radio program for three years. He was a regular contributor to the CFU official organ, the *Zajedničar*, writing particularly about episodes in Croatian or Croatian-American history, pieces that were widely read and used as historical references. He also wrote about his travels to Croatia, the Holy Land, and to Croatian settlements in the United States.

For his contributions to ethnic heritage and culture and his extensive writings on Croatian and Croatian-American history, he received the Heritage Award from the Slavic Educational Society in Pittsburgh. Moreover, Badovinac attended all of the CFU's conventions, from the first one, held in Cleveland in 1926, until his death in 1981.

Matjaž Klemenčič

REFERENCES
"About JayBee." *Zajedničar* (Croatian fraternal union), 25 February 1981, 2.

Čizmić, Ivan. *History of the Croatian Fraternal Union of America 1894–1994.* Zagreb: Golden Marketing, 1994.

Luketich, Bernard M. "JayBee Passes Away in Florida." *Zajedničar* (Croatian fraternal union), 18 February 1981, 1, 4.

Prpić, Jure. *Hrvati u Americi.* (Croats in America). Zagreb: Hrvatska Matica Iseljenika, 1998.

Balanchine, George (né Georges Melitonovitch Balanchivadze) (1904–1983)

Choreographer
Russian

George Balanchine was born Georges Melitonovitch Balanchivadze in St. Petersburg, Russia, in 1904. He established himself as one of Europe's foremost choreographers before coming to the United States in 1934. Here he became the country's leading choreographer, defining the American-style ballet.

Balanchine's father, Meliton Balanchivadze, was a composer born in Kutais, Georgia, on the east coast of the Black Sea. Balanchine said: "We Georgians are not Russians in culture, not at all. We are Mediterranean people, like Italians." His mother, Maria Nikolayevna Vassilyeva, was Russian and she wanted one of her children to be a ballet dancer. In 1914, when Balanchine was nine, he and his older sister, Tamara, auditioned for the Maryinsky School in St. Petersburg. Only he was accepted. The school survived World War I and under the Soviet Union was state sponsored; thus young Balanchivadze's training was scarcely interrupted.

In 1924 Balanchivadze was part of a small group that toured Europe as the Soviet State Dancers. He remained in Western Europe, joining the Serge Diaghilev Ballet Company as a dancer and choreographer. He changed his name to Balanchine and made a name for himself as a choreographer. When he choreographed a dance to Igor Stravinsky's *Apollon Musagéte* in 1928, he felt he had reached a turning point. He had choreographed a ballet to music without a narrative story line. The dance was a hit, and since then the "abstract,"

or plotless, ballet has become a significant part of the ballet repertoire.

Balanchine came to the United States at the end of 1933 at the invitation of Lincoln Kirstein, who invited him to found a ballet school and a company. The school and company changed names and homes several times in the ensuing years. First called the School of American Ballet, it eventually became the New York City Ballet, with a permanent home at Lincoln Center. In the intervening years, Balanchine was associated with the Metropolitan Opera and also went to Hollywood to choreograph dances for the film industry.

In 1954 Balanchine choreographed his first full-evening ballet, a version of *The Nutcracker.* In 1962 he toured the Soviet Union with his New York City Ballet. It was his first visit since 1924. On that tour, he directed his second full-evening ballet, *A Midsummer Night's Dream.*

Balanchine continued working on plotless ballet and in 1967 directed *Jewels,* the first full-evening plotless ballet. It was first performed at the Saratoga Performing Arts Center in Saratoga Springs, New York. During his tenure as artistic director, Balanchine choreographed all or part of most of the ballets produced by the New York City Ballet. Consistent with his childhood training in music, Balanchine appreciated good music and especially enjoyed setting it to dance without feeling that it needed a story line. Dance, he thought, like music, did not need words to be understood.

Although Balanchine was not active within the Russian-American community, it has been said that he was a devout Russian Orthodox and that, despite not possessing any aristocratic lineage so common among many Russian émigrés, he was well regarded by them. Balanchine died in April 1983.

Keith P. Dyrud

REFERENCES

McDonagh, Don, ed. *George Balanchine.* Boston: Twayne Publishers, 1983.

Taper, Bernard. *Balanchine, a Biography.* Berkeley: University of California Press, 1996.

———. *Portrait of Mr. B.: Photographs of George Balanchine,* with an essay by Lincoln Kirstein. New York: Viking Press, 1984.

Bambace, Angela (1898–1975)

*Labor organizer, civil rights activist,
and union official
Italian-American*

Angela Bambace, champion of workers' rights and organizer of the 1919 New York City needle workers' strike, helped establish the International Ladies' Garment Workers' Union (ILGWU) Local 89, a separate, Italian-speaking one. In 1957, she was elected vice president of the ILGWU, the first woman to penetrate the union's all-male leadership. Her successes came at a time when unions were skeptical about organizing women, and Italian women in particular, who were considered "unorganizable."

Bambace was born to Antonio and Giuseppina Bambace on 14 February 1898, in Santos, Brazil, where her immigrant parents owned a small fishing fleet. They repatriated to Italy when her father's health failed but, in 1901, emigrated again, this time settling in East Harlem, New York. After completing high school in 1916, Angela and her younger sister, Maria, took jobs in the garment industry, where they joined the ranks of union organizers demanding better working conditions and fair wages. Because of their Italian identity and bilingual abilities, the sisters were instrumental in recruiting Italian-American women workers to join the union movement. They even won the support of their mother, who took an active role in organizing and accompanying them on their union rounds, armed with a rolling pin to ward off thugs who threatened the female organizers. As a result of their tireless efforts, Local 89, with 40,000 members, had become the largest local in the United States by 1934.

In 1920, Bambace married Romolo Camponeschi and remained at home to have two sons. However, dissatisfied with a traditional domestic role, she returned to work in 1925 and moved toward greater labor militancy. Her husband, using her radical activities to brand her an unfit mother, sued for divorce and won custody of their children. Bambace was allowed visitation with her children until her former husband accepted shared custody.

In 1942, Bambace was appointed manager of the Maryland-Virginia district of the ILGWU and began working to fight prejudice in the upper South, especially the anti-Semitism directed against the union's largely Jewish leadership and the racism encountered by the black workers it recruited. Her success gained her recognition; and in 1957, she became the first female vice president of the ILGWU. Her selection, moreover, represented the increasing role of Italian-Americans in union leadership. She retired in 1972.

Although her closest friends and union colleagues were Jews, Bambace continued her ties with the Italian-American community throughout her life. She was a champion of Italian causes, speaking out against the execution of Sacco and Vanzetti and taking a public stand against fascism. During World War II and after, she retained her contacts with anti-Fascist organizations and Italian war relief groups. She was also active in war relief programs, Histadrut (the Zionist labor movement), the Italian American Labor Council, the Americans for Democratic Action, and the American Civil Liberties Union.

Bambace's activism, ambition, and sense of herself as an Italian-American woman and a female trade unionist are representative of the many Italian women garment workers who followed, rising within the ranks of the union to become prominent organizers and leaders. She died in Baltimore in April 1975.

Diane C. Vecchio

REFERENCES

Fenton, Edwin. "Immigrants and Unions: A Case Study: Italians and American Labor, 1870–1920." Ph.D. diss., Harvard University, 1957.

Mangione, Jerre, and Ben Morreale. *La Storia. Five Centuries of the Italian American Experience.* New York: Harper Perennial, 1992.

Scarpaci, Jean A. "Angela Bambace and the International Ladies' Garment Workers Union: The Search for an Elusive Activist." In *Pane e Lavoro: The Italian American Working Class,* edited by George E. Pozzetta. Toronto: The Multicultural History Society of Ontario, 1980.

Zappia, Charles, "Unionism and the Italian American Worker: A History of the New York City 'Italian Local' in the International Ladies' Garment Workers Union." Ph.D. diss., New York University, 1979.

Baraga, Frederic Irenej (1797–1868)
Catholic bishop, missionary, and scholar
Slovene

Frederic Irenej Baraga, Catholic bishop, missionary among American Indians, and author, achieved recognition in the United States and then in the Habsburg Empire as the missionary bishop of Marquette (Michigan) and author of books on Chippewa (Ojibwe) Indians.

Baraga was born in the village of Mala vas pri Dobrniču, in what was Carniola under the Habsburgs and today the Republic of Slovenia. After studying law at the University of Vienna (1816–1821), he entered Ljubljana Catholic seminary and became a priest. He served as chaplain in Šmartin pri Kranju and Metlika. He left for the United States in 1830 and served as a Catholic missionary among the Indians in the Great Lakes region. In 1853 the Northern Peninsula of Michigan was detached from the Diocese of Detroit and elevated into an apostolic vicariate with the seat in Sault St. Marie (the seat of the diocese was transferred to Marquette in 1866). Baraga was appointed its first bishop. Shortly after he became a bishop, Baraga issued two circulars, one in English and one in the Chippewa language. The circular in Chippewa was the first and only Catholic bishop's circular written in an Indian language in the United States during the nineteenth century.

Baraga brought Christianity to many of the Chippewa and Ottawa Indians. He also promoted the drainage of swamps to provide farmland for Indians and taught them to read and write. He tried to accustom them to European work habits and culture and encouraged abstinence from liquor. Bishop Baraga will always rank among the foremost authors in American Indian literature. He wrote six books on and for American Indians. The most important of them are the *Prayer* and *Catholic Enamiad,* a short survey on the Catholic faith and/or doctrine. Having studied Ojibwe (Chippewa) for twenty years, Baraga wrote a dictionary and a grammar book on the language for missionaries. It was published in 1850 and reprinted several times, most re-cently in 1978. Both the grammar and the dictionary were highly prized and constantly used by Indian missionaries and others. He also wrote books in Ottawa Indian language, with his Ottawa prayer book, which included prayers, songs, and catechism, appearing in 1832. He even translated that volume into Ojibwe. His last book in Ojibwe was published in 1855, when he was already a bishop.

In addition to those works, Baraga wrote *On the Manners and Customs of the Indians,* which he published in German and in French in 1837. A shortened version of it was published in Slovene. This book is really an ethnological study on Indian culture, describing Indians from an anthropological point of view, including their material culture, social life, religion, and treatment of diseases. Even today, Slovene-Americans consider Bishop Baraga one of the most important Slovenes to have come to the United States, and some have even initiated the process of his beatification.

Matjaž Klemenčič

REFERENCES

Baragov Simpozij v Rimu. Simpoziji v Rimu 17 (Baraga's symposium in Rome. Symposiums in Rome 170). Celje: Slovenska teološka akademija v Rimu, Inštitut za zgodovino cerkve, 2000.

Ceglar, Charles A. *Baragiana Collection,* Part 1: *The Works of Bishop Frederic Baraga.* Hamilton, Ont.: Baragiana Publishing, 1991.

———. *Baragiana Collection,* Part 2: *Bishop Frederic Baraga Bibliography.* Hamilton, Ont.: Baragiana Publishing, 1992.

Granda, Stane, Marjan Zupančič, and Pavle Rot, eds. *Baraga in Trebnje: predavanja na Baragovem simpoziju v Trebnjem, 9. januarja 1998* (Baraga and Trebnje: Lectures at the Baraga Symposium, 9 January 1998). Trebnje: Obèina Trebnje, Baragov odbor, 1998.

Jaklič, Franc, and Jakob Šolar. *Friderik Baraga.* Celje: Mohorjeva družba, 1968.

Jezernik, Maksimiljan. *Frederik Baraga: A Portrait of the First Bishop of Marquette, Based on the Archives of the Congregation de Propaganda Fide.* New York and Washington, DC: Studia Slovenica, 1968.

Walling, Regis M., and Rev. N. Daniel Rupp, eds. *The Diary of Bishop Frederic Baraga.* Detroit: Wayne State University Press, 1990.

Barolini, Helen (1925–)
Writer
Italian-American

Since the 1970s, Italian-American women scholars and creative writers have turned to the Italian-immigrant women and the Italian-American women who write about them as the focus of a new and growing literary genre. Helen Barolini, one of the first women writers who represents this "new breed" of Italian-American novelists, is an award-winning novelist, critic, translator, essayist, and one of the first to write a novel about contemporary Italian-American women.

Barolini, a third-generation Italian-American, was born in Syracuse, New York, in 1925. A graduate of Syracuse University, she received a *diploma di profitto* from the University of Florence and a master's degree from Columbia University. Her marriage to Italian writer Antonio Barolini in 1950 provided her with the opportunity to live in Italy for more than ten years, an experience that greatly influenced her writings.

After receiving a National Endowment of the Arts grant for fiction writing, Barolini completed *Umbertina* (1979), a novel that explores on an epic scale the lives of three women of the same family, each of whom is conflicted by Old and New World values. *Umbertina* covers four generations of women's development, from 1860 through approximately 1975. This pivotal novel delicately intertwines the subjects of family and immigrant saga with a distinctively feminist perspective. Barolini's insights into Italian-American life reveal how ethnic women from one generation to the next retrieve the past through their grandmothers and enter adulthood with a fuller understanding of their cultural identity.

In 1985, Barolini published the first anthology solely dedicated to Italian-American women writers, for which she won an American Book Award. *The Dream Book: An Anthology of Writings by Italian American Women* presents their literary contributions, discusses the historical and social context in which the writers worked, and examines the barriers they had to break through in their struggle against silence and invisibility. Barolini's publication of *The Dream Book* has created an increased awareness of—and discussion about—the literary talent of Italian-American women and has given them a voice in literature.

Celebrating her rediscovery of Italian food and its meaning in Italian-American life, Barolini published *Festa: Recipes and Recollections of Italian Holidays* (1988). A cookbook that combines recipes with descriptions and stories related to the holidays and saints' days, *Festa* takes the reader on a culinary journey marking the feast days of Saint Joseph to Pasqua (Easter) and Natale (Christmas). Barolini's creative interests have taken her into other genres, including the essay. Her most recent publication includes topics as wide ranging as the Italian literary prize business, which she humorously portrays in "Neruda vs. Sartre at the Sea," and her mother's inclination for collecting Americana in "The Finer Things in Life," both published in *Chiaroscuro: Essays on Italian American Culture.*

The literary contributions of Helen Barolini reflect the works of second- and third-generation writers who return to their parents' and grandparents' homeland, seeking a better understanding of the immigrant experience. As a result, Barolini's writings have been recognized by Italian-Americans as an important literary contribution to the Italian-American experience.

Diane C. Vecchio

REFERENCES

Ahearn, Carol Bonomo. "Interview: Helen Barolini." *Fra Noi,* September 1986, 47.

Barolini, Helen. *The Dream Book: An Anthology of Writings by Italian American Women.* New York: Schocken Books, 1985.

———. *Festa: Recipes and Recollections of Italian Holidays.* New York: Harcourt, Brace, 1988.

———. "Heritage Lost, Heritage Found." *Italian Americana* 16.2 (Summer 1998).

———. "Italian American Women Writers." In *The Italian American Heritage,* edited by Pellegrino D'Acierno, 193–265. New York: Garland Publishing, 1999.

———. *Umbertina.* New York: Feminist Press, 1979.

Bona, Mary Jo. "Women Writers." In *The Italian*

American Experience: An Encyclopedia, edited by Salvatore LaGumina, 694–701. New York: Garland Publishing, 2000.

Mangione, Jerry, and Ben Morreale. *La Storia. Five Centuries of the Italian American Experience.* New York: Harper Perennial, 1992.

Bartók, Béla (1881–1945)

Pianist, composer, teacher, and ethnomusicologist

Hungarian

Béla Bartók was born on 25 March 1881 in Nagyszentmiklos, Hungary (Sinnicolau Mare, Romania, today). He was one of the twentieth century's greatest composers.

Bartók inherited his talent from both of his parents, who were teachers and amateur musicians. His father died when Béla was eight years old, and after that his mother persuaded him to pursue the musical field. He studied at the University of Pressburg and the Royal Academy in Budapest (also known as the Liszt Academy). In 1907, he became a professor of piano at the university and, while teaching, composed dozens of concertos, operas, ballets, and other pieces that would later make him famous. Some of his most acclaimed works include: *Kossuth, Bluebeard's Castle, The Wooden Prince, Piano Concertos Nos. 1–3, Mikrokosmos,* and *String Quartets Nos. 1–6.* In collaboration with his colleague Zoltan Kodaly, Bartók also traveled throughout the country collecting regional music. He incorporated these folk elements, atonality, and traditional techniques into his own works, making his sound unique, though uncelebrated at that time.

After the *Anschluss* in March 1938 (when Hitler took control of Austria), Bartók expressed his fears that Hungary would be the next to succumb to Germany. He was an avid anti-Fascist but could not leave Hungary, for he had a family, including an elderly mother, to support. In 1939, after his mother died, Bartók and his second wife, Ditta, immigrated to the United States. Leading schools offered him high-paying positions in composition, although Bartók had never taught that subject, and he did not wish to do so at his age. Rather, he took a position at Columbia University, where he did research on Southern European musicology and taught piano.

Although Bartók expressed his frustration at Hungary's alliance with the Axis, he refused to take part in any Hungarian-American organizations, for his son Peter was still in Hungary and he did not want to jeopardize his son's safety. However, in 1942, after Peter arrived in the United States, Bartók gradually became involved in efforts to free Hungary. On 16 July 1942, he became leader of the Free Hungary Movement (FHM), after Tibor Eckhardt, a controversial political émigré, resigned. Bartók attempted to recruit his fellow Magyar-American musicians and other friends to join in his efforts, yet they refused, fearing that those still in Hungary would face punishment for their participation. One week after Bartók accepted his position, the FHM disintegrated because of incessant infighting with other Hungarian movements, which had begun well before he accepted his post.

Bartók did express his concerns about the ascending Communist movement in Hungary after the war, and some Magyars—both in the United States and Hungary—urged him to return to his homeland to assume the post of prime minister, but he no longer desired to participate actively in politics. He had fallen ill, and although his doctors never informed him that he had leukemia, he preferred to work tirelessly to compose more music. On 26 September 1945, he died. After a lifetime of composing, Bartók had received praise for his works only during the last few years of his life. Many musicians proclaimed him, posthumously, as one of the greatest composers of his time.

Judith Fai-Podlipnik

REFERENCES

Antokoletz, Elliott. *The Music of Bela Bartok.* Berkeley: University of California Press, 1984.

Deak, Zoltan, ed. *This Noble Flame: An Anthology of a Hungarian Newspaper in America, 1902–1982.* New York: Columbia University Press, 1984.

Ewen, David, ed. *The Book of Modern Composers.* New York: Alfred A. Knopf, 1942.

Gillies, Malcom. *Bartok Remembered.* New York: W. W. Norton, 1990.

Juhasz, Vilmos. *Bartok's Years in America*. Washington, DC: Occidental Press, 1981.

Schonberg, Harold C. *The Lives of the Great Composers*. New York: W. W. Norton, 1997.

Stevens, Halsey. *The Life and Music of Bela Bartok*. New York: Oxford University Press, 1964.

Suchoff, Benjamin, ed. *Bela Bartok Essays*. Lincoln: University of Nebraska Press, 1976.

Bassiouni, Mahmoud Cherif (1937–)
Professor of law and human rights advocate
Egyptian

M. Cherif Bassiouni, a native of Egypt, has achieved worldwide recognition for his work in international law and human rights, from pro bono work for Arab-American groups to investigating war crimes in Bosnia for the United Nations. In 1999 he and the Association International de Droit Penal, of which he is president, were nominated for the Nobel Peace Prize for their single-minded efforts to establish the International Criminal Court.

Bassiouni, son of a career diplomat and grandson of the former president of the Egyptian Senate, was born in Cairo, Egypt. After legal studies in France, he joined the Egyptian army in 1956 and was wounded in battle at the Suez Canal, receiving the highest medal of military valor. Soon after, he was invited to work in the office of President Gamal Abdel Nasser, but his questioning of arbitrary arrests and detentions led to his being put under house arrest for seven months. He then resumed his legal studies at the University of Cairo and managed to join his mother, who had immigrated to California and was undergoing treatment for cancer. He became a U.S. citizen in 1967.

Graduating from Indiana University's law school in 1964 and obtaining a doctorate in law from George Washington University in 1973, Bassiouni joined the faculty at De Paul University College of Law, specializing in international criminal law. He is the author of 42 books and 167 law review articles, published in six different languages. Moreover, he has been very active for years in the Arab and Muslim communities, helping Chicago-area Palestinians retain legal claim to property in Israel and handling extradition cases, such as that of Mousa Mohammed Abu Marzouk, a Hamas leader accused of terrorism. He helped found or served on the boards of numerous organizations, including the Association of Egyptian-American Scholars, the Mid-America Arab Chamber of Commerce, the Association of Arab-American University Graduates, and the Arab-American Anti-Discrimination Committee. He also helped establish and sat as chairman of the board of the Islamic Center of Chicago.

He has, in addition, carved a place for himself in national and international government affairs, testifying before Congress on the Middle East and extradition reform legislation and working as a consultant for the State and Justice Departments on diverse Middle Eastern, Arabic, and Islamic affairs. After being invited back to Egypt by Anwar Sadat in 1973, he served as an independent adviser to the Egyptian government on a variety of issues, including the Camp David Accords. In 1993 and 1994 Bassiouni served as chair of the United Nations (UN) commission investigating human rights violations in the former Yugoslavia. Subsequently, he chaired the Drafting Committee of the United Nations Diplomatic Conference on the Establishment of an International Criminal Court and in 1995 was elected chairman of the UN General Assembly committee to lay the foundation for establishing an international criminal court. It was for this work that he was conominated for the Nobel Peace Prize in 1999.

Elizabeth Plantz

REFERENCES

Bassiouni, M. Cherif. Interview by author, 11 January 2000.

Flaherty, Roger. "De Paul Prof. Roots Out War Crimes." *Chicago Sun-Times,* 8 February 1993, 10.

Fornek, Scott. "Professor's Work Helps Spur War Crimes Tribunal." *Chicago Sun-Times,* 31 May 1999, 20.

"M. Cherif Bassiouni." In *Contemporary Authors,* new rev. series, vol. 34. Detroit: Gale Research, 1991.

"M. Cherif Bassiouni." In *Who's Who in Finance and Industry,* 30th ed. Chicago: Marquis Who's Who, 1998–1999.

"M. Cherif Bassiouni." In *Who's Who in the World,*
    14th ed. Chicago: Marquis Who's Who, 1996.
Sula, Mike. "On Top of the World." *Reader* 28.22
    (5 March 1999): 1, 16, 18, 20, 22, 26–28.
Wilson, David L. "A Victim of Oppression Probes
    War Crimes." *Chronicle of Higher Education* 68.16
    (9 December 1992): A5.

Beck, Mary (née Mariia Bek) (1908–)
*City and county elected official and
community activist*
Ukrainian-American

The "Lady of Many Firsts," Mary Beck was
the first woman elected to Detroit's city council, the first chosen as Detroit's acting mayor, and
the first elected a supervisor for Wayne County.
She accomplished all that while remaining active within the Ukrainian community.

Beck was born Mariia Bek on 29 February
1908, in Ford City, Pennsylvania. Her parents
were immigrants from the Lemko region in
Ukraine. In 1920, when she finished eighth
grade, her parents sent her to school in Western Ukraine. She perfected her Ukrainian language, gained considerable knowledge of
Ukrainian history and literature, and witnessed
repressive measures against Ukrainians. She returned to the United States in 1924, graduated
from high school, and enrolled at the University of Pittsburgh. There, she and her brother
John organized evening classes for the local
Ukrainian community and encouraged young
people to participate in community activities.

In 1932, Beck, affectionately known among
Ukrainians as Marusia, was the first American-
born Ukrainian woman to obtain a law degree.
In 1933–1934, she worked as general manager
of the Ukrainian Pavilion at the Century of
Progress Exposition in Chicago and in 1932
had started to publish the first regular Ukrainian-American women's journal, *Zhinochyi Svit*
(Woman's world). She was its first editor
(1933–1934). In 1934, she moved to Detroit,
where she worked for twelve years in the
Wayne County Juvenile Court.

Beck was a brilliant speaker. Despite the
strong prejudice against women in politics and
the fact that she was an active member of an
ethnic community, she decided on a political
career. In 1949, she was the first woman elected
to the Detroit City Council, the first woman
elected as head of the council (1952–1962),
and the first woman to be the acting mayor
(1958–1962). Prior to 1958, she served for
nineteen years on the Wayne County Board of
Supervisors. She has received many awards: In
1953, she was proclaimed a Woman of
Achievement by Detroit newspapers; in 1955,
Woman of the Year by Zeta Phi Beta; and, in
1991, she was inducted to the Michigan
Women's Hall of Fame. Detroit proclaimed 29
February, her birthday, Mary Beck Day.

For Beck, there was no dichotomy between her American and Ukrainian identities.
In City Hall she fought for programs concerning law and order, human rights, and
public welfare. Her activities in the Ukrainian
community basically had the same foundation: human rights and public welfare. She was
involved in Ukrainian women's organizations,
especially the Ukrainian Women's League of
North America and the World Federation of
Ukrainian Women's Organizations. In 1959
she established and financed a literary contest
for Ukrainian Women Authors and, in 1979, a
contest for young people. An avid promoter of
music, art, ethnic traditions in American and
Ukrainian communities, she sponsored a
World Wide Ukrainian Art Exhibit in 1960.

A visit to Soviet Ukraine in 1963 reinforced her dedication to the cause of
Ukraine's independence, and she often spoke
about the suppression of freedom in her ancestors' homeland. Integrating two worlds in
her life, American and Ukrainian, she set a
prominent example that American and ethnic
values need not be mutually exclusive.

Daria Markus

REFERENCES
"Detroit Newspaper Profiles Atty. Mary Beck."
    Svoboda, 14 February 1976.
"Lady of Many Firsts Inducted to Michigan
    Women's Hall of Fame." *Ukrainian Weekly,*
    15 December 1991.
"Mary Beck." *Forum,* no. 57 (Winter 1984): 1–8.

Bednarik, Charles "Chuck" (1925–)
Athlete, football player
Slovak-American

Chuck Bednarik, a member of the Pro Football Hall of Fame, played for the Philadelphia Eagles. During college and professional careers spanning the years 1946 to 1962, Bednarik was consistently awarded national honors for athletic achievements. The last professional football player to play both offense and defense for an entire game, he is known as "the last of the sixty-minute men."

Born in 1925 in Bethlehem, Pennsylvania, Bednarik, the son of Slovak immigrants, did not learn English until he went to the Slovak elementary school, Saints Cyril and Methodius. He attended Bethlehem Catholic High School but subsequently transferred to public institutions with broader athletic programs. He played three sports, but his football talents drew the attention of college coaches. Turning eighteen in May 1943, he was, however, immediately drafted into military service. He chose the U.S. Army Air Force, became a B–24 waist gunner, and flew thirty combat missions.

After the war, Bednarik returned to Bethlehem. As a second-generation Slovak growing up in Bethlehem's working-class community, he had assumed that, like his father, he was destined for the mill. But rather than becoming a mill worker, he decided to attend college; the GI Bill and his athletic talents having provided the means. He went to the University of Pennsylvania, where in 1947 and 1948 he was chosen All-American center. In 1948, he won the Maxwell Award, given to the college player deemed the nation's best, and was runner-up for the Heisman Trophy. The first player picked in the 1949 professional draft, he went to the Philadelphia Eagles. During his career Bednarik played both center and linebacker and, in 1960 and 1961, did "double duty" at both positions. Twice in the 1960 regular season, he stayed on the field for entire games. His most famous "sixty-minute game" occurred in Philadelphia's 1960 championship win over Green Bay. Among his numerous distinctions, he was selected "All-Pro" eight times. Retiring from athletics in 1962, he was inducted into the Pro Football Hall of Fame in 1967, his first year of eligibility. In 1969 the National Football League (NFL) further recognized Bednarik by naming him the NFL all-time center.

By graduating from college and choosing professional sports, Chuck Bednarik deviated from the life pattern typically followed by second-generation Slovak males raised in industrial towns. Certainly, his successes were not as an ethnic American. Nevertheless, he continued to identify with his ethnic heritage. References to his ancestry as well as to Slovak traditions, values, history, and even stereotypes permeate the pages of his biography, written in collaboration with him. He sees his principles as rooted in Slovak values. "I'm primarily an American, but I am Slovak too, and I always will be," he declared. He maintained membership in Slovak organizations and has achieved significant recognition among Slovak-Americans, especially those in Pennsylvania. The final sentence of his biography is a telling commentary regarding his own ethnicity: He had to rush off to a speaking engagement because "the First Catholic Slovak Ladies Union was not a group to be kept waiting."

June G. Alexander

REFERENCES

Carroll, Bob, et al., eds. *Total Football: The Official Encyclopedia of the National Football League.* New York: HarperCollins, 1997.

McCallum, Jack, with Chuck Bednarik. *Bednarik: Last of the Sixty-Minute Men.* Englewood Cliffs, NJ: Prentice Hall, 1977.

National Football League. *Official 1999 National Football Record and Fact Book.* New York: Workman Publishing, 1999.

Bell, Alexander Graham (1847–1922)
Inventor and educator
Scottish

Alexander Graham Bell, the inventor of the telephone and many other important devices, was also an educator. He devoted himself to helping the deaf.

Bell was born in Edinburgh, Scotland, the

son of Alexander Melville Bell and Grace Symonds. Bell's father and grandfather were teachers of speech, his mother was a pianist interested in sound communication, and Edinburgh was one of the world's centers of science and technology—all of which prepared Alexander Graham Bell for a life of research and invention, his greatest being the telephone.

Precocious as a child, Bell showed an early interest in invention. He was encouraged by his grandfather and his father to create a "speaking machine," which could reproduce vocal sounds. This initiated a lifelong fascination with the mechanism of sound and speech that involved experiments with everything that could produce sound. His goal was to teach the deaf to speak, though along the way he would become better known as an inventor.

Bell migrated with his parents in 1871 at age twenty-four, first to Canada, and then in the same year to Boston, when he was invited to teach at a school for deaf children. The next year he opened his own private teacher-training classes, and in 1873 Boston University hired him as professor of vocal physiology. By day he taught classes and attended lectures at Massachusetts Institute of Technology; by night he performed his experiments. Bell's earlier interest in the possibility of sending several messages at once on the same telegraph line, combined with his experiments to make speech visible by tracing sound vibration mechanically, led him to the basic principles behind the telephone. In 1875 he hired an assistant, Thomas A. Watson, who accidentally touched a steel reed that was attached to an electromagnet, which produced a sound on a reed and an electromagnet on the other end of the wire. After more experimentation, the first sentence was transmitted over a line on 10 March 1876: "Mr. Watson, come here, I want to see you." Bell, only twenty-nine years old, was issued one of the most valuable patents in history.

Bell spent the next years refining the telephone, promoting it in public demonstrations, and defending his patents against counterclaimants. He became a U.S. citizen in 1882,

the same year he moved to Washington, D.C. But Bell never slowed down as an inventor or as an advocate for the deaf. He created the audiometer, studied the inherited propensity to deafness, directed schools for the deaf, became a friend and mentor to Helen Keller, and gave a considerable part of his money to helping the deaf. He even invented the precursor to the iron lung, improved on Edison's phonograph, and experimented with heavier-than-air flight and hydrofoil boats. Bell was highly honored for his achievements. He was elected to the National Academy of Sciences and served as president of the National Geographic Society.

In 1886 Alexander Graham Bell purchased an estate near Baddeck, Nova Scotia, where he spent much of his leisure time. And although he loved the place and was buried there after his death in 1922, he had these words carved on his gravestone: "Died a Citizen of the United States."

William E. Van Vugt

REFERENCES
Bruce, Robert V. *Alexander Graham Bell and the Conquest of Solitude.* Boston: Little, Brown, 1973.
Costain, Thomas B. *The Chord of Steel: The Story of the Invention of the Telephone.* Garden City, NY: Doubleday, 1960.

Bell, Thomas (né Belejčák) (1903–1961)
Novelist
Slovak-American

Thomas Bell was a writer whose books sensitively portrayed the life of ordinary people. He is known particularly for *Out of This Furnace,* a novel about Slovak immigrants and their descendants in industrial America. "Bell" was a pseudonym that Belejčák adopted, but it is not known if he ever legally changed his name.

Thomas Bell (Belejčák), a second-generation Slovak, was born in Braddock, Pennsylvania, in 1903. His father had immigrated to the United States at fifteen; his mother, the daughter of Slovak immigrants, was born in Whitehaven, Pennsylvania. His father died of tuberculosis on Thomas's eleventh birthday, and five years later, his mother succumbed to the same disease. Bell quit school, probably at fifteen, and held jobs in a glass factory, as an apprentice electrician, and later in his hometown's steel mill.

In 1922, Bell went to New York to pursue a writing career. His first novel, an adventure, *The Breed of Basil* (1930), was not particularly successful. In 1932, he married Marie Benedetti, an Italian whose parents had immigrated when she was two. Marie became the breadwinner so that Thomas could write full-time. They had no children.

His happy marriage and his decision to write from firsthand experience, imbuing his stories with social commentary, were pivotal to Bell's ultimate success as a novelist. He set his second novel, *The Second Prince* (1935), in a mill town. One of its chief characters was a second-generation Slovak steelworker and union activist. *All Brides Are Beautiful* (1936) ignored issues of ethnicity and depicted two years in the life of a newlywed couple during the Great Depression. It revealed his talent for writing about common people living ordinary lives and established his reputation as a writer. A decade later it was made into a movie, *From This Day Forward*.

Bell produced his acknowledged masterpiece, *Out of This Furnace,* in 1941. Partially autobiographical, this powerful novel spans three generations of a Slovak family. The tale begins with a man's departure for the United States in 1880 and ends with his grandson's participation in efforts to organize a steel union in the 1930s. Prominently reviewed in 1941, the novel has accorded Bell lasting recognition as a novelist of the immigrant and working-class experience. The book also offers a second-generation view of ethnic life and American society. Neither of Bell's subsequent two novels achieved comparable success (*Till I Come Back to You* [1943] and *There Comes a Time* [1946]). After 1946, Bell published short stories but no more novels. When told he had terminal cancer, he wrote *In the Midst of Life* (posthumously published in 1961), which he described as "the journal of a dying man." He died on 17 January 1961.

Belejčák's Americanized name and marriage to an Italian woman did not signify a rejection of his ethnic identity. He was acutely aware and proud of his Slovak ancestry. Nonetheless, although he wrote vividly about the experiences of Slovak-Americans and achieved recognition outside his ethnic community, he has not enjoyed great acclaim among Slovak-Americans, in part because of his political views and his rejection of religion. However, his novels did bring him success in mainstream America.

June G. Alexander

REFERENCES

Berko, John F. "Thomas Bell (1903–1961): Slovak-American Novelist." *Slovak Studies* 15 (1975): 143–158.

Demarest, David P., Jr. Afterword to *Out of This Furnace,* by Thomas Bell. 1941. Reprint, Pittsburgh: University of Pittsburgh Press, 1976.

Fadiman, Clifton. "Mixed Bag." Review of *Out of This Furnace,* by Thomas Bell. *New Yorker* 5 (April 1941): 73.

"The Writer Who Taught Us about Ourselves." *Národné Noviny,* July 1987.

Bellow, Saul (1915–)
Author
Jewish-American

Saul Bellow, born in 1915 in Lachine, Quebec, near Montreal, to Russian-Jewish immigrants who had arrived in Canada in 1913, became the preeminent writer of fiction in the post–World War II era in the United States. He won wide recognition and many prizes, including the Nobel Prize in literature, three National Book Awards, and the Pulitzer Prize for fiction.

Raised in Montreal until the age of nine and then in Chicago, Bellow had a trilingual childhood: Yiddish, English, and French. Yiddish apparently continued to resonate in his inner ear and has permeated most of his writing. After studying at the University of Chicago and Northwestern University, Bellow combined writing with a teaching career at various institutions, among them University of Minnesota, Princeton, New York University, Bard College, the University of Chicago, and Boston University.

He won some early recognition with his first two novels, *Dangling Man* (1944), which depicted the intellectual and spiritual vacillations of a young man waiting to be drafted, and *The Victim* (1947), a study of a convoluted relationship between a Jew and a Gentile and an insightful treatment of the theme of anti-Semitism. *The Adventures of Augie March* (1953), a picaresque tale of a poor Jewish youth, won wider acclaim as well as a National Book Award.

Bellow was intensely interested in Jewish concerns but he could be, and very much wanted to be, appreciated outside of the Jewish-American community as an unhyphenated American novelist. He succeeded and, in so doing, prepared the way for others as part of the movement of Jews from the periphery to the center of American life. After *Seize the Day* (1956) and *Henderson the Rain King* (1959), Bellow wrote *Herzog* (1964; National Book Award 1965), his most widely acclaimed work and an international best-seller. In *Herzog* and in later works—*Mr. Sammler's Planet* (1970; National Book Award 1971); *Humboldt's Gift* (1975; Pulitzer Prize 1976); *The Dean's December* (1982); *Him with His Foot in His Mouth* (1984); *More Die of Heartbreak* (1987), *A Theft* (1989), *Bellarosa Connection* (1989), and a novella, *The Actual* (1997)—Bellow showed himself to be a consistently brilliant writer and social critic, exploring traditional morality's claim on human behavior. That is true, too, for Bellow's nonfiction, *To Jerusalem and Back* (1976) and *It All Adds Up* (1994).

Throughout his work, including *Ravelstein* (2000), his first full-length novel in more than a decade and one in which questions of Jewish identity again play an important role, Bellow recognizes the incomparable value of intelligence but also its frailty in the face of sensual demands. He seems to have an irrepressible faith in a moral ethic, perhaps even in God, that he has difficulty justifying rationally.

His typical hero struggles with alienation and marginality, constantly trying to reconcile a Jewish upbringing and a memory of intense, complex, but nurturing immigrant family life with the reality of being an uprooted "intellectual" in a world full of frenzy and artificial relationships. In the process, Bellow has presented a fuller picture of the modern Jewish-American experience than any other writer as well as depicting a social context in the United States devoid of spaces where a "religious" or moral spirit could be nourished and sustained. Bellow has thus proven himself the major representative of the Jewish-American writers who have significantly influenced American literature since World War II.

Gerald Sorin

REFERENCES

Brans, Jo. "Common Needs, Common Preoccupations: An Interview with Saul Bellow." *Southwest Review* 62.1 (1977): 1–19.

Clayton, John Jacob. *Saul Bellow: In Defense of Man.* 2d ed. Bloomington: Indiana University Press, 1979.

Fuchs, Daniel. *Saul Bellow: Vision and Revision.* Durham, NC.: Duke University Press, 1984.

Miller, Ruth. *Saul Bellow: A Biography of the Imagination.* New York: St. Martin's Press, 1991.

Rovit, Earl, ed. *Saul Bellow: A Collection of Critical Essays.* Englewood Cliffs, NJ: Prentice Hall, 1975.

Rubin, Derek. "Marginality in Saul Bellow's Early Novels," Ph.D. diss., Free University, Amsterdam, 1995.

Shechner, Mark. *After the Revolution: Studies in the Contemporary Jewish American Imagination.* Bloomington: Indiana University Press, 1987.

Belpré, Pura (1899?–1982)
Librarian, author, and community activist
Puerto Rican

With no prior training, Pura Belpré discovered her love for children's literature in general and Puerto Rican children's literature in particular. Reading programs that she developed in New York City libraries—and similar projects with other institutions—have had an important cultural impact. Many of the stories that she herself wrote in an effort to preserve and disseminate her cultural heritage have been republished as well as performed on television.

Belpré may have been born in February 1899, or in December 1901, or February 1903, but we do know she was born in Cidra, Puerto Rico. In 1920 she did enter the University of Puerto Rico, but she left the following year to attend a wedding in New York City and remained there. Like most Puerto Rican women, Belpré began working in New York's garment industry. However, her keen language skills soon earned her a position as Hispanic assistant in a branch of the New York Public Library in Harlem. She was the first Puerto Rican hired within that system. While working in the children's division, she discovered her passion for storytelling and her love of children's literature.

In 1926, she began her formal studies to become a librarian. As a course requirement she wrote her first folktale, based on a childhood story told to her by her grandmother. It became the first story she read during the children's reading hour begun by her at the Harlem branch library. Because of the increasing number of Spanish-speaking arrivals, she was transferred in 1929 to the 115th Street branch, where she instituted bilingual story hours. Under her direction, the branch library became an important cultural center for the city's Spanish-speaking residents. In 1940, she was invited to present a paper on her work with the Spanish-speaking community to the American Library Association meeting in Cincinnati, Ohio.

While there, she met her future husband, violinist and composer Clarence Cameron White. They were married in December 1943. Belpré soon resigned her position and went on tour with her husband, devoting her time to writing children's books. Her first was *Perez and Martina: A Portorican Folktale.* "The Three Magi" was published as part of an anthology, *The Animal's Christmas,* and, later, Belpré did a series called *The Tiger and the Rabbit and Other Tales.* That was the first collection of Puerto Rican folktales published in English. In addition, one of her best-known stories,

"Juan Bobo and the Queen's Lace," has been performed on children's television shows in Puerto Rico.

Although Belpré collected stories from all parts of the world, her focus remained on the preservation and dissemination of Puerto Rican folk culture. In 1960 her husband died, and she returned part-time to her library work as a Spanish children's specialist, working all over the city. She retired in 1968 after launching the new South Bronx Library Project, a community outreach effort for the Latino/a community. Belpré's activities also included her work with various grassroots and civic agencies, particularly the Association for the Advancement of Puerto Rican People—where she helped establish the "Archivo de Documentacion Puertorriqueña"—and her development of the children's program at the "Museo del Barrio."

Belpré died in July 1982. In 1996 the Pura Belpré Award was established by the Association for Library Service to Children, a division of the American Library Association, to honor a writer or illustrator whose work for children best affirms or celebrates Latino/a cultural experiences.

Linda Delgado

REFERENCES

Belpré, Pura, papers, collected at the Center for Puerto Rican Studies, Hunter College, CUNY, New York. See also www.centropr.org/lib-arc/archives/belpre.html (accessed 21 December 2000).

Berger, Victor (1860–1929)
Journalist and U.S. House representative
German

A native of Austria-Hungary, Victor Luitpold Berger attended Budapest and Vienna Universities. After completing his education, he immigrated to the United States in 1878 and settled in Milwaukee. A German enclave thrived there, providing Berger with an outlet for his political and journalistic ambitions. In 1892 he established *Vorwarts* (Forward), a Socialist German-language newspaper. Subsequently, Berger published two English-language weeklies, the *Social*

Democratic Herald and the *Milwaukee Leader.*
Political life also beckoned through an ac-
quaintanceship with Eugene V. Debs. The two
men were instrumental in forming what
would become the American Socialist Party
in 1901. Within ten years Socialists would
control the city of Milwaukee. However,
Berger was not an ideologue but a practical
reformer who helped bring efficient government to the midwestern city.

Local political maneuvering led to Berger's
running for Congress in 1910. He won, the
first Socialist (he preferred to be called a Social Democrat) to achieve that. Yet Berger's
experience in Washington was not without
drama. As World War I loomed, he proclaimed
his pacifist beliefs openly and outspokenly opposed U.S. participation in the conflict. His
speeches sparked outrage among colleagues,
and in 1919, shortly after winning reelection,
the antiwar candidate was denied his seat and
indicted under the Espionage Act of 1917,
charged with aiding the enemy by obstructing
the war effort. Berger was found guilty and
given a twenty-year prison term. But the U.S.
Supreme Court reversed the sentence in
1921, and in 1922 the unrepentant Socialist
successfully ran once more for a seat in the
House of Representatives. He was reelected
twice, then defeated in 1928. Berger never lost
his enthusiasm for socialism or for the political process. In 1929 he returned to Wisconsin
to resume his editorial work and to serve as
Debs's successor as chairman of the Socialist
Party's executive committee, a post that he
would hold until his death in 1929.

Victor Berger inspires admiration for both
his journalist achievements and his service in
Congress. He remained devoted to the tenets
of socialism and pacifism despite their un-
popularity with powerful segments of U.S.
society and the pressure to support a world
war. Prosecution and prison did not dampen
his commitment to his ideals. Thus, Berger
stands not only as a prominent German-
American but also as a man of integrity and
conviction.

Susanne M. Schick

REFERENCES

Berger, Victor. *The Victor Berger Papers.* 55 microfilm reels. Wilmington, DE: Scholarly Resources, 1994.

———. *Voice and Pen of Victor L. Berger: Congressional Speeches and Editorials.* Milwaukee: n.p., 1929.

"Berger, Victor Luitpold." *Biographical Directory of the U.S. Congress:* bioguide.congress.gov/scripts/biodisplay. pl?index=B000407 (accessed 29 June 2000).

Miller, Sally. *Victor Berger and the Promise of Constructive Socialism, 1910–1920.* Westport, CN: Greenwood Press, 1973.

Preston, William, and Paul Buhle. *Aliens and Dissenters: Federal Suppression of Radicals, 1903–1933.* 2d ed. Urbana: University of Illinois Press, 1995.

Salvatore, Nick. *Eugene V. Debs: Citizen and Socialist.* Urbana: University of Illinois Press, 1982.

Stevens, Michael, ed. *The Family Letters of Victor and Meta Berger, 1894–1929.* Madison: State Historical Society of Wisconsin, 1995.

Bergman, Ingrid (1915–1982)
Film and stage actress
Swedish

Ingrid Bergman was one of the most versatile, accomplished, charismatic, and im-
mensely popular stars of her time on screen
and stage. Her career spanned more than four
decades in both Europe and the United
States. Altogether she played in more than fifty
productions in Sweden, Germany, Italy,
Britain, and the United States.

Bergman was born in Stockholm, Sweden,
the daughter of a Swedish photographer and
portrait painter and a German mother. She
grew up in an artistic milieu. In 1933 she entered the Royal Dramatic Theater School but
left to make her first movie with the Swedish
studio Svensk Filmindustri (1935), which was
followed by several others, including one
made in Germany in 1938. In 1937 she married Petter A. Lindström. Two years later, she
departed for Hollywood, invited by David O.
Selznik to star in *Intermezzo.* There followed
a series of films that won her great critical
and popular success, including *Casablanca*
(1942), with Humphrey Bogart; *For Whom the
Bell Tolls* (1943), with Gary Cooper; Alfred

Hitchcock's *Gaslight* and *Spellbound* (1945); *The Bells of St. Mary's* (1945), with Bing Crosby; and Hitchcock's *Notorious* (1946). She conveyed a radiant image of Nordic health, sincerity, and wholesomeness, in contrast to the glitter and artificiality of Hollywood at that time.

In 1949, Bergman played in the Italian film, *Stromboli,* directed by Roberto Rosselini. This role resulted in a passionate and much-publicized love affair between them, leading to her divorce from Lindström. The episode caused enormous disillusionment and indignation in the United States, where she had been idolized. In 1950 Bergman married Rosselini, with whom she had three children. The scandal compelled her to relocate to Europe, where she appeared in several Italian and French films.

She subsequently separated from Rosselini, and in 1958, following an annulment of her marriage to him, Bergman married the Swedish theatrical producer Lars Schmidt. During that time, she was able to return in triumph to the United States, where she starred in *Anastasia* (1956). Her later film roles included *Indiscreet* (1957), *Murder on the Orient Express* (1974), and the Swedish director Ingmar Bergman's *Autumn Sonata* (1978).

Bergman meanwhile had won acclaim in several stage productions, among them Ferenc Molnár's *Lilliom* (1940), Sherwood Anderson's *Joan of Lorraine* (1946), and W. Somerset Maugham's *The Constant Wife* (1975), in New York; Henrik Ibsen's *Hedda Gabler,* in Paris (1962); and Ivan Turgenev's *A Month in the Country* (1965) and George Bernard Shaw's *Captain Brassbound's Conversion* (1971), in London. Bergman likewise appeared in television plays, including her last performance, as Golda Meir, in *A Woman Called Golda,* in 1981. She was widely honored internationally, receiving three Academy Awards.

Bergman had become a U.S. citizen in 1945 but had kept close personal and professional ties with her homeland. Although she was not active in the Swedish-American community, it keenly followed her controversial life and rejoiced in her artistic triumphs. By the early 1970s Bergman was already afflicted with cancer, from which she died in London in 1982.

H. Arnold Barton

REFERENCES

Bergman, Ingrid, with Alan Burgess. *My Story.* New York: Delacorte Press, 1980.

Leamer, Laurence. *As Time Goes By: The Life of Ingrid Bergman.* New York: Harper & Row, 1986.

Spoto, Donald. *Notorious: The Life of Ingrid Bergman.* New York: HarperCollins, 1997.

Bethune, Mary McLeod (1875–1955)
Educator, community activist, and public official
African American

Mary McLeod Bethune served as an adviser to four U.S. presidents, was the first African American woman to head a federal agency, founded a school, and worked actively to advance the lives of African American men and women. By 1932, in a newspaper article by journalist Ida Tarbell, she ranked Bethune tenth among America's fifty greatest women.

McLeod was born in Mayesville, South Carolina, the fifteenth of seventeen children of former slaves Samuel and Patsy McLeod. Although impoverished, she was able to use her intelligence and leadership skill to secure an education that culminated at the Moody Bible Institute for missionary training in Chicago. But with no posts available for African American missionaries in Africa, she returned to the South to teach, marrying Albertus Bethune in 1898. They had one child in 1899. They formally separated in 1907 but never divorced.

In 1904 Bethune had moved to Daytona, Florida, and, with $1.50, established a school, the Daytona Educational and Industrial Institute School for Training Negro Girls. Through aggressive fund-raising, she expanded the school so that it offered a broad curriculum of courses even at the college level. In 1923, it merged with the Cookman Institute and was renamed the Bethune-Cookman College.

Bethune was also actively involved in black

women's organizations and became president of the Florida Federation of Colored Women, president of the Southeastern Federation of Women's Clubs, twice president of the 200,000-member National Association of Colored Women, and was elected to the executive board of the National Urban League. In 1935, she formed the National Council of Negro Women and, in 1940, was elected vice president of the National Association for the Advancement of Colored People (NAACP). In addition, she served as president of the National Association of Teachers in Colored Schools.

A leading educator and black women's activist, she became involved with the federal government. President Calvin Coolidge invited her to attend his Child Welfare Conference in 1928, and Herbert Hoover appointed her to the White House Conference on Child Health in 1930. From 1936 to 1944, under Franklin Delano Roosevelt, she held the position of director of the Division of Negro Affairs of the National Youth Administration, the first African American woman to head a federal agency. She was also Roosevelt's special adviser on minority affairs (1935–1944) and worked closely with Eleanor Roosevelt on minority issues. During World War II she served as consultant to the U.S. secretary of war for selection of the first female officer candidates. After the war, she was one of three African American consultants to the U.S. delegation involved in writing the UN charter. In 1951, she served on President Harry Truman's Committee of Twelve for National Defense.

Bethune's activism fighting against racism and discrimination won her both national and international recognition and honors, including the NAACP's Spingarn Medal in 1935, the Thomas Jefferson Award for Leadership in 1942, the Medal of Honor and Merit from the Republic of Haiti in 1949, and the Star of Africa from the Republic of Liberia in 1952. In 1974 a statue of Mary McLeod Bethune was placed in Lincoln Park in Washington, D.C.; she was the first woman and the first African American to receive that honor.

Juliet E. K. Walker

REFERENCES

Fleming, Sheila Y. "Bethune-Cookman College." In *Black Women in America: An Historical Encyclopedia,* edited by Darlene Clark Hine, Elsa Barkley Brown, and Rosalyn Terborg-Penn, 127–128. Brooklyn, NY: Carlson Publishing, 1982.

Holt, Rackham. *Mary McLeod Bethune: A Biography.* Garden City, NY: Doubleday, 1964.

LeFall, Delores C., and Janet I. Sims. "Mary McLeod Bethune—the Educator." *Journal of Negro Education,* Summer 1976.

Ross, Joyce B. "Mary McLeod Bethune and the National Youth Administration: A Case Study of Power Relationships in the Black Cabinet of Franklin D. Roosevelt." In *Black Leaders of the Twentieth Century,* edited by John Hope Franklin and August Meier, 191–219. Urbana: University of Illinois Press, 1982.

Smith, Elaine M. "Bethune, Mary McLeod." In *Black Women in America: An Historical Encyclopedia,* edited by Darlene Clark Hine, Elsa Barkley Brown, and Rosalyn Terborg-Penn, 113–127. Brooklyn, NY: Carlson Publishing, 1993.

Sterne, Emma Gelders. *Mary McLeod Bethune.* New York: Alfred A. Knopf, 1957.

Bierstadt, Albert (1830–1902)
Painter
German-American

For about two decades in the final third of the nineteenth century, Albert Bierstadt's grand vistas of the American West and Native-Americans there captured the imaginations of Americans. With shifts in public tastes regarding painting styles, his reputation diminished, yet a century later, his masterpieces were rediscovered and found even greater admiration.

Born in Solingen, Germany, Albert Bierstadt immigrated with his parents to the United States in 1832. The family settled in New Bedford, Massachusetts. His fascination with painting led the young man to travel to Düsseldorf to study art at the academy. Although only twenty-three years old at the time, Bierstadt was an apt pupil and quickly developed his own style. After spending four years traveling and painting in Italy, he returned to the United States determined to explore the Western frontier and to capture this exotic new world on canvas. Bierstadt's style, a combination of naturalism and luminism (a school of art that stressed the qualities of light), would be perfectly realized in his landscape paintings of the West.

Bierstadt made several trips to the frontier, sometimes in the company of government surveyors and cartographers. In the years between 1859 and 1889, the artist made six trips to the Rocky Mountains and on to Yosemite in California. Accompanied by his brother, a photographer, Bierstadt also experimented with the new medium of photography. He was repeatedly awed by the vistas and the Native Americans that the expeditions encountered. The artist came to believe that he had to share these natural wonders with the average American. Bierstadt's method involved making small sketches that were brought home to his New York studio to be translated into mammoth landscape paintings (known as "machine paintings"). Enthusiastic and curious easterners queued up to study these compelling, exotic images.

Bierstadt's powerful skills made him one of the most popular painters of the 1860s and 1870s. Unfortunately, art critics were a fickle lot, and the Romantic vision of Bierstadt and his contemporaries fell out of favor. A devastating review appeared in an exhibition catalogue for the Centennial Exhibition in 1876. Clearly, Bierstadt had been eclipsed by other artists and changing attitudes toward landscape painting. All prominent luminists fell into disfavor during the 1880s, and their important works were ignored and forgotten. Bierstadt stubbornly continued traveling and painting. He died in 1902.

Albert Bierstadt's works were "rediscovered" in the mid–twentieth century. Today, he is considered one of the premiere landscape painters of the West. His romantic vision and attention to detail make his paintings historically important as well. Hundreds of his canvases and sketches are on regular exhibit across the country, providing new generations of art lovers with a view of a frontier that no longer exists but continues to fascinate.

Susanne M. Schick

REFERENCES

Anderson, Nancy, and Linda Ferber. *Albert Bierstadt: Art and Enterprise.* New York: Hudson Hills Press, 1990.

Biagell, Matthew. *Matthew Bierstadt.* New York: Watson-Guptill Publications, 1981.

Hedgepeth, Don. "The Emergence of Western Art." *Southwestern Art* 6 (1977–78): 4–18.

Hendricks, Gordon. *Albert Bierstadt: Painter of the American West.* New York: Harry N. Abrams, 1974.

———. "Roaming the West with Albert Bierstadt." *American West* 12 (1975): 22–29.

Ogden, Kate Nearpass. "God's Great Plow and the Scripture of Nature: Art and Geology at Yosemite." *California History* 71 (1992): 88–109.

Wickham, Christopher. "Oil and Water: The Development of the Portrayal of Native Americans by Nineteenth-Century German Painters." *Yearbook of German-American Studies* 31 (1996): 63–106.

Bikel, Theodore (1924–)
Stage and screen actor and folksinger
Israeli

Theodore Bikel is internationally known as an actor and singer. Born into a Jewish family in Vienna in 1924, he immigrated to Palestine with his parents when he was thirteen years old.

At the age of nineteen, he began his acting career in Israel and helped found the Israeli Chamber Theater (the Cameri) in 1944. In 1946, he entered London's Royal Academy of Dramatic Art. Appearing in several small London productions, he was "discovered" by Sir Laurence Olivier, who offered him a role in his production of *A Streetcar Named Desire* with Vivien Leigh. Since that time, Bikel has appeared in many plays, musicals, and operas in London, on Broadway, and internationally. He is best known for his starring roles in *Zorba* and as Tevye in *Fiddler on the Roof.* He has performed the latter more than 1,600 times since 1967.

In addition to his stage career, Bikel has been featured in numerous film roles, many of which are now classic, including *The African Queen* (1951), *The Defiant* Ones (1958) (for which he received the Academy Award nomination for best supporting actor), *The Rus-*

sians Are Coming, the Russians Are Coming (1965), Frank Zappa's *200 Motels* (1970), and *Shadow Conspiracy* (1996). He has also been featured on many television and radio programs. He is noted for his wide array of characters, ranging from a Hungarian-language expert in *My Fair Lady* to an Indian doctor in *The Sands of the Kalahari* to the American folklorist in *My Side of the Mountain.* His skill in accents and dialects is rooted in his real-life fluency in seven languages.

One of the world's best-known folksingers, he cofounded the Newport Folk Festival in 1961, the same year he became a U.S. citizen. Between 1959 and 1992, he recorded around three dozen albums, including folk music, sound tracks, a variety of Jewish and Israeli songs, and many books on tape. He has performed at nightclubs and with symphony orchestras throughout the United States and internationally.

Active in the Civil Rights movement and a supporter of the arts, he was an elected delegate to the historic 1968 Democratic National Convention in Chicago. He was president of Actor's Equity (1973–1982) and a board member of Amnesty International. By presidential appointment, he became a member of the National Council on the Arts (1977–1992). He has also served as a senior vice president of the American Jewish Congress.

Bikel's love for theater and folk culture and commitment to social activism and Jewish music and tradition are clearly linked to his experiences as a Jewish refugee from Austria and his life in Palestine (later Israel). Reflecting on the relationship of his work to his life, he claims, "Many people these days insist that their birth was like the birth of the Phoenix: suddenly, one day they sprang out in the middle of the desert without memory or parentage." Impossible, Bikel maintains. "You must explore your roots in the past in order to pinpoint your place in the present or to be entitled to a future. It doesn't work any other way."

Steven J. Gold

REFERENCES

Bikel, Theodore. *Theo.* New York: HarperCollins, 1994.

"Biography for Theodore Bikel": us.imdb.com/Name?Bikel (accessed 29 June 2000).

"Theodore Bikel: Biographical Information": www.bikel.com/biographical_information.html (accessed 19 June 2000).

Birkerts, Gunnar (1925–)
Architect and professor
Latvian

Gunnar Birkerts, professor emeritus of architecture at the University of Michigan, is a successful and celebrated architect with a career spanning more than fifty years. His designs reflect a classical training tempered by the influences of some of finest architectural minds of the twentieth century. The result has been the development of his own distinctive, internationally successful style.

Birkerts was born on 17 January 1925 in Latvia. He grew up there in the interwar period, when the tiny nation was at peace. A teenager when World War II broke out in Europe, Birkerts eventually became, like many other Latvians, a displaced person (DP), but one fortunate enough to be in the western sector of occupied Germany, controlled by the United States, Britain, and France. Birkerts's architectural training began in 1945 at the Stuttgart Technical College, in West Germany. Finishing in 1949, he immediately left for the United States, a turning point in his life, for he was able to continue his architectural career there.

Birkerts's career encompasses more than fifty years of architectural excellence. He is now professor emeritus of architecture at the University of Michigan, where, from 1959 to 1990, he was active in training a new generation of architects. He is a fellow in the American Institute of Architects, the Latvian Architects Association, and the Graham Foundation. Some of his most famous designs include the Federal Reserve Building in Minneapolis, Minnesota, and the U.S. Embassy in Caracas, Venezuela. He has also designed several museums and thirteen libraries in the United States. Among these are the Corning Museum of Glass in Corning, New York; the Kemper Museum of Contemporary Art and Design in Kansas City; the Law Library addition, University of Michigan; the Contemporary Art Museum, Houston, Texas; and the Geisel Library Addition, University of California at San Diego.

In addition to work in the United States and Latvia, Birkerts has been prominent in architecture in Italy, a country he particularly loves. He was at one time architect in residence at the American Academy in Rome. Besides being inspired by Italy's classic architecture, he was also involved with the design of a project for the University of Turin, a stadium in Venice, and a civic center in Florence. For his native Latvia, Birkerts has been designing the expansion of the classic central market in Riga, part of the city's redevelopment plan. The most ambitious current project for Latvia is the proposed Latvian National Library in Riga. For Birkerts it is especially thrilling to be able to create a potential landmark building for the Latvian people.

Birkerts has contributed greatly to both U.S. and international architecture, as well as enhancing the civic reputation of the Latvian-American community with his outstanding scholarship and artistic talent. His presence and his works are a constant reminder of the contributions of a relatively small ethnic group to the richness of American society. Birkerts is often a guest lecturer at universities, professional associations, and public organizations in the United States, Canada, Mexico, and Europe.

With his wife, Silvija, Birkerts has raised two sons and a daughter.

Paul Sando

REFERENCES

"Birkerts, Gunnar." In *Who's Who in America,* 55th ed., 2001. New Providence, NJ: Marquis Who's Who, 2000.

"Birkerts, Gunnar." In *Who's Who in the Midwest,* 28th ed., 2000–2001. New Providence, NJ: Marquis Who's Who, 2000.

"Birkerts, Gunnar." In *Who's Who in the World,* 18th ed., 2001. New Providence, NJ: Marquis Who's Who, 2000.

Gunnar Birkerts Architect. Personal and professional Web site: *www.gunnarbirkerts.com/index.html* (accessed 20 June 2000).

Gunnar Burkerts Associates. Gunnar Birkerts's archival material, Bentley Historical Library, University of Michigan, Ann Arbor: mirlyn. web.lib.umich.edu/WebZ/SearchOrScan? sessionid=01–49184-1571285749 (accessed 19 December 2000).

"Profile—Gunnar Birkerts." *World Architecture* 36 (1995): 22–53.

Blades, Ruben (1948–)
Singer, actor, and political activist
Panamanian

Ruben Blades, an internationally recognized musician, actor, and activist, has consistently used his position to raise awareness about social justice issues that affect Latinas/os. He has released more than fourteen albums and starred in numerous Hollywood films. Yet, in 1994 he put his career on hold and ran for the presidency of Panama. In his various endeavors, he has continually crossed borders in order to redefine traditional notions of Latino identity, music, and politics.

Blades was born in July 1948 in Panama City, Panama, and he grew up there. His family heritage reflects a mixed ancestry of Cuban, North American, Colombian, and St. Lucian. Blades became involved with music as a youth and formed part of a salsa music duo with Willie Colon. They were among the first to present politically charged lyrics through salsa. Their albums introduced that music to an international audience and presented it as an important avenue to represent and speak to the disempowered.

Blades's aim as a musician has been to reach as wide an audience as possible while creating music that reflects the political concerns and urban folklore of Latinas/os. When Blades went solo, his first album with his own group, Seis del Solar, was entitled *Buscando América*. Nominated for a Grammy Award in 1984, *Buscando* represents political themes that express solidarity with the "disappeared" and the conflicts in Central America of the time. (*Desaparecidos,* or "disappeared," refers to persons seized by paramilitary or progovernment forces and never again seen alive.) Although Blades was working with a major record label, he maintained the focus on Spanish-language lyrics and Latino-oriented themes throughout his many subsequent records. He won a Grammy in 1987 for his album *Escenas.*

Because spreading political ideas was so important to Blades, he went back and forth between music and the study of law. He received a law degree from the University of Panama in 1972 and a master's in international law from Harvard in 1985. In 1992, Blades formed Papa Egoro, an alternative Panamanian political party that means the Mother Earth; it was under that party that he ran for president of Panama in 1994. Having lived in New York and Los Angeles, he briefly moved to Panama in 1993 to launch his campaign. Coming in third, Blades's party won six legislative seats.

He is again living in Los Angeles and has been actively supportive of Latino-owned and Latino-run media, such as Fresno's Radio Bilingüe and *Latina Magazine.* Throughout his career, Blades has often participated in benefit concerts and political protests for international causes, notably human rights abuse, and such national issues as drug abuse and immigration.

Along with these activities, beginning in 1986, Blades appeared in a number of films. Despite the fame he has obtained through his music and acting career, Blades speaks with the press on limited occasions and engages the media mostly to promote important issues, among them HIV awareness or literacy programs. This man of many trades has consistently allowed his name to be used for the benefit of Latinos everywhere in helping educate them and others through music, organize them through politics, and encourage them through positive representations in film.

Leticia Hernández-Linares

REFERENCES

Cruz, Barbara. *Ruben Blades: Salsa Singer and Social Activist.* Springfield, NJ: Enslow Publishers, 1997.

Lopetegui, Enrique. "From Pop to Populism." *Los Angeles Times,* 12 September 1993.

———. "'Something to Defy All Definitions': After Losing Election, Blades Returns to Music, Ready to Explore." *Los Angeles Times,* 23 January 1995.

Marton, Betty. *Ruben Blades.* New York: Chelsea House Publishing, 1992.

Wilentz, Amy. "Slippery Blades." *New Republic* 209.8 (1 November 1993).

Bok, Edward William (1863–1930)
Magazine editor
Dutch-American

Edward Bok achieved prominence as the editor of *Ladies' Home Journal (LHJ)* from 1889 to 1919. During Bok's tenure, the magazine's circulation grew to an unprecedented 2 million copies.

Bok was born 9 October 1863, in Helder, the Netherlands. His well-to-do parents suffered major financial reversals and chose to start over in the United States. The family emigrated in 1870, settling in Brooklyn. Bok and his brother spent considerable time doing "women's work," helping their mother keep house—an experience Bok found useful years later as editor of a women's magazine. The family's economic circumstances prompted Bok to leave school at age twelve, after six years of public school, to work as an office boy for Western Union Telegraph Company. Nonetheless, Bok maintained a lifelong interest in self-education, nurtured by reading about and corresponding with prominent achievers. This correspondence led to a renowned collection of personal letters from such notables as Rutherford B. Hayes and Louisa May Alcott.

When his father died, eighteen-year-old Bok took a job as a stenographer at Henry Holt and Company, his first exposure to publishing, moving on to Charles Scribner's Sons in 1884. At the same time, he and a partner founded and edited *Brooklyn Magazine.* Bok convinced several of his eminent acquaintances to contribute articles gratis, and the little magazine gained favorable notice. Later, Bok and his partner sold their interests in the magazine. It eventually became *Cosmopolitan*.

In 1889, Bok became editor of the *Ladies' Home Journal* and instituted several practices that were new to magazine publishing. He refused to accept advertising for patent medicines, lucrative though it was. He spoke out against advertising and billboards that spoiled the landscape. He published controversial photographs of neglected and trash-strewn urban areas, resulting in cleanups by embarrassed city officials. He offered college and music school scholarships as magazine premiums, giving many young people access to higher education.

Fostered by a lifelong belief in giving back to the country that had given him much, Bok encouraged civic involvement, helping to form the Merion [Pennsylvania] Civic Organization in his own town. During World War I he served as state chairman for both the War Work Council of the Young Men's Christian Association (YMCA) and the United War Work Committee. He retired from *LHJ* in 1919 and then wrote his autobiography, *The Americanization of Edward Bok,* which won a Pulitzer Prize in 1921. He died in 1930.

Bok credited his success to the career opportunities, idealistic spirit, and freedom from social barriers he found in American culture, although he was critical of Americans for their wasteful habits and emphasis on quantity of production over quality. He believed that immigrants were responsible for learning the language, culture, and political system of their adopted country but felt that U.S. institutions, particularly public schools, fell short in teaching these. He saw his magazine as a means of helping both the American-born and immigrants educate themselves on the finer points of American life. In addition, throughout his career, Bok expressed pride in his Dutch heritage, which he credited for his personal characteristics and common sense. In 1910, he was awarded an honorary degree by Hope College in Holland, Michigan, a Dutch institution.

Jennifer Leo

REFERENCES

Bok, Edward W. *The Americanization of Edward Bok.* New York: Scribner's, 1920.

———. *A Dutch Boy Fifty Years After.* New York: Scribner's, 1921.

"Bok, Edward William." In *Concise Dictionary of American Biography,* 5th ed., 116. New York: Scribner's, 1997.

Doezema, Linda Pegman, ed. *Dutch Americans: A Guide to Information Sources.* Detroit: Gale Research, 1979.

Mulder, Arnold. *Americans from Holland.* New York: J. B. Lippincott, 1947.

Booth, Evangeline Cory (1865–1950)
Social worker and Salvation Army general
English

Evangeline Cory Booth was one of the most important social reformers and supporters of the urban poor, commanding the Salvation Army in the United States and extending its redemptive influence throughout the nation.

Evangeline Cory Booth was born in London, daughter of William Booth, a Methodist minister and the founder of the Salvation Army, and Catherine Mumford. She attended private schools but from the start devoted her life to her father's mission. As a teenager she lived among the people of London's slums, dressed in rags, so that she could gain their confidence and understand their plight. She became known as the White Angel, helping to feed the hungry and comfort the sick and dying, while also preaching the gospel. It was this form of "social gospel"—by which the poor were helped before they were preached to—that Booth would build upon in the United States. With it, she helped transform the attitudes and methods by which Americans addressed their own poor people. By her early twenties she was principal of the Salvation Army's International Training College and commander of field operations in London. In 1896 she moved to Canada to take command of the Salvation Army there and then, in 1904, took command of the Salvation Army in the United States, which had been established by emigrant Salvationists in 1880.

Booth reorganized the U.S. Salvation Army

and made it more effective, acquiring new buildings and properties in which to house and train the army's officers. By 1927 the organization owned 1,220 buildings in the United States. She was also responsible for changing the army's practice from offering "bread lines" for the poor during Christmas to providing them with Christmas baskets so that they could eat at home with their families. Booth also enhanced the army's work in U.S. prisons. During World War I she created the war auxiliary movement, which collected cloth for bandages for wounded soldiers, and she headed the Salvation Army's war board, in which capacity she sent personnel and supplies to the front. Afterward, she instituted new methods of annual drives for financial support from the public and successfully convinced many that such expenditure was a good investment in business and society, as well as an important form of altruism. In 1919 she was awarded the U.S. distinguished service medal in recognition of her "exceptionally meritorious service" as commander of the Salvation Army.

During the 1920s and 1930s Booth traveled throughout the world, establishing and nurturing branches of the Salvation Army and meeting heads of state. Although she had been romantically linked with several men, she never married, preferring to devote her entire life to her work. She was in England when World War II broke out but returned to the United States in 1940. In retirement she remained active as an adviser and an inspiration to the organization.

Booth died at age eighty-four, full of honors and hailed throughout the world as the "friend of the friendless" and the "White Angel of the Slums."

William E. Van Vugt

REFERENCES

Booth, Evangeline Cory. *The Harp and the Sword.* West Nyack, NY: Salvation Army, Literary Dept., 1992.

Troutt, Margaret. *The General Was a Lady: The Story of Evangeline Booth.* Nashville: A. J. Holman Co., 1980.

Wilson, Philip Whitwell. *General Evangeline Booth of the Salvation Army.* New York: Scribner's, 1948.

Borge, Victor (né Borge Rosenbaum) (1909–2000)

Pianist, comedian, conductor, and philanthropist Danish

Victor Borge entertained Americans with his zany mixture of music and comedy for sixty years. In December 1999, the "Great Dane" was honored at the Kennedy Center in Washington with the nation's highest honor for the performing arts.

Born Borge Rosenbaum in Copenhagen, on 3 January 1909, he changed his name to Victor Borge shortly after his arrival in the United States. His father, Bernard Rosenbaum, was a violinist for the Royal Danish Opera Orchestra, and his mother, Frederikke Lichtinger, was a talented pianist. By the age of ten, Borge was an accomplished pianist and, four years later, he gave a solo performance with the Copenhagen Philharmonic Orchestra. Blessed with an impish sense of humor and a talent for satire, he enjoyed playing musical jokes and gradually his concerts became a mixture of classical music and comedy. Before long, he was also performing in films and on the radio and soon became one of Denmark's leading entertainers. When Germany invaded and occupied Denmark in 1940, Borge, a Jew, who had often ridiculed Hitler and the Nazis in his performances, fled to the United States.

Initially handicapped by his limited knowledge of English, Borge was hired to do the warm-up for Rudy Vallee's popular radio show. This led to his big break, a guest appearance on Bing Crosby's *Kraft Musical Hall* show. Borge's performance, which centered around reading a story with sounds assigned to each punctuation mark, was a huge success, and during the next eighteen months he returned to the Crosby program fifty-four times. Appearances on other programs followed, and soon the National Broadcasting Company (NBC) signed him to the *Victor Borge Show,* which also featured Benny Goodman's orchestra. Eventually, however, Borge grew weary of the time constraints imposed by radio and took his act on the road, where the reaction of the audience would determine the nature and length of each routine. Encouraged by the critical and financial success of his concerts, Borge decided to take his road show to Broadway. Opening in October 1953 at the Golden Theater, his *Comedy in Music,* with 849 performances, still holds the record for the longest-running one-man show on Broadway. Borge returned to the concert tour in 1956 and, with exception of some extended vacations, never left it. In his ninetieth year he performed nearly 60 shows.

Over the years he made numerous television appearances, including several recent specials for the Public Broadcasting Service (PBS). One of the most popular was with the Chicago Symphony Orchestra, hosted by Itzhak Perlman. Another was *Victor Borge: Then and Now,* which combined recent concert footage and early television and movie performances. Beginning in the 1970s Borge returned to conducting, the love of his youth, and premier orchestras throughout the world followed his baton.

Throughout much of his life, Borge was uncommonly generous. He gave many concerts to benefit worthy causes, particularly scholarships at universities and colleges. In 1963 he joined with Richard Netter, a prominent New York lawyer, to create the "Thanks to Scandinavia Scholarship Fund," in gratitude for the actions of Scandinavians in saving the lives of thousands of Jews during World War II. This multimillion-dollar fund has supported the study in the United States of more than a thousand students from the Scandinavian countries. Although he became a U.S. citizen in 1948, he remained a popular figure in Denmark. His 1933 marriage to American Elsie Chilton ended in divorce, and in 1953 he wed Sanna Roach, his manager. She died in September 2000, and Borge died December 23, 2000.

Peter L. Petersen

REFERENCES

Blumenthal, Ralph. "Still Going Like Sixty at Ninety: Borge Is as American as a Cheese Danish." *New York Times,* 21 January 1999, E1.

Borge, Victor, with Dean Jennings. "Everybody Laughs at Me." *Saturday Evening Post* 299.3 (16 February 1957): 19ff (the first part of a extensively illustrated memoir that ran in seven consecutive issues of the magazine).

Borge, Victor, with Niels Jorgen Kaiser. *Smilet erden korteste afstand . . .* (A smile is the shortest distance . . .). Copenhagen: Gyldendal, 1997. (An English version of this Borge autobiography was scheduled for publication in the United States in late 2000.)

Hellman, Geoffrey T. "Profile: Birds in the Hand." *New Yorker* 31 (7 May 1955): 51ff.

Holden, Stephen. "Victor Borge: Pianist Who Combined Comedy and Classical Music, Dies at 91." *New York Times,* 25 December 2000, A19.

Oliver, Myrna. "Victor Borge, Pianist, Comedian." *Los Angeles Times,* 24 December 2000, B6.

Borglum, Gutzon (1867–1941)
Sculptor
Danish-American

One of the country's most prolific and controversial sculptors, Gutzon Borglum is best remembered for carving the faces of George Washington, Thomas Jefferson, Abraham Lincoln, and Theodore Roosevelt on Mount Rushmore, in South Dakota. He attributed his art to both his Danish heritage and his American experience.

Borglum was born in Ovid, Idaho Territory, on 25 March 1867, the son of Jens de la Mothe Borglum and Christina Mikkelsen, Mormon converts who had recently emigrated from Denmark. Jens Borglum was also married to Christina's sister, Ida. Eventually Christina withdrew from the household, and Gutzon was reared by Jens and Ida. Jens left the Mormon church and went to study medicine in St. Louis, after which he moved his family to Fremont, Nebraska. Young Borglum attended a Catholic boarding school in Kansas and schools in Fremont and nearby Omaha. In 1883 the family moved to Los Angeles, and seventeen-year-old Borglum went to work as an apprentice lithographer while taking art lessons. He studied with Elizabeth Jaynes Putnam, whom he married in 1889, even though she was eighteen years older. They went to Paris, London, and California, where he studied painting and sculpture. After that he left his wife and moved to New York.

A talented artist, Borglum received many commissions, including a statue of Philip Sheridan in Washington, D.C., and a bust of Lincoln for the Rotunda of the U.S. Capitol. Eventually, he would create more items for Statuary Hall in the Capitol than any other artist. But Borglum had many interests besides art. He dabbled in politics, and at times his speeches and writings suggested a streak of racism and anti-Semitism, but he was also an early critic of Nazi Germany's racial policies.

In 1909 Borglum divorced Putnam and married Mary Montgomery. They had two children, James Lincoln and Mary Ellis.

Borglum had been commissioned to carve a giant memorial to the Confederacy on the side of Georgia's Stone Mountain but had managed to finish only a twenty-foot head of Robert E. Lee before repeated clashes with the memorial's sponsors prompted the hot-tempered artist to smash his models and abandon the project in 1925. By this time he was already in contact with a group of South Dakotans, who envisioned a stone sculpture somewhere in the state's Black Hills. Borglum leaped at the opportunity and, after much study, chose Mount Rushmore as the location for his work. Like many of Borglum's projects, this one was fraught with difficulties and controversies, but with financial support from Congress and the State of South Dakota, the artist, aided by a small army of workers, was able to create a sixty-foot face of Washington by 1930. Slowly the other faces took form and were dedicated: Jefferson in 1936, Abraham Lincoln in 1937, and Roosevelt in 1939. Borglum died in 1941, and his son, Lincoln, who had been supervising the project for years, added the finishing touches to "The Shrine of Democracy."

Borglum was proud of his Danish heritage. He once said that "whatever is good in my art came from my mother and the old Danish race to which she belonged, but whatever gives my art strength, which makes it prevail here, comes from the courage imparted by the West."

Peter L. Petersen

REFERENCES

Casey, Robert J., and Mary Borglum. *Give the Man Room: The Story of Gutzon Borglum*. Indianapolis: Bobbs-Merrill, 1952.

Fite, Gilbert C. *Mount Rushmore*. Norman: University of Oklahoma Press, 1952.

Shaff, Howard, and Audrey Karl Shaff. *Six Wars at a Time: The Life and Times of Gutzon Borglum, Sculptor of Mount Rushmore*. Sioux Falls, SD: Center for Western Studies, 1985.

Smith, Rex Alan. *The Carving of Mount Rushmore*. New York: Abbeville Press, 1985.

Brzezinski, Zbigniew "Zbig" (Kazimierz) (1928–)
Professor and foreign policy consultant
Polish

In addition to being a distinguished university professor, Zbigniew Brzezinski was one of America's leading national security analysts of the Cold War era. He served as adviser to Presidents Lyndon Johnson and Jimmy Carter.

Brzezinski was born in Warsaw, the son of a Polish nobleman and diplomat, Tadeusz Brzezinski, and Leonia (Roman) Brzezinski, who helped Jews escape Nazi Germany. Brzezinski accompanied his parents to Canada in 1938, where his father served as Polish consul in Montreal. When a Communist Polish government was created in 1945, his father retired and the family settled in Canada. Brzezinski received his B.A. and M.A. from McGill University and his Ph.D. (1953) in political science from Harvard. He was appointed associate professor of law and public government at Columbia University, became director of its new Institute on Communist Affairs in 1961, and then full professor.

In the 1960s Brzezinski found his way into the Democratic foreign policy establishment. Until 1968, he supported U.S. engagement in Vietnam and, during then President Lyndon B. Johnson's administration, took leave from Columbia (1966–1968) to work on the State Department's Policy Planning Council and serve as adviser to Vice President Hubert H. Humphrey. He was the first director of the Trilateral Commission and President Jimmy

Carter's national security adviser (1977–1981). After leaving office, Brzezinski held positions at the Center for Strategic and International Studies and the Paul Nitze School for Advanced International Studies at Johns Hopkins University.

Brzezinski's intellectual output and foreign policy commentary have been enormous and influential. President Johnson in 1966 used Brzezinski's term *peaceful engagement* to announce the U.S. initiative toward the Soviet Bloc. Brzezinski advocated initiatives to bring Russian-controlled Eastern Europe closer to the West as well as to secure German reunification. He was a constant advocate of the need to maintain U.S. military superiority; nevertheless, during the Carter administration, he emphasized human rights as a means of enhancing America's ideological and political appeal and improving its strategic position relative to the Soviet Union. In his 1989 book, *The Grand Failure: The Birth and Death of Communism in the Twentieth Century,* Brzezinski maintained that the Soviet Union was already a spent ideological and political force. Subsequent to the collapse of communism, he argued for Polish, Czech, and Hungarian admission to the North Atlantic Treaty Organization (NATO) (which did occur in 1999) and the extension of European security to eastern European countries in the post-Soviet age. Brzezinski had also argued that the United States was the first to enter the postindustrial age, where society is shaped by computers, electronics, and technology.

Brzezinski has received several honorary degrees and, in 1981, was awarded the Presidential Medal of Freedom by President Carter. He was a director of the Polish American Enterprise Fund and one of the few to receive the Order of the White Eagle, the highest decoration of the Republic of Poland. Although not actively engaged in the Polish-American community, Brzezinski has maintained links with it as vice president of the Polish Institute of Arts and Sciences in America and in periodic addresses before such groups as the Polish American Congress.

In 1955 Brzezinski married Emilie Benes. They have three children.

Stanislaus A. Blejwas

REFERENCES

Andrianopolous, Gerry. *Kissinger and Brzezinski: The NSC and the Struggle for Control of U.S. National Security Policy.* New York: St. Martin's Press, 1991.

Brzezinski, Zbigniew. *The Grand Failure: The Birth and Death of Communism in the Twentieth Century.* New York: Scribner's, 1989.

———. *Power and Principle: Memoirs of the National Security Adviser, 1977–1981.* New York: Farrar, Straus & Giroux, 1983.

———. *The Soviet Bloc: Unity and Conflict,* Cambridge, MA: Harvard University Press, 1960.

Brzezinski, Zbigniew, and Samuel P. Huntington. *Political Power: USA/USSR.* New York: Viking, 1964.

"Brzezinski, Zbigniew." In *The Cold War 1945–1991: Leaders and Other Important Figures in the United States and Western Europe,* edited by Benjamin Frankel. Detroit: Gale Research, 1992.

"Brzezinski, Zbigniew." In *Current Biography Yearbook 1970,* edited by Charles Moritz, 53–55. New York: H. W. Wilson, 1970.

Bulosan, Carlos (1911–1956)
Writer
Filipino

Carlos Bulosan was the most notable American literary figure who was Filipino. A highly regarded young writer in the 1930s and 1940s, he suffered from tuberculosis and died in obscurity. By the 1970s his reputation had rebounded as post-1965 immigrants from the Philippines and their children hailed his works.

Like many of his generation, Bulosan left Pangasinan Province, in the northern Philippines, for California in the early 1930s. There, he found few opportunities for employment and suffered the effects of racial prejudice against "Pinoys." Unlike most of his cohort, Bulosan found opportunities to write. He wrote both about life in the Philippines and about the Filipino experience in the fields and canneries of the western United States. His first book-length work, *The Laughter of My Father* (1944), included stories and folktales from his home province, some previously published in such magazines as the *New Yorker* and *Harper's Bazaar*. It received respectful reviews and sold well, though Bulosan later claimed, "I am not a Laughing Man."

Bulosan's most significant work, *America Is in the Heart,* appeared in 1946. In that book, he offered a first-person tale of the harrowing life faced by immigrant-Filipino workers—brawls, beatings, and even murder—against a backdrop of depression-era California. Described by a close friend as "30 percent auto-biography, 40 percent case history of Pinoy life in America, and 30 percent fiction," the book's narrator does not give way to despair, however. Bulosan proclaimed high aspirations, and his protagonist prevailed over oppressive conditions through writing, the help of American and Filipino friends, and participation in the left wing of the U.S. labor movement.

Although he wrote in English and was perhaps the first Filipino writer to attract an audience that extended beyond his compatriots, Bulosan retained his national identity. In 1946, granted along with other Filipinos the right to apply for U.S. citizenship, he declined to do so. Although Bulosan never returned to the Philippines, much of his later writing—largely unpublished in his lifetime—centered on the islands' recent past. In failing health, he moved to Seattle in 1950, where he died.

Bulosan's reputation revived with the republication of *America Is in the Heart* in 1973. It soon became a staple of college classes in Asian American literature on the West Coast and has sold more than 25,000 copies since its reissue. In the early 1990s Filipino-American community theater groups across the nation performed a play drawn from it, *America Is in the Heart,* by Chris Millado.

In recent years several collections of Bulosan's poetry, short fiction, essays, and letters have appeared, including *On Becoming Filipino: The Selected Writings of Carlos Bulosan* (1995). The same year also saw the publication in the United States of Bulosan's manuscript novel, *The Cry and the Dedication,* with an introduction by E. San Juan, Jr. The book is set in the Philippines at the time of the Huk rebellion of the late 1940s and early 1950s.

Controversial during his lifetime, Bulosan has been celebrated in recent years. Friends from Seattle provided a new gravestone with appropriate ceremonies in 1984. In fact, in the 1990s, Philippine President Fidel Ramos saluted Bulosan during a visit to the United States.

Roland L. Guyotte

REFERENCES

Anderson, Rick. "American's Grave: New Awareness of Filipino History Casts Light on Carlos Bulosan." *Seattle Times,* 1 October 1984.

Bulosan, Carlos, *America Is in the Heart.* New York: Harcourt, Brace, 1946.

———. *On Becoming Filipino: The Selected Writings of Carlos Bulosan.* Edited by E. San Juan, Jr. Philadelphia: Temple University Press, 1995.

Evangelista, Susan. *Carlos Bulosan and His Poetry: A Biography and Anthology.* Quezon City, Philippines: Atenes de Manila University Press, 1985.

Guyotte, Roland L. "Generation Gap: Filipinos, Filipino Americans, and Americans, Here and There, Then and Now." *Journal of American Ethnic History* 17 (Fall 1997): 64–70.

Morantte, P. C. *Remembering Carlos Bulosan.* Quezon City, Philippines: New Day Publishers, 1984.

"Ramos Emphasizes the U.S.–Philippine Connection." *Seattle Post-Intelligencer,* 22 November 1993.

San Juan, E., Jr., "Bulosan as a Revolutionary." *Philippine News,* 30 January–5 February 1985, 13.

Bunkse, Edmunds (1935–)

Geographer, educator, and journalist
Latvian

Edmunds Bunkse has been a professor of geography at the University of Delaware since 1969. He has also been the director of the Cultural Programmes Department of Latvian TV. He has distinguished himself through his scholarship and professionalism and is internationally recognized for his work in the Baltic states. Moreover, he exemplifies the ability of the human spirit to overcome the hardships that war refugees face.

Bunkse was born in Latvia in 1935, amidst a period of "golden years" peace. During

World War II, in June 1941, his family was deported by the occupying Soviet forces. His father scattered the family in hiding places. Edmunds stayed with a Latvian nationalist group living in the forests. Food was scarce, and he developed symptoms of malnutrition. In early 1944, the family fled attacking Russians, going by sea to Danzig, Poland (now Gdansk). Upon arrival, they were placed by German officials in a labor camp, alongside Russian prisoners of war, but they escaped during an air raid and, after more perilous episodes, arrived at a UN Refugee Association camp, or Displaced Persons camp, in Lübeck, Germany.

In June 1950, the family was allowed to immigrate to the United States, despite the fact that his father was then sixty years old. Four years later, Edmunds entered the University of Illinois but withdrew to serve two years in the U.S. Army Medical Corps. Subsequently, he completed both a master's degree and a doctorate in geography at the University of California at Berkeley (1969, 1973) and began teaching at the University of Delaware in 1969. He has been visiting professor in Sweden, London, and the University of Latvia, where he holds an adjunct professorship. After the collapse of communism in Europe and Russia, Bunkse also became involved with Latvian Television and its Cultural Programmes Department. The programs produced by Bunkse and Latvian Television have educated viewers about the culture and politics of many Western countries and about issues of international communications. He was the U.S. representative to a conference sponsored by the George C. Marshall Center for Security Studies, participating in discussions concerning the recent expansion of NATO to include Poland, Hungary, and the Czech Republic, and other possibilities.

For ethnic Latvians in the United States and abroad, Bunkse is considered a highly professional scholar and promoter of cultural understanding, nationally and internationally. His work with the Marshall Center has helped shape the perception of Latvia and Latvians as members of the community of nations. His presence in several professional societies has raised awareness of the character of the Latvian people and other Latvian causes. He is also a member of a learned society in Toronto, Canada, called "Lidums," which promotes Latvian culture and contact among immigrants to North America.

Married to a producer for Latvian Television and father of two children, Bunkse continues his scholarship and service. Along with the "privilege of serving" the United States in NATO, he cites his two books on "humanistic geography"—*Siren Voices: Geography as a Humanistic Erudition* and *Geographic Sensibilities* (forthcoming)—among his proudest achievements. He believes that the hardships of his early life experiences helped prepare him to succeed.

Paul Sando

REFERENCES

"Bunkse, Edmunds." In *Who's Who in America 2001*, 55th ed. New Providence, NJ: Marquis Who's Who, 2000.

"Bunkse, Edmunds." In *Who's Who in the East 1999–2000*, 28th ed. New Providence, NJ: Marquis Who's Who, 1998.

"Bunkse, Edmunds." In *Who's Who in the World 2001*, 18th ed. New Providence, NJ: Marquis Who's Who, 2000.

University of Delaware, Department of Geography, Web site: *www.Udel.edu/Geography/framefac.html* (accessed 20 June 2000).

Burton, Richard Walter (Jenkins) (1925–1984)

Actor
Welsh

Richard Burton, son of a Welsh coal miner and one of the most gifted stage actors of the twentieth century, won seven Academy Award nominations for his film roles. He became an international celebrity but was also known for his extravagant living and widely publicized love affairs.

Burton was twelfth of thirteen children born to Dic and Edith Jenkins in the South Wales mining village of Pontrhydyfen. Alienated from his alcoholic father, at age eighteen he became the ward of Philip Burton, his boyhood teacher, drama coach, and mentor, whose last name he took for his own. Burton taught Richard to speak without a Welsh accent and helped him spend a year at Exeter College, Oxford, where he attracted attention for his acting abilities.

In 1947, following service in the Royal Air Force, Richard Burton received stage roles and a part in a Welsh film, launching his acting career. While making that film, he met and married Sybil Williams, also from a Welsh mining valley, with whom he had two children. A season of Shakespeare at Stratford-upon-Avon in 1951 established him as the most promising classical actor of his time. During his two seasons in London with the Old Vic Company he played in *Hamlet, Coriolanus, The Tempest, Henry V,* and *Othello.* His stage charisma attracted the attention of Hollywood, and he was contracted by Twentieth Century Fox for roles in *My Cousin Rachel* (which earned him the first of seven Academy Award nominations), *The Desert Rats,* and *The Robe.*

During the filming of *Cleopatra* in Rome in the early 1960s, his reputation for sexual escapades was firmly established by his well-publicized affair with the actress Elizabeth Taylor. Their stormy romance was complicated by Burton's alcoholism. Hollywood studios capitalized on the couple's notoriety by casting them together in several films. *Who's Afraid of Virginia Woolf* (1966) was their greatest joint critical success. Between 1964 and 1976 they married, divorced, remarried, and again divorced. Burton subsequently married twice again.

Burton acted in sixty films, many of them undistinguished, but he did enjoy success on the American stage in the musical *Camelot* and won praise for his role in the stage play *Equus,* receiving an Academy Award nomination and a Golden Globe when he repeated the role on film. Although Burton felt that his true calling lay in the theater, he performed only four stage roles during his last twenty years.

Burton clung to his Welsh roots and working-class background, drawing on his Welshness, both as an actor and as a celebrity, cultivating the romantic image of the alternately brooding and boisterous, hard-drinking Celt, and maintaining his connections with his family and such notable Welsh intellectuals as the poet Dylan Thomas. He insisted on celebrating the Welsh national day, reserving it as a holiday in his acting contracts. He gave Welsh-Americans an example of both heroic qualities and lamentable flaws.

Burton died in Geneva, Switzerland, in 1984 and was buried, according to his wishes, in clothes the color of the dragon on the Welsh national flag, while his family sang his favorite Welsh hymns and songs.

D. Douglas Caulkins and Lorna W. Caulkins

REFERENCES

Bragg, Melvyn. *Richard Burton: A Life.* Boston: Little, Brown, 1988.

Ferris, Paul. *Richard Burton.* New York: Coward, McCann & Geoghegan, 1981.

Jenkins, David, with Sue Rogers. *Richard Burton—A Brother Remembered.* London: Century, 1993.

Jenkins, Graham, with Barry Turner. *Richard Burton, My Brother.* New York: Harper & Row, 1988.

Steverson, Tyrone. *Richard Burton: A Bio-Bibliography.* Westport, CN: Greenwood Press, 1992.

Cabet, Étienne (1788–1856)
Utopian thinker
French

Étienne Cabet, a French utopian thinker, came to the United States to establish the communities he had envisioned. However, his success in Texas, Illinois, Iowa, and Missouri was more limited than he had anticipated.

Cabet was born in Dijon on 1 January 1788. His father was a cooper. At Dijon University, he studied law under Pierre-Joseph Proudhon, an early French anarchist. Cabet received his doctorate of law in 1812, moved to Paris in the 1820s, and joined the French *charbonnerie,* a republican movement inspired by the Italian *carbonari.* In July 1831 he was elected to the French National Assembly, but he was brought before French judges in 1834 for opposing the government during the 1830 uprising and was condemned to two years in prison. He chose exile and left for Great Britain, settling in London and writing books. He met Robert Owen, and Owen's ideas and Thomas More's *Utopia* helped Cabet write his own utopian novel, *Voyage to Icaria.* After Cabet returned to France in 1840, his novel attracted followers and his popularity grew; he eventually agreed to establish a utopian settlement in the United States in 1848.

The departure of Cabet's advance guard in early 1848 was poorly timed. A republican uprising in France had prompted many Icarians, as they called themselves (based on his novel), to stay and push for the creation of a republic. Meanwhile, the advance guard in Texas failed because they had not cleared land for settlement; they were former city dwellers whose careers had been in industry, not agriculture. When Cabet arrived in New Orleans in 1849, he found several hundred followers there. About half of them demanded a refund of the money they had paid to participate in the venture and returned to France. Cabet and his followers moved to Nauvoo, Illinois, where they had bought land from the Mormons who had left for the western territories.

Cabet created and organized his utopian settlement in Nauvoo with fewer than 200 Icarians. In the early 1850s, French followers arrived, but most did not stay; they were surprised by the backward appearance of the Nauvoo settlement and the children's being housed away from their parents. Dissension and opposition to Cabet arose because the Icarians realized that their life in Nauvoo was much different from the descriptions in his novel. Icarians still in France declined to leave since the news from Nauvoo was disappointing. Furthermore, Cabet's departure had diminished his popularity in France, and the financial support for his efforts declined significantly. Many Icarians had returned to France by the end of the decade, and others settled outside the Icarian community.

In 1853, Cabet's community bought lands in western Iowa in order to create a new community, and a new Icarian village was constructed in Adams County. Three years later, the Nauvoo community formally divided, with Cabet and his followers moving to St. Louis, and the others settling in Iowa. Cabet died in St. Louis on 7 November 1856.

Cabet's projects hardly survived his demise. The Iowa colonies divided in the 1870s and were finally dissolved in 1898. The last Icarian community created was in California in the 1870s, but it lasted only a few years. By 1900 Icarianism had ended in both the United States and France.

André J. M. Prévos

REFERENCES

Bonnaud, Félix. *Étienne Cabet et son œuvre.* Paris: Société libre des Gens de Lettres, 1900.

Prudhommeaux, Jules. *Icarie et son fondateur Etienne Cabet. Contribution à l'étude du Socialisme Expérimental.* Paris: Édouard Cornély et Cie., 1907.

Rude, Fernand, ed. *"Allons en Icarie." Deux ouvriers isérois aux États-Unis en 1855.* Grenoble: Presses Universitaires de Grenoble, 1980.

Cabrini, Francesca Xavier (1850–1917)

Missionary, religious order leader, and first American saint
Italian

As mother superior of the Missionary Sisters of the Sacred Heart, Francesca Cabrini was commissioned by Pope Leo XIII to minister to the Italian immigrants in the United States, where she founded orphanages, hospitals, and schools. Having established sixty-five convents and hundreds of schools and orphanages on three continents, Mother Cabrini was beatified, and she was made a saint by the Catholic church in 1946. Thus, the first American saint was an immigrant who had become a naturalized citizen.

Born on 15 July 1850 in Sant'Angelo (Lombardy), Italy, Cabrini was the youngest of thirteen children. Inspired by her uncle, a missionary priest, and by her father, she was motivated to become a missionary. She was educated by the Daughters of the Sacred Heart and became a schoolteacher at eighteen. Two years later she became a nun, taking as her middle name that of the great missionary Saint Frances Xavier.

Cabrini committed herself to working with orphans and had established eight orphanages by 1887. Her request to do missionary work in China having been denied in 1887, she established the Missionary Sisters of the Sacred Heart in Rome. There, she met Bishop Giovanni Scalabrini, founder of the Scalabrinian Fathers, who asked Mother Cabrini to bring her mission to New York and to establish orphanages and schools in the immigrant neighborhoods.

Convinced by the pope to go, Cabrini and six of her nuns left and, in May 1889, settled among the Italians on the Lower East Side, where they found many suffering immigrants. Within two weeks, Cabrini had gathered 200 children to attend her religious education classes and opened an orphanage for Italian children. Her missionary activities spread to other Italian communities, and Cabrini made the first of many trips to Italy for more sisters to help her missions. With them, she started Catholic hospitals across the country, from New York to Chicago to Seattle, even organizing fund-raisers.

Despite her small stature and physical frailty, Cabrini established a network of religious and service institutions spanning Europe and the Americas. Her work became so well known that she was asked to found schools and orphanages in France, Spain, England, and Latin America, but she remained committed to her work among Italian immigrants in the United States. In 1892, for example, she traveled to New Orleans to arrange for nuns to meet returning plantation workers as well as a priest to say mass for families on isolated plantations. In addition, they worked with prison inmates in Louisiana and later at Sing Sing and Chicago prisons.

In 1902, after a half dozen years abroad, Mother Cabrini returned to the United States, summoned by the bishop of Denver, who requested her aid for Italian miners. She and her nuns descended deep into mine shafts to offer aid and spiritual comfort; and she extended her various efforts to Seattle and Los Angeles. In the midst of all this, she took the time to become a U.S. citizen.

Mother Cabrini died in Chicago on 22 December 1917. In 1928, the investigations concerning her sanctity opened. Her beatification took place in the Vatican Basilica on 13 November 1938. On 7 July 1946, Francesca Xavier Cabrini was canonized a saint by the Catholic church.

Diane C. Vecchio

REFERENCES

Caliaro, Marco, and Mario Francesconi. *John Baptist Scalabrini: Apostle to Emigrants.* Staten Island, NY: Center for Migration Studies, 1977.

DiDonato, Pietro. *Immigrant Saint: The Life of Mother Cabrini.* New York: McGraw-Hill, 1960.

DiGiovanni, Stephen Michael. "Mother Cabrini: Early Years in New York." *Catholic Historical Review* 77 (January 1991): 56–77.

Maynard, Theodore. *Too Small A World: The Life of Francesca Cabrini.* Milwaukee, WI: Bruce Publishing, 1945.

Cahan, Abraham (1860–1951)
Journalist, author, and socialist labor leader
Jewish

Abraham Cahan was an immigrant who, through his renowned journalism, used Yiddish to Americanize the new Jewish immigrants and English to bring their experiences to the wider American community. He is remembered as a great journalist, a legendary teacher to a people in the process of acculturation, and an indefatigable defender of the cause of labor and socialism.

Cahan was born in 1860, in Byelorussia, the only child of Shachne Cahan, a relatively poor shopkeeper and Hebrew teacher, and Sarah Goldarbeter. When he was under six, the family moved to Vilna, the capital of rabbinic learning and the seat of a growing modernization movement. He went to religious school but also devoured the secular works in the Vilna Public Library. He mastered Russian and gained admission to the Vilna State Teachers' Training College in 1878, a center for student radicalism. Within two years Cahan had converted to socialism. By 1881 he was a certified schoolmaster and a member of an underground revolutionary cell. Having to flee the police, Cahan joined an Am Olam group that, in the wake of pogroms in Ukraine, was going to the United States to experiment with Jewish agricultural communalism.

Cahan arrived in New York on 6 June 1882. He worked at odd jobs, but his joy came from teaching English to his Lower East Side neighbors at night, work he continued to do for ten years. Cahan also began to deliver political harangues in Yiddish and, lecturing in Yiddish and English in 1884 and 1885, he helped organize a Jewish tailors' union and a Jewish cloak makers' union, marking the beginning of his lifelong association with the labor movement.

Cahan's main contribution, however, came in journalism, particularly in pioneering popular Yiddish journalism. The Yiddish *Daily Forward,* which he edited at its founding in 1897 and to which he returned in 1903, under his leadership became the educator of the Jewish-immigrant masses. A critical component of the Jewish labor movement and Jewish socialism and a defender and patron of Yiddish literature and modern culture, it elevated Yiddish to journalistic and literary heights. Among the authors sustained by the *Forward* were Sholem Asch and Isaac Bashevis Singer. The circulation of this socialist paper, from Boston to Los Angeles, at its height in 1920 was close to 300,000. Yet Cahan also tried to reach beyond his community with articles and stories in the English press and in several books, among them *Yekl: A Tale of the New York Ghetto* (1896) and his classic novel of the urban-immigrant experience, *The Rise of David Levinsky* (1917).

Cahan was a moderate Socialist whose anticapitalist views were tempered by conditions in the United States and the excesses of Soviet authoritarianism. After the 1917 revolution, and in the face of militant Bolshevism, the *Forward* became increasingly anti-Communist. In addition, although not considered a Zionist, Cahan paid tribute to the courage and idealism of Zionist pioneers.

Throughout the 1930s and 1940s Cahan continued to be productive and creative. Only after suffering a stroke in 1946 did he reduce his activities. He died five years later.

Gerald Sorin

REFERENCES

Cahan, Abraham. *Bleter fun mayn lebn* (Leaves from my life). 5 vols. New York: Forward Association, 1926–1931.

Chametzky, Jules. *From the Ghetto: The Fiction of Abraham Cahan.* Amherst: University of Massachusetts Press, 1977.

Howe, Irving. *World of Our Fathers.* New York: Harcourt Brace Jovanovich, 1976.

Rischin, Moses. *Grandma Never Lived in America: The*

New Journalism of Abraham Cahan. Bloomington: Indiana University Press, 1985.

———. *The Promised City.* Cambridge: Harvard University Press, 1962.

Sanders, Ronald. *The Downtown Jews.* New York: Harper & Row, 1969.

Stein, Leon, et al., trans. *The Education of Abraham Cahan.* Philadelphia: Jewish Publication Society, 1969.

Callas, Maria (née Maria Kalogeropoulos) (1923–1977)

Opera singer
Greek-American

Maria Callas is regarded as simply one of the finest opera singers of the twentieth century. She set new standards for opera performances.

Callas was born to Greek parents in New York City on 2 December 1923. When she was thirteen, her family returned to Greece, which gave her the opportunity to study with soprano Elvira de Hidalgo at the Athens Conservatory. There, she performed her first major role as *Tosca* in July 1942. She was eighteen years old.

Callas returned to New York during the German occupation of Greece. She auditioned for, and was offered a contract by, the Metropolitan Opera but decided instead to go to Italy after the war. She made her formal operatic debut with Ponchielli's *La Gioconda,* in Verona, on 3 August 1947. It was there that she also met and married Giovanni Battista Meneghini. Her Italian husband became her business manager and helped her financially. During the years they lived together, she sang 475 operatic performances. Callas was also encouraged by Tullio Serafin to sing *Isolde* and *Aida* in various Italian productions. In 1951 she became a member of La Scala in Milan. In the tragic role of *Medea* in Cherubini's opera, Callas mesmerized the audience with her interpretation of pity and terror. Through the power of her voice, Callas was acknowledged as the greatest dramatic singer of the century. She had legions of admirers, despite frequent temper outbursts during which she would walk off the stage and cancel appearances.

For many years Callas's name was linked romantically with that of shipping magnate Aristotle Onassis. This relationship proved to be a source of disappointment to the great singer and was destined to be fodder for the world's tabloid industry. Moreover, Callas continually battled obesity, which handicapped her career. At one point her weight burgeoned to 210 pounds, but she was able to reduce it to 135 pounds. Despite her weight, she possessed a classical Greek profile, which made a great impression on the stage.

In 1958 Callas left La Scala but returned there from 1960 to 1962. She performed at London's Covent Garden (1952–1953 and 1957–1959), in Chicago (1954–1956), and in Dallas (1958–1959). Nonetheless, the peak of her success may well have been her brilliant debut at the Metropolitan Opera in New York, as Norma, on 29 October 1956. In 1971–1972 Callas taught a seminar on opera at the Julliard School of Music in New York, which was enthusiastically received. In 1974 Callas gave her final public performance in a series of concerts with Giuseppe di Stefano.

Callas returned to Europe, where she suffered a fatal heart attack in her Paris apartment on 16 September 1977. Her body was cremated and the ashes were scattered on the Aegean Sea. But her legend lives on. When people speak of Rossini, Bellini, Donizetti, and Verdi, they remember Callas, for she dominated the opera stage and set new standards in the world of opera with the dramatic power of her voice, acting, and intelligence.

George A. Kourvetaris

REFERENCES

"Callas Divina. The Official Maria Callas Web Site": www.callas.it (accessed 15 June 2000).

"Callas, Maria." *Encarta Online Encyclopedia 2000:* encarta.msn.com/find/Concise.asp?ti= 03B84000 (accessed 15 June 2000).

"Maria Callas." In *Baker's Biographical Dictionary of Twentieth-Century Classical Musicians,* edited by Laura Kuhn, 205–206. New York: Schirmer Books, Prentice Hall International, 1997.

"Maria Callas. 1977–1997. 1st International Congress, September 1997, Athens Greece": www.mariacallas97.ids.gr (accessed 15 June 2000).

Pilichos, G. K. "The Eternal Maria Callas!" (1997): www.mariacallas97.ids.gr/docs/pilichos.htm (accessed 15 June 2000).

Scott, Michael. *Maria Meneghini Callas.* Boston: Northeastern University Press, 1991.

Calleros, Cleofas (1896–1973)

*Community and civil rights leader
and historian*
Mexican-American

Cleofas Calleros had a significant impact within the city of El Paso, Texas, organizing many community institutions—particularly for the Mexican-American community. He also wrote extensively on the history of El Paso and south Texas and fought discrimination against Mexicans and Mexican-Americans.

Calleros was born in 1896 in Río Florido, Chihuahua, Mexico, to Ismael and Refugia Perales Calleros. In 1902, the family immigrated to El Paso. Calleros enrolled in Sacred Heart School and graduated as class valedictorian in 1911, later attending Draughton Business College. He was initially employed as a printer and a dispatcher for the Southern Pacific Railroad but joined the army in 1917. The following year, he became a U.S. citizen and married Benita Blanco; they had one daughter. Calleros was wounded in action overseas but remained to serve in Germany with the Army of Occupation and continued thereafter in the U.S. Army Officers Reserve Corps (1920–1938).

In the early 1920s, Calleros began his many community projects. He was hired as the southwest representative for the U.S. Catholic Welfare Conference and worked there for more than twenty years. He organized free citizenship-preparation classes for Mexican immigrants; helped establish the El Paso Boy's Club and the El Paso chapter of the League of United Latin American Citizens (LULAC); served as president of the Sociedades Latino-Americanas (Latin American societies); and was a founding member of the first chapter of the Texas Knights of Columbus and numerous chapters elsewhere in Texas (and wrote a history of the knights for the organization's sev-entieth anniversary). In turn, the Knights of Columbus honored Calleros by inducting him as a knight commander of St. Gregory the Great. Among his other community efforts, in 1936 he and other Mexican-Americans fought to repeal the classification of Mexicans as colored on birth and death records held by the El Paso City-County Health Unit.

Calleros was also an award-winning writer. He earned the Daliet Award and trophies in 1935 through 1938 for his writings celebrating the 1936 Texas Centennial. In 1952 he was cowinner with the *El Paso Times* of first prize and the award of merit from the American Association for State and Local History for feature articles on the history of West Texas. He coauthored the book *Historia del Templo de Nuestra Señora de Guadalupe* (1953) and coauthored *El Paso—Then and Now* (1954), based on his newspaper article series on late-nineteenth-century El Paso and early Texas settlements. In the same year he helped organize the El Paso County Historical Society and, afterward, the Chihuahua State Historical Society and the Western History Association.

The Spanish government named Calleros a knight of the Order of Isabella for his work on Spanish Southwestern history. In addition, he was awarded an honorary doctorate from New Mexico State University and an honorary master's of fine arts from the University of New Mexico.

Calleros died on 22 February 1973 and was buried with military honors at Fort Bliss National Cemetery.

Zaragosa Vargas

REFERENCES

Calleros, Cleofas, Collection. Special Collections, University of Texas, El Paso.

García, Mario T. *Desert Immigrants: The Mexicans of El Paso, 1880–1920.* New Haven: Yale University Press, 1981.

———. "Mexican Americans and the Politics of Citizenship: The Case of El Paso, 1936." *New Mexico Historical Review* 59.2 (1984): 187–204.

Calvin, William Austin (1898–1962)
Labor leader
Canadian

William Calvin spent his life in service of others, both his union—the International Brotherhood of Boilermakers and Blacksmiths—and his adopted country, serving in various capacities in government and sharing his labor expertise.

Born in St. John, New Brunswick, in 1898, Calvin was educated in public schools in Grand Bay, New Brunswick, and Brooklyn, New York. He was employed as a boilermaker first by the Canadian National Railway and then by the Bartlett Hayward Company of Baltimore. Joining the Canadian army in 1915, Calvin served through World War I, receiving serious wounds a month prior to the armistice. At the time of his discharge from the army he had achieved the rank of captain. He immigrated to the United States in 1919. For reasons of health he choose to settle in Jacksonville, Florida. He continued as a boilermaker, working for the Seaboard Airline Railroad. He also boxed professionally during the 1920s.

Calvin's union career began when he was elected chairman of his local shop committee of the Union of Boilermakers and Blacksmiths in 1921. He rose among the ranks to the post of vice president of the International Brotherhood of Boilermakers and Blacksmiths in 1930. Three years later, he was lent to the American Federation of Labor, where he served as secretary-treasurer for seven years. In 1933, he was also appointed to the Industrial Relations Committee for the Shipbuilding and Repairing Industry and was responsible for drafting the 1936 Merchant Marine Act. In 1940 he was appointed to the General Naval Wage Board of Review and in 1942 became a member of the Shipbuilding Commission as well as an alternate on the National Defense Mediation Board. In 1951 he was employed as a labor specialist in the National Production Authority, a post he held until 1952. He then returned to the union as an international representative.

In 1953 Calvin was appointed as assistant to the international president, Charles McGowan. The following year he was chosen to complete McGowan's term of office. He was subsequently elected to the post in both 1957 and 1961. He continued to serve the U.S. government, with trips to India and South America on behalf of the State Department. In 1961, in addition to his election as international president of the International Brotherhood of Boilermakers and Blacksmiths, he was elected to the executive council of the American Federation of Labor and Congress of Industrial Organizations.

He and his wife Nancy had three daughters: Elaine, Marilyn, and Katherine. They lived in Kansas City. His death in 1962, after a meeting in Washington, D.C., left the union shocked. He was eulogized as a dedicated member of the labor movement and a great leader. He made significant contributions to his union and to the labor movement, and his work with the U.S. government gave him much prestige among union leaders.

Gillian Leitch

REFERENCES

"Death Takes International President." *Boilermakers Blacksmiths Journal* 74.3 (1962): 4–8.

Fink, Gary M., ed. *Biographical Dictionary of American Labor.* Westport, CT: Greenwood Press, 1984.

"W. A. Calvin Dies; a Labor Leader." *New York Times,* 28 January 1962, 74.

Campbell, Alexander (1788–1866)
Religious reformer
Scotch-Irish

Alexander Campbell was a major religious reformer who promoted the interrelationship of religion, education, and republican political reforms. He played a decisive role in the development of the Disciples of Christ church.

Campbell was born in County Antrim, Ireland, the son of Thomas Campbell, a Presbyterian clergyman. It was in Ulster that he developed his lifelong dedication to religious reform, freedom, and education, receiving a strict religious and moral education, including a year at Glasgow University. Among Campbell's important intellectual sources were the Scottish Common Sense Realists, who believed that moral and religious questions could be answered only by examining and classifying evidence. Faith, for Campbell, was the result of rational, intelligent comprehension of the scriptures.

Campbell's father left for the United States in 1807 to pave the way for the family. The family, however, was shipwrecked off the Scottish coast and wintered in Glasgow, where Alexander committed his life to the ministry. After the family reunited in the United States in 1809, Campbell joined his father's new evangelical society, the Christian Association of Washington, Pennsylvania, which was dedicated to Christian unity and the restoration of early New Testament practices. In 1811, the association was reorganized into the Brush Run Church, the first church of the Disciples of Christ. By 1814 Campbell had replaced his father as the Disciples' leader.

Campbell's postmillennialist beliefs—"that progress in science, technology, republican institutions, and the Christian religion would bring in a golden age before Christ's second coming"—were the foundation for all of his work. He believed that the American Revolution was an important step toward the new millennium and that educational and political reform and the emancipation of the slaves were additional preparatory steps. Campbell toured extensively throughout the United States and in Britain during a return trip in 1847, and he wrote widely about the coming utopian age. He started a monthly journal, the *Christian Baptist,* in 1823 and another, the *Millennial Harbinger,* in 1830. Because his essays were also published in Britain, his influence on both sides of the Atlantic was considerable. In 1835 he wrote *Christianity Restored,* revised as *The Christian System* (1839), which became a widely read summary of his teachings. The Disciples established conventions in several states during the 1840s.

As a critic of U.S. educational institutions, Campbell in 1840 established Bethany College in Virginia (now West Virginia), dedicated to preparing people for a responsible, moral life in a democratic society. Though he spent much of the remainder of his life working for Bethany College, he got entangled in the slavery issue. He had owned slaves but freed them early on, afterward preaching that slavery was antidemocratic and a barrier to the millennium. He also supported the American Colonization Society and a constitutional ban on slavery yet refused to become an active abolitionist and continued to work with slave-owning colleagues. He died in 1866.

Today, nearly 5 million members of churches in more than 100 nations have their religious roots in Campbell's ministry. He changed and democratized American religion more than any other immigrant in the first half of the nineteenth century.

William E. Van Vugt

REFERENCES

Campbell, Alexander, Collection. Bethany College, Bethany, West Virginia.

Hatch, Nathan O. *The Democratization of American Christianity.* New Haven: Yale University Press, 1989.

Campos, Patricia (1973–)
Labor rights and community activist
Salvadoran

Patricia Campos began to take an interest in labor rights and advocacy at an early age. Despite her youth, she has achieved renown for the depth of her commitment to several major Salvadoran associations as well as to labor unions representing the more recent waves of immigrant workers.

Campos was born in 1973 in Chirilagua, San Miguel, El Salvador. In 1988, she left her small town for the Washington, D.C., metropolitan area. At her high school in Alexandria, Virginia, Campos helped restart the International Student Organization, for which she served as president. The organization was responsible for establishing the International Hall of Flags at T. C. Williams High, where, currently, 125 different flags acknowledge immigrant history in the United States. As a sophomore, she worked with teachers to restructure the English as a second language (ESL) program to better serve her and her fellow students. She also helped set up Bienvenidos, a community group for parents that facilitated their school involvement through translation, meetings, and progress reports.

Her passion for economic equality having come from her experience in El Salvador, where some of her family members were involved in community and union organizing, Campos was soon a labor and community activist as well. She combined these efforts with her academic pursuits by attending Cornell University and receiving her B.S. degree in industrial and labor relations in 1996 and, the following year, a master's degree in public administration from Cornell's Institute for Public Affairs. Meanwhile, she had continued to demonstrate her commitment to social justice in college through her participation in numerous organizations. She was cofounder and president of the Latino Labor Education Coalition, cofounder and director of Students Stop Sweatshops, and the national coordinator for the latter group's Back-to-School Boycott of Guess clothing.

Campos is currently the assistant director of the Labor Council for Latin American Advancement (LCLAA), a national organization of Latino trade unionists who belong to the affiliated unions of the American Federation of Labor and Congress of Industrial Organizations (AFL-CIO). Assisting with program development and implementation at local and national levels, she participates in policy-related dialogue with AFL-CIO officials, government officials, and members of Congress. Prior to this position, she worked as an associate field director with the Union of Needle Trade Industrial and Textile Employees (UNITE) and oversaw institutional and community support for ongoing worker-organizing campaigns by doing media outreach and producing educational materials for public distribution.

Campos has served as the president of the Salvadoran American Organization (OSA) and continues to chair its political mobiliza-

tion committee. She is also currently on the national executive committee of the Salvadoran American National Network. Her graduate thesis, "Building the Singapore of the West: Industrial Development vs. Workers Rights in El Salvador," in which she examines the new global economic order and its impact on Salvadoran workers, is under review for publication. A public speaker on such issues as student activism, Latinos in the labor movement, immigrant rights, the Salvadoran-American experience, and youth leadership development, Campos has already claimed her own power and fought to help others do the same since she came to the United States.

Leticia Hernández-Linares

REFERENCES

Campos, Patricia. Interview by author, 13 August 1999.

Huang, Fung-Yea. *Asian and Hispanic Immigrant Women in the Work Force: Implications of the United States Immigration Policies since 1965.* New York: Garland Publishing, 1997.

Repak, Terry. *Waiting on Washington: Central American Workers in the Nation's Capital.* Philadelphia: Temple University Press, 1995.

Suarez-Orozco, Marcelo. *Central American Refugees and U.S. High Schools: A Psychosocial Study of Motivation and Achievement.* Stanford: Stanford University Press, 1989.

Carnegie, Andrew (1835–1919)
Industrialist and philanthropist
Scottish

Andrew Carnegie's life exemplifies the poor immigrant who rose to fantastic wealth and power in the United States. He made important contributions to industrialism, philanthropy, and pacifism, thereby shaping American life and institutions more than almost any other immigrant.

Carnegie was born in Dunfermline, Scotland, son of William Carnegie, a handloom weaver who prospered until steam-powered looms displaced him in the 1840s. In winter 1847, the family decided to immigrate to the United States. In mid-1848 they joined the two sisters of Andrew's mother, Margaret, in Pittsburgh. There, Carnegie's "rags to riches" life would embody the myth of the poor immigrant who "made it" in the United States.

Carnegie quickly became completely Americanized—later, he was known as the Star-Spangled Scotsman—and he rose with astonishing speed. Starting out in the textile mills and then as a steam engine tender and messenger boy at a telegraph office, he became a telegraph operator and one of the first who could translate messages directly from the clicks rather than from the printed tape. This enabled him to become the telegrapher and secretary to Thomas A. Scott, one of the superintendents of the Pennsylvania Railroad. He quickly learned about stock investments and business management and in 1859, at age twenty-four, became Scott's successor.

Carnegie helped form the Pullman Palace Car Company in 1867. He invested in telegraph companies and iron bridge companies and sold railroad bonds. But it was in steel that Carnegie would make his lasting mark. In England, he learned about the new Bessemer process for mass-producing steel and, in anticipation of the railroads' shift from iron rails to the stronger steel, brought the process to the United States. He built the J. Edgar Thompson mill near Pittsburgh during the depression of 1873, capitalizing on cheap labor and construction costs. He pioneered vertical integration and was obsessed with the costs of production. Unfortunately, he often reduced workers' wages and smashed their attempts at unionization with brutality, as he did in 1892.

It may have been in an attempt at moral recovery and to ease his conscience that he turned his great wealth to philanthropy, particularly after he sold his steel empire to J. P. Morgan for nearly $500 million. "The man who dies thus rich, dies disgraced" was a motto he lived up to rather well, giving away roughly nine-tenths of his fortune. He provided nearly 3,000 free public library buildings to the English-speaking world. He also established a pension fund for his former workers and, through the Carnegie Foundation for the Advancement of Teaching, for

college teachers. He formed the Carnegie Institution of Washington in 1902 to promote scientific discovery. He pioneered modern philanthropy by forming the Carnegie Corporation of New York, with an endowment of $125 million. Finally, he turned his attention and wealth toward the quest for world peace and international justice by advocating summit meetings of the great powers and the international arbitration of disputes. But his ideals were dashed by the ghastly bloodletting of World War I. Carnegie died a year after the Great War ended.

William E. Van Vugt

REFERENCES
Livesay, Harold C. *Andrew Carnegie and the Rise of Big Business.* Boston: Little, Brown, 1975.
Wall, Joseph Frazier. *Andrew Carnegie.* New York: Oxford University Press, 1970.

Carnegie, Henrietta "Hattie" (née Henrietta Kanengeiser) (1889–1956)

Fashion designer and entrepreneur
Austrian

In November 1945 Russell Maloney's feature story in *Life* magazine was titled "Hattie Carnegie. With a 'Look', a Little Suit and a Knowledge of All the Angles, She Has Risen from Poverty to be Absolute Boss of a $6,500,000 Dress Business."

Born in Vienna, the second of seven children of Hannah Känzer and Isaac Kanengeiser, Henrietta moved to the United States in 1892 with her family, which then changed its name to Carnegie. They settled in New York's Lower East Side, near St. Mark's Place. She attended public school until 1902, when her father died. To help support the impoverished family, she became a messenger at Macy's, where she observed upper-class tastes and became familiar with the new retailing business methods.

At age fifteen, she modeled and trimmed hats in a millinery wholesale enterprise, became fascinated with fashion, and in 1909 established with Rose Roth the shop "Carnegie—Ladies' Hatter." By 1919, Hattie, as she called herself, had bought out her partner, created her own fashion designs, which were sought after by numerous wealthy clients, and moved her shop from East Tenth to West Eighty-sixth Street. In 1926 she moved it to the fashionable East Forty-ninth Street area. She traveled regularly to Paris to examine firsthand French haute couture, which she adapted to American upper-class expectations with a unique creative touch.

"We are living in an era of good sense, good taste, sound judgment," Carnegie observed in 1942. She abhorred fads and theatrics in fashion, insisted that the particular role of women's clothing was to enhance charm, and claimed that a "too often admired dress" was suspicious. Fashion was to be neither cute nor playful but elegant. It was to express "classic care for line, color, and the natural contours of the body." To reach her goals, Carnegie hired some of the most talented designers of her generation, among them such noted artists as Norman Norell, the first American to win the coveted Parisian Coty Prize. During the 1920s and 1930s "the Carnegie look" dominated U.S. fashion, and it remained influential until the 1960s. Carnegie counted among her customers many famous contemporaries, including the American actress Joan Crawford, the British film star Gertrude Lawrence, her favorite, and Harry L. Hopkins, President Roosevelt's secretary of commerce.

Carnegie also became a successful entrepreneur. During the depression years she added the "ready-to-wear" and the lucrative "spectator sports ready-to-wear" departments to her expensive custom-design enterprise. By the 1940s more than 100 stores carried her collections, and she employed more than 1,000 people. By the time of her death she had established an $8 million family business in which her siblings played an important part, too: Cecilia, for example, served as the firm's director, Herman as secretary-treasurer, and Abe as manager of the wholesale department. Hattie, an indomitable immigrant entrepreneur, is supposed to have remarked occasionally, "I've had three husbands, but my

romance is my work." Inspired by classical Viennese forms and admiring the Parisian haute couture, she ingeniously adapted both to the demands of American sensibility.

Leo Schelbert

REFERENCES

Bauer, Hambla. "Hot Fashions by Hattie." *Collier's* 123.16 (16 April 1949): 26–27.

"Carnegie, Hattie, 1889—Dress Designer." In *Current Biography 1942,* 136–138. New York: H. W. Wilson, 1942.

Kenny, Alma L. "Carnegie, Hattie." In *Notable American Women: The Modern Period. A Biographical Dictionary,* edited by Barbara Sicherman et al., 135–136. Cambridge, MA: Belknap Press of Harvard University, 1980.

Maloney, Russell. "Hattie Carnegie." *Life* 19.20 (12 November 945): 62–70.

Carse, Matilda Bradley (1835–1917)
Temperance leader and editor
Scotch-Irish

Matilda Bradley Carse contributed significantly to women's equality through her leadership of the temperance and other reform movements. She was also a strong advocate of women's suffrage.

Carse was born in the Belfast area, the daughter of merchants John Bradley and Catherine Cleland, whose ancestors had left Scotland in the 1600s and settled in Ulster. She received a good education in Ireland, and in 1858 the twenty-two year old immigrated to Chicago and quickly assimilated into American life. Three years later, she married railroad engineer Thomas Carse, and together they had three sons. A tragic and formative event in her life occurred in 1870, when a drunken cart driver struck and killed her youngest son, inspiring her to join the newly organized Woman's Christian Temperance Union (WCTU) and work with its leader, Frances Willard. Carse became president of the Chicago Central Union, one of the most active branches of the WCTU, and until 1913 supervised its many reform and charitable activities, such as establishing nursery schools, libraries, and shelters for prostitutes and runaway girls.

With her remarkable energy and vision, Carse was also able to establish and serve as president of the Woman's Temperance Publishing Association (WTPA), a publishing company that was owned and operated almost exclusively by women. Perhaps its most famous publication was the *Union Signal,* the weekly paper of the WCTU, but the company also published many pamphlets and books that advocated temperance and the reform of the social ills that marred the Gilded Age. The ideas and passion that Carse and her publishing company brought to the public consciousness contributed to the reforms that occurred in the Progressive Era of the early twentieth century.

Carse began another visionary project in 1887: to build a thirteen-story office building in the Chicago Loop, to be called the "Woman's Temple," which would be the national headquarters of the WCTU and the WTPA. The original capital was provided by leading businessmen of the city and the supporters of the WCTU, and the building was supposed to make a profit by renting its office space while serving as a symbol of the power of American women. However, the project was too grandiose and was completed during the panic of 1893. It proved to be a financial burden to the WCTU. It also caused much dissension within the ranks and led to personal attacks against Carse's integrity, which she defended but with much pain. After Willard's death in 1898, Carse lost the support of the national union and, with the financial problems continuing, the temple was purchased by Marshall Field. Carse's presidency of the WTPA soon came to an end, and her publishing company was dissolved a decade later.

Carse continued her work in Chicago, maintaining her leadership of the Chicago Central Union. She was selected to be one of the managers of the Columbian Exposition of 1893, and she became the first woman to be appointed to the Chicago Board of Education. She retired from her professional duties in 1913 to live with her son in New York, where she died in 1917 at the age of eighty-one.

William E. Van Vugt

REFERENCES

Bordin, Ruth. *Frances Willard: A Biography.* Chapel Hill: University of North Carolina Press, 1986.

———. *Woman and Temperance: The Quest for Power and Liberty, 1873–1900.* Philadelphia: Temple University Press, 1981.

Cayetano, Benjamin J. (1939–)

Governor of Hawai`i
Filipino-American

Democrat Benjamin J. Cayetano became the highest elected official of Filipino ancestry in the United States when he won Hawai`i's governorship in 1994. He is now in his second term, having been reelected in 1998.

Cayetano, who was born in Hawai`i in 1939, often encountered as a youth the racial discrimination against Filipinos that was typical in Hawai`i at midcentury. After becoming governor, he vividly recalled the lack of respect that his Filipino-immigrant father, a waiter, had faced: "I remember going to places when I was a kid where no one would even speak to my father. . . . It was humiliating for him, but he would just take it. . . . He'd been conditioned to think that was his station in life." Raised in the "tough" Kalihi district of Honolulu, Cayetano tried during his teen years "to fit the stereotype of the Kalihi kid—to be rough and not afraid to use your dukes." More interested in fast cars and pool halls than in school, he almost became a dropout, but marriage at eighteen to Lorraine Guico and the birth of the first of three children prompted him to "wise up." He graduated from high school in 1958 and, after a series of dead-end jobs—"In those days, I never met a Caucasian who wasn't a boss"—he moved to Los Angeles in 1961. By 1971, he had earned a B.A. in political science from UCLA and a law degree from Loyola University Law School.

Two years after Cayetano's return to Hawai`i in 1971, Governor John A. Burns, a Democrat, named him to the Hawai`i Housing Authority Commission. Burns said, "Ben, there are not too many young Filipinos who come out of Kalihi and become lawyers." In 1975, Cayetano won a seat in the state house of representatives. Never losing an election, he followed two terms there with two in the state senate and two as Hawai`i's lieutenant governor before winning a three-way gubernatorial race in 1994 with 37 percent of the vote. Proud of his Filipino-American identity, Cayetano nonetheless maintained: "The only way to overcome the racial issue is to find common ground. . . . My campaigns have always been mixed—issue-oriented and performance-based"—not just tied to the Filipino community.

As Hawai`i's economy plummeted during the persistent Asian economic crisis of the late 1990s, Cayetano struggled to cut massive state deficits by enacting severe cuts in state employment and public spending. Running for reelection in 1998, Cayetano faced a serious Republican challenge from Maui mayor Linda Lingle and often trailed in preelection polls. Stressing such accomplishments as "the only mandatory prepaid health care in the country," his campaign relied on traditional Democratic support from labor unions and Japanese Americans as well as from Filipino Americans. After his slim victory by 5,254 votes over Lingle, Cayetano proclaimed: "Democrats, wake up . . . we'd better do what needs to be done to get this state together. Forget about everything else."

During his first term, Cayetano and his wife of thirty-seven years were divorced, and he married Philippine-born Vicky Tiu Liu.

Barbara M. Posadas

REFERENCES

Arguelles, J. R. Lagumbay. "Ben Cayetano: Breaking Stereotypes." *Filipinas,* October 1992, 11–13.
"Benjamin J. Cayetano: Governor of Hawaii." *Heritage,* Spring 1996, 15–16.
Borreca, Richard. "From Kalihi to Hawaii's Top Job." *Honolulu Star-Bulletin,* 23 October 1998.
Ige, Ken. "'The Democrats Built This State,'" *Honolulu Star-Bulletin,* 23 October 1998.
Kakasako, Gregg K. "Ben—Barely." *Honolulu Star-Bulletin,* 4 November 1998.
Silva, John L. "Straight Outta Kalihi." *Filipinas,* May 1996, 32–34, 57.

Cenarrusa, Pete (1917–)
Politician and philanthropist
Basque-American

Pete Cenarrusa's initial political effort, election to the Idaho state House, began his political life. For more than forty-five years, he never lost a political election, either in contests for the legislature or for the seven quadrennial races for Idaho's secretary of state. Notwithstanding those successes, he continued to demonstrate a concern for issues affecting Basques.

The child of immigrant Basque parents, Joe and Ramona Gardoqui Cenarrusa, Pete Cenarrusa has dedicated his life to public service in Idaho. In the midst of the Great Depression, in 1936, he left his hometown of Bellevue, Idaho, in pursuit of a degree from the University of Idaho. That same year the Spanish Civil War broke out, turning Cenarrusa's attention to the land of his parents' birth. His mother's hometown, Gernika, Spain, was the site of the first military bombing of a civilian population, and several members of his extended family had been affected by the hostilities. He considered joining the fighting forces in Spain but chose to finish his college degree. However, the Spanish Civil War left a lasting mark on him.

After graduation, Cenarrusa taught high school for two years until the attack on Pearl Harbor prompted him to enlist. After serving in the marines from 1942 to 1946, he returned to rural Blaine County, Idaho. There, he began working as a vocational agriculture instructor and giving flying and boxing lessons in his spare time. In 1947, he met and married Freda B. Coates.

Soon, his nascent interest in politics surfaced. A heated debate about local-option gambling caught his attention. His friends convinced him to run for a seat in the state legislature. He won and remained an Idaho state representative from 1951 through 1967. From 1963 through 1967, Cenarrusa served as speaker of the house. In 1967, he was named secretary of state, a tenure that ended in 1998, when he was over eighty years old. During those years, he was a member of Idaho's Commission on Human Rights, the state Purchasing Advisory Board, a delegate to the Republican National Convention of 1976, Citizens for Reagan-Bush in 1980 and 1984, and the Board of Land Commissioners. Cenarrusa's career in Idaho politics was longer than that of any other politician in the state.

Moreover, no other political leader in Idaho has kept such a watchful eye on issues related to Basques in the state and in Europe. When the Spanish government was about to open the trial in Burgos, wherein sixteen young Basques were accused of terrorist activity and murder, Cenarrusa convinced the governor of Idaho and the U.S. State Department to intervene and seek guarantees for an impartial and fair trial. He often stated that his decision to act on their behalf dated back to 1936, when, as a youth, he was unable to aid the Basque cause. He was also very active in the Boise Basque Club, especially in its charitable and community-building efforts. In 1998, the Society for Basque Studies in America honored Cenarrusa with membership in the Basque-American Hall of Fame.

Jeronima Echeverria

REFERENCES

Bieter, J. Patrick. "Pete Cenarussa: Idaho's Champion of Basque Culture." In *Portraits of Basques in the New World,* edited by Richard W. Etulain and Jeronima Echeverria, 172–191. Reno: University of Nevada Press, 1999.

Douglass, William A., and Jon Bilbao. *Amerikanuak: A History of Basques in the New World.* Reno: University of Nevada Press, 1975.

Cermak, Anton "Tony" Joseph (1873–1933)

Entrepreneur, politician, and mayor
Czech-American

Only one person died from a bullet meant to end the life of President-elect Franklin D. Roosevelt in early 1933. That person was the mayor of Chicago, Anton (Tony) Cermak.

Antonín J. Čermák was born on 9 May 1873 in the mining town of Kladno, northwest of Prague. In 1874 his father, a miner, moved his family to the United States. The Cermak family (the spelling of the name was simplified) headed for Chicago, home to the largest population of Czech immigrants, before settling in Braidwood, a coal-mining town about sixty-five miles to the southwest.

Cermak dropped out of school before his twelfth birthday to help his parents. He held a number of jobs, including driving a mule team at a local coal mine. His propensity toward action became evident in his midteens, when he became the leader of a strike for higher wages by the mule teamsters. He lost his job and, at sixteen, moved to Chicago. After working at several jobs, he began his own business at the age of nineteen. Starting with one horse and wagon, he hauled furniture, kindling wood, coal, and other materials. In a few years he was said to own forty teams. During evenings he studied business and law. In 1894 he married a Czech-born seamstress from his neighborhood in Lawndale and steadily prospered. By 1907 he was president of the Lawndale Building and Loan Association and soon a senior partner in a real estate firm.

His political career advanced just as rapidly. After six years as aide to a local Democratic Party official of Czech origin, by 1900 Cermak had become a precinct captain and, within two years, was both secretary and chair of his Democratic Party ward organization. That year he was elected to the state legislature and reelected three times. In 1909 he filled a vacancy on the city council as alderman, later served as bailiff of the municipal court, and returned to the city council in 1919. Three years later Cermak became chair of the Cook County Board of Commissioners and by 1928 was consolidating his hold on the Democratic Party leadership in Chicago. He was elected mayor in 1931 by the largest majority ever polled in a Chicago mayoral election.

In early February 1933, in the depths of the Great Depression, Cermak traveled to Miami, Florida, to speak with President-elect Franklin D. Roosevelt, eager to extract the promise of a federal loan. On 15 February, Roosevelt gave a short speech from his automobile and then engaged in a brief conversation with Chicago's mayor. Just as the automobile was about to proceed, shots rang out, and Cermak and several others were hit. Cermak was rushed to the hospital in Roosevelt's car. When Roosevelt spoke with him there, Cermak is quoted as having told the president-elect, "I am glad it was me instead of you." He died from complications on 6 March 1933.

Although of humble immigrant background and with little formal education, Cermak had become a successful businessman, an influential politician, and mayor of the nation's second-largest city. His death was mourned not only in the United States but in his native Czechoslovakia as well.

Zdenek Salzmann

REFERENCES

Allswang, John M. *A House for All Peoples: Ethnic Politics in Chicago 1890–1936.* Lexington: University Press of Kentucky, 1971.

Drnec, Gustav. [Kdo je] *Antonín J. Čermák.* Praha: Orbis, 1948.

Gottfried, Alex. *Boss Cermak of Chicago: A Study of Political Leadership.* Seattle: University of Washington Press, 1962.

Chandrasekhar, Subrahmanyan "Chandra" (1910–1995)

Astrophysicist and Nobel laureate
Asian Indian

Subrahmanyan Chandrasekhar, a native of India and astrophysicist, became a Nobel Prize winner. He was also known for his concern for students, his mentoring, his broad knowledge base outside of science, and his superb writing ability.

Chandrasekhar, known as Chandra throughout the scientific world, was born in Lahore, India, in 1910. His father was a civil servant, his grandfather a scholar, and his uncle, C. V. Raman, a Nobel Prize winner in physics. In 1930, at the age of nineteen, he sailed to England to do postgraduate study at Cambridge University. While on the voyage, he developed a theory about the nature of stars for which he would be awarded the Nobel Prize fifty-three years later, in 1983. He challenged the theory of

the 1930s that held that for all stars, after burning up, their fuel becomes faint, planet-sized remnants known as white dwarfs. Chandra determined that stars with a mass greater than 1.4 times that of the sun—now known as the "Chandrasekhar mass"—must eventually collapse past the stage of a white dwarf into an object of such enormous density that "one is left speculating on other possibilities."

Not only was Chandra's theory rejected by peers and professional journals in England but he was also publicly ridiculed by the distinguished astronomer Sir Arthur Eddington. Disappointed and not willing to engage in public debate, Chandra moved to the United States in 1937 and joined the faculty at the University of Chicago. There, he immersed himself in teaching and research and wrote over a half dozen definitive books, ranging in subjects from radiative transfer of energy of stars through the atmosphere to the motions of stars within galaxies, and from magneto-hydrodynamics to Einstein's theory of general relativity and black holes. His success is measured by the fact that his books have sold over 100,000 copies; he was editor of *Astrophysical Journal,* the field's leading journal, for almost twenty years; and he presided over 1,000 colloquia and supervised the research of more than fifty Ph.D. students. His dedication to teaching was illustrated during the time he was based at the university's Yerkes Observatory. He drove 100 miles round-trip each week to teach two students. The entire class—T. D. Lee and C. N. Yang—won the Nobel Prize in physics in 1957.

Chandra also received twenty honorary degrees, was elected to twenty-one learned societies, and received numerous awards in addition to the Nobel Prize, including the Gold Medal of the Royal Astronomical Society of London; the Royal Medal of the Royal Society, London; the National Medal of Sciences; and the Henry Draper Medal of the National Academy of Sciences.

Chandra and his wife, Lalitha, became U.S. citizens in 1953. At that time he stressed that he had a sense that humanity is not defined by national boundaries and that he was "not necessarily committed to the old-fashioned concept of 'Right or Wrong, my country.'" He added: "My loyalty is not the parochial or flag-waving type of thing. My first loyalty is to Science."

Subrahmanyan Chandrasekhar died on 28 August 1995. The legacy he left behind was that of an exemplary and dedicated individual mentoring, researching, and making life better for humankind.

Arthur W. Helweg

REFERENCES

Kamath, M.V. *The United States and India, 1776–1976*. Washington, DC: Embassy of India, 1976.

Wali, Kameshwar. *Chandra: A Biography of S. Chandrasekhar*. Chicago: University of Chicago Press, 1991.

———. *S. Chandrasekhar: The Man Behind the Legend*. London and Rivers Edge, NJ: Imperial College Press, 1997.

Chaplin, Charlie (1889–1977)
Movie actor and director
English

During the forty years after his immigration to the United States, Charlie Chaplin, the consummate comedic actor and director, created probably the most renowned film character, the little tramp. Chaplin remained one of the most famous and beloved people in the entertainment world.

Chaplin was born in London, the son of English music hall singers. His father, an alcoholic, left the family, and his mother was hospitalized for emotional and physical problems. Chaplin was placed in institutions, receiving little education. His first performance occurred at age five. A few years later he worked with a dancing group, then acted in plays and, in 1908, joined a comic pantomime group that toured North America. During its second tour in 1913, Mack Sennet, head of Keystone Studio, offered Chaplin a contract for $150 per week to act in his short comic movies. Within five years Chaplin became one of the wealthiest and most popular stars of cinema.

Chaplin's popularity resulted in unprece-
dented contracts. In 1917 he signed to make eight short films with full creative control for over $1 million. He built his own studio and maintained artistic control for the rest of his career. In 1919 he teamed up with Douglas Fairbanks, Sr., D. W. Griffith, and Mary Pickford to form United Artists. Chaplin's own phenomenal popularity was based on his unique screen persona: the "little tramp" in oversized clothes, with a cane, wearing a derby hat, down on his luck—a persona that combined delightful comedy with pathos and often insightful social commentary. Such films as *The Tramp* (1915), *Gold Rush* (1925), and *City Lights* (1931) remain classics.

After the success of *City Lights*, Chaplin toured the world, meeting with leaders and observing the devastating effects of the worldwide depression. He subsequently put many of his observations and concerns into his art. *Modern Times* (1936) is about the homelessness, police violence, and soul-crushing effects of modern technology. His most daring and successful film, *The Great Dictator* (1940)—an obvious attack on the rise of Hitler—ends with a four-minute speech calling for resistance to totalitarianism and inhumanity.

Chaplin's later career and life were marked by controversy, with the media casting him as a womanizer. But it was his positive comments about the Soviet Union, U.S. allies during the war—as well as the fact that he had not become a U.S. citizen—that led some to charge him with being a Communist sympathizer. Others led boycotts against his films. In 1952, during a trip to England, his reentry permit was revoked, effectively banishing him from the United States, pending his answering moral and political questions from the Immigration and Naturalization Service. He decided to live in Vevey, Switzerland.

Though his later films never had the box office success of his earlier ones, *Limelight* (1952) won the Foreign Film Critics' Best Film Award. During a 1972 visit to the United States, he was honored at Lincoln Center in New York and given a special Oscar for his formative role in the movie industry. In 1975, he was knighted by Queen Elizabeth. He died two years later.

William E. Van Vugt

REFERENCES

Maland, Charles J. *Chaplin and American Culture.* Princeton, NJ: Princeton University Press, 1989.

Lynn, Kenneth S. *Charlie Chaplin and His Times.* New York: Simon & Schuster, 1997.

Robinson, David. *Chaplin: His Life and Art.* New York: McGraw-Hill, 1985.

Cherian, Joy (1942–)

*Lawyer, immigrant rights activist,
and federal official*
Asian Indian

Joy Cherian, a native of India, was a presidential appointee to the U.S. Equal Employment Opportunity Commission (EEOC). He is an activist in the Asian Indian community and an advocate for immigrant rights.

Cherian was born in Cochin, Kerala, India, on 18 May 1942. While attending parochial schools, he was active in anti-Communist demonstrations before the Communists came to power in Kerala. He attended the University of Madras for one year and then entered the University of Kerala, where he earned a B.S. degree in 1963 and a law degree in 1965. After briefly practicing law in India, he immigrated to the United States in 1967 to attend the Catholic University of America, in Washington, D.C., where he obtained his M.A. (1970) and Ph.D. in international law (1975). His revised Ph.D. thesis, published as *Investment Contracts and Arbitration,* is still found in most law school libraries. Cherian also obtained an M.A. in comparative law from the National Law Center, George Washington University, in 1978.

While working on his doctorate, Cherian joined the American Council of Life Insurance, for which he traveled in Asia, Europe, and North America promoting international trade and services. He became its director of international insurance law in 1982 and a registered lobbyist for the life insurance industry. He was instrumental in the enactment of several trade bills and treaties affecting U.S. trade in services. He was also appointed as an adviser to the National Associations of Insurance Commissioners' task force on international insurance relations.

The following year, President Ronald Reagan appointed Cherian to the EEOC, the first Asian American to serve on it. During his tenure, he championed many causes and published widely in law journals concerning equal opportunity, focusing especially on national origin–based discrimination. As a result of his efforts, the EEOC increased its efforts to defend such cases. For example, in 1987, when Cherian was first appointed, there were 9,653 complaints that dealt with national origin–based complaints, or 8.8 percent of the EEOC's caseload. By 1990, the number had increased to 11,688, or 11.1 percent of the caseload. Besides pursuing several high-profile discrimination cases, Cherian also advocated the protection of Americans' civil rights abroad, contributing to the Civil Rights Act of 1991, extending extraterritorial protection in such matters for all Americans.

When Cherian's term on the EEOC ended in 1993, he returned to the private sector. He established a consulting firm that offers a variety of services. Besides being active in the legal community and continuing to write on legal issues, he has been especially successful in areas of diversity training, targeting workforce diversity, harassment based on race, color, or national origin, and other related topics.

During this professional career, Cherian has been active in Asian-American and Asian-Indian affairs. He founded the American Indian Forum for Political Education (AIFPE), a nonprofit organization working with branches of the federal government to increase political awareness and participation of young Asian Indians in the United States. In 1986, he was elected national chairman of the Asian American Voters Coalition (AAVC), an umbrella organization representing a dozen national ethnic organizations. He has continued to consult and publish and frequently speaks at Asian Indian events, often as a keynote speaker at such functions as well as for those in the business and legal community.

Arthur W. Helweg

REFERENCES

Cherian, Joy. *Investment Contracts and Arbitration: The World Bank Convention on the Settlement of Investment Disputes.* Leyden: A. W. Sijthoff, 1975.

———. *Our Relay Race: A Compilation of Selected Articles and Speeches.* Lanham, MD: University Press of America, 1997.

Cherian, Joy, Consultants, Inc. "Joy Cherian, Ph.D." Press release, Washington, DC, 1994.

Henry, Jim. "Joy Cherian." In *Notable Asian Americans,* edited by Helen Zia and Susan B. Gall, 46–47. Detroit: Gale Research, 1995.

Chin, Frank (1940–)
Playwright and author
Chinese-American

The first Chinese- or Asian American playwright to have a New York stage production (*The Chickencoop Chinaman*), Frank Chin was also coeditor of what is considered the seminal text of Asian American literature, *Aiiieeeee!* Since then, Chin has written other equally thought-provoking, politicized works that attempt to assert a male-oriented, Asian American heroic identity shorn of old stereotypes.

Chin's creativity was nurtured by his family and by the emergence of the Asian American movement in the 1960s. Born in Berkeley, California, in 1940, he is a fifth-generation Chinese-American on his mother's side of the family. His father was an immigrant, but his maternal grandfather worked in the steward service of the Southern Pacific Railroad. For a few years Chin followed his grandfather, working for a railroad in Oakland but left that for the University of California, Berkeley, where he earned a degree in English in 1966. He moved to Seattle, Washington, initially working for a television station filming documentaries, including a few on Chinese-American life. He then became a story editor and scriptwriter for *Sesame Street*.

Chin's big break came in 1972, when *Chickencoop Chinaman* was staged off-Broadway. An irreverent work, the play satirizes media images of Chinese-Americans. Far from being servile, the characters are outspoken in their search for a viable identity in a racially divided society. Inspired by the Black Power movement of the 1960s and resisting Euro-American cultural hegemony, Chin continued to project an anti-assimilationist sensibility. His next play, *The Year of the Dragon* (1974), focuses on the disintegration of a Chinese-American family because of the pressures of capitalism and popular culture. They must escape Chinatown to find a new identity. The play was a PBS production in 1975.

In 1974 Chin helped edit *Aiiieeeee!* He and his colleagues issued a follow-up volume in 1991, *The Big Aiieeeee!* Chin's contributions have also included establishing the Asian American Theatre Workshop (AATW) in 1973, which he headed until 1977. AATW showcased new, cutting-edge works. After Chin's departure, AATW became the Asian American Theatre Company (AATC), which remains a stalwart part of the Asian American community. After his AATW years, Chin was invited by universities to teach Asian American history and offer literature workshops, using storytelling, theater, and writing exercises.

By the late 1980s, frustrated with rejections from mainstream theatres, he turned to fiction, writing *The Chinaman, Pacific and Frisco R.R. Co.* (1988), a collection of short stories inspired partly by his family's history, and two novels, *Donald Duk* (1991) and *Gunga Din Highway* (1994). Although in *Donald Duk* he takes a lighthearted look at a Chinese-American adolescent, in *Gunga Din Highway* he draws from the heroic tales of Chinese classics to fashion a brooding narrative.

Chin, with his emphasis on a native-born, English-speaking, masculine ethos, is generally considered a controversial writer, and he has stirred controversy by attacking such Asian American women authors as Maxine Hong Kingston and Amy Tan, accusing them of having "sold out" to the mainstream market. Yet Chin has infused Chinese-American literature with an identity that is neither "Chinese" nor "American" but unique and fluid.

Benson Tong

REFERENCES

Chin, Frank. "BackTalk." In *Counterpoint: Perspectives on Asian America*, edited by Emma Gee, 556–557. Los Angeles: Asian American Studies Center, University of California, Los Angeles, 1976.

———. "This Is Not an Autobiography." *Genre* 18.2 (1985): 105–130.

Chin, Frank, et al. *Aiiieeeee! An Anthology of Asian-American Writers.* Washington, DC: Howard University Press, 1974.

Chisholm, Shirley
(née Shirley St. Hill) (1924–)

Politician and U.S. House representative
Barbadian-Guyanese-American

Shirley Chisholm rose from teacher's aide to congresswoman. She was the first black—and first woman—whose name was put in nomination at a major party convention for president of the United States.

Chisholm was born Shirley St. Hill, in Brooklyn, New York, the oldest of four daughters of a Barbadian mother and a Guyanese father. Shirley's mother returned to Barbados in 1928, leaving the children with their grandmother until her mother could save enough money to provide for them adequately in New York. Chisholm credits her strict schooling on Barbados for her later success. Her father, a follower of Marcus Garvey, imbued his children with an awareness of issues affecting blacks and the poor. Her mother, a very religious woman, took her daughter to church three times every Sunday.

In 1934 the family returned to Brooklyn. Following high school there, Chisholm attended Brooklyn College, majoring in sociology. She joined the Brooklyn chapter of the NAACP and worked at the Urban League Settlement House before graduating in 1946 and enrolling in a Columbia University master's program, which she completed in 1952. In 1949 she married Conrad Chisholm, a Jamaican. For a dozen years she worked in education, beginning as a teacher's aide and ending as supervisor of ten child care centers and a consultant to the City of New York on day care for children.

In 1964 she was elected to the New York assembly. Of fifty bills introduced by Chisholm during her four years in the assembly, eight were passed. In 1968 redistricting enabled Chisholm to run for a seat in the U.S. House of Representatives. She did not have money for a conventional campaign, so she took to the streets with the slogan "Fighting Shirley Chisholm—Unbought and Unbossed." Winning handily, she joined eight other black members of the House of Representatives, of which she was the only woman. She represented New York's Twelfth Congressional District from 1969 to 1983.

Once in Congress, Chisholm was a maverick. For instance, she challenged the tradition of new members' accepting whatever assignment they were given, requesting a change from the House Agriculture Subcommittee on Forestry and Rural Villages. Her complaint was heeded: She received a new assignment to the Committee on Veterans' Affairs. She was an original promoter of the Head Start Program and later a member of the House Education and Labor Committee. In 1972 Chisholm became the first woman and first black to run for U.S. president. She did not believe she would win but sought to pave the way for women and blacks to run successfully in the future.

Leaving Congress after seven terms, she divorced her husband and remarried. In 1983 she taught at Mount Holyoke College and Spellman College. She served as chair of the National Political Congress of Black Women from its founding in 1984 until 1992. She considered running for mayor of New York in 1989 but did not. In the 1992 presidential campaign Chisholm was a potential running mate for independent candidate Ross Perot. In 1993 President Clinton offered her the ambassadorship to Jamaica, but a progressive eye disorder caused her to decline. Since 1993 Chisholm has lived in Palm Coast, Florida.

Rhys James

REFERENCES

Brownmiller, Susan. *Shirley Chisholm.* Garden City, NY: Doubleday, 1970.

Chisholm, Shirley. *The Good Fight*. New York: Harper & Row, 1973.

———. *Unbought and Unbossed*. Boston: Houghton Mifflin, 1970.

"Chisholm, Shirley Anita." *Biographical Directory of the U.S. Congress:* bioguide.congress.gov/scripts/biodisplay.pl?index=C000371 (accessed 30 June 2000).

Colemen, Seth. "Q & A [with Shirley Chisholm]." *Atlanta Journal and Constitution,* 13 January 1996, 2A.

Hinckley, David. "Shirley Chisholm Riding Alone." *New York Daily News,* 9 March 1999, 19.

"Shirley Anita Chisholm. United States Representative. Democrat of New York . . .": www.usbol.com/ctjournal/Schisholmbio.html (accessed 5 July 2000).

Christopher (né Christophorides), Philip (1948–)

Business executive and community activist
Cypriot

Philip Christopher provides an outstanding example of an immigrant who achieved success in business as a corporate executive while maintaining an active involvement in his ethnic community. He was a leader in a variety of Greek Cypriot organizations.

Christopher was born in 1948 in the picturesque town of Keryneia (under Turkish occupation since 1974), on the northern coast of Cyprus. He was the youngest in a family of six children. As a young boy in Upper Keryneia, he would gather neighborhood kids to play soccer, which became one of his life's passions. The team, however, did not have money to buy a soccer ball. In order to earn enough, he organized a patriotic show, which were very popular in those days because Cyprus was embroiled in an anticolonial campaign against the British rulers of the island. The show was a success, and the team raised the needed funds.

The episode underscores not only Christopher's leadership qualities but also the enterprising spirit that would become such an important part of his adult life. He arrived in the United States with his mother and three sisters on 19 October 1959, joining his father and older sister, who had immigrated in 1952. Once in the United States, Christopher attended St. Demetrios Greek American school and William Cullen Bryant High School, where he was captain of the soccer team, earning All-State honors and a scholarship to New York University. In 1970 he graduated with honors, having again been captain of the soccer team and an All-American selection. Following a brief stint as a teacher, he joined the Audiovox Corporation, an electronics company, later becoming the executive vice president and a stockholder, a position he still holds.

At the same time, Christopher has been a true champion of Cypriot and Hellenic causes in the United States. He is the president of the Pancyprian Association of America and the International Coordinating Committee of Justice for Cyprus (PSEKA), which was founded in 1976 to coordinate the struggle of the Cypriots for freedom and justice. PSEKA has its headquarters in Lefkosia, Cyprus, and offices in the United States, Canada, Australia, Greece, the United Kingdom, France, and Africa. Every spring, Christopher, as president of PSEKA, leads a delegation of the most important activists of the Hellenic community to Washington to inform members of the House and Senate about the Cyprus issue. In addition to his PSEKA presidency, he has served as national cochair of the Democratic National Committee Greek American Leadership Council and as cochairman of the finance committee for the Dukakis presidential campaign in 1988 and the Tsongas presidential campaign in 1992.

Christopher has also served the Cypriot and Hellenic communities in other capacities. He has been president of the Cyprus Federation, chairman of the Justice for Cyprus Committee, as well as a member of the board of directors of the Cyprus Children's Fund, the American Hellenic Alliance, and the United Hellenic American Congress. He remains dedicated to the cause of his native island of Cyprus.

Stavros T. Constantinou

REFERENCES

Christopher, Philip. Resume.

Pancyprian Association of America Program for
Freedom Award 1988 Ceremony (including a
special album published on the occasion of
honoring Christopher), 14 May 1988, New
York City.

Christowe, Stoyan (1898–1995)

Writer and state legislator
Macedonian

Stoyan Christowe, born in the Ottoman
Empire, achieved recognition in Macedonia
and in the United States as a reporter for the
Chicago *Daily News* and the North American
Newspaper Alliance and as the author of diverse works. He also served as a state legislator in Vermont.

Christowe was born and raised in Aegean
Macedonia, at that time an ethnically mixed
area of Slavic Macedonians and Greeks, today
part of Greece. In his autobiography, *This Is My
Country* (1938), he described the reaction in his
own village in Macedonia when an immigrant
to the United States sent back a relatively large
sum of money and later returned dressed in
American clothes. Everyone wanted to follow
his path, including young Stoyan Christowe,
who, with the help of his father, borrowed
money for the fare and joined his uncle in St.
Louis in 1911. He first settled in with a group
of older men from his village, taught himself
English, and was educated in the public schools.

Cristowe became a U.S. citizen in 1924
and was admitted to Valparaiso University in
Valparaiso, Indiana. After he graduated, he became a reporter for the Chicago *Daily News*
and in 1928 was sent to the Balkans as a foreign correspondent for the *Daily News* and
the North American Newspaper Alliance. He
visited the Greek part of Macedonia and the
vicinity of his own village but could not enter it, as he was afraid of being drafted since he
was technically a dual citizen. After he came
back to the United States, he settled down in
Dower (Windham County), Vermont, and,
during World War II, served in military intelligence in the Pentagon.

In 1961, Christowe was elected as a Republican representative to the state house in
Vermont, serving two two-year terms, and he
was a state senator from 1965 until 1972. He
served on many committees concerning education and social welfare; for example, he was
chairman of the Legislative Council's Higher
Education Study Committee and a member
of the National Committee for Support of the
Public Schools. After retiring from the state
senate, he served as chairman of the advisory
board to Vermont's Office on Aging.

Christowe's eventful life provided excellent
material for his books, which include memoirs, novels, and a volume about Macedonia.
In his autobiography he described his fellow
immigrants' life in the United States, his efforts to educate himself, and his life as a correspondent in Sofia. While there, he interviewed, among other prominent people, Ivan
Michailoff, leader of the Inner Macedonian
Revolutionary Organization, one of the oldest and most dreaded revolutionary societies
in the world, and King Boris of Bulgaria. Out
of his associations with Michailoff's *comitadjis*
(members of his organization) and terrorists
(among whom was the future assassin of King
Alexander of Yugoslavia) grew his book *Heroes
and Assassins.* However, Macedonians found
the book objectionable because they saw it as
too objective: Christowe had become an
American and a writer first and a Macedonian second. Other books in which he described his life in the United States and issues
of Americanization of immigrants are *My
American Pilgrimage* (1947) and *The Eagle and
the Stork* (1976). He died 28 December 1995
in Brattleboro, Vermont.

Matjaž Klemenčič

REFERENCES

Christowe, Stoyan. *The Eagle and the Stork.* New
York: Harper's Magazine Press, 1976.

———. *My American Pilgrimage.* Boston: Little,
Brown, 1947.

———. *This Is My Country: An Autobiography by
Stoyan Cristowe.* New York: Carrick & Evans,
1938.

Dzhukeski, Aleksandar. "Stoyan Christowe—a
Worthy Representative of the Macedonian

People in the USA." *Macedonian Review* (Skopje, Republika Makedonija), 15.2 (1985): 201–205.

Stefanija, Dragi. "Macedonia vo delata na Stojan Hristov i Luj Adamiè" (Macedonia in the works of Stoyan Christowe and Louis Adamic). In *Louis Adamič Simpozij* (Louis Adamic Symposium), 298–300. Ljubljana: Univerza Edvarda Kardelja v Ljubljani, 1981.

Cifuentes, Claire (1967–)
Attorney, activist, and educator
Guatemalan-American

Claire Cifuentes was born in Guatemala City and lived there until the age of three. Her family then relocated to the United States, and Cifuentes grew up in the metropolitan Los Angeles area. Although initially she had aspirations of being a physician or veterinarian, her early participation in student government in high school foreshadowed an important career in law. Majoring in economics, she graduated from University of California in Los Angeles in 1990 and went on to Loyola Marymount Law School, passing her bar exam in 1994.

Cifuentes's law practice focuses primarily on immigration law, and she has worked closely with members of Congress, advising on and reviewing changes in the Nicaragua Adjustment and Central American Act (NACARA). Her lobbying efforts in Washington, D.C., resulted in significant amendments to the bill. At the request of the Immigration and Naturalization Service, she has participated in the NACARA Working Group Committee, the planning group for the implementation of the law in Los Angeles.

Overall, Cifuentes works in various aspects of immigration law. One of her main efforts involves the Central American Resource Center (CARECEN), where she volunteers as an attorney and consultant. As the cochair of the Immigration Law Committee for the Mexican American Bar Association, she helped establish a pro bono representation panel for NACARA immigrants. The program, funded by the American Bar Association and CARECEN, provides assistance for families affected by the new law. The program has helped about 100 families in its two-year existence. Tracing her community work in part to her college experience, Cifuentes first began working with CARECEN through its subsidiary on campus, the Central American Refugee Association (CARA). She was also active with Latinas Guiding Latinas, a group that counseled young women about college. In addition, Cifuentes takes pro bono cases on her own and speaks publicly in an effort to inform the Latina/o community about various aspects of immigration law and their rights in general.

Her Guatemalan heritage is important to her, but Cifuentes stresses that she sees herself more as a Latina than as strictly a Guatemalan. Her hope is that her work extends to all Central Americans and Latinos in general because no one group should benefit over another. She has helped in establishing a Guatemalan-led, nonprofit organization that provides services similar to those of CARECEN, providing immigration information and tax and GED (high school equivalency diploma) preparation. Also, Cifuentes is currently attempting to establish a Central American Political Action Committee (PAC). There is already a Salvadoran PAC, and Cifuentes hopes that a more general committee will offer political agency to more Central American communities in the United States.

Another important organization that Cifuentes works with is the American Immigration Lawyers' Association. She holds two positions with them: as the asylum liaison and the immigration court liaison. Cifuentes has demonstrated a commitment to immigration rights through her impressive list of accomplishments. In the short time that she has been a lawyer, she has been able to effect important changes in the law and promises to fill an important gap as a politician in the near future.

Leticia Hernández-Linares

REFERENCES
"ABA Awards MABA a $40,000 Grant for Pro-bono Project." *Mexican American Bar Association News,* September 1998.
"Actúe ya: tramite su residencia antes del

30 septiembre" (Act Now: Process your residency before 30 September). *La Opinion,* 11 July 1997.

"El Asilo: solo se concede cuando se demuestre un miedo credible" (Asylum: It is only awarded when a reasonable fear is demonstrated). *La Opinion,* 2 May 1997.

"Más difícil suspender deportaciones y ganar apelación" (More difficult to suspend deportations and win appeals). *La Opinion,* 23 October 1994.

Cohan, George M. (Michael) (1878–1942)

Actor, dancer, composer, and playwright
Irish-American

George Michael Cohan was responsible for more than eighty shows in his fifty-year theatrical career. He defined a genre of theater in addition to inspiring Americans with numerous rousing songs.

Cohan's proudest claim in a distinguished career was that he was born on the fourth of July—in 1878—in Providence, Rhode Island. His parents, Jeremiah Cohan and Helen Frances Costigan, had a successful minstrel act. Cohan had little formal education because he joined his parents' vaudeville act by the time he was seven. With his sister, Josephine, the Four Cohans toured the North American vaudeville circuit. By seventeen he was writing songs and sketches and managing the act. In 1901 his first play, *The Governor's Son,* opened on Broadway, using comedy, dance, melodrama, and lively popular songs; the script was sentimental, as was the fashion. His first successful show, *Little Johnny Jones* (1904), introduced two of his many hit songs, "I'm a Yankee Doodle Boy" and "Give My Regards to Broadway."

In 1899 Cohan married Ethel Levey, a comedienne, and the act became the Five Cohans. Following their divorce in 1907, Cohan married Agnes Nolan, an actress. Cohan's business partner for sixteen years (1904–1920) was Sam H. Harris. Together, they produced at least fifty plays; owned theaters in several cities, a music publishing firm, and a minstrel show; and had five road companies at one time.

In 1917 Americans marched to war singing other enduring Cohan songs, "Over There" and "You're a Grand Old Flag." After a final spoof on the Irish-American family in *The Merry Malones* (1927), Cohan went to Hollywood but disliked the studio's treatment of him and abruptly ended his film career. He turned to dramatic acting in Eugene O'Neill's *Ah, Wilderness!* (1933), one of his most successful leading roles, and followed that with his acclaimed performance of President Franklin D. Roosevelt in *I'd Rather Be Right* (1937).

When Cohan retired in 1940, Congress awarded him a medal for his patriotic songs. Hollywood also celebrated Cohan's career in the film *Yankee Doodle Dandy* (1942), starring James Cagney, another Irish-American New Yorker, who won an Oscar as best actor for his dynamic portrayal of Cohan. That film and *The Seven Little Foys* (1955) both celebrate Irish contributions to the American musical theater, as did Joel Grey's performance as Cohan in the Broadway musical, *George M* (1968).

In 1959 New York City honored Cohan with a statue on Times Square. His contributions to American popular entertainment were considerable and, perhaps—because he exercised unusual creative control—his most important was that he developed a unified format for light comedic drama. Moreover, though a third-generation Irish-American, Cohan created a memorable place in the American ethnic mosaic, and his contributions to U.S. culture, suffused as they were with elements of the Irish-American character, are unique, for he deftly blended his Irishness with his Americanness. "The Man Who Owned Broadway" died in New York City on 5 November 1942.

Peter C. Holloran

REFERENCES

Cohan, George M. *Twenty Years on Broadway.* New York: Harper and Brothers, 1924.

Cohan, George M., Collection. Museum of the City of New York.

Ewen, David. *Great Men of American Popular Song.* Englewood Cliffs, NJ: Prentice Hall, 1972.

McCabe, John. *George M. Cohan: The Man Who*

Owned Broadway. Garden City, NY: Doubleday, 1973.

Morehouse, Ward. George M. Cohan, Prince of the American Theater. Philadelphia: J. B. Lippincott, 1943.

Colón, Jesús (1901–1974)
Community activist
Puerto Rican

Jesús Colón spent decades writing, lecturing, and organizing on behalf of Puerto Rican workers' rights in New York City. During the 1930s and 1940s, he helped establish many of the institutional foundations for the Puerto Rican community. In his writings he powerfully depicted the challenges confronting newcomers trying to adapt to the city.

Colón was born in the town of Cayey, Puerto Rico, on 20 January 1901. By age fourteen, he was an active member of the Socialist Party. In 1917, Colón arrived in New York City. He saw himself as a chronicler of his times, and his colorful narratives, commentaries, and essays include the difficulties of just surviving; of dealing with the unsavory traps set for naïve and desperate newcomers; of living in slum conditions and the competition for work in a city teaming with immigrants. In letters to his family and friends and in those especially written to his fiancée, Rúfa Concépcion "Concha" Fernandez (whom he married in 1925), Colón also described the loneliness of migrant life and warned her to complete her education before coming to New York.

In 1918, Colón and his cohorts created the Puerto Rican Committee of the Socialist Party in New York City. He founded Alianza Obrara Puertorriqueña and Ateneo Obrara (Alliance of Puerto Rican Workers and Workers' Forum), where, in keeping with the Latin American/Caribbean tradition of "El lector," Colón taught classes in English to the workers. He was a founding member of Sol Naciente (The Risen Sun), one of the earliest Hispanic benevolent societies as well as a founding member of the most important civic organization in the community, La Liga Puertorriqueña (The Puerto Rican League). He also served for

a time as the editor of La Liga's publication, Boletin. Throughout the 1920s and 1930s, Colón was an active participant in community activities and a popular labor organizer. He was national head of more than thirty Spanish- and Portuguese-speaking lodges of the International Workers' Order (IWO).

Some of his work also centered around cultural activities for children and youths. He organized drama clubs, sports clubs, and choral groups. In addition, during the 1930s and 1940s he wrote for various Spanish-language publications in New York, including Gráfico and La Voz. In 1955 he became a regular columnist for the two Communist newspapers, the Daily Worker and the Daily World. In 1961, his first book, A Puerto Rican in New York City, and Other Sketches, was published (it was reprinted in 1984); his second, The Way It Was and Other Writings, appeared posthumously in 1993. Many of the vignettes from the first book have been translated into various languages, and although some are humorous, most are poignant portrayals of a life in New York that vastly differs from the more traditional stereotypic representations. Although didactic at times, Sketches gives a realistic snapshot of the world of New York City's Puerto Ricans during the transition "from colonia to community."

In addition to his writings, in 1953 Colón was a candidate for the city council and, later, for assemblyman under the banner of the American Labor Party. He ran for city comptroller in 1969 on the Communist Party ticket. Colón died in 1974.

Linda Delgado

REFERENCES

Colón, Jesús. A Puerto Rican in New York, and Other Sketches. New York: Mainstream Publishers, 1961.

———. The Way It Was and Other Writings. Edited by Virginia Sánchez Korrol and Edna Acosta Belén. Austin: University of Texas Press, 1993.

Colón, Jesús, Writings. Archival collection of the Center for Puerto Rican Studies, Hunter College, City University of New York.

Delgado, Linda. Jesús Colón: A Political Biography of a Puerto Rican Activist, 1901–1974. Forthcoming.

James, Winston. "Afro-Puerto Rican Radicalism in the U.S." *Journal del Centro de Estudios Puertorriqueños* (Hunter College, New York), Spring 1996.

Korrol, Virginia Sánchez. *From Colonia to Community: The History of Puerto Ricans in New York City.* Westport, CT: Greenwood Press, 1983. Reprint, with new introduction, Berkeley: University of California Press, 1994.

Conein, Lucien E. (1919–1998)
Soldier and spy
Franco-American

Lucien E. Conein's life has been seen as a model for one of the foreign spies that served in the Office of Strategic Services (OSS) and the Central Intelligence Agency (CIA). What Conein said about himself may have been closer to what his supervisors wished to hear or what Conein wanted to be repeated than it was to reality.

Conein was born in Paris in 1919. In 1924, his widowed mother sent him to Kansas City to live with an aunt. He retained his French citizenship and, when World War II began in 1939, he joined the French army. Returning to the United States after the fall of France in 1940, Conein was assigned to the OSS, the predecessor of the CIA. In late 1944, he landed in Nazi-occupied France to deliver weapons to the French Resistance forces preparing to attack the German army.

After the war, Conein was assigned to the newly formed CIA but kept his military rank and position as a cover. He infiltrated saboteurs into Eastern Europe and trained paramilitary forces in Iran. In 1954, he was sent to Saigon, where he prepared caches of arms for anti-Communist uprisings that never came. In Vietnam, he met and married his third (and last) wife. During his stay in South Vietnam in 1962, as the CIA's liaison between Ambassador Henry Cabot Lodge and South Vietnam's top generals, he delivered the message that the generals took to mean that the United States would not object if they assassinated the president, Ngo Dinh Diem. Conein retired in 1968 and, three years later, declined

an offer from E. Howard Hunt to join President Nixon's team of "plumbers," who later carried out the Watergate burglary.

Many tales of war, death, and sex form an enduring legend associated with Conein. Some of his claims cannot be proven. Stanley Karnow interviewed him at length for a proposed biography but abandoned the project when he decided that Conein could not differentiate between his cover stories and the story of his life. For example, Conein had lost two fingers of his right hand and claimed that he had lost them in a dangerous secret mission; in fact, he had lost them while fixing the engine of a car carrying him and his best friend's wife to a spy's assignation. (There was a basis in truth to that part of the story.) However, from 1973 until 1984, Conein did run secret operations for the Drug Enforcement Agency (DEA). In the mid-1970s he was in the headlines when allegations were made that a DEA unit was preparing to assassinate drug lords, and he became a public figure of sorts in 1975 when he candidly testified about his role in the assassination of President Diem to a Senate committee investigating the U.S. role in the assassination of foreign leaders.

Conein lived in MacLean, Virginia, with his wife. He died on 3 June 1998 and was buried with full military honors at Arlington National Cemetery.

André J. M. Prévos

REFERENCES

Barnes, Bart. "Lucien E. Conein Dies at Seventy-nine; Fabled Agent for OSS and CIA." *Washington Post,* 6 June 1998, B6.

Horrock, Nicolas. "Senate Panel, Reporting on CIA, Asserts US Aides Were Involved in Plots to Kill Foreign Leaders. Data Made Public. No Evidence That US Actions Resulted in Deaths Is Found." *New York Times,* 21 November 1975, 1, 53–54.

———. "US Aide Was Briefed on Assassination Equipment." *New York Times,* 23 January 1975, 38.

Weiner, Tim. "Lucien Conein, Seventy-nine, Legendary Cold War Spy." *New York Times,* 7 June 1998, 35.

Cordova, Dorothy Laigo (1936–), and Cordova, Fred (1931–)

Community activists and historians
Filipino-Americans

Married in 1953, Dorothy Laigo Cordova and Fred Cordova began their activism in Seattle's Filipino community in 1957 with the founding of Filipino Youth Activities (FYA), an organization dedicated to providing Filipino-American youth with "wholesome activities . . . that would also teach them about Filipino culture." In the mid-1970s, even as FYA flourished, Dorothy and Fred Cordova began to reclaim the sources of Filipino-American history in work with the Washington State Oral/Aural History Program, the Demonstration Project for Asian Americans (DPPA), and the Filipino American National Historical Society (FANHS).

Born in Selma, California, on 3 June 1931, Fred Cordova received a bachelor of social sciences degree from Seattle University in 1952. Dorothy Laigo Cordova was born in Seattle on 6 February 1936; she also studied at Seattle University, earning a B.A. in sociology in 1953. While raising a family that would ultimately include eight children, the Cordovas began FYA to provide recreational activities for Filipino-American teens in Seattle's central area. Over the years, the organization's most notable activity has been its drill team, with its precision marchers of both sexes garbed in costumes reminiscent of the southern Philippines. In addition to the drill team, which has involved hundreds of Filipino-American youth since its founding, FYA has offered basketball and volleyball, folk dancing, drama, language classes, and a job placement office.

Because of Dorothy Cordova's work with the Washington State Oral/Aural History Program and the DPPA, the couple's focus moved to history; they began to collect oral interviews with Filipinos and Koreans in Seattle and elsewhere on the West Coast. These interviews showed the early Filipino-immigrant experience to be more varied than that presented in Carlos Bulosan's *America Is in the Heart*. As they gathered the interviews, the couple also began collecting Filipino-American photographs, clippings, and manuscript materials, and in 1983, Fred published *Filipinos: Forgotten Asian Americans—A Pictorial Essay / 1763–Circa 1963*.

Chartered in Washington in 1984, the Filipino American National Historical Society (FANHS) housed the Cordovas' expanding collection, now named the Pinoy National Archive. FANHS, which operates on a shoe-string budget, with assistance from trustees scattered throughout the United States, has emphasized support for the organization of local chapters that will collect the raw materials of Filipino-American history. Some chapters also offer speakers, workshops, newsletters, and publications. Every two years FANHS organizes and sponsors a conference that showcases the local chapter that is the conference site. At the meeting, those interested in Filipino-American history present their work to an audience drawn from chapters throughout the country. These papers and presentations then provide the material for the organization's journal.

Since its founding, FANHS has become parent to twenty local chapters, including New England, Metropolitan New York, and Hampton Roads in the East; the Midwest chapter; and in the West, Alaska, Seattle, Oregon, Rio Grande (New Mexico), and twelve chapters in California. FANHS has raised consciousness about Filipino-American history among Filipino Americans throughout the nation.

In 1998, the Cordovas were honored for their work with honorary doctorates from their alma mater, Seattle University.

Barbara M. Posadas

REFERENCES

Cronin, Mary Elizabeth. "Marriage in the Nineties: Marriage Matters." *Seattle Times,* 28 July 1996.

De Leon, Ferdinand M. "Forty Years of Drilled-in Memories." *Seattle Times,* 21 February 1997.

Evangelista, Oscar and Susan. "Continuity and Change among the Second-Generation Filipino-Americans in Seattle, Washington." *Philippine Historical Association Historical Bulletin* 27.1–4 (1982): 164–177.

"Filipino American Faces of the Century." *Filipinas,* January 2000, 39.

Cormier, Robert (1925–2000)
Writer
Franco-American

Robert Cormier, whose father emigrated from Quebec and whose mother was an Irish-American, was born in 1925. He is known worldwide for more than twenty works of fiction, essays, and blank verse that have been translated into more than a dozen languages.

A journalist by profession, Cormier graduated from Fitchburg College, in Massachusetts, but had begun writing at a very young age. His first novel, *Now and at the Hour* (1960), is poignant and moving, revealing a lesser known side of this author. In *The Chocolate War* (1974), Cormier begins his depiction of a fictional universe that continues to unfold to this day, a universe made up largely of bullies and their victims, an institution's demands for conformity, and the individual's sense of integrity.

Focused on adolescents, his novels are usually assigned to the "Young Adult" category, which is distressing because his works, with their universal themes, can be read with profit by people of all ages. In Cormier's fictional world, evil takes many forms. Far from being an abstraction, evil lurks in the hearts of many characters as well as in institutions, against which adolescents sometimes rebel, though seldom with impunity. Because most of his novels are sophisticated psychological thrillers in which the suspense often begins on the first page, they are riveting, compelling, and unsettling. The story lines are well crafted, with intriguing characters and provocative and controversial themes that have prompted some to try to ban his works from high school reading lists. Therefore, the statement he made to an interviewer in 1998, "I write to upset the reader—to shake up the sensibilities," is understandable.

Two other aspects of this fictional oeuvre should be mentioned: The town of Monument, the setting for most of his stories, is a thinly disguised version of Leominster, Massachusetts, the author's hometown. The other is his ethnic group, an issue he addressed in a letter in September 1999: "I still identify very much with my French Canadian background, am still a member of St. Cecilia's parish where I was baptized, confirmed and married. Many of my books have a strong French Canadian background and most of my characters are of Franco-American descent. . . . I have written 18 books. To a great extent they reflect the Franco-American experience here in New England." In addition, he remained a member of the Leominster chapter of Union Saint Jean Baptiste. Indeed, *Fade* (1988), which may be his most complex novel, seems to include in its multiple layers of meaning the theme of the slow disappearance of the Franco-Americans as an ethnic group. His ethnicity is also a major aspect of his most recent book, *Frenchtown Summer* (1999), a memoir in blank verse.

Although Cormier made creative use of his French Canadian background in the course of a highly successful writing career over nearly a half-century, it is that career that was his life, and he was not active within the Franco-American community itself. Indeed, he was perhaps better known within mainstream society—and internationally—than within that Franco-American community. However, Cormier did receive a *certificat de merite* from the Institut français at Assumption College in Worcester, Massachusetts. He died in Leominster, Massachusetts, on November 2, 2000.

Armand Chartier

REFERENCES
Campbell, Patricia. *Presenting Robert Cormier.* Rev. ed. New York: Twayne Publishers, 1985; New York: Dell, 1990.
Concise Dictionary of American Literary Biography: Broadening Views, 1968–1998. Detroit: Gale Research, 1989.
"Cormier, Robert." In *Who's Who in America,* 54th ed., 984. New Providence, NJ: Marquis Who's Who, 1999.

Coryn, Edward (1857–1921)
Corporate executive, civic leader,
and community activist
Belgian

Edward Coryn, a native of Belgium, was a self-made businessman, politician, and influential immigrant leader. He achieved wide recognition for his activities in his adopted hometown and in the Belgian-American community.

The son of farmers, Coryn was born in Lotenhulle, a small town in the Belgian province of East Flanders, on 2 September 1857. At age twenty-four, he immigrated with his family to the United States. They settled in Moline, Illinois, where he worked for ten years as a laborer. In 1892 he quit his job at a factory and opened a grocery store in Moline, which he managed for fourteen years. In 1907, he became a shareholder and manager of the Moline Trust and Savings Bank and a month later its vice president. At various stages, he was also the director of several other businesses.

In 1896, Coryn was elected alderman from the Sixth Ward and for eight years served on Moline's city council. He was chairman of the public library's executive committee for several years and in 1914 was appointed postmaster for Moline.

Although a successful and well-integrated local businessman and civic leader, Coryn remained loyal to the Belgian-American community, ready to assist his countrymen and eager to extend a helping hand to new arrivals. He assumed a leadership role to help realize these goals among the Belgian-Americans in Moline. In 1890, he was one of the principal organizers of the Belgian Working Men's Union, a sick-benefit society to assist Belgian workingmen's families. He also helped found the first Belgian-American Club in Moline in the early 1900s and served as its first president. The club's foremost function was social, but it also sponsored English-language lessons and citizenship classes and owned its own library. Under Coryn's leadership, the Belgian-American Club was instrumental in petitioning the bishop of Peoria for a Belgian church in Moline, which was granted in 1906.

A year later, Edward Coryn was one of the shareholders and first president of the Moline Gazette Publishing Company, which was created primarily to publish the country's first Flemish newspaper, the *Gazette van Moline.* The first issue appeared 15 November 1907. The *Gazette,* a weekly, enjoyed a substantial circulation during the 1910s and was particularly popular during World War I, its coverage extending across various Belgian settlements in the United States and Canada. Reflecting Coryn's views, the paper encouraged strong cooperation among the Belgians in the United States. Finally, on a national level, Coryn was a tireless promoter and first president of the National Belgian-American Alliance, a loose federation of Belgian-American organizations in the United States, founded in 1910. It created the Belgian Bureau in New York City to assist immigrants and rescue friends and family from occupied Belgium during World War I.

The Belgian government recognized Edward Coryn's contributions to the Belgian-American community, awarding him the Knight's Cross of the Order of Leopold in 1913. In 1919 he was also appointed honorary vice-consul of Belgium. He died two years later.

Kristine Smets

REFERENCES

Baert, Gaston Pieter. "Uitwijking naar Amerika Vijftig Jaar Geleden," (Emigration to America fifty years ago). *Bijdragen tot de Geschiedenis der Stad Deinze en van het Land aan Leie en Schelde* (Contributions to the History of the Town of Ghent and the Region of the Leie and Schelde Rivers), 22 (1955): 9–72; reprint, Deinze: n.p., 1956.

"Coryn, Edward." In *Historic Encyclopedia of Illinois and History of Rock Island County,* edited by Newton Bateman and Paul Selby, 1077–1978. Chicago: Munsell Publishing, 1914.

Houthaeve, Robert. *Camille Cools en zijn "Gazette van Detroit": Beroemde Vlamingen in Amerika* (Camille Cools and his "Gazette van Detroit": Famous Flemish in America). Moorslede, Belgium: Author, 1989.

Smets, Kristine A. J. "The Gazette van Moline and the Belgian-American Community, 1907–1921." Master's thesis, Kent State University, 1994.

Cotton, John (1584–1652)
Clergy and colonial leader
English

John Cotton was an important leader of England's Puritan movement and of the settlement of Boston, Massachusetts. His scholarly sermons and writings shaped the history and culture of Puritan New England.

Cotton was born in Derby, Derbyshire. The son of Roland Cotton, a successful lawyer, and Mary Hurlbert, John Cotton was a gifted student at Trinity College, Cambridge, earning his B.A. and M.A. there. He became a fellow at Emmanuel College in 1606, where he taught and preached for six years, during which time he adopted Puritanism. A decade later, he accepted a call to serve as vicar in Boston, Lincolnshire, where he prepared other young Cambridge graduates for ministry in the Puritan movement. He avoided ecclesiastical punishment for his nonconformity for several years, but in 1632, with the rise of Archbishop William Laud and his policy enforcing stricter conformity, Cotton was compelled to go into hiding from time to time. In 1633 he resigned his vicarage and set sail with his family to join the new Puritan settlement in Boston, Massachusetts Bay Colony.

Cotton arrived in the colonies already recognized as a leading Puritan preacher and thinker, but it was there that his sermons were published and that he flourished as a writer. Initially, in the late 1630s, he became embroiled in the trial of Anne Hutchinson, John Wheelwright, and some others of his Lincolnshire followers, who were charged with antinomianism. According to this belief, "free grace" was accessible to an individual directly from God, thus de-emphasizing good works as evidence of salvation and the role of the minister as mediator between God and the sinner. Cotton initially supported Hutchinson and was opposed by most of the other clergy in Boston, but as the antinomian faction grew and adopted views that he saw as clearly heretical, he distanced himself from Hutchinson and the rest and supported their exile to Rhode Island.

Soon, the rise of Puritans in England during the Civil War and then Oliver Cromwell's rule gave Cotton and other Puritans the freedom and exposure to extend their influence on both sides of the Atlantic. Cotton had become the teacher of the first church in Boston, a prominent position in the most important town in New England, and he remained one of the leading spokesmen for Puritan New England for the rest of his life. He was also frequently asked for advice on church practice by Puritans who had remained in England. Nevertheless, he spent much of his energy in his later years in debate with the exiled Roger Williams over religious authority and discipline. This debate, known as the "Bloody Tenent Controversy," was published in a series of tracts and books that were widely read by subsequent generations of New England Puritans.

Among Cotton's the most influential publications were *The Keyes of the Kingdom of Heaven* (1644) and *The Way of the Churches of Christ in New England* (1645). These helped define what became known as the New England Way, the set of beliefs that guided and shaped Puritan New England in the seventeenth century. John Cotton died in 1652.

William E. Van Vugt

REFERENCES
Emerson, Everett H. *John Cotton*. New York: Twayne Publishers, 1967.
Gallagher, Edward J., and Thomas Werge. *Early Puritan Writers: A Reference Guide*. Boston: G. K. Hall, 1976.
Ziff, Larzer. *The Career of John Cotton: Puritanism and the American Experience*. Princeton, NJ: Princeton University Press, 1962.

Cronyn, Hume (1911–)
Actor, director, and writer
Canadian

Hume Cronyn has enjoyed a long career in the theater and screen, having begun in the 1930s. He has been rewarded with accolades and nominations for Academy Awards, Tonys, Golden Globes, and Emmys. He was inducted into the American Theater Hall of Fame in 1979.

Cronyn was born in London, Ontario, to a prominent, prosperous family. His father was Hume Blake Cronyn, a financier and politician, and his mother, Frances A. Labatt. While studying at McGill University in Montreal, Quebec, for a law degree, he joined the Montreal Repertory Theatre and the McGill Players Club. Realizing that he was more interested in acting than in the law, he left McGill and studied at the New York School of Theater, the Mozarteum in Salzburg, Austria, and the American Academy of Dramatic Arts. He settled in New York.

In 1942 he married the English actress Jessica Tandy, marking the beginning of what would become a long and successful union, professionally and personally. They raised three children and worked together on stage and screen until her death in 1994.

Cronyn's professional acting debut was in Washington, D.C., in 1931, and his Broadway debut in 1934. His initial directorial effort was the Los Angeles production of *Portrait of a Madonna,* in 1946. His film career began in 1943, as Herbie Hawkins in Alfred Hitchcock's *Shadow of a Doubt.* He was nominated for an Academy Award for his supporting role in the film *The Seventh Cross* in 1944. His movies include *Lifeboat* (1944), *A Letter for Evie* (1945), *Sunrise at Campobello* (1960), *Cleopatra* (1963), *Rollover* (1981), *Brewster's Millions* (1984), *Cocoon* (1984), and *Cocoon, the Return* (1988).

Cronyn has enjoyed much acclaim in television, too, beginning with his appearance in 1949 in NBC's production of *Her Master's Voice.* He and his wife had a television series called *The Marriage* in 1954 (begun on radio in 1953), which he also produced. He has made many appearances on established television programs, such as *Omnibus* and the *Ed Sullivan Show,* along with such specials as *Juno and the Paycock* (1960), *The Gin Game* (1979), *Foxfire* (1987), which he also cowrote, *Broadway Bound* (1991), *To Dance with the White Dog* (1993), and *Twelve Angry Men* (1998).

During World War II he entertained troops under the auspices of both the United Service Organization (USO) and the Canadian Active Service Canteen. He has served as a director of the Screen Actors' Guild, council member of Actors' Equity, trustee of the American Academy of Dramatic Arts, and board member of the Yale University School of Drama and the board of governors of the Stratford Festival, Canada.

Along with his Academy Award nomination, Cronyn has been nominated five times for the Tony Award, winning it for *Hamlet* in 1964. He has been nominated seven times for the Emmy, once for his script of *The Dollmaker* (1984), which he cowrote. He has won three times for his acting: in *Age Old Friends* (in 1990), *Broadway Bound* (in 1992), and *To Dance with the White Dog* (in 1994). Among his numerous awards, he was a recipient of the Kennedy Center Honors in 1986 and the National Medal of Arts, presented by the president of the United States in 1990, and he was invested as an officer of the Order of Canada in 1988.

Gillian Leitch

REFERENCES
Atkinson, Brooks. *Broadway.* New York: Macmillan, 1974.
Cronyn, Hume. *A Terrible Liar: A Memoir.* Toronto: Key Porter Books, 1991.
"Cronyn, Hume." In *The Biographical Encyclopedia and Who's Who of the American Theatre,* edited by Walter Ridgon. Clifton, NJ: James T. White, 1990.
"Cronyn, Hume." In *Canadian Who's Who 1997.* Toronto: University of Toronto Press, 1997.
"Cronyn, Hume." In *Contemporary Theatre, Film and Television,* vol. 1, edited by Monica A. O'Donnell. Detroit: Gale Research, 1984.
"Hume Cronyn": www.emmys.org (Primetime Emmy Award database, accessed 10 June 2000).
"Hume Cronyn": www.gg.ca (Governor General of Canada: Order of Canada index, accessed 10 June 2000).
"Hume Cronyn": www.oscars.org (Academy Awards database, accessed 10 June 2000).

Cuesta, Angel L. (1858–1936)
Cigar manufacturer and philanthropist
Spanish

Angel L. Cuesta, who emigrated from Spain at age ten, ultimately created an enormously successful business. He used his wealth to help fellow immigrants, their children, and his fellow villagers in Spain.

Cuesta was born in Colosía, a small village in the mountains of Asturias, Spain, on 21 December 1858. As a young boy, he worked as a shepherd tending flocks of sheep and cows. Attracted by the stories told by returned emigrants, when he was ten he begged his parents to allow him to go to Cuba with a family friend who was returning to the island. They agreed, and in Cuba Cuesta lived with his godfather, who helped him find a job as an apprentice in a cigar factory. In 1875, already a skilled cigar maker, he moved to Key West and later to New York City and Chicago. In 1884, he settled in Atlanta and opened a small cigar factory. There, he met his wife, Marie Binder. They were married in 1888 and had four children.

In Atlanta, Cuesta employed a fellow Spaniard, Peregrino Rey, as foreman in Cuesta's cigar factory. Enticed by news of the cigar industry boom in Tampa, Cuesta decided in 1892 to move there. The firm of Cuesta & Rey, dubbed "the truly Spanish house," was established three years later. It was so successful that after just six years Cuesta & Rey opened a factory in Jacksonville, Florida. The firm soon achieved renown for the high quality of its cigars and it became even more prominent in 1915, when King Alfonso XIII named it the official purveyor of Havana cigars to the royal court of Spain.

Throughout his adult life, Cuesta contributed to a variety of civic and philanthropic projects in both the United States and Spain. He was a long-standing member and president of the Centro Español, the Spanish mutual aid society in Tampa. He belonged to civic clubs and Masonic lodges. He joined the Rotary Club in 1914 and was instrumental in the establishment of the club in Cuba (Ha-

vana, 1916) and in Spain (Madrid, 1920). In recognition of his services to his fellow countrymen, Cuesta was knighted and decorated by the Spanish monarch three times, in 1908, 1913, and 1925.

Cuesta, who had received very little formal schooling as a child, was especially committed to promoting education both in Tampa and in Spain. In 1911, he funded the construction in West Tampa of a grammar school, where generations of Spanish-immigrant children were educated. In his native village, he donated money to build an elementary school and establish a small library. The grant also paid the teacher's salary for several years, until the school was integrated into the national education system. Cuesta's contributions to his village also funded the construction of new roads, the establishment of a water system, and the building of a public market. In 1935 his fellow villagers honored him by erecting a monument with his bust in a public park that bears his name. Cuesta died in Tampa on 30 July 1936.

Ana M. Varela-Lago

REFERENCES
Cuesta, Angel L. "Memorias del Excmo. Sr. D. Angel L. Cuesta." *El Eco de los Valles,* 10 January 1936.
Hawes, Leland. "Education Was a Serious Business at Cuesta School." *Tampa Morning Tribune,* 19 March 1983.
Licht, Cindy. "He Came in Quest of Knowledge." *Tampa Times,* 6 July 1974.
Manteiga, Victoriano. *Centro Español de Tampa, Bodas de Oro, 1891–1941. Reseña Histórica de Cincuenta Años.* Tampa: n.p., 1941.
Mormino, Gary R., and George E. Pozzetta. *The Immigrant World of Ybor City. Italians and Their Latin Neighbors in Tampa, 1885–1985.* Urbana: University of Illinois Press, 1987.
Murray, Jock. "Angel L. Cuesta, Sr., One of the Cigar Trade's Pioneers, Passes Away in Tampa at Seventy-eight." *Tobacco Leaf,* 1 August 1936, 1.

Daignault, Elphège J.
(1879–1937)

Lawyer, journalist, and community activist
Franco-American

Immediately after World War I, the decades-long animosity that existed between some native-born Americans and immigrants exploded into a full-blown Americanization movement. At that time, Elphège J. Daignault, founder and publisher of the French-language newspaper, *La Sentinelle,* of Woonsocket, Rhode Island, stood at the forefront of those who fought for the linguistic and cultural rights of the New England Franco-American population.

One of eleven children of an immigrant grocer from Quebec and his wife, Daignault was born on 8 June 1879, in Woonsocket, Rhode Island. He received a classical education in Quebec and, upon his return to the United States, earned a B.A. degree at Boston College in 1900 and a law degree at Columbia University in 1903.

Subsequently, he resettled in Woonsocket and married Florina Gaulin, the daughter of a local merchant. Together they raised ten children. Daignault held a succession of professional and political positions, including those of Rhode Island state legislator, Providence County judge of probate, and Woonsocket district attorney. Meanwhile, he also became active in several Franco-American organizations, including the Association Canado-Américaine (ACA), a New England and Quebec-wide fraternal life insurance society. In 1922, he became its third president.

That same year, Daignault and other Franco-American activists founded Les Croisés (The crusaders), a secret society dedicated to the preservation of the language and culture of their compatriots. In 1924, Daignault launched the society's mouthpiece, *La Sentinelle,* through which he attacked the Roman Catholic church's Irish-American–dominated hierarchy and, in particular, Monsignor William A. Hickey, bishop of Providence. Daignault accused Hickey of trying to destroy the French language in Rhode Island. Soon, the militant tone of *La Sentinelle* divided French-language activists. There were many pro-*Sentinellistes* but also many anti-*Sentinellistes.* In Manchester, where Daignault served as ACA president, Bishop George A. Guertin revoked the society's chaplains and thus its status as a Catholic organization.

The polemic raged until 1928, when Daignault and sixty-one other *Sentinellistes* were excommunicated by the ecclesiastical courts in Rome and *La Sentinelle* was placed on the Church's Index of banned publications. Although Daignault and his colleagues eventually were pardoned by Church authorities, he remained militant to the end. He also continued as ACA president until 1936, at which time his bid for reelection was thwarted in order to bring about the reinstatement of the society's chaplains.

Daignault died suddenly of a heart attack in Woonsocket on 25 May 1937. Since his death, Daignault has remained a controversial figure in the New England Franco-American community. It is safe to say that Franco-Americans in general believed in the cause for which he fought. However, only those who saw a necessity for his militant tactics considered him a hero, whereas moderates viewed him as a hothead who went beyond the bounds of propriety, behavior that discouraged future activists from joining in the struggle to keep the French language alive in New England. Consequently, today, except for

Franco-American activists and historians, the children and grandchildren of Daignault's contemporaries have largely forgotten him and the *Sentinelliste* movement.

Robert B. Perreault

REFERENCES

Adolphe Robert, ed. *Les Franco-Américains peints par eux-mêmes (*Self-portraits of Franco-Americans). Montréal: Editions Albert Lévesque, 1936.

Daignault, Elphège J. *Le vrai mouvement sentinelliste en Nouvelle-Angleterre (1923–1929) et l'affaire du Rhode Island* (The real Sentinelliste movement in New England [1923–1929] and the Rhode Island Affair). Montréal: Editions du Zodiaque, 1936.

Foisy, J. Albert. *Histoire de l'Agitation sentinelliste dans la Nouvelle-Angleterre 1925–1928* (History of the Sentinelliste agitation in New England, 1925–1928). Woonsocket: La Tribune Publishing Co., 1928.

Perreault, Robert B. *Elphège J. Daignault et le mouvement sentinelliste à Manchester, New Hampshire.* Manchester, NH: National Materials Development Center for French and Creole, 1981.

———. "The Franco-American Press." In *The Ethnic Press in the United States: A Historical Analysis and Handbook,* edited by Sally M. Miller, 115–130. Westport, CT: Greenwood Press, 1987.

Rumilly, Robert. *Histoire des Franco-Américains.* Montréal: Robert Rumilly, 1958.

Sorrell, Richard S. "The Sentinelle Affair (1924–1929) and Militant *Survivance:* The Franco-American Experience in Woonsocket, Rhode Island." Ph.D. diss., State University of New York, Buffalo, 1975.

Damrosch, Walter Johannes (1862–1950)

Conductor and composer
German-American

Walter Damrosch is remembered for bringing serious music to a wide public audience. As one of several immigrant musicians who introduced German music traditions, he influenced American musical life.

Damrosch was born in 1862 into a family of musicians in Breslau, Prussia. His father, Leopold Damrosch, was a well-known orchestra conductor; his mother, Helene Damrosch, was an opera singer. The family circulated among the highest musical circles in Germany, with acquaintances including Richard Wagner, Franz Liszt, and Clara Schumann. When Walter Damrosch was nine, the family came to the United States, where his father took up a conducting post. Walter began his music training under his father and later studied in Germany.

Upon his return to the United States, Damrosch worked as a church organist and violinist. He began to conduct in 1881, assisting his father, and traveled again to Europe on conducting assignments. The illness and death of his father in 1885 allowed Walter to assume some of his father's conducting duties. While his father was in his final illness, Damrosch took over conducting a performance of Wagner's *Tannhäuser* at the Metropolitan Opera in New York. He was frequently called upon thereafter to conduct German operas at the Metropolitan from 1885 to 1891 and from 1900 to 1906. During the 1890s he formed his own Damrosch Opera Company, which traveled widely in the United States.

Damrosch had also taken over his father's position as principal conductor of the New York Symphony Society orchestra. He continued to be associated with that orchestra until it was dissolved in 1926, when many of its players were absorbed into the newer New York Philharmonic. During his long tenure with the New York Symphony Society, Damrosch cultivated wealthy patrons for classical music culture. His biggest achievement was in persuading Andrew Carnegie to build Carnegie Hall as a home for the orchestra. For the opening of Carnegie Hall in 1891, Damrosch invited Peter Ilyich Tchaikovsky to conduct his own works at the inaugural concert.

Damrosch saw himself as a missionary, introducing serious music to a wide public. His own concerts frequently had him explaining the principal works for the benefit of first-time concertgoers. When the New York Symphony Society came to an end in 1926, he turned to the new field of radio broadcasting, where he was a pioneer in the broadcasting of classical music. He had conducted a broadcast by the New York Symphony Society in 1923, and he conducted the first symphony broadcast over a network, NBC, in 1926. He became the principal music adviser to NBC, continuing concerts of classical music and innovating an educational program, the *Musical Appreciation Hour,* from 1928 to 1942. During his career he wrote a number of dramatic operas and other works, which were deemed successful in their time.

Damrosch was president of the National Institute of Arts and Letters from 1937 to 1941 and received numerous awards and honorary degrees for his contributions to U.S. musical culture. Although never regarded as among the first rank of American conductors for his interpretation, he was unexcelled in his steadfast dedication to bringing serious music to a wider public audience. And although his musical connections extended far beyond the German-American community, he was particularly recognized by German-Americans for his role in bringing German musical culture to the United States.

James M. Bergquist

REFERENCES

Damrosch, Walter. *My Musical Life.* New York: Scribner's, 1924.

Finletter, Gretchen Damrosch. *From the Top of the Stairs.* Boston: Little, Brown, 1946.

Martin, George. *The Damrosch Dynasty: America's First Family of Music.* Boston: Houghton Mifflin, 1983.

Das, Taraknath (Tarak Nath Das) (1884–1958)

Political activist and writer
Asian Indian

Taraknath Das (also known as Tarak Nath Das), a native of India, was a political activist and writer who fought anti–Asian Indian legislation and discrimination in Canada and the United States.

Das was born in Majhipara, a village near Calcutta, on 15 June 1884. Even in high school he joined an underground revolutionary cell, where he studied and espoused revolutionary propaganda against British rule of India. In college, he remained involved in anti-British politics and left the university in order to share his political ideas with the people. When a warrant was issued for his arrest, he fled to Japan in 1905 and linked up with Indian students there. After the British ambassador requested that they be deported because of their anti-British activities, Das and others left for the United States.

At age twenty-two in 1906, Das was one of the first activists in the United States for Asian Indian rights. He studied at the University of California, Berkeley, and published the first nationalistic newspaper in the United States, *Free Hindustan.* He moved to the University of Washington, in Seattle, acquiring a B.A. in political science in 1910 and an M.A. in 1911. After several attempts, he became a U.S. citizen in 1914. Meanwhile, as part of the Ghadr (or Gadar) movement, *Free Hindustan* and many Asian Indian activists were vehement in linking the struggle for Asian Indian equality in the United States to the issue of India's independence, condemning Canadian and U.S. immigration exclusion laws and urging Asian Indians to fight such laws. This struggle led Das to Berlin during World War I, where he became enmeshed in revolutionary activities against British India.

When the United States entered the war, Asian Indians and Germans plotting for India's independence, including Das, were arrested. He returned to the United States and stood trial with other coconspirators in the Ghadr Party, in the "Hindu Conspiracy" case of 1917. He was convicted and served eighteen months. After his release, Das earned his Ph.D. (1923) from Georgetown University and married Mary Keating, of a prominent Quaker family. Following the 1923 U.S. Supreme Court ruling that South Asians could not be citizens because they were not considered white persons, he was denaturalized. Das's wife lost her citizenship as a result of the 1922 Cable Act, stripping American women married to men ineligible for citizenship of their citizenship. They both had their citizenship reinstated after numerous petitions and changes in the law in 1931 (for wives) and 1946 (for men).

Das and his wife set up student-exchange programs and, in 1930, cofounded the Taraknath Foundation, which is still housed at Columbia University and issues grants supporting Indian studies. Das became a traveling lecturer, a radio commentator on contemporary politics, in 1948 an adjunct professor at New York University, and, in 1949, a lecturer in history at Columbia University. In 1952, he embarked on a lecture tour of Japan, Israel, India, and Germany. Returning to India after forty-six years, he was greeted by large crowds and glowing press editorials. Das taught and gave public lectures until his death in New York City on 22 December 1958.

Arthur W. Helweg

REFERENCES

Cao, Lan, and Himilce Novas. *Everything You Need to Know about Asian-American History.* New York: Plume, 1996.

Gordon, Leonard A. "The Taraknath Foundation." New York: Taraknath Das Foundation, n.d.

Jensen, Joan M. *Passage from India: Asian Indian Immigrants in North America.* New Haven and London: Yale University Press, 1988.

Kamath, M.V. *The United States and India, 1776–1976.* Washington, DC: Embassy of India, 1976.

Mukherjee, Tapan. "Taraknath Das." In *Distinguished Asian Americans: A Biographical Dictionary,* edited by Hyung-chan Kim, et al., 81–83. Westport, CT, and London: Greenwood Press, 1999.

Davis, James John (1873–1947)
Community leader and U.S. senator
Welsh-American

Davis rose from working-class origins to become one of the few Welsh immigrants in high political office in the United States. At the same time, he was an influential cultural leader in the Welsh ethnic community.

Born in the iron-producing town of Tredegar, South Wales, Davis immigrated to the United States with his family in 1881, eventually settling in Sharon, Pennsylvania. Like many Welsh-immigrant children, he left school early, going to work in the local iron industry, although he continued his education by attending evening school. In 1893, following a period of tramping across the country in search of work, he secured employment in a tin-plate works in Elwood, Indiana.

In Elwood, Davis entered public life, becoming president of the local lodge of the Amalgamated Association of Iron and Steel Workers and—having joined the Republican Party—getting elected as Elwood city boss in 1898 and as recorder of Anderson County, Indiana, in 1902. Although Davis had by that time left the ranks of manual labor, he would always proclaim his belief in the value of hard work and learning a trade.

In 1907, he became director-general of the Loyal Order of Moose. He had a spectacular impact: Membership mushroomed, and he initiated the establishment of new headquarters in Pittsburgh, various commercial enterprises, and a vocational school for orphans at Mooseheart, Illinois. The order became a major money-making concern, and it rewarded Davis substantially. He settled in Pittsburgh, married in 1914, and had five children.

In 1921 Davis's already colorful life took another turn. Invited by President Warren G. Harding to be his secretary of labor, he continued to serve under Presidents Calvin Coolidge and Herbert Hoover. Then, in 1930 he was elected U.S. senator for Pennsylvania by an overwhelming margin and remained in the Senate until 1944, when he narrowly lost his seat and his health was declining. His record in office was relatively undistinguished, and subsequent historians have rightly seen him as a minor figure. Yet in his time, he was very popular, especially among sections of the industrial working class, who were attracted by his homespun philosophy, his pride in his lowly origins, and his folksy populism.

Davis is an exemplar of the immigrant success story, and the core of his politics was his faith in what he described as America's "boundless opportunities." But his pursuit of the American Dream was not accompanied by a downplaying of his ethnicity. To the contrary, he was the promoter, organizer, and financier of a number of Welsh cultural activities and organizations: He served as president of the Pittsburgh International Eisteddfod (of 1913), was archdruid of the American Gorsedd of Bards (1940–1941), and was co-owner of *The Druid [The Welsh-American]* (1912–1939), the major English-language Welsh newspaper in the United States. By the second decade of the twentieth century Davis had emerged as one of the most active and influential leaders of the Welsh among the sizable—and largely English-speaking—contingents of Welsh people in the Pennsylvania and Ohio coalfields. That was his cultural as well as his political power base. Davis died in November 1947.

Bill Jones

REFERENCES

Davis, James J. *The Iron Puddler. My Life in the Rolling Mills and What Came of It.* Indianapolis: Bobbs-Merrill, 1922.

"Ex-Secretary James J. Davis Passes Away in Washington." *Y Drych* [The mirror]: *The American Organ of the Welsh People,* 15 December 1947, 1.

The Royal Blue Book: Prize Productions of the Pittsburgh International Eisteddfod. Pittsburgh: American Printing Company, 1916.

"Secretary of Labor for Three Presidents Dies." *New York Times,* 22 November 1947, 15.

"Yr Ysgrifennydd Llafur." *Y Drych* [The mirror]: *The American Organ of the Welsh People,* 10 March 1921, 4.

Zieger, Robert H. "The Career of James J. Davis." *Pennsylvania Magazine of History and Biography* 48.1 (January 1974): 67–89.

———. "David, James John." In *Dictionary of American Biography.* Supplement 4 (1946–1950), edited by John A. Garraty and Edward T. James, 219–220. New York: Scribner's, 1973.

———. *Republicans and Labor, 1919–1929.* Lexington: University of Kentucky Press, 1969.

De Kooning, Willem (1904–1997)
Artist
Dutch

Willem de Kooning was one of the major American abstract impressionist painters of the twentieth century. Along with Jackson Pollack and others, he broke new artistic ground.

Born 24 April 1904, in Rotterdam, the Netherlands, to parents who owned a water-front bar, de Kooning experienced an unhappy childhood marked by his parents' divorce, an acrimonious custody battle, and his mother's tyrannical abuse. Eager to be on his own, de Kooning apprenticed himself as a teenager to a commercial art and design firm and began attending art classes in the evening. In 1926, with the help of some sailors he met in his mother's bar, he immigrated to the United States as a stowaway and began working as a housepainter in New York City, doing some freelance artwork on the side. Initially, he lodged with a Dutch sailor in Hoboken, New Jersey, in a heavily Dutch community. Later, he moved to New York City.

In the 1930s de Kooning became acquainted with other artists, including Arshile Gorky, John Graham, and Jackson Pollack. Together, these artists formed the nucleus of the burgeoning modern art scene in Greenwich Village, later dubbed the New York School. For a short time in the heart of the Great Depression of the 1930s, de Kooning found work with the Federal Art Project of the Works Progress Administration (WPA). His status as an illegal alien, however, jeopardized that source of funds. Nonetheless, his experience in the Federal Art Project convinced him to devote himself full-time to his art. He supported himself with odd jobs in carpentry and painting, commercial art work, and store displays. Occasionally, he was commissioned to paint a mural, such as one he painted for the Hall of Pharmacy at the New York World's Fair. He also taught briefly at Black Mountain College and at Yale University.

Influenced by such diverse masters as Michelangelo, Rubens, and the Cubists, de Kooning became best known for his distorted, brightly colored paintings, including controversial images of women. By the 1950s he had become considered one of the foremost artists in the United States. Later in life, de Kooning branched out from painting to work in clay and other media.

In 1936, de Kooning married Elaine Fried, also an artist. Although marred by alcohol abuse and infidelity, the tumultuous marriage endured until Elaine's death in 1989. The couple had one daughter, Lisa.

With the exception of the Dutch-American neighbors in Hoboken who helped the young artist get acclimated to his new country, de Kooning did not have any significant dealings with the Dutch-American community. He formed his alliances within artistic circles in New York, and his unconventional lifestyle was very different from that of the typical God-fearing Dutch immigrant. He owed much of his career, however, to the solid background and training in art that he had received as a young apprentice and art student in Rotterdam and the strong work ethic he developed there. De Kooning died of Alzheimer's disease at age ninety-two in 1997.

Jennifer Leo

REFERENCES

"de Kooning, Willem." In *A Biographical Dictionary of Artists,* edited by Sir Laurence Gowing, 357. New York: Facts on File, 1995.

Hall, Lee. *Elaine and Bill: Portrait of a Marriage.* New York: HarperCollins, 1993.

De la Renta, Oscar (né Oscar Arístides de la Renta Fiallo) (1932–)

Fashion designer
Dominican

Oscar de la Renta is a renowned fashion designer and a well-known name in many parts of the world. His designs have been worn by such celebrities as Hillary Rodham Clinton, who wore de la Renta designs for the 1993 presidential inauguration ceremony and ball.

Oscar Arístides de la Renta Fiallo was born in Santo Domingo, Dominican Republic. He studied at the School of Fine Arts in Santo Domingo, and at the age of seventeen moved to Madrid to study art in hopes of becoming a painter. There, he began doing fashion illustrations to support himself and became interested in design. He was asked to design a debut gown for the daughter of the U.S. ambassador to Spain, and quite soon de la Renta was working for Spanish designer Cristóbal Balenciaga.

In 1961 de la Renta moved to Paris to fur-

ther his career and the next year went on to New York City, where he began working for Elizabeth Arden on her ready-to-wear collection. By 1967 Oscar de la Renta had established a name for himself in the fashion design industry and owned his own company, which carried his name. That same year he married Françoise de Langlade, the editor-in-chief of the French *Vogue.* Her connections to the rich and famous helped boost de la Renta's career, and by 1991 his company was grossing an average $450 million a year. Françoise died in 1983, and six years later de la Renta married multimillionaire Annette Reed. Both are now part of New York City's high society; de la Renta himself is on the board of trustees of the Metropolitan Opera and of Carnegie Hall.

In 1993, at the height of his career, de la Renta was asked to take over the classic house of Pierre Balmain. De la Renta thus became the first American (he had been naturalized in 1971) to administer a French couture business, and his debut was a huge success, rescuing Balmain from economic decline. De la Renta's success has been based on hard work, designing skills, and business acumen. Like many other haute couture designers, his fame has come from designing for the wealthy and famous, but his profits are mostly from his ready-to-wear clothing, accessories, and perfume. His net worth was estimated in 1997 at $47 million.

But de la Renta's work goes beyond his fashion success; he is also involved in several charity projects. In his native Dominican Republic, he supports La Casa del Niño (founded in 1982), an orphanage in La Romana that houses and educates around 400 children. Every year de la Renta organizes a fashion show to benefit the orphanage, and one of the orphans, Moises, was adopted by the de la Rentas when he was a two-month-old abandoned baby. De la Renta has been recognized for his charitable work in the Dominican Republic, where he was awarded two of the nation's top honors: the Order of Juan Pablo Duarte and the Order of Cristóbal Colón. He has also been recognized by the

Panamerican Development Foundation, which bestowed on him the Lifetime Achievement Award in 1992.

Oscar de la Renta represents a success story among the Dominican-American community. He has made a name for himself in the field of fashion designing and as a recognized social benefactor and New York socialite.

Ernesto Sagás

REFERENCES

Molina Morillo, Rafael. *Personalidades dominicanas 1993.* Santo Domingo: Molina Morillo & Asociados, 1993.

"1997 Hispanic Business Rich List." *Hispanic Business,* March 1997, 24.

Novas, Himilce. *The Hispanic 100: A Ranking of the Latino Men and Women Who Have Most Influenced American Thought and Culture.* New York: Carol Publishing Group, 1995.

Debas, Haile T. (1937–)
Scientist, surgeon, and educator
Eritrean

Haile T. Debas has achieved an outstanding career as a surgeon, professor, and dean of surgical medicine. At the same time, he has been immersed in the affairs of his ethnic community and homeland.

Debas was born in Asmara, Eritrea, in 1937. After receiving his undergraduate training in biology at University College of Addis Ababa in 1958, he went to McGill University, Montreal, receiving his M.D. degree in 1963. He completed his residency at the University of British Columbia in Vancouver General Hospital. His postgraduate work included a research fellowship at the University of Glasgow in Scotland and two years at the University of California, Los Angeles, as a medical research council scholar in gastrointestinal physiology. Between 1971 and 1993, he held teaching and research positions at the University of British Columbia, UCLA, University of Washington (Seattle), and University of California, San Francisco (UCSF). In 1993, he was appointed UCSF's dean of medicine and the Maurice Galante Distinguished Professor of Surgery.

Debas is one of two people of African descent who are deans in highly recognized medical schools in the United States. In 1997–1998, he served as interim chancellor of UCSF and, in 1997, also held the position of president of the Association of Minority Physicians in the United States. Debas has been honored for his academic and scientific accomplishments. He is a member of the Institute of Medicine and the American Board of Surgery. He is an elected fellow of the National Academy of Science and has been the director of the American Board of Surgery. He is recognized for his research on gastrointestinal hormones, which has led to the discovery of new approaches to the treatment of intestinal diseases.

With all that, Debas has never lost touch with his African ancestry and has a deep commitment to underprivileged communities in the United States. An outspoken supporter of affirmative action, he is committed to training doctors who will serve the state's diverse populations. He has been a source of inspiration and pride for Eritrean professionals in the health care field. In spring and summer 1992, Debas was instrumental in obtaining from UCSF donations of medical supplies and equipment for Eritrea with an estimated value of $250,000. He contributed his own money for the shipment.

He has also helped Eritrean physicians come to the United States for advanced studies and training and has performed major surgeries for free in Eritrea for veterans of war who could not afford medical treatment abroad. He is a member of the Eritrean Medical Association (EMA) and served as its honorary president in 1986. In 1994, he hosted a reception at UCSF to honor Issaias Afworki, the president of the newly independent Eritrea, inviting Eritreans, friends of Eritrea, dignitaries in the Bay Area, and officials of UCSF. In 1995, Debas visited Eritrea and participated in a strategy session with the Ministry of Health on the future training of Eritreans in the health care profession; he is currently involved in planning for training Eritreans in various medical fields.

Tekle M. Woldemikael

REFERENCES

Burdman, Pamela. "Med School Chief Set to Become UCSF Chancellor. Surgeon Said to Be in Line for Interim Appointment." *San Francisco Chronicle,* 9 April 1997, A13.

Debessay, Araya. "A Profile of a Remarkably Distinguished Eritrean Surgeon." 19 March 1996. Unpublished [personal correspondence to author].

Fox, Carol. "UCSF Press Release—Haile T. Debas, M.D. 10 April 1997": www.ucsf.edu/press-rel/1997/04/0410deba.html (accessed 13 June 2000).

Mebrahtu, Tomas. "Eritrean Professionals and Scholars in the Diaspora: Rising up to the Challenge." Report on Dr. Haile T. Debas's Keynote Address at the AEPAD Annual meeting 16 August 1997, Washington, DC: www.wam.umd.edu/~demoz/dkeynote.html (accessed 12 June 2000).

Seligman, Katherine. "UCSF Dean Takes Top Post Reluctantly: Interim Chancellor Haile Debas Would Rather Be Teaching." *San Francisco Examiner,* 11 April 1997, 6.

Deer, Ada E. (1935–)

Community activist and U.S. assistant secretary for Indian affairs
Native American (Menominee)

For nearly four decades Ada Deer has struggled to preserve Menominee sovereignty and the historic trust relationship between Indian nations and the United States. Her life serves as a window into the major events of recent Native American history, the history of ethnic activism, and the progress of women in the late twentieth century.

Deer was born in 1935 in Wisconsin, on the Menominee Reservation. Her mother was an Anglo-American nurse who worked for the Bureau of Indian Affairs (BIA) and her father a Menominee employee of Menominee Indian Mills. She was one of the growing number of Native Americans to attend college in the post–World War II years, receiving a B.A. from the University of Wisconsin in 1957 and a master's in social work from Columbia University in 1961. Initially employed as a social worker in New York, she was a Peace Corps volunteer in Puerto Rico and then in Minnesota as a BIA community ser-

vice coordinator. However, her commitment to tribal and national politics drew her away from her quest for a law degree.

Deer's leadership abilities faced a crucial test in the late 1960s and early 1970s. Congress had passed the Menominee Termination Act in 1954, ending the tribe's federal status in 1961. Tribal members lost health care, education benefits, and trust status for reservation land, and the 230,000-acre reservation in central Wisconsin became Menominee County, subject to state jurisdiction. Menominee Enterprises, Inc., a corporation established to manage tribal properties and economic development, mishandled assets and then sold or developed valuable waterfront land to replace lost revenue, worsening the financial situation.

In 1970, Deer and other concerned Menominees established Determination of Rights and Unity for Menominee Shareholders (DRUMS). DRUMS sought to repeal the Menominee Termination Act and restore tribal-federal relations. Their 1971 testimony before the U.S. Senate Committee on Interior and Insular Affairs, their letter-writing campaigns, and their public demonstrations culminated in the Menominee Restoration Act in 1973, renewing federal recognition. Deer chaired the tribe and the Menominee Restoration Committee until the drafting of a new constitution in 1976.

Simultaneously, Deer continued to bridge the cultural gap between her tribe and the surrounding society by teaching in the School of Social Work and Native American Studies at the University of Wisconsin, Madison, and by serving on the American Indian Policy Review Commission (AIPRC). The latter was established in 1975 in response to confrontational events during the 1960s and 1970s and emphasized self-determination, health care, education, and the quality of life for urban Native Americans. Although the AIPRC served mainly as an advisory body, its 900-page study influenced legislation for decades.

In 1993, Deer became the first female assistant secretary of the interior for Indian affairs—the position previously known as the commissioner of Indian affairs. During her tenure, she accomplished much, such as the inclusion of Alaska Natives as federally recognized groups. Her work in the Department of the Interior illustrated how Native Americans could make the system benefit them. Her life stands as a tribute to tribal sovereignty and self-determination in the late twentieth century.

Jeffrey P. Shepherd

REFERENCES

Bataille, Gretchen M., ed. *Native American Women.* New York: Garland Publishing, 1993.

Carter, Christina E. "Ada E. Deer." In *Notable Native Americans,* edited by Sharon Malinowski, 111–113. New York: Gale Research, 1995.

Hoikkala, Paivi. "The Hearts of Indian Nations: American Indian Women in the Twentieth Century." In *Indians in American History,* 2d ed., edited by Frederick E. Hoxie and Peter Iverson, 263–264. Wheeling, IL: Harlan Davidson, 1998.

Iverson, Peter. *"We Are Still Here": American Indians in the Twentieth Century.* Wheeling, IL: Harlan Davidson, 1998.

Peroff, Nicolas. *Menominee DRUMS: Tribal Termination and Restoration, 1954–1974.* Norman: University of Oklahoma Press, 1982.

Philp, Kenneth, ed. *Indian Self-Rule: First Hand Accounts of Indian-White Relations from Roosevelt to Franklin.* Salt Lake City: Howe Brothers, 1986.

Prucha, Francis Paul. *The Great Father: The United States Government and the American Indians.* Lincoln: University of Nebraska Press, 1986.

Delany, Martin Robinson (1812–1885)

Abolitionist, black nationalist, and writer
African American

Martin Robinson Delany, a leading African American intellectual of the nineteenth century, was active in the abolitionist movement. He is best known for his black nationalism, writing and lecturing extensively on race pride, and urging African American emigration to a more congenial homeland.

Delany was born in May 1812 to a free black mother and an enslaved father in Charles Town, Virginia (now West Virginia). Both parents traced their ancestry to African princes, and Martin was raised with a strong sense of pride in his African heritage. Because

he and his siblings were taught to read, local whites threatened the family, and they moved to Pennsylvania in 1822. His father purchased his freedom the next year and joined them. At the age of nineteen, Delany left for Pittsburgh to study, where he met and married Catherine Richards in 1843. They had eleven children, seven surviving. Her earnings were the primarily support for the family, as Delany continued his political work.

In 1843 Delany, an active abolitionist, supporter of fugitive slaves, temperance worker, and moral reformer, founded *The Mystery,* the first black newspaper west of the Alleghenies. After it folded in 1847, he became coeditor of Frederick Douglass's *North Star,* which advocated political action to achieve abolition. Throughout, Delany traveled extensively to lecture on abolition, often at great risk. He had also been studying medicine and, in 1850, was accepted by Harvard's medical school. Although classmates' protests convinced Harvard to bar him after one semester, Delany had accumulated enough medical knowledge to return to Pittsburgh and begin practicing. (No licensing was required.)

He remained politically active, organizing resistance to the new Fugitive Slave Act (1850), heading an underfunded black school, and beginning to question the prospects for blacks in the United States. His books, *The Condition, Elevation, Emigration and Destiny of the Colored People of the United States, Politically Considered* (1852) and *Blake* (1859), a novel about a slave rebellion, established him as a nationalist and separatist. He argued that African Americans should leave the United States for a homeland, whether in Canada, Latin America, or Africa. Although few other black leaders endorsed emigration, Delany enjoyed substantial support in black communities. In 1854, he organized the first of several National Emigration Conventions, attended by over 100 delegates. He visited various countries, including what is now Nigeria, in search of a homeland.

Though he moved to Ontario, Canada, Delany also helped recruit men and support for John Brown's efforts. After the Civil War began, the Delanys returned to the United States, to Brooklyn and later Ohio. When the Union army finally agreed to accept African Americans, Delany became a recruiter and was commissioned a major. Sent to South Carolina, he remained there after the war in the Freedmen's Bureau, becoming enmeshed in party politics, first as a Republican and, when that party's local fortunes waned, as a Democrat. Appointed a trial judge, he continued writing and supporting emigration efforts. His *Principia of Ethnology* (1879) argued for greater race pride, using history and archeology to demonstrate the preeminent role Africans played in the development of civilization.

In 1880 he resumed the lecture circuit. He returned to Ohio in 1884, and died there in January 1885.

Cheryl Greenberg

REFERENCES

Delany, Martin. *Blake; or The Huts of America*. Edited by Floyd Miller. 1859. Reprint, Boston: Beacon Press, 1970.

———. *The Condition, Elevation, Emigration and Destiny of the Colored People of the United States*. 1852. Reprint, New York: Arno Press, 1968.

Griffith, Cyril. *The African Dream: Martin R. Delany and the Emergence of Pan African Thought*. University Park: Pennsylvania State University Press, 1975.

Levine, Robert. *Martin Delany, Frederick Douglass and the Politics of Representative Identity*. Chapel Hill: University of North Carolina Press, 1997.

Sterling, Dorothy. *The Making of an Afro-American: Martin Robinson Delany*. Garden City, NY: Doubleday, 1971.

Ullman, Victor. *Martin R. Delany, The Beginnings of Black Nationalism*. Boston: Beacon Press, 1971.

Delerue, Georges (1925–1992)

Composer
French

Georges Delerue was famous in France and in the United States. He composed major musical scores for French (e.g., François Truffaut, Pierre Schoendorfer), U.S. (e.g., George Roy Hill, Oliver Stone), and other movie directors.

Delerue was born in Roubaix, France, in 1925. He showed an early interest in music and earned a scholarship to study at the renowned Paris Conservatory with Darius Milhaud, who encouraged him to write music for films. His career began in France in the 1950s, with Alain Resnais's *Hiroshima Mon Amour*. He wrote the scores for sixteen films directed by Philippe de Broca, beginning in 1956. Other memorable work of Delerue's was for François Truffaut's *Jules and Jim, Day for Night, The Last Métro*, and for other French so-called new-wave directors (Agnès Varda, Alain Robbe-Grillet, Jean-Luc Godard). In 1959, he married Micheline Gautron; they had a daughter, Claire; Gautron also had a child from a previous marriage.

Delerue's renown spread outside France. He scored films for British directors beginning in 1963 (Ken Russel, *French Dressing*) as well as for Italian directors (Bernardo Bertolucci, *The Conformist*). Around 1970, Delerue began scoring American films, dividing his time between France and the United States. During the 1970s he scored Paul Mazurski's *Willie and Phil*, a homage to *Jules and Jim*, and Mike Nichol's *Silkwood* and *Biloxi Blues*. Delerue moved to Los Angeles in the early 1980s, during which time he scored a wide variety of films, from George Cukor's *Rich and Famous* to Norman Jewison's *Agnes of God*, from Bruce Beresford's *Crimes of the Heart* and *Her Alibi* to Herbert Ross's *Steel Magnolias*, and the epic *The French Revolution*. Among his later works were the scores for *Joe Versus the Volcano, Black Robe, Mister Johnson*, and Bruce Beresford's *Rich in Love*. Delerue also wrote music for television productions, such as *The Borgias, Escape from Sobibor, Deadly Intentions*, and *Queenie*, as well as for commercials.

His achievements brought him success and renown. In 1969, Delerue won an Emmy for the music for the television documentary *Our World*, an Academy Award in 1979 for best original soundtrack, for George Roy Hill's *A Little Romance*, and an Oscar nomination in 1969 for *Anne of the Thousand Days*, in 1973 for *The Day of the Dolphin*, and in 1977 for *Julia*. Finally, in 1987, he received much praise for the music he wrote for the restoration of the 1927 silent film *Casanova.* However, in 1986, Delerue found himself at the center of a controversy about the soundtrack for the movie *The Color Purple,* composed by Quincy Jones. It was said that sections of Jones's music resembled Delerue's for a 1967 British film, *Our Mother's House.* Delerue was "bemused," for his own accomplishments included scores for about 200 films, and several of his soundtracks had been on records.

France also honored him by naming him a commander of arts and letters, one of France's highest honors for an artist. He died in Los Angeles on 20 March 1992.

André J. M. Prévos

REFERENCES

Carlson, Peter. "As It Ponders *The Color Purple's* Sound Track, Hollywood Hums, 'I've Heard That Song Before.'" *People,* 31 March 1986, 38–41.

Cohn, Lawrence. "Georges Delerue." *Variety,* 30 March 1992, 68.

Folkart, Burt. "G. Delerue: Maestro of Film Scores." *Los Angeles Times,* 23 March 1992, 20.

"Georges Delerue, Sixty-seven, a Composer on Truffaut and Stone Films, Dies.*" New York Times,* 23 March 1992, B10.

Delgado, Marcel (1898?–1976)
Film special effects pioneer
Mexican

Marcel Delgado is best remembered as a model maker for special effects master Willis O'Brien in such classic fantasy films as *The Lost World* (1925) and *King Kong* (1933). He has been called the Father of King Kong.

Delgado was born in La Parrita, Mexico, a village near the Texas border. At the age of six, he developed a love for sculpting toys. In 1909, in order to find work in agriculture, his father moved the family to California, but he died two years later. Marcel was forced to quit school and take various jobs to help support his mother and three siblings. He did not speak English until he was seventeen.

After World War I, Delgado enrolled as an art student at the Otis Institute in Los Angeles. While there, he met Willis O'Brien, a film-maker who had shot several experimental animated shorts. O'Brien was scouting for a sculptor to create nearly fifty models of dinosaurs for a film version of Sir Arthur Conan Doyle's novel *The Lost World.* Delgado spent more than two years making realistic dinosaur models in metal and textured rubber—one to two feet in length—that could be posed incrementally and shot frame by frame to give the illusion of life and, when projected on the screen, seemed to tower over the actors. The effects were so convincing that Conan Doyle himself borrowed an advance print of the film and showed it to a crowd of skeptics of psychic phenomena, claiming that a medium had enabled humanity to capture on film beasts of bygone ages. The practical joke astounded American critics. The film was released in 1925.

Delgado continued to work for O'Brien, contributing models and animation skills to a total of nine film projects, including *King Kong, Son of Kong, The Last Days of Pompeii,* and *Mighty Joe Young,* a film for which O'Brien won an Academy Award in 1949. In the 1950s and 1960s, Delgado branched out on his own. As a creator of special visual effects, he contributed models to *The Beast of Hollow Mountain, Master of the World* (with Vincent Price), *Jack the Giant Killer, Dinosaurus, Fantastic Voyage,* and *It's a Mad, Mad, Mad, Mad World.* Of his work in films, Delgado once observed: "I was never taught how to make models. . . . I had to rely on my own imagination. And, by God, I produced the first ones!"

Fantasy author Ray Bradbury noted: "To think of Marcel's name is to think of *King Kong*—the original. One hundred years from now the film which his unique artistry helped create will still be running—and there couldn't be a better monument than that, could there?" Mexico's "greatest gift to fantasy films" left an enduring legacy of inspiration for special effects creators the world over.

Delgado died in November 1976; he was survived by four daughters and eleven grandchildren. Other details about his personal life and community involvement are uncertain.

John F. Crossen

REFERENCES

Ackerman, Forrest J. "Delgado Dies: King Kong's Creator Succumbs." *Famous Monsters of Filmland* 133 (April 1977): 30–32.

Archer, Steve. *Willis O'Brien: Special Effects Genius.* Jefferson, NC: McFarland, 1993.

Schmidt, Richard J., Jr. "Master Monster Maker: His Children: Great Apes and Dinosaurs." *Famous Monsters of Filmland* 127 (August 1976): 35–38.

Simonson, Si, [special] effects technician and associate of Delgado's on *King Kong* and *Mighty Joe Young.* Interview by Jay Gowey, March 1999.

Deloria, Vine, Jr. (1933–)
Lawyer, scholar, and community activist
Native American (Yankton Sioux)

The preeminent Native American scholar of his generation, Vine Deloria, Jr., came of age as an activist as Native Americans in the United States pushed for recognition and rights after World War II. A dynamic advocate and accomplished public intellectual, he has been a part of contemporary Native American politics for more than thirty-five years.

Deloria's participation in Native American affairs follows a family tradition spanning generations. His great-grandfather, Saswe, was a healer and leader with the Yankton Sioux's White Swan band; his grandfather, Philip Deloria, was an Episcopal missionary; his aunt, Ella C. Deloria, was a prominent tribal ethnographer; and his father, Vine Deloria, Sr., was the first Native American to hold a national post within the Episcopal church in the United States. Thus, for Deloria, born in Martin, South Dakota, in 1933, Sioux traditionalism and Christianity were equally familiar cultural milieus. Like his father and grandfather, he initially pursued a religious career. In 1963, by which time he was married, he earned a master's degree in theology at Augustana Lutheran Seminary. But a growing disenchantment with the Episcopal church's relationship with Native Americans drew him away from religion.

Deloria's move toward a career in politics roughly coincided with the emergence of the Red Power movement. Fish-ins, (protests comparable to sit-ins), the occupations of Alcatraz, and the organization of such groups as the National Indian Youth Council and the American Indian Movement all signaled that Native Americans refused to wait quietly for the federal government to address their concerns. Deloria entered this highly charged arena when he became executive director of the National Congress of American Indians (NCAI) in 1964. Deloria's experiences helping Indian communities defend their sovereignty from federal, state, and private encroachments persuaded him to pursue a career in the field of Native American law. He left the NCAI in 1967 to attend the University of Colorado Law School.

In the thirty years since his graduation from law school in 1970, Deloria's career has followed three distinct paths: litigation on behalf of Native peoples, teaching at the university level, and scholarship. In the 1970s he defended fishing rights for tribes in the Pacific Northwest; during that decade he also chaired the Institute for the Development of Indian Law. As Native American studies gained recognition and legitimacy as an academic discipline in the 1970s and 1980s, major research institutions, including the University of Arizona and the University of Colorado, sought him out for faculty appointments. Moreover, his reputation as an author reached international proportions with the publication of such books as *Custer Died for Your Sins* (1969), *The Nations Within* (1984), and *Red Earth, White Lies* (1997). His literary style is sophisticated and polemical; his sharply honed critiques range across topics as diverse as Indian stereotypes, federal assimilation policies, "New Age" religions, and the Bering Straits Land Bridge migration theory. Like his father, aunt, grandfather, and great-grandfather before him, Deloria has kept faith with his tribal heritage throughout his long career as a Native American public intellectual.

Lisa E. Emmerich

REFERENCES

Deloria, Vine, Jr. *Behind the Trail of Broken Treaties.* New York: Delacorte Press, 1974.

———. *For This Land.* Edited by James Treat. New York: Routledge, 1999.

———. *God Is Red: A Native View of Religion.* 2d ed. Golden, CO: North American Press, 1992.

Deloria, Vine, Jr., and David E. Wilkins. *Trials, Treaties, and Constitutional Tribulations.* Austin: University of Texas Press, 1999.

Warrior, Robert Allen. *Tribal Secrets: Recovering American Indian Intellectual Traditions.* Minneapolis: University of Minnesota Press, 1995.

DeVos, Richard (1926–), and Van Andel, Jay (1924–)

Entrepreneurs and philanthropists
Dutch-Americans

Richard DeVos and Jay Van Andel, co-founders of Amway Corporation, have been lifelong friends and have led such parallel lives that they have been called America's Dutch Twins. In addition to being major employers and remarkably wealthy, they became the principal benefactors in their community.

Both Van Andel and DeVos were born to middle-class immigrant parents in the heavily Dutch community of Grand Rapids, Michigan—Van Andel in 1924 and DeVos in 1926. Their families were deeply religious in the Reformed faith, which for the boys meant catechism on Saturday, church all day Sunday, and a private Christian school during the week. The Calvinist doctrine in which they were steeped emphasized the responsibility of man to adhere to God's word in every facet of life. The church highly valued hard work as the duty of every Christian and as a means of bringing glory to God. In later life Van Andel wrote, "All my political, economic, and entrepreneurial beliefs came from these two tenets of my religious upbringing."

Growing up during the depression taught DeVos and Van Andel about financial devastation and the value of a dollar. Each showed an early bent for entrepreneurship by doing odd jobs for money. In high school Van Andel charged a small fee to drive a group of neighbors to school, one of whom was DeVos. The two became fast friends. In 1947, following military service, Van Andel and DeVos purchased Wolverine Air Service, a chartered plane service and flight school. Both attended Calvin College but did not graduate, choosing to put the interests of business ahead of formal education.

In 1949, at the suggestion of a Dutch relative of Van Andel's, the two formed Ja-Ri Corporation, through which they distributed food supplements manufactured by Nutrilite. By 1959, they had broken away from Nutrilite and formed the American Way Association, later renamed Amway Corporation. Initially, Amway sold household cleaners. The company has since expanded into many diverse product lines, is active worldwide, and is considered a model of multilevel marketing. It is located in Ada, Michigan—a heavily Dutch community that is a Grand Rapids suburb.

Both men married Dutch-American women from the Grand Rapids community and had four children each. In 1992, the founders' sons, Dick DeVos and Steve Van Andel, took over as Amway's president and chairman respectively.

The two families have been labeled the Fords of west Michigan for their economic impact and substantial community support. Although Amway's pseudoevangelistic corporate culture has been criticized by some, DeVos and Van Andel's contributions to their community are undeniable. Under their leadership, Amway became one of the first companies to express concern for environmental issues by producing biodegradable, phosphate-free, fluorocarbon-reduced, concentrated products. In 1992, the company planted 100 million trees to promote forestry issues.

Among many institutions underwritten by the men and their wives in Grand Rapids and its environs are an arts museum and arts council, the Gerald R. Ford Presidential Museum, the Van Andel Institute for Education and Medical Research, the DeVos Graduate School of Management at Northwoods University, and several area colleges—as well as the Van Andel Arena, home to three minor league teams. In addition, Van Andel served as chairman of the U.S. Chamber of Commerce, and DeVos forged alliances with Republican leaders and contributed significant funds in support of political causes.

The men have also maintained ties to their Dutch roots, including long-term, active membership in a Dutch Reformed congregation, LaGrave Christian Reformed Church, and have made sizable contributions to it. Furthermore, to build unity between the United States and the Netherlands, Van Andel chaired the Netherlands-American Bicentennial Commission, and Amway sponsored an art exhibit at Amsterdam's Stedelijk Museum. Each man credits his Dutch-American upbringing with giving him the tools for success in business and in life.

Jennifer Leo

REFERENCES

Butterfield, Steve. *Amway: The Cult of Free Enterprise.* Boston: South End Press, 1985.

Conn, Charles Paul. *The Possible Dream: A Candid Look at Amway.* Old Tappan, NJ: Fleming H. Revell, 1977.

Hamilton, Neil A. *American Business Leaders: From Colonial Times to the Present.* Santa Barbara: ABC-CLIO, Inc., 1999.

Hast, Adele, ed. *International Directory of Company Histories.* Chicago: St. James Press, 1991.

Van Andel, Jay. *An Enterprising Life.* New York: HarperCollins, 1998.

Young, Dale G. "Amway Founders Reshape Hometown with Millions." *Detroit News,* 18 October 1998: www.detnews.com/1998/specials/amway/981018a/981018a.htm. (Accessed 20 May 2000.)

Devoy, John (1842–1928)

Political activist, newspaper reporter, and editor
Irish

John Devoy was considered by the British to be one of their most dangerous enemies. He played out the role as a political activist and newspaper reporter and editor.

Devoy was born on 3 September 1842 in the parish of Kill, County Kildare. His father was principally a railroad laborer. His mother was Elizabeth Dunn. The Devoy cottage was said to be a meeting place for revolutionary nationalists. During "Black '47," following the failure of the Devoy potato crop, the family moved to Dublin. John attended school taught by the Christian Brothers and later took classes at the Catholic University.

By 1861, John Devoy had taken the oath of the Irish Republican Brotherhood (IRB). Between 1862 and 1865, he was its leader for the district surrounding Naas, in County Kildare, and Republican organizer for Irish soldiers in the British army. Devoy began to draw up a strategy to capture army barracks, and, in September 1865, the British attempted to arrest Devoy. In February 1866 he was finally captured. He was convicted of a felony and treason and sentenced to fifteen years. However, in January 1871, after five years, he was released on the condition that he go to the United States. Along with fellow Fenians, Devoy arrived in New York to a hero's welcome.

In 1873, Devoy joined the Clan na Gael, an Irish-American revolutionary organization. He drew up plans for an Irish revolution, sent money and arms to the IRB, and formulated plans for a rescue of Fenian prisoners in Australia. As chairman of the rescue committee, he used $15,000 donated by the Clan na Gael to purchase a whaling boat, the *Catalpa*. It left in April 1875, under clan leadership, and when the boat arrived in New York in August 1876 with six prisoners, Irish New Yorkers went wild.

To make a living, Devoy pursued a newspaper career. He worked for eight years for the *New York Herald,* first as a reporter, then as telegraph editor, and eventually as head of the foreign desk. He had shorter stints with the *Daily Telegraph* and the *Morning Journal* in New York, as well as *The Herald* and *Evening Post* in Chicago. In 1881 he founded the short-lived (1881–1885) *Nation,* a New York weekly with an Irish nationalist focus.

Irish nationalism was Devoy's life, supporting Parnell's fight against landlordism; helping the Land League and cofounding an American affiliate; and developing the "New Departure" policy, which combined militant republicanism with constitutional nationalism. Devoy reentered publishing in 1903, editing *The Gaelic American Newspaper* until his death in 1928. It was a strong supporter of the Irish-language movement, the Sinn Fein, and the Irish Volunteers. With the start of the Anglo-Irish war in 1916, Devoy helped organize the Friends of Irish Freedom and raise funds for the new Irish Republic's struggle against Britain.

Devoy returned to Ireland only twice after his imposed exile, in 1879 and again in summer 1924, to visit his old home. He spent his life fighting for Irish freedom and died penniless on 29 September 1928.

Seamus P. Metress

REFERENCES

Devoy, John. *The Land of Eire and the Irish Land League.* New York: Patterson and Neilson, 1882.

———. *Recollections of an Irish Rebel.* New York: Charles Young, 1929.

Golway, Terry. *Irish Rebel: John Devoy and America's Fight for Irish Freedom.* New York: St. Martin's Press, 1998.

O'Brien, William, and Desmond Ryan, eds. *Devoy's Post Bag.* 2 vols. Dublin: C. J. Fallon, 1948, 1953.

O'Luing, Sean. *John Devoy.* Tralee, Ireland: Anvil Books, 1961.

Di Loreto, Edward (1913–)

Entrepreneur, community activist, and philanthropist
Italian-American

Edward Di Loreto exemplifies the immigrant work ethic. For more than fifty years the guiding principles in his business and public service have been "success through hard work and concern for others."

Di Loreto was born in Prato, Italy, in 1913. Shortly thereafter, his father, Joseph, immigrated to Boston to establish a language school. Nearly six years later, his mother, Michelina, took Edward and his five siblings and joined her husband. The family moved to Connecticut, and Joseph began publishing *Il Sole,* a magazine for Italian-Americans, while his wife worked as a seamstress and dress designer and Edward held odd jobs and took night classes. Following high school, Di Loreto attended trade school and one year of business college. During World War II he worked in a submarine factory. He had two children in his first marriage; in 1954, he married Jill Krause, with whom he had four children.

In 1946 Di Loreto moved to Downey, California, where he capitalized on his technical and business education. First employed by Douglas Aircraft, in the mid-1950s he established the Downey Screw Products in a one-car garage. The company quickly expanded under his direction and became the Yale Engineering Company. With the financial success of his company, he began a long career in public service.

For more than thirty years Di Loreto has dedicated his time and resources to local, national, and international causes. He served on the boards of many Southern California organizations, among them the Downey Symphony Orchestra, Red Cross, St. Francis Medical Center Foundation, and United Way. He was twice honored with the Rockwell International Man of the Year Award for his community service. In addition, in 1969 he was instrumental in giving the law school to Pepperdine College, and later the Joseph and Michelina Di Loreto undergraduate scholarship fund and the Di Loreto–McConnell law school scholarship. He also contributed $1,000,000 to renovate the Pepperdine University Italian Study Center in Florence, Italy, and helped establish a cultural exchange program between Italy and Pepperdine.

Such contributions illustrated Di Loreto's attachment to his heritage. He has given generously to Italian and Italian-American causes; acted as a guiding force behind committees to raise funds for the Florence Flood Relief Drive, Sicilian Earthquake Relief Drive, and the Italian Earthquake Relief Drive; and served as chairman of the fund-raising campaign for the Casa Italian Cultural and Social Center (connected with St. Peter's Catholic Church, Los Angeles) and the Villa Scalabrini Retirement Center in Sun Valley. He helped the endowment fund for the Italian Heritage Cultural Foundation in Los Angeles, chaired a $1,000,000 campaign for the National Italian American Foundation in Washington, D.C., and remains a supporter of Southern California's Italian newspaper, *L'Italo-Americano.*

In recognition of his contributions, the

Italian government awarded him the Cavalliere Award and the Commendatore Award. In 1996 he received the Italian Catholic Federation's Pope John XXIII Award, given to an outstanding layperson who "best exemplifies the spirit and tradition of the late Pope John." More than 100 awards testify to Di Loreto's guiding belief: "Give something in return for the blessings you have received and leave something for the generations to come."

Kenneth Scambray

REFERENCES

Barbera, Robert. "Special Celebration Prepared by Patrons of Italian Culture." *L'Italo-Americano,* 18 May 2000, 14.

Henegar, Bill. "An American Love Affair." *Pepperdine People* (alumni magazine), Winter 1996, 2–5.

Perniciaro, Gianvittorio. "Edward Di Loreto, Philanthropist." *L'Italo-Americano,* 10 October 1996, 7–8.

Veneracion, Henry C. "Di Loreto Family's Story of Success." *Downey Eagle* (California), 9 December 1994, 3.

DiMaggio, Joseph Paul (1914–1999)
Baseball player
Italian-American

Joe DiMaggio was the greatest representative of Italian descent in the most popular American sport—baseball. His stature as one of baseball's greatest players made him a cultural hero for second-generation Italian-Americans.

Born in Martinez, California, on 14 November 1914, DiMaggio was one of nine children of Giuseppe and Rosalie DiMaggio, who had emigrated from Sicily in 1898. Descended from generations of Sicilian fishermen, his father continued his trade in California, later moving his family to North Beach, San Francisco, where Joe was one of three brothers who became major league baseball players.

By the early 1920s there were several Italian-American players in the major leagues, but it was not until the mid-decade that the sons of Italian immigrants achieved widespread prominence. DiMaggio started his baseball career in the Boys Club League and later played for the San Francisco Seals, a minor league team. The New York Yankees signed him in 1935, and he was the team's superstar for thirteen seasons between 1936 and 1951. Called the Yankee Clipper, in 1,736 games DiMaggio had a career batting average of .325, hitting 361 home runs and striking out only 369 times. With a gliding stride, deep range, one of the most powerful and precise throwing arms, he was credited with 153 assists in his thirteen seasons. In December 1942, he enlisted in the U.S. Army Air Force, resuming his career in 1946 and leading the Yankees back into the World Series a year later. He was voted his league's Most Valuable Player (MVP) in 1939, 1941, and 1947. He played in ten World Series, nine of which the Yankees won. He was admitted into the Baseball Hall of Fame in 1955.

But DiMaggio was more than a great baseball player; he became a cultural icon, possessing qualities that were widely respected and admired. He was elegant both on and off the field and carried himself like a hero. David Halberstam wrote that DiMaggio "guards his special status carefully, wary of doing anything that might tarnish his special reputation." He knew what his fans wanted and what children expected of him, and he always lived up to that image. The private, the silent, "the great DiMaggio," as Ernest Hemingway called him in *The Old Man and the Sea,* did indeed become the designated hero of the postwar era, even the catch phrase in popular songs. As singer Paul Simon phrased it: "Where have you gone, Joe DiMaggio? A nation turns its lonely eyes to you." The esteem with which he was regarded was further acknowledged in 1969, when he was named the Greatest Living Baseball Player.

His personal life, however, especially his nine-month marriage to Marilyn Monroe in 1952, brought him much unwanted public attention. Yet in his own way, he remained devoted to her for many years following her August 1962 death.

Although DiMaggio was not active within the Italian-American community, his success as a sports hero and, perhaps even more important, the dignity with which he conducted his life made him a source of great ethnic pride for Italian-Americans. He died in March 1999.

Diane C. Vecchio

REFERENCES

Allen, Maury. *Where Have You Gone, Joe DiMaggio?* New York: E. P. Dutton, 1975.

DeGregorio, George. *Joe DiMaggio: An Informal Biography.* New York: Stein and Day, 1981.

Herbert, Bob. "A Designated Hero." *New York Times,* 10 March 1999.

"Joe DiMaggio, Yankee Clipper, Dies at Eighty-four." *New York Times,* 9 March 1999.

Douglass, Frederick (né Frederick Bailey) (1818–1895)

Abolitionist, social activist, and journalist
African American

Frederick Douglass was a leading African American abolitionist and human rights activist from the early 1840s until his death in 1895. His writings and public speeches made him a preeminent spokesman for African Americans during those decades.

Frederick Douglass, the son of a slave mother and a white father, escaped to freedom in 1838. He was born in Tuckahoe, Maryland, and named Frederick Bailey. While a slave he was taught to read and write by a slave mistress. When he was sent to Baltimore to sell his own time (masters occasionally allowed some slaves to hire themselves out as long as they gave part of the pay back to the master) and tried to escape, he was sent to a "slave breaker," where he was brutally whipped. When he fled, Douglass was assisted by a free black woman, Anna Murray (1813–1882), whom he subsequently married. They moved to New Bedford, Massachusetts, and had five children. There, Frederick changed his surname to Douglass.

Douglass came to public notice in 1841 when he addressed a meeting of the Massachusetts Anti-Slavery Society in Nantucket. A brilliant speaker, he was hired by the American Anti-Slavery Society but was so impressive that few believed he had ever been a slave, which led him to write his first autobiography. Although its publication in 1845 catapulted Douglass to great prominence, it also revealed that he was a fugitive, which forced him to flee to England. In 1847 friends purchased Douglass's freedom, and he returned. He and his family then moved to Rochester, New York, where he launched a career as a journalist with the publication of the *North Star,* begun in 1847 (the paper was renamed twice during the 1851–1863 period).

Douglass continued his abolitionist activities, spoke out against other injustices and on behalf of women's rights, and was active in the Underground Railroad as well as the National Negro Convention Movement, which denounced slavery, opposed the colonization of free blacks, and promoted the advancement of free blacks. However, in the 1850s he began to move from his position that slavery had to end through legal means and even supported the raid on Harper's Ferry, led by John Brown in 1859. When the Civil War began, Douglass escalated his activities to end slavery, served as Lincoln's adviser, and, after the Emancipation Proclamation became effective on 1 January 1863, became a recruiter for the all-black 54th and 55th Massachusetts Regiments. After the Civil War, he was a major spokesman for the freedmen and supported the three Civil War amendments to the U.S. Constitution.

During the next two decades, Douglass was president of the Freedmen's Bank (1874), secretary of the Santo Domingo Commission (1871), U.S. marshal of the District of Columbia (1877–1881), recorder of deeds for that district (1881–1886), and minister to Haiti (1889–1891). In 1884 Douglass, whose first wife had died, married Helen Pitts, a white woman. Although the marriage was criticized by both whites and blacks, it did not diminish Douglass's prominence. Until his death in 1895, he continued to speak out against the increasing racial iniquities, segregation, and the discrimination that would be given constitutional sanction a year later, in *Plessy v Ferguson,* hastening the rise of Jim Crow.

Juliet E. K. Walker

REFERENCES

Andrews, William L., ed. *Critical Essays on Frederick Douglass.* Boston: G. K. Hall, 1991.

Blassingame, John W., et al., eds. *The Frederick Douglass Papers.* New Haven: Yale University Press, 1979.

Foner, Philip S. *The Life and Writings of Frederick Douglass: Pre–Civil War Decade, 1850–1860.* New York: International Publishers, 1950.

Huggins, Nathan Irvin. *Slave and Citizen: The Life of Frederick Douglass.* Boston: Little, Brown, 1980.

McFeely, William S. *Frederick Douglass.* New York: W. W. Norton, 1991.

Quarles, Benjamin. *Frederick Douglass.* Washington, D.C.: Associated Publishers, 1948.

Waldo, Martin E., Jr. "Frederick Douglass: Humanist as Race Leader." In *Black Leaders of the Nineteenth Century,* edited by Leon Litwack and August Meier, 59–84. Urbana: University of Illinois Press, 1988.

Draves, Victoria "Vicki" Manalo (1924–)

Diver and Olympic gold medalist
Filipino-American

In 1948, at the first Olympic games held after World War II, twenty-four-year-old Victoria Manalo Draves became the first female to win gold medals in both the ten-meter platform and the three-meter springboard diving competitions. Her achievements boosted Filipino-American self-esteem and came after years of her being forced to hide her Filipino heritage in California's discriminatory prewar environment. Today, she is recognized not only for her accomplishments as a diver but also as an early Filipino-American heroine whose story illustrates the era of prejudice against Filipinos.

The daughter of a Filipino-immigrant father, Theodore Manalo, and an English-immigrant mother, Gertrude Taylor, Victoria Manalo was born in San Francisco, California, on 31 December 1924. With her parents and her two sisters, she grew up in the low-income South Market neighborhood and rode a streetcar to a public seawater pool. There, she practiced diving and was discovered by the coach of the Fairmont Hotel Swimming and Diving Club. In order to practice at the Fair-

mont, which would not allow a teenager with a Filipino name to use its pool, she became Victoria Taylor, using her mother's maiden name. "It surprised me . . . I didn't like it at the time. I didn't think what it would do to my father," she said later. To earn money while still in high school, she held "a part-time job passing out towels and mending suits in the Fairmont's locker rooms" and, after her high school graduation, worked as a secretary. The need to earn a living often left her too tired to train or compete effectively.

In 1943, after working with several coaches, Victoria Taylor Manalo turned to Lyle Draves, at the Athens Athletic Club, in Oakland. Then coaching Zoe Ann Olsen, who would win the 1948 silver medal in springboard diving, Lyle Draves took Vicki, as she was nicknamed, as a pupil in 1943. Three years later—and one year after her father's death—Vicki married her coach. They moved to Pasadena, where, in the less-hostile post–World War II atmosphere, she won Pasadena Athletic Club sponsorship. While training for the Olympics under her husband's dogged prodding, Draves did more than 100 dives during six hours of practice each day.

Following her Olympic victories, Draves retired from competition and, in 1949, spent over a month in the Philippines, where she was entertained by President Elpidio Quirino at Malacañang Palace and visited her father's hometown of Orani, Bataan. Turning down B-movie offers of roles playing a stereotypical native girl—"I wasn't about to make a fool of myself"—she toured with various water shows until 1953, when she left public view to raise a family of five children.

In 1994, while living in retirement with her husband in Palm Springs, California, Draves was honored by the Filipino American National Historical Society (FANHS) with its Gold Very Important Pinoy/Pinay (VIP) Award. It appears that older members of the San Francisco FANHS chapter had remembered her achievements, although she had not been active in the Filipino community.

Barbara M. Posadas

REFERENCES

Ayuyang, Rachelle Q. "Catch a Diving Star." *Filipinas,* July 1996, 28–30.

"Draves, Victoria (Manalo)" (1999): www. hickoksports.com/biograph/dravesvi.shtml (accessed 19 June 2000).

Posadas, Barbara M. *The Filipino Americans.* Westport, CT: Greenwood Press, 1999.

"Very Important Pinoy/Pinay Award [Program]." Filipino American National Historical Society, Fifth National Conference, San Francisco, CA, 6 August 1994.

Drewsen, Gudrun Løchen (1867–1946)

Community activist and suffragist
Norwegian

When the premier Norwegian-language newspaper in the United States announced Gudrun Løchen Drewsen's death in 1946, it emphasized the qualities and achievements then considered important for a woman of her class in Norway and the United States. For her great charitable work among her needy countrymen in the United States, the king of Norway had awarded her the country's Royal Service Medal of Gold, the newspaper noted, saying nothing about her career as a path-breaking activist on behalf of women's suffrage.

Gudrun Løchen was the tenth child of a rural entrepreneur and member of Norway's parliament, Hermann Løchen. After his death, she lived in Trondheim with her uncle, one of the city's most highly regarded businessmen. She associated with young people who discussed the radical ideas concerning the equality of the sexes that were in the work of Norwegian authors Camilla Collett and Henrik Ibsen. Nevertheless, her uncle announced that university study was inappropriate for a girl and instead provided private tutors at his home until business difficulties necessitated her finding paid employment.

For a year she worked while privately struggling against the limits put on women's opportunities. She was sent to Kristiana (Oslo) to study with several famous Norwegian artists after she abruptly decided to become engaged and marry Viggo Drewsen, a Danish-American chemist. As part of an agreement, she lived with her future mother-in-law while engaged in her studies, even holding a public exhibition as a painter before her wedding day.

She became a devoted wife and mother, bearing three children and then following her husband to New York when he saw greater opportunities as a chemist in the United States. In 1902, she was asked by one of Norway's most famous women's suffragists, Fredrikke Kvam, to represent the country's women in Washington, D.C., at the first international conference devoted to women's suffrage. Once she represented her countrywomen, spoke to meetings of congressmen, and met the president, she found returning to private life impossible. The encouragement she received to function as a spokeswoman for Norwegian, Norwegian-American, and U.S. groups propelled her, she claimed, to become an activist. Eventually a recognized leader of the women's suffrage movement, she worked nationally and internationally until the vote was won in the United States in 1920.

Starting in 1903, she mobilized women in her ethnic community in Brooklyn and some of its leading men to participate in annual suffrage marches along Manhattan's Fifth Avenue. She was an efficient strategist and recruiter, spearheaded campaigns petitioning for women's rights, and arranged lectures and events in support of the cause. She was also instrumental in winning the support of Brooklyn's leading Norwegian-language newspaper, *Nordisk Tidende.* That the U.S. women's suffrage movement made a habit of putting her on its programs is a convincing tribute to her abilities as a platform speaker.

Drewsen succeeded in combining the roles of suffragist leader, wife, mother, club woman, and hostess for increasing numbers of international celebrities. After 1920, she retired to private life, first in Larchmont, New York, and, after her husband's death, with her daughter in San Francisco.

David C. Mauk

REFERENCES

Bakken, Anja. "'Our Country Gives Us the Vote—America Refuses It': Norwegian-American Suffrage Workers in Brooklyn and Minneapolis, 1880–1920, and Their Gendered Sense of Ethnicity." Master's thesis, University of Trondheim, Norway, 1998 [available at the Norwegian American Historical Association (NAHA) Archives and the Minnesota Historical Society].

Drewsen, Gudrun Løchen. *Man minnes mangt* (One remembers a great deal). Oslo: Crydendal, 1937.

Nordisk Tidende (Norwegian times) (Brooklyn, NY), 1902, 1913–1916.

"Fru Gudrun Løchen Drewsen." *Decorah-Posten*, 27 June 1946, under "Viggo Drewsen," Roberg Files and "Gudrun Löchen Drewsen" in the Knut Gjerset Collection, NAHA, Northfield, MN.

Du Bois, W. E. B. (William Edward Burghardt) (1868–1963)

Scholar, editor, and human rights activist
African American

The nation's first African American to receive a Ph.D. from Harvard, W. E. B. Du Bois is recognized as one of the foremost intellectuals in this nation's history. Along with Frederick Douglass and Booker T. Washington, he is considered one of the three leading African Americans in the century prior to 1960.

Du Bois was born in Great Barrington, Massachusetts, the son of Alfred and Mary Burghardt Du Bois. The town was primarily white, and he attended integrated schools. He earned B.A. degrees from Fisk University and Harvard, as well as a Ph.D. in history from Harvard in 1895. Du Bois's career began at Wilberforce University, in Ohio, where he was a professor of Latin and Greek (1894–1896) and where he married Nina Gomer. They had a son and a daughter, but his son died. Hired in 1896 by the University of Pennsylvania to conduct a one-year study, he published *The Philadelphia Negro: A Social Study*. In 1897 he went to Atlanta University as professor of economics and history, where he continued his social study of black America. From 1897 to 1914 he convened conferences and edited the studies known as the Atlanta University publications.

It was his 1903 *Souls of Black Folk,* a literary masterpiece, that gave Du Bois a national audience. He emphasized the "double consciousness" of black Americans as both black and American, "two warring souls." His critique of the accommodationist policy of Booker T. Washington set the stage for a black national debate. He vehemently opposed African Americans' giving up their political and civil rights and denounced Washington's emphasis on industrial education, advocating instead a strong liberal arts education, particularly for black leaders, whom he called the "Talented Tenth." In an attempt to counter Washington's influence, in 1905 he founded the Niagara movement, the goals of which were incorporated in the agenda of the NAACP, organized in 1909. Du Bois became its director of research and publications and established its journal, *Crisis,* which he edited until 1934. The journal provided a forum for his views, particularly his opposition to Washington and denunciation of Marcus Garvey. As the only national journal that provided information on the progress of African Americans, it rapidly increased its circulation.

In the early 1930s, his increasingly radical editorials and promotion of a black separate economy prompted the integrationist NAACP to seek his resignation. He had moved to the left politically and had begun to denounce capitalism and laud Marxism. He was also an ardent Pan-Africanist, perceiving the condition of black America within the context of worldwide imperialism. After World War II, he focused on the international peace movement, but his comments favorable to the Soviet Union made him suspect. He became isolated from African American civil rights activities during the 1950s and, completely disillusioned, formally joined the Communist Party in 1961, moved to Ghana with his second wife, Shirley Graham Du Bois, renounced his U.S. citizenship, and became a citizen of Ghana. Du Bois was ninety-four when he died on 27 August 1963.

Juliet E. K. Walker

REFERENCES

Andrews, William L., ed. *Critical Essays on W. E. B. Du Bois.* Boston: G. K. Hall, 1985.

DeMarco, Joseph P. *The Social Thought of W. E. B. Du Bois.* Lanham, MD: University Press of America, 1983.

Harris, Thomas E. *Analysis of the Clash over the Issues between Booker T. Washington and W. E. B. DuBois.* New York: Garland Publishing, 1993.

Horne, Gerald. *Black and Red: W. E. B. Du Bois and the Afro-American Response to the Cold War, 1944–1963.* Albany: State University of New York Press, 1986.

Lewis, David Levering. *W. E. B. Du Bois—Biography of a Race, 1868–1919.* New York: Henry Holt, 1993.

Marable, Manning. *W. E. B. Du Bois: Black Radical Democrat.* Boston: Twayne Publishers, 1986.

Reed, Adolph L., Jr. *W. E. B. Du Bois and American Political Thought: Fabianism and the Color Line.* New York: Oxford University Press, 1997.

Rudwick, Elliott. "W. E. B. Du Bois: Protagonist of the Afro-American Protest." In *Black Leaders of the Twentieth Century,* edited by John Hope Franklin and August Meier, 63–83. Urbana: University of Illinois Press, 1982.

Du Pont de Nemours, Éleuthère Irénée (1771–1834), and Du Pont de Nemours, Pierre Samuel (né Pierre Samuel Du Pont) (1739–1817)

Industrialist and diplomat, respectively French

Pierre Samuel Du Pont's life was spent mostly in France, but he corresponded with Benjamin Franklin and Thomas Jefferson, worked to develop commercial and diplomatic relations between France and the United States, and played a role in the Louisiana Purchase. He settled in Delaware with his sons, Victor-Marie and Éleuthère Irénée. The latter son started the Du Pont company, which began as a gunpowder manufacturer.

The elder Du Pont was born in Paris, in 1739, the son of Samuel Du Pont, a watchmaker, and Anne Alexandrine de Montchanin. Although he was baptized in the Roman Catholic Church in order to secure a "civil status," he was later baptized a Huguenot. In January 1766, Du Pont married Marie Le Dée, a Catholic. Their first son, Victor-Marie, was born in 1767, and their third son, Éleuthère Irénée, in 1771. In 1767, Du Pont published *Physiocratie,* a collection of the works of François Quesnoy, the founder of physiocracy. The following year he corresponded with Ben Franklin and, seven years later, asked to be sent to America as a French secret agent. Between 1781 and 1787, Du Pont worked with Charles Gravier, Comte de Vergennes, who was promoting relations between France and the United States. Three years after being named a noble in 1783 (becoming Du Pont de Nemours), Du Pont was raised to councilor of state and worked with the Marquis de Lafayette and Jefferson on increasing trade between France and the United States.

Du Pont continued to remain active during the French revolutionary period. He was elected a deputy of the Loiret in 1795 and was chosen to sit on the Council of Elders. He was also selected to be a member of the Institut de France, a division of the French Académie des Sciences. However, because he had expressed opposition to Napoleon Bonaparte, he was briefly arrested in September 1797.

At that point, worried about further arrests, Du Pont decided to transfer all the members of his family to the United States. As a member of the Institut, Du Pont had the status of a "traveling scientist," guaranteeing him a safe departure and the right to return to France. The family landed in Newport, Rhode Island, in January 1800, moved to New York, and settled on the Bergen Point estate. Du Pont hoped to launch a new company in order to help the settlement of French farmers, a project based on physiocratic ideas that emphasized the vital importance of agriculture for a "healthy society." But he was unfamiliar with the way lands were "grabbed" in the United States, and his plans failed. Éleuthère Irénée and Victor sailed back to France. Éleuthère Irénée, who had studied with Lavoisier, "the father of modern chemistry," inquired about the manufacture of gunpowder and obtained financial help to launch his gunpowder-manufacturing company near Wilmington, Delaware. Meanwhile, Victor tried in vain to convince investors of the soundness of his father's plans.

After meeting with President Jefferson, the elder Du Pont returned to France in 1802 with papers from the president. Although Du Pont played only an unofficial role in the Louisiana Purchase, Jefferson formally thanked him in a letter dated 1 November 1803. Nevertheless, Du Pont's stay in France was a period of frustration, for he could not complete any of his projects, nor could Victor raise any money for them. Du Pont left France after the return of Napoleon in February 1815 and spent his last years in Wilmington, writing and living with Éleuthère Irénée's family. He died on 7 August 1817.

Éleuthère Irénée, as noted, had first come to the United States with his father and his brother Victor-Marie. In 1800, he was told about gunpowder manufacturing in the United States, and in 1803, he started a gunpowder plant in Wilmington, Delaware. Éleuthère Irénée tried to manufacture the highest possible grade of gunpowder and tested his production extensively. He then contacted Thomas Jefferson, who decided that the United States should buy all its gunpowder from the Du Pont company. This de facto exclusivity caused serious financial woes to the company. During the War of 1812, the Du Ponts lost large amounts of money because the government was paying its bills late or not at all. Meanwhile, Éleuthère Irénée improved the manufacture of gunpowder by building new workshops along the Brandywine River. They were constructed with three thick masonry walls and one light wooden wall so that, in case of explosion, the wooden wall would be blown away and the rest of the building would be left standing.

Among his other activities, Éleuthère Irénée had started a woolen mill in 1810 but without much success and soon closed it. He also focused on plants and flowers and established a continuous exchange with France. In 1822, President James Monroe appointed Éleuthère Irénée to the board of directors of the United States Bank. The Du Pont company that he had started as a gunpowder manufacturer diversified in the nineteenth and twentieth centuries and became a major U.S. company. Éleuthère Irénée died in Philadelphia on 31 October 1834.

André J. M. Prévos

REFERENCES
Dorian, Max. *The du Ponts: From Gunpowder to Nylon.* Boston: Little, Brown, 1961.
Du Pont de Nemours, Pierre Samuel. *The Autobiography of Du Pont de Nemours.* Translated and Introduction by Elizabeth Fox-Genovese. Wilmington, DE: Scholarly Resources, 1984.
Gates, John D. *The du Pont Family.* Garden City, NY: Doubleday, 1979.
Saricks, Ambrose. *Pierre Samuel Du Pont de Nemours.* Lawrence: University of Kansas Press, 1965.
Wilkinson, Norman B. *E. I. du Pont, Botaniste. The Beginning of a Tradition.* Charlottesville: University Press of Virginia, 1972.

Dukakis, Michael Stanley (1933–)
Professor, state representative, governor, and presidential candidate
Greek-American

The son of Greek immigrants, Michael Dukakis rose from local Democratic politics to become a three-term governor of the state of Massachusetts. He was the Democratic candidate for president of the United States in 1988, losing his bid to George H. W. Bush.

Michael Dukakis, an only child, was born in Brookline, Massachusetts, on 3 November 1933. His father, Panos, a Boston obstetrician, and his mother, Euterpe (Boukis), a teacher, both emigrated from Greece, going to the mill cities of Lowell and Haverill, Massachusetts, early in the twentieth century. After graduating from Swarthmore College in 1955 with a degree in political science, Dukakis served with the U.S. Army in Korea. He then entered Harvard Law School, earning his J.D. degree in 1960 and joining a Boston law firm. In 1963 he married the former Katherine (Kitty) Dickison.

Dukakis began his political career as a member of the Brookline town meeting in 1959. During the scandal-ridden administration of Governor Foster Furcolo, a Democrat, he led a reform movement and was elected four times to the state house of representatives during the 1960s. Dukakis set himself apart as a reform-oriented politician, sponsoring a number of consumer housing and environmental protection measures, most notably the nation's first no-fault auto insurance law. Then, losing his bid for lieutenant governor in 1970, he organized a Ralph Nader–type organization to monitor state agencies, while developing a power base for a bid for the governorship. Relying on volunteers from the 1972 McGovern presidential campaign and those of the anti–Vietnam War movement, Dukakis launched a campaign to unseat the Republican governor, Francis W. Sargent. He stressed the need for "efficiency and fiscal responsibility" in government. He became an advocate for the working and lower-middle classes, answering the grievances of "ethnics," including black Americans. On 5 November 1974, Dukakis won with 56 percent of the vote. He was reelected in 1982 and 1986. During the hiatus between his first and second terms, he taught at Harvard University's Kennedy School of Government.

Dukakis's fiscal and other successes, which, in his third term, he labeled the Massachusetts Miracle, attracted many liberals, progressives, and minorities. In 1986 his colleagues in the National Governors' Association voted him the most effective governor in the nation. He won the Democratic nomination for president in 1988. However, a combination of media attacks by his opponent and many tactical mistakes led to his defeat by George H. W. Bush. After leaving the governorship, Dukakis taught at five different universities and published a number of articles on public health policies.

In the minds of many voters, Dukakis epitomized the American Dream, the son of Greek immigrants who made it big. He spoke Greek and Spanish fluently and attracted many so-called ethnic voters. However, although, according to Archbishop Iakovos, Dukakis was a member of the Orthodox church, in fact Dukakis was not actively involved in the Greek community before he began to pursue the presidency. Although his participation in the Greek-American community has been casual, he remains highly respected in that community, and most Greek-Americans are proud of his accomplishments in Massachusetts. Moreover, in Thessaloniki, Greece's second-largest city, Anatolia College recently named a chair in his honor.

George A. Kourvetaris

REFERENCES

Dukakis, Michael, and Rosabeth Moss Kanter. *Creating the Future: The Massachusetts Comeback and Its Promise for America.* New York: Summit Books, 1987.

Kenney, Charles, and Robert L. Turner. *Dukakis: An American Odyssey.* Boston: Houghton Mifflin, 1988.

"Michael S. Dukakis. Biographical information": www.hri.org/hri/dukakis.html (accessed 15 June 2000).

Moskos, Charles C. *Greek Americans: Struggle and Success.* 2d ed. New Brunswick, NJ: Transaction Publishers, 1989.

Rossides, Eugene. *The American Hellenic Who's Who.* Washington, DC: American Hellenic Institute, 1990.

UCLA School for Public Policy and Social Research. "Michael Dukakis Appointed Visiting Professor of Policy Studies": www.sppsr.ucla.edu/dean's/bulletin/dukakisa.htm (accessed 15 June 2000).

Edison, Thomas Alva (1847–1931)

Inventor and entrepreneur
Canadian-American

Thomas Edison's inventions and innovations revolutionized the way people live. From the incandescent light bulb to recorded sound, his 1,093 patents have contributed enormously to modern technological development.

Edison was born in Milan, Ohio, to Canadian parents. His father, Samuel, a supporter of the rebel cause, had fled Upper Canada after the Rebellion of 1837. Edison had very little formal schooling, his entry to school having been delayed until 1855 by scarlet fever. He left school to work on the Grand Trunk Railway in 1862, selling food and newspapers to the passengers. He soon began his own newspaper and employed other boys to sell them on the trains. He then began working as a telegraph operator, although he was hard of hearing.

Unsupervised, his job allowed him the luxury of studying as well as the opportunity to experiment with the machines. His experimenting was not always appreciated, and he changed jobs often, working as a telegraph operator in various locales. It was during this work that he improved the design of the "duplex" telegraph machine in 1867. His first patent was for the legislative vote recording machine in 1868. The next year he began to invent full-time. He moved from Boston to New York and, after working for a time with a telegraph company, became a partner in Pope, Edison and Company. He concentrated first on the improvement of the telegraph system, developing the "quadruplex" telegraph system, allowing for the transmission of four messages simultaneously. He also worked on the Edison pen, marketed in the 1880s as the "Edison Mimeograph." The invention allowed the reproduction of written material. Although Edison developed an "acoustic telegraph," which was much like a telephone, Alexander Graham Bell held that first patent. However, Edison later developed the carbon-button transmitter, which was licensed to Bell for use in the telephone. Edison's work on the recording telegraph led him to the development of the phonograph in 1877. He then developed a cylinder on which the sound was recorded.

In 1879 Edison revolutionized lighting by developing the carbon filament incandescent lamp. This led to his interest in electric lighting and electric power. He built the first electricity-generating station in New York City in 1882 with his Edison Electric Illuminating Company. In the 1890s, Edison developed an iron mining and ore concentrating process and opened a plant near Ogdensburg, New Jersey. During this same period he also began experimenting with moving pictures and developed the roll film peephole Kinescope in 1894. At the turn of the century he researched and developed storage batteries. He also began to search for a natural substitute for rubber, identifying latex from goldenrod, which was made into tires for him by Firestone in 1928.

During World War I, Edison headed a group of inventors and businessmen who formed the Naval Consulting Board. For the U.S. government he experimented with sonic devices designed to detect German submarines.

Edison was married twice, first to Mary Stilwell in 1871. They had three children, but she died in 1884. He next married Mina Miller in 1886 and had three more children. He died on October 18, 1931.

Gillian Leitch

REFERENCES

Clark, G. Glenwood. *Thomas Alva Edison*. New York: E. P. Dutton, 1950.

Clark, Ronald W. *Edison: The Man Who Made the Future*. New York: Putnam, 1977.

Jenkins, Reese V. "Edison, Thomas Alva." In *American National Biography*. Vol. 7: 310–315. New York & Oxford: Oxford University Press, 1999.

Kaplan, Fred. "Inventor of the Century." *Edmonton Journal*, 26 December 1999, E5.

Millard, Andre. *Edison and the Business of Innovation*. Baltimore & London: John Hopkins University Press, 1990.

Edwards, Henry Morgan (1844–1925)
Jurist, writer, and community leader
Welsh

In his role as one of Pennsylvania's foremost jurists and through his services to the people of Lackawanna County, Henry Morgan Edwards became the most respected and the best-known Welshmen in the state. He was also one of the most active and influential Welsh community leaders in the United States during his time.

Edwards was born into an Ebbw Vale, South Wales, coal mining family in 1844. His intellectual gifts manifested themselves early, and he earned a B.A. at the University of London. In 1864, he immigrated to Scranton, Pennsylvania, a move he described as inspired by "the principles of American Civil Liberty" and the conviction that "America was the land of the greatest Opportunity (a big O, please)."

His dream of becoming a lawyer would be triumphantly realized, but not until after a brief stint as a journalist in New York City. Returning to Scranton in 1868, he studied law and entered the Luzerne County bar in 1871 (Lackawanna County after 1878). Until 1885, he practiced privately and thereafter enjoyed dazzling success in public office. He served as Republican district attorney for Lackawanna County (1885–1901) and in 1893 was elected unopposed as county judge, and also in 1903, 1913, and 1923. A kindly, gentle man, he won extensive respect and admiration for his fairness, learning, and elo-

quence. He also gave long and devoted service to a variety of Scranton committees and public and charitable bodies, prompting a 1924 reference to him as "an institution."

Among the Welsh, Edwards's stature was immense, and he was widely regarded as being one of the foremost Welsh bards and orators in Welsh and English in the United States. In the 1860s and 1870s he had published a play and essays in Welsh and contributed to the Scranton newspaper *Baner America* (Banner of America), as well as editing a short-lived literary journal. Throughout his life he would write for the local and Welsh-American press in both languages. Edwards was also a major figure in Scranton's Welsh-immigrant financial and benevolent institutions and cultural societies, among them the *Gymdeithas Athronyddol Gymreig* (Welsh philosophical society) and, later, the English-language Druid Society. On the wider Welsh-American stage, he became deputy archdruid of the American Gorsedd of Bards in 1913, while retaining his membership in the Gorsedd of Bards of Great Britain. Above all, he was a passionate promoter of the Welsh literary and musical competitive festival, the *eisteddfod,* and was so recognized in Wales and the United States.

Though he acquired wealth and power, Edwards remained a resident of the Welsh section of Scranton, where he and his wife brought up their five children. He also continued to attend his Welsh church and speak Welsh to the end of his life. He never wavered in his conviction that a love of Welshness was compatible with being a good American and constantly proclaimed in his speeches and writings that the Welsh should "Americanize" but not forget their Welsh origins. As a close friend remarked in 1907, he was "the handle between the old and the new."

Bill Jones

REFERENCES

Edwards, H. M. "Eisteddfodic Reminiscences." *Druid,* 9 September 1909–30 June 1910, passim.

"H. M. Wedi Myned." *Y Drych* [The mirror]: *The American Organ of the Welsh People,* 17 December 1925, 8.

Jones, William D. *Wales in America: Scranton and the Welsh 1860–1920.* Cardiff, Wales, and Scranton, PA: University of Wales Press/University of Scranton Press, 1993.

———. "The Welsh Language and Welsh Identity in a Pennsylvanian Community." In *Language and Community in the Nineteenth Century. A Social History of the Welsh Language,* edited by Geraint H. Jenkins, 261–286. Cardiff, Wales: University of Wales Press, 1998.

"Marwolaeth yr Anrh. H. M. Edwards." *Y Drych* [The mirror]: *The American Organ of the Welsh People,* 3 December 1925, 1, 8.

"Remarkable Career of a Distinguished Jurist." *Druid,* 15 December 1925, 9.

Stoddard, Dwight J. *Prominent Men of Scranton and Vicinity.* Scranton: Tribune Publishing Co., 1906.

Ellis, Rowland (1650–1731)
Quaker minister and community leader
Welsh

Emigration to America provided Rowland Ellis an escape from religious persecution in his homeland and enabled him to continue to be a much respected and devoted servant to his faith and people. He, like other Welsh immigrants, made a major contribution to the early history and development of Pennsylvania.

Ellis was born in 1750 into a prominent family of gentry at Bryn Mawr Farm, near Dolgellau, in Meirioneth, North Wales. At an early age he married a rich heiress and acquired great wealth and influence in the area where he lived. Around 1672 he joined the Society of Friends and later became a minister. He suffered greatly for his faith during the persecution of religious dissenters that followed the restoration of the monarchy in Britain in 1660. Imprisoned, he narrowly escaped being hanged in 1676.

As with many other Quakers in Wales at the time, continued persecution, the fear of property confiscation, and news of William Penn's "Holy Experiment" in Pennsylvania convinced Ellis that emigration to North America was the only way he and his family could practice their faith in peace. In 1682 he purchased a large property in the "Welsh Barony," a tract of land on the outskirts of Philadelphia that Penn had set aside for Welsh dissenters. Along with his eldest son and about 200 of his neighbors, Ellis arrived in Pennsylvania in 1687; he stayed there for nine months preparing his plantation. He finally settled permanently in America with his second wife (his first had died young) in 1697. Soon after his arrival, he lost much of his fortune through land speculation and eventually sold the Bryn Mawr plantation. Today, Bryn Mawr College, established in the nineteenth century, partly occupies the site of his original estate.

Ellis's distinction lies in his considerable, zealous service to the Society of Friends, his fellow Welsh, and to the wider civic life. He was regarded as one of the four most important Welshmen in the Pennsylvania of his time, but his multiple roles gave him a position of prominence within both the general and the Welsh communities. A man of great intellectual ability, sound judgment, and good education, he was also an accomplished writer and speaker. In 1700 he was elected to represent Philadelphia County in the colonial assembly but gave that up after a few years, preferring to devote his time to religious service. He preached regularly in Welsh and English in the Philadelphia area and also acted as interpreter for Welsh-speaking immigrants in various religious and public gatherings.

A fine example of Ellis's many public works was his patronage of the Welsh Quaker preacher and writer Ellis Pugh, author of *Annerch i'r Cymry* (1721), the first Welsh book printed in America. Ellis translated Pugh's book into English so that it might achieve a wider circulation. This important translation, entitled *A Salutation to the Britains,* was first published in Philadelphia in 1727, with subsequent editions published in London throughout the eighteenth century.

Bill Jones

REFERENCES
Browning, Charles H. *Welsh Settlement of Pennsylvania.* Philadelphia: W. J. Campbell, 1912.
Davies, Hywel M. *Transatlantic Brethren: Rev. Samuel Jones (1735–1814) and His Friends.* Bethlehem, PA: Lehigh University Press, 1995.
Dodd, A. H. "The Background of the Welsh Quaker Migration to Pennsylvania." *Journal of the*

Meirioneth Historical and Record Society 3.2 (1958): 111–127.

Glenn, Thomas A. *Meirion in the Welsh Tract, with Sketches of the Townships of Haverford and Rador.* Norristown, PA: Printed for the subscribers, 1896.

Owen, Bob. "Rowland Ellis." In *Dictionary of Welsh Biography Down to 1940,* 212. London: Blackwell, 1959.

Rees, T. Mardy. *The Quakers in Wales and Their Emigration to North America.* Carmarthen, Wales: W. Spurrell and Son, 1925.

Emeagwali, Philip (1955–)

Scientist

Nigerian

Currently a computer scientist at the University of Michigan, Philip Emeagwali has been called the Bill Gates of Africa because of his achievements in the field of supercomputing. His many awards include being voted Africa's Best Scientist, America's Best and Brightest Inventor, and Computer Scientist of the Year. In 1989, he won the Gordon Bell Prize, the computing world's equivalent of the Nobel Prize.

Emeagwali was born in western Nigeria, the oldest of nine children. His father, James, was a nurse, and his mother, a homemaker. Emeagwali credits his father with recognizing his intelligence and nurturing the mathematical ability that led to his later success. Unfortunately, the Nigerian civil war derailed his formal education after less than nine years, for his family fled to eastern Nigeria in 1967. As horrifying as those years were, they taught Emeagwali to be a survivor.

This lesson led him to further his own education. He passed the U.S. Scholastic Aptitude Tests with top grades and, in 1974, won a scholarship to attend Oregon State University (OSU). During the early, difficult years in the United States—beginning at OSU in Corvallis, Oregon—he was at times unemployed, homeless, and hungry—almost as bad as when he had been a refugee. But he drew on that prior experience, and his academic achievements grew. He now holds five degrees in four fields: one bachelor's, three master's, and a doc-torate in scientific computing, ocean and marine engineering, civil and environmental engineering, and applied mathematics. It was as a doctoral student at the University of Michigan that Emeagwali won the Gordon Bell Prize. He had programmed a computer to work faster than any other computer in the world—at a rate of 3.1 billion calculations per second. His accomplishments in supercomputing have wide-ranging scientific, technical, and medical applications, including finding oil, improving the accuracy of weather predictions, and tracking the flow of blood in the heart.

Emeagwali's African background has had a profound impact on his outlook as a scientist. He sees his work as a means to help people, especially those of African descent. His "Africa One" project is designed to bring fiber optics technology to forty-one locations along the African coast in order to facilitate the information revolution on the continent. He also strives to be a role model for future African and African American scientists. In his interviews with African and American journalists and in his work visiting disadvantaged, largely minority, schools in the United States, he stresses the importance of education and technology for improving the quality of life for individuals and communities. His hope is to see more scientists of African descent, and he stresses that poor children can succeed if their intelligence is nurtured, as was his. He believes in helping others to succeed.

Emeagwali has also brought twenty-one relatives to the United States, including his parents. Five of his brothers and sisters have graduated from college. He is married to African American molecular biologist, Dale Brown, herself an award-winning scientist. They have a ten-year-old son, and Emeagwali strives to instill in his son a recognition that, despite racism or other obstacles, he and other black children can make scientific and other contributions to mankind.

April Gordon

REFERENCES

Cho, David. "He's an Intellectual Inspiration." *Philadelphia Inquirer,* 26 February 1999.

Emeagwali, Philip. Personal correspondence with author, 12 December 1999 and 19 April 2000.

Morgan, Barry. "Nature's Own Numbers Man." *Upstream* 2 (Week 4, January 1997).

O'Hagan, Tim. "Superbrain of Africa. *Drum* (South Africa), 19 March 1998.

Enander, Johan Alfred (1842–1910)

Journalist, historian, and educator
Swedish

Johan Alfred Enander, in his day the leading Swedish-American opinion maker, was a major figure in the Swedish-American community, for his writings and his journalism inspired much ethnic pride among Swedes. In addition, he was a founder and first president of the Swedish Historical Society of America.

Enander was born in Västergötland Province, in Sweden. After some secondary schooling and journalistic experience, he immigrated to the United States in 1869 to attend the Swedish Augustana Lutheran Seminary. Once there, however, he was persuaded to become editor of the Swedish-language newspaper *Hemlandet* (The homeland) in Chicago.

From the beginning, Enander sought to instill in his countrymen pride in both their old and new homelands. Between 1874 and 1880 he brought out a massive history of the United States in Swedish, particularly emphasizing the Viking discoveries and Sweden's seventeenth-century colony on the Delaware River. He thus sought to legitimize his countrymen as "colonists," rather than simply "immigrants," as well as to reveal an essential similarity between Swedish and Anglo-American values.

Enander preached this message throughout his career in innumerable articles and speeches, some of which he published in book form in 1891. In 1893, in connection with Chicago's World Columbian Exposition, he brought out a book asserting that the New World had actually been discovered nearly 500 years before Columbus by the Northmen, who indeed had first heard of the land to the west on an earlier voyage to Iceland. Enander thereby challenged not only the Italian-Americans but, stressing that the "Northmen" came from all of Scandinavia, also the Norwegian-Americans, who were inclined to monopolize the Viking heritage.

Increasingly, Enander came to see his immigrant countrymen as a "nationality" of its own. Neither purely Swedish nor purely American, they combined the best qualities of both to the benefit of the republic. From this viewpoint, he could often be sharply critical of Sweden itself. He declared his credo in 1899: It was not to Sweden's but to Swedish America's cause that he had devoted his life. In 1889, Enander was appointed U.S. ambassador to Denmark but declined for personal reasons. The following year he became professor of Swedish language and literature at Augustana College, Rock Island, Illinois. Between 1893 and 1896, he edited the Swedish-language *Svenska Journalen* in Omaha and then returned to *Hemlandet* in Chicago.

As an historian in the grand filiopietistic manner, Enander powerfully influenced most of his contemporaries who wrote about the Swedes in the United States, including sympathetic Anglo-Americans. In 1888, he was the featured speaker at the celebration in Minneapolis of the 200th anniversary of the founding of Sweden's colony on the Delaware. In 1905, he was a founder and first president of the Swedish Historical Society of America, which survived until 1934.

Enander exemplifies Swedish America's remarkably flourishing journalistic life. No one had greater influence in arousing the Swedish-Americans' ethnic pride and in creating their self-image. Following his death in 1910, through public subscription, a stately monument with a suitable quasi-runic inscription was raised to him in Chicago's Oak Hill Cemetery.

H. Arnold Barton

REFERENCES

Barton, H. Arnold, *A Folk Divided*. Carbondale: Southern Illinois University Press, 1994.

Blanck, Dag, *Becoming Swedish American*. Uppsala, Sweden: Acta Universitatis Upsaliensis, 1998.

Ericsson, John (1803–1889)

Inventor
Swedish

John Ericsson was one of the great mechanical geniuses of the nineteenth century, particularly with regard to ship construction and propulsion. It was he who designed the *Monitor,* which won a decisive victory during the Civil War, influencing the course of that conflict.

Ericsson was born in Värmland Province, Sweden, the son of a mine superintendent. Although he lacked theoretical background, he was apprenticed early in the construction of the Göta Canal. In 1820 he received an army commission, eventually being promoted to captain, the title he thereafter used.

Following a tragic love affair, Ericsson took leave from the Swedish army in 1826 to pursue his mechanical interests in England. There, he designed a locomotive, the "Novelty," which in the Liverpool and Manchester Railway's competition in 1829 only narrowly lost out to George Stephenson's "Rocket" because of mechanical problems. In 1833 Ericsson patented a hot-air, or "caloric," engine and in 1836 the first practical screw propeller. From his tubular steam boiler, important for ship propulsion, he also developed a fire engine. However, lacking business sense, he was twice imprisoned for debt.

Ericsson's reputation meanwhile had spread to the United States, especially when the steamship *Robert F. Stockton,* equipped with Ericsson's new propeller, crossed the Atlantic in 1839. He, himself, followed that same year, settling in New York. In partnership with De Lamater's Mechanical Works, he designed the world's first ironclad, propeller-driven warship, the *Princeton,* with cannon of his own model. Unfortunately, on its maiden cruise on the Potomac in 1844, a gun exploded, killing six dignitaries, including two cabinet secretaries. In 1853, he suffered another serious blow when the *Ericsson,* an experimental vessel with a caloric engine, foundered in a storm in New York harbor.

Ericsson offered the design for an armored gunboat, low in the water and with a revolving turret mounting a large-bore cannon, to Emperor Napoleon III of France, who refused it in 1854. His breakthrough came during the American Civil War, when the Confederate ironclad *Merrimack* devastated the Union fleet in Chesapeake Bay. Ericsson was commissioned on short order to construct a gunboat of his new type, the *Monitor,* which decisively defeated the *Merrimack* at Hampton Roads, Virginia, in March 1862. This victory assured the Union's naval superiority early in the war, significantly affecting its outcome. Ericsson proudly claimed that his *Monitor* "broke the chains of 4 million slaves."

During his later years, Ericsson invented a torpedo and a compressed-air underwater cannon to propel it. A prototype vessel so equipped, the *Destroyer,* was constructed during the 1870s. He also carried out forward-looking experiments with solar power. During his lifetime, Ericsson took out some 500 patents.

In later years, Ericsson became ever more reclusive, devoting himself single-mindedly to his work. His reputation was immense, and he received numerous honors. However, he had almost no contact with his fellow Swedish-Americans, although for them he had great symbolic value. Nonetheless, although he had become a U.S. citizen in 1848 and never revisited Sweden, he always remained a strong Swedish patriot. Upon his death in 1889, his remains were conveyed to Sweden, as he had wished, by an American warship. He was buried in state in Filipstad, near his birthplace, where his mausoleum remains a monument to close Swedish-American relations.

H. Arnold Barton

REFERENCES
Church, William Conant. *The Life of John Ericsson.* 2 vols. New York: Scribner, 1890.

Erikson, Erik H. (Homburger) (1902–1994)

Psychologist and author
German-Jewish

Erik Erikson was a pioneer in the field of child psychology and the effects of culture on child development. The "eight psychosexual stages" of development he delineated and his insights about childhood, culture, and identity are considered by some people required reading for parents and caregivers wishing to understand children.

Erikson was born in Frankfurt, Germany, to Karla Abrahamsen, who was married to someone other than Eric's father. Her extramarital affair led to the breakup of her marriage, and Erik would never meet his biological father. In 1905, his mother married Theodore Homburger, who adopted the boy. His mother and stepfather, both Jews, raised Erik as a Jew, but he was not accepted by either German or Jewish children. Feeling like an outsider, he was obsessed all his life about his father.

After graduating from high school, Erikson spent seven years traveling around Europe. In 1927, he met Anna Freud, who asked him to teach at her school in Vienna. He accepted and also began psychoanalysis with her. Psychology fascinated him, and he matriculated at the Vienna Psychoanalytic Institute. The study of children and their development would occupy Erikson's attention for much of his life.

Erikson also found time to marry Joan Serson, an artist and dancer, in 1930. In 1933, after completing his training, they immigrated to the United States, settling in Boston, where Erikson began work in child psychoanalysis with a position at Harvard Medical School. He entered a Ph.D. program at Harvard but never completed the degree. Nevertheless, he was considered an expert in his field. He began to focus his attention on the effects of culture on child development and the ways child rearing was affected by cultural differences and practices, continuing his research at Yale in 1936.

Upon becoming a U.S. citizen in 1939, he officially took the name he had invented and used: Erik Erikson. During the next decade Erikson did some of his most influential work, including the famous "experimental play" studies, "identity crisis" research with adolescents, and the formulation of his theory of the "eight psychosexual stages" of human development. Erikson would expand on the life stages in his landmark book, *Childhood and Society* (1950). He also became interested in the psychological lives of famous men, writing two best-sellers—"psychological histories"—*Young Man Luther* (1958) and *Gandhi's Truth* (1969). *Gandhi's Truth* received both a National Book Award and a Pulitzer Prize. After retirement in 1970, Erikson turned his attention to the study of the elderly and the struggles of the last stages of life. His final two books dealt with the subject and were cowritten with his wife.

Joan Erikson collaborated with her husband throughout his career, acting as his unofficial editorial assistant. She also served as primary caregiver to the couple's four children, for it appears that Erikson was emotionally removed from his children's lives. Besides being criticized for his less-than-perfect behavior as a father, he was accused of denying his Jewish heritage by choosing the name Erikson. Some colleagues noted his lack of academic credentials, and Freudians decried his theories as heretical. Nonetheless, he remained convinced of his competence. Erikson died at age ninety-one, never having discovered the secret of his paternity.

Susanne M. Schick

REFERENCES
Bloland, Sue Erikson. "Fame: The Power and Cost of a Fantasy." *Atlantic Monthly* 284 (November 1999): 51–62.
Coles, Robert. *Erik H. Erikson: The Growth of His Work.* New York: Da Capo Press, 1987.
Evans, Richard. *Dialogue with Erik Erikson.* New York: Praeger, 1981.
"Featured Author: Erik H. Erikson, With News and Reviews from the Archives of the New York Times." *New York Times* on the Web (1999): www.nytimes.com/books/99/08/22/specials/erikson.html (accessed 7 July 2000).
Friedman, Lawrence. *Identity's Architect: A Biography of Erik H. Erikson.* New York: Scribner, 1999.

Goldberger, Leo, and Robert Wallerstein, eds. *Ideas and Identities: The Life and Work of Erik Erikson.* International Universities Press, 1998.

Gross, Francis. *Introducing Erik Erikson: An Invitation to His Thinking.* Lanham, MD: University Press of America, 1987.

Escalante, Jaime Alfonso (1930–)

Educator
Bolivian

Jaime Escalante, teaching in an inner-city Los Angeles school, motivated his students to excel in math to such a remarkable degree that a film was made about his achievements and he became an inspiration and model for others.

Escalante was born in La Paz, Bolivia, into a family of teachers. During his childhood, Bolivia was in a state of turmoil—politically, economically, and socially—and he developed four natural "talents for survival" that would remain with him: a love of mathematics, a feel for showmanship, an impatience with rules, and *ganas*—a spirit of competitiveness and intense urge to win.

In his native country, Escalante was a successful mathematics teacher, motivating his students to have faith in themselves, to be focused, disciplined, and dedicated. He immigrated to the United States in 1963, but without U.S. teaching credentials, was forced to take menial jobs until 1974. He then secured a teaching position at Garfield High School in East Los Angeles, an inner-city school with a high drop-out rate. More than 95 percent of the student body was Latino, with many coming from poor immigrant families. That was the challenge that Escalante needed.

With Escalante's bantering style of teaching—a mixture of chastisement and praise, cajoling and entertainment—he once more helped his students believe in themselves and succeed in the classroom. Both his and his students' efforts came to fruition between the years 1979 and 1992, as 711 of his students passed the rigorous Advanced Placement Test in calculus. Escalante inspired his students to become disciplined and to know that, with serious work and dedication, they could overcome almost any obstacles. His work at Garfield in 1982—the subject of Edward James Olmos's 1988 film *Stand and Deliver*—meant that fifteen of his eighteen students were able to go to college. And of this number, only two dropped out.

In 1991, Escalante moved to Hiram Johnson High School in Sacramento, California, where he taught only briefly. According to Escalante, faculty policies and petty jealousies in the mathematics department prompted his departure. Nonetheless, in addition to classroom teaching, he worked with the Foundation for Advancement in Science and Education to develop the video series, *Futures,* for PBS. This program, a recipient of two Peabodys and numerous other awards describes how science and math in school relate to real-world careers.

In 1997, Escalante was named honorary chairman of "English for the Children," a group that was working to rid California public schools of bilingual education. Having to learn English as an adult was a difficult experience for Escalante, and he believed that bilingual education only serves to hold children back. Though an unpopular stand in much of the Latino community, Escalante, true to his nature, did what he believed was right.

Escalante's success and that of his students won him many awards, including the Presidential Medal for Excellence in Education, a Special Recognition Award for Teaching Excellence from the American Association of Community and Junior Colleges, and the Andres Bello Prize of the Organization of American States.

Kathleen Paparchontis

REFERENCES

Hopkins, Kevin R. "The Escalante Math Program." *Business Week,* 25 November 1997: ED67.

"Jaime Escalante." In *Notable Latino Americans, A Biographical Dictionary,* edited by Matt S. Meier, with Conchita Franco Serri and Richard A. Garcia, 46. Westport, CT: Greenwood Press, 1997.

Mathews, Jay. *Escalante: The Best Teacher in America.* New York: Henry Holt, 1988.

Meek, Anne. "On Creating GANAS: A Conversation with Jaime Escalante." *Educational Leadership* 46.5 (February 1989): 6.

Espaillat, Rhina P. (1932–)
Writer

Dominican-American

Although her books of poetry have appeared only since her retirement, Rhina Espaillat had already accrued considerable prestige through her frequent publications in highly regarded poetry magazines. She has received numerous awards, including both the T. S. Eliot Poetry Prize and the Howard Nemerov Sonnet Award in 1998.

Espaillat was born in 1932 in Santo Domingo and raised in La Vega, Dominican Republic. When she was seven, her parents immigrated to New York City. Her father, a political exile, encouraged her to regard U.S. society as a temporary abode and English as "the medium of the outer world" and he stressed the importance of her mastering "pure" Spanish. But the political dictatorship of Generalissimo Trujillo lasted longer than her father had expected.

By then, the family had deep roots in the United States. An adult with a remarkable command of English, Espaillat had already distinguished herself as a young American poet, earning an induction into the Poetry Society of America at the age of sixteen. However, although a proponent of "genuine bilinguality," she fears the mix of Spanish and English might impoverish both languages, yet finds it perfectly natural for the two to coexist in the poetic text, as, for example, in *Lapsing to Grace* (1992) and *Where Horizons Go* (1998).

After Espaillat completed B.A. and M.A. degrees in the 1950s, she worked as an English and social studies junior high school teacher and then spent ten years rearing her three sons, after which she returned to high school teaching. When her husband, the Jewish-American painter Alfred Moskowitz, chose to retire from teaching, Espaillat left teaching to resume writing, and they moved to Newburyport, Massachusetts.

Years of teaching and child rearing notwithstanding, Espaillat has amassed an impressive output, as judged by the numerous literary magazines that have carried her poems, including *Poetry, Encore, America, Plain Poetry Journal,* the *New Press, Commonweal, Orphic Lute, Croton Review, Voices International, Bronte Street, Poetry Digest,* and the *American Scholar.* Her poetry has also appeared in various anthologies, among which are *Looking Home: Women Writing about Exile* (1990), *A Formal Feeling Comes: Poems in Form by Contemporary Women* (1994), and *Sarah's Daughters Sing: A Sampler of Poems by Jewish Women,* the latter especially pleasing as she is the only non-Jew in the collection.

Before leaving New York, Espaillat became cofounder of a Queens group called the Fresh Meadows Poets, going strong since 1986. In New England, she has assumed the directorship of the Powow River Poets, a poetry workshop open to the public. Often, when she reads, she makes a point of reciting poems in Spanish and their English translations. She has helped organize the Latino Arts Month Festival at Northern Essex Community College, while frequently interacting with Dominicans and other writers of Hispanic descent. Since her inclusion by Mexican-American author Roberta Fernandez in the anthology *In Other Words: Literature by Latinas in the United States* (1994), Espaillat has become increasingly more visible to her Dominican compatriots as well as to readers and scholars of Latino literature in general.

Silvio Torres-Saillant

REFERENCES

Aleman, Manuel, ed. *Las caras del amor: Antologia poetica contemporanea* (The faces of love: An anthology of contemporary poetry). Andover, MA: Versal Editorial Group, 1999.

De Roche, Joseph, ed. *The Heath Introduction to Poetry.* 6th ed. Boston and New York: Houghton Mifflin, 2000.

Espaillat, Rhina P. *Lapsing to Grace.* East Lansing, MI: Bennet & Kitchel, 1992.

———. "Selected Poems." In *Landscapes With Women: Four American Poets. Martha Bosworth, Rhina P. Espaillat, Barbara Loots, and Gail White,* edited by Gail White. Canton, CT: Singular Speech Press, 2000.

———. *Where Horizons Go.* Kirksville, MO: New Odyssey Press, 1998.

Fernandez, Roberta, ed. *In Other Words: Literature by Latinas in the United States.* Houston: Arte Publico Press, 1994.

Torres-Saillant, Silvio, and Ramona Hernández. *The Dominican Americans.* Westport, CT: Greenwood Press, 1998.

Estefan, Gloria Fajardo (1957–)
Singer
Cuban-American

Gloria Estefan has achieved outstanding success as a singer. Her music is well known around the world and in her native Cuba. She has served as a bridge not only between Cubans of different generations and ideological outlooks but also between Anglos and Latinos.

Gloria Fajardo was born in Havana on 1 September 1957. Her family fled Fidel Castro's revolutionary Cuba with her in 1959. As a member of the 1961 failed Bay of Pigs invasion, her father returned to the island and was imprisoned for a time. Gloria's childhood was far from happy, as the family struggled with separations, illness, exile, and poverty. She found consolation in playing her guitar.

One day she sang at a friend's wedding. Listening was bandleader Emilio Estefan, who immediately recruited her. In September 1978, they wed, and two years later their son, Naybi, was born. Meanwhile, the Miami Sound Machine, with which she was performing, was becoming increasingly popular among Latinos in the United States and released several Spanish-language pop albums. In 1984 Epic released Miami Sound Machine's first album in English, *Eyes of Innocence,* an attempt to cross over into the mainstream pop market. The group gained a growing Anglo following. In 1989, Estefan formally launched her solo career—with the Miami Sound Machine backing her—with *Cuts Both Ways,* a top-ten platinum debut.

The following year, in March 1990, just after having been hosted at the White House, Estefan was critically injured when her tour bus was hit by a trailer. Many feared she would not walk again. With the support of her husband and son, her extended family, and thousands of letters and good wishes from fans, she underwent intensive physical therapy and, less than a year later, she was back on the stage, releasing *Into the Light* in 1991.

After being one of the first Latino singers to cross over successfully, Estefan has released three Spanish-only albums (1993, 1995, and 2000). In 1994 she took a break to give birth to her second child, Emily, often seen with her mother on the set.

In spite of Estefan's international fame, meetings with heads of states, appearances on the cover of major magazines, and budding acting career, the Estefans have remained a very Miamian couple, supporting many community projects through the Gloria Estefan Foundation. When Hurricane Andrew hit the area in 1992, the couple personally delivered food supplies to the homeless. She has received many well-deserved awards, including an honorary doctorate of music from the University of Miami and the Hispanic Heritage Award.

Gloria Estefan's Cuban roots are reflected not only in her music, her strong family values, and her community service but also in her involvement in political exile issues. Faithful to her father's staunch anti-Castro stand, she often voices her hopes for democratic changes in her country of origin and brings the plight of the Cuban people to the attention of international media. In a recent interview, Gloria Estefan fantasized about the day Cuba would be free and expressed a wish shared by many of her compatriots: "I long to return to *mi tierra.*" She still holds the return ticket to her native island.

Uva de Aragón

REFERENCES

Doria, Luz María. "El alma de Gloria" (Gloria's souls). *Cristina Magazine,* Spring 2000, 24.

"Estefan Online Page" (18 May 2000): www.estefan.net (accessed 26 June 2000).

"Gloria Estafan's Glory Days." *People Weekly,* 12 August 1996: 61–66.

Farley, Christopher John, and Michael S. Serril. "From a Cuban Heart." *Time,* 12 August 1996, 45.

Flick, Larry. "Epic's Estefan Blends Caribbean Sounds on Set." *Billboard,* 6 May 2000, 1.

"Latinas of the Year." *Latina,* September 1999, 64–66.

Seal, Mark. "Gloria Estefan's Miami." *American Way,* 15 April 2000, 31.

Etzioni, Amitai (1929–)
Sociologist and political adviser
Israeli

Amitai Etzioni is a sociologist, political activist, adviser to U.S. presidents, and a prominent leader of the communitarian movement. The latter, in an effort to achieve a balance between individual rights and collective responsibilities, stresses core American values to benefit all members of society.

Born in Cologne, Germany, Etzioni (whose original family name was Falk) escaped Nazi persecution by moving with his Jewish family to Palestine prior to World War II. There, he lived in a cooperative settlement populated by German refugees. He traces his valuation of community to life to this small community wherein every face was familiar, values and belongings were shared, and neighbors solved common problems at community meetings. Later, young Etzioni fought within a small unit in the Israeli war of independence, an experience he considers to be "a most dramatic example" of the bonds of community. Prepping for college, he attended an institute run by Martin Buber and was profoundly influenced by his dialogic "I and thou" philosophy. These many experiences in the Jewish State left Etzioni with a lifelong appreciation of benefits of communal affiliation.

After receiving his B.A. and M.A. at the Hebrew University of Jerusalem, he came to the United States, where he earned a Ph.D. in sociology in only two years at the University of California, Berkeley. From the late 1950s to the 1970s, Etzioni was a member of the sociology department at Columbia University before becoming university professor at George Washington University. He went on to serve as senior adviser to Richard Harden, special assistant to President Jimmy Carter, as a guest scholar at the Brookings Institution, and on the president's Council on Foreign Relations.

With modesty, Etzioni says he came up with the broadly influential communitarian approach simply by taking ideas widely discussed among academics and projecting them on the screen of national attention. He seeks to build a new consensus between the polarities of right and left. "We don't want to take anybody's rights away," he says, "but strong rights presume strong responsibilities." Moreover, our liberties are rooted in our civil institutions and hence will not survive if those institutions fall apart. "If society does not have shared values, if there is no sense of community, then it dies." Amitai Etzioni has thus forged a new approach to mediating between rights and responsibilities, between individualism and collectivism—among the most pressing issues in contemporary American life.

Expressing his ideas in newspaper columns, his editing of a communitarian quarterly, *The Responsive Community: Rights and Responsibilities,* and nineteen books, including *The New Golden Rule: Community and Morality in a Democratic Society* (1996), Etzioni's influence is far-reaching among academics and the general public. A 1982 study ranked Etzioni as the leading expert among a list of thirty who had made "major contributions to public policy in the preceding decade." He was president of the American Sociological Association in 1994–1995.

Etzioni also remains connected to Israeli and Jewish communities, writing articles about Israel and the Middle East and serving on the boards of Israeli academic publications and universities. He received a book award from the Simon Wiesanthal Center and regularly publishes essays in the American-Jewish magazine *Tikkun.*

Steven J. Gold

REFERENCES

D'Antonio, Michael. "Tough Medicine for a Sick America" *Los Angeles Times Magazine,* 22 March 1992, 32, 34, 50.

Etzioni, Amitai. *The Limits of Privacy.* New York: Basic Books, 1999.

———. *The New Golden Rule: Community and Morality in a Democratic Society.* New York: Basic Books, 1996.

———. *Public Policy in a New Key.* New Brunswick, NJ: Transaction Publishers, 1993.

———. *The Spirit of Community: Rights, Responsibilities and the Communitarian Agenda.* New York: Crown Publishers, 1993.

Ross, Warren R. "Are You a Communitarian without Knowing It?" *World: The Journal of the Unitarian Universalist Association,* September/October 1994, 13–17.

Eu, March Fong (née Kong) (1922–)

State assembly member, state secretary of state, and ambassador
Chinese-American

In 1994, March Fong Eu capped a distinguished political career that extended more than four decades. Having been California's first Asian American assembly member and secretary of state, she was appointed U.S. ambassador to Micronesia.

The daughter of hand laundry owners, Eu (her family name is Kong) was born on March 29, 1922, to Yuen and Shu Kong, in the small farming community of Oakdale, California; and, like so many Chinese Americans of that era, her grandparents hailed from Guangdong, China. Soon after her birth, the Kongs moved to Richmond, California. They were the only Chinese in town.

Eu was active in high school government, which gave her a taste for politics. However, she had a conversation with a high school bus driver that reminded her of her "perpetual alien" status. When she told him she planned to pursue a career in the sciences, he replied that she could then help China's modernization. That incident impressed upon Eu that Chinese Americans, including herself, had to strive to succeed in order to constantly prove to the larger society that they do have a legitimate claim to citizenship.

After earning a bachelor of science degree at the University of California, Berkeley (1943), and working for some time as a dental hygienist, she decided to become a professional health educator. She secured a master's in education from Mills College (1947) and a doctoral degree in education from Stanford (1956). Raising a family of two children interrupted her career, but she did begin lobbying the California legislature on educational issues. Her interest in politics was rekindled, and she won a seat in 1956 on the Alameda County Board of Education, where she served for three full terms. Ten years later, she was elected to the state assembly and, after four terms, ran successfully for California secretary of state, winning the 1974 election with a unprecedented margin of 3 million votes.

She remained in the secretary of state office for twenty years, during which time she also earned a law degree from Lincoln University (1984). Under her direction, voting reforms were introduced, including voter registration by mail, bilingual ballots, and a voter outreach program, all of which set nationwide trends. She also fought for the creation of a new home for the state archives, which came to fruition in the mid-1990s, and, after being attacked in 1996 by a robber in her home, made fighting crime a high priority. In addition, Eu championed women's rights, initiating bills related to child-care facilities and fair pregnancy leave. Most of all, she streamlined complex governmental policies and procedures, thereby increasing the efficiency of the bureaucracy. In 1994, Eu was nominated by President Bill Clinton to be ambassador to the Federated States of Micronesia, and her appointment was confirmed by the U.S. Senate.

On 31 August 1973, March Fong wed Henry Eu. A third-generation Californian, March Fong Eu has integrated her Asian ancestry and her American experience in a life and career centered around service and stewardship. In 1988 *Ladies' Home Journal* named her one of America's 100 Most Important Women.

Benson Tong

REFERENCES

Lyons, Steve. "March Fong Eu, Ed.D.: Breaking Barriers to Serve." *ACCESS,* July 1992.

"March Fong Eu: The First Woman in the State Assembly." www.chineseinc.com/37005.htm (accessed 18 December 2000).

Maxwell, Jacqueline. "Color March Fong Eu Successful." *Ledger Dispatch,* 26 September 1990.

Wong, Jerrye. "Supporters Gather to Hear Eu Take Oath for Fifth Term." *AsianWeek,* 1 January 1991.

Farrell, James Thomas (1904–1979)
Author and literary critic
Irish-American

James Thomas Farrell gained renown for his realistic fiction documenting the urban experience of the Irish in the United States. His more than fifty published works focused on the struggle of an Irish working-class community in an economically stratified society, expanding this segment of the immigrant experience in Irish and American literature.

Farrell said: "[I felt that] the past was dragging through my boyhood and adolescence. Horatio Alger, Jr., died only seven years before I was born. The climate of opinion . . . was one of hope. But for an Irish boy born in Chicago in 1904, the past was a tragedy of his people." Son of James Frances, a teamster, and Mary Daly, a domestic servant, Farrell was sent at the age of three to live in the middle-class household of his maternal grandparents because of economic hardships at home. This early experience of two different households and two very different sets of lifestyles for the Irish in Chicago fostered an awareness of class and society that would weigh heavily on his writing.

Farrell studied at both De Paul University and the University of Chicago but set off at twenty-three to be a writer before receiving any degree. He noted that his Catholic schooling had a profound effect on his career, supplemented by his introduction to Irish nationalism by Father Albert Dolan, a Carmelite priest and teacher at St. Cyril High School. Through Father Dolan's history lessons, Farrell began to see where his teamster father and grandfather fit in the social history of the Irish working class.

Farrell also became heavily influenced by Marxist and Trotskyist materialist thinking. During the 1930s and 1940s he became active in the Socialist Party as well as with several left-wing political journals. After a visit to Ireland in 1938, he felt that the trip helped him understand and describe the lives of his fellow Chicago Irish but he was taken aback at the Irish working class's prioritizing of nationalism over Socialist politics. He also encountered a literary tradition that insisted that a writer should not concern himself with social questions and realistic writing.

Farrell is best known for his two cycles of novels depicting the American experience of the Irish-American community: the Studs Lonigan trilogy—*Young Lonigan* (1932), *The Young Manhood of Studs Lonigan* (1934), and *Judgment Day* (1935)—and the O'Neill-O'Flaherty pentology: *A World I Never Made* (1936), *No Star Is Lost* (1938), *Father and Son* (1940), *My Days of Anger* (1943), and *The Face of Time* (1953). These eight novels present a hyperrealist portrait of the Irish-American experience. With an unprecedented candidness, Farrell worked to create a corpus of novels that paid close attention to a community whose identity as Catholic, working class, and urban, within a class-stratified society, he felt was largely ignored. James Farrell died in 1979.

Former U.S. ambassador to Ireland, Walter V. Shannon, wrote: "Few college-educated Irish Catholics reach manhood without making Studs Lonigan's acquaintance twice, once in life and once in the pages of Farrell's novel. It . . . has become part of a young Irishman's coming of age."

Michael L. Murray

REFERENCES

Branch, Edgar M. *James T. Farrell*. New York: Twayne Publishers, 1971.

———. *Studs Lonigan's Neighborhood and the Making of James T. Farrell*. Newton, MA: Arts End Books, 1996.

Ebest, Ron. "The Irish Catholic Schooling of James T. Farrell, 1914–1923." *Éire-Ireland* 30.4: 18–32.

Farrell, James T. *On Irish Themes*. Edited by Dennis Flynn. Philadelphia: University of Pennsylvania Press, 1982.

Flynn, Dennis. "Appréciation: Farrell in Ireland." 18.1 *Éire-Ireland*: 109–131.

Salzman, Jack. "James T. Farrell: An Essay in Bibliography." *Resources for American Literary Study* 6 (Autumn): 131–163.

Wald, Alan M. *James T. Farrell: The Revolutionary Socialist Years*. New York: New York University Press, 1978.

Fermi, Enrico (1901–1954)
Physicist and Nobel laureate
Italian

Italian-born American physicist Enrico Fermi pioneered work in nuclear physics, fission reaction, and atomic energy that contributed to the development of the atomic bomb. His work earned him worldwide recognition both in Italy and in the United States.

Fermi was born in Rome on 29 September 1901, to schoolteacher Ida de Gattis and Alberto Fermi, a railroad department head. In 1918, Fermi enrolled in the Reale Scuola Normale Superior in Pisa, graduating with a doctor of physical science degree in 1922. He earned a fellowship and continued his study of physics in the laboratory of Max Born, in Göttingen, Germany. Following a lectureship in Rome and a position in mechanics and mathematics at the University of Florence, he was appointed chair of the newly developed Institute of Physics in Rome and given tenure for life. During the early 1930s, he published papers on radioactivity and began to experiment with the effects of modulated neutron bombardment of various elements.

At the midpoint of a rising and distinguished career, Fermi married Laura Capon, an Italian Jew, in 1928, an event that would have been inconsequential during any other period in Italian history. However, Mussolini's rise, followed by his creation of a fascist state and a treaty with Hitler, led to anti-Semitic laws influencing Fermi's decision to emigrate with his wife.

In 1938, Fermi was awarded the Nobel Prize in physics for his work on radioactive substances. Instead of returning to Italy after accepting the award in Stockholm, he and his family took a circuitous route to the United States. Having become an exile from Fascist Italy, he accepted a position in research at Columbia University in New York. The research team eventually moved to the University of Chicago, where, in 1942, Fermi supervised the first self-sustaining nuclear chain reaction. But the U.S. entry into World War II had created serious problems for Fermi, who was officially classified as an enemy alien. His movements were curtailed and his mail censored, and he had to secure a special travel permit for each research trip taken from New York to Chicago. On Columbus Day 1942, U.S. Attorney General Francis Biddle announced that Italians would no longer be considered enemy aliens, and Fermi resumed his work without further incident.

Fermi was sent to Los Alamos, New Mexico, where he became an important part of the Manhattan Project, a research and engineering endeavor to construct a nuclear bomb. In August 1945, the United States dropped the first two atomic bombs developed by the Manhattan Project scientists on Hiroshima and Nagasaki, forcing Japan's surrender and bringing World War II to an end. In May 1946, Fermi received the Congressional Medal for Merit for his work in developing the atomic bomb. He left Los Alamos in 1946 and returned to the University of Chicago, where he resumed teaching and research on nuclear accelerators. He continued to serve as an adviser on the board of the Atomic Energy Commission from 1947 to 1950.

Enrico Fermi's work in physics earned him worldwide recognition both in Italy and in the United States. After his death in Chicago in November 1954, his wife, Laura, featured his achievements in her own publications, *Atoms in the Family* (1954) and *The Story of Atomic Energy* (1961).

Diane C. Vecchio

REFERENCES

De Latil, Pierre. *Enrico Fermi, the Man and His Theories.* New York: Paul S. Erikson, 1966.

Fermi, Laura. *Atoms in the Family.* Chicago: University of Chicago Press, 1954.

Segre, Emilio. *Enrico Fermi, Physicist.* Chicago: University of Chicago Press, 1970.

Ferraro, Geraldine Anne (1935–)

Lawyer and U.S. House representative
Italian-American

As the Democratic vice presidential candidate of the United States in 1984, Geraldine Ferraro was the first woman—and the first Italian-American—to run on a national ticket of a major party. Her career opened doors for other women and reflects a political coming of age in state and national arenas of Italian-Americans, especially Italian-American women.

Geraldine Ferraro was born in Newburgh, New York, on 26 August 1935, to Dominick and Antoinette Corrieri Ferraro. Her parents, who owned a restaurant and a five-and-dime store, encouraged Geraldine in her educational pursuits. She earned a B.A. in 1956 from Marymount Manhattan College. From 1956 to 1960 she taught school in Queens, New York, while attending night classes at Fordham University Law School, where she earned a J.D. degree in 1960.

Ferraro married businessman John Zaccaro and raised three children while practicing civil law. She began her career in government service as assistant district attorney in Queens County and headed the Special Victims Bureau for cases dealing with child abuse, domestic violence, and rape. In 1978 she won election from a conservative Queens district to the U.S. House of Representatives. As a member of Congress, Ferraro focused on the needs of senior citizens and women's issues. Reelected in 1980 and 1982 by ever-increasing margins, Ferraro quickly gained influence within the Democratic Party, where she was respected for her intelligence and political sophistication. She became the first woman in 1984 to head the party's platform committee.

Concerned with the public image of Italian-Americans, Ferraro frequently spoke at Italian-American organizations, addressing them on Italian heritage, Italian education, and speaking out against discrimination and ethnic stereotyping by the media. She helped form the National Organization of Italian American Women and worked on immigration issues with Father Cogo of the American Committee on Italian Immigration. She also fought to get Italian-Americans into government positions and onto the judicial bench.

Shortly before the Democratic National Convention in July 1984, presidential candidate Walter F. Mondale selected Ferraro as his vice presidential running mate, the first time a woman—or an Italian-American—had been nominated for such high public office by one of the major parties. However, she immediately felt the stigma of Mafia attached to her name, for newspapers around the country insinuated that her family was connected with organized crime. Despite her previous work with the Italian-American community, Ferraro did not receive the support of Italian-American leaders, who, intimidated by the accusations, remained silent. The alleged association of the Ferraro-Zaccaro family with organized crime led Italians in New York to pull their support from the Mondale-Ferraro ticket. As a woman's rights activist, Ferraro was also attacked by religious extremists, who could not accept a prochoice Catholic.

In November, the Democratic slate was defeated, and Ferraro returned to private life. In 1992, she ran for the New York State Senate and was defeated but has remained active. In 1993, for example, President Clinton appointed her to the U.S. delegation of the United Nations Human Rights Commission. She has also been a commentator and cohost of CNN's *Crossfire* and has lectured extensively around the country.

Diane C. Vecchio

REFERENCES

Berry, Dawn Bradley. *The Fifty Most Influential Women in American Law.* Los Angeles: Lowell House, 1996.

Ferraro, Geraldine A. *Ferraro, My Story.* New York: Bantam, 1985.

———. *Framing a Life. A Family Memoir.* New York: Prentice Hall, 1998.

"Ferraro, Geraldine." Biographical profile. U.S. Congressional Directory: bioguide.congress.gov/ scripts/biodisplay.pl?index=F000088 (accessed 21 June 2000).

Figueroa, Elizabeth (1951–)
State assembly member and senator
Salvadoran-American

Elected to the California State Senate in November 1998, Elizabeth Figueroa is the Democratic representative for the Tenth District. She was the first northern California Latina to be elected to the California State Assembly and is the highest-ranking Central American official in the state.

Figueroa was born on 9 February 1951 in San Mateo, California. At the age of eighteen, she was the youngest member of the San Mateo Human Relations Commission. Through political organizing and advocacy, she has been representing the voice and interest of her various communities since then. By the time she became involved with the Democratic Party Central Committee in the mid-1980s, she had served on many boards and commissions, including the American Civil Liberties Union (ACLU) Earl Warren Chapter of Berkeley. Because of her own experiences with conservative companies that neglect workers' needs, she started her own business, Figueroa Employment Consultants, a company that ensured that workers were informed of their rights. For seventeen years the business placed injured workers in jobs.

Figueroa served as the chair of Alameda County ACLU chapter for eight years. When she was not able to find someone to run for the assembly, she decided to run herself and won in 1994. During her time in the assembly, Figueroa was named Legislator of the Year by eight organizations, including groups as diverse as the American Academy of Pediatricians, the Association of Retarded Citizens, and the California National Organization for Women. She helped nine bills become laws during her first term in the assembly. After serving four years as an assemblywoman, she ran for the state senate and won in 1998.

Figueroa maintains her ties with the Salvadoran and Latina/o community and has supported events and efforts to organize the U.S. Central American community in California. In March 1999, she was invited to observe the elections in El Salvador and was recognized as an important Salvadoran representative in the United States. In the United States, she has worked with the Salvadoran American Leadership and Education Fund (SALEF) and Latina/o politicians to encourage more Latinas/os to vote. In 1998, she was marshal of the Central American independence parade and celebration in Los Angeles. The Los Angeles Spanish-language newspaper, *La Opinion,* has followed the senator's activities and lauded her as a role model for Latina women.

Within a broader context, Figueroa views the objective of her work as encouraging the traditionally disempowered to exercise their collective voice: workers, minority groups, women, the elderly, and the sick. On any given day, she can be found sitting in on a naturalization class, sharing a traditional celebration of one or another cultural group, or observing a procedure in an emergency room. Figueroa is committed to seeing the way that the legislature affects people's daily lives and personally getting to know the communities that she serves. She has also involved California in the international human rights struggle against female genital mutilation, political prisoners, and unfair labor practices. Figueroa has thus served the needs of her local and state communities and demonstrated a greater vision for change, paving the way for other Latina women in international politics.

Leticia Hernández-Linares

REFERENCES

Barabak, Mark. "California's New Breed of Latino Lawmakers." *Los Angeles Times,* 16 July 1997.

Figueroa, Elizabeth, Senator. California State Senate Web site: www.sen.ca.gov/figueroa (accessed 4 July 2000).

Figueroa, Liz. Interview with author, 8 February 2000.

Linares, Jesse J. "Liz Figueroa: triunfo de la mujer latina; asambleista es ejemplo de lo que pueden alcanzar los hijos de inmigrantes" (Liz Figueroa: Triumph of the Latina woman; assemblywoman is an example of how the children of immigrants can attain). *La Opinion* 72.362 (September 1997).

Olivo, Antonio. "Issues May Be Scarce, but Passion and Politics Aren't." *Los Angeles Times,* 11 April 1999.

Silva, Héctor Avalos, and Bóris Zelada. "Los hermanos se acercan" (The relatives come closer). *La Prensa Gráfica* (San Salvador), 5 March 1999.

Fischer-Galati, Stephen (1924–)
Historian
Romanian

Stephen Fischer-Galati is one of the world's foremost specialists on East European history. He has held many prestigious positions and received many awards and honors for the breadth of his scholarship.

Born in Bucharest, Romania, in 1924, Fischer-Galati escaped from Romania in the early stages of World War II. After a year of high school in Massachusetts, he entered Harvard University, where he received his B.A. in 1945, M.A. in 1946, and Ph.D. in 1949. (He also met his future wife at Harvard in 1944.) He was awarded a doctorate *honoris causa* by Romania in 1994.

Partly because of his linguistic qualifications, partly because the Cold War directly involved Eastern Europe, he became interested in the evolution of East-West relations and the interaction of major Western and Eastern cultural and political developments in early modern and modern times. He became fascinated by the similarities between the "cold war" of the sixteenth century, involving Christian Europe and the "infidel" Ottoman Empire, and that between the "democratic" West and the "heathen" Communist Soviet empire. His doctoral dissertation on the Turkish impact on the German Reformation, later published as *Ottoman Imperialism and German Protestantism,* launched what turned out to be a successful professional career as an historian of, primarily, Eastern Europe.

Fischer-Galati has been Distinguished Professor of History at the University of Colorado since 1966. He has also held positions as assistant professor in history at Harvard University; intelligence research specialist in East European Affairs at the U.S. Department of State; research director at the Mid-European Studies Center; professor of history at Wayne State University; visiting professor of history at Indiana University, the University of South Florida, Graduate School of International Studies (University of Denver), and at Central European University, Budapest; and as the John D. and Catherine T. MacArthur Professor at New College of the University of South Florida.

He has received numerous fellowships and grants, including awards from the Guggenheim Foundation, American Council of Learned Societies, International Research and Exchanges Board, and National Endowment for the Humanities. He has also directed the Center for Slavic and East European Studies at the University of Colorado and been a consultant for East European affairs to the White House, Department of State, Ford Foundation, American Council of Learned Societies, Social Science Research Council, Library of Congress, National Endowment for the Humanities, Canada Council, and Columbia University Press. Fischer-Galati is the author of more than 250 papers and articles and 6 books. For the past thirty years he has been editor of *East European Quarterly* and the East European Monograph Series of Columbia University Press, which has published more than 500 scholarly books on Eastern Europe.

Although he knows many Romanians across the United States, the fact that Fischer-Galati came to this country when he was still a teen-ager largely accounts for his having substantially assimilated and not gotten more involved with the Romanian community. He divides his time between Florida, Colorado, and Eastern Europe. Officially retired from the University of Colorado, he continues to teach part-time in Boulder and Bucharest, edit his journal and book series, and publish his own works.

G. James Patterson

REFERENCES

Fischer-Galati, Stephen. *The Balkan Revolutionary Tradition.* New York: Columbia University Press, 1981.

———. Curriculum vitae, 1999.

———. *Eastern Europe and the Cold War.* New York: East European Monographs, Columbia University Press, 1994.

———. Interviews with author, 1999.

———. *Ottoman Imperialism and German Protestantism, 1521–1555.* Cambridge: Harvard University Press, 1959.

Flynn, Elizabeth Gurley (1890–1964)
Labor and political activist, feminist, and writer
Irish-American

One of the great public speakers in U.S. history was an Irish-American radical, Elizabeth Gurley Flynn. Active in various political groups, notably the Communist Party, Flynn devoted her life to fighting for the rights of workers and women.

Flynn was born on 7 August 1890 in Concord, New Hampshire. Her father, Thomas Flynn, was a second-generation Irish-American, and her mother, Anne Gurley, was an Irish Presbyterian immigrant. The family moved to the South Bronx, New York, in 1900. Her father was a member of the Industrial Workers of the World (IWW), and her mother, a tailor, was a member of the Knights of Labor and the Irish Feminist Club of New York. Both were ardent Irish nationalists. Their daughter was raised on stories of the Irish, and the Flynn children were encouraged to get involved in political and social issues. In 1906 the family joined the Harlem Socialist Club, and it was there that Elizabeth made her first public speech, "What Socialism Will Do for Women."

In 1907 Flynn left school to work for women's and workers' rights. She had already joined the IWW and in 1907 was elected a delegate to the IWW convention, where she was appointed a traveling labor organizer. From 1908 to 1909 she participated in the labor struggles in Montana and Washington. Flynn played a major role in most of the significant labor actions of the early twentieth century, including the New York waist makers' strike of 1909; the Lawrence, Massachusetts, textile strike of 1912; the 1913 Patterson, New Jersey, silk strike; and the Mesabi Range strike of 1916. Between 1910 and 1917, she worked as an IWW organizer and at the same time, she forcefully pressed women's issues. She organized the first "united" labor defense group in 1914, providing public support to fight repression against immigrants and African Americans and was involved during the 1920s in the fight to save Nicola Sacco and Bartolomeo Vanzetti from execution. Failing health then forced her from public life for ten years.

In 1937, she joined the Communist Party and became a columnist for the *Daily Worker*. She was then expelled from the American Civil Liberties Union (ACLU), although she had been a founding member of the ACLU (after her death it reversed its action). In 1961 she became the first woman to chair the National Communist Party Committee, yet feminists criticized her for participating in organizations that were often sexist in principles and actions. However, she felt that the improved status of women at work was dependent upon all workers achieving their rights. Flynn was also arrested many times, but on 20 June 1951, she was arrested for violating the Smith Act and was convicted of teaching the violent overthrow of the U.S. government. In 1955, she began serving a twenty-eight-month sentence.

Flynn was also an excellent writer and wrote many articles and editorials in a variety of publications as well as two major books, *I Speak My Own Piece: Autobiography of a Rebel Girl* (1953) and *The Alderson Story* (1963). Flynn died on a visit to Moscow on 5 September 1964 and was given a full state funeral.

Seamus P. Metress

REFERENCES

Baxandall, Rosalyn F., ed. *Words on Fire: The Life and Writings of Elizabeth Gurley Flynn.* New Brunswick, NJ: Rutgers University Press, 1987.

Camp, Helen C. *Iron in Her Soul: Elizabeth Gurley Flynn and the American Left.* Pullman: Washington State University Press, 1995.

Flynn, Elizabeth Gurley. *The Alderson Story: My Life as a Political Prisoner.* New York: International Publishers, 1963.

———. *I Speak My Own Piece: Autobiography of a Rebel Girl.* New York: Masses and Mainstream, 1955.

Lamont, Corliss, ed. *The Trial of Elizabeth Gurley Flynn by the American Civil Liberties Union.* New York: Horizon Press, 1968.

Ford, Patrick (1837–1913)
Editor and political activist
Irish-American

Many Irish-American newspapers had controversial editors, but one of the most controversial of all was Patrick Ford, of the *Irish World.* He was a strong advocate of Irish national independence.

Ford was born in Galway, Ireland, in 1837. His parents, Edward and Anne Ford, immigrated with their family to the United States in 1845 because of the potato-crop failure. They settled in Boston, where Patrick was educated, worked as a printer at William Lloyd Garrison's *Liberator,* and later became editor of the *Boston Tribune.*

When the Civil War began, Ford enlisted for two years in a Massachusetts regiment. He married an Irish-American woman, Odele McDonald, and, at the war's end, settled in Charleston, South Carolina, working initially for the *South Carolina Leader,* a paper that promoted the rights of African Americans. In 1866 he founded the *Charleston Gazette,* which was primarily concerned with Irish-Catholic affairs.

Four years later, in 1870, the Fords moved to Brooklyn, New York. There, Ford founded the *Irish World,* which he continued to edit until his death. The paper dealt with Irish Catholic and labor news and at one point reached a circulation of 100,000. Ford was acutely aware of the inferior status afforded the Irish in the United States and used his paper to uplift and help them become acceptable Americans, couching his approach to Irish nationalism in the context of the American experience. The early years of the *Irish World* coincided with the depression of the 1870s and gained Ford a reputation as a radical. He strongly defended labor unions and even violent labor activities. He supported socialist ideas, identified with the philosophy of Henry George, and worked against prejudice, linking the struggle of African Americans for land in the South to the struggles in Ireland.

Ford had a strong Catholic system of values but was very critical of the Church because he felt it was too aristocratic, unsympathetic to the poor, and indifferent to its social responsibilities. He also chided the Irish Americans for their almost serf-like support of the Democratic Party; in 1874, he helped found the Greenback-Labor Party. However, by 1884 he began to develop connections with the Republican Party. Criticism from the Irish-American middle class and increasing labor violence seemed to move Ford away from his earlier radicalism. Following the Haymarket Riot of 1886, he increasingly called for class harmony, urging his readers to look toward the lifestyle of the growing Irish-American middle class—notably emphasizing self-help and education as the road to acceptability in the United States. At the same time, Ford is best remembered for his support of Irish national independence, pushing land reform as the key to raising the laboring classes from poverty, collecting money for the Irish National Land League, and eventually organizing 2,500 branches of his Irish World Land League before the need for the league dwindled in the mid-1880s.

Between 1890 and his death in 1913 Ford continued to attack Britain as the cause of oppression in Ireland. He also tried to get the Ancient Order of Hibernians to follow the path of the United Irish League rather than that of Sinn Fein. Ford died on 23 September 1913, but his family continued to maintain control of his newspaper until the 1980s.

Seamus P. Metress

REFERENCES

Ford, Patrick. "The Irish Vote in the Pending
    Presidential Election." *North American Review* 47
    (1888): 185–190.
Rodechko, James P. "The Irish American Journalist
    and Catholicism: Patrick Ford of the *Irish
    World*." *Church History* 39(4) (1970): 524–540.
———. *Patrick Ford and the Search for America: A Case
    Study in Irish American Journalism, 1870–1913.*
    New York: Arno Press, 1976.
Taylor, Sabina C.. "Patrick Ford and His Pursuit
    of Social Justice." Master's thesis, St. Mary's
    University (Halifax, Nova Scotia, Canada), 1994.

Forman, Miloš (1932–)
Filmmaker
Czech

The "new wave" of Czech filmmakers during the first half of the 1960s consisted of a
handful of men and a woman who decided to
tell the truth about contemporary life in
Czechoslovakia and express it in a nontraditional and nonschematic manner. One of the
filmmakers of that time whose films are still
shown, enjoyed, and discussed is Miloš Forman, who has lived mainly in the United
States since 1969. In 1975 he became a U.S.
citizen. Several of his films are already considered classics of the genre.

Forman was born on 18 February 1932 in
Čáslav, a small city east of Prague, Czechoslovakia, the youngest son of parents who would
both die in concentration camps during
World War II. Cared for by relatives and family friends and attending schools in a half-
dozen Bohemian cities, he was accepted in
1950 in the screenwriting program of the
Prague Academy of Musical and Dramatic
Arts. After graduating in 1954, Forman began
his career by working for Czech Television.
Continuing to live in Prague, he took advantage of the city's cultural life, especially its
avant-garde aspects. In 1958, he had the good
fortune to assist Alfred Radok with the multimedia spectacle *Magic Lantern,* which was a
huge success at the Brussels World's Fair that
year. However, Forman's dream of directing a
film of his own did not materialize until the
early 1960s, when he made the short semi-
documentary film *Competition.*

Forman's talents were soon recognized, and
during the period 1963–1967 he directed several films, two of which became well known
abroad—*Loves of a Blonde* (1965) and *Firemen's
Ball* (1967). The former won the jury prize at
the 1965 Venice Film Festival, the 1966 best-
film award of the French Film Academy, and
the West German Academy Award; the latter
had its U.S. premiere at the New York Film
Festival in 1968 and was shown at festivals at
Cannes and San Francisco.

By this time Forman's satirical view of the
foibles and small-mindedness of the presumably ideal Communist society had spelled
trouble for him in his native country. When
Forman received an offer from a U.S. film
company to produce a picture about American youth culture, he eagerly accepted it. *Taking Off,* released in 1971, was Forman's lightest
American film and in its style closest to his
Czech work. It was chosen as the official U.S.
entry at the 1971 Cannes Film Festival and received a special jury prize. A succession of
films followed, two of which are now considered classics: *One Flew over the Cuckoo's Nest*
(1975) and *Amadeus* (1984). For each of them,
Forman received the Academy of Motion
Pictures Award for best director. Together,
these two films were honored with more than
a dozen Oscars. Among his other films, mention should be made of *Hair* (1979), *Ragtime*
(1981), and *The People vs. Larry Flynt* (1996),
which received the Golden Globe Award.

Zdenek Salzmann

REFERENCES

Barson, Michael. "The Sound Era." In *The Illustrated
    Who's Who of Hollywood Directors, vol. 1,* edited
    by Michael Barson, 158–159. New York: Farrar,
    Straus, and Giroux, 1995.
Hames, Peter. "Forman." In *Five Filmmakers,* edited
    by Daniel J. Goulding, 50–91. Bloomington:
    Indiana University Press, 1994.
Hillstrom, Laurie Collier, ed. *Directors.* Vol. 2 of
    International Dictionary of Films and Filmmakers.
    3d ed. Detroit: St. James Press, 1997, 340–343.
Liehm, Antonín J. *The Milos Forman Stories.*
    Translated by Jeanne Nemcova. White Plains,
    NY: International Arts and Sciences Press, 1975.
"Milos Forman." *Current Biography,* December
    1971, 8–10.

Thomson, David. *A Biographical Dictionary of Film.* 3d ed. New York: Alfred A. Knopf, 1995, 259–260.

Friml, Rudolf (1879–1972)
Composer
Czech

Some of the most popular tunes of the second and third decades of the twentieth century were composed by Czech-born Rudolf Friml. His operettas were successful both in the United States and in Europe. *Rose Marie* was on the stage in Paris for three years without interruption.

Friml was born in Prague on 7 December 1879, the son of a baker who loved music and himself played the accordion and zither. At a very early age Friml began the study of piano and was ten years old when his first composition, a piano piece, was published. He was fourteen when he began his studies at the Prague Conservatory of Music, with Antonín Dvořák himself as his composition teacher. After completing his conservatory work at seventeen, Friml was asked by violinist Jan Kubelík to be his assisting artist in appearances throughout Europe. It was while accompanying Kubelík that he made his first visit to the United States, in 1901.

Friml was, however, above all, a composer, with such compositions as a song cycle, piano etudes, a piano trio, several suites, two piano concertos, and a symphony already to his credit. In 1906 he returned to the United States, this time as a soloist, for a successful performance of his B Major Piano Concerto with the New York Symphony Orchestra. He decided to remain as a pianist and teacher. His entry into the world of Broadway musical theater came about serendipitously in 1912 when he was asked to replace Victor Herbert in writing the music for a planned operetta, *The Firefly*. The operetta opened on 2 December 1912 and was an immediate success—in no small part because of his score.

Friml's melodic and romantic music soon became well known. He himself said his operettas were characterized by "a full-bodied libretto with luscious melody, rousing choruses and romantic passions." Between 1912 and 1947 he composed more than thirty operettas as well as music for films. *The Firefly* was followed by, among others, *High Jinks* (1913), *Katinka* (1915), *You're in Love* (1917), *The Little Whopper* (1919), *June Love* (1921), *Rose Marie* (1924), *The Vagabond King* (1925), *The Wild Rose* (1926), and *The Three Musketeers* (1928). The 1936 film version of *Rose Marie* with Jeanette MacDonald and Nelson Eddy made their duet, "Indian Love Call," one of the best-known songs of the time. For the film version of *The Firefly* (1937), Friml added the popular "Donkey Serenade" to his already rich and varied score. Among his other operettas that were filmed was *The Vagabond King* (1930 and 1956).

Friml, some of whose compositions were published under the pseudonym Roderick Freeman, was active throughout his long life as a pianist, conductor, and arranger. He became a U.S. citizen in 1925 and was married to Kay Ling in 1952. Their son, Rudolf Friml, Jr., became an orchestra conductor. Friml died in Hollywood, California, on 12 November 1972.

Zdenek Salzmann

REFERENCES
Kennedy, Michael. *The Oxford Dictionary of Music.* 2d ed. Oxford and New York: Oxford University Press, 1994.
"Rudolf Friml." In *The Encyclopedia of Popular Music,* 3d ed., compiled and edited by Colin Larkin, vol. 3: 2036. London: Muze, 1998.
"Rudolf Friml." In *1973 Britannica Book of the Year,* 511. Chicago: Encyclopaedia Britannica, 1973.
"Rudolf Friml 1879– ." In *Popular American Composers: From Revolutionary Times to the Present,* compiled and edited by David Ewen, 65–67. New York: H. W. Wilson, 1962.
Slonimsky, Nicholas. *Baker's Dictionary of Music.* Edited by Richard Kassel. New York: Schirmer Books, 1997.

Furuseth, Andrew (né Anders) (1854–1938)
Union leader and Washington lobbyist
Norwegian

Years as a seaman convinced Anders Furuseth of the pressing need to organize seamen, improve their conditions, and protect their rights. He successfully led the movement that achieved those goals.

By the time Furuseth was eight, his parents, Marthe Jensdatter and Andreas Nilsen, had ten children to feed. Lacking adequate resources, they sent him, their fifth child, to work on a farm some distance away. He must have shown uncommon promise, for although he was the son of landless farmworkers, his employer paid for his education at a private parish school until his fifteenth birthday. In 1873 he completed three years' study at the noncommissioned officers' school in Norway's capital, Christiana (later renamed Oslo), an institution offering many poor boys a way to rise in society. For Furuseth, however, completing its course failed to open a military career, and in frustration he apparently went to sea as an ordinary sailor.

During sixteen years as a deep-water and coastal sailor, Furuseth jumped ship many times to escape the abuse of harsh captains. Claiming that the brutal discipline and injustice he experienced at sea awoke in him a passion to improve the lot of seamen everywhere, he settled in San Francisco and joined the San Francisco Coast Seamen's Union in 1885 and two years later became its only paid officer. Radically democratic, he resigned his position several times because he believed in rotation of officeholders and viewed career union officials as threats to working-class solidarity. But he proved so indispensable to the union that the members reelected him and insisted he remain in office from 1892 until his death in 1938.

His local office became mostly a symbol of his local base of support as he traveled the nation's coasts and the Great Lakes, organizing locals and advising them to join forces with others as the only way to become an effective force for change. Tirelessly speaking and writing about the "slavery of the sea," which denied sailors a voice in their hiring and working conditions, he led the various regional seamen's unions into a national and then an international organization, guiding it into membership in the American Federation of Labor. In addition, he attended international conferences to make the case for cooperation among the seamen's unions of the world. For decades he also pursued legal remedies for the men's plight by lobbying Congress. Eventually, with Senator Robert La Follette's support, he was instrumental in the writing and passage of the Seamen's Act of 1915, which gave sailors the same rights as other workers and became a model for the revision of other nations' maritime statutes.

Since he viewed Viking society as the birthplace of democracy, Furuseth was pained by Norway's complicity in denying seamen's rights. Asserting that he settled in the United States because its democracy offered the best chance to improve seamen's lot, he was nonetheless a life member of San Francisco's Norwegian Club and resided there when he was in town. He steadfastly praised Norwegian traditions of skilled seamanship and, inspired by his idealism and career, Norwegian-Americans proudly called him the Abraham Lincoln of the Sea.

David C. Mauk

REFERENCES

Axtell, Silas B., compiler. *A Symposium on Andrew Furuseth*. New Bedford, CT: Darwin Press, 1948.

"Furuseth, Andrew." In *Dictionary of America Biography,* supplement 2, edited by Allen Johnson. New York: Scribner's, 1958.

Gjerseth, Knut. *Norwegian Sailors in American Waters.* Northfield, MN: Norwegian-Amercan Historical Association, 1933.

Weintraub, Hyman. *Andrew Furuseth: Emancipator of the Seamen.* Berkeley: University of California Press, 1959.

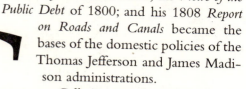

Jeffersonian Republicans. His 1796 *Sketch of the Finances of the United States;* his *Views of the Public Debt* of 1800; and his 1808 *Report on Roads and Canals* became the bases of the domestic policies of the Thomas Jefferson and James Madison administrations.

Gallatin, Albert (1761–1849)
Secretary of the treasury, diplomat, and scholar
Swiss

For six decades, beginning in 1789, Albert Gallatin contributed to the shaping of institutions and events in the American republic, based on firmly held moral and political convictions that derived from the Enlightenment and Gallatin's Calvinist heritage. During twelve years as secretary of the treasury (1801–1813), Gallatin pursued the goal of a diversified economy. He also participated in the negotiations to end the War of 1812 and wrote scholarly works on American issues.

Born into an established family of Geneva, Gallatin was orphaned at age nine. Nevertheless, in 1774 he entered the city's academy, graduating at the top of his class. Rejecting several career options, he immigrated in 1780 to the United States and, after three years in New England, bought land in western Pennsylvania, about sixty miles south of Pittsburgh. In 1789 he was chosen delegate of Fayette County to the state constitutional convention and served from 1790 to 1793 in the state assembly. Elected to the U.S. Senate in 1793, he was disallowed his seat on a technicality regarding his citizenship. In August 1794 he helped prevent bloodshed between federal troops and rebellious western farmers over the whiskey tax, was elected to Congress, and initially denied a seat because of his pro-farmers stance in the rebellion. Reelected twice, Gallatin served from 1795 to 1801, during which time he emerged as a powerful leader of the

Gallatin served as secretary of the treasury during Jefferson's administration and in Madison's administration until 1814. He opposed Jefferson's agrarianism and slave holding, yet shared his trust in the people, his fear of a centralized government, and his will to maintain the balance of power among the House, Senate, and the Executive. Among other things, Gallatin was particularly noted for his advocacy that the Bank of the United States be preserved. He was thus neither unqualifiably anti-Hamilton nor unquestioningly pro-Jefferson; his outlook was "Gallatinian"—he was a middle-of-the-roader. In foreign policy Gallatin opposed jingoism and, with the British and French, pursued a diplomatic course to keep the United States from being drawn into European conflicts. Although denied official status, Gallatin was an influential member of the peace delegation meeting with British negotiators at Ghent to end the War of 1812. As ambassador to France in 1815 and to Great Britain in 1824 he laid the groundwork for solving the disputes with Great Britain that threatened war over the Pacific Northwest, settled in 1846 in favor of the United States.

In 1830 Gallatin retired from public office, yet published *Considerations of the Currency and Banking System of the United States* in 1831 and was a cofounder of New York University, which opened in 1832. In 1836 he published *A Synopsis of Indian Tribes in North America* and later was a founding member and first president of the American Ethnological Society. His final publication, opposing the 1846 U.S. war against Mexico, found a wide audience. Thus, Gallatin always took positions that were original, independent, and, in their impact, enduring.

Leo Schelbert

REFERENCES

Adams, Henry, ed. *The Writings of Albert Gallatin.*
3 vols. Philadelphia: J. B. Lippincott, 1879; New
York: Peter Smith, 1943.

Ferguson, E. James, ed. *Selected Writings of Albert
Gallatin.* New York: Bobbs-Merrill, 1967.

Kuppenheimer, L. B. *Albert Gallatin's Vision of
Democratic Stability: An Interpretive Profile.*
Westport, CT: Praeger, 1996.

Merk, Frederick. *The Oregon Question: Essays in
Anglo-American Diplomacy and Politics.* Cambridge,
MA: Belknap Press of Harvard University, 1967.

Walters, Raymond, Jr. *Albert Gallatin: Jeffersonian
Financier and Diplomat.* Pittsburgh, PA:
University of Pittsburgh Press, 1957.

Garbo, Greta (née Greta Lovisa Gustafsson) (1905–1990)

Film actress
Swedish

A film legend in her time, Greta Lovisa
Gustafsson—who became Greta Garbo—rose
from poverty to great renown for her twenty-
four films. She made the transition from silent
movies to sound and created a mystique that
would long survive her death.

Garbo was born to a poor family in Stockholm. After her father's death, she left school
at fourteen to become a barber's helper and a
department store clerk. After appearing in an
advertising film, she attended the Royal Dramatic Theater School from 1922 to 1924. She
played a bathing beauty in the 1922 film *Luf-
far-Petter.* Mauritz Stiller, one of Sweden's
leading directors, discovered her and gave her
a leading role in his classic film dramatization
of Selma Lagerlöf's *The Story of Gösta Berling*
(1924). Garbo would go on to the United
States and star in a number of classic American films.

Louis B. Mayer, after seeing *The Story of
Gösta Berling,* engaged Stiller in 1925 for the
Metro-Goldwyn-Mayer (MGM) Studio in
Hollywood. Stiller insisted on a contract for
Garbo as well, after she completed a film in
Germany. Stiller was soon sidelined, whereas
Garbo quickly became MGM's most valuable
property, appearing in a long line of its films:
twenty-four over the next sixteen years. Many
were superficial potboilers, saved only by
Garbo's great beauty, expressiveness, and charm.

The change from silent to sound films—
the nemesis of many earlier stars of the silver
screen—only enhanced her allure with her
dark, sensual voice and subtle accent, first
heard in the movie version of Eugene
O'Neill's *Anna Christie* in 1930. With her
cool, classic features and large soulful eyes,
Garbo was increasingly typecast as the femme
fatale in such films as *Flesh and the Devil*
(1927), *Wild Orchids* (1929), *Mata Hari* (1932),
and *Grand Hotel* (1932). By the mid-1930s she
was able to command the grand dramatic
roles that fully revealed her mastery, above all,
Queen Christina (1934), in which she played a
seventeenth-century Swedish monarch, and
the film versions of Leo Tolstoy's *Anna Karen-
ina* (1935) and Alexandre Dumas's *Camille*
(1936). In *Ninochka* (1939) she showed a previously unrevealed talent for comedy.

Unrelenting work and frustrating require-
ments from the studio took their toll. An intensely private person who shunned publicity,
Garbo became widely known for a line from
one of her films, "I want to be alone," which
only added to her mystique. Her name was
linked romantically with various men, but she
never married. Garbo made her last movie in
1941. For a time she considered further roles,
none of which worked out, and she withdrew
into carefully guarded seclusion. The public's
fascination with the "Divine Garbo" has survived her death in New York in 1990.

Although she became a U.S. citizen in
1951, Garbo was deeply attached to her old
homeland, which she frequently visited. She
had little contact with Swedish Americans as
such, but she heightened their pride in Sweden's cultural eminence. For the American
public, she came to symbolize the remote and
timeless beauty of the Land of the Midnight
Sun amid the rush and clamor of early-twen-
tieth-century life.

H. Arnold Barton

REFERENCES

Bainbridge, John. *Garbo.* New York: Holt, Rinehart
& Winston, 1971.

Paine, Robert. *The Great Garbo.* New York: Praeger, 1976.

Paris, Barry. *Garbo: A Biography.* New York: Alfred A. Knopf, 1995.

Geiringer, Hilda (1893–1973)
Mathematician
Austrian

Although two ills of the times—anti-Semitism and androcentrism—overshadowed her career, Hilda Geiringer pursued mathematical research with undaunted devotion. Her investigations in applied mathematics centered on three main issues: probability theory, mathematical dimensions of plasticity, and biometrical issues.

Geiringer grew up in Vienna, the second of four children of Martha (Wertheimer) and Ludwig Geiringer, a textile manufacturer, and she early developed a talent for numbers. After attending the gymnasium (high school), she took up graduate study in theoretical mathematics at the University of Vienna, which she concluded in 1917 with a dissertation published as "Trigonometrische Doppelreihen" (Trigonometric double rows) in the *Monatshefte* [Monthly journals] *für Mathematik und Physik* 29 (1918). Until 1921 she assisted Leon Lichtenstein, editor of an influential yearbook for mathematics, then moved to Berlin to become assistant *(Assistent)* of the Vienna-born Richard von Mises (1883–1953), at the Institute for Applied Mathematics of the University of Berlin. In the same year she married Felix Pollaczek, with whom she had a daughter, Magda. They divorced in 1923. In 1927 she became a lecturer *(Privatdozent)* at the university and in 1933 was nominated an associate professor *(Extraordinarius),* yet denied the position because of Hitler's infamous policies.

Consequently, she moved with her daughter to Belgium to teach at a school in Brussels and then in 1934 went to Turkey to assume a professorship at the University of Istanbul. After five years she left for the United States to teach at Bryn Mawr College, where the algebraist Anna Wheeler, a daughter of Swedish immigrants, helped her adapt to the American way of teaching. In 1943 Hilda Geiringer married Richard von Mises, who also had fled Germany and also had arrived in 1939 in the United States via Turkey. A member of the Vienna Circle, which advocated positivism, a convert to Catholicism, and an interpreter of the German poet Rilke—but above all a gifted mathematician—von Mises received a position at Harvard, where in 1944 he became Gordon McKay Professor of Aerodynamics and Applied Mathematics. On leaving Bryn Mawr to be near her husband, Hilda Geiringer, however, could find a teaching position only at Wheaton College in Norton, Massachusetts, since, as she was told, administrators preferred men in research. Yet, in 1954 she received a grant from the Office of Naval Research, was named a research fellow at Harvard University, and in 1956 elected a salaried professor emerita of the University of Berlin. She was honored by the University of Vienna in 1967.

Despite setbacks, Hilda Geiringer steadily published scholarly papers that eventually numbered more than seventy. She also wrote several books, among them *Die Gedankenwelt der Mathematik* (The thought-world of mathematics) (Berlin, 1922) and *Geometrical Foundations of Mechanics* (Providence, Rhode Island, 1942). After von Mises's death, she published his manuscripts and several revised editions of his works, among them his book *Mathematical Theory of Probability and Statistics* (1964), "edited and complemented" by her. She vigorously defended von Mises's controversial view that probability theory was based on induction and grounded in the objective exploration of frequency. Her numerous scholarly contributions have undoubtedly advanced the field of applied mathematics in the United States.

Leo Schelbert

REFERENCES

Moite, Sally M. "Hilda Geiringer." In *Notable Mathematicians: From Ancient Times to the Present,* edited by Robyn V. Young, 197–198. Detroit: Gale Research, 1998.

Richards, Joan L. "Geiringer, Hilda." In *American National Biography.* Vol. 8, 832. New York: Oxford University Press, 1999.

———. "Hilda Geiringer von Mises (1893–1973)." In *Women of Mathematics: A Biobibliographical Sourcebook,* edited by Louise Grinstein and Paul J. Campbell, 41–46. New York: Greenwood Press, 1987 [contains an extensive selected list of H. Geiringer's publications].

Giannini, Amadeo P. "A. P." (1870–1949)

Banker and entrepreneur
Italian-American

Amadeo Peter "A. P." Giannini, a great innovator in modern banking, created the Bank of America, the largest banking institution in the world. Giannini's entrepreneurial talents contributed greatly to the economic development of the American West. His concept of branch banking and his economic policies helped democratize banking practices by providing services to immigrants, farmers, and working-class people.

Born in San Jose, California, on 6 May 1870, Giannini was the son of Luigi and Virginia Giannini, Italian immigrants who managed a hotel in the Santa Clara valley. As a young man, he entered banking with money from his wealthy father-in-law, who started him out on the board of a savings and loan association. Indignant at the neglect of the needs of Italians in San Francisco's Italian colony by other banks, Giannini formed, in 1904, the Banca d'Italia in a remodeled saloon in North Beach.

His unorthodox approach to the services banks could provide immigrants, wage earners, and farmers helped him transform banks from elitist institutions to democratic ones. Committed to serving "the people," Giannini traveled throughout California to meet with farmers and sign contracts to bring their crops to market. He shocked customers and bankers alike by lending money without collateral.

Giannini expanded his mostly Italian clientele through such innovations as longer hours, savings deposits, and the extension of small and low-cost loans. Giannini's Banca d'Italia became a household name following the San Francisco earthquake of 1906, when he opened a makeshift bank on the Washington Street wharf, lending money to help rebuild the city. The bank's post-earthquake success encouraged him to expand to other California locations. In 1924, he acquired the Bank of America Los Angeles and several others in southern California, institutionalizing branch banking. His acquisitions expanded into New York with the purchase of several more banks, which he used to create a network of banks that served immigrants. By 1929, Giannini emerged with the Bank of America, the world's largest commercial bank.

During the 1930s, Giannini helped finance California's new industries, notably motion pictures, and kept pace with the West's urban expansion by extending loans for purchasing homes, farms, and automobiles. During World War II his bank provided much-needed capital to West Coast shipbuilders and, afterward, it made 1 million residential loans to individuals migrating to California. Under the postwar Marshall Plan, the Bank of America was one of the banks that supported Western European nations with generous economic aid, providing the majority of funds for the reconstruction of Italy.

In May 1945, Giannini resigned his position as chairman of the board. He died four years later, on 3 June 1949. One-half of his personal fortune was given to the Bank of America–Giannini Foundation for employee scholarships and medical research; he gave $1.5 million to the University of California for agricultural research through the Banc-Italy Corporation. The Bank of America was then the world's largest bank, with 517 branches, more than $6 billion in assets, and nearly 40 percent of its shares owned by its employees.

A true son of the West, Giannini's style of entrepreneurship reflected not only his immigrant heritage but also his belief in growth, unlimited opportunities, and innovation.

Diane C. Vecchio

REFERENCES

Bonadio, Felice. *A. P. Giannini. Banker of America.* Berkeley: University of California Press, 1994.

Dana, Julian. *A. P. Giannini, Giant in the West.* New York: Prentice Hall, 1947.

James, Marquis, and Bessie R. James. *Biography of A Bank. The Story of Bank of America.* New York: Harper & Brothers, 1954.

Nash, Gerald. *A. P. Giannini and the Bank of America.* Norman: University of Oklahoma Press, 1992.

Gibran, Kahlil (1883–1931)
Poet and artist
Syrian

Kahlil Gibran is best known as the author of *The Prophet,* first published in 1923. He ultimately became the best-selling poet in the United States. His inspirational book, although not highly regarded by critics, remains popular throughout the United States and elsewhere, having sold more than 9 million copies in North America alone. In 1991, President George H. W. Bush dedicated the Kahlil Gibran Memorial Garden in Washington D.C., built on federal land after a 1984 legislative authorization. Many Arab-American leaders were involved in raising money for the garden, which features a bronze bust of the poet.

In 1895, as a boy of twelve, Gibran immigrated with his mother, Kamila Rhamé Gibran, and three siblings to Boston. Gibran's father remained in Bsharri (in present-day Lebanon), where Kahlil had been born. His family settled in an established Syrian community in Boston's South End. Workers at the Denison House Settlement in Boston recognized Gibran's talent. That led to an introduction to Fred Holland Day, a Boston photographer and luminary, who encouraged Gibran to read, helped him develop as a book illustrator, and provided him with connections to artistic patrons.

Gibran, who was raised as a Maronite, returned to Lebanon in 1898 to attend high school in Beirut, while his mother struggled to support her family in Boston. Shortly before his return to the United States in 1902, his sister died, and in 1903 his half-brother and mother also died, leaving Gibran and his younger sister, Marianna, to care for each other. Nevertheless, Gibran continued to pursue his artistic endeavors. In 1908, under the patronage of Mary Haskell, a Boston educator, confident, onetime fiancée of Gibran, and longtime correspondent, he moved to Paris to study at the Académie Julian. In 1910 his work was exhibited at a Société Nationale des Beaux-Arts salon.

The following year Gibran moved to Greenwich Village, in New York City, where he was greatly influenced by various writers. He is generally classified as part of the Symbolist movement, which emphasized ideal beauty and the inspirational over the intellectual. Gibran also wrote for several Arab-language publications in New York, including *Al-Mohajer,* and later published in such English-language literary publications as the *Dial.* He became increasingly well known in the Arab-American community, among readers in the Middle East, and finally to a more general American audience. His first book, *Broken Wings,* a novella written in Arabic, appeared in 1912. Gibran joined an international Syrian group, the Golden Links Society (Al-Halaqat al-Dhahabiyyah), and was also known for his leadership of the Pen League (Arrabitah Al-Qalamiyyah), established in 1920, whose members experimented with new Arabic literary styles. *The Prophet* (1923), written and illustrated by Gibran, is a spiritual meditation on topics that include marriage, children, friendship, sorrow, and death, a meditation that has appealed to millions of persons of various religious backgrounds.

Gibran died in 1931, succumbing to health problems stemming from alcoholism, which developed during the 1920s. He bequeathed his future royalties to charities in his hometown of Bsharri, to which his remains were returned and where a tomb and museum were built in his honor. Gibran became a vital figure both in the Arab-American community and in the Arab literary world, and his major book remains a best-seller almost eighty years after its publication.

Deirdre M. Moloney

REFERENCES

Haiek, Joseph R. *Arab-American Almanac.* 4th ed. Glendale, CA: News Circle Publishing, 1992.

Waterfield, Robin. *Prophet: The Life and Times of Kahlil Gibran.* New York: St. Martin's Press, 1998.

Goizueta, Roberto (1931–1997)

Corporate executive and philanthropist
Cuban

A refugee from Cuba, Roberto Goizueta worked his way up through the Coca Cola corporate structure, becoming its chairman just twenty years after settling in the United States. At his funeral, his son Roberto S. eulogized him for his integrity and recalled the words he often repeated: "A company must have a soul; it must have a heart."

The son of a wealthy Cuban sugar magnate, Goizueta was born in Havana on 18 November 1931. At Belen Jesuit School, he captured the title of brigadier, the highest honor awarded a student each year for academic achievement and character traits. He completed his education in the United States and returned to his hometown with a degree in chemical engineering from Yale University. But instead of entering the family business, in 1954 he answered a help-wanted ad for a chemist. He started working at the Coca-Cola Company on 4 July.

Less than five years later, Castro marched triumphantly into Havana, and the life of Goizueta and of many of his compatriots changed forever. In 1961, the revolution began nationalizing many businesses, including that of the Goizueta family and Coca Cola. Goizueta and Olga, his wife of eight years, sent their children to the United States, and the parents followed, pretending to be on vacation. A suitcase and $40 in cash was all they had to begin a new life. But Goizueta knew he could count on some valuable assets. "I came to this country with two possessions," he reflected years later, "my education and a job with the Coca Cola Company."

His managerial skills were soon recognized, and Goizueta started rising through the ranks of the Coca Cola's technical division, first in Miami and the Caribbean, then at headquarters in Atlanta. By 1966 he had become the youngest vice president in the company's history and, by 1979, as vice-chairman, he had vast responsibility over administration, external affairs, legal, and technical matters. In May 1980, Goizueta was elected president and chief operating officer and a director. Ten months later, he became chairman, heading one of the U.S. companies most widely known around the world, an icon of the country's culture and economic system.

During his tenure, his passionate commitment and what he called "intelligent risk taking" triggered a period of astounding growth for the company and its share owners. When he turned sixty-five, the customary retirement age, he was asked to stay indefinitely. However, just a few months later, in August 1997, he was diagnosed with lung cancer. Seven weeks later, on 18 October 1997, he died in the arms of his wife, Olguita.

Fortune magazine described Goizueta as one of "America's Greatest Wealth Creators." During his life, Goizueta prided himself that—through the philanthropic work of the Robert W. Woodruff Foundation, named for Goizueta's predecessor and mentor—part of such wealth went to those in greater need. Among those institutions he favored was the Belen Jesuit School, which had reopened in Miami in 1961.

Uva de Aragón

REFERENCES

Allen, Frederick. *Secret Formula: How Brilliant Marketing and Relentless Salesmanship Made Coca Cola the Best-Known Product in the World.* New York: HarperCollins, 1994.

The Life and Legacy of Robert C. Goizueta. A Special Publication of *Journey, the Magazine of the Coca Cola Company,* 1997.

Goldman, Emma (1869–1940)

Political activist and writer
Jewish

Emma Goldman is best known for her anarchist politics and the considerable influence that she had on leaders of the American labor movement and, specifically, on leaders of Jewish immigrant workers at the turn of the century. She was especially famous for her fiery speeches against social controls and the coercive authority of the state.

Born in Kovno, Lithuania, Goldman immigrated to the United States with her impoverished family in 1885, at the age of sixteen. Inspired by the nihilist ideals of Russian intelligentsia, she followed the labor strikes for decent working conditions with great interest. After a brief marriage and a job in the garment industry in Rochester, Goldman moved to New York City, where she emerged as an impressive speaker. She first addressed Jewish immigrant workers in German and Yiddish, lecturing about decent working conditions and, as she put it, "freedom, the right to self-expression, [and] everybody's right to beautiful, radiant things."

As she went beyond these themes to advocate sexual and reproductive freedom, she shifted her focus to wider audiences, who swelled in number as her notoriety grew. She traced her interest in social justice and radical causes to her Jewish cultural roots, arguing that Jews had developed a universalistic vision of equality and freedom for all without distinction of ancestry or race. In 1893 she was sentenced to a year in prison for defying government control of her freedom of speech. A decade later, she continued to agitate on behalf of the idea of freedom of speech and expression.

She became well known for both her speeches and her equally incisive essays, most of which have been collected in *Anarchism and Other Essays* (1911) and the two volumes of *Living My Life* (1931). She helped found the Free Speech League in 1903 and was the editor of the anarchist magazine *Mother Earth* (1906–1917). In 1917 Goldman was imprisoned for speaking out against conscription, and in 1919 she was deported along with her comrade and lover, Alexander Berkman, and other immigrant radicals. She toured Russia and delivered defiant speeches against communism and totalitarianism, but Goldman and Berkman eventually left Russia, disappointed and dispirited. She spent the rest of her life in exile, first in Spain and later in Canada, writing extensively on the rise of Nazism and fascism in the early 1930s.

In her autobiography, *Living My Life* (1931), Goldman concedes that her Jewish cultural roots inspired her defiance of authority and her questioning mind. At the same time she was critical of the repressive moralism of all religious systems, including Christianity and Judaism. Although rejecting the religious and nationalist aspects of Judaism, she endorsed what she understood as Jewish cosmopolitanism, arising from a condition of statelessness. With the rise of Nazism she softened her anti-Zionist stance, though she never modified her rejection of traditional Judaism as merely repressive atavism. Though she benefited from the lasting support of liberal elements in the Jewish community, she achieved notoriety and impact well beyond the Jewish community in the United States and around the world. Goldman died in 1940.

Esther Fuchs

REFERENCES

Falk, Candace. *Emma Goldman: A Guide to Her Life and Documentary Sources.* Alexandria, VA: Chadwyck-Healey, 1995.

———. *Love, Anarchy, and Emma Goldman.* New York: Holt, Rinehart & Winston, 1984.

Goldman, Emma. *Anarchism and Other Essays.* 1911. Reprint, New York: Dover, 1969.

———. *Living My Life.* 2 vols. 1931. Reprint, New York: Dover, 1970.

———. *Nowhere at Home: Letters from Exile of Emma Goldman and Alexander Berkman,* edited by Richard and Anna Maria Drinnon. New York: Schocken Books, 1975.

"Goldman, Emma." In *Jewish Women in America: A Historical Encyclopedia,* edited by Paula E. Hyman and Deborah Dash Moore, 526–530. New York: Routledge, 1998.

Shulman, Alix Kates. *Red Emma Speaks: An Emma Goldman Reader.* New York: Schocken Books, 1982.

Gompers, Samuel (1850–1924)
Labor leader
English

Samuel Gompers influenced the American labor movement more than any other immigrant. He was cofounder and first president of the American Federation of Labor (AFL).

Gompers was born in the East End of London, the son of Dutch Jewish immigrants Solomon Gompers, a cigar maker, and Sarah Rood. By age eleven he was forced by his family's poverty to quit school and become apprenticed as a shoemaker and then cigar maker. At thirteen, he and his family immigrated to the United States, arriving in 1863, during the height of the American Civil War.

Gompers started out working as a cigar maker with his father in a tenement on New York's Lower East Side. Though uninterested in the labor movement, he did join other immigrant workers in social groups and fraternal orders, thereby becoming aware of the need for worker solidarity. Cigar makers hired one of their own to read while the others worked, and in that way Gompers was introduced to political issues affecting the condition of labor. He soon became committed to creating a successful American labor movement, in fact so committed that he rejected an attractive position at the Treasury Department in Washington and became involved with the new Cigar Makers' International Union (CMIU).

Gradually, he began to change the union's style and structure. Using the stronger British unions as an example, Gompers demanded higher dues to cover such benefits as sick relief, unemployment compensation, and especially a strike fund. He strengthened and centralized the union structure so that it could weather economic slumps and provide workers with a sense of class consciousness. In Pittsburgh in 1881 Gompers helped establish the Federation of Organized Trades and Labor Unions and was chosen president. Five years later, Gompers and his allies transformed it into the American Federation of Labor, focusing on organizing skilled labor and dispelling the notion that unions were anarchistic, which had become common

after the 1887 Haymarket Riot in Chicago. Gompers served as AFL president during all but one of the next thirty-eight years.

The AFL prospered under Gompers's leadership. He lobbied New York legislators to regulate the conditions of work in the tenements and he constantly traveled to organize workers and increase the AFL's membership. He also encouraged unskilled workers to organize and opposed those who tried to exclude workers of color. By 1893 the AFL included 250,000 members; by 1904, nearly 1,750,000. Gompers gradually came to see that the Democratic Party was more friendly to labor than the Republicans. He supported the election of Woodrow Wilson in 1912 and celebrated the flood of Progressive legislation that followed. The AFL continued to flourish through World War I, with membership rising to over 4 million by 1920. Gompers also served as an adviser to the Paris Peace Conference for matters concerning international labor.

With the return of Republican administrations and new fears of Bolshevism and immigration, as well as increased antilabor activism among employers, AFL membership declined during the 1920s. Not until the New Deal would organized labor once again experience the kind of influence and dignity for which Gompers had fought. Gompers died in 1924.

William E. Van Vugt

REFERENCES
Gompers, Samuel. *Seventy Years of Life and Labor.* 2 vols. 1925. Edited with an introduction by Nick Salvatore. Ithaca, NY: ILR Press, 1984.
Livesay, Harold C. *Samuel Gompers and Organized Labor in America.* Boston: Little, Brown, 1978.
Mandel, Bernard. *Samuel Gompers: A Biography.* Yellow Springs, OH: Antioch Press, 1963.
Reed, Louis S. *The Labor Philosophy of Samuel Gompers.* New York: Columbia University Press, 1930.

Gonzales, Rodolfo "Corky" (1928–)
Community activist
Mexican-American

Rodolfo "Corky" Gonzales was one of the most influential and charismatic community leaders during the 1960s Chicano movement

(Chicano is the term of self-identification adopted by young Mexican-American activists beginning in the 1960s). He and his independent organization, the Crusade for Justice, worked for civil rights and equity for Mexican Americans and inspired a generation of young Chicanos/as.

Gonzales was born on 18 June 1928 in Denver, Colorado, to Mexican-immigrant parents. His father worked in Colorado's coal mines and as a farmworker in the sugar beet fields. His mother died when Gonzales was three. By the age of ten, he was working in the fields alongside his father and siblings, migrating and changing schools many times before graduating from high school. To escape the poverty, he became a boxer, winning the Golden Glove amateur championships. Turning professional at nineteen, he won sixty-five out of seventy-five fights and was considered a major contender but stopped because of his wife's opposition. He went into business (a bar and, later, insurance), gained a reputation as an honest and committed member of Denver's Mexican-American community, and entered Democratic politics, becoming the first Mexican-American elected district captain. During the 1960 race, he served as Colorado's state coordinator for the Viva Kennedy! campaign.

After Kennedy's election, Gonzales began working for community social services agencies, particularly those with poverty programs. His eventual disillusionment with bureaucracies led him to organize a community-based Mexican-American organization, the Crusade for Justice. He built one of the most effective grassroots organizations, mobilizing community groups for numerous civil rights causes and establishing a cultural center noted for its support of aspiring Chicano artists.

Following his participation in the Poor Peoples' March in Washington, D.C., in 1968, Gonzales organized one of the most influential conferences of the 1960s. In March 1969, he brought 1,500 Chicanos and Chicanas together in the first Chicano Youth Liberation Conference. The agenda included political, economic, educational, and social issues affecting Chicano youth. Delegates drafted their demands in "El Plan Espiritual de Aztlán," calling for ethnic self-determination and envisioning a Mexican-American national homeland in the Southwest. It is considered a major document of the Chicano movement. Gonzales became one of the major figures in Chicano politics. The 1972 presidential campaign brought Chicanos and Chicanas together at a national political conference in El Paso, Texas, organized by a nascent third party, La Raza Unida. Gonzales brought his Crusade for Justice delegation, but a bitter political struggle ensued, with Gonzales vying for political control with the La Raza Unida Party (United People's Party, LRUP) leader, José Angel Gutiérrez. Gutiérrez emerged as victor and became the national spokesperson for the party.

Gonzales returned to Colorado and continued his work mobilizing the Mexican-American community. His brand of ethnic nationalism proved highly effective in the early years, but eventually, with Gutiérrez's strong influence, a more pragmatic political agenda opposed to Gonzales's ethnic separatism won the support of a new generation of Mexican-American activists. By the mid-1970s, Gonzales's Crusade for Justice had lost its appeal and support.

He retreated from his work as a community activist and turned to training amateur boxers. In 1987, Gonzales was involved in a serious car accident that left him with permanent medical problems. However, his life remains emblematic of the ethnic movements that developed during the turbulent 1960s.

Alma M. Garcia

REFERENCES

Garcia, Ignacio M. *United We Win: The Rise of La Raza Unida Party*. Tucson: University of Arizona Mexican-American Studies & Research Center, 1989.

Gomez-Quiñones, Juan. *Chicano Politics: Reality and Promise, 1940–1990*. Albuquerque: University of New Mexico Press, 1990.

Muñoz, Carlos, Jr. *Youth, Identity, Power: The Chicano Movement*. New York: Verso, 1989.

Rosales, F. Arturo. *Chicano: The History of the Mexican American Civil Rights Movement*. Houston: Arte Publico Press, 1996.

Gonzalez, Henry B. (1916–2000)
City council member, state senator, and
U.S. House representative
Mexican-American

Henry B. Gonzalez was elected to the Texas State Senate in 1956, the first Mexican American to hold such a seat in 100 years. In 1961 he was elected to the U.S. House of Representatives, the first Mexican American from Texas elected to national office.

Gonzalez was born in San Antonio, Texas, on 3 May 1916, his upper-middle-class parents having fled the turmoil of the Mexican Revolution. His father had been the mayor of a small town in Durango and, after his migration to Texas, continued his public career as editor of *La Prensa,* a Spanish-language newspaper in San Antonio. Despite that professional status, Gonzalez's parents experienced economic hardship and difficulties providing financial support for their six children. Nonetheless, they instilled in them the value of education as a key to upward mobility. In 1936, Henry Gonzalez accomplished the first of many lifelong successes as a second-generation Mexican American, earning admission to the University of Texas at Austin. However, the Great Depression made it impossible for him to continue working to pay for his college expenses. Returning to San Antonio, he eventually attended St. Mary's University and received his degree, later being awarded an honorary doctor of jurisprudence from his alma mater.

After World War II, Gonzalez left his position as a nonenlisted employee in the offices of both Army and Navy Intelligence. He began his long and illustrious political career in 1953 when he was elected a member of San Antonio's city council. Three years later, he was elected to the state senate, the first Mexican American in a century. By the end of the 1950s, he had gained a respected reputation and, in 1961, won a special congressional election, the first Mexican American in Texas to do so. He would achieve a national reputation, for throughout his political life, he devoted his legislative energies to the struggle for social justice. He was at the forefront of efforts to end segregation, improve housing conditions, increase educational opportunities and civil rights for his constituency in the Twentieth Congressional District of Texas, a predominantly Mexican-American district. One of his major victories, occurring in late 1964, was his role in ending the Bracero program, wherein there were sustained violations of the civil rights of hundreds of Mexican-immigrant workers. That program was also responsible for keeping a ceiling on agricultural wages.

As a result of his political successes and seniority in Congress, Gonzalez was appointed chair of the House Banking and Currency Committee. His political philosophy led him to focus on the need to pass specific legislative reforms and monitor the policies of the Federal Reserve System Board in order to expand economic opportunities for minority populations. He also became a voice for such issues as the abolition of both poll taxes and restrictive covenants in housing and for reform of mortgage constraints aimed at economically marginal groups. Together with Edward Roybal, congressman from California, Gonzalez founded the Congressional Hispanic Caucus.

Congressman Gonzalez retired in 1999 and died on November 28, 2000, in San Antonio, Texas. His son was elected to Congress from the same Texas district.

Alma M. Garcia

REFERENCES
Chacon, Jose. *Hispanic Notables in the United States of North America.* Albuquerque: Saguaro Publications, 1978.
Ehrenhalt, Alan, ed. *Politics in America.* Washington, DC: Congressional Quarterly, 1983.
"Gonzalez, Henry Barbosa, 1916– ." Biography, U.S. House of Representatives: bioguide. congress.gov/scripts/biodisplay.pl?index=G000272 (accessed 20 June 2000).
Rodriguez, Eugene. *Henry B. Gonzalez: A Political Profile.* New York: Arno Press, 1976.

Gregorian, Vartan (1934–)
Educator and university president
Armenian

Vartan Gregorian was born into an Armenian family in the provincial town of Tabriz,

Iran. Having arrived in the United States in 1956 on a university scholarship, he went on to become one of the most noted educators and leaders in higher education in the country. He has been honored worldwide for his intellectual contributions and leadership in the fields of education and philanthropy.

Gregorian received his elementary education in Iran and his secondary education in Beirut, Lebanon. He earned his B.A. and Ph.D. in history from Stanford University and began an illustrious academic career. He taught or held administrative positions at the University of California, Los Angeles, the University of Texas, and the University of Pennsylvania, where he became the dean of arts and sciences and eventually provost.

Gregorian earned a reputation for his curricular innovations and reforms and as an effective leader. In 1981, he was appointed president of the New York Public Library and, within a few years, transformed what was then a decaying and underfinanced institution into a center of New York cultural life. During his eight-year tenure as president, $400 million was raised in support of the library. In 1989, Gregorian was chosen to be the sixteenth president of Brown University and, with the same enthusiasm that he had demonstrated at the New York Public Library, embarked on a successful $535 million fund-raising drive, raising the total endowment to more than $850 million. He also led several major initiatives to maintain and enhance the traditional academic strengths of the university, including its excellent faculty and its diverse and talented student body. After eight years at Brown, Gregorian was selected to head the Carnegie Corporation, where he has pushed initiatives in teacher education, international peace, and cooperative efforts with other foundations.

In 1986, Gregorian was awarded the Ellis Island Medal of Honor, and in 1989 he received the American Academy and Institute of Arts and Letters' Gold Medal for Service to the Arts, having, in addition to his administrative posts, written extensively on various aspects of Armenian history and culture. In a White House ceremony in 1998 he was named a recipient of a National Humanities Medal, representing "virtuosity in the humanities in a variety of ways—through writing and teaching, scholarship and literary creation, and public outreach and philanthropy." Indeed, Gregorian has regarded his life's work as bringing knowledge and light to the society at large. He continues that mission today.

Furthermore, within the Armenian community he has been active as well. He is seen as a highly visible model for Armenians and is a much-sought-after keynote speaker at Armenian events, particularly the annual Armenian Genocide Day commemorations on April 24. In addition, on 10 February 1999, Gregorian received the St. Gregory the Illuminator Medal, the highest award that the Armenian church bestows on its laity, conferred at the direction of the supreme patriarch and Catholicos of all Armenians, His Holiness Karekin I. Gregorian, together with his wife, Clare, whom he met at Stanford four decades ago, have raised three sons.

Barlow Der Mugrdechian

REFERENCES

Arenson, Karen. "Gregorian, Ending an Eight-Year Tenure at Brown, Is Leaving 'a Hot College Even Hotter.'" *New York Times*, 8 January 1997.

Dreifus, Claudia. "It Is Better to Give Than to Receive." *New York Times*, 14 December 1997.

Lieberman, Paul. "Vartan Gregorian: A Fund-Raiser in an Age of New Money Learns to Give in the Old Style." *Los Angeles Times*, 18 July 1999.

"Vartan Gregorian Receives Bezalel Jerusalem Prize for Arts and Letters." *Armenian Reporter* 26.8 (28 November 1992): 11.

Groth, Dijana (1963–)
Journalist, editor, and publisher
Bosnian

Recognizing the need for the peoples of the fractured former Yugoslavia to center on their strengths as a united community and to leave the poison of division behind, in 1997 Dijana Groth created PLIMA, a bimonthly native-language magazine. With an entertaining and informative format, Groth uses PLIMA, which means Ocean (New) Tide, to

address the needs and concerns of newly arrived refugees from her home country. As a
national publication, it reaches into major
U.S. cities as well as small towns, thereby becoming a networking vehicle for refugees and
immigrants from the former Yugoslavia.
PLIMA became their voice, whatever their
ethnicity and wherever they reside.

Groth came to St. Louis, Missouri, with her
parents, Ivanka and Zlatko Mruckovski, and
her younger sister, Patricia, on 21 December
1978. She was fifteen years old. In time she
graduated from Maryville University in St.
Louis, Missouri, with a double major in mass
communication (stressing written journalism)
and international understanding (Political Science Department). At the same time, she
started working at a variety of jobs at the *St.
Louis Post-Dispatch* newspaper. She married
Charles Groth, a graphic artist, in 1989.

Soon, refugees from Yugoslavia started
coming to St. Louis, the second-biggest reset-
tlement area for Bosnians in the United
States. Although Groth remembered her
home country as sophisticated and heterogeneous, she found people coming to the
United States in great physical need, but also
showing signs of being divided along ethnic
and religious lines. Deeply troubled, she felt
there must be something she could do to help.
She constantly received calls seeking aid, such
as directions for turning on the heat. While assisting in as many ways possible, she decided
that the community needed a magazine to
educate and encourage the incoming refugees
to value their multiethnic roots and, at the
same time, adapt to their host country. She
started publishing PLIMA.

In the beginning people were cautious. As
Groth noted, "Their wounds were so fresh."
But she persisted. She and her friends did the
writing, and her husband did the graphic design work for the first issues. She did everything from selling advertising and subscrip-
tions to writing and editing the materials.
However, within two years she needed a paid
staff, and today she has subscribers in more
than forty U.S. cities.

Groth realized music also played a role in
people's lives, providing the glue to bind
people together. In 1997 she decided to bring
a famous Bosnian singer to St. Louis. She
thought, "It has to be possible." After struggling with monetary and logistical issues, such
as finding a neutral place for the concert, she
again succeeded. People came from all over
the Midwest. Since then she has sponsored
other concerts in St. Louis and in Chicago,
Illinois. As with her magazine, she stresses
unity, picking artists reflecting the total multiethnic community.

If PLIMA is the voice of her community,
the concerts are its heart. Behind these powerful tools, PLIMA and the concerts, which
forge a sense of unity and allow people to adjust to their new environment, stands a young
woman making her dreams a reality.

Pamela A. DeVoe

REFERENCES
Bertelson, Christine. "As Modern Fools Rush In,
    Angels Get Their Bread." *St. Louis Post-Dispatch,*
    19 January 1995, 1B.
Flannery, William. "Magazine Reaches Bosnians,
    Croats Here." *St. Louis Post-Dispatch,* 26 May
    1997, Business Plus, 12.
Groth, Dijana. Interview with author, 16 April
    1999.
"MetroWatch." *St. Louis Post-Dispatch,* 1 June 1999,
    Metro, B2.

Gutiérrez, José Angel (1944–)

*Lawyer, professor, judge, and political activist
Mexican-American*

José Angel Gutiérrez personifies the confrontational politics of the 1960s Chicano
movement and remains a symbol of successful
grassroots political mobilization. As founder of
the La Raza Unida Party, he earned a prominent place in Chicano history.

Gutiérrez was born on 25 October 1944 in
Crystal City, Texas, a town of about 10,000
people. His father, Angel, was a medical doctor who moved north during the Mexican
Revolution but died when Gutiérrez was still
in grade school. His mother, Concepción
Fuentes, raised José and his siblings. The entire

family worked in the agricultural fields of south Texas, but they were not migrant laborers, and he was able to attend regularly elementary and high school, excelling and becoming an avid debater and student body president.

Gutiérrez completed a B.A. in political science in 1966 at Texas Arts and Industries University, Kingsville, Texas. He earned an M.A. at St. Mary's University and a doctorate in 1976 at the University of Texas, Austin, followed in 1988 by a doctorate in law at the University of Houston.

When he was a student leader, Gutiérrez started his political activism, establishing a chapter of the Mexican American Youth Organization (MAYO) at St. Mary's. Elected president, he mobilized Chicano students to achieve educational reforms. After graduation he returned to Crystal City to continue his political mobilization, for Mexican Americans constituted about 80 percent of the population. Long-standing problems in the public high schools erupted in 1969 when students staged a walkout in protest of Anglo control of the schools and discrimination patterns against Chicano students. These events convinced Gutiérrez to found La Raza Unida Party (LRUP). LRUP succeeded in tapping into the electoral strength of Crystal City's Chicano community and it ran a slate for city council and the school board. It gained national attention in 1970 with its electoral victories. The rise to local community power in a historically Anglo-controlled city represented a major victory in Chicano history.

Gutiérrez and LRUP soon became a significant force on the national Chicano political scene. A keen political negotiator and power broker, he soon faced political opponents, such as Corky Gonzalez, from Denver, Colorado, but won the party's leadership during its national convention in 1972 in El Paso, Texas. He blended an oppositional political style with a pragmatic, mainstream political machine, yet was never able to build LRUP into an institutionalized national third party. He often alienated a generation of Mexican Americans who distanced themselves from militant politics. He was elected to a judgeship in Zavala County, Texas, in 1974, only to encounter constant attacks from Anglos. Facing criticism for an injudicious trip to Cuba, he eventually resigned in 1981.

Gutiérrez then became a university professor in Oregon. However, he returned to Texas in 1986 to become the director of the Greater Dallas Legal and Community Development Foundation, reentering political life when he became an administrative law judge in 1988. After Lloyd Bentsen left the U.S. Senate in 1993, Gutiérrez ran unsuccessfully for his seat. He has since continued to work in the legal field in Texas, teach, and lecture for community and student groups.

Alma M. Garcia

REFERENCES

Garcia, Ignacio M. *United We Win: The Rise of La Raza Unida Party.* Tucson: University of Arizona Mexican-American Studies and Research Center, 1989.

Gomez-Quiñones, Juan. *Chicano Politics: Reality and Promise, 1940–1990.* Albuquerque: University of New Mexico Press, 1990.

Muñoz, Carlos, Jr. *Youth, Identity, Power: The Chicano Movement.* New York: Verso, 1989.

Shockley, John S. *Chicano Revolt in a Texas Town.* Notre Dame, IN: University of Notre Dame Press, 1974.

Hagedorn, Jessica (1949–)
Writer
Filipino

Jessica Hagedorn's writings and performances have attracted attention outside the Filipino-American community as well as within it. She is currently the most recognized Filipino-American literary figure. Her first novel, *Dogeaters* (1990), was a finalist for the National Book Award and her anthology of Asian American writers, *Charlie Chan Is Dead* (1993), has become the standard work in its field.

Born in the Philippines but uprooted from Manila at fourteen when her parents divorced and her mother brought her to the United States, Hagedorn grew up in San Francisco and later moved to Greenwich Village, in New York City. In the Philippines Hagedorn had learned about the United States from American movies and rock music on the radio. Themes drawn from both media characterize her writing. As a teenager in San Francisco she met writer Kenneth Rexroth, who encouraged her literary aspirations. She attended the American Conservatory Theater for two years and subsequently gave poetry readings, sang in her own rock band, the Gangster Choir, and collaborated with figures from the Black Arts Movement in the Bay Area and in New York.

Hagedorn writes about life in both the United States and the Philippines, stressing the difficulties of growing up in either setting: "I have a dual sense of home." But it is a contemporary, mostly urban world that she writes about, not an idealized old-country village life or one of an earnest immigrant striving toward the American Dream. Her characters seem often to be between identities in a kaleidoscopic world of constant change. Both *Dogeaters* (1990), set in the Marcos-era Philippines of the 1970s and 1980s, and her second novel, *The Gangster of Love* (1996), careening between the U.S. West and East Coasts, reflect the influence of such Latin American novelists as Manuel Puig and Mario Vargas Llosa.

Hagedorn is no stranger to controversy. Some Filipinos claimed that *Dogeaters,* whose title derives from a negative stereotype of Filipinos, focused only on corruption and cruelty. A *New York Times* reviewer criticized her frequent use of Tagalog words and phrases without a glossary, ignoring Filipinos' and Filipino-Americans' usage of "Taglish" in their communication. Hagedorn has defended herself against both charges, retorting to one Filipino-American questioner: "I know, I know. I set the race back 400 years." She added later, "You don't go to literature and say I need to feel good about my race, so let me read a novel."

Nevertheless, for all her willingness to shock and outrage, Hagedorn has contributed significantly to Filipino-American literature and has offered generous aid to beginning writers, whatever their ancestry. Although she is considered the preeminent Filipino-American fiction writer today and, for example, is regarded by the Filipino American National Historical Society as a most important cultural figure, she has become increasingly Americanized. Yet, her perspective is not all that different from many other immigrants, literary or otherwise. Wondering whether the United States "is the country where I want to die and be buried," she observed, "if so, maybe it's because this is a country that allows you to reinvent yourself."

Roland L. Guyotte

REFERENCES
Almendraia, Laarni C. "Don't Fence Her In: Author Jessica Hagedorn." *Filipinas,* November 1997, 50–53.

Alpuget, Blanche d'. Review of *Dogeaters,* by Jessica Hagedorn. *New York Times Book Review,* 25 March 1990, 1–2, 38.

"An Interview with Jessica Hagedorn." *Mosaic,* Fall 1993, 25.

Bonetti, Kay. "An Interview with Jessica Hagedorn." *Audio Prose Library,* 1994.

Hagedorn, Jessica, ed. *Charlie Chan Is Dead: An Anthology of Contemporary Asian American Fiction.* New York: Penguin, 1993.

Sengupta, Somini. "Jessica Hagedorn: Cultivating the Art of the Melange." *New York Times,* 4 December 1996, C1.

Updike, John. "Farfetched." *New Yorker,* 18 March 1991, 102–106.

Hakim, Thomas (né Tobia Jajoo) (1884–1972)

Merchant and religious and community leader
Chaldean

Thomas Hakim was one of the earliest immigrants to the United States from what is now the nation of Iraq. He was a major figure in the establishment of the Chaldean Iraqi community of Detroit, Michigan, a community that numbered over 70,000 members in the mid-1990s.

Hakim was born on 22 April 1884 in the village of Telkaif, near the city of Mosul, in what was the ancient region of Mesopotamia, at that time part of the Ottoman Empire. He farmed a considerable portion of land and took advantage of the location of Telkaif—near the borders of Turkey, Syria, and Iran—to develop diverse trade ties and, in the process, to acquire a fluency in English, Arabic, and Turkish besides his native Aramaic. After the British mandate expired, he felt compelled to leave and entered the United States illegally through Mexico in 1923 (his status was later legalized to refugee). Journeying to Detroit, Hakim found a Chaldean community of only ten adults, a community that lacked ethnic institutions to maintain itself and carry on its heritage. Hakim contributed particularly to the development of community business and religious institutions and to assisting those with immigration problems.

Chaldean immigrants who had preceded him had become involved in retail groceries, basically a few small "Mom and Pop" stores that served the workers in Detroit's burgeoning automobile business. Initially, Hakim used his prior contacts to import Russian furs but with the stock market crash, he, too, moved into the grocery business. Then, drawing upon his old-country experiences, he helped his fellow Chaldeans develop and expand those businesses. He assisted many new immigrants in selecting appropriate locations and gaining financial support for new stores. He also encouraged other community business owners to move into new auxiliary enterprises, such as the wholesale grocery field and commercial real estate sales and management, or simply to add items to their merchandise lines, such as beer, liquor, and prescription drugs.

In addition, Hakim was instrumental in the establishment of the Chaldean church in the United States following World War II. He was one of a small group of Chaldean men who negotiated with the Roman Catholic archbishop of Detroit, Edward Cardinal Mooney, and the leader of the Chaldean Rite in Mosul, Iraq, Patriarch Joseph Emmanuel Thomas II, to appoint a priest to serve Chaldean people in the United States and to establish a Chaldean church. He then used his business skills and contacts in the community to collect funds for the church in order to establish it on a sound financial basis.

Finally, having worked with the British colonial officials in Iraq prior to his emigration as well as having had immigration problems of his own, Hakim was more knowledgeable about such issues than were many American lawyers. He was aware of the major immigration provisions, from the quotas to family preferences to student visas, and was able to assist other Chaldeans in determining the most effective means for facilitating the chain migration of family members. Hakim died on 25 November 1972.

Mary Cay Sengstock

REFERENCES
"Our Chaldean Pioneer in the Land of Opportunity (America): Tom Hakim." *Chaldean Detroit*

Times, 1 September 1996, 2; and 15 September 1996, 2.

Sengstock, Mary C. *Chaldean-Americans: Changing Conceptions of Ethnic Identity.* New York: Center for Migration Studies, 1999.

———. "Telkaif, Baghdad, Detroit—Chaldeans Blend Three Cultures." *Michigan History,* Winter 1990, 293–310.

Hall, Gus (né Arvo Halonen) (1910–2000)
Political activist
Finnish-American

Gus Hall was the longtime head of the Communist Party, USA, having held the position of general secretary since 1959. He was the product of, and one of the last remnants of, the radical legacy of Finnish America. During his entire adult life, Hall was a proponent of Marxist-Leninist orthodoxy and was—until the collapse of the Soviet Union—one of its most fervent supporters.

Born Arvo Halonen in 1910 in Minnesota, Hall grew up on Minnesota's Mesabi Range, one of the most important places of immigrant settlement for Finns. It was a hotbed of labor militancy and political radicalism and, in this milieu, Finns constituted perhaps the most radical ethnic group. Hall grew up in a Communist home and came of age during the 1920s, the so-called Red decade, during which, in the wake of the Russian Revolution, many Finns shifted toward communism. They came to constitute 45 percent of the membership of the Communist Workers Party. It was at this time that Hall began his long career in the Communist movement.

While still in his teens, he began to work for the Young Communist League as an organizer in the upper Midwest. He became involved in labor struggles in Minneapolis, taking part in hunger marches, demonstrations on behalf of farmers, and various strikes. He was jailed for six months for his involvement in the 1934 teamsters' strike. Shortly thereafter, he was appointed head of the Communist Party in Ohio. At the same time, Hall worked as a union organizer from his base in

Youngstown, helping to found the United Steelworkers of America. He was a leader of the little steel strike in 1937.

Hall joined the navy during World War II and spent time in the Pacific. During this period, he was elected to the national committee of the Party. Seen as a loyalist, his reputation rose in the years immediately following the war, and in 1946 he was elected to the national executive board. Three years later, he was arrested and sentenced to a five-year prison term under the provisions of the 1940 Smith Act. During the height of the McCarthy era, there were renewed efforts to jail Hall. Failing in an attempt to flee to Moscow, he was again sent to prison, ultimately serving a total of eight years in Leavenworth Prison.

During these years, the Communist Party experienced mass defections. The Soviet invasion of Hungary in 1956 prompted many to exit the Party. When Hall took over, the Party was no longer the organization it had been during the 1930s. The rise of the New Left and the hostility on the part of many American leftists toward the Soviet invasion of Czechoslovakia in 1968 served to further marginalize the Party.

Beginning in 1972, Hall ran for U.S. president several times, seeing his attempts as symbolic protests. He remained committed to the Soviet brand of Marxism and thus resisted such liberalizing efforts as Eurocommunism. Despite the decline of the Party's fortunes and the collapse of the Soviet Union, Hall remained a true believer and an influential figure among the dwindling remnant of Finnish-American "true believers." He died in New York City on October 13, 2000.

Peter Kivisto

REFERENCES

Georgakas, Dan. "Gus Hall." In *Encyclopedia of the American Left,* 2d edition, edited by Mari Jo Buhle, Paul Buhle, and Dan Georgakas, 285–286. New York: Oxford University Press, 1998.

Kivisto, Peter. *Immigrant Socialists in the United States: The Case of Finns and the Left.* Rutherford, NJ: Fairleigh Dickinson University Press, 1984.

Klehr, Harvey. *Far Left of Center: The American*

Radical Left Today. New Brunswick, NJ: Transaction Publishers, 1988.

Scott, Janny. "Comrades up in Arms." *New York Times,* 21 December 1994, B1.

Tanenhaus, Sam. "Gus Hall, Unreconstructed American Communist of Seven Decades, Dies at 90." *New York Times* (17 October 2000): C300.

Hancock, Ian F. (1942–)

Professor, writer, and political activist
Roma

Ian Hancock has achieved distinction for his efforts to preserve and teach Romani language and culture and for his participation in the international struggle to gain recognition for the Romani (Gypsy) peoples. They consider him a hero for their cause.

Hancock was born in London in 1942, the offspring of marriages between at least three Romani families from Hungary and Britain during the prior century. In the late 1950s Hancock's family immigrated to Vancouver, Canada, where he soon dropped out of school to work. In 1961, he returned to London, met a student from Sierra Leone, was introduced to the Sierra Leonean community, learned to speak Krio, and began to compile a grammar and dictionary. After briefly moving back to British Columbia, where he continued to work on Krio, Hancock returned to London in 1965 with a book manuscript and was soon introduced to David Dalby, of the University of London, who offered him the opportunity to enroll in a doctoral program there. He was sent to Sierra Leone in 1968 and also married in that year; he and his wife had three children prior to divorcing. He successfully defended a 758-page dissertation in December 1971 and left for Canada.

Hancock had never lost touch with his Romani roots and regularly visited his relatives in England. In 1969 a Romani family was subjected to police harassment there, which resulted in the deaths of small children. Enraged, Hancock became involved in the Romani community. He attended the First World Romani Congress in London, in 1971,

becoming a member of the International Romani Union. In 1972, he was offered a position at the University of Texas, Austin, as specialist in creole languages. He accepted and, after a few years, he began teaching courses on Romani language and culture, making that university the only U.S. institution regularly offering such courses.

Following the Second World Romani Congress in 1978, Hancock, together with Yul Brynner and other Roma activists, went to the UN headquarters to present a petition for recognition of the Romani people. It was approved, and the International Romani Union was granted membership in the UN Economic and Social Council as a nongovernmental organization (NGO). Later, he obtained membership in the United Nations International Children's Emergency Fund (UNICEF).

Hancock is the author of more than 300 publications, mostly dealing with Romani self-determination, antigypsyism, and civil and social issues. His book *The Pariah Syndrome: An Account of Gypsy Slavery and Persecution* (1987) sold out in two editions, and his language text, *A Handbook of Vlax Romani* (1995), sells widely. He regularly travels to Europe, giving workshops on racism or meeting with government representatives to discuss the Roma situation. He lectures often in the United States on the Romani victims of the Holocaust and on Romani history and migration. In 1997 President Clinton appointed him to the U.S. Holocaust Memorial Council, and in the same year Norway awarded him the Rafto Foundation's prestigious International Human Rights Prize. In 1998 he was awarded the University of Wisconsin's Gamaliel Chair in Peace and Justice. He and his second wife have one child.

William A. Duna

REFERENCES

Fonseca, Isabel. *Bury Me Standing: The Gypsies and Their Journey.* New York: Alfred A. Knopf, 1995.

Hancock, Ian. Interviews by author periodically during the 1990s.

Hanson, Howard Harold
(1896–1981)
Composer, conductor, and music educator
Swedish-American

A major twentieth-century composer, Howard Harold Hanson was born on October 28, 1896, to immigrant parents near Wahoo, Nebraska, in an area of Swedish settlement. His varied accomplishments over a long life made him one of the century's most prominent figures in American musical life.

From his early childhood, Hanson showed precocious musical talent. He attended the Swedish-American Luther Academy in Wahoo (no longer existing), the Institute of Musical Art (which became the Juilliard School) in New York, and Northwestern University, from which he graduated in 1916. After teaching for three years at College of the Pacific in Stockton, California, Hanson went to Rome in 1921 on the first Prix de Rome fellowship for composition awarded by the American Academy there.

Following a stint as a guest conductor for various musical ensembles, in 1924 Hanson was appointed dean of the Eastman School of Music in Rochester, New York. He held that position for the next forty years, during which the school developed into one of the most prestigious U.S. conservatories. Also in that time he initiated the American Composers Concerts in 1925 and an annual Festival of American Music in 1930. Hanson was an outspoken supporter of arts education in public schools, particularly music education, giving speeches and writing numerous periodical articles to promote it, even after his retirement in 1964. He also served on the boards of several music education organizations, on government commissions on the arts, and in the United Nations Economic, Scientific, and Cultural Organization (UNESCO).

Hanson was a prolific composer. His numerous compositions include four symphonies as well as symphonic poems and works for chorus, piano, chamber ensembles, and concert band. His music is generally described as neoromantic in character but it reveals varied influences and experimentation in modern idioms. He is probably best known today for his Symphony no. 2 (*Romantic*). His opera *Merry Mount*, based on Nathaniel Hawthorne's tale of colonial New England, received particular acclaim in 1934 when it premiered at the Metropolitan Opera in New York.

Hanson was a powerful promoter of American music. Yet, he always remained warmly attached to his Swedish and broader Nordic heritage. His earliest works include his "Scandinavian Suite" and "Three Swedish Folk Songs" in 1919. Hanson's 1922 Symphony no. 1 (*Nordic*) shows strong Scandinavian influences. His Symphony no. 3, first performed in 1938, commemorated the 300th anniversary of Sweden's colony on the Delaware River, as did his "Hymn to the Pioneers" the same year, which he dedicated to "the epic qualities of the Swedish pioneers in America." Hanson's choral compositions reflected and sometimes directly incorporated themes from Swedish Lutheran hymnody. A strain of Nordic austerity in his music caused him to be regarded as the "American Sibelius."

As composer, conductor, and music educator, Howard Hanson held a position in American musical life equaled by few in his time. He received many distinctions, both in the United States and abroad, including a Pulitzer Prize and thirty-six honorary degrees from U.S. institutions. Although his music may nowadays seem somewhat conservative, it has enjoyed a growing revival in recent years. He died on February 26, 1981.

H. Arnold Barton

REFERENCES

Heglund, Gerald. "The American Sibelius." *Sweden and America,* Winter 1998, 10–15.

Perone, James E. *Howard Hanson: A Bio-Bibliography.* Westport, CT: Greenwood Press, 1993.

al-Hibri, Azizah Y. (1943–)
Professor of law and Muslim women's
rights advocate
Lebanese

In defiance of what others thought a Muslim woman should do, Azizah al-Hibri has found success as a professor of law and an advocate for the Muslim community. Founder and former president of Karamah: Muslim Women Lawyers for Human Rights, she has taken an active role in defending Muslim women's rights in the United States and abroad.

Al-Hibri, who was born in Lebanon in 1943, grew up in a "house of learning." Her family always encouraged her studies and, after graduating with a B.A. in philosophy from the American University of Beirut in 1966, she came to the United States to continue her education. Struggling against the prevailing attitude that a Muslim woman should stay at home, al-Hibri received a Ph.D. in philosophy from the University of Pennsylvania in 1975. After teaching for several years at Texas A&M University and Washington University, St. Louis, she decided to become a lawyer in order to have a more concrete impact on women's lives. In 1985 she earned her J.D. from the University of Pennsylvania Law School. Following a short stint in corporate law in New York, al-Hibri joined the faculty at the T. C. Williams School of Law, University of Richmond, in 1992, specializing in securities regulation, corporate finance, and Islamic jurisprudence. Widely published, she also serves on a number of editorial boards, including those of the *Journal of Law and Religion* and the *American Journal of Islamic Social Sciences*.

Al-Hibri is active in a variety of projects and organizations that promote religious tolerance and human rights. She is codirector of the Religious Assembly on Uniting America, organized by the American Assembly, Columbia University. She also is a member of the advisory board of the Pluralism Project, Harvard University, and the Religion and Ethics News Weekly, PBS. She serves on the board of the Interfaith Alliance Foundation and, until recently, was a member of the Virginia State Advisory Committee to the U.S. Commission on Civil Rights. She is frequently interviewed on CNN and PBS on issues relating to American Muslims and Islam. In May 2000, she was the first Muslim woman to re-

ceive the Outreach Award from the Islamic Information Service.

As founder and former president of Karamah: Muslim Women Lawyers for Human Rights, al-Hibri has placed herself at the forefront of the fight for human rights for Muslims. Established on the ideal that education, dialogue, and action can counter the destructive effects of ignorance and prejudice, Karamah is dedicated to providing the Muslim community—in particular, Muslim women—with the tools necessary to exercise their rights in accordance with Islamic as well as U.S. law. This includes working on a model Islamic marriage contract enforceable in U.S. courts and the development of an alternative dispute resolution project to solve common legal issues in the American-Muslim community. In addition to her work with Karamah, al-Hibri travels extensively to discuss the issues of Islam, democracy, and women's rights with religious and political leaders and women from all walks of life. In 1999 she visited nine Muslim countries as part of the U.S. Information Agency Speakers' Program.

Elizabeth Plantz

REFERENCES

"al-Hibri, Azizah Y." In *Directory of American Scholars,* edited by Jaques Cattell Press, 8th ed. New York: R. R. Bowker, 1982.

"al-Hibri, Azizah Yahra." In *Who's Who in American Law 1994–1995,* 8th ed., 12. Chicago: Marquis Who's Who, 1994–1995.

"al-Hibri, Azizah Y." In *Who's Who of American Women 1981–1982,* 12th ed., 11. Chicago: Marquis Who's Who, 1981.

al-Hibri, Azizah Y. Faculty information from T. C. Williams School of Law Web site: www.law.richmond.edu/faculty/al-hibri.htm (accessed 16 June 2000).

———. Telephone interview by author, 28 February 2000.

"Welcome to Karamah: Muslim Women Lawyers for Human Rights," Karamah home page: www.karamah.org/karamah/default. htm (accessed 14 June 2000) (biographical information and publications).

Hill, James Jerome (1838–1916)
Entrepreneur
Canadian

James Hill possessed the vision, drive, and business acumen to foresee the integration of the regional economies of Canada and the northern United States extending west to the Pacific. He spearheaded the development of the transcontinental Great Northern Railroad, which he then managed with great efficiency.

Hill was born in Eramosa Township, Upper Canada. His parents had come to British America from County Armagh, Ireland, to farm in 1829. Young James attended William Wetherald's academy (later Rockwood Academy) but left school at his father's death in 1852 to clerk in a store. In 1856 he traveled to New York and from there to St. Paul, Minnesota, where he found a job clerking with a shipping firm, Borup and Champlin. Hill was soon integrated into the community, joining the volunteer fire department in 1858 and the militia in 1859.

Hill tried his hand as an independent freight agent in 1865, handling the local affairs of both the Northwest Packet Company and the Milwaukee and Mississippi Railroad. He soon acquired the agency for the St. Paul and Pacific Railroad, building a warehouse in St. Paul. He understood from the beginning the need for volume and control of a trade as well as the desirability of the horizontal integration of transportation facilities and of detailed accounting practices. Much of his attention turned north to the new Canadian province of Manitoba, where Ontarians were opening an agricultural frontier. He worked to establish control of steamboating on the Red River, forming the Red River Transportation Company in 1872, and in partnership with Norman Kittson and Donald B. Smith (later Lord Strathcona), he acquired the St. Paul and Pacific Railroad in 1874. With the completion of rail lines across the border, the St. Paul, Minneapolis, and Manitoba Railroad Company began operation in 1879, with Hill as general manager and, three years later, president. The railroad was able to tap into a

period of great expansion in a region spanning both sides of the border.

In 1880, at the same time that he became a U.S. citizen, Hill entered into a scheme to construct a Canadian transcontinental railroad but never happy with it, he left it in 1883 and concentrated on his own railroad interests. In 1885–1886 he joined his railroad with the Chicago, Burlington, and Quincy and in 1889 determined to build a railroad across the northern United States to the Pacific. This line, known as the Great Northern, was extremely well managed by Hill and served as the basis for further expansion on both sides of the border. However, his Northern Securities Company Limited, which held the shares of several major railroads, was dissolved by the U. S. Supreme Court in 1904 as part of its trust-busting operations.

Nevertheless, in alliance with the Morgan and Vanderbilt interests, Hill continued to expand his railroad and transportation investments throughout his life. He was always an economic integrationist, viewing Canada as "a portion of our own Western country cut off from us by the accidents of original occupation and subsequent diplomatic agreement." He also became active philanthropically in support of charities. Hill died in 1916.

J. M. Bumsted

REFERENCES
Greenberg, Dolores. "A Study of Capital Alliances: The St. Paul and Pacific." *Canadian Historical Review* 57 (1976): 25–39.
"Hill, James Jerome." In *Dictionary of Canadian Biography*. Vol. 14: 491–495. Toronto: University of Toronto Press, 1998.
Martin, Albro. *James J. Hill and the Opening of the Northwest*. New York: Oxford University Press, 1976.

Hill, William (1741–1816)
Iron maker, industrialist, patriot, and politician
Scotch-Irish-American

William Hill was one of the most important iron makers and industrialists of America's colonial and early national period. He serves as a good example of the importance of British immigrants to America's early industrial development.

Hill was born in Belfast. Little is known about his parents or his early life in Ulster, but he immigrated as a child with his family to York County, Pennsylvania, where he learned the trade of iron making. Hearing rumors that a place called Nanny's Mountain (near the Catawba River) in South Carolina had vast, accessible iron deposits, he moved there and built his home, several mills, and a forge designed to make bar iron. He also invested in lands and came to own over 5,000 acres by the 1770s.

The Revolutionary War highlighted the limitations of colonial America's industrial capacity, and William Hill responded by accepting the South Carolina governor's request to build a new and larger furnace that could produce cannonballs, grape shot, and tools and utensils for the revolutionary army. He had become the only manufacturer of weapons and munitions south of Virginia, and his production proved important for the survival of the region during the conflict. So important was Hill's enterprise that in 1780 British forces burned the ironworks, mills, and dwellings to the ground. They also confiscated ninety of Hill's slaves, for he had come to rely on them for skilled and unskilled labor. Hill was so enraged that he joined the revolutionary army as a lieutenant colonel. He served in several local battles and was wounded.

Hill also was a prominent politician, representing his area in both the South Carolina General Assembly and the State Senate during the 1770s and 1780s. He was elected again to the General Assembly, 1800–1808 and 1812–1813, and held the posts of justice of the peace and tobacco inspector. He also became known for being an effective orator and, as a champion of states' rights, fought the ratification of the new federal Constitution. Hill's main contribution after the Revolution, however, was in the economic development of the region. He supported many transportation projects, especially inland navigation

projects involving canal companies, and he superintended projects to open the Broad and Pacolet Rivers to navigation. But his main goal was to rebuild South Carolina's iron industry. Although he subsequently encountered financial troubles, he rebuilt his furnaces with the help of the South Carolina legislature, which provided him with fifty slaves to do much of the work. Hill also pioneered the use of new smelting techniques and devices that had been developed in Europe and thus laid the foundation for the iron industry of the antebellum American South.

In 1812 the legislature acknowledged Hill's losses and service during the Revolutionary War by forgiving him the balance of his financial debt. When Hill died four years later, he was a wealthy and influential leader of his community.

William E. Van Vugt

REFERENCES
Cowan, Thomas. "William Hill and the Aera Ironworks." *Journal of Early Southern Decorative Arts* 13 (November 1987): 1–32.
Lander, Ernest M., Jr. "The Iron Industry in Ante-Bellum South Carolina." *Journal of Southern Industry* 20 (August 1954): 337–355.

Howe, Irving (né Irving Horenstein) (1920–1993)
Editor, author, educator, and literary critic
Jewish-American

Irving Howe was one of the towering intellectual figures in Jewish-American literature during much of the second half of the twentieth century. He produced seminal works of literary criticism, political thought, history and politics, and Jewish culture.

Howe was born in the Bronx, New York, in 1920 to David and Nettie (Goldman) Horenstein. The family grocery store went bankrupt in 1930, and the Horensteins were forced to move in with relatives in an impoverished neighborhood in the East Bronx, deeply paining their son, Irving. By the time he was fourteen, he was committed to political radicalism and in 1934 joined the Young People's Socialist League. Although his political radicalism would go through a number of creative changes over time, it was an ideology—a moral influence—to which he would remain committed.

Beginning in 1936, Howe attended City College of New York (CCNY), where he became a prominent anti-Stalinist Socialist youth leader who spent more time with other children of immigrants than attending classes. By the time he graduated in 1940 (still as Horenstein), Howe had concluded that the Soviet Union was neither democratic nor a workers' state. He would continue to believe that democracy was an absolute prerequisite for any society and that socialism without democracy would not be socialism at all.

During World War II Howe was stationed in Alaska, where, with little else to do, he read voraciously and wrote pieces for radical periodicals under a variety of assumed names. In 1946 he resumed writing under his own name (officially changed to Howe), contributing reviews and essays. From 1948 to 1952 he worked for *Time* magazine as a book reviewer and in 1949 published his first book, with B. J. Widick, *The U.A.W. and Walter Reuther,* followed by *Sherwood Anderson* (1951) and *William Faulkner* (1952).

As his literary output increased, Howe became less and less politically active. In 1953, he became an associate professor of English at Brandeis University, where he remained until 1961. After two years at Stanford University, he became, from 1963 to 1986, Distinguished Professor of English at the City University of New York (CUNY).

In 1954 Howe cofounded *Dissent,* with Lewis Coser. Howe would edit that democratic-socialist periodical for forty years. During the 1950s, he published several more important works in the political realm, including his still influential *Politics and the Novel* (1957). In other studies, he hammered home the idea that democracy was the essence of socialism and that there was room for viable cooperation between socialism and liberalism. Howe also moved more deeply into Yiddish literature and Jewish communal creativity. In 1954

he coedited *A Treasury of Yiddish Stories,* the first of six such collections, and helped introduce Isaac Bashevis Singer to the American public. His interest in things Jewish was manifest, too, in his attack on Hannah Arendt's *Eichmann in Jerusalem* (1963), which tended to blame Jews for their victimization in the Holocaust; in his coedited anthology *Israel, the Arabs, and the Middle East* (1972); and in his monumental *World of Our Fathers* (1976), a history of the Jewish-immigrant generations in the post–1881 United States, for which he won the National Book Award.

Concurrently, Howe continued his intensive effort as a literary critic, publishing six prominent books in this field between 1963 and 1993. He was the quintessential New York intellectual, rising from poverty to preeminence in the study of ideas, literature, and politics. He died in 1993.

Gerald Sorin

REFERENCES

Alexander, Edward. *Irving Howe: Socialist, Critic, Jew.* Bloomington: Indiana University Press, 1998.

Bloom, Alexander. *Prodigal Sons: The New York Intellectuals and Their World.* New York: Oxford University Press, 1986.

Dissent 40:4 (1993): 514–551.

Howe, Irving. *A Margin of Hope: An Intellectual Autobiography.* New York: Harcourt Brace Jovanovich, 1982.

Pinsker, Sanford. "Lost Causes/Marginal Hopes: The Collected Elegies of Irving Howe." *Virginia Quarterly Review* 65 (Spring 1989): 585–599.

Hrdlička, Aleš (1869–1943)
Scientist
Czech

Toward the end of the nineteenth century, modern anthropology was in its infancy. Among those who helped lay the foundations of one of its subfields, physical anthropology, was Czech-born Aleš Hrdlička.

Hrdlička was born on 29 March 1869 in Humpolec, in southeastern Bohemia. At the age of thirteen he immigrated with his father, a cabinetmaker, to the United States, and the rest of the family joined them later. As a young boy, he worked for six years during the day in a New York City cigar factory and at night attended school to learn English. In 1888, when he suffered a serious attack of typhoid fever, the attending physician persuaded him to begin the study of medicine. Hrdlička graduated at the top of his class from the Eclectic Medical College in New York in 1892 and then, while practicing medicine in the evenings, went on to graduate from the New York Homeopathic Medical College in 1894. That same year he accepted a research internship in the new State Homeopathic Hospital for the Insane in Middletown, north of New York City.

In 1895 Hrdlička published an article based on his study of hospital patients, which led to his being invited to join the newly established Pathological Institute of New York State Hospitals as an associate in anthropology. He chose to go first to Paris in 1896 to gain more experience in medicine and to study physical anthropology. His scholarly introduction to Native Americans took place when he accompanied the Norwegian explorer Carl S. Lumholtz to Mexico in 1898. His fieldwork in Mexico and subsequently in the U.S. Southwest brought Hrdlička to the attention of the Smithsonian Institution. In 1903 he was invited to form a Division of Physical Anthropology at the United States National Museum and to serve as its curator.

Hrdlička traveled widely, assembled a very large collection of American Indian physical remains for research, and published numerous books and articles, thereby helping to found physical anthropology in the United States. In 1918 he established the *American Journal of Physical Anthropology,* which he edited for more than twenty years. Eleven years later, he founded the American Association of Physical Anthropologists and became its first president. One of his greatest contributions was his conclusion that the Americas were peopled by populations from Asia who had entered the New World via the Bering Strait. Among the many awards Hrdlička earned was the Huxley Memorial Medal of the Royal Anthropological Institute of Great Britain and Ireland,

which he received in 1927. On that occasion he gave a lecture in which he maintained that all humans have a common origin.

Hrdlička was first married in 1896 to a young Frenchwoman whom he had met in New York. Two years after her death in 1918 he married a woman of Czech descent. He died on 5 September 1943, at his home in Washington, D.C. He was always proud of his Czech background, visited his native country many times, and, with his gifts, made possible the Hrdlička Museum of Man at Charles University in Prague.

Zdenek Salzmann

REFERENCES

Montagu, M. F. Ashley: "Aleš Hrdlička, 1869–1943." *American Anthropologist* 46 (1944): 113–117.

Schultz, Adolph H. "Biographical Memoir of Aleš Hrdlička, 1869–1943." *National Academy of Sciences, Biographical Memoir* 23.12 (1945): 305–338.

Stewart, T. D. "Hrdlička, Aleš." In *Dictionary of American Biography.* Supplement 3 (1941–1945): 371–372. New York: Scribner's, 1973.

Hughes, John (1797–1864)
Roman Catholic archbishop
Irish

Archbishop John Hughes was one of the most influential churchmen in nineteenth-century America. However, he never lost touch with his Irish roots, playing a major role in the Americanization of the Irish Americans.

John Hughes was born in Annaloghan, County Tyrone, Ireland, on 24 June 1797. His father, Patrick, a small farmer, immigrated to the United States in 1816. The next year John followed. Margaret McKenna Hughes, his mother, and the rest of the family came the year after and settled in Chambersburg, Pennsylvania. In 1819 Hughes was accepted into Mount St. Mary's Seminary, in Emmitsburg, Maryland, and was ordained a priest in October 1826.

He started his career as a parish priest in Philadelphia at a time of great conflict between the hierarchy and the parish trustees. Hughes had no tolerance for trustees' meddling in church affairs and ruled from the start with a firm hand. In 1838 he became the coadjutant of the Diocese of New York. When Bishop John Du Bois suffered a stroke in 1838, Hughes ran the diocese until December 1842, when he became bishop of New York. In July 1850, New York was made an archdiocese and Hughes its first archbishop.

In 1840, Hughes became embroiled in a dispute with the Public School Society of New York, a private organization that ran the New York public schools. He suggested that Catholic schools be given a proportionate share of the state's funds. Protestants denounced Catholic schools as purveyors of alien ideas and barriers to assimilation, and Hughes's agitation resulted in the state's passage of the Maclay Act of 1842, barring all religious instruction from public schools and contributing to a permanent separation of religion and public education in the United States. The episode led Hughes to build a Catholic school system. He also established St. John's College (which eventually became Fordham University), a hospital, two orphanages, and the Irish Emigrant Society to aid in job procurement and to protect immigrants against exploitation.

During a period of anti-Catholic nativist violence in the 1840s, Hughes prevented further attacks on Catholic neighborhoods by surrounding his churches with mostly Irish armed guards and threatening retaliation if one more Catholic church was destroyed. During the Civil War, Hughes supported the Union cause and urged his fellow Irish Americans to do the same. When the infamous Draft Riots of 1863 occurred in New York City, it was Hughes who helped quell the angry mobs.

Archbishop Hughes was an ardent Irish nationalist. He supported the Young Ireland Movement of the 1840s. In August 1848, at a huge rally to raise funds for weapons, the archbishop contributed $500, but the revolution of 1848 failed. A newspaper writer once described Hughes as "more a Roman gladiator than a devout follower of the meek founder of Christianity." Hughes's combativeness in defense of the Church and of his flock earned him the nickname Dagger John. His frontal attack on the horrendous social conditions that confronted Irish immigrants in New York at midcentury ultimately changed the fortunes of New York. Hughes died on 3 January 1864.

Seamus P. Metress

REFERENCES

Connor, Charles P. "Archbishop Hughes and the Question of Ireland, 1829–1862." *Records of the American Catholic Historical Society of Philadelphia* 95 (1984): 1–4, 15–26.

Hassard, John R. *Life of the Most Reverend John Hughes, D.D, First Archbishop of New York.* New York: Appleton, 1886.

Kehoe, Lawrence. *Complete Works of the Most Reverend John Hughes, First Archbishop of New York.* New York: Catholic Publication House, 1865.

McCadden, Joseph J. "Bishop John Hughes Versus the Public School Society of New York." *Catholic Historical Review* 50.2 (1964): 188–207.

Shaw, Richard. *Dagger John: The Unquiet Life and Times of Archbishop John Hughes of New York.* New York: Paulist Press, 1977.

Hurja, Emil (1892–1953)

Pollster and political adviser
Finnish-American

Emil Hurja, the first important pollster in U.S. politics, was considered to be the person most responsible for introducing survey research into national political campaigns. Hurja led a peripatetic life, working in a wide variety of occupations ranging from journalist to stock market analyst, but it was for his work as a political analyst during the 1930s that he is best remembered.

Hurja was born in Crystal Falls, Michigan—in a major region of Finnish settlement in the United States—into a working-class immigrant family. Working his way through school with such jobs as grocery delivery boy and printer's devil, Hurja earned a journalism degree from the University of Washington. After graduation, he dabbled in several jobs, as a gold miner in Alaska, a journalist in Texas, and a Wall Street oil stock analyst, among others.

He also served in World War I, rising to the rank of captain in the army's air service.

Without any formal training as a statistician, the self-taught Hurja nonetheless became convinced that he could use polling data to forecast electoral support for political candidates. In 1928, he offered his services to Alfred E. Smith's presidential campaign but was rebuffed. Four years later, through the intervention of a Wall Street contact with close ties to the Roosevelt campaign, Hurja was hired to provide predictions that could be used to plan the campaign. His forecasts proved to be remarkably accurate. Two years later, when most analysts thought Democrats would win very few Senate seats and lose House seats, Hurja contended that the Senate gain would be ten and that Democrats would actually pick up House seats. The results were very close to his predictions and, as a consequence, his stature in the Democratic Party rose and his duties expanded to include directing the distribution of political patronage jobs.

No longer working behind the scenes, he became known to the public as the Crystal Gazer from Crystal Falls. Indeed, an enduring interest in his ancestral homeland prompted Hurja to lobby for the ambassadorship to Finland, but because he was so valuable in Washington, the administration refused to grant his request. However, by the early 1940s, Hurja had become disillusioned with the Roosevelt administration and left to work as a financial analyst in New York and to serve as the editor of *Pathfinder* magazine. In fact, he had switched to the Republican Party, backing the bid of Herbert Hoover for the nomination in 1940. In part, this was due to the fact that Hoover's sympathy for Finland was clear, having served as chair of the Finnish Relief Fund during the Winter War. Hurja contracted his services to the presidential campaigns of Thomas Dewey and Dwight Eisenhower.

In an expression of his continued efforts on behalf of Finland, Hurja still harbored a desire to serve as ambassador to Finland but before his dream could be pursued further, he died in 1953 of a heart attack at the National Press Club. Finnish Americans regarded Hurja's life as an American success story. As adviser to the Roosevelt administration and consultant for the Democratic National Committee between 1932 and 1937, he was a precursor to the contemporary phenomenon of the pollster as key political adviser.

Peter Kivisto

REFERENCES

Eisinger, Robert M., and Jeremy Brown. "Polling as a Means toward Presidential Autonomy: Emil Hurja, Hadley Cantril, and the Roosevelt Administration." *International Journal of Public Opinion Research* 10.3 (1998): 1–13.

Holli, Melvin. "Emil Hurja: Michigan's Political Pollster." *Michigan Historical Review* 21.2 (Fall 1995): 125–138.

Johnson, Alva. "Professor Hurja, the New Deal's Political Doctor." *Saturday Evening Post* 208 (13 June 1936): 9.

Tucker, Ray. "Chart and Graph Man." *Colliers* 95 (12 January 1935): 28.

Hutchinson, Anne (1591?–1643)
Religious dissenter and colonial leader
English

Anne Hutchinson was one of the most influential religious leaders and dissenters in colonial New England. She was persecuted for her religious views and for violating the limitations placed on women at the time.

Hutchinson was born in Alford, Lincolnshire, the daughter of a minister of the Church of England, Francis Marbury, and his wife, Bridget Dryden. From her father, Anne learned much about theology as well as what it meant to be persecuted for one's religious beliefs: Anne's father was imprisoned for criticizing the inadequate training of English clergymen.

In 1612 Anne married William Hutchinson, a successful merchant. They had fourteen children. In Lincolnshire, Anne and William Hutchinson heard the preaching and teaching of John Cotton, a leading Puritan, and joined the religious movement. After Archbishop William Laud began his campaign to enforce religious conformity through the persecution of Puritans, the Hutchinsons immigrated to

Boston, Massachusetts, in 1634 to join Cotton and other leading Puritans who had immigrated the year before. There, Anne began to hold prayer meetings at her home, where she came to embrace and develop the view of Cotton and others about the Covenant of Grace, which taught the complete reliance on God's grace rather than on good works as a sign of salvation.

Anne's intelligence and articulate leadership proved threatening to Puritan leaders, especially when she attracted other women, whose roles in colonial society were customarily restricted. Although Cotton originally supported Anne, he eventually joined the majority who denounced her, particularly when she claimed that the spirit of God, through his immediate revelation, gave her the authority to preach. The authorities derisively called Hutchinson and her followers antinomian, which means "against customary law," in an attempt to crush her movement. John Winthrop led the attack during her trial and later wrote the official record—destroying contrary evidence—which has misrepresented her as unstable, a woman threatening the established order. In 1637 she and her family were banished from Massachusetts and later she was excommunicated. She joined Roger Williams's dissenter group in Rhode Island, where she attracted merchants wishing to be free from Puritan restrictions.

The Puritans of Massachusetts were not content, however, with merely getting rid of Hutchinson, for they sent delegations of Puritan leaders to silence her even in Rhode Island. In an attempt to escape this form of persecution, Anne and her family moved again in 1642, this time to Dutch-held Long Island. The following year, she and her entire family, save one daughter, were massacred by Indians. The detailed reports about the attack clearly suggest that Puritans were present, convincing some scholars that this dreadful event was incited by Puritan authorities, who were still concerned about Hutchinson's teachings. As the testimony given at her earlier trial makes clear, the Puritan leaders were fighting what they considered the unbiblical influence of women, as evidenced by Anne's audacity in teaching men.

Some modern scholars regard Anne Hutchinson as the first feminist in America. She challenged the social conventions that kept women in subordinate roles and the religious restrictions that were created by the Puritan leadership in New England.

William E. Van Vugt

REFERENCES

Barker-Benfield, Ben. "Anne Hutchinson and the Puritan Attitude toward Women." *Feminist Studies* 1 (Fall 1972): 65–96.

Battis, Emery John. *Saints and Sectaries; Anne Hutchinson and the Antinomian Controversy in the Massachusetts Bay Colony.* Chapel Hill: University of North Carolina, 1962.

Hall, David D., ed. *The Antinomian Controversy, 1636–1638: A Documentary History.* Middletown, CT: Wesleyan University Press, 1968.

Huber, Elaine. *Women and the Authority of Inspiration: A Reexamination of Two Prophetic Movements from a Contemporary Feminist Perspective.* Lanham, MD: University Press of America, 1985.

Idar, Jovita (1885–1946)
Feminist and community activist
Mexican-American

Teacher, journalist, political activist, feminist, Mexican-American, Jovita Idar gained national prominence as a political and feminist activist and as a journalist during the 1910s. These activities sharply set her apart from the vast majority of contemporary Mexican and Mexican-American women.

Idar was born in Laredo, Texas, in 1885, one of eight children of Jovita and Nicasio Idar, a politically prominent family. The younger Jovita attended the Methodist Holding Institute in Laredo and earned a teaching certificate in 1903. She taught at a small school in Ojuelos, Texas. However, school conditions were so disconcertingly poor that she resigned. She returned to Laredo and, along with two of her brothers, became a writer for *La Crónica,* her father's weekly newspaper. In 1910 and 1911 *La Crónica* was critical of Mexican-Anglo relations in south Texas, featuring stories on the rampant racial discrimination against Texas Mexicans, their poor economic conditions, the attacks on their use of Spanish, the loss of Mexican culture, and the lynching of Texas Mexicans.

In September 1911, Idar and other Texas Mexicans met in Laredo at El Primer Congreso Mexicanista (the first Mexican congress), an organization that addressed the educational, social, labor, and economic issues affecting the Texas Mexican community. Idar and other Texas Mexican women participated as speakers. A consequence of El Congreso that year was Idar's formation in Laredo of Liga Femenil Mexicanista (Mexican feminist league) in support of the educational and economic advancement of women. She served as its first president. Like its counterpart El Congreso, La Liga was founded as a benevolent, cultural, and political organization, operating its own schools, providing food and clothing to the poor, and sponsoring literary readings and theatrical productions to raise funds for its charities. Its main goal was to provide for the educational needs of poor children.

During the Mexican Revolution, Idar was a member of a pacifist organization calling for an end to the fighting in Mexico. She crossed into Mexico to care for the injured, later joining La Cruz Blanca (the White Cross) and, as a nurse in the company of revolutionary forces, traveled throughout northern Mexico. Returning to Laredo, she joined the editorial staff of *El Progreso* and wrote editorials critical of President Woodrow Wilson's deployment of U.S. Army troops to the border to reinforce the Texas Rangers and of the general maltreatment of Mexicans in Texas. When the Texas Rangers tried to shut down *El Progreso,* Idar blocked the doorway in defiance, preventing the officers from entering. The Texas Rangers did finally close the newspaper, and Idar returned to *La Crónica.* She took charge of the paper upon the death of her father in 1914.

In 1917, Idar married Bartolo Juárez, and the couple moved to San Antonio. There, she became active in the Democratic Party and also established a free nursery school, worked as an interpreter for patients in a county hospital, and was an editor of *El Heraldo Christiano,* a publication of the Rio Grande Conference of the Methodist Church. Jovita Idar died in San Antonio in 1946.

Zaragosa Vargas

REFERENCES

Cotera, Martha P. *Diosa y Hembra: The History and Heritage of Chicanas in the U.S.* Austin: Information Systems Development, 1976.

Limón, José E. "El Primer Congreso Mexicanista de 1911." *Aztlán* 5 (Spring, 1974): 85–117.

Rogers, Mary Beth, et al., *We Can Fly: Stories of Katherine Stinson and Other Gutsy Texas Women*. Austin: Texas Foundation for Women's Resources, 1983.

Ruiz, Vicki L. *From Out of the Shadows: Mexican Women in Twentieth Century America*. New York: Oxford University Press, 1998.

Zamora, Emilio. *The World of the Mexican Worker in Texas*. College Station: Texas A&M Press, 1995.

Inouye, Daniel Ken (1924–)

Politician, U.S. senator, and Medal of Honor recipient
Japanese-American

Following a term in the U.S. House of Representatives, Daniel K. Inouye, a decorated veteran in World War II, was elected to the U.S. Senate to represent the state of Hawai`i. He has served seven terms.

Inouye was born in Honolulu on 7 September 1924, the son of Japanese immigrants. He attended public schools in Honolulu, graduating in 1942 from McKinley High School—nicknamed Tokyo High for its high concentration of Japanese-American youth. After the attack on Pearl Harbor, Inouye, who had dreams of becoming a doctor, served for a week as part of a first-aid team attending the many casualties.

In February 1943, while Inouye was a freshman at the University of Hawaii, the formation of the all-Japanese-American 442d Regimental Combat Team was announced. Inouye was one of the first to enlist. He and his Nisei compatriots went overseas and established a sterling war record in some of their most difficult battles, including the Rome-Arno campaign and the famed rescue of the "Lost Battalion" in October 1944.

In the closing months of the war, Inouye lost his right arm when he was hit by a German rifle grenade at close range while leading an assault up a heavily defended hill in Italy. He spent twenty months in army hospitals recovering. He was promoted and awarded the Distinguished Service Cross, the second-highest award for military valor.

During his recuperation, he and a fellow wounded Nisei soldier, recalling the racial discrimination they had faced in Hawai`i and their record of military service—as well as having witnessed Nisei friends killed in action—vowed to work to change things when they returned home. To that end, Inouye attended school on the GI Bill and eventually earned a law degree from George Washington University. Subsequently, working as a public prosecutor for the City of Honolulu, he was part of the 1954 Democratic revolution that swept through Hawaiian politics, winning election to the territorial house of representatives. When Hawai`i became a state in 1959, he won a seat in the U.S. House of Representatives and was elected to the Senate in 1962. He has won reelection six times.

Inouye is perhaps best remembered for his keynote address at the 1968 Democratic National Convention in Chicago. He was also a member of Senate committees that investigated the Watergate and Iran/Contra Affairs, serving as the chairman of the latter. He has also served as chairman of the Committee on Indian Affairs, Select Committee on Intelligence, and the Democratic Steering Committee.

Inouye has retained his ties with the Japanese-American community, participating in the fight for reparations for Japanese Americans interned during World War II and playing an active role in such organizations as the Japanese-American National Museum, for which he is chair of the board of governors.

Inouye has been married since 1949 to Margaret Awamura. The couple has one son.

On 21 June 2000, more than a half century after he lost his arm in battle, Inouye was among twenty-one Japanese-American veterans awarded the Congressional Medal of Honor by President Clinton for bravery during World War II.

Brian Niiya

REFERENCES

Inouye, Daniel K., with Lawrence Elliot. *Journey to Washington*. Englewood Cliffs, NJ: Prentice Hall, 1967.

———. Official U.S. Senate biography: www.senate.gov/~inouye (accessed 20 June 2000).

Richter, Paul. "Twenty-one Asian Americans to Get Medal of Honor for WWII." *Los Angeles Times,* 13 May 2000, A16.

Ivask, Ivar Vidrik (1927–1992)
Poet, scholar, and artist
Estonian

Ivar Ivask helped define Estonian culture and identity in exile after World War II. He introduced Americans not only to the literature of his Baltic homeland but also to the prose and poetry of many of the world's finest writers.

Ivask was born in Riga, Latvia, the son of an Estonian father and Latvian mother. In 1944, when the Soviet army reoccupied the Baltic states, his family fled to Germany. As a refugee after the war, he graduated from the Estonian gymnasium in Wiesbaden and studied art history and comparative literature at the University of Marburg. In 1949, he met and married Astrid Hartmanis, a Latvian poet and writer, and they immigrated to the United States.

Ivask earned advanced degrees in German literature and art history from the University of Minnesota and began teaching in the German Department at St. Olaf College in Northfield, Minnesota, in 1952. Three years later, while serving in the army, he became a U.S. citizen, returning after his military service to St. Olaf.

In 1967, he moved to the University of Oklahoma, Norman, where he became a professor of modern languages and literatures and editor of the international literary quarterly *Books Abroad.* He expanded its coverage and eventually guided its transition to a new format and new name, *World Literature Today,* in 1977. He also organized the Puterbaugh Conference on Writers of the French-Speaking and Hispanic World in 1968. The following year, he founded the biennial Neustadt International Prize for Literature, which, given the high quality of its recipients, has often been described as an American Nobel. Also in 1969 he helped found the Association for the Advancement of Baltic Studies, an academic organization dedicated to advancing scholarship on the Baltic states. He would later serve as the organization's president.

A prolific scholar and writer and conversant in at least ten languages, Ivask edited numerous critical anthologies and wrote more than 150 book reviews and a dozen volumes of poetry in Estonian, German, and English—the latter including perhaps his best-known work, *Baltic Elegies* (1987, 1990). Besides being a scholar and poet, Ivask was also an accomplished pen-and-ink and collage artist, and his works were exhibited in the United States, Canada, and Europe.

Although geographically isolated from much of the Estonian-American community, he nonetheless maintained a connection with it through his work. His poetry abounds with images of his lost Baltic homeland and the loneliness of exile. In one of the first poems he read on Estonian soil, he wrote: "I have learned other languages along the way. / It is in Estonian I still count my annual rings." Ivask received many honors over the course of his distinguished career, including the Henrik Visnapuu Prize in 1973 for the best Estonian poetry, the Award of the Foundation for Estonian Arts and Letters in the U.S.A. in 1975, and Estonian Culture Council in Canada Prizes in 1976 and 1981. The Estonian House in Stockholm, Sweden, and the Tallinn Art Salon in Estonia exhibited his artworks. In 1991, Ivask retired to Fountainstown, County Cork, Ireland, where he died in 1992.

Bernard Maegi

REFERENCES
Aspel, Alexander. "Ice, Stars, Stones, Birds, Trees: Three Major Postwar Estonian Poets Abroad." *World Literature Today* 63 (Spring 1989): 227–231.
Ivask, Ivar. *Baltic Elegies.* Norman: University of Oklahoma Press, 1987, 1990.
———. *Oklahoma October.* Norman: University of Oklahoma Press, 1984.
———. *Verandaraamat ja teisi luuletusi* (The veranda book and other poems). Tallinn, Estonia: Eesti Raamad, 1990.
Riggan, William. "In Memoriam: Ivar Ivask." *World Literature Today* 66 (Fall 1992): 791–792.
Talvert, J. "Along the Annual Rings of the Heart: The Poetry of Ivar Ivask." *Journal of Baltic Studies* 30 (Spring 1999): 40–52.
Tucker, Martin, ed. *Literary Exile in the Twentieth Century: An Analysis and Biographical Dictionary.* New York: Greenwood Press, 1991.

Jalali, Reza (1944–)
Human rights activist
Kurdish-Iranian

Having experienced poverty, persecution, and threats on his life for being a Kurd, Reza Jalali has devoted himself to aiding fellow Kurds. He has fought injustices in the United States and abroad and promoted intergroup harmony and cooperation.

Reza Jalali was born in Qasre-Shirin, a Kurdish town in Iran located near the Iraqi border. The youngest of nine children, he grew up experiencing the dangers of being Kurdish, with memories of family members being forced into hiding or being arrested for opposing the shah's policies toward the Kurds. When he was an adolescent, his parents, fearing for his life, sent him to India, where, in 1981, he was arrested and held in solitary confinement for seven months at the request of Iran, which wanted him extradited. Jalali then spent one year as a street person, which "opened [his] eyes to the real world of human rights violations."

On Memorial Day 1985, granted admission as a refugee, he arrived in Portland, Maine, "having packed [his] life into one suitcase"—but unable to leave the past behind. By the time Jalali became a U.S. citizen in February 1991, he was a vocal spokesman for Amnesty International, for after he was arrested in India it had provided him with "life insurance" by means of a letter-writing campaign publicizing his name to deter his captors from killing him. He is currently one of Amnesty International's national directors.

In Portland, where Jalalai lives with his wife and child, he is actively involved in organizing events to provide humanitarian aid to the many thousands of Kurdish refugees in Iran, as well as in Iraq, Turkey, Syria, and the former Soviet Union. In June 1993, as a survivor of state violence, he testified at the UN World Conference on Human Rights to demand accountability from governments, reminding those in power that his "people live their lives in fear solely because they want to remain Kurds." Along with four other survivors, he founded the Survivors' Committee, which emphasizes the importance of survivors' accounts at international conferences on human rights issues.

By 1991, in the aftermath of the Persian Gulf war, Jalali, who identifies as an American Kurd, established the Maine Kurdish Relief Fund, a grassroots volunteer organization, gathering support from churches, schools, corporations, and private citizens in order to provide materials and raise money for Kurdish refugees. One of his most successful efforts has been "Project Tired Feet," wherein Maine shoe companies donated over 5,000 pairs of shoes and transportation companies volunteered to ship them, along with other items, to the refugees. Jalali has also focused locally on raising awareness of the increasing levels of hate crimes targeting immigrant and refugee populations. His experiences as a refugee and human rights activist led him to create the Ethnic Minority Coalition in 1994 in an effort to combat distrust among different immigrant and ethnic communities in Maine.

Currently, Jalali coordinates multicultural services for Maine's Department of Mental Health, Mental Retardation, and Substance Abuse Services, Region 1. He has participated in UN-sponsored international conferences in Korea, Japan, and Austria. His essays, articles, and commentaries have appeared in many publications; he writes a monthly column in "Maine's Multicultural Heritage" section for the region's largest newspaper, the *Portland Press Herald.*

Arlene Dallalfar

REFERENCES

Cohen, William S. "A New Citizen Seeks Help for Kurds." *Hroostook Republican,* 21 August 1991.

Harper, Judith. "'Born with a Curse,' OOB [Old Orchard Beach, Maine] Man Knows Kurds' Plight Too Well." *Journal Tribune,* 8 May 1991.

Jalali, Reza. "Immigrants' Children Face Obstacles to Fluency in Parents' Tongue." *Portland Press Herald,* 27 August 1998.

———. Interview by author, 11 November 1999.

———. "Richness of Many Cultures Enhances the Good Life in Southern Maine." *Portland Press Herald,* 1 October 1998.

———. "Right to Cast Ballot Leads to Reflections on Democracy and Change." *Portland Press Herald,* November 1998.

———. "Winter of Discontent." *Paivand* (Persian journal, Montreal) 5.133 (15 February 1999).

Jao, Frank (1949–)

Entrepreneur

Chinese-Vietnamese

Chairman of the board of Bridgecreek Group, a real estate company with $250 million worth of properties, Frank Jao arrived in the United States with nothing but the clothes on his back. By constructing more than two-thirds of the commercial and industrial space in Little Saigon in Westminster (Orange County, California), Jao is considered the builder of the biggest Vietnamese business enclave in the world.

Frank Jao was born in 1949 in Haiphong, Vietnam, a harbor city in North Vietnam. His grandparents emigrated from China at the turn of the twentieth century. The seventh of eleven children whose father was an insurance clerk, Jao already possessed business skills at the age of twelve when, to help his family, he had a job handling the town's newspaper account. In 1954, along with his family, he moved to Da Nang, South Vietnam, and completed his secondary education there in 1967. Although reared in a traditional Chinese family environment, he quickly adapted to the so-

cial expectations of Vietnamese society and joined the South Vietnamese Army immediately after he graduated from high school. He was soon transferred to U.S. Special Forces units, where he worked as interpreter for the U.S. government in Saigon while attending night college at Van Hanh University. In 1972, he earned a bachelor's degree in business and worked as a sales and services representative for several American companies, including Xerox and 3M.

When the South Vietnamese government collapsed in 1975, Jao left Vietnam and arrived at Camp Pendleton Marine Base, in Orange County, California. His first job in the United States was selling vacuum cleaners door-to-door, but he quickly saw his future career in real estate when he foresaw that the Vietnamese community would grow fast and Vietnamese Americans would need businesses to meet their various cultural needs. After receiving his real estate license in 1976, Jao went to work for a broker in Westminster. Two years later, he founded his own company, Bridgecreek Realty, on Bolsa Avenue, in the heart of the Vietnamese community, and developed the idea of building a centralized Vietnamese shopping complex. In 1979, with financing from a Chinese investor in Indonesia, Jao created the Far East Shopping Plaza, the first Asian shopping center in the area. Since then, in partnership with other Chinese merchants, he has built nearly two dozen shopping centers, including the largest facilities in Orange County. By the end of 1990s, he had expanded to the San Francisco–San Jose Bay Area.

Although Jao is married, has two daughters, and runs extensive, far-flung enterprises, he has not overlooked his responsibility to his fellow Asians and has established a strong record of community services. He was a founding member of the Chinese American Lions Club of Orange County, has been a member of the Vietnamese Chamber of Commerce, and has joined and provided support for numerous other Asian organizations. Without his development of Vietnamese business centers in Westminster, the formation of Little Saigon would, in all likelihood, not have been possible.

Hoan N. Bui

REFERENCES

Do, Quyen. "O.C. Developer Jao Looking to Asia." *Orange County Register,* 26 December 1996, 1, 24.

Gonzales, J. L., Jr. *The Lives of Ethnic Americans.* Dubuque, IA: Kendall/Hunt, 1991.

Higgs, D. A. "The Builder of Little Saigon." *Orange County Business Journal,* 17 May 1993, 1, 12.

Ibrahim, N. M. "Bridgecreek on Expansion." *Orange County Business Journal,* 20 April 1998, 1, 9.

———. "Little Saigon Developer Jao Prepares to Expand." *Orange County Business Journal,* 24 April 1995, 3.

Lee, D. "Power Broker Has New Plan for Little Saigon." *Los Angeles Times,* 5 August 1997, A1, 16.

Sullivan, J. L. "How Now Frank Jao?" *Orange County Business Journal,* 10 February 1997, 1, 30.

Jean, Nelust Wyclef (1970–)
Musician

Haitian-American

With his origins in a poor Haitian family, Wyclef Jean, as he is popularly known, has lived the American Dream and achieved international fame in the process. Using his celebrity status as a platform, Jean has provided opportunities and renewed hope to thousands of young people.

Jean emigrated from Haiti to New York at the age of nine. Raising children in the inner city proved challenging for his mother, and she steered him toward the world of music by providing him with an acoustic guitar. A few chords taught to him at age thirteen jumpstarted Jean's interest, and he has been playing ever since.

Jean's father, who was a preacher, forbade him to listen to rap music. Instead, Jean listened to Christian rock and anything else that he could disguise as Christian music. He also developed a love of his native Haitian music. While still in high school, Jean and two other young musicians, Prakazrel "Pras" Michel and Lauryn Hill, formed a hip-hop group they called "The Fugees—Tranzlator Crew." The

band's debut album in 1993 met with limited success, and they simplified their name to "The Fugees"; released a second album in 1996, "The Score"; and sold over 16 million copies, catapulting them into stardom.

One year later, Jean released his first solo album, "The Carnival," to critical acclaim, establishing him as a multitalented artist, writing and producing a diverse mélange of songs, including four in his native Creole. For example, the song "Gone 'til November" was recorded with a modern hip-hop edge. The eclectic solo effort yielded over $1 million in sales and two Grammy nominations. Subsequently, having worked on a number of movie soundtracks, he was asked to score the Eddie Murphy film *Life*.

In an effort to share his success, Jean founded the Wyclef Jean Foundation in 1997. Through the foundation, he organizes a variety of urban and pop artists to perform an annual benefit concert, the first of which took place in Haiti. The proceeds provide musical instruments to poor children in Haiti and are contributed to VH-1's Save the Music Program, which is dedicated to improving music education in schools. In 1999, Jean recorded "New Day," with Irish singer Bono, the proceeds of which benefited Kosovo relief efforts as well as the Wyclef Jean Foundation. Later that year, Jean received the Do Something Award, which honors America's top young community leaders, for his efforts to support music education and provide opportunity for underprivileged children through his foundation.

Wyclef Jean's success has had an impact on the self-esteem of hundreds of young Haitian immigrants, who look to him as a role model and a hero. For these young people, who are often faced with negative stereotypes, insults, and rejection from many of their American peers, Jean serves as a symbol of Haitian pride and acceptance. Popular Haitian-American writer Edwidge Dandicat has indicated that young Haitian identity can be classified as "before Wyclef" and "after Wyclef," indicating the profound sociological effect he has had on the young Haitian community.

Jean discovered his love of music at an early age and never lost sight of his goal, despite poverty and the temptation of drugs and quite a lot of money. He hopes to ensure that other young people are able to achieve their dreams as well.

Nancy C. Lespérance

REFERENCES

Charles, Pat. "Wyclef Honored with 'Do Something' Award." *Rolling Stone.com* (29 October 1999): www.rollingstone.com/sec-tions/news/text/newsarticle.asp?afl=&NewsID=9602&LookUpString=2125 (accessed 19 June 2000).

Ewey, Mo. "Wyclef's World: Carnival CD Highlights Passions and Problems of Fugee's Star Wyclef Jean." *Ebony* 53 (May 1998): 120–123.

Johnson, B., Jr. "The Carnival Barker Speaks." Interview with Wyclef Jean. Launch.com: www.launch.com/Promotional/wyclef_jean_qa.html (accessed 19 June 2000).

Oumano, E. "Wyclef Jean Foundation Plans Fund-raiser." *Billboard* 111 (11 September 1999): 100.

Pierre-Pierre, G. "A Hip-Hop Idol Is the Pride of a People; Young Haitian Americans Hope for an End to Taunts and Fights." *New York Times,* 28 March 1998, A10, B1.

Smith, S. "Jean Looks Past 'Carnival' Season." *Billboard* 110 (21 March 1998): 35.

Touré. "Wyclef." *Rolling Stone,* (29 October 1998): 38.

Johnson, John Harold (1918–)

Publisher and cosmetics manufacturer
African American

John H. Johnson was the leading black entrepreneur of the late twentieth century, with business achievements in a predominantly African American consumer market. He founded the Johnson Publishing Company in 1942, launching the most successful black magazine, *Ebony,* in 1945. He became the first African American to become prominent in U.S. magazine publishing. He also succeeded with his Fashion Fair cosmetics, the world's largest black-owned cosmetic firm.

Johnson was born in Arkansas City, Arkansas, to Leroy and Gertrude Jenkins Johnson. The family was poor, and when he was eight, his father was killed in a work-related accident. After Johnson finished eighth grade, his mother moved to Chicago, for she wanted Johnson to get a high school education and there were no black high schools in Arkansas City. He attended Du Sable High School, one of the two all-black high schools in the city at that time, and graduated in 1936 with honors and a scholarship. He went to the University of Chicago while working part-time at the all-black Supreme Liberty Life Insurance Company.

Johnson eventually left school to work full-time until he launched his publishing venture in 1942 with his magazine *Negro Digest,* a black counterpart to *Reader's Digest.* He began this business venture with $500 borrowed from a loan company, using his mother's furniture as collateral. *Negro Digest* was a success and, within six months, had a circulation of 50,000. Then, with *Life* magazine as a model, Johnson began publication of *Ebony* in 1945, also an immediate success. By 1967 it had a circulation of more than 1 million. Over the years, Johnson expanded with publications of several magazines, such as *Tan Confession,* a black woman's true-confession genre magazine, and *Jet,* which is still in publication after a half century. In 1962, Johnson began publishing books with a focus on African American history.

Within seven years of beginning his publications, Johnson was a millionaire. He would eventually build the first black-business office building in Chicago's downtown South Michigan Avenue. Eunice Walker, a graduate of Talladega College whom he married in 1941, has been involved in the company as secretary-treasurer since his first business venture. In the early 1990s, their daughter Linda Johnson Rice, a Northwestern University business school graduate, was made chief operating officer (COO) of Johnson Publications.

While he was building his publishing empire, Johnson developed businesses in several areas, including Supreme Beauty Products, radio stations in Chicago and Kentucky, and syndicated television programs. In African American business history, the black publishing industry remains virtually the only area that has a black consumer market, where there are no black-oriented publications owned and published by whites. In other industries, especially hair care and cosmetics, black enterprises face greater competition from white-owned companies.

In 1958, Johnson started Ebony Fashion Fair, with showings of the latest couturier fashions in 190 cities and the proceeds going to the United Negro College Fund. He has received numerous awards for his achievements and contributions, among them the Horatio Alger Award, the NAACP Spingarn Medal, and the National Newspaper Publishers Association's Henry Johnson Fisher Award for outstanding contributions to publishing.

Juliet E. K. Walker

REFERENCES

Berry, William E. "Johnson, John Harold." In *Succeeding against the Odds: The Inspiring Autobiography of One of America's Wealthiest Entrepreneurs,* edited by Juliet E. K. Walker and John H. Johnson, with Lerone Bennett, 331–335. New York: Warner Books, 1989.

Walker, Juliet E. K. *The History of Black Business in America: Capitalism, Race, Entrepreneurship.* New York/London: Macmillan/Prentice Hall International, 1998.

Water, Enoch, *American Diary: A Personal History of the Black Press.* Chicago: Path Press, 1987.

Wilson, Clint C. *Black Journalists in Paradox.* Westport, CN: Greenwood Press, 1991.

Jones, Mary Harris "Mother Jones" (1830–1930)

Union organizer and labor leader
Irish

From the 1870s to the 1920s "Mother Jones" traveled the United States working to improve labor conditions for all workers, including children. She became one of the best-known labor leaders of her time.

Jones was born 1 May 1830 into a poor farming family in rural County Cork, Ireland. Her father, Richard, immigrated to the United States first and sent for his family in 1850. They lived for a time in Toronto, Ontario, Canada, and Jones attended the Toronto Normal School in preparation for a teaching ca-

reer. After a job in a Michigan elementary school and a stint in Chicago as a dressmaker, she moved to Memphis and resumed teaching. In 1861, she married George Jones, an iron molder. She had four children, but all of them died, along with her husband, in a yellow fever epidemic in 1867. Jones returned to Chicago and resumed dressmaking until her business was consumed in the Great Fire of 1871.

In the years of toil that followed, Jones grew increasingly concerned about the growing gap between the rich people, for whom she worked, and the poor people, with whom she lived. She began to attend labor rallies and read labor-related literature. As the Knights of Labor grew in size and influence in the 1870s and 1880s, Jones took to organizing. The first strike she helped organize occurred in 1877 in Pittsburgh, against the Baltimore and Ohio Railroad. The local government's decision to call in the state militia led to a bloody riot and pushed her into full-time labor activism.

For the rest of her life she traveled the country, from trouble spot to trouble spot, organizing unions, leading strikes, and giving inspirational speeches. She was especially active among railroad workers and miners. By the late 1890s she was one of the best-known figures in the labor movement, and one of its most controversial. Small in stature, she stood large in the eyes of both the workers she served and the employers she chastised. One of her most effective initiatives involved a crusade against child labor. In 1903, to dramatize the plight of thousands of children toiling long hours in unsafe working conditions, she organized a march of thousands of maimed children from Pennsylvania to the summer home of Theodore Roosevelt, on Long Island. President Roosevelt refused to meet her, but dozens of states subsequently passed laws against child labor.

In 1905 she spoke at the founding convention of the Industrial Workers of the World (IWW) and in 1913 played a key role in the Ludlow, Colorado, copper mine strike. That event led to her testifying at several congressional hearings on the conditions of labor. Throughout her career she was repeatedly arrested and confronted with threats against her life. Jones always attributed her fearlessness and radicalism to her Irish heritage and the Ireland of her childhood.

She was ninety-one years old when she worked her last strike. The "Angel of the Mines" died on November 30, 1930, seven months after her one-hundredth birthday. In his eulogy the Reverend J. W. McGuire said: "Wealthy coal operators and capitalists throughout the United States are breathing sighs of relief. . . . Mother Jones is dead."

Edward T. O'Donnell

REFERENCES

Fetherling, Dale. *Mother Jones: The Miners' Angel.* Carbondale: Southern Illinois University Press, 1974.

Hawoe, Mary Lou. "Mother Jones: The Miners' Angel." Illinois Labor History Society website: http://www.kentlaw.edu/ilhs/majones.html (accessed 19 December 2000).

Jones, Mary. *The Autobiography of Mother Jones.* Edited by Mary Field Parton. Chicago: C. H. Kerr, 1925.

K

Kahanamoku, Duke
(1890–1968)

*Champion Olympic swimmer, actor,
and surfer
Hawaiian*

Enshrined in the U.S. Olympic Swimming and Surfing Halls of Fame, Duke Kahanamoku is remembered as Hawai`i's greatest ambassador of goodwill and as an embodiment of Aloha.

A pure-blooded Hawaiian, Duke Paoa Kahanamoku was born amid the duck ponds and palm groves of Waikiki in the Kingdom of Hawai`i in 1890. He was the eldest of the fourteen children of Duke and Julia Paakania Kahanamoku. His family called him Paoa (his mother's family name) to avoid confusing him with his father, who was named after the Duke of Edinburgh (who had arrived in Hawai`i on the day Duke Sr. was born).

The younger Duke spent much of his youth fishing and swimming in the seas of Waikiki. In 1911, without ever having had instruction or training, he swam competitively in an American Amateur Union meet in Honolulu Harbor. He shattered the official American 100-yard freestyle record, cutting off more than four seconds with a stroke he invented himself. Duke went on to Stockholm, taking the Olympic gold medal for the 100-meter freestyle the following year. He would compete in four Olympic games (1912, 1920, 1924, and 1932), winning three gold and two silver metals. The handsome, dark-skinned, 6-foot 2-inch 210-pound athlete was the most famous swimmer in the world at the time. Kahanamoku is remembered for his sportsmanship, gentlemanly qualities, personality, and warmth. He often held back when he swam as he wanted to make the races interesting, giving a thrill to the spectators, and making his competitors look good.

Kahanamoku was a water person who enjoyed swimming, body surfing, water polo, paddling, rowing, sailing, and fishing, but his most enduring legacy is as the international father of modern surfing. The Hawaiian pleasure of *he'e nalu*, or wave sliding, was virtually unknown outside of Hawai`i before Kahanamoku's efforts to popularize the sport. By the end of his life, there were surfers everywhere in the world where there were waves. His 1914 visit to Australia established surfing as a new international sport. He taught Australians how to fashion surfboards on the beach by hewing planks with an adze. His surfing prowess, which often included stunts like standing on his head, jumping from one board to another, and tandem surfing, attracted fascinated crowds and caught the attention of the Australian press, which widely reported the new sport of "board walking," or "shooting the breakers."

Kahanamoku had a nine-year career in Hollywood, with roles in about thirty movies. Acting and surfing took him all over southern California. When the Huntington Beach Surfing Walk of Fame was established, the Father of Surfing was honored with the first tile laid. In 1953, Duke was proclaimed a national hero for having saved the lives of eight men at Newport Beach, California, paddling out three times through the raging surf to their capsized fishing boat.

Kahanamoku's popularity enabled him to be elected to thirteen consecutive two-year terms as sheriff of the City and County of Honolulu. From 1960 until his death in 1968, he was officially appointed official greeter and ambassador-at-large. His statue graces Waikiki Beach, where he surfed.

David W. Shideler

REFERENCES

Brennans, Joseph L. *Duke: The Life Story of Duke Kahanamoku.* Honolulu: Ku Pa'a Publishing, 1994.

Hall, Sandra K., and Greg Ambroses. *Memories of Duke: The Legend Comes to Life.* Honolulu: Bess Press, 1995.

Karimi, Mansoorali (1929–)

Entrepreneur and philanthropist
Pakistani-Burmese

Mansoorali Karimi is an outstanding example of an immigrant who identified a significant commercial niche in the United States and used his entrepreneurial skills to achieve great success. He accomplished that while also maintaining a firm commitment to serve his ethnic community.

Like his father, Karimi found success not in his country of birth but in his adopted country. Driven by the abject poverty of Kathiawar, India, Karimi's father, Jivabhai Bhanji, embarked on a search for a better life, eventually settling in Rangoon, Burma, in the early 1880s. He became one of the most prosperous Indians in Burma and rapidly attained leadership positions in the growing Ismaili Muslim community of Rangoon. His piety, voluntary service, and charitable activities earned him the trust of Aga Khan III, the forty-eighth imam (spiritual leader) of the Ismaili Muslims, who appointed him to several posts and gave him the honorific title of *vazir.*

In the wake of military rule and nationalization in the early 1960s, Burma's Indian and Pakistani-immigrant population dwindled. Bhanji had had twelve sons and nine daughters, and his descendants were among the emigrants, adopting the surname Karimi and resettling in Pakistan.

Mansoorali Karimi was Bhanji's second-youngest child. From his father he acquired business acumen, a charitable outlook, and the habit of daily attendance at a *jamatkhana* (the multipurpose religious, educational, cultural, and social center) as well as voluntary service *(seva)* to the community.

Immigrating to the United States in the late 1970s, Karimi, his wife Noorjehan, and their two sons and three daughters made Atlanta, Georgia, their new home. Their first investment was leasing a restaurant in a truck stop. They then acquired the truck stop itself and sold it at a handsome profit. Within a decade, Karimi and his two sons—Ramzanali and Malik—had bought and built a convenience store empire with more than fifty locations in the metropolitan Atlanta area. In addition, they have expanded into Tennessee and diversified into real estate, land development, and jewelry stores.

The remarkably rapid success of Karimi, a pioneer among South Asian immigrants in the convenience store business, generated an unmistakable interest in this field among them. That there were over 600 Ismaili-owned convenience stores in the greater Atlanta region at the beginning of 2000 is a tribute to Karimi, for many current owners acquired their exposure to and training in operating this business as his employees.

Furthermore, in keeping with the teachings of Islam, more particularly its Ismaili *Tariqa* (interpretation), and the guidance of Prince Karim Aga Khan IV, the forty-ninth imam, the Karimi family has shared its good fortune with others. Besides substantial annual donations to the Aga Khan Foundation U.S.A., the family endowed the Mansoorali J. Karimi Scholarship Fund at the Aga Khan University in Karachi, Pakistan, in 1994. Karimi also attends a *jamatkhana* daily and renders *seva* at the local level, whereas his sons and sons-in-law—who are in the convenience store business as well—serve at the local, regional, and national levels. Karimi's philanthropy and *seva* were recognized by Aga Khan IV in 1997 with the bestowal of the honorific title *Alijah.*

Nizar A. Motani

REFERENCES

Ali, Mumtaz Ali Tajddin S. *"Vazir Mukhi* Jivabhai Bhanji." Karachi, Pakistan: n.p., n.d.

Charney, Michael W. "Burmese." In *American Immigrant Cultures: Builders of a Nation,* edited by David Levinson and Melvin Ember. Vol. 1: 115–118. New York: Macmillan, 1997.

Karimi, Mansoorali. Interview by author, 7 March 2000, and several other times, March–May 2000.

Malik, Salahuddin. "Pakistanis." In *American Immigrant Cultures: Builders of a Nation,* edited by David Levinson and Melvin Ember. Vol. 2: 674–678. New York: Macmillan, 1997.

Motani, Nizar A. "Ismailis." In *American Immigrant Cultures: Builders of a Nation,* edited by David Levinson and Melvin Ember. Vol. 1: 469–474. New York: Macmillan, 1997.

Kaupas, Casmira (née Kazimiera Kaupaitë) (Mother Maria) (1880–1940)

Founder of the Sisters of St. Casimir Lithuanian

Casmira Kaupas was the founder of the largest women's religious community among Lithuanian immigrants to the United States. Having grown up in a village, she became the most prominent Lithuanian woman in the United States. Membership in her Sisters of St. Casimir would one day reach nearly 500.

Kaupas was born in Lithuania, in Gudeliai village, County of Panevežys, on 6 January 1880. Her brother, Father Antanas Kaupas, invited her to his parish in Scranton, Pennsylvania, where she served as housekeeper from 1897 to 1901. In these new surroundings, observing women who had taken religious vows and were in nuns' communities, the devout young woman became acquainted with religious life, suppressed in czarist-occupied Lithuania. In 1902 she studied at the Congregation of the Holy Cross in Ingenbohl, Switzerland, to prepare for such a life. Clinging to her dream to start a Lithuanian sisterhood, she returned to Scranton in 1905 to accept further tutelage from the Immaculate Heart Sisters.

Kaupas's stirrings coincided with a decade-long discussion among Lithuanian clergy about the need for a Lithuanian women's community. Father Antanas Staniukynas was cofounder of the fledgling Sisters of St. Casimir in 1907, when two other aspirants joined Kaupas in pledging their vows. Relieved of his parish duties, Staniukynas successfully recruited candidates and collected funds, prompting a move in 1911 to Chicago, the center of Lithuanian life. There, Casmira, whose name was Maria in religious life, became mother general, a post she held until her death. Her lengthy tenure stemmed from the universal admiration of her sisters, despite her willingness to step aside at the 1934 election, prior to her death.

During her tenure, she showed remarkable organizational skills: opening twenty-nine primary schools, three high schools, and two hospitals. During World War I, bishops in Lithuania showed great interest in her work. Accordingly, Mother Maria obtained Pope Benedict XV's consent in 1920 to begin a branch in Lithuania at the Pažaislis Monastery, in Kaunas. Under Mother Maria's guidance, and supported by funding from Chicago, the branch prospered and, in 1934, became autonomous. Beyond these building accomplishments, Mother Maria demonstrated great tact and wit in dealing with Irish bishops as well as with the Lithuanian clergy. On 14 June 1933, the Lithuanian government awarded Mother Maria the Order of Gediminas in recognition of her contribution to the homeland.

Meanwhile, her uncommon holiness left an indelible impression on her followers, who have introduced proceedings in Rome for beatification. In 1989–1990 eye-witness testimony about her heroic virtuous life, secretly taken in emerging Soviet-occupied Lithuania, was brought to the United States. It has taken nine years since then to translate more than 1,000 pertinent letters, as her sisters pursue their cause.

William Wolkovich-Valkavičius

REFERENCES

Brizgys, Vincentas. *Kazimiera Kaupaitë—Motina Marija* (Casimira Kaupas—Mother Maria). Chicago: Draugas, 1982.

Journeys (Sisters of St. Casimir newsletter), 1988 to present, passim.

Kazimiero seserų kongregacija (Congregation of the St. Casimir Sisters). Mount Carmel, PA: Končius, J. Šv., 1932.

Kuzmickus, Sr. Marilyn, and Sr. Agnes Dering, eds. *The Founding of the Sisters of St. Casimir: Mother Maria Kaupas*. Chicago: Claret Center for Resources in Spirituality, 1981.

Wolkovich-Valkavičius, William. *Lithuanian Religious Life in America*. Vol. 3:177–190. Norwood, MA: Lithuanian Parish History Project, 1998.

Kazan, Elia (né Elia Kazanjoglou or Kazanjouglous), (1909–)

Writer and director for stage and cinema
Greek-American

Elia Kazan was a genius of twentieth-century filmmaking and theater. His many fiction and nonfiction works have commanded great attention. His directorial achievements received long-overdue recognition in March 1999, when the Academy of Motion Picture Arts and Sciences bestowed on him its Lifetime Achievement Award.

Elia Kazanjoglou (shortened to Kazan) was born in Constantinople, Asia Minor (modern Turkey), on 7 September 1909, to Greek parents. The family immigrated to the United States when he was four. After living initially in a Greek neighborhood in New York City, his father, a successful rug merchant, moved the family to suburban New Rochelle. Kazan graduated from Williams College and, for a time, attended Yale School of Drama, before returning to New York in 1933. In 1932 he married Molly Day Thatcher and, after her death in 1963, Barbara Loden, an actress-director.

Following a brief acting career with New York's Group Theatre, Kazan became a director. His first major recognition came with Thornton Wilder's *The Skin of Our Teeth* in 1942, which won a Pulitzer Prize and a New York Drama Award for Kazan. He directed *One Touch of Venus* (1943) and *Jacobowsky and the Colonel,* for which he received a Drama Critics' Circle Award in 1944. In 1947, he reached another milestone with his coproduction and direction of Arthur Miller's *All My Sons.* He then began working with Tennessee Williams on the award-winning *Streetcar Named Desire.*

By 1948 Kazan was an influential force in American theater. In that year he, Lee Strasberg, and a number of alumni from the old Group Theater founded the Actors Studio, which nurtured such actors as Paul Newman, Marlon Brando, and James Dean. Kazan continued working on Broadway, directing Arthur Miller's award-winning *Death of a Salesman.* Between 1945 and 1957 Kazan also directed two critically acclaimed films and won Academy Awards as best director for *A Gentlemen's Agreement* (1947) and *On the Waterfront* (1954) and was nominated for two others—*A Streetcar Named Desire* (1951) and *East of Eden* (1955)—followed by only seven other films during the next twenty years, including two based on his own writings, for Kazan had begun to devote more time to writing fiction and nonfiction. His nonfiction book, *America, America* (1962), which also became a movie, marked Kazan's search for his Greek roots and the immigrants' dream of passage to the New World. His novel *The Arrangement* (1967) also was a best-seller and a movie. Kazan wrote seven other books.

Kazan's name, however, was embroiled in the politics of the Cold War and McCarthyism in the 1950s. In his testimony before the House Committee on Un-American Activities, on 10 April 1952, Kazan identified eight people who had been members of the Communist Party with him in the mid-1930s. He became a pariah thereafter, and his Lifetime Achievement Award in 1999 came only after the end of the Cold War.

In recent years he has appeared occasionally in documentaries about Greece. Although he was not involved with the Greek-American community, his career made Greek Americans proud of his accomplishments, and he will definitely leave a legacy in the world of popular arts.

George A. Kourvetaris

REFERENCES

Berlin Film Festival. "Hommage to Elia Kazan." Press Conference, 18 February 1996: www.tinet.ch/VOI/96/berlino/kazan_e.htm (accessed 15 June 2000).

Kazan, Elia. *A Life.* New York: Alfred A. Knopf, 1988.

"The Kennedy Center Honors Elia Kazan." 1983:

www.kennedy-center.org/honors/years/
kazan.html (accessed 15 June 2000).

Kolitsas, Constantine. "Defending Kazan." *Greek American Review,* April 1999, 7.

Kunsankosken Kaupunginkirjasto [Finland]. "Elia Kazan (1909–) Elia Kazanjoglous, 'Gadge.'" [2000]: www. kirjasto.sci.fi/kazan.htm (accessed 15 June 2000).

Mills, Michael. "Elia Kazan: Postage Paid" [1999]: www.moderntimes.com/palace/kazan (accessed 20 June 2000).

Sarris, Andrew. "Kazan's Cold War." *Odyssey,* March/April 1999, 58–61.

Walsh, David. "Hollywood Honors Elia Kazan, Filmmaker and Informer." *World Socialist Web Site Arts Review* (20 February1999): wsws.org/articles/1999/feb1999/kaz1-f20.shtml (accessed 15 June 2000).

Kerkorian, Kerkor "Kirk" (1917–)
Entrepreneur, investor, and philanthropist
Armenian-American

Rising from very humble origins with great business acumen, Kerkor "Kirk" Kerkorian had become the fortieth-wealthiest American by 1999 as well as the single most important donor to Armenian causes in the world. Much of his philanthropy is anonymous.

Kerkorian was one of four children born to an Armenian-immigrant family in Fresno, California, on 6 June 1917. His father, Ahron, was a farmer; his mother, Shushan, was a homemaker. The family had emigrated from Kharpert (Harput), Armenia, in 1905. His father made a fortune but lost it in the agricultural depression of 1921–1922, and the family moved to Los Angeles, eking out a precarious existence. At age sixteen, Kirk dropped out of school and made his way boxing but was not physically big enough to be a pro.

In 1939 Kerkorian fell in love with planes and became a professional pilot, serving in World War II by flying bombers to England and earning $1,000 a month, tax free. Afterward, he made his first million dollars buying and selling surplus air force planes and operating a charter flight business. Armenians helped him by investing in the fledgling company. When he sold Trans International Airlines in 1966, his profit was $104 million.

In 1954 Kerkorian married Las Vegas showgirl Jean Maree Hardy, and had two daughters, Linda and Tracy. A daughter, Kira Rose, was born in 1998 from a second marriage. His close attachment to Las Vegas soon led to his purchasing hotel sites, then movie studios, a one-seventh ownership of Chrysler, and other businesses. In 1999 he continued to have interests in hotels, casinos, a luxury airline, and a Las Vegas theme park. *Forbes* magazine estimated his wealth in 1999 at $7.3 billion dollars.

With all that, Kerkorian, an intensely shy man, developed a reputation as an honest businessman but one who jealously guarded his privacy. He has given millions anonymously to Armenian causes and more than 20 percent of his net worth to charities, schools, old-age homes, and so on. Consistent with his desire to stay out of the spotlight, no buildings bear his name. It was also through the efforts of Kerkorian's Lincy Foundation that the United Armenian Fund (UAF) was founded in 1989 to bring humanitarian and rehabilitation aid to Armenia. The UAF is composed of many of the principal Armenian secular and religious organizations in the United States; since 1989, it has sent over $235 million in humanitarian supplies to Armenia. During the energy crisis in 1993 and 1994, Kerkorian contributed $14 million dollars to enable fuel to reach Armenia's homes and offices. "I just want to help Armenia in any way I can," he said. "It's a wonderful country; they're wonderful people." Indeed, Kerkorian made other contributions worth over $200 million.

Kerkorian's commitment is not limited to the Republic of Armenia. He has become the largest donor to Armenian-American causes in the history of the community, donating great sums to the Armenian church, Armenian day schools, the California Armenian Home in his birthplace, Fresno, California, and to a myriad other causes. Not surprisingly, in 1993 *Armenian International Magazine* named Kerkorian "Man of the Year" for his philanthropy to Armenian causes.

Barlow Der Mugrdechian

REFERENCES

Arax, Mark. "Uncommon Impact, Kirk Kerkorian: Man of the Year." *Armenian International Magazine,* December 1993.

Asatrian, Hagop, and Salpi Haroutinian Ghazarian. "Kerkorian's Newest Bold Venture." *Armenian International Magazine,* November/December 1997.

Haroutinian Ghazarian, Salpi. "Mr. Kerkorian Goes to Yerevan." *Armenian International Magazine,* August 1998.

McClintock, David. "Third Try at the Club." *Forbes* 160.13 (15 December 1997).

Torgerson, Dial. *Kerkorian: An American Success Story.* New York: Dial Press, 1974.

Kerouac, Jean-Louis "Jack" (1922–1969)

Novelist, poet, and essayist
Franco-American

Known to the reading public as a founding member of the Beat Generation of the 1950s, Jack Kerouac possessed a less visible identity as a working-class, Roman Catholic Franco-American. In fact, he recounted that early life in various novels that are deeply rooted in his ethnic, religious, and familial background.

Born in Lowell, Massachusetts, on 12 March 1922, the third child of immigrants from Quebec, Jean-Louis Kerouac spoke only French until the age of six. Although he was an athlete who harbored dreams of becoming a famous writer, Kerouac's athletic career at Columbia University came to an end after a gridiron injury, but it was there that his writing career began to take shape. After brief stints in the Merchant Marine and in the U.S. Navy during World War II, Kerouac returned to New York, where he met Allen Ginsberg, William Burroughs, and others with whom he would found the Beat Generation.

Bored or frustrated by the postwar attitudes of U.S. society, Kerouac and his Beat colleagues led bohemian lifestyles that included vagabond wanderings, the study of Eastern religions, free sex, listening to jazz, and the use of alcohol and drugs. Kerouac served as a chronicler of these adventures in *On the Road* (1957) and similar novels. It was also in this setting that he met his first two wives, Frankie Edith Parker and Joan Haverty, the latter with whom he had a daughter, Janet Michelle (1952–1996), who herself became an author. Still, ever faithful to the motto on the Lebris de Keroack family crest—*aimer, travailler, souffrir* (love, work, suffer)—Kerouac had one true love in life, his writing, at which he worked constantly and prolifically, and which caused him great suffering whenever it was rejected, altered, panned, or misinterpreted by readers.

In an equally spiritual quest to better understand his youth in Lowell and his identity as a Franco-American and Roman Catholic, Kerouac related his feelings about faith, ethnic values, family ties, and so on, in such novels as *The Town and the City* (1950), *Doctor Sax* (1959), *Maggie Cassidy* (1959), *Visions of Gerard* (1963), and *Vanity of Duluoz* (1968). Collectively referred to as the Lowell novels, these works reveal the more quiet, private, conservative working-class hometown boy. Nevertheless, as a Franco-American, Kerouac's connection with and image within his ethnic community remain ambiguous. Having had close ties to the community during his formative years, he saw these ties weaken during his adulthood. Despite that, in 1950, in a letter to critic Yvonne Le Maître (a reviewer for *Le Travailleur,* of Worcester, Massachusetts), Kerouac proudly declared, "All my knowledge rests in my 'French Canadianness' and nowhere else."

Although in his lifetime he drew criticism from many French-speaking-community leaders for both his unconventional lifestyle and his choice of English rather than French as his language of literary expression, after his death Kerouac gained the respect of most Franco-American activists, who recognize the community's evolution toward a more bilingual and bicultural status. Some even consider him an icon, the community's most famous writer.

In 1966, his health declining, Kerouac married Stella Sampas. They and his elderly mother returned to live in Lowell but eventually moved to St. Petersburg, Florida, where Kerouac died on 21 October 1969, at the age of forty-seven, the victim of alcoholism. He is buried in Edson Cemetery in Lowell.

Robert B. Perreault

REFERENCES

Anctil, Pierre, et al., eds. *Un homme grand: Jack Kerouac at the Crossroads of Many Cultures/Jack Kérouac à la confluence des cultures.* Bilingual edition. Ottawa: Carleton University Press, 1990.

Beaulieu, Victor-Lévy. *Jack Kérouac: Essai-poulet.* Montréal: Editions du Jour, 1972; *Jack Kerouac: A Chicken-Essay,* translated by Sheila Fischman. Toronto: Coach House Press, 1976.

Nicosia, Gerald. *Memory Babe: A Critical Biography of Jack Kerouac.* New York: Grove Press, 1983.

Perreault, Robert B. "Au-delà de la route: L'identité franco-américaine de Jack Kerouac" (Beyond the road: The Franco-American identity of Jack Kerouac). In *La littérature franco-américaine: Écrivains et écritures* (Franco-American literature: Writers and writings), edited by Claire Quintal, 88–107. Worcester, MA: Institut français, Collège de l'Assomption, 1992.

Sorrell, Richard S. "Kerouac's Lowell: 'Little Canada' and the Ethnicity of Jack Kerouac." *Essex Institute Historical Collections* 117.4 (October 1981): 262–282.

Turner, Steve, *Angelheaded Hipster: A Life of Jack Kerouac.* New York: Viking Penguin, 1996.

Woolfson, Peter. "The French-Canadian Heritage of Jack Kerouac as Seen in His Autobiographical Works." *Louisiana Review* 5.1 (Summer 1976): 35–43.

Kilian, Jan (1811–1884)
Clergy
Wend (Sorb)

Jan Kilian was a moving force in the migration of the largest single group of Wends, or Sorbs (550), from Europe to the United States. Once the group was established, he provided religious guidance as well as leadership to preserve the Wendish language and culture. In the United States members of this ethnic group are called Wends; the people are called Sorbs in Europe. They are the remnants of the Slavs in central Europe who resisted removal or assimilation by the Germans. Their homeland is in Germany, roughly between Dresden and the Polish and Czech borders.

Kilian, born in Germany, in a village east of the city of Bautzen, Saxony, grew up in a bilingual environment. He attended the gymnasium in Bautzen, where he developed his skills in Wendish, even though the instruction was largely in German. After graduation he studied theology at the University of Leipzig and eventually became the pastor of a small parish near his birthplace.

Kilian took an active interest in the improvement of the Wendish people of his parish and participated in the movement to preserve the Wendish language and culture against German assimilation. He was especially active in translating such religious materials as Luther's *Catechism* and the *Augsburg Confession* from German into Wendish. He also composed hymns and songs in Wendish. The desire to preserve the Wendish language was a factor in the group migration to Texas in 1854. But even more important than language maintenance was the religious motive. Some Wends in Prussia objected strenuously to the efforts of the Prussian government to force a union between the Lutheran church and the Reformed church in order to create a single state church. Kilian was the pastor of an independent congregation in Prussia, and the goal of these dissidents became the establishment of a Wendish Lutheran congregation and settlement in Texas.

An association of lay leaders purchased a league of land in present-day Lee County. Most of the Wends became farmers, and some resided in their village, called Serbin. They built a church and school, and Kilian served as both as pastor and teacher. Whereas in Germany Kilian's adversaries had been state and ecclesiastical officials, in Texas the adversaries were often members of his own flock. Methodists attempted to convert them, and even though nearly all remained Lutheran, the stage was set for individuals who preferred greater fervor within church services and a greater emphasis on German in church and school. Although Kilian did preserve a large central core of his membership and continued to preach and teach in Wendish, individuals and groups left and formed their own congregations. Nonetheless, the rural congregation in

Serbin still worships in the stone church erected during Kilian's time. However, Wendish language succumbed to German as more Germans moved into the area, and even Kilian's use of German increased over time. Eventually, especially during World War I, German gave way to English.

Within the context of dramatic changes and adaptation to Texas life, Kilian served as a stabilizing force in the cultural and religious aspect of the Wends' lives. He died in 1884.

George R. Nielsen

REFERENCES

Malinkowa, Truda. *Ufer der Hoffnung* (Shore of hope). Bautzen, Germany: Domowina Verlag, 1995.

Nielsen, George R. *In Search of Home: Nineteenth-Century Wendish Migration.* College Station: Texas A&M University Press, 1989.

Wilson, Joe. "Pastor John Kilian." In *The New Handbook of Texas,* edited by Ron Tyler, 3:1094. Austin, TX: State Historical Association, 1996.

King, Martin Luther, Jr. (1929–1968)

Minister, civil rights leader,
and Nobel laureate
African American

The 1964 Civil Rights Act and the 1965 Voting Rights Act were the results of the Civil Rights movement and the leadership of Dr. Martin Luther King, Jr., whose strategy of nonviolent civil disobedience was that movement's dominant force. For his achievements King was awarded the Nobel Peace Prize in 1964.

King was born in Atlanta, Georgia, on 15 January 1929, one of three children of Martin Luther King, Sr., pastor of Ebenezer Baptist Church, and Alberta (Williams) King, a former schoolteacher. The family was already prominent as civil rights activists. King attended segregated schools and entered Morehouse College. Before receiving his B.A. in sociology in 1948, King was influenced by Morehouse's president to pursue a career in the ministry. He attended Crozer Theological Seminary, in Chester, Pennsylvania, and completed a doctoral program at Boston University in 1955. In 1953, he married Coretta Scott; they had four children.

In 1954, King accepted the pastorate of Dexter Avenue Baptist Church in Montgomery, Alabama. The Montgomery bus boycott in December 1955—which lasted 328 days and resulted in a November 1956 U.S. Supreme Court action affirming a lower court decision declaring segregated intrastate buses unconstitutional—marked the beginning of King's leadership of the modern Civil Rights movement. He became nationally recognized and, in 1957, one of the founders— and president—of the Southern Christian Leadership Conference (SCLC). The ideals of this organization drew on King's philosophy of social justice, Christian principles, civil disobedience, and nonviolence. From then on, King traveled more than 6 million miles, spoke publicly more than 2,500 times, was arrested about 30 times, and assaulted at least 4 times. His writings include *Why We Can't Wait* (1964) and *Where Do We Go from Here: Chaos or Community?* (1967).

It was King's involvement in the 1963 Birmingham protest to desegregate department stores and encourage fair hiring practices that demonstrated the extent of southern resistance to racial justice. The brutal assault on blacks by the police and their dogs, captured on television, horrified the nation and the world. While in jail for leading the demonstration, King wrote "Letter from a Birmingham Jail," which became a classic defense of the Civil Rights movement. The same year, standing at the Lincoln Memorial during the 28 August 1963 March on Washington, he delivered his famous "I Have a Dream" speech. By then, federal officials had recognized that the government had to respond to the Civil Rights movement. King's prominence and philosophy of civil rights protest, along with the efforts of several black activist groups, led to the passage of the Civil Rights Act of 1964. And in that year, King, at age thirty-five, became the youngest man to receive the Nobel Peace Prize. In 1965, he challenged the limited voting rights of blacks and led the five-day Selma to Montgomery (Alabama) march, which resulted in the 1965 Voting Rights Act.

Not long afterward, with Black Power gaining ascendancy and the violence of the urban riots, even King, assessing his failed 1966 Chicago campaign, began to realize that nonviolent civil disobedience was not sufficient to fight institutional racism. And foreseeing that the struggle against racial injustice was being undermined by war, he escalated his anti–Vietnam War protest. Also, in 1967, he initiated a multiethnic Poor People's campaign as his new civil rights agenda. In Memphis to support a sanitation workers' strike, he was assassinated on 4 April 1968. Black America was devastated and expressed its rage in riots.

It was in death that his opponents finally understood the significance of King's nonviolent civil disobedience. Thus, in 1986, his birthday was designated a federal public holiday.

Juliet E. K. Walker

REFERENCES

Albert, Peter J., and Ronald Hoffman. *We Shall Overcome: Martin Luther King, Jr., and the Black Freedom Struggle.* New York: Pantheon Books, 1990.

Branch, Taylor. *Parting the Waters: America in the King Years, 1954–1963.* New York: Simon & Schuster, 1988.

Burns, Stewart. *Daybreak of Freedom: The Montgomery Bus Boycott.* Chapel Hill: University of North Carolina Press, 1997.

Cone, James H. *Malcolm and Martin and America: A Dream or a Nightmare?* Maryknoll, NY: Orbis Books, 1991.

Garrow, David J. *Bearing the Cross: Martin Luther King, Jr., and the Southern Christian Leadership Conference.* New York: Random House, 1988.

———. *The FBI and Martin Luther King, Jr.* New York: W. W. Norton, 1981.

Lewis, David Levering. *King: A Biography.* Urbana: University of Illinois Press, 1978.

Morris, Aldon D. *The Origins of the Modern Civil Rights Movement: Black Communities Organizing for Change.* New York: Free Press, 1984.

Kingston, Maxine Hong (1940–)
Author and professor
Chinese-American

Maxine Hong Kingston is perhaps the most celebrated Asian American author. Through her well-crafted, riveting works she has played an instrumental role in introducing Asian American literature to the American public.

Kingston was born on 27 October 1940 in Stockton, California. Both of her parents—Chew Ying Lan and Tom Hong—were immigrants from China who were well educated but suffered from occupational downgrading in the United States. In Stockton they ran a laundry with the help of their six children. Kingston spent her free time reading Chinese literary classics, which her parents had brought from China, and attending Chinese operas. The myths and family history passed down by the Hongs would eventually make their way into Kingston's novels. At home Kingston conversed mainly in Cantonese; English was her second language. Yet, by the age of nine she had made sufficient progress in mastering English to begin composing poetry in that language.

When she first attended the University of California, Berkeley, she majored in engineering but soon switched to English literature. However, although she did not find such studies useful for her own creative writing, Berkeley was seething with political protest, which did profoundly affect her. Echoes of that era would surface in her writings. In between earning her undergraduate degree in 1962 and moving to Hawai'i in 1967, she married Earl Kingston and gave birth to a son, Joseph. In Hawai'i, as she had in California, she taught at the high school and college levels.

Teaching—and perhaps raising a family—seemed to be her destiny until the publication of her first book, *The Woman Warrior: Memoirs of a Girlhood among Ghosts* (1976). Since the narrative centers on a mother-daughter relationship and the influence of sexism in Chinese-American life, it seems to be part of the then-burgeoning feminist scholarship. But the book is also about the struggle to reconcile the tension between her Chinese ancestry and her American upbringing. Because of its original narrative style and provocative issues, *The Woman Warrior* won numerous honors, culminating with the 1976 National Book Critics Circle Award for nonfiction. It has sold more than 500,000 paperback copies.

Four years later, Kingston published *China Men,* which is seen as a response to allegations that the first work, supposedly anti-male, was an attempt to cash in on the "feminist fad." *China Men* focuses on the men and their historical deeds and explores themes of emigration, struggle, oppression, and assimilation. Kingston again won the National Book Critics' Circle Award for general nonfiction. Fewer accolades greeted Kingston's first full-fledged work of fiction, *Tripmaster Monkey: His Fake Book* (1989), for it was overshadowed by the publication of Amy Tan's *The Joy Luck Club* (1989). Since Kingston's success with her first book, works by women writers that deal with Asian American, female-centered issues have indeed proliferated. Today, Kingston's works remind Americans of the willpower of early Chinese immigrants even as they endured manifold sufferings. Her innovative narratives also challenge the parameters of the genre and, thus, have encouraged writers to experiment and defy conventions.

Benson Tong

REFERENCES

Kim, Elaine H. "Visions and Fierce Dreams: A Commentary on the Works of Maxine Hong Kingston." *Amerasia Journal* 8.2 (1981): 145–161.

Ling, Amy. *Between Worlds: Women Writers of Chinese Ancestry.* New York: Pergamon Press, 1990.

Skandera-Trombley, Laura. *Critical Essays on Maxine Hong Kingston.* New York: G. K. Hall, 1998.

Knudsen, William S. (né Signius Wilhelm Poul Knudsen) (1879–1948)

Corporate executive
Danish

Described by Henry Ford as "a wizard of mass production," William S. Knudsen was a major contributor to the automobile revolution. He rose from poor immigrant to president of General Motors. So great was his reputation as a "production genius" that Franklin D. Roosevelt named him to a variety of posts during World War II and awarded him the rank of lieutenant general, the highest military rank ever given a civilian.

Born in Copenhagen in 1879 to customs inspector Knud Peter Knudsen and his wife, Augusta Zoller, he was christened Signius Wilhelm Poul Knudsen. The family was poor, and young Knudsen went to work after school at age six. He was a strong student, particularly in mathematics, and graduated from a technical school with honors. In 1900, Knudsen immigrated to New York, seeking work as a bicycle mechanic.

In 1902, he finally found employment with a bicycle manufacturer, the John R. Keim Mills, in Buffalo, New York. But the bicycle craze was fading, and the Keim plant was beginning to manufacture automobile parts. In 1906, Keim obtained a large order from the Ford Motor Company and soon became one of its major suppliers. In 1911, Ford bought the company and soon called Knudsen to Detroit. By 1916 he was in charge of twenty-eight assembly plants. During World War I, he was superintendent of Ford's war production and afterwards supervised the company's renewed production of the Model T. However, tensions between Ford and Knudsen increased, and Knudsen resigned in 1921.

Rather quickly he was named vice president of operations for the Chevrolet Division of General Motors (GM). Two years later, he became president and general manager of Chevrolet and a GM vice president and director. He pioneered "flexible" mass production techniques, creating greater options in body styles, colors, and power train. Soon, Chevrolet surpassed Ford in sales. In October 1933, Knudsen began coordinating production for all of GM's car-manufacturing divisions and, four years later, became president of General Motors.

In May 1940, shortly after Germany occupied Denmark, President Roosevelt asked Knudsen to chair the National Defense Advisory Council (NDAC). Knudsen resigned his $459,000 position and went to work for the government at no salary. In January 1941, he and Sidney Hillman, president of the Amalgamated Clothing Workers Union, were named codirectors of the Office of Production Management (OPM). After the United States entered the war, Knudsen was appointed lieutenant general in the army and director of war production for the War Department, remaining in that position until 1945. He then returned to General Motors as a member of the board of directors and consultant. He died in 1948.

Knudsen had become a U.S. citizen in 1914 and was honored by both his homeland and his adopted country. In 1932, the king of Denmark knighted Knudsen. During World War II, the United States awarded him two Distinguished Service Medals, the nation's highest noncombat-earned military honor.

In 1911 Knudsen had married Clara Elizabeth Euler. Their only son, Semon Emil, served as president of GM's Pontiac and, later, Chevrolet Divisions and, in 1968, became president of the Ford Motor Company.

Peter L. Petersen

REFERENCES

Beasley, Norman. *Knudsen: A Biography.* New York: Whittlesey House, 1947.

Borth, Christy. *Masters of Mass Production.* Indianapolis: Bobbs-Merrill, 1945.

Cray, Ed. *Chrome Colossus: General Motors and Its Times.* New York: McGraw-Hill, 1980.

Flink, James J. "William Signius Knudsen." In *The Automobile Industry, 1920–1980,* edited by George S. May, 265–283. New York: Facts on File, 1989.

Kochiyama, Yuri (1921–)
Community and political activist
Japanese-American

Since her politicization in the 1960s, Yuri Kochiyama has been active in championing the rights of the oppressed all over the world. Active in the Civil Rights and Black Liberation movements, she became known to the general public in 1965 when a *Life* magazine cover showed her holding Malcolm X's head after he was shot.

Kochiyama was born as Mary Nakahara in San Pedro, California, in 1921, the home of a substantial Japanese-American community, most of whom were involved in the fishing industry, including her father. Young Mary attended San Pedro High School, where she was active in such typical small-town activities as sports and Sunday school.

One of the turning points of her life came with the Japanese attack on Pearl Harbor on 7 December 1941. That evening government officials came and took away her father, Seiichi Nakahara, despite his having just been released from the hospital after surgery the day before. He died after six weeks in detention. The remaining family members were forcibly removed from the West Coast in spring 1942, along with all other Japanese Americans. The Nakaharas were first incarcerated in Santa Anita "Assembly Center," then taken to the Jerome internment camp in Arkansas in fall 1942. In Jerome, Nakahara taught school and Sunday school and also organized young women in camp to write letters to Japanese-American soldiers stationed overseas. Through this letter-writing endeavor, she met a handsome GI from New York named Bill Kochiyama, whom she would subsequently marry.

The couple moved to New York after the war and had six children. A second turning point in her life came when the growing family moved to Harlem in 1960. Her first experience with activism came with the Harlem Parents Committee and their demands for more traffic lights at an intersection where several children had been hit by cars. She soon became caught up in the Civil Rights and Black Liberation movements during the 1960s, as did her entire family. Three of her children attended the Harlem Freedom School and often accompanied her to demonstrations, sometimes being arrested with her.

Kochiyama is perhaps best known for her friendship with Malcolm X. A famous *Life* magazine cover shows her holding Malcolm's head in her hands after he had been shot at the Audubon Ballroom in Harlem in 1965. She was a member of Malcolm's Organization of

Afro-American Unity and also was active in the Puerto Rican independence movement.

In the years since, she has been active in the anti–Vietnam War movement, in support of ethnic studies on college campuses, and in support of political prisoners around the world. She has taught and lectured all over the country and also remained active in the Japanese-American community, especially in the movement for reparations for Japanese-American internment during World War II. She has often implored other Japanese Americans, particularly those who have experienced the racism of mass internment, to support other people's fights for freedom and justice. Most recently, she has been one of the leading figures in the efforts to free activist and death row inmate Mumia Abu-Jamal.

Kochiyama has inspired a generation of young activists of all ethnic backgrounds and has been the subject of two documentary films and two forthcoming biographies. In 1999, a residence hall lounge at the University of Michigan was named in her honor.

Brian Niiya

REFERENCES

Fujino, Diane. "The Making of an Asian American Woman Activist: Revolutionary Soldier Yuri Kochiyama." In *Dragon Ladies: Asian American Feminists Breathe Fire,* edited by Sonia Shan, 169–181. Boston: South End Press, 1997.

Kochiyama, Yuri. *Discover Your Mission: Selected Speeches and Writings of Yuri Kochiyama,* edited by Russell Muranaka. Los Angeles: UCLA Asian American Studies Center, June 1998.

Kochiyama, Yuri (as told to Sasha Hohri). "Because Movement Work Is Contagious." *Gidra, 1990,* 6, 10.

My America . . . Or Honk If You Love Buddha (1996; directed by Renee Tajima Peña): www.pbs.org/myamerica/honk/ (accessed 20 June 2000).

Yuri Kochiyama: A Passion for Justice (1993; directed by Pat Saunders and Rea Tajiri).

Kohut, Rebekah Bettelheim (1864–1951)
Educator and social work activist
Jewish-American

Rebekah Bettelheim Kohut made her mark as a social welfare activist and educator. She took "pride in her people" and "glory in [her] religion," and dedicated herself to fulfilling the obligations of *tsedakah* (righteousness) by working for the "betterment of the general Jewish lot" and for a "humane civilization."

Bettelheim was born in Kaschau, Hungary, to Albert Siegfried Bettelheim, a rabbi and physician, and Henrietta Weintraub, a schoolteacher, who immigrated to the United States with their five children in 1867. Her later pursuit of higher education at the University of California, Berkeley, aroused "considerable objection" from the board of the synagogue her father served, but he championed her cause.

Inspired by her mother, Bettelheim aspired to "a career of service" and "significant work" rather than "a life limited to housewifely duties." However, on a trip to New York City in 1886, she met Alexander Kohut, a distinguished rabbi and scholar of Hungarian origin, twenty-two years older than she and a widower with eight children. She and Kohut soon married. Besides running a household of ten people, Kohut instituted and ran the sisterhood of her husband's synagogue, did volunteer work for the Women's Health Protective Association, and directed a kindergarten on the Lower East Side of New York. Although rebelling against the unequal treatment of women in the synagogue, she still fulfilled the traditional roles of wife and mother but interpreted these broadly.

It was her husband's death in 1894 and the prospect of gradual impoverishment that moved Kohut to pursue a more active public life and a career. She became a well-known speaker on cultural and literary topics. In 1899, with the aid of Jacob Schiff, the New York banker and philanthropist, she opened the Kohut College Preparatory School for Girls, a day and boarding institution that enrolled over 100 students per year. Throughout her life, Kohut remained an advocate of Jewish causes and reform. As president of the New York Council of Jewish Women (1897–1901), she promoted Jewish women's activism, spoke for women's suffrage, and was committed to religious "suffrage" for Jewish women and better education and broader social opportunities than were usually accorded them at that time. In the Hebrew tradition of *tikkun olam* (the obligation to repair or improve the world), she continued to be a model of the productive Jewish woman involved in constructive social purposes.

Beginning in 1914, Kohut headed the Young Women's Hebrew Association employment bureau and, during World War I, chaired the employment committee of the Women's Committee for National Defense. In 1917, she was appointed to the Federal Employment Clearing House. After the war, under her direction, the National Council of Jewish Women began its relief work for Jewish refugees. In 1923 in Vienna she was elected president of the World Jewish Congress for Women.

Kohut's interests and activities in the area of unemployment intensified during the Great Depression. In 1931 she was appointed to the New York State Advisory Council on Employment and, in 1932, served on the Joint Legislative Commission of Unemployment. Until her death in 1951 at age eighty-seven, Kohut remained active and effective in philanthropic and social welfare organizations.

Gerald Sorin

REFERENCES

Baum, Charlotte, Paula Hyman, and Sonya Michel. *The Jewish Woman in America.* New York: Dial Press, 1976.

Kohut, Rebekah. *More Yesterdays: An Autobiography (1925–1949).* New York: Bloch Publishing Co., 1950.

———. *My Portion (An Autobiography).* New York: T. Seltzer, 1925.

Marcus, Jacob Rader. *The American Jewish Woman: A Documentary History.* New York: Ktav Publishing Co., 1981.

Rogow, Faith. *"Gone to Another Meeting": The National Council of Jewish Women, 1893–1993.* Tuscaloosa: University of Alabama Press, 1993.

Kolff, Willem Johan (1911–)
Physician and biomedical engineer
Dutch

Willem Kolff is a notable physician and biomedical engineer. Among his many accomplishments, he is best known for his work on the artificial kidney and kidney dialysis and for leading the medical team that implanted the first artificial heart in a human.

Kolff was born in Leiden, the Netherlands, in 1911. His father was a physician specializing in the treatment of tuberculosis. The elder Kolff encouraged his son's interest in medicine and instilled in him a lifelong desire to alleviate suffering. Fond of animals, young Kolff thought he might become a zoologist before eventually dedicating himself to the care of people.

Because he was dyslexic, Kolff did not enjoy reading, nor did he have an easy time at school. He loved carpentry, however, and working with his hands, building things and tinkering with machinery. The unusual combination of medical expertise and mechanical dexterity eventually led him to invent extraordinary biomedical devices that would improve the quality of life for countless people.

Kolff graduated from the University of Leiden medical school in 1938 and did postgraduate study at the University of Groningen. One of his first patients was a twenty-two-year-old man slowly dying from kidney disease and toxins in his bloodstream. After helplessly watching the young man die, Kolff searched for a way to purify the blood of poisonous wastes. Originally, he planned to work in Indonesia, but World War II intervened and he was forced to stay in the Netherlands. In 1940, as Germany bombed Holland, Kolff organized a blood bank in the Hague, the first blood bank in continental Europe (the concept came from England). In 1943, while working in a small-town hospital in Nazi-occupied Holland, he quietly developed, using smuggled materials, the first kidney dialysis machine. To prevent the Nazis from taking credit for his discoveries, he published his research findings in Scandinavian journals. His fierce loyalty toward the Dutch cause in World

War II led to his receiving the Landsteiner Silver Medal in 1942 from the Red Cross of the Netherlands.

After the war, at age thirty-nine, Kolff immigrated to the United States with his wife and children, becoming a naturalized citizen in 1956. He began work at the Cleveland Clinic Foundation, developing artificial organs. In 1967 he joined the University of Utah faculty and was named director of the Institute for Biomedical Engineering. At the institute, Kolff worked on developing an implantable human heart. On 2 December 1982, he led the surgical team that implanted the Jarvik-7 artificial heart in Barney Clark.

In addition to the kidney dialysis machine and artificial heart, Kolff has also made significant contributions to intra-aortic balloon pumping, organ preservation for transplants, and the development of other artificial organs and prostheses. He has published more than 600 papers and several books. Among his many honors, he was inducted into the Inventor's Hall of Fame and was named one of *Life* magazine's 100 Most Important Americans of the Twentieth Century. Although Kolff has not been closely allied with the Dutch-immigrant community in the United States, he is nonetheless proud of his Dutch heritage and the rigorous education he received in the Netherlands.

Jennifer Leo

REFERENCES

Adler, Jerry, and Jeff B. Copeland. "The Trio Who Did It." *Newsweek,* 13 December 1982, 73.

Keck, Patricia S., and John J. Meserko. "Willem J. Kolff: Pioneer in Artificial Organ Research." *Proceedings of the American Academy of Cardiovascular Perfusion* 6 (January 1985). Available online: members.aol.com/amaccvpe/history/history.htm (accessed May 20, 2000).

"Kolff, Willem Johan." *American Men and Women of Science.* 18th ed. 4:454. New Providence, NJ: R. R. Bowker, 1992.

McMurray, Emily J., ed. *Notable Twentieth Century Scientists.* Detroit: Gale Research, 1995.

Saari, Peggy, and Stephen Allison, eds. *Scientists: The Lives and Works of 150 Scientists.* Detroit: Gale Research, 1996.

Kono, Tamio "Tommy" (1930–)
Weightlifter, bodybuilder, and coach
Japanese-American

A world champion eight times and an Olympic gold medalist twice, Tommy Kono is probably the greatest American weightlifter of all time. His achievements have helped reduce the stereotypes of Japanese Americans as nonathletic and, in so doing, served as a role model for Japanese-American males, significantly encouraging them to develop more positive self-images.

Kono was born in Sacramento, California, the youngest of four sons of Kanichi and Ichibi Kono. In 1942, the Konos, along with other Japanese Americans who lived on the West Coast, were forcibly removed and sent to American internment camps. The family ended up at the Tule Lake center, in northern California, near the Oregon border. As a boy, Kono had been plagued with chronic asthma. However, the dry weather at Tule Lake helped relieve his condition, and he began to lift weights, encouraged by a neighbor and other weightlifters in the camp.

In 1945, Kono and his parents returned to Sacramento, where he graduated from high school. (His older brothers had earlier "resettled" in the Midwest and East.) He began training with weights at the Sacramento Young Men's Christian Association (YMCA) and was coaxed into his first competition at age seventeen, where he took second place in his weight class. For the next two years, he continued to train. In his first national championship meet in 1950 he placed second in the lightweight (148-pound) division. Drafted in 1951, he continued to compete while in the army and was, in fact, sent to local and national competitions by the army once his Olympic potential was noted.

In 1952, he set his first world record, won his first national title, and made the U.S. Olympic team. At the games in Helsinki, Finland, Kono won the gold medal in the lightweight division, the first of eight consecutive world championships he would win. In part to challenge himself, Kono moved up and down in weight class. After winning the 1953 world title in the middleweight (165-pound) division, he moved up to the light-heavyweight division (181 pounds) in 1954 and won his next three world championships in that division, including his second Olympic gold medal in 1956, setting a world record in the process. He won his next three world championships as a middleweight.

In the 1960 Olympics, he finished second in the middleweight division, ending his world championship string. Coming back stronger than ever in 1961, he set a world record in the light-heavyweight division at the Prize of Moscow meet. Primed to regain the world title in the middleweight division, he failed to make weight in a hotly disputed judgment. Forced to compete in a higher weight class, he finished third. In between these many major weightlifting meets, Kono also entered bodybuilding contests and won four major titles, including "Mr. Universe" three times.

Throughout his career, Kono's exploits were closely followed in the Japanese-American popular press, and he remains one of the best-known athletes within his ethnic group. He retired from competition in 1965 and opened a gym in Maui. He later coached the Mexican national team for the 1968 Olympics and the German national team for the 1972 Olympics. Still active in weightlifting circles today as a coach, official, and promoter of the sport, Kono lives on the island of Oahu in Hawai`i.

Brian Niiya

REFERENCES

Day, A. Grove. "America's Mightiest Little Man." *Coronet*, July 1960, 106–110.

Fair, John D. "Bob Hoffman, the York Barbell Company, and the Golden Age of American Weightlifting, 1945–1960." *Journal of Sport History* 14.2 (Summer 1987): 164–188.

Mason, William Reynolds. "A History of Men's Competitive Weightlifting in the United States from Its Inception through 1972." Master's thesis, University of Washington, 1973.

Krol, John Joseph (1910–1996)
Roman Catholic priest, bishop, and cardinal
Polish-American

John Cardinal Krol, the son of immigrant parents, became a prince of the Roman Catholic church, the first Polish-American cardinal. He was also an elector of the first pope from Poland.

The fourth of eight children, Krol was born in Cleveland, Ohio, to John and Anna (Pietruszka) Krol, who were from Poland's Tatra Mountains. His father was a machinist. Krol attended the Latin School and Polish Seminary in Orchard Lake, Michigan, and Cleveland's St. Mary's Seminary. He was ordained in 1937. Krol's career followed a classic career track for American prelates. He studied canon law at Rome's Gregorian University and earned his doctorate in canon law from the Catholic University of America. He taught at St. Mary's seminary, served in various administrative capacities in Cleveland dioceses, and was consecrated auxiliary bishop in 1953. In 1961 Pope John XXIII named Krol the archbishop of Philadelphia, the fourth-largest diocese in the United States. He was the first Polish American to lead a major U.S. diocese and to be an archbishop.

At the Second Vatican Council (1962–1965), Krol was one of the council's six permanent undersecretaries. Pope Paul VI elevated him to cardinal in 1967. He served on several pontifical commissions and chaired (1982–1992) the Prefecture of Economic Affairs of the Holy See. He was equally prominent in the American Catholic hierarchy, serving as vice president (1966–1971) and president (1971–1974) of the National Conference of Catholic Bishops and in 1976 as host of the Forty-first Eucharist Congress in Philadelphia. A formidable administrator and a person of compassion, Krol restored Philadelphia's diocesan school system, was an advocate for government funds for religious-affiliated schools, expanded the number of parishes and the services for refugees, the hungry, and the old, and promoted ecumenism and racial understanding. Although a politically conservative churchman, he also supported nuclear disarmament and the "moral imperative" of preventing the use of nuclear weapons.

Cardinal Krol was a defender of the integrity of traditional theology, denouncing birth control and abortion as "an unspeakable tragedy for this nation," insisting upon respect for hierarchical authority, and, in the years after Vatican II, criticizing Catholic clergy and laity who insisted upon even greater democratization and social relevance. He was also critical of priests who left the priesthood, and he opposed the easing of regulations about marriages between Catholics and non-Catholics.

Krol was unique in an Irish-dominated American Catholic church. He was the first Polish-American cardinal, one involved in Polish issues. He spoke to the Polish American Congress, criticized violations of human rights in Poland, spoke on Radio Free Europe and the Voice of America, and raised funds for the Catholic League for Religious Assistance to Poland. In 1966 he was prominent in commemorations of the Millennium of Poland's Christianity and later rescued the Czçstochowa Shrine in Doylestown, Pennsylvania, from financial ruin. Following martial law in Poland in 1981 and the crackdown on Solidarity, Krol supported relief efforts and was involved in quiet diplomacy. He accepted the Catholic faith as an integral element of Polish ethnic identity and also believed that ethnic identity responded to the need to enrich "mature pluralism" with one's ancestral cultural heritage. Krol retired in 1988 and died in 1996.

Stanislaus A. Blejwas

REFERENCES

"John Cardinal Krol. Twenty-five Years in Philadelphia." *Catholic Standard and Times* (Philadelphia, PA; Commemorative Edition), 3 April 1986.

"Krol, John Cardinal." In *Current Biography Yearbook 1969,* edited by Charles Moritz, 251–253. New York: H. W. Wilson, 1969.

"Krol, John Cardinal." *In Who's Who in America 1995,* 45th ed., vol. 1: 2095. New Providence, NJ: Reed Reference Publishing, 1995.

Nir, Reverend Roman. "Wielki Kardynał, Wielki Polak." *Przegląd Polski in Nowy Dziennik* (Polish daily news, New York), 14 March 1996, 4.

Steinfels, Peter. "John Cardinal Krol, Pivotal Catholic Figure, Dies at Eighty-five." *New York Times,* 4 March 1996.

Kübler–Ross, Elizabeth (1926–)
Psychiatrist
Swiss

Her assistance to people in war-torn Europe between 1944 and 1951 and service as a country physician in a Swiss farming village led Elizabeth Kübler-Ross to focus her American career on three concerns: the personalized, loving approach to patients beyond the mere application of medical technology; the existential needs of the insane, imprisoned, and the dying; and the probing of the nature of death. Kübler-Ross's efforts eventually fostered the Hospice movement and brought renewed attention to near-death experiences and phenomena explored by parapsychology.

Kübler-Ross was born 8 July 1926 to Ernst Kübler and Emma Villiger in Zurich, Switzerland. That she was born one of triplets intensified her search for personal identity and independence. Early on she became an advocate for the mistreated and discovered the healing power of the beauty found in nature. Working as a young woman in a hospital, she approached the dying as well as the shunned, such as prostitutes, with listening and caring warmth. From 1944 to 1951 she volunteered in various war-ravaged countries, which intensified her understanding of human suffering and the need for a person-oriented care of patients in combination with medical technology. From 1951 to 1957 she completed her medical studies at the University of Zurich, married Emanuel Ross in 1958, an American fellow student, and moved with her husband to New York City, where she completed her residency in psychiatry and applied her unorthodox personalist approach to the mentally ill. From 1962 to 1965 both took positions in Denver, Colorado, and after 1965, in Chicago.

At La Rabida Children's Hospital and at Billings Hospital of the University of Chicago, Kübler-Ross developed seminars on death and dying for students in medicine, nursing, theology, and social work, with terminally ill patients present as the main teachers. A November 1967 article in *Life* magazine and the publication of *On Death and Dying* led not only to an avalanche of mail, invitations to lecture in the United States and abroad, translations of her writings, honorary degrees, and prizes, but also to ostracism. Fellow physicians complained that her work was exploitative of terminally ill patients and was turning attention away from the physician's calling of healing to a preoccupation with death. Undaunted, Kübler-Ross turned to the study of death itself and in 1977 founded a center in Escondido, California, where she also probed spirit appearances.

In 1983 she moved to Headwaters, Virginia, where she transformed a farm into a healing center, hoping to use it also as a hospice for unwanted AIDS babies. Local opposition, however, turned violent and in 1994 culminated in the burning of her center and the loss of her vast documentary collections. Saddened but unbroken, she moved to Scottsdale, Arizona, where she was paralyzed by a stroke in 1995, yet published her autobiography in 1997.

Although one may disagree with her views about the certainty of a personal afterlife, the determining force of destiny, and the wrongness of assisted suicide, her concern for the terminally ill and for a personalized health care, derived from her experiences in Europe and refined in the experiment-friendly atmosphere of the United States, remain influential.

Leo Schelbert

REFERENCES

Gill, Derek. *Quest: The Life of Elizabeth Kübler-Ross.* Epilogue by E. Kübler-Ross. New York: Harper & Row, 1980.

Kübler-Ross, Elizabeth. *Death, the Final Stage of Growth.* Englewood Cliffs, NJ: Prentice Hall, 1975.

———. *On Children and Dying.* New York: Simon & Schuster, 1983.

———. *On Death and Dying.* New York: Macmillan, 1969.

———. *The Wheel of Life. A Memoir of Living and Dying.* New York: Simon & Schuster, 1997.

Kuniyoshi, Yasuo (1889–1953)
Artist and art teacher
Japanese

Japanese-born artist Yasuo Kuniyoshi became a highly respected and beloved figure in the New York art world from the 1920s until his death. His paintings have been regularly exhibited since 1922 and are of continually escalating value to art collectors in the United States and Japan. For many years he also was known in New York City as a fine photographer and art teacher.

Born an only child in Okayama prefecture, on 1 September 1889, Yasuo Kuniyoshi decided early on that he wanted either to enter military school or to go to the United States. Discouraged from the military by his father, he journeyed to the United States at age sixteen in 1906. Arriving in Seattle with little English and no money or friends, he, like many other Issei (Japanese immigrants), took odd jobs to support himself.

In spring 1907 he moved to Los Angeles, attending the Los Angeles School of Art and Design for three years while working as a hotel bellboy and picking fruit. He then went to New York to pursue a career in art. Enrolling at the Art Students League in September 1916 was the key event, for there he found friendship and a direction in art and life. He studied there until 1920, the last three years on scholarship, and he met and married fellow artist Katherine Schmidt in 1919. He also gained the sponsorship of Hamilton Easter Field, an arts patron.

By 1922, Kuniyoshi had had his first one-man exhibition at the prestigious Daniel Gallery in New York City. Although selling many paintings, he supported himself until 1925 as a photographer, gaining a reputation for photographing works of art. In 1931, he returned for the first time to Japan to visit his ailing father and for a one-man exhibit organized by the National Museum of Modern Art. The following year, he and Schmidt were divorced; in 1935, he married Sara Mazo.

Two years before, he had begun teaching at the Art Students League, where he would remain. He continued to exhibit and teach throughout the 1930s and 1940s and, in 1944, took first prize in the prestigious annual exhibition of American painting at the Carnegie Institute of Art in Pittsburgh. A major retrospective of his work was mounted at the Whitney Museum of American Art in 1948, the first one-man exhibition of a living American artist ever presented there. Kuniyoshi died of stomach cancer on 14 May 1953.

Although he came to the United States as a teenager, his paintings do not depict identifiably Japanese or Japanese-American experiences. Moreover, Kuniyoshi did not appear to have close ties with the Japanese-American community, nor was he covered much in the Japanese-American press, perhaps because he lived in New York City, away from the major concentrations of Japanese Americans. Nevertheless, his work has continued to be exhibited, including a major retrospective put together by the University of Texas in 1975, which toured the United States and Japan, followed by a 1989–1990 retrospective in Japan.

Brian Niiya

REFERENCES

Goodrich, Lloyd. *Yasuo Kuniyoshi.* New York: Macmillan, 1948.

Kuniyoshi, Yasuo. *Yasuo Kuniyoshi.* New York: American Artists Group, 1945.

Sakurai, Josephine. "Kuniyoshi: Artist, American." *Scene* 5.5 (September 1953): 13–16.

Wolf, Tom. *Kuniyoshi's Women.* San Francisco: Pomegranate Art Books, 1993.

Yasuo Kuniyoshi 1889–1953: A Retrospective Exhibition. Austin: University of Texas at Austin, 1975.

Kviklys, Bronius (1913–1990)

Journalist, editor, chronicler, and archivist Lithuanian

A refugee after World War II, Bronius Kviklys immigrated to the United States with an unwavering ethnic-religious intensity. His legacy to Lithuanian culture is monumental. His two series on Lithuanian geography and homeland churches solidified his reputation.

Kviklys was born on 10 November 1913, in Zastronas village, Utena County, Lithuania. He received a degree in economics at Vytautas Magnus University, Kaunas, and then studied law at Kaunas and Vilnius Universities, 1938 to 1941. He became administrator and technical editor of *Mūsų Sportas* (Our sport) and *Kūno ir Kulturos Sveikata* (Physical and cultural health), 1932 to 1934, and *Policija* (Police), 1942 to 1944. He also edited *Policijos kalendorius* (Police calendar), 1936 to 1940, and other publications in Lithuania and abroad.

After fleeing from the Soviets to Germany, he and others organized a displaced persons society, *Illertissene,* and he was a deputy for the Lithuanian Red Cross. On coming to the United States in 1951, he became a consultant to the Lithuanian Bibliographic Service and, with Aleksandras Ruzančov, prepared a bibliography of refugee literature. Under a variety of pseudonyms, Kviklys contributed to numerous Lithuanian newspapers and journals. Meanwhile, he wrote many entries for the thirty-seven-volume *Lietuvių enciklopedija* (Boston, 1955 to 1969, 1985). Kviklys also published a comprehensive four-volume geography, *Mūsų Lietuva* (3,037 pages), profusely illustrated from his archival collection and supplemented both by pictures smuggled out of Soviet-occupied Lithuania by hired photographers and by data from 100 oral histories and 200 correspondents. A few copies were smuggled into Lithuania, helping to raise national spirits in the late 1980s. The original volumes, having proven invaluable for their details about locations and monuments destroyed by the Soviets, were reissued in Lithuania.

Much of this was done while Kviklys adhered to a semiascetic daily routine, supporting his family as a daytime carpenter and then, from 1968 to 1980, as a member of the editorial staff of the Chicago daily, *Draugas* (Friend). At the same time, for decades he salvaged archival material in Germany and in the United States, accumulating a vast and rare collection about the czarist press ban era, 1864–1904, and the period of resistance by freedom fighters, 1942–1948. His holdings included coins, banknotes, commemorative medals, postage stamps, autographs, photographs, unpublished manuscripts, letters, and the papers of exiled President Antanas Smetona—in all totaling around 10,000 items. From time to time, he staged exhibits of his uncommon holdings, and researchers often visited his archives.

The magnum opus crowning his extraordinary career was his seven-volume series on the Roman Catholic church in Lithuania, diocese by diocese (3,556 pages, with hundreds of photos), appended by brief biographical sketches of priests. In recognition of Kviklys's unparalleled undertakings, Pope John Paul II awarded him the Pro Ecclesia et Pontifice [For church and pontiff] Medal on 24 January 1984.

"If I myself cannot return to Lithuania, then at least my archival holdings will do so," Kviklys remarked before his unexpected death on 28 August 1990. On 27 April 1995, his collection was given to the Center for the Study of the Diaspora, at Vytautas Magnus University. Although he had managed to solicit some financial aid and find a score of volunteers, he practically single-handedly succeeded in leaving an extraordinary legacy to his homeland.

William Wolkovich-Valkavičius

REFERENCES

"Apie Bronių Kviklį—Lietuvos bažnyčių autorių" (Concerning Bronius Kviklys—Author of Churches of Lithuania). *Katalikų pasaulis* (Catholic world), December 1995.

"Kviklys, Bronius." In *Encyclopedia Lituanica,* edited by Simas Sužiedelis and Antanas Kučas, 3:256. Boston: Juozas Kapočius Publisher, 1975–1978.

"Kviklys, Bronius." In *Lietuvių enciklopedija* (Lithuanian encyclopedia), vol. 13: 472; vol. 36: 330; vol. 37: 319. Boston: Lithuanian Encyclopedia Press, 1953–1969, 1985.

Kviklytė–Kulikauskienė, Rūta (Kviklys's daughter). Interview by Regina Dringelienė, in *Katalikų pasaulis* (Catholic world), December 1995.

La Guardia, Fiorello Henry (Enrico) (1882–1947)

Politician, mayor, and U.S. House representative

Italian-American

A three-term congressman and a three-term mayor of New York City, Fiorello La Guardia was a progressive urban reformer. He emerged as the first Italian American to challenge the political reign of Irish Americans in New York City.

Fiorello La Guardia was born in 1882 in Greenwich Village, New York City, to accomplished and talented Italian-immigrant parents. His father, Achille, was a composer, conductor, and cornetist, and his mother, Irene Luzzatto-Coen, an Italian Jew, was accompanist to the celebrated diva Adelina Patti. After his father's death in 1904, Fiorello's mother took him to Budapest, where he worked in the consulate. Later, he was employed as an interpreter in Trieste and as a U.S. consular agent in Fiume, positions that sensitized him to the plight of immigrants.

In 1906, La Guardia returned to New York and began studying law at New York University, while working at Ellis Island as an interpreter in seven languages, including Italian and Yiddish. In 1910, degree in hand, he started practicing law. His resentment against corruption and special privilege provided the foundation for his progressive thinking. For example, he offered free legal advice to push-cart peddlers and shopkeepers on the Lower East Side and later represented striking garment workers in the 1911–1912 strikes.

His distaste for Tammany Hall (the Irish-run, Democratic political machine) fueling his political ambitions, La Guardia joined the Republican Party. After losing two races, he became the third Italian American elected to Congress, serving from 1917 to 1919, and continued to champion immigrant causes. But after the U.S. entry into World War I, he absented himself from the House in order to serve in the armed forces. When he returned, he founded an Italian-language magazine, *L'Americolo*, worked tirelessly to organize New York City's Italian Americans, and, with their support, was elected again to Congress in 1922 and reelected four times, serving until 1933. In 1932, his efforts to protect workers culminated in the passage of the Norris–La Guardia Act, a far-reaching law that placed restrictions upon the use of the injunction and rendered yellow-dog provisions in contracts unenforceable. The following year, with strong backing from Italians, Jews, and blacks, La Guardia won the first of three mayoral elections in New York City (serving 1934–1945). In an effort to reform city politics, he removed much of the political influence involved in securing civil service positions, labored to end graft and discrimination in city government, and helped increase the representation of blacks in city jobs and the political role of Italians and Jews.

During the depression years, La Guardia put people back to work by creating federally funded jobs through public works projects, rebuilding highways and bridges, and constructing new schools, hospitals, parks, and airports. He also worked with New Deal officials to clear slums and build safe public housing. As mayor, La Guardia implemented philosophies of good government inspired by nineteenth-century reformers together with twentieth-century ideas of progressivism and New Deal programs. He was a fighter against machine politics, a champion of immigrants and workers, and a symbol of the process through which Italian Americans came of political age. La Guardia died in 1947.

Diane C. Vecchio

REFERENCES

Bayor, Ronald H. *Fiorello La Guardia: Ethnicity and Reform.* Wheeling, IL: Harland Davidson, 1993.

Garrett, Charles. *The La Guardia Years: Machine and Reform Politics in New York City.* New Brunswick, NJ: Rutgers University Press, 1961.

Kessner, Thomas. *Fiorello H. La Guardia and the Making of Modern New York.* New York: McGraw-Hill, 1989.

"La Guardia, Fiorello Henry." Biographical profile. U.S. Congressional Directory: bioguide.congress. gov/scripts/biodisplay.pl?index=L000007 (accessed 21 June 2000).

Mann, Arthur. *La Guardia: A Fighter against His Times, 1882–1933.* Philadelphia: J. B. Lippincott, 1959.

———. *La Guardia Comes to Power, 1933.* Philadelphia: J. B. Lippincott, 1965.

Zinn, Howard. *La Guardia in Congress.* Ithaca, NY: Cornell University Press, 1959.

LaFlesche Picotte, Susan (1865–1915)

Physician and community activist
Native American (Omaha)

Susan LaFlesche Picotte, the Omaha chief's daughter who became the first Native American woman trained as a physician, lived during a period of tremendous change for her people and all Native Americans. Although parts of her public story read like a nineteenth-century assimilation success tale, it was Omaha, not American, culture that grounded her professional and personal identities.

Susan LaFlesche grew up in a world shaped by the clash of Native and American customs. Her father regarded acculturation as the best survival strategy for the Omaha people and encouraged Susan and her four sisters and brother to lead their community on this difficult road. Her childhood and youth symbolized this determined parting with traditionalism. Schooled first at the local Presbyterian mission, she then attended the Elizabeth Institute for Young Ladies in New Jersey and the Hampton Institute in Virginia. Under the sponsorship of the Connecticut Indian Association, she matriculated at the Women's

Medical College of Pennsylvania, graduating first in her class in 1889.

LaFlesche remained firmly tied to her family and tribal community, returning to Nebraska as the Bureau of Indian Affairs (BIA) physician on the Omaha Reservation. Her tenure required all of her professional acumen and her skills as a cultural mediator. As a physician, she fought the ravages of poverty as well as the epidemic diseases that afflicted the community. As a representative of a once-traditional family dedicated to "walking the white man's road," she urged the Omaha she treated as patients to accept some degree of Americanization.

In 1894, Susan LaFlesche married Henry Picotte, a mixed-blood Lakota man. After her marriage and the birth of her sons Caryl and Pierre, she began a small private medical practice in Bancroft, Nebraska. Henry Picotte's death in 1905 left her as the sole support for her children and aged mother. LaFlesche Picotte accepted a position with the Presbyterian Board of Home Missions in Walthill, Nebraska. Her stylish two-story home, boasting an extensive library and modern conveniences, became the center for her work with the Omaha tribe. For a decade, evangelism for the Presbyterians was only one small facet of her life, for, following her father's example, she sought to protect her community's rights through activism. Her efforts proved especially important in 1910, when the BIA attempted to extend the trust period over tribal lands. With the Omaha land base at stake, she successfully lobbied the Department of the Interior to uphold tribal sovereignty.

LaFlesche Picotte's political advocacy paralleled her efforts on behalf of community health care. After years of work, she established a hospital in Walthill that initially served Native Americans and, later, others as well. She died there on 15 September 1915. That hospital, renamed the Susan LaFlesche Picotte Center, is now a National Historic Landmark. The small building overlooking Walthill memorializes the Omaha woman whose journey of acculturation made her an effective advocate for her tribe.

Lisa E. Emmerich

REFERENCES

Green, Norma Kidd. "Four Sisters: Daughters of Joseph LaFlesche." *Nebraska History* 45, (June 1964): 165–176.

———. *Iron Eye's Family: The Children of Joseph LaFlesche.* Lincoln, NE: Johnsen Pub., 1969.

Mathes, Valerie Sherer. "Dr. Susan LaFlesche Picotte: The Reformed and the Reformer." In *Indian Lives: Essays on Nineteenth and Twentieth-Century Native American Leaders.* New ed., edited by L. G. Moses and Raymond Wilson, 61–90. Albuquerque: University of New Mexico Press, 1993.

———. "Susan LaFlesche Picotte, M.D.: Nineteenth-century Physician and Reformer." *Great Plains Quarterly* 13, (Summer 1993): 172–186.

Tong, Benson. *Susan LaFlesche Picotte, M.D.: Omaha Indian Leader and Reformer.* Norman: University of Oklahoma Press, 1999.

Laurens, Henry (1724–1792)
Merchant and diplomat
Franco-American

Henry Laurens began as a merchant and became a planter. He rose in South Carolina politics to become a member, and then president, of the Continental Congress during the American Revolution.

Laurens, born in Charleston on 6 March 1724, was the son of Jean Laurens and Esther Grasset, two French Huguenots. He was raised to be a merchant and, in 1748, started his career in this city of some 7,000 inhabitants. He was in partnership until 1762. He married Eleanor Ball in 1750, and by 1764, Laurens and his wife and children had moved to his new house and plantation in Ansonboro. He then devoted himself to his plantation, slowing his mercantile activities. In the meantime, Laurens had entered South Carolina's Common House of Assembly in 1757 and was regularly reelected (except once) between 1757 and the American Revolution.

In 1770, Lauren's wife died and, a year later, seeking an adequate college for his children and finding none in South Carolina, he sailed to England with his sons. During his three-year stay in England, Laurens was a vocal defender of the American colonies. By the time he returned in September 1774, resistance to British rule had grown in South Carolina. Four months later, he was elected to South Carolina's First Provincial Congress, representing Charleston. At the second meeting he was elected the congress president and, in January 1777, was chosen for the Continental Congress. Following John Hancock's resignation, Laurens was elected president of the Continental Congress, but in December 1778, he, too, resigned as a result of the Deane-Lee diplomatic controversy. It was also during this period that Laurens and the Marquis de Lafayette developed a friendship. He recognized, like Washington, that French help sprang more from a hatred of England than from any love of America.

In May 1780, the British captured Charleston, along with 5,000 men, and Laurens argued that Charleston could have been saved if the army had armed "trusty Negroes" to fight against the British. Two months later, the Continental Congress sent him to Europe, but he was captured by the British and jailed in the Tower of London. Laurens was released in May 1782 and traveled to Holland and France, where he was asked to join the peace commissioners. He sailed back to America in June 1784. As one of his sons had died during a battle in 1782, Laurens returned to Charleston with his only surviving son in January 1785. His two daughters arrived afterward from London. (Of the twelve children born to the Laurenses, four survived childhood, but only three outlived their father.)

Disgusted with public life, Laurens retired to his plantation, refusing all offices to which he was elected, including Congress, the state legislature, and the Constitutional Convention in 1787. The war had cost him large amounts of money; indeed, he had to rescue his Georgia estates from public seizure, and the British Treasury as well as the U.S. government were his debtors. Nonetheless, the cause of South Carolina and of the United States had been well served by Laurens, who died on 8 September 1792.

André J. M. Prévos

REFERENCES

"Laurens, Henry." In *Biographical Directory of the United States Congress, 1774–1989,* edited by Kathryn Allamond Jacob and Bruce A. Ragsdale. Washington, DC: Government Printing Office, 1989.

Laurens, Henry. *Papers of Henry Laurens.* Edited by Philip M. Hamer, George C. Rogers, Jr., and David R. Chestnutt. 10 vols. Columbia: University of South Carolina Press, 1968.

Ramsay, David. *Memoirs of the Life of Martha Laurens Ramsay.* 3d ed. Boston: Samuel T. Armstrong, 1812.

Wallace, David Duncan. *The Life of Henry Laurens. With a Sketch of the Life of Lieutenant-Colonel John Laurens.* New York and London: Putnam and Knickerbocker Press, 1915.

Lausche, Frank J. (1895–1990)

Mayor, governor, and U.S. senator
Slovene-American

The career of Frank J. Lausche took him from a Cleveland municipal judgeship to being the mayor of Cleveland, governor of Ohio, and U.S. senator from Ohio. During the 1950s, his name was frequently mentioned as a possible presidential candidate.

Lausche, who was born in Cleveland on November 14, 1895, to parents who had both come from what is today the Republic of Slovenia, graduated from the John Marshall School of Law and was admitted to the bar in 1920. In 1932, he was appointed and then elected judge of the Cleveland Municipal Court; in 1937, he moved to the court of common pleas. Resigning from the court, Lausche ran for mayor in 1941, won, and was reelected in 1943. Lausche's election was a high point in the success of Slovene Americans in city politics, the result of his political education during the 1920s and 1930s on the streets of the Slovene neighborhood around St. Clair Avenue, in Cleveland's Twenty-third Ward. Slovene Americans supported his mayoral candidacy as well as his campaigns for governor and U.S. senator.

Although nominally a Democrat, Lausche operated outside of the Democratic Party organization throughout his political career. As mayor, he strove for lower taxes and was noted for having a clean and frugal administration. Spurred partly by antipathy to Nazi racial doctrines, his municipal government moved to address the needs of its black constituents with a Committee on Democratic Practice, aimed at preserving minority rights during wartime and developing an educational program to combat discrimination and racial intolerance. Concerned about Cleveland's postwar development, he also organized the Postwar Planning Council in 1944 to identify major problems and coordinate future planning in such areas as public transportation, public works, labor-management relations, and the needs of returning servicemen.

Lausche successfully campaigned for the governorship of Ohio in 1944. Although defeated in 1946, he was subsequently reelected from 1948 to 1956. Under Lausche's leadership, the long-neglected state welfare program was rehabilitated, and he fought for increased aid to local governments, increased state investment in transportation and education, and a statewide civil defense organization. In 1950, he was elected chairman of the U.S. Governors' Conference and, during the early 1950s, was repeatedly mentioned as a possible candidate for president or vice president of the United States.

Lausche was elected to the U.S. Senate from Ohio in 1956 and served two terms until 1969. (He failed to win renomination in 1968). In the Senate, he thundered against national debt increases and supported President Lyndon Baines Johnson during the Vietnam War as part of his own anti-Communist ideology. While he was in the Senate, there were varying opinions regarding his condemnation of the Communist regime in Slovenia and Yugoslavia, and opposing views were frequently expressed about him within the Slovene-American community. Nevertheless, in the 1960s, he sponsored a bill that prevented the closure of the Slovene section of Voice of America radio, when the management wanted to close the section down and combine it with Serbian and Croatian broadcasts. Lausche died on April 21, 1990, in Cleveland.

Matjaž Klemenčič

REFERENCES

Bitter, William. *Frank J. Lausche, A Political Biography.* New York: Studia Slovenica, 1975.

Gobetz, Edward Giles. *Frank Lausche, Lincoln of Ohio.* Willoughby Hills, OH: Slovenian Research Center of America, 1987.

Klemenčič, Matjaž. *Slovenes of Cleveland: The Creation of a New Nation and a New World Community, Slovenia and the Slovenes of Cleveland, Ohio.* Novo Mesto: Dolenjska založba, 1995.

"Lausche, Frank John." Biographical Directory of the United States Congress, 1774–Present. http://bioguide.congress.gov/scripts/biodisplay.pl?index=L000122 (Accessed 19 December 2000).

Laxalt, Paul (1922–), and Laxalt, Robert (1923–)

Governor and U.S. senator; novelist and journalist, respectively

Basque-American

Robert Laxalt is the most significant of all Basque-American authors, having written on a full range of topics relating to Basque life in Europe and in the American West. Robert's older brother, Paul, became a nationally known politician and the governor of Nevada as well as a U.S. senator. Owing to the efforts of Robert, Paul, and Robert's daughter, Monique Laxalt Urza, the Laxalt family is probably the most highly visible Basque family in the United States.

Robert Laxalt was born to Basque immigrants, Dominique and Teresa Laxalt, in Alturas, California, in 1923. In his early years he lived on Basque sheep ranches in northern California and Nevada until moving to Carson City, Nevada, where he spent his boyhood and public school years. In 1940, he enrolled in Santa Clara University. Following a few years in college, he unsuccessfully attempted to join the armed forces, being rejected for medical reasons. However, he landed a State Department position in the Belgian Congo. Thereafter, needing to recover from numerous tropical maladies, including malaria, dysentery, and yellow jaundice, young Laxalt returned home and majored in English at the University of Nevada, Reno. While in Reno, he

worked part-time, writing United Press International stories. Although he was grateful for those early experiences as a journalist, since his youth he had dreamed of becoming a more serious writer and, for the next ten years or so, would attempt historical sketches and popular short fiction based on Nevada scenes. But it was *Sweet Promised Land,* in 1957, that would established him as the leading interpreter of the Basque experience in the American West.

The subject of *Sweet Promised Land* is his father, Dominique Laxalt. In the book, the son tells the story of his father's adaptation to sheepherding on the high desert plains of northern Nevada, his becoming a successful sheep and cattle rancher, and his solitary return visit to the land of his birth. The poignant, novelized story of his father's life launched Robert Laxalt's literary career. After completing several other novels, such as *Man in the Wheatfield* (1964) and *In a Hundred Graves* (1972), and assisting his brother's campaign efforts, Laxalt returned to writing fictionalized themes relating to his own immigrant family. In *The Basque Hotel* (1989), he tells the story of a young man who grew up in a Carson City, Nevada, Basque boardinghouse, just like the one owned by his parents. In *Child of the Holy Ghost* (1992), he turned his attention to a woman named Maitia, telling the story of a young woman like his own mother, who had been rejected by her native village because she was born out of wedlock. The novel culminates when the Maitia's two sons (presumably Robert and Paul Laxalt) return triumphantly to the Basque village of her birth—one a novelist, journalist, and college professor; the other, the U.S. senator from Nevada.

Among other aspects of Robert Laxalt's career, he started the University of Nevada Press (1961), wrote articles on Basques for *National Geographic* during the 1960s, and a history of Nevada (1977). Among other awards, he received one from the Nevada State Council of the Arts (1978) and he was inducted into the Basque Hall of Fame (1989).

The life and career of Robert's brother, Paul, who was born in August 1922 and received his degree from the University of Denver Law School, is given a fictionalized treatment in another of Robert's books, *The Governor's Mansion* (1994). In the book, the author reveals details about the Laxalt clan as they deal with their brother, the governor. In fact, when Paul, who had been a district attorney for Ormsby County (1950–1954), initially decided to run for lieutenant governor in 1963, the Laxalt family met to weigh the possibility of reissuing *Sweet Promised Land* for Paul's campaign year. (In 1993, the story of that meeting was told by Robert's daughter, Monique Laxalt Urza, in *The Deep Blue Memory*, a novel on the life of a child growing up with an author-father and a politically prominent family.) *Sweet Promised Land* made it easy for Paul Laxalt, the candidate, to claim "native son" status, and he was elected. In the following year, he nearly won Nevada's U.S. Senate seat, losing by only eighty-four votes. A few years later, the lieutenant governor convinced his brother to reissue *Sweet Promised Land* with a new introduction praising the values of hard work, honesty, and integrity found among Basques, as well as noting their contributions to the State of Nevada. The reissued novel assisted Paul in his successful campaign against Governor Grant Sawyer in 1966.

As governor from 1967 to 1971, Paul Laxalt continued a strong pattern of executive leadership and fiscal conservatism, despite having to work with a divided legislature. He worked to organize state and regional leadership of the Republican Party during his years in office as well as during his candidacy. Perhaps the most important measure passed during his administration was a corporate gambling law that made entering Nevada gambling industry more attractive to large corporations. He also fought a tough but unsuccessful battle for a fair housing bill for the state.

Despite his popularity and expected reelection, Laxalt decided not to run for a second term. But in 1974, Nevada's "Basque native son" entered the U.S. senatorial campaign. That year marked the first such election in Nevada without an incumbent as a candidate. The decision opened the field for Paul Laxalt and Harry Reid, then lieutenant governor. The campaign was an intense and controversial one, with Reid attacking the entire Laxalt family. The strategy backfired, and Laxalt defeated Reid by 624 votes. Laxalt served as U.S. senator from 1975 through 1981 and actively supported Ronald Reagan's bid for the presidency in 1980 and 1984, serving as director of the Republican National Campaign in 1984. In the subsequent presidential season, there was some discussion of Paul Laxalt as a candidate for the presidency. However, he retired from politics and moved east. Because of the accomplishments of Robert, Paul, and Monique, the Laxalt family remains the most highly visible Basque family in United States.

Jeronima Echeverria

REFERENCES

Douglass, William A., and Jon Bilbao. *Amerikanuak: A History of Basques in the New World*. Reno: University of Nevada Press, 1975.

Echeverria, Jeronima. *Home Away from Home: A History of Basque Boarding Houses*. Reno: University of Nevada Press, 2000.

Etulain, Richard W. "Robert Laxalt: Basque Writer of the American West." In *Portraits of Basques in the New World*, edited by Richard W. Etulain and Jeronima Echeverria, 212–229. Reno: University of Nevada Press, 1999.

Hulse, James. *The Nevada Adventure: A History*. Reno: University of Nevada Press, 1981.

Laxalt, Paul. *Nevada's Paul Laxalt: A Memoir*. Reno: Jack Bacon and Co., 2000.

"Laxalt, Paul Dominique." U.S. Senate Biographical Directory: bioguide.congress.gov/scripts/biodisplay.pl?index=L000148 (accessed 1 August 2000).

Laxalt, Robert. *The Basque Hotel*. Reno: University of Nevada, 1989.

———. *Child of the Holy Ghost*. Reno: University of Nevada, 1992.

———. *The Governor's Mansion*. Reno: University of Nevada, 1994.

———. *Sweet Promised Land*. Reno: University of Nevada, 1957.

Urza, Monique Laxalt. *The Deep Blue Memory*. Reno: University of Nevada, 1993.

Lazarus, Emma (1849–1887)
Poet and writer
Jewish-American

Emma Lazarus won universal recognition for her poem "The New Colossus," in which she affirms the idea that the United States provides opportunity and freedom for Jews and other persecuted and impoverished immigrants, the "wretched refuse" and "huddled masses." The final four and one-half lines were engraved on the pedestal of the Statue of Liberty.

Lazarus was born in New York City in 1849, to Moses and Esther Lazarus. Both sides of the family had been in the United States since the Revolution. Her father was a successful merchant and provided Emma with private tutors and emotional and financial support for her writing. Free of obligations, she studied various fields and was tutored in German, French, and Italian. In 1866, when Emma was only seventeen, her father had *Poems and Translations Written between the Ages of Fourteen and Sixteen* printed "for private education." Soon after, Lazarus met Ralph Waldo Emerson, who was highly supportive of her work. "Colossus" is included in *Poems and Translations*.

In 1882 Lazarus published *Songs of a Semite: The Dance to Death and Other Poems,* in which she speaks out as a self-identified Jew as well as an American writer. In this volume she challenges both anti-Semitism and Jewish apathy, encouraging Jews to "recall today the glorious Maccabean rage." Many poems in that volume proclaim Lazarus's identity as a Jewish poet. In one of a series of impassioned essays written that year, "Russian Christianity vs. Modern Judaism," she pleads for an understanding of Russian Jewry and its political predicament. In "The Jewish Problem" she argues that Jews, who are always a minority, "seem fated to excite the antagonism of their fellow countrymen." Her solution is the founding of a state by Jews for Jews in Palestine. Lazarus promoted Zionism during the 1880s.

In addition to Ralph Waldo Emerson, Lazarus conducted a correspondence with other writers, among them Ivan Turgenev and Henry James. Lazarus's zeal for poetic expression was equaled by her passion for social justice. She was involved with the founding of the Hebrew Technical Institute for Vocational Training and tried to form a Committee for the Colonization of Palestine. In 1883 she sailed to London armed with letters of introduction from well-placed people who could help her in her work toward the establishment of a Jewish national homeland. Thus, a decade before Theodor Herzl's launching of political Zionism, Lazarus would argue in her own poetic voice and in powerfully persuasive prose for the Land of Israel as a safe haven for oppressed Jews everywhere.

Lazarus never married and died childless. Consequently, she had to contend with American and Jewish middle-class prescriptions for womanly behavior, gender expectations that imposed limitations on a woman artist's expressions. In "Echoes" she describes some of them. More than any other Jewish woman of the nineteenth century, Lazarus identified herself and was recognized as an *American* writer. Nevertheless, she was also outspoken in her roles as both a Jew and a woman writer, combining a passionate identification with her people and a deep belief in the United States as the epitome of all freedoms.

Esther Fuchs

REFERENCES

Kessner, Carole S. "Matrilineal Dissent: The Rhetoric of Zeal in Emma Lazarus, Marie Syrkin and Cynthia Ozick." In *Women of the Word: Jewish Women and Jewish Writing,* edited by Judith R. Baskin, 197–215. Detroit: Wayne State University Press, 1994.

Lazarus, Emma. *An Epistle to the Hebrews.* New York: Federation of American Zionists, 1900.

———. *The Poems of Emma Lazarus.* 2 vols. New York: Houghton Mifflin, 1888.

"Lazarus, Emma." In *Jewish Women in America: An Historical Encyclopedia,* edited by Paula E. Hyman and Deborah Dash Moore, 806–810. New York: Routledge, 1998.

Lichtenstein, Diane. *Writing Their Nations: The Tradition of Nineteenth Century American Jewish*

Women Writers. Bloomington: Indiana University Press, 1992.

Merriam, Eve. *Emma Lazarus: Woman with a Torch.* New York: Citadel Press, 1956.

Schappes, Morris U., ed. *Letters of Emma Lazarus.* New York: New York Public Library, 1949.

Lee, Ang (1954–)
Filmmaker
Chinese

Ang Lee is a highly acclaimed filmmaker whose award-winning films are warmhearted tales of ordinary joy and sorrow. A sensitivity to social nuance and the workings of human relationships has enabled him to produce movies with universal appeal, some of which have played a role in demystifying the "Orient" and Asian Americans.

Lee's inspiration for earlier films partly came from dynamics within his family. Born in Taiwan on 23 October 1954, Lee was the son of a high school principal. His father expected him to do well academically, but he failed the critical annual college final examination. Tension developed between son and father, a family dynamic later explored in his films. Fleeing this disgrace, Lee in 1978 went to the United States to study. After graduating from the theater arts program at the University of Illinois, he entered the New York University (NYU) film school. At NYU, he won the best-student-film award for his master's project, *Fine Line*, a comedy about an Italian trying to escape the Mafia and a Chinese woman hiding from the Immigration and Naturalization Service. But breaking into the film business would not be easy; studio executives often questioned his talents and his command of English.

Finally, in 1990 Lee entered two screenplays in the Taiwanese government's annual screenplay contest. He swept both first and second prize, with *Pushing Hands* receiving first place. Filmed in the United States but never released here, it recounts the travails of a retired *tai chi* master when he moves to New York from Beijing to live with his son and contentious Euro-American daughter-in-law.

When *Pushing Hands* became a success in Taiwan, that nation's largest studio urged Lee to make *The Wedding Banquet,* the second-prize winner in the 1990 contest. Costing only $750,000 to produce, this art-house smash is a riotous yet touching farce about a Chinese-American gay man who fakes a wedding in order to satisfy his parents' wish for a grandson. Some of the comic scenes at the wedding reception were inspired by the mayhem of Lee's own marriage to Taiwan-born Jan Lin. His next film in this trilogy of intergenerational and cultural conflicts in Chinese family life, the Oscar-nominated *Eat Drink Man Woman* (1995), also explores human relations, as a widowed father, who is a master chef, struggles to come to terms with his grown daughters' sexuality. That same fascination with social codes amid rapid change then led Lee to take on the filming of Jane Austen's *Sense and Sensibility* (1996). Its phenomenal success gave Lee the opportunity to recruit a star-studded cast to make *The Ice Storm* (1997), another crowd pleaser, which opened the prestigious New York Film Festival in 1997. In 2001, Lee won the best director and best foreign film Golden Globe awards for *Crouching Tiger, Hidden Dragon.*

A humble person, Lee is uncomfortable with being labeled as a role model for Asian Americans; he sees himself as a filmmaker trying to produce all kinds of movies rather than one simply with an Asian sensibility. Nevertheless, his status and influence in the United States show that Chinese Americans can overcome structural barriers in their search for self-expression.

Benson Tong

REFERENCES

Hornaday, Ann. "A Director's Trip from Salad Days to a 'Banquet.'" *New York Times,* 1 August 1993, H25.

Neumann, Lin. "Cultural Revolution: Taiwan Director Ang Lee Takes on Jane Austen." *Far Eastern Economic Review,* 28 December 1995/4 January 1996, 97–98.

Powers, John. "The Ice Cometh." *Vogue* 187 (October 1997): 230, 232.

Lee Bing (1873–1970)
Merchant and entrepreneur
Chinese

A Chinese pioneer, Lee Bing was one of the most important Chinese merchants in late-nineteenth-century rural California. (Since Lee Bing was addressed and referred to in the traditional Chinese manner, namely, with family name first, followed by the given name, that format is used here for his name.) He established numerous businesses and helped finance the establishment of Locke, California, the only town built by and for Chinese. His life illustrated how the merchant elite attained success during an era of anti-Chinese sentiments and exclusion.

Born in 1873, in Guangdong Province, China, Lee grew up in an impoverished family of eight children. His mother died when he was seven. At the age of twenty-one—like so many other immigrants—he borrowed money for a voyage to the United States. Upon arrival, Lee befriended a Chinese merchant who took him to Walnut Grove, California, which then had a flourishing Chinatown. Initially employed as a farm laborer, he studied English at night; he then worked at a local hotel, where he was soon promoted to be the hotel's cook.

Lee saved enough money and eventually started a restaurant. He invested in a hardware store, an apothecary, and a gambling house. With the sizable presence of Chinese in Walnut Grove, his diverse enterprises flourished and his socioeconomic status rose. During the early 1900s, he was a heavy contributor when Sun Yat Sen visited California to raise funds for his revolutionary movement in China. In 1900 he returned to China to marry Lum Bo-ying. However, like other immigrants who had to contend with gender-biased immigration laws and a culture that proscribed women's mobility, he did not bring her to the United States until ten years later.

After a fire in 1915 destroyed most of Walnut Grove's Chinatown, Lee and a few other merchants rebuilt their enterprises at a new site. Locke, a small riverside, rural town, was the first Chinese community built by and for Chinese, and Lee was one of its chief financiers. He constructed a restaurant, boardinghouse, two gambling joints, a dry goods store, and a hardware store, and he contributed to the building of a community hall and home for the destitute. In 1919 Lee also bought a meat market in downtown Sacramento. He leased land nearby to raise poultry for the market and soon produced enough to supply chicken and meat for the three branch markets he had established elsewhere in the city.

Not long after the 1929 stock market crash Lee recovered his losses and by 1932 had begun acquiring businesses all over northern California and Oregon. Many of these, such as bars, dance halls, and restaurants, almost exclusively served whites, an indication he had broken out of the ethnic enclave economy.

At seventy-five Lee Bing went into retirement, and he died in 1970 at the age of ninety-seven. Lee's life attests to the fact that for the ruling Chinese elite in the United States their social origins in China had little to do with the positions they secured in California. Yet few other Chinese merchants in rural California rivaled Lee in the array of enterprises undertaken. He succeeded economically and became a community leader mainly on the basis of his managerial abilities.

Benson Tong

REFERENCES

Chan, Sucheng. *This Bittersweet Soil: The Chinese in California Agriculture, 1860–1910.* Berkeley: University of California Press, 1986.

Gillenkirk, Jeff, and James Motlow. *Bitter Melon: Stories from the Last Rural Chinese Town in America.* Seattle: University of Washington Press, 1987.

Lee, Choua Eve (in Hmong, Cua Lis) (1970–)
Teacher, business owner, and public official
Hmong-American

Choua Eve Lee was elected in 1992 to the St. Paul Board of Education, despite being Hmong, a woman, and only twenty-two years old. She thus became the first Hmong and one of the first former refugees from Indochina to be elected to local public office in the United States. She has been recognized for her roles as a teacher, entrepreneur, mother, wife, Hmong woman, and community leader.

In 1975, following the Secret War in Laos, during which the Central Intelligence Agency recruited the Hmong to fight, more than 10 percent of that population began fleeing the country, with Lee's family among them. After one year in a Thai refugee camp, they were resettled in Chicago, Illinois. Choua Lee started school there as a second grader. By 1983, she was fluent in English and doing well. After living briefly in Ohio and Wisconsin, the family moved to St. Paul, Minnesota, in 1984. Lee went off to college and two years later married another Hmong college student, who soon graduated with a degree in electronic engineering. They decided to open an insurance agency in St. Paul. Postponing her education, Lee was hired as executive director of the Women's Association of Hmong and Lao (WAHL). Learning especially about the educational needs of the youth, she resigned one year later to run for a seat on the St. Paul Board of Education. Her concerns reflected those of many groups, and the Democratic Party supported her candidacy. She was elected easily. However, after one four-year term she decided to devote more time to her young son and her education.

Lee had taken a risk that many Hmong at the time thought impossible. In Hmong traditional culture, politics and leadership are the province of the older men, and in Hmong-American society, leadership remains in the hands of men. Second, Lee was only twenty-two and pregnant when she ran for the board; in Hmong culture, respect, dignity, and wisdom are equated with age. And finally, Hmong culture had been shaped by the people's long history as oppressed. They did not have a written language until the early 1950s. Given all these disadvantages, it was extraordinary that a Hmong woman would be one of the first Indochinese to run successfully for public office in the United States.

Lee's victory marked the beginning of a new period in the Indochinese refugee community: Its members are now active participants in U.S. social, economic, and political processes. Her victory empowered many Hmong to take control of their own destiny. Since her 1992 victory, three Hmong have been elected to local city councils (Appleton and Eau Claire, Wisconsin; and Omaha, Nebraska), and three others to local school boards (La Cross and Wausau, Wisconsin; and St. Paul, Minnesota) as of 1999. Many women have, since 1992, played important leadership roles in the Hmong-American community.

In 1997 Lee received her B.A. in elementary education and two years later completed her master's in education. She is currently an elementary school teacher in St. Paul, helps her husband run their several small businesses, and continues to teach her son to speak Hmong and to learn many Hmong traditional values.

Kou Yang

REFERENCES

Barney G. Linwood. "The Hmong of Northern Laos." Master's thesis, University of Minnesota, 1957.

Donnelly, Nancy D. *Changing Life of Refugee Hmong Women.* Seattle: University of Washington Press, 1994.

Hein, Jeremy. *From Vietnam, Laos, and Cambodia.* New York: Twayne Publishers, 1995.

Lee, Choua Eve. Interview by author, 16 January 1999.

Olney, D. P. "We Must Be Organized: Dual Organizations in an American Hmong Community." Ann Arbor, MI: University Microfilm International, 1993.

Yang, Dao, and North, David. "Profile of the Highland Lao Communities in the United States." Washington, DC: U.S. Department of Health and Human Services, Family Support Administration, Office of Refugee Settlement, November 1988.

Yang, Kou. "Hmong Men's Adaptation to Life in the United States." *Hmong Studies Journal* 1.2 (Spring 1997): 1–21.

Lee, Sammy (1920–)

Olympic gold medalist and physician
Korean-American

Sammy Lee is best known for his Olympic gold medalist performances in diving both in 1948 and in 1952. He has also left a lasting mark as a respected physician, goodwill ambassador for the United States, and diving coach.

Lee was born on 1 August 1920 in Fresno, California. Son of Soonkee and Eunkee Lee, he grew up in a Korean-immigrant family with his two older sisters, Dolly and Mary. Like many Asian Americans of his era, Lee encountered racial prejudice on many fronts but he was determined to succeed. He was a top student and enrolled at Occidental College in southern California. Upon graduation in 1942 he entered the medical school at the University of Southern California (USC), joining the U.S. Army specialized training program in order to help finance his education.

Ten years earlier, Lee had attended the 1932 Olympics, held in Los Angeles, where his family had settled. He aspired to compete and win, and his interest and budding ability in diving brought him into contact with Jim Ryan, a former Olympic coach, who worked with Lee to shape him into a world-class athlete. By the time that Lee departed for the 1948 Olympics, the twenty-eight year old had graduated from Occidental College and USC medical school. In London that summer, Lee took the gold in platform diving and, four years later, repeated the feat in the 1952 games in Helsinki on his thirty-second birthday. In 1953, Lee became the first American of Asian descent to receive the prestigious James E. Sullivan Award, given to the outstanding U.S. amateur athlete.

Although Lee gained widespread recognition as an Olympic champion, he also found respect as a medical doctor specializing in the treatment of ear diseases. Yet, despite such international success and professional accomplishment, he faced the continuing hardships of racial prejudice when restrictive housing covenants barred him and his wife, Roz, from purchasing a home in Orange County. Journalist friend and CBS news correspondent Robert Pierpont used his contacts to publicize the Lees's fate, enabling Sammy Lee to break yet another barrier.

Lee's optimism and staunch belief in the opportunities that the country afforded him and his family paved the way for his many years as a goodwill ambassador for the United States. The State Department as well as Presidents Eisenhower, Nixon, and Reagan called upon Lee to represent the United States. In addition, for many years Lee coached aspiring American divers, taking hopefuls into his own home and working with them despite his busy medical practice. He helped guide future champions, including Olympic gold medal winners Bob Webster and Greg Louganis.

Lee is currently retired from his medical practice and from coaching but has continued to grant interviews and to speak at a wide range of conferences and other gatherings. He has long been active within the Korean-American community and in other civic affairs. In looking back on his life, Lee has tried to remember his father's advice that he would not be accepted as an American if he were not proud of the color of his skin and of his ancestral heritage.

David Yoo

REFERENCES

Hong, Terry. "Sammy Lee." In *Notable Asian Americans,* edited by Helen Zia and Susan B. Gall, 201–203. Detroit: Gale Research, 1995.

Kim, Hyung-chan, ed. *Dictionary of Asian American History.* Westport, CT: Greenwood Press, 1986.

Wampler, Molly Frick. *Not without Honor: The Story of Sammy Lee.* Santa Barbara, CA: Fithian Press, 1987.

Lee Tsung-Dao (1926–)

Physicist and professor
Chinese

A physicist, Lee Tsung-Dao (in the traditional Chinese-name format, which he used) is a pioneer in his field of study. In 1957 he shared the Nobel Prize with Chen Ning Yang for having refuted the long-held scientific hypothesis about the conservation of parity (regarding the interactions of colliding sub-atomic particles), a tenet in nuclear physics that had gone unchallenged since its formulation in the 1920s.

Born on 25 November 1926 in Shanghai, China, Lee Tsung-Dao was the son of Lee Tsing-Kong, a businessman, and Chang Ming-Chan. The family had their lives disrupted by the outbreak of the Sino-Japanese War. Lee had to flee in 1945 to the south when National Chekiang University at Kweichow, which he was attending, relocated and consolidated with other colleges and universities. In spite of the interruption, Lee did succeed the following year in earning a bachelor's degree in physics.

After graduation, Lee came to the United States on a Chinese government scholarship to study physics at the University of Chicago. While there, he studied under Enrico Fermi, a prominent nuclear physicist. After earning his Ph.D. in 1950, Lee was hired as a research associate by the Yerkes Astronomical Observatory, Lake Geneva, Wisconsin. By then, Communists ruled Mainland China, and Lee, like many other stranded Chinese students, applied for political refugee status, which allowed him to remain in the United States. In 1951 he joined University of California, Berkeley, as a research associate. A year later he moved to Princeton's Institute for Advanced Study.

At Princeton, Lee was reunited with Chen Ning Yang, a fellow student from his undergraduate days in China. Through their close study of other scientists' past experimentation, Lee and Yang solved a puzzling deadlock in elementary particle physics. Basically, when subatomic particles were placed in high-speed accelerators, the scientists discovered two new particles called K-mesons. One K-meson would decay into two pi-mesons and the other would decay into three. This was contrary to the laws of conservation of parity, which deemed that the natural world behaves in symmetrical ways. The two men paved the way for the rejection of those laws. They designed experiments to prove their hypothesis, and those experiments, as carried out by other

physicists at Columbia University and by government scientists, validated that hypothesis. For their work, they were awarded the 1957 Nobel Prize in physics. Lee and Yang were among the youngest (and the first from Mainland China) ever to receive the Nobel Prize. Since then Lee has done substantial theoretical work in such areas as statistical mechanics, astrophysics, hydrodynamics, and turbulence.

While working on his path-breaking project, Lee in 1953 had joined the Columbia University faculty, returned to Princeton, and finally went back to Columbia to take an endowed chair as the Enrico Fermi Professor of Physics. Lee has received numerous other honors and awards, including an honorary degree from Princeton. In addition, in 1980 Lee spearheaded efforts to set up the China–United States Physics Examination and Application (CUSPEA) program to enable talented Chinese physics students to pursue doctoral studies at U.S. universities. This project grew out of his personal life journey; the fellowship for American study that a Chinese physics teacher had helped him to secure in 1946 had changed his life, and he hoped to do the same for others.

Benson Tong

REFERENCES

Magill, Frank N. *The Nobel Prize Winners: Physics.* Vol. 2. Pasadena: Salem Press, 1989.

Wasson, Taylor, ed. *Nobel Prize Winners.* Princeton, NJ: Visual Education Corporation, 1987.

Lennon, John (1940–1980)
Musician
English

John Winston Lennon, founder of the Beatles music group, proved to be a creative giant in the music world. He took contemporary music in dramatically new directions and inspired many people around the world.

Lennon was born in Liverpool during a German bombing raid in 1940, son of Julia Stanley and Alfred Lennon, a merchant sailor who abandoned him and his mother. As a student at Quarry Bank High School, Lennon formed his first band, the Quarrymen, and invited his younger school friend, Paul Mc-Cartney, to join. Lennon quit the Liverpool College of Art in the late 1950s to turn his full attention to the band. Renaming themselves the Beatles in 1960, the members of the band developed their talents playing in the rough clubs in Hamburg, Germany, and in northern England.

In 1961 they signed with Liverpool businessman Brian Epstein, who cleaned up their rough image and introduced them to George Martin, the producer of the Beatles' recordings. By 1963 Beatlemania was sweeping Britain, and after their performance on the *Ed Sullivan Show* in the United States in 1964, the Beatles became an unparalleled force in popular culture throughout the world. Lennon and McCartney would become among the most successful and important rock musicians of all time.

By 1966 the Beatles had tired of touring, especially after Lennon made a comment about the Beatles being "more popular than Jesus," which resulted in protests and death threats in the United States. Also in that year, the Beatles became the first rock group to criticize the Vietnam War, a theme that Lennon would return to with great passion and conviction in later years. The Beatles decided to quit performing and concentrate on developing their music in the studio, and their musical development was astonishing. The albums *Rubber Soul* and *Revolver* included lyrics with serious social commentary and darker, more introspective melodies, much of which came from Lennon's influence. *Sergeant Pepper's Lonely Hearts Club Band* (1967), widely considered the most brilliant and significant rock album ever, included Lennon's songs "A Day in the Life," "Lucy in the Sky with Diamonds," and "Being for the Benefit of Mr. Kite." The Beatles revolutionized popular music. Moreover, Lennon's single *All You Need Is Love* became an anthem for the "summer of love" in 1969.

One important source for Lennon's new direction and the breakup of the group in 1970 was his relationship with Japanese-American avant-garde artist, Yoko Ono, whom he met in 1968 and married in 1969. In the early 1970s they lived in the United States, while Lennon applied for permanent-resident status. But his continued war protests and the potential embarrassment for Richard Nixon's reelection campaign in 1972 prompted surveillance and deportation orders. After Nixon's resignation, Lennon was finally granted permanent residency.

Determined to destroy his own legend as a rock superstar, Lennon quit music to be a househusband and raise his son, Sean, while Yoko attended to their business matters. The Lennons returned to the studio in 1980 to record their last album, *Double Fantasy*. In December 1980 he was assassinated by a deranged fan. The worldwide outpouring of grief revealed the depths to which John Lennon moved the soul of so many of the world's youth.

William E. Van Vugt

REFERENCES
Coleman, Ray. *John Winston Lennon*. London: Sidgwick & Jackson, 1984.
Wiener, Jon. *Come Together: John Lennon in His Time*. New York: Random House, 1989; Urbana: University of Illinois Press, 1991.

Lewis, John L. (Llewellyn) (1880–1969)

Labor leader
Welsh-American

John Llewellyn Lewis was one of the most important labor leaders in U.S. history. From lowly origins he rose to achieve wealth, power, influence, fame, and notoriety. He represents the significant Welsh contribution to the American labor movement, and in 1960 he was awarded the Presidential Medal of Freedom, the nation's highest civilian decoration, by President John. F. Kennedy.

Lewis was born in Lucas County, Iowa, in 1880. His parents were Welsh immigrants, his father a miner and farm laborer. In the late 1890s Lewis began working in local coal mines and, between 1901 and 1905, worked in mining and construction in the West. Returning to Lucas County, he established a business, but it soon failed. He married Myrta Bell, and they had three children. In 1908 they moved to the new mining town of Panama, in south-central Illinois. Lewis obtained a minor office with the United Mine Workers of America (UMWA) in 1901, and thus his union career was launched.

From 1911 on, Lewis rose rapidly. In 1920 he was elected president of the UMWA and would hold that office for forty years, ruthlessly maneuvering himself into a position of unassailable power. When Franklin D. Roosevelt became president in 1933, the political climate became far more favorable to labor than it had been during the 1920s, and Lewis exploited it. He revitalized the UMWA and devoted himself to successfully establishing unions among workers in the hitherto unorganized mass production industries. Between 1935 and 1940 he was president of the new Congress of Industrial Organizations (CIO), making him one of the most powerful men in the United States—and, in certain circles, one of the most hated. He played a crucial role in many strike victories for both his own union and the CIO, particularly the dramatic one following the General Motors sit-down strike at Flint, Michigan, in February 1937. He retired in 1960 but remained chair of the UMWA Welfare and Retirement Fund, his greatest legacy, until his death in 1969.

A great deal has been written about Lewis. He was a complex, charismatic, even contradictory character, whose massive physical presence alone ensured he could not be ignored. A great orator, negotiator, and strike tactician, he built the UMWA into a powerful, financially secure union, winning higher wages and improved working conditions. Thus, although he was a poor financial manager, had strong despotic tendencies, amassed great wealth, and lived opulently, he remained the champion of the miners, who stayed loyal to him because of the gains he secured for them.

Although Lewis grew up in the Welsh-speaking cultural milieu steeped in the mining and union traditions that his family brought over from Wales, its influence on him is uncertain. During his adult life he neither made much of his Welshness nor became involved in Welsh cultural activities. He was certainly aware of his roots and occasionally did express pride in his Welsh heritage. Some contemporaries associated his fighting spirit and championing of labor as proof that he was "a chip off the old Cymric block." Thus, even though Lewis's own relationship with his Welshness was ambivalent, on both sides of the Atlantic he remains one of the best-known Welsh Americans of all time.

Bill Jones

REFERENCES
Dubovsky, Melvyn. "Lewis, John Llewellyn." *Dictionary of American Biography*. Supplement 8 (1966–1970), edited by John A. Garraty and Mark C. Carnes, 374–377. New York: Scribner's, 1988.
Dubovsky, Melvyn, and Warren Van Tine. *John L. Lewis: A Biography*. New York: Quadrangle Books, 1977.
"John L." *Western Mail* (Wales), 13 June 1969, 10.
"John L. Lewis Dies." *New York Times,* 12 June 1969, 1, 34.
Roberts, Ron E. *John L. Lewis: Hard Labor and Wild Justice*. Dubuque, IA: Kendall/Hunt, 1994.
Zieger, Robert H. *John L. Lewis: Labor Leader*. Boston: Twayne Publishers, 1988.

Lewis, Loida Nicolas (1942–)
Corporate executive, immigration lawyer, and writer
Filipino

Between 1994 and 1999, Loida Nicolas Lewis won acclaim in corporate America as chair of the board and chief executive officer of TLC Beatrice International Holdings, a food distribution company with holdings in thirty-one countries and—with annual revenues of over $2 billion—the nation's largest African American–owned business in 1995. Simultaneously, she retained strong connections to Filipinos in the United States.

Born in Sorsogon Province on Luzon, in the Philippines, Nicolas enjoyed "privileged security" as the daughter of a wealthy furniture manufacturer. She received a B.A. degree from St. Theresa's College in Manila in 1963 and an LL.B. from the University of the Philippines in 1967. Given a world tour as a reward for passing the Philippine bar exam, Nicolas stopped in New York City, where a blind date with Reginald F. Lewis in 1968 changed the direction of her life.

In August 1969 Nicolas married Lewis, an African American with roots in the Baltimore ghetto and a law degree from Harvard. Two daughters were born to the couple during the next decade. Although Nicolas Lewis consistently put her husband's career before her own during their twenty-four-year marriage, she nonetheless carved a niche for herself in immigration law. In 1975, the year of her naturalization, she passed the New York State bar exam and applied for a job with the Immigration and Naturalization Service (INS). When the position was awarded to someone with lesser qualifications, she sued, won a judgment against the INS, and finally became an INS attorney in 1979. During the 1970s, with financial support from her husband, she also published *Ningas Cogon* (Brush fire), a magazine critical of Philippine president Ferdinand Marcos's martial law regime. Working a "nine to five" schedule during these years, Nicolas Lewis acknowledged her husband as the family's primary source of income.

In 1987, after Reginald Lewis's highly publicized $985 million leveraged buyout of TLC Beatrice, the family moved temporarily to Paris, where Loida Lewis drafted two books on immigration law: *How the Filipino Veteran of World War II Can Become a U.S. Citizen (According to the Immigration Act of 1990)* (1991) and *101 Legal Ways to Stay in the U.S.A., or How to Get a Green Card according to the Immigration Act of 1990* (1992).

When Reginald Lewis died of brain cancer in January 1993, his widow and their daughters inherited 51 percent of TLC Beatrice. After observing the yearlong period of mourning traditional in the Philippines, Loida Lewis took control of the company and, despite her lack of business experience, reversed its financial slide. From 1997 through 1999, she oversaw the liquidation of the company's holdings.

During the late 1990s, Loida Lewis also maintained her Filipino-American connections and her earlier interests. She supported the campaign for benefits for Filipino veterans of World War II, paying $50 fines for protestors who chained themselves to the White House fence in August 1997. The fourth edition of her book *How to Get a Green Card: Legal Ways to Stay in the U.S.A.*, coauthored with Len T. Madlansacay, appeared in August 1999.

Barbara M. Posadas

REFERENCES

Ciria-Cruz, Rene P. "Ready to Rumble." *Filipinas,* October 1997, 35, 52.

Dingle, Derek T. "TLC's Final Act." *Black Enterprise,* September 1999, 117.

"The Glass Ceiling." *Economist,* 26 August 1995, 59.

"Lewis, Loida Nicolas." In *Current Biography Yearbook 1997,* 321–324. New York: H. W. Wilson, 1997.

McCarroll, Thomas. "A Woman's Touch." *Time* 28 (October 1996): 60–62.

Silva, John L. "On Her Own." *Filipinas,* February 1996, 30–33.

Solomon, Jolie. "Operation Rescue." *Working Woman,* May 1996, 54–59.

Liam, Alison Prapaislip (1956–)
Merchant
Thai

How much impact can a small-business person have? The answer lies in the personal attributes of that individual and the particular historical characteristics of his or her business geography. Alison Prapaislip Liam represents a small-business person who has made a difference in the larger community in which she lives. Quietly, over a number of years, she has had a sociocultural impact on the St. Louis area, both as an individual and as a member of an extended family.

In Thailand, a multiethnic country, Liam grew up in an entrepreneurial family. Both her grandmother and her mother owned and operated grocery stores. Her father was in the mining industry and had a large number of employees. Liam recognized early that although there were people of many different ethnic backgrounds, they were all of one nation and should be treated equitably and respectfully. Today, she continues to build on this perspective in her personal and business relationships.

After finishing her political science degree in Thailand, Liam moved to the United States in 1982. The rest of her family was already in St. Louis, and there shet met and marreid Vinoi ("Noy") Liam. She immediately became engaged in the enterprises they had and continued to establish (Asian imports, an international foods grocery store, and a Thai restaurant). Many of these are now considered landmark businesses in an area known as the International Business District. Liam and her family have had a major impact on the character and development of that St. Louis area, contributing greatly to the revitalization of a dying urban zone by starting and maintaining businesses. Although for about twenty years Vietnamese and other refugees have been settling in the area, helping to stabilize the residential surrounding neighborhoods, it took entrepreneurs like the Prapaislip family to rejuvenate the commercial area and to remain committed to it. Once a declining neighborhood and business district, it is now prospering. Today, all types of businesses have moved into the area: upscale boutiques as well as restaurants, grocery stores, video stores, hair salons, and shops representing Middle Eastern, Latin American, Southeast Asian, and Far East–Asian traditions.

As a businessperson, Liam has had a dual impact on the larger community. First, she is a member of an extended family and of a family corporation, where she shares the responsibility of participating in the local business community. Second, through her own gregarious, energetic personality, she creates an environment of open engagement for her and her customers of different ethnic backgrounds. Her shop attracts people of every ethnicity, with the majority being black and white Americans. In a city where there is often tension between the races, Liam embodies the integrationist attitude and behavior actively espoused by community

and business leaders. Always curious about what others think and how they behave, she engages her customers in conversations reaching beyond the level of conventional communication, making her shop a "meeting place of the minds" as well as a business establishment.

Thus, Liam, through her family and as an individual, has added significantly to an urban neighborhood's growth and development and to ethnic understanding in her new St. Louis, Missouri, home. Moreover, the influence of Liam and her family has spread beyond the International Business District to nearby towns.

Pamela A. DeVoe

REFERENCES
Flannery, William. "Ethnic Stores Thrive in South Grand Area." *St. Louis Post-Dispatch,* 14 June 1993, Business, 12.
———. "Thai Restaurant, Food Store Anchor South Grand Boom." *St. Louis Post-Dispatch,* 8 January 1996, Business, 3.
Gross, Thom. "Special Blend: The Grand–Oak Hill Neighborhood Has a Strong, International Flavor." *St. Louis Post-Dispatch,* 26 April 1994, D1.
Liam, Alison. Interview with author, 14 May 1999.
Nguyen, My Linh. "Dream of Business Brings Taste of Asia to Main Street." *St. Louis Post-Dispatch,* 28 October 1996.
O'Neil, Tim. "A Distinctive Regional Culture Was Built with Influences from Foreign Places." *St. Louis Post-Dispatch.* 3 October 1999, B1.
VandeWater, Judith. "'Asiatown' Emerges on South Side." *St. Louis Post-Dispatch,* 24 July 1989, Business, 1.

Lieberman, Joseph Isadore (1942–)
Lawyer, politician, U.S. senator
Jewish-American

Joseph Isadore Lieberman has risen from state office in Connecticut to U.S. senator. In 2000 he was nominated for the U.S. vice presidency by the Democratic Party, the first Jewish American so chosen.

Lieberman was born in Stamford, Connecticut, in 1942 to Marcia (Manger) Lieberman and Henry Lieberman, a liquor-store owner and realtor. Raised in an Orthodox Jewish home, he attended the public schools and graduated from Yale University in 1964 and Yale Law School in 1967.

Although not especially religiously observant while in college, he saw Judaism as the foundation of a progressive political outlook, particularly the prophetic commandment *tikkun olam*, to repair the world. As editor of the *Yale Daily News,* he used his position to promote liberal activism, including voter registration drives in the Deep South. In 1963 he was himself active in Mississippi. He also worked in Washington, D.C., as a summer intern. After graduating from law school, Lieberman practiced law for several years until, in 1970, he won a seat in the Connecticut State Senate. After a decade there, including six years as majority leader, he ran unsuccessfully for Congress but he was elected Connecticut's attorney general in 1982. Popular as an environmentalist and consumer advocate, he was easily reelected in 1986.

In the middle of that second term he defeated three-term incumbent Republican Lowell P. Weicker, Jr., for the U.S. Senate, becoming that body's first Orthodox Jew. He proved to be a moderate liberal, voting with the Democrats on civil rights and environmental issues and supporting abortion rights, gun control, tax increases, welfare reform, minimum-wage increases, and consumer protections. On several issues, however, such as foreign policy and military defense spending, he joined the Republicans. A strong supporter of Israel, he was one of only ten Democratic senators to support U.S. involvement in the 1991 Persian Gulf war. Lieberman also departed from Democrats on other high-profile issues, especially those involving so-called family values. He has been an outspoken critic of sexual explicitness and violence in the arts and media and has supported tuition vouchers for children attending private schools. Moreover, he broke ranks again in 1997 by raising tough questions during hearings on charges of fund-raising abuses by the 1996 Clinton-Gore campaign. In 1998, once more demonstrating his political independence and moral sensitivity, Lieberman, a friend and ally of Bill Clinton for thirty years, publicly denounced the president's extramarital sexual encounters in the White House and their cover-up as not just inappropriate but immoral.

Lieberman has been as independent in his Orthodox Judaism as in his liberalism. Reflecting the relatively liberal standards of Modern Orthodoxy, he does not always wear a skullcap, is clean shaven, and, although avoiding campaigning and purely political activities on the Jewish Sabbath, has often felt obliged to serve, attending meetings and legislative sessions and voting. Sometimes criticized as a moralizer but more often dubbed "the conscience of the Senate," in 2000 Lieberman became the first Jew nominated for vice president on a major national ticket, a confirmation of the steady decline in anti-Semitism in the United States since 1945. Following an unprecedented election process, the Gore-Lieberman ticket had a popular vote majority but lost in the Electoral College. Lieberman retained his U.S. Senate seat.

Gerald Sorin

REFERENCES

"Lieberman, Joseph I." U.S. Congressional Directory: bioguide.congress.gov/scripts/biodisplay. pl?index=L000304 (accessed 18 September 2000).

Lieberman, Joseph I., with Michael D'Orso. *In Praise of Public Life.* New York: Simon & Schuster, 2000.

McFadden, Robert. "A Man of Steady Habits— Joseph Isadore Lieberman." *New York Times,* 8 August 2000, 1.

Turque, Bill. "The Running Mate: Joe Lieberman, Moralist and Politician." *Newsweek,* 21 August 2000, 26–31.

Lin, Maya (1959–)

Architect

Chinese-American

Maya Lin is an architect but also a sculptor and ultimately an artist. Her contributions embody a vision that strives for positive change. Since her controversial role in designing the unconventional Vietnam Veterans Memorial, Lin has a presence in the annals of American visual history and continues to hone her skills for artistic excellence.

Born on 9 October 1959 in Ohio, Lin is the daughter of Henry Huan Lin, a fine arts professor, and Julia Chang, who taught Asian and English literature. Both were refugees who had fled to the United States to escape from Communist rule in Mainland China and then joined the faculty of Ohio University, Athens, Ohio. Living in a small Midwest college town, Lin grew up with little Chinese-American sensibility. And yet, like her parents, she never felt really at home in Athens, sharing her parents' sense of displacement. But she also shared her parents' passion for the arts. Encouraged by them, she dabbled in ceramics, sculpture, and silversmithing. The time spent in the nearby hilly woods also nurtured an interest in nature; her later designs would always be site oriented, keeping intact the natural setting. The confluence of those experiences led her to pursue an architectural degree at Yale University.

At twenty-one, Lin submitted a design to a national contest for the Vietnam Veterans Memorial, a contest that attracted 1,421 entries. Her winning entry, now located between the Washington Monument and the Lincoln Memorial, involved two highly polished walls of black granite in the shape of a chevron that delved into the earth—symbolizing death—and then rose to meet at an angle, calling thus for remembrance. On these walls the names of the almost 58,000 dead or missing veterans of the Vietnam War would be inscribed.

Controversy quickly broke out, with a few even questioning the appropriateness of allowing an Asian American woman to design a national memorial to a U.S. military action in Asia. Lin was being seen as a "foreigner." A compromise of an additional statue and flag was worked out, although Lin was never consulted. She passionately spoke out against this threat to her artistic integrity. However, the memorial, dedicated on Veterans Day in 1982, has fulfilled Lin's aspirations. Thousands of visitors have been deeply moved, for it evokes reconciliation even as it memorializes losses. In 1987, just a year after she earned her master's degree in architecture, Yale conferred upon her an honorary doctorate of fine arts, and the following year she received the Presidential Design Award.

Since the Vietnam controversy, Lin has created a wide variety of projects, including the biblically inspired Civil Rights Memorial in Montgomery, Alabama; the Peace Chapel at Juniata College, Huntington, Pennsylvania; the "Women's Table" at Yale University; and the philanthropic Gleitsman Foundation sculpture in Malibu, California. More recently, Lin has also revamped museum spaces and designed client-oriented architectural and sculptural works.

Lin has acknowledged that her artistic vision is distinctly Asian in its simplicity and tendency to look inward. She is also aware that her works come from a female aesthetic and that she draws inspiration from her parents' fortitude and love for knowledge. She described herself as Chinese American with unique values.

Benson Tong

REFERENCES
Malone, Mary. *Maya Lin: Architect and Artist.* Springfield, NJ: Enslow Publishers, 1995.
Ng, Franklin. "Maya Lin and the Vietnam Veterans Memorial." In *Chinese America: History and Perspectives 1994,* 201–223. San Francisco: Chinese Historical Society of America, 1994.
Zinsser, William. "I Realized Her Tears Were Becoming Part of the Memorial." *Smithsonian* 22 (September 1991): 32–43.

Linares, Guillermo (1951–)
Educator and politician
Dominican

Guillermo Linares was the first Dominican American elected to public office in the United States, when in 1991 he was elected to the New York City Council. Linares's election marked the first major step in the political participation of the Dominican community in the United States.

Linares was born in Cabrera, a small town on the northern coast of the Dominican Republic. He lived on a farm until his family moved to New York City in 1965. A resident of the Bronx, Linares attended school while working at a number of odd jobs (e.g., supermarket clerk, taxi driver). He earned B.A. and M.S. degrees from City College of New York and became a teacher in 1975. During the 1970s, Linares also became increasingly politically aware as a result of the Civil Rights movement. He was president of City College's Dominican Students Association and lobbied for the creation of courses related to the Dominican Republic. In 1979, Linares and a group of Dominican professionals created the Community Association of Progressive Dominicans, a nonprofit community service organization located in Washington Heights, Manhattan, in the heart of New York's Dominican community.

His career as an educator led him to get involved with the school board, to which he was later elected. In 1989, he became the first Dominican to be elected president of a New York City school board (Community School Board 6). In 1991, New York City's council districts were reorganized, and a predominantly Dominican district was created in northern Manhattan. Linares was urged to run for the council and he was elected on the Democratic Party's ticket, thus becoming the first Dominican American to be elected to office in the United States. He was reelected in 1993 and 1997.

Linares represents the political emergence of the Dominican-American community, particularly in New York City, where the majority of U.S. Dominicans reside. In 1992, Linares had to face riots in the Dominican community of Washington Heights, sparked by the death of a Dominican man at the hands of the police. Thus, Linares's main priorities have become public safety and police relations as well as improving the deteriorated public image of his impoverished district. Linares introduced legislation for the creation of a police precinct in Washington Heights (the Thirty-third Precinct), which has drastically reduced crime levels in a neighborhood known for its drug problems. More recently, he was involved in a

bitter controversy over the establishment of a Pathmark supermarket in Harlem, as his opponents accused him of siding with big-business interests.

As the first Dominican American elected to office in the United States, Linares has come to represent more than his local constituents. To a certain extent, he also represents the interests of all Dominicans in the United States. As a result of his political prominence in the Dominican-American community, Linares is also usually courted by Dominican politicians visiting the United States, who see in him a liaison between the Dominican Republic and the U.S. political system.

Ernesto Sagás

REFERENCES

"District 10: Guillermo Linares (D)": www.council.nyc.ny.us/council/mh_lin_b.htm (accessed 13 June 2000).

Graham, Pamela M. "The Politics of Incorporation: Dominicans in New York City." *Latino Studies Journal* 9.3 (Fall 1998): 39–64.

Molina Morillo, Rafael. *Personalidades dominicanas 1993*. Santo Domingo: Molina Morillo & Asociados, 1993.

Perez, Luis. "El Político: Guillermo Linares": newmedia.jrn.columbia.edu/1997/projects/Weekly/Issue_3-Dominican/Linares/index.html (accessed 13 June 2000).

Lindbergh, Charles Augustus, Sr. (1859–1924)

U.S. House representative
Swedish-American

One of the leading representatives of his ethnic group in U.S. politics, Charles A. Lindbergh was born in Skåne Province, Sweden, and brought to the United States at the age of one. His father, Ola Månsson, took the name Lindbergh in the United States. Between 1847 and 1858, he had been a leading advocate of farmers' interests in the Swedish parliament; he immigrated to Minnesota due to political harassment. His son, Charles, would go on to become a prominent Progressive in the U.S. Congress.

Charles Lindbergh grew up on his family's farm and in 1883 earned a law degree at the

University of Michigan. He practiced law in Little Falls, Minnesota, becoming increasingly interested in politics. In 1906 he was elected for the first of five terms as a Republican to the U.S. House of Representatives.

A leading member of his party's Progressive wing, Lindbergh was particularly concerned with the economic problems caused by trusts and monopolies, banking and currency. In Congress and in his writings he worked for antitrust legislation, regulation of railroads, utilities, and banks, and improved working conditions, as well as female suffrage, conservation, and Prohibition. He staunchly supported President Theodore Roosevelt. When the latter's successor, William Howard Taft, appeared to align himself with the conservative Republicans, Lindbergh backed Roosevelt's unsuccessful bid for the Republican presidential nomination and subsequent campaign in 1912 as presidential candidate for the short-lived Progressive Party.

From the beginning of World War I in Europe in 1914, Lindbergh determinedly opposed U.S. intervention and war preparations. As American opinion became increasingly anti-German, his antiwar position cost him support. When he declined to run again for the House and instead sought nomination to the U.S. Senate in 1916, he lost to a more militant, prointerventionist candidate. In April 1917, a month after Lindbergh's congressional term expired, the United States declared war on Germany. Although Lindbergh recognized that Americans had no choice but to support their government, he privately published *Why Is Your Country at War?* three months later. In that book he predicted that the war's only beneficiaries would be financiers and large corporations, particularly the armaments manufacturers. The book aroused a furor, and most of the edition was seized and destroyed by the government. (It was reprinted in 1934 at a time of renewed isolationism in the United States.)

Undeterred, Lindbergh sought the Republican nomination for governor of Minnesota in 1918 against another Swedish American,

J.A.A. Burnquist, a vocal supporter of the war and "100 percent Americanism." Lindbergh lost the nomination in a bitter struggle, but by a narrow margin, showing the tacit support he still commanded among the state's largely Scandinavian- and German-American voters. Overall, his progressive Republicanism appears to have been characteristic of his mainly Protestant, rural, and small-town ethnic supporters. In 1924, he was nominated for governor by the Farmer-Labor Party but died in May, during the campaign.

Two years later, his son, Charles A. Lindbergh, Jr., became undoubtedly the most celebrated American of Swedish descent after he accomplished the first solo flight across the Atlantic. Yet, he was already too thoroughly assimilated to be considered an "ethnic" American.

H. Arnold Barton

REFERENCES
Larson, Bruce L., *Lindbergh of Minnesota*. New York: Harcourt Brace Jovanovich, 1971.
Lindmark, Sture. *Swedish America, 1914–1932*. Stockholm: Läromedelsförlaget, 1971.

Loewy, Raymond (1893–1986)
Industrial designer
French

Raymond Loewy helped to establish the profession of industrial design. His work for numerous American companies during more than three decades led to his renown (including being on the cover of *Time,* 31 October 1949). His work for U.S. institutions, ranging from the Super Market Institute to the National Aeronautics and Space Administration (NASA), made him a recognized figure in industrial design.

Loewy was born in Paris on November 5, 1893, the son of a managing editor of a financial journal. During his studies Loewy developed a taste for physics and drawing, inventing a prize-winning toy model airplane in 1908. Both his brothers had already left France for the United States when he decided to emigrate after serving in the French army during World War I. He arrived in the United

States in September 1919. Throughout the 1920s he found freelance illustration jobs for fashion magazines in New York City.

Loewy's 1929 Gestetner design for a new duplicator launched his career. In the 1930s he established himself as an industrial designer. Success came when he and other designers were able to convince industrialists that a good appearance, such as with the Sears Roebuck Coldspot refrigerator in 1934, was a sellable factor. In the 1940s, he worked for the U.S. war effort. Because of the shortage of metal, he designed a cardboard container for lipstick that sold in the millions. After the war, Loewy worked for Frigidaire, Greyhound Bus, Shell, BP, Coca-Cola, TWA, and United Airlines. (During this time he married Viola Erickson, following his divorce from Jean Thomson, whom he had wed in 1931.)

In the 1950s the field of industrial design blossomed in the United States, enabling Raymond Loewy Associates to grow. Their range extended from developing the "ranch station" for Shell to their highly successful packaging for Nabisco, to working on a safety car for the U.S. Department of Transportation, as well as cargo ships and nuclear transatlantic vessels. In 1952, Lowey created the Compagnie de l'Esthétique Industrielle, the Paris branch of his New York company; He also worked for European firms, and his designs included the French helicopter Alouette and a BMW racecar. He also visited Japan in the 1950s on a government-sponsored trip, and he contributed to establishing a blueprint for Japan's postwar industry.

In the early 1960s Loewy designed the new exterior for Air Force One. In fact, he was on friendly terms with President Kennedy and later designed the Kennedy commemorative stamp. He worked for NASA as a habitability consultant for the Saturn-Apollo-Skylab projects, and it was he who demanded that a porthole be fitted on the Skylab shuttle so that the astronauts could see the earth. In the 1970s Loewy transferred his offices to Europe because he thought that his U.S. division focused too heavily on store design. He then worked for the Soviet Union, the French railways, and for Air France, redesigning the interior of the Concorde.

In 1975, Loewy was honored with an exhibition at the Smithsonian Museum. Five years later, he retired and sold Raymond Loewy International to Farrell and Riedel, the directors of his London office. In 1983, he sold them the Paris branch. Loewy died in Monaco on July 14, 1986.

André J. M. Prévos

REFERENCES

Jodard, Paul. *Raymond Loewy*. Marlboro: Taplinger Publishing, 1992.

Loewy, Raymond. *Industrial Design*. London: Fourth Estate, 1980.

————. *Never Leave Well Enough Alone. The Personal Record of an Industrial Designer.* New York: Simon & Schuster, 1951.

Raymond Loewy Corporation. *Super Markets of the Sixties.* Vol. 1, *Findings and Recommendations.* Vol. 2, *Floor Plans and Sketches.* Chicago: Super Market Institute, 1960.

Schönberger, Angela, ed. *Raymond Loewy. Pioneer of American Industrial Design.* Munich, Germany: Prestel-Verlag, 1990.

Lopez, Alfonso "Al" Ramón (1908–)
Baseball player and manager
Spanish-American

Al Lopez's major league baseball career spanned thirty-nine years, half of them as catcher, the other half as manager. Inducted into both the national and Florida Halls of Fame for sports figures, he has been a local hero—a model of success—and an inspiration to "Latins" in his community. (In Tampa, the term *Latin* was used to describe the mixed ethnic backgrounds of the immigrant enclaves of Ybor City and West Tampa, which included Spanish, Cuban, and Italian immigrants and their descendants.)

Alfonso Ramón Lopez was born in Tampa, Florida, on 20 August 1908, the youngest of the nine children of Modesto and Faustina Lopez. His parents were Spaniards who had immigrated to Cuba at the turn of the century and moved from Cuba to Tampa in the 1900s to work in the booming cigar industry in Ybor City. Lopez became interested in baseball during the 1920 World Series. As a teenager, he played on several local baseball teams, for it was one of the most popular sports in the immigrant enclave. In 1925, he left high school and a job at a local bakery to sign a minor league contract. At sixteen, he was one of the youngest catchers in professional baseball. After a year with the Jacksonville Tars, he left in 1927 to play with the Brooklyn Dodgers.

In his nineteen years as catcher, he played for the Brooklyn Dodgers (1928–1935), the Boston Braves (1936–1940), the Pittsburgh Pirates (1940–1946), and the Cleveland Indians (1947). At the end of his playing days, Lopez held the record for the most games as catcher in a career (1,918), as well as the record for most games as catcher in the National League (1,861). After his playing career, Lopez then worked nineteen years as a manager, sixteen of them in the majors: the Indianapolis Indians (1948–1950)—the top farm club of the Pittsburgh Pirates—which won the American Association pennant in 1948 and finished second in the next two seasons; the Cleveland Indians (1951–1956); and the Chicago White Sox (1957–1965 and 1968–1969). While he was a major league manager, his teams won pennants twice, the Cleveland Indians in 1954 and the Chicago White Sox in 1959, and finished second ten times. Lopez was the only manager to interrupt the New York Yankees' pennant dynasty (1949–1964). He was inducted into the National Baseball Hall of Fame in 1977.

Throughout his career, Lopez maintained his links to Tampa, where he was a local hero for the Latin community. When he returned to Tampa at the end of each season, he was greeted by fans and friends and paraded down Ybor City's main thoroughfare. Tampa Latins felt very proud that the immigrant enclave had produced the city's first professional baseball player. His success paved the way for a new generation of Latin players. It also helped to break down some of the social barriers separating the immigrant enclaves from the larger Tampa community. Since his retirement, Lopez has made Tampa his permanent residence. He was inducted into the State of Florida Sports Hall of Fame and, in 1989, received an honorary doctorate from the University of South Florida. In 1992, the City of Tampa, the county, and the state paid tribute to his achievements by proclaiming 3 October 1992 "Al Lopez Day" and renaming a Tampa city park after him.

Ana M. Varela-Lago

REFERENCES

Brandmeyer, Gerard A. "Baseball and the American Dream: A Conversation with Al Lopez." *Tampa Bay History* 3 (Spring/Summer1981.): 48–74.

Frommer, Harvey. *Baseball's Greatest Managers*. New York: Franklin Watts, 1985.

Karst, Rene. *Who's Who in Professional Baseball*. New Rochelle, NY: Arlington House, 1973.

Mormino, Gary R., and George E. Pozzetta. *The Immigrant World of Ybor City: Italians and Their Latin Neighbors in Tampa, 1885–1985*. Urbana: University of Illinois Press, 1987.

Singletary, Wes. *Al Lopez: The Life of Baseball's El Señor*. Jefferson, NC: McFarland, 1999.

Smith, Myron J., Jr., compiler. *Baseball: A Comprehensive Bibliography*. Jefferson, NC: McFarland, 1986.

Luahine, Iolani (née Harriet Lanihau Makekau) (1915–1978)

Dancer and dance teacher
Hawaiian

Iolani Luahine, dancer, chanter, teacher, was the undisputed priestess of the ancient hula and an authentic living link to traditional Hawaiian culture. She has been called the last handmaiden to the Hawaiian gods.

Born in the small fishing village of Napo`opo`o, near Captain Cook, Hawai`i (the "big island"), Harriet Lanihau was the youngest of five daughters of Manasseh and Ko`olani "Mama Bessie" Makekau. She could trace her genealogy to dancers and keepers of the ancient Hawaiian rituals and chants. Her father decreed that she would carry on the Kaua`i traditions. Following the Hawaiian custom of having close relatives bring up one's children, she was sent to Honolulu to her great aunt, Keahi Juliet Luahine, who had been a dancer at the court of King David Kalakaua. When she was an infant, Makekau fell ill, and a seer declared that she had the wrong name and should be called Iolani Luahine. Her name was changed, and the illness passed.

Luahine's training began at age four, and her life was dedicated to Laka, the goddess of the hula. "The hula," she said, declaring it as a complete sentence, a single topic. Eating, sleeping, awake, it was always the hula. She attended Kamehameha School, a school for Hawaiian children, until her great aunt learned that the hula was forbidden there. She attended other schools, all the while training in the ancient forms of dance.

In 1940, Luahine received considerable attention as Hawai'i's representative at the National Folk Festival, in Washington, D.C. She appeared there again in 1946 and in 1971. In 1947, she organized a *halau* (a hula school) and made her professional debut in Honolulu. She was immediately hailed as a master—a position she held until her death. Yet during the 1940s, having danced for money, Luahine was tormented by the lapse of her vows to Laka, which prohibited the hula as entertainment. Similarly, she was unsuccessfully married to artist James McMahon (1951–1953), another breach of her vows, for, dedicated to the hula, she was forbidden to marry.

At that time there was little financial compensation for dancers, and at one point, Luahine worked as a telephone operator. In 1956, she took a position as curator at Hulihe'e Palace in Kailua-Kona, afterward becoming a custodian of the Royal Mausoleum in Nu'uanu and a guide at the Throne Room of Iolani Palace. She retired to Hawai'i Island in 1966, dividing her time between her volunteer work at Hulihe'e Palace and her childhood home in Napo'opo'o.

Luahine was uniquely creative and spirited in her dance. She was transformed in dance, as though she lent her form to the world of the past. "When Iolani dances," said dancer Ted Shawn, "you feel the thousands of years of dancing ancestors concentrated in this one body for their outlet and immortality. She is no longer just Iolani. She is Hawaii." Luahine was awarded the first State of Hawai'i Order of Distinction for Cultural Leadership in 1970 by the governor and in 1974 was named a Living Treasure of Hawai'i as the world's greatest exponent of Hawaiian dance. Luahine died in 1978.

David W. Shideler

REFERENCES

Cooks, Christina M. "The Art of the Hula as Seen in the Dance of 'Iolani Luahina." Dance Research, Fall 1983. Manuscript, Hamilton Library, University of Hawai'i at Manoa.

Haars, Francis. *Iolani Luahine*. Honolulu: Topgallant Publishing, 1985.

von-Garske, Elizabeth. *Iolani Luahine: The Lost Art of Hula as Seen in the Dance of 'Iolani Luahine, Handmaiden to the Gods,* an annotated bibliography. Hamilton Library, University of Hawai'i, 1988.

Lugosi, Bela (né Béla Blasko) (1882–1956)

Actor

Hungarian

Bela Lugosi has long been associated with the character he portrayed on the Broadway stage in 1927 and in a 1931 film, the romantic vampire Count Dracula. To this day, he is a bona fide American cinematic icon.

Béla Blasko was born on 20 October 1882 in Lugos, Hungary, the son of a baker turned banker. Blasko dreamed of being an actor and left home at age eleven to pursue his aspirations. In 1902, he secured a major stage role and started using various stage names, including Béla Lugosi. In 1910, he drew positive reviews for his lead role in *Romeo and Juliet* and became a matinee idol in his country.

Following military service in World War I, Lugosi debuted in a feature film in 1917. In 1918, he found himself participating in labor movements opposing the dictatorship of Michael Karolyi and marching for the establishment of unions for actors. When the Communist leader, Béla Kun, was ousted in 1919, Lugosi fled Hungary, settling in Berlin and continuing his film work there. He then decided to seek a new life—and greater fame—in the United States. Arriving in New Orleans in late 1920, he gained admission with the help of other Hungarian émigrés, for this artist was warmly welcomed by the Hungarian-American community.

Throughout the 1920s, Lugosi secured various supporting roles on the New York stage and starred in his first American film in 1923, *The Silent Command*. In 1927, following rave reviews for his performance in *The Werewolf*, he was offered the role that would mean stardom but also typecasting: the titular part in the Deane-Balderston play based on Bram Stoker's novel *Dracula*. The Broadway play with Lugosi was a sensation, running more than 1,000 performances. In 1930, Lugosi brought the vampire count to movie screens, and the next year *Dracula* was a box-office hit. Lugosi, however, rejected the role as the Monster in *Frankenstein*, which established Boris Karloff as the King of Horror. During that decade, Karloff and Lugosi would star together in several classic chillers, including *Son of Frankenstein,* in which Lugosi created his second-most-famous horror character, the sinister, broken-necked villain Igor.

In 1931 Lugosi became a U.S. citizen but would remain active on behalf of his native country. In World War II, as a self-proclaimed Socialist, he objected to Hungary's alliance with Germany, organized a short-lived American-Hungarian Defense Federation, participated in fund-raisers for refugees, and often spoke out on behalf of anti-Fascist forces in Hungary. He would also maintain his ties to the Hungarian community in southern California, supporting Hungarian sports leagues and entertaining other Hungarian notables in the entertainment industry, including actor Peter Lorre.

At the same time, Lugosi struggled to obtain important roles in Hollywood. Despite participation in major films, he found himself starring mostly in cheap films, which continued in the 1950s, for he was the victim of both changing tastes among filmgoers and a morphine addiction.

Lugosi died of a heart attack in August 1956 and was buried in his Dracula cape, tuxedo, and medallion. He was survived by his fifth wife, Hope, and one son, Bela Lugosi, Jr. (born in 1938).

John F. Crossen and Judith Fai-Podlipnik

REFERENCES

Beck, Calvin. *The Heroes of the Horror.* New York: Macmillan, 1975.

Bojarski, Richard. *The Complete Films of Bela Lugosi.* New York: Citadel Press, 1992.

Edwards, Larry. *Bela Lugosi, Master of the Macabre.* Brandenton, FL: McGuinn & McGuire Publishing, 1979.

Gordon, Richard, "An Appreciation of Bela Lugosi." In *Bela Lugosi*, edited by Gary J. and Susan Svehla, 209–217. Baltimore: Midnight Marquee Press, 1995.

Grey, Rudolph. *Nightmare of Ecstasy: The Life and Art of Edward Wood, Jr.* Los Angeles: Feral House, 1992.

Lenning, Arthur. *The Count: The Life and Films of Bela "Dracula" Lugosi.* New York: Putnam, 1974.

Rhodes, Gary Don. *Lugosi: His Life in Films, on Stage, and in the Hearts of Horror Lovers.* Jefferson, N.C.: McFarland, 1997.

Skal, David J. *Hollywood Gothic.* New York: W. W. Norton, 1990.

U.S. Department of State. Records of the Department of State Regarding the Internal Affairs of Hungary, 1933–1956. Washington, DC: GPO, 1984.

MacNeil, Robert Breckenridge Ware (1931–)
Journalist and author
Canadian

Best known for his work on the MacNeil-Lehrer News Hour, Robert MacNeil has enjoyed much acclaim in an interesting career that has spanned more than forty years. That is quite an accomplishment for someone who stumbled into journalism and intended to stay in it only until his first play had been produced.

MacNeil, born in Montreal, Quebec, was raised in Halifax, Nova Scotia. He first went to Dalhousie University but received his B.A. in 1955 from Carleton University, in Ottawa, Ontario. His broadcast career started in 1952, when he was working the night shift at CJCH radio, Halifax. In 1954 he worked for the Canadian Broadcast Corporation. He moved to London in 1955, getting a job as a subeditor at Independent News and then shifting to Reuters that same year. He advanced in Reuters, researching and writing important news stories. He became a foreign correspondent for NBC television and was based in London. He was transferred to Washington, D.C., in 1963. It is during this period that he gained some distinction for being one of the first to report that President Kennedy had been shot, making his call from the Texas Book Depository and running into Lee Harvey Oswald. Another moment of personal notoriety was when he visited Cuba during the missile crisis. He and other foreigners present there were detained by the authorities for nine days. Despite being in detention, he was still able to send out a report on the conditions there.

He moved to NBC radio in 1967, doing work on the program *Emphasis.* He then joined BBC London's program *Panorama,* doing various documentaries. He moved back to the United States in 1971 to work as a coanchor with Sander Vanocur on the newly created National Public Affairs Center for Television. Because of interference by the Richard Nixon administration, the job did not last long. He returned to London and the BBC. In 1973, he and Jim Lehrer were offered the opportunity to create a news broadcast program on the PBS network, to be called the *Robert MacNeil Report.* It became the *MacNeil-Lehrer News Report* and, in 1983, the *MacNeil-Lehrer Newshour.* MacNeil left the program in 1996.

While working for PBS, he cowrote and narrated the documentary *The Story of English,* which earned him an Emmy in 1987. He has also written several books. His first was *The People Machine: The Influence of Television on American Politics* (1968). He has since written two memoirs and two novels and has edited a book on the Kennedy years.

For his efforts, MacNeil has been greatly rewarded. He has received several honorary doctorates in Canada, the United States, and Britain, including one from his alma mater: Carleton University. He has four Emmy Awards, a Peabody, a George Dupont Award from the Columbia School of Journalism, and he is a fellow of the American Academy of Arts and Sciences. He was inducted as an officer in the Order of Canada in 1998. He and his third wife live in New York.

Gillian Leitch

REFERENCES

MacNeil, Robert. *Breaking News.* Garden City, NY: Doubleday, 1998.
———. *Burden of Desire.* Harvest Books, 1992.
———. *The People Machine: The Influence of Television on American Politics.* New York: Harper & Row, 1968.

———. *The Right Place at the Right Time.* New York: Penguin Books, 1982.

———. *Wordstruck: A Memoir.* New York: Viking, 1989.

"Robert MacNeil": www.emmys.org/awards/results.asp (Primetime Emmy Award Database). (Accessed 15 June 2000.)

"Robert MacNeil": www.gg.ca/cgi-bin/oc_details.pl?lang=e&rec_id=2525 (Order of Canada database). (Accessed 15 June 2000.)

Makemie, Francis (1658?–1708)

Presbyterian minister and leader
Scotch-Irish

Francis Makemie was Presbyterianism's most important leader and advocate in colonial America. He was also its most successful defender, apologist, and overseer of congregations.

Makemie was born near Ramelton, in County Donegal, Ireland. He was of Scottish ancestry, but little is known about his parents or early life. However, as a youngster during the 1660s, he did witness the persecution of Presbyterians in Ulster, which probably instilled in him a strong sense of religious independence. In 1676 he was admitted to the University of Glasgow, where he studied theology. He was ordained and licensed to preach in 1682. He immigrated to the Chesapeake region in 1683 because of restrictions against Presbyterians in Ulster and because he was attracted there by letters of invitation from a member of Lord Baltimore's council.

Makemie served as an itinerant minister in Maryland, Virginia, and North Carolina, and in 1687 he made his home in Accomack Country, Virginia, where, in addition to preaching, he acquired land and engaged in trading. During the 1690s he served as a minister in Barbados. He also engaged in trade there but retained his residence in Virginia, which he regarded as his true home. He was Virginia's second licensed dissenting minister. Makemie married Naomi Anderson, daughter of a rich landowner and merchant, from whom the couple inherited much property. He continued to combine his ministry with the promotion of trade and commerce in Virginia.

Makemie returned to England in 1704 in order to build his trading connections but, more important, to find some assistance for his ministry. In one of his first publications, *Truths in a True Light* (1699), he had stressed what Presbyterianism and Anglicanism had in common. But he had become concerned that Anglicanism was growing too fast in America at the expense of Presbyterianism. In 1705, when he returned to the Chesapeake with two new ministers to assist him, he encountered Anglican hostility and competition. He organized the first American presbytery in 1706 and served as its first moderator.

When in 1707 Makemie traveled to New York with a colleague in an attempt to expand the presbytery, they were arrested by the royal governor, Edward Hyde, Lord Cornbury, for preaching without permission. At his trial, Makemie claimed not only that he was protected by England's Act of Toleration of 1689 but also that the Church of England did not extend to the colonies and, therefore, the demand for toleration was not even necessary. The jury sided with Makemie, and thus the trial was a step toward greater religious freedom in the colonies. He wrote about the trial in his most important publication, a call for religious toleration, *A Narrative of a New and Unusual American Imprisonment of Two Presbyterian Ministers: And Prosecution of Mr. Francis Makemie* (1707).

Makemie, who died near his home in Virginia, was later called the Father of American Presbyterianism. He succeeded not only as a minister but also as a landowner. His estate included 5,000 acres—making him the second-largest landowner in Accomack county—and thirty-three slaves, indicative of the fact that many southern clergymen strongly believed in religious and political freedom yet supported slavery.

William E. Van Vugt

REFERENCES

Schlenther, Boyd S. *The Life and Writings of Francis Makemi.* Philadelphia: Presbyterian Historical Society, 1971.

Makino, Fred Kinzaburo (1877–1953)

Newspaper publisher and community leader
Japanese

Fred Kinzaburo Makino was an editor and community activist. He was the leading spokesperson of a vision of Americanism for Hawai`i's Japanese Americans that did not shy away from the fight for equal rights.

Makino was born on 28 August 1877 in Yokohama, the son of a British trader, Joseph Higgenbotham, and a Japanese woman from Kanagawa prefecture, Kin Makino. After the death of his father when Makino was only five, he and his four siblings were raised by his mother. He learned to read, write, and speak both Japanese and English from an early age, a skill that would prove invaluable.

In time, one of his older brothers, Eijiro, sent him to the "big island" of Hawai`i, where their eldest brother, Jo, operated a store. Makino arrived in April 1899. He first worked for his brother, then on two sugar plantations, and, in 1901, moved to Honolulu and opened Makino Drug Store. Two years later, he married Michie Okamura, a Nisei from Kapaa, Kauai.

Because Japanese immigrants were prohibited from practicing law, there was a legal services void. Makino opened a "law office" above his store. Dispensing legal advice and helping with paperwork made him keenly aware of the issues facing the immigrants, especially wages and conditions on the plantations. In 1908, he helped found the Higher Wage Association, which led a large-scale plantation workers' strike in 1909. Although the strike was eventually broken, many of the changes fought for were later granted. Makino and three other strike leaders were imprisoned, but they emerged from prison four months later as heroes in the community.

Makino then decided to start a newspaper not beholden to the planters, and began publishing the *Hawaii Hochi* on 7 December 1912. Despite its owner's financial hardship, the newspaper took difficult stands from the outset, supporting unity between Japanese and Filipino plantation workers and the Great 1920 Plantation Strike. It advocated citizenship for Issei veterans of World War I and fought attempts by the territorial government to regulate Japanese-language schools. Led by Makino, the fight went all the way to the U.S. Supreme Court. This effort split the Japanese-American community, but in a landmark 1927 decision, the court rejected all such regulation, a great victory for Makino. *Hochi*'s popularity soared.

When World War II came, Makino was one of the few Issei leaders not arrested by authorities, in part because he consciously rejected any connection to the Japanese consulate, never visited Japanese naval ships, and discouraged the purchase of Japanese war bonds, in contrast to the vast majority of Issei. Still, all Japanese-American newspapers were taken over by the military government during the war, and Makino's influence waned after the war, as many of his key aides died.

In 1949, he and his wife went to Maui and climbed to the top of Haleakala crater. Two days later, he suffered a heart attack, never fully recovered, and died at age seventy-six, in 1953. The *Hawaii Hochi* and its sister publication, the exclusively English-language *Hawaii Herald*, continue to be published in Hawai`i.

Brian Niiya

REFERENCES

Compilation Committee for the Publication of Kinzaburo Makino's Biography. *Life of Kinzaburo Makino.* Honolulu: Hawaii Hochi, 1965.

Kitano, Harry H. L. *Japanese Americans: The Evolution of a Subculture.* 2d ed. Englewood Cliffs, NJ: Prentice Hall, 1976.

Kotani, Roland. *The Japanese in Hawaii: A Century of Struggle.* Honolulu: Hochi, Ltd., 1985.

Ogawa, Dennis M. *Kodomo No Tame Ni, for the Sake of the Children: The Japanese American Experience in Hawaii.* Honolulu: University Press of Hawaii, 1978.

Malcolm X (El Hajj Malik El Shabazz) (né Malcolm Little) (1925–1965)

Nationalist leader
African American

Malcolm X (El Hajj Malik El Shabazz) was one of the most vital African American political leaders of the latter half of the twentieth century. His iconic stature often obscures the contributions he made. He transmitted a militant black nationalist tradition to a new generation of activists during the 1960s.

Born Malcolm Little on 19 May 1925 in Omaha, Nebraska, he was one of eight siblings. Both parents were members of Marcus Garvey's Universal Negro Improvement Association (UNIA), and Malcolm's father led local UNIA meetings until 1931, when he mysteriously died. Devastated by the Great Depression, Malcolm's mother suffered a mental collapse, and authorities separated the children.

In Boston and later in Harlem, Malcolm was drawn to the flamboyant aspects of the zoot-suit culture of the early 1940s. But like a number of African American youth who adopted this lifestyle, he became immersed in illegal activity and in 1946 received a ten-year prison sentence for breaking and entering. While an inmate, he molded himself into a disciplined intellectual and became acquainted with the Lost-Found Nation of Islam (NOI). Formed in Detroit around 1931, the NOI was an amalgam of unorthodox Muslim religion and Garveyite nationalism. Malcolm, after his release in 1952, began his ministry in the NOI, dropped his last name, and adopted an "X" to signify black people's severed ties to their African past. In 1958, he married fellow Muslim Betty X.

By addressing the frustrations of black urban working people, Malcolm helped transform the NOI by the early 1960s into a national organization with over 200 temples. As national spokesman and editor of NOI's newspaper, *Muhammad Speaks,* he became the most visible and eloquent proponent of the organization's worldview. Nevertheless, he was becoming skeptical of the NOI's racialist doctrines and increasingly frustrated with the NOI's lack of involvement in secular politics, envisioning a fusion of black nationalist strategies and the mass direct action taking place during the period. Because of policy differences and internal scandals, in 1963 Elijah Muhammad, NOI's leader, suspended Malcolm.

After leaving the organization in 1964, Malcolm made two tours of Africa and during a religious pilgrimage to Mecca assumed the name El Hajj Malik El Shabazz. He also met several leaders of African nations, prompting him to form the Organization of Afro-American Unity (OAAU). He drew analogies between racial oppression in the United States and colonialism and imperialism abroad in an attempt to force the Civil Rights movement to adopt a more internationalist, pan-African orientation. He courted the young activists of the militant Student Nonviolent Coordinating Committee and built a working relationship with the Revolutionary Action Movement. But this all was aborted on 21 February 1965, when two NOI gunmen assassinated him during an OAAU meeting in Harlem. He left a widow and four young daughters.

Malcolm paved the way for the Black Power movement, and the OAAU became an antecedent to a series of black nationalist groupings during the 1970s. In the late 1980s and early 1990s, a new generation of black youth was introduced to Malcolm through music and other cultural items and a major motion picture directed by Spike Lee in 1992.

Clarence Lang

REFERENCES

Cone, James H. *Martin and Malcolm and America: A Dream or a Nightmare.* Maryknoll, NY: Orbis, 1992.

Evanzz, Karl. *The Judas Factor: The Plot to Kill Malcolm X.* New York: Thunder's Mouth Press, 1992.

Goldman, Peter. *The Death and Life of Malcolm X.* 2d ed. Urbana: University of Illinois Press, 1979.

Malcolm X. *February 1965: The Final Speeches.* New York: Pathfinder, 1992.

Malcolm X and Alex Haley. *The Autobiography of Malcolm X.* New York: Ballantine Books, 1965.

Sales, William W., Jr. *From Civil Rights to Black Liberation: Malcolm X and the Organization of Afro-American Unity.* Boston: South End Press, 1994.

Wood, Joe, ed. *Malcolm X: In Our Own Image.* New York: St. Martin's Press, 1992.

Mallet, Edmond (1842–1907)
Historian, community activist,
and federal official
French Canadian

Edmond Mallet is remembered as a Civil War hero, ethnic activist, historian, and bibliophile. He also took photographs of various Native American families, which have not yet been published.

Born in Montreal, Mallet accompanied his family in their immigration to Oswego, New York. The Civil War having begun, he left his study of law at age nineteen to join the Eighty-first Regiment of New York Volunteers. He participated in about twenty-two battles and in numerous skirmishes. Wounded almost fatally during the Battle of Cold Harbor, Virginia (3 June 1864), he received a rarely given double promotion on the same day: from lieutenant to captain to major, for "distinguished gallantry in battle." After the war, he completed his studies at Columbian College, in Washington, D.C., and received his law degree "with high honors." He then embarked on a long career as a civil servant, beginning in the Treasury Department.

Contacts with French Canadians and their writings revived his interest in his ethnic heritage, and he soon became a zealous campaigner in the effort to preserve that heritage in the United States. A gifted orator, he was invited to every large French Canadian gathering in the United States and Canada. He became known as a pillar of *survivance,* an ideology whose main tenets were the cultivation of the French language, of French Canadian customs and traditions, and of a form of militant Catholicism, one goal of which was to convert non-Catholics through constant prayer. In addition, his was a major voice in Washington, where he was ever ready to help his fellow immigrants in every possible way.

Mallet also proved to be a skilled mediator between Native Americans and the federal government. Appointed U.S. Indian inspector by President Grover Cleveland (1888) after serving as a U.S. government agent for the District of Puget Sound (1887), he developed amicable relations with Arapahos, Omahas, Sioux, Winnebagos, and others. The photographs he took of various Native American families have been awaiting publication for the past century. His objectives regarding the Native Americans were clear: pacification, temporization, and slow, gradual assimilation into the American mainstream. He also strove to preserve what little was left of the multifarious Native American heritage.

A born researcher, he published substantive articles on French and French Canadian explorers and military men, several of whom he perceived as heroic figures. This research led him to acquire a sizable collection of books, brochures, newspaper articles, letters, and other priceless manuscript materials. Fortunately, this collection was acquired and preserved by Union Saint Jean Baptiste, a Franco-American fraternal and cultural insurance society headquartered in Woonsocket, Rhode Island, where it is made available to researchers. This trove is clearly the outstanding element of his legacy. Edmund Mallet died in 1907.

Armand Chartier

REFERENCES

Anctil, Pierre. "Les letters de Gabriel Dumont au Major Edmond Mallet." *Recherches amerindiennes au Quebec* 10.1–2 (1980): 53–66.

Belisle, Alexandre. *Histoire de la presse franco-americaine.* Worcester, MA: L'Opinion publique, 1911.

Nadeau, Gabriel. "L'oeuvre historique d'Edmund Mallet." *Bulletin de la Société Historique Franco Américaine,* 1941, 49–60.

Manoogian, Alex (1901–1996)
Industrialist, inventor, and philanthropist
Armenian

Alex Manoogian, an enterprising immigrant and modest manufacturer, transformed an unsuccessful household plumbing design into a major manufacturing empire. With that success, he became the principal philanthropist in the Armenian-American community as well as a major contributor to numerous projects worldwide.

Manoogian was born in an Armenian village near the ancient Greek city of Smyrna (now Izmir), in the Ottoman Empire. The son of Tacouhie and Takvor Manoogian, a prosperous grain and raisin merchant, he attended the rural Jevahirjian School and then the Greek and Jewish Schools in Smyrna, learning five languages in the process. Foreseeing trouble (Smyrna would be sacked by Turkish nationalist forces in 1922), Manoogian came to the United States in 1920, intending to establish himself and then send for his family.

He first settled in Connecticut, learning English in the process, and then went to Detroit, Michigan, to be near the high-wage automotive industry. Manoogian taught himself mechanical skills and gained insights into manufacturing processes. In 1929 he and two partners (whom he soon bought out) founded Masco Screw Products, which began as a supplier to the automotive industry. Growth was slow but steady until Manoogian purchased the rights to a failed single-handed faucet design. Redesigning and then marketing the Delta faucet in 1954 turned Masco into a major international success.

In 1931 Manoogian was able to bring his parents and siblings to the United States. He married Marie Tatian, an Armenian who had arrived in the United States in 1910 at the age of eight. Their marriage lasted sixty-two years, until her death in 1993. They had two children.

Manoogian's commitment to Armenian Americans extended past mere philanthropy. In his early years in the United States he taught Armenian to immigrants who had become so denationalized by oppression they had forgotten their native tongue. However, his greatest impact was through his philanthropy, for either directly or through the Armenian General Benevolent Union (AGBU), the Alex Manoogian Cultural Fund, and the Alex and Marie Manoogian Foundation, he gave away $90 million to organizations and people in the United States and worldwide. He donated considerable sums in the United States to the Eastern and Western Dioceses of the Armenian Apostolic church; many of the local Armenian churches; the AGBU; the Manoogian Manor, an Armenian senior citizens' home in Livonia, Michigan; and to the Alex Manoogian Chair of Modern Armenian History and the Marie Manoogian Chair of Modern Armenian Language and Literature at the University of Michigan, Ann Arbor. In addition to grants to several major universities and hospitals, he contributed to the Ford and Carter presidential libraries as well as donating his home to Detroit as the mayor's official residence.

Unsurprisingly, he was a leading member of many Armenian-American organizations: grand commander of the national Grand Lodge of the Knights of Vartan (similar to the Knights of Columbus); president, and then life president, of the Armenian General Benevolent Union; and president of the Armenian Apostolic Society. No project of any sizable monetary amount would even be considered by Armenian Americans before they had consulted him.

Manoogian died in 1996. His son, Richard, became chairman of Masco, and his daughter, Louise, became president of the AGBU.

Dennis R. Papazian

References

Alex Manoogian: The Man, the President, the Humanitarian. Saddle Brook, NJ: Armenian General Benevolent Union, n.d.

Azadian, Edmond. *Alex Manoogian—An Armenian Hero.* Southfield, MI: Alex Manoogian Tribute Committee, 1995.

Azadian, Edmond, and Gary Zamanigian. *Alex Manoogian: Eighty Years of Service to the Armenian Church.* Southfield, MI: St. John's Armenian Church, 1994 program booklet.

Dekmejian, R. Hrair, et al., eds. *Who's Who among Armenians in North America.* Pasadena, CA: Millennia Publishers, 1995.

Hoffman, Gary. "Inventor Alex Manoogian, Founder of the Manoogian Empire, Is Dead at Ninety-five." *Detroit News,* 12 July 1996, A1.

Musial, Robert. "He Reached U.S. with $50; He's Given Away 50 Million." *Detroit Free Press,* 1 April 1990.

Vlasic, Bill. "Manoogian's Quest: From Faucets to Fortunes, MASCO Empire Flourishes." *Detroit News,* 20 August 1988.

Marohnič, Josip (1866–1921)
President of the National Croatian Society and publisher
Croatian

Josip Marohnič achieved recognition within the U.S. Croatian community and in Croatia as a publisher, writer, and leader of the fraternal movement among Croatian Americans. He was president of the National Croatian Society (NCS), the predecessor of the Croatian Fraternal Union, still the largest Croatian fraternal organization in North America.

Marohnič was born in Hreljin, in the Croatian coastland. He immigrated to the United States at the age of twenty-eight, in 1904, after serving in the Austrian navy. He settled in Chicago and worked as a printer-typographer but soon moved to Pittsburgh, where the NCS was headquartered. He became treasurer of the society until he was elected president in 1909, and he was re-elected president at successive conventions until he died in 1921.

In the late 1890s, Marohnič built his own printing house and established a Croatian bookstore. At first he sold only books and newspapers from Croatia. Later, he published books in which he offered advice to Croatian-American immigrants; the *Hrvatski Glasnik* (Croatian herald), a weekly Croatian newspaper; annual almanacs, beginning in 1898 with *Hrvatska vila-Kalendar* (Croatian village-calendar) and later *Domobran i Orao* (Defender of the home and eagle); in 1899, the first Croatian-American humorous monthly, *Brico* (Funny); the first English-language textbook for the use of Croatian immigrants; the first anthology of Croatian poetry in the United States, *Amerikanke* (American women); and in 1913 *Velika narodna hrvatska pjesmarica* (Grand anthology of Croatian poetry), a 700-page collection of Croatian-American art and people's poetry. Moreover, in 1904 he published the first Croatian-English/English-Croatian dictionary as well as one by Croatian lawyer Francis Bogadek (1908), which Croatian Americans are still using.

As treasurer of the NCS, Marohnič re-formed the way insurance was collected by the society, for, at first, the fraternal organizations collected no assessments. When a member died, the other lodge members gathered money to pay $400 or $600 to the remaining family members. That was acceptable when members were relatively young and planning to return home to Croatia. However, it was not attractive to younger members with families who wanted to stay in the United States, for they ended up paying for older members. Marohnič very quickly proposed regular assessments, with differing amounts based on the age of the member. However, it took some time—and fights within the society—before the plan was implemented at the 1912 convention.

During World War I, Marohnič, as president of the NCS, initiated a fund to help Croatian orphans in Croatia. The society contributed $15,000 to that fund; individual lodges and members contributed more than $50,000. The NCS also financially supported the Yugoslav Committee, an organization of émigré politicians who fled Austria-Hungary during World War I and gathered in London to work for the unification of Austria-Hungary's South Slavs with Montenegro and Serbia. The society gave $10,000 to support that effort. Marohnič was likewise instrumental in organizing political gatherings of Croatian and other South Slavic immigrants in the United States to support the cause of the Yugoslav Committee.

Matjaž Klemenčič

REFERENCES

Čizmić, Ivan. *History of the Croatian Fraternal Union of America, 1894–1994.* Zagreb: Golden Marketing, 1994.

Lupis-Vukić, Ivan. "Josip Marohnič—najzaslužniji predsjednik Narodne Hrv. Zajednice, Uz 60-godisnjicu H.B.Z" (Josip Marohnič, the most deserving president of the National Croatian Society—on the occasion of the Sixtieth Anniversary of the Croatian Fraternal Union). *Matica, List Matice iseljenika Hrvatske* (Bee, paper of the Croatian Emigrant Society), 4 June 1954, 126–128.

Prpić, Jure. *Hrvati u Americi.* (Croats in America). Zagreb: Hrvatska Matica Iseljenika, 1998.

Marshall, Louis (1856–1929)
Attorney, philanthropist, and community leader
Jewish-American

Louis Marshall, the son of German Jewish immigrants, was a believer in the concept of noblesse oblige, or "stewardship," and went on to become a brilliant attorney, philanthropist, civil servant, and perhaps the most capable communal leader of his era. He met with President Benjamin Harrison in 1891 on behalf of Russian Jewry and presided over the Jewish delegation to the Paris Peace Conference in 1919.

Marshall was born in Syracuse, New York, in 1856 and graduated from Columbia Law School. Between his graduation in 1877 and 1894, he argued more than 150 cases before the New York State Court of Appeals, while also taking up the burdens of communal leadership in his early thirties and playing a prominent role in Syracuse's Jewish community. Marshall's stature and reputation were already such that he was included in a delegation that visited President Benjamin Harrison in 1891 on behalf of a Russian Jewry beleaguered by pogroms and anti-Semitic decrees.

Marshall became preeminent in his service to fellow Jews, serving several terms as president of Manhattan's Temple Emanu-El, the flagship Reform synagogue in the United States. In 1902, he recognized that a more traditional Judaism than Reform was needed to serve eastern European Jews as a bridge to the U.S. mainstream. Together with Jacob Schiff, Cyrus Adler, and others, he raised $500,000 to reenergize New York's Jewish Theological Seminary in order to train a religious leadership that would be more attractive to these newcomers. Indeed, Marshall felt little of the disdain for the new Jewish immigrants typical of the German Jews in the United States and he even learned Yiddish in order that he might serve as a link between the German Jewish community and the new arrivals.

Moreover, as president of the Jewish delegation to the Paris Peace Conference in 1919, Marshall was instrumental in securing protection for the Jews in eastern Europe through the incorporation of minority rights clauses in the constitutions of the newly created states there. Although not a political Zionist, he also understood the need for Palestine as a center of Jewish culture and settlement, especially after the United States severely limited immigration from southern and eastern Europe in the 1920s.

Marshall had helped establish the American Jewish Committee (AJC) in 1906 and served as its president from 1912 to 1929, defending the causes of American Jews. His leadership was crucial in the AJC's successful lobbying effort on behalf of New York's Civil Rights Act of 1913. Furthermore, Marshall believed in the indivisibility of civil rights and was a consistent champion of other minorities, fighting major legal battles on behalf of blacks and in a number of watershed cases affecting such important social issues as alien migration, child labor laws, and church-state relations. His most noteworthy victory came in 1925, when the U.S. Supreme Court upheld Marshall's contention that an Oregon law denying Catholics the right to send their children to parochial schools was unconstitutional. In the same decade Marshall continued to battle an increasing anti-Semitism, including Harvard University's plan to institute a quota limiting the admission of Jews. He was central to the public exposure of the anti-Semitic forgery, "The Protocols of the Learned Elders of Zion," published in Henry Ford's newspaper, the *Dearborn Independent*. In 1927, Ford apologized for his anti-Semitic agitation. Louis Marshall died in 1929.

Gerald Sorin

REFERENCES
Cohen, Naomi. *Not Free to Desist: The American Jewish Committee, 1906–66.* Philadelphia: Jewish Publication Society, 1972.
Goren, Arthur. *The New York Jews and the Quest for Community.* New York: Columbia University Press, 1970.
Reznikoff, Charles, ed. *Louis Marshall: Champion of Liberty.* 2 vols. Philadelphia: Jewish Publication Society, 1957 [selected papers and addresses].
Rosenstock, Morton. *Louis Marshall: Defender of Jewish Rights.* Detroit: Wayne State University Press, 1965.

Rosenthal, Jerome C. "The Public Life of Louis Marshall." Ph.D. diss., University of Cincinnati, 1983.

Marshall, Thurgood (né Thoroughgood) (1908–1993)

Civil rights lawyer, U.S. solicitor general, and U.S. Supreme Court justice
African American

Thurgood Marshall, U.S. Supreme Court justice, fought for civil rights causes all his life. As special counsel for the National Association for the Advancement of Colored People (NAACP), Marshall argued such cases as *Brown v. Board of Education of Topeka, Kansas* and, as solicitor general, argued the Miranda case, protecting suspects' rights. At the NAACP and on the bench Marshall never wavered from his liberal and egalitarian political commitments and proved a determined— and sometimes lonely—defender of civil rights and civil liberties.

Thoroughgood Marshall was born in Baltimore on 2 July 1908. He was named after a paternal grandfather who had chosen that name when joining the Union army, but by the third grade, he had shortened it to Thurgood. For his frequent rambunctiousness in school Marshall was punished by having to read the U.S. Constitution; he had it memorized by the time he graduated. In 1925 he left to study at Lincoln University, near Philadelphia, where he married Vivian Burey in 1929. The next year he graduated and attended Howard University Law School. He studied there with prominent civil rights jurist Charles Houston and earned his LL.B. in 1933.

While employed by a private Baltimore law practice, Marshall found time to work for the local NAACP, where he fought against employment and education discrimination. In 1936 the NAACP invited him to join its national office in New York as assistant special counsel, working alongside mentor Charles Houston and others. Two years later, he became head special counsel and, in 1940, director of the NAACP's Legal Defense and Education Fund.

Marshall argued civil rights cases until 1961. He challenged segregation and discrimination in voting, higher education, jury selection, and, most famous, public school segregation, which culminated in the stunning victory in *Brown v. Board of Education of Topeka, Kansas* (1954). When the Civil Rights movement employed civil disobedience, Marshall defended demonstrators, protests, and boycotts. In every instance he continued Houston's legal strategy of using each case as a stepping-stone to reach broader civil rights goals. Of the thirty-two cases he and the NAACP argued before the Supreme Court, the association won twenty-nine.

Marshall's wife died in 1955; almost a year later he married Cecilia Suyat, with whom he had two children. In 1961, John Kennedy named Marshall to the U.S. Court of Appeals. Four years later Marshall became the first African American solicitor general, representing the government before the Supreme Court. Lyndon Johnson nominated Marshall to the Supreme Court in 1967, and despite the fierce opposition of several southern senators, he was confirmed. He joined the Court as its first African American justice on 2 October 1967.

He remained on the Court through its era of liberal activism in the 1960s and 1970s and its conservative retrenchment thereafter. Ill health forced his retirement in 1991. Throughout, he remained a champion of individual rights, civil rights, and civil liberties, sometimes as a minority of one. Thurgood Marshall died on 24 January 1993.

Cheryl Greenberg

REFERENCES

Ball, Howard. *A Defiant Life: Thurgood Marshall and the Persistence of Racism in America.* New York: Crown Publishers, 1998.

Davis, Michael, and Hunter Clark. *Thurgood Marshall: Warrior at the Bar, Rebel on the Bench.* Secaucus, NJ: Carol Publishing Group, 1992.

Goldman, Roger. *Thurgood Marshall: Justice for All.* New York: Carroll and Graf, 1992.

Rowan, Carl. *Dream Makers, Dream Breakers: The World of Justice Thurgood Marshall.* Boston: Little, Brown, 1993.

Tushnet, Mark. *Making Civil Rights Law: Thurgood Marshall and the Supreme Court, 1936–1961*. New York: Oxford University Press, 1994.

———. *Making Constitutional Law: Thurgood Marshall and the Supreme Court, 1961–1991*. New York: Oxford University Press, 1997.

Williams, Juan. *Thurgood Marshall: American Revolutionary*. New York: Times Books, 1998.

Martí, José (1853–1895)
Writer and activist
Cuban

José Martí was born on 28 January 1853 in Havana, Cuba. From his youth he devoted himself to fighting Spanish colonialism and building the foundations for a democratic, free Cuba. At age seventeen, he was deported to Spain. He made his way to the United States in 1880 and spent almost the rest of his short life in New York City. Fifteen years of cease-less activity made him a commanding figure in Cuba's struggle for independence.

For years Martí's significance as a writer was overshadowed by his fame as a political leader; today, he is recognized as a leading fig-ure of Modernism, the literary movement that asserted the maturity of Latin American let-ters. Indeed, shortly after his arrival in New York, he started contributing articles revealing a profound understanding of Hispanic culture to the *Hour* and the *New York Sun*. His vision of "Nuestra América," as he called the nations south of the Río Grande, led several Latin American republics to name him their official representative.

For *La Nación,* a widely read Argentine newspaper, Martí chronicled life in the United States. The electoral process and the ritual of inauguration inspired many of his stories. Besides the political climate of the United States, episodes from New York City to the Far West were immortalized in his "Es-cenas norteamericanas," (North American scenes) including the installation of the Statue of Liberty and the opening of the Brooklyn Bridge. Ralph Waldo Emerson, Walt Whitman, Edgar Allan Poe, Mark Twain, Washington Irving, and other authors were made known in South America through his writings.

Like many exiles, Martí held odd jobs, working as a translator, a teacher of French, Spanish, and oratory at a night school, and even as a bookkeeper. But he maintained two undying passions: freeing Cuba and literature. Whether in his office on Front Street, on board the ferry shuttling across the East River, or on a train to Tampa or Key West to meet Cuban tobacco workers, he was writing.

Although he was frail and small in stature, Martí's personality drew people to him like a magnet. The immigrant seeking employment, the cigar maker from Havana on vacation, a friend bringing a relative to the United States for an operation, a young poet eager to publish a new book often crowded his tiny office in downtown Manhattan. Nevertheless, his life in the "Iron city" was lonely. His wife and young son joined him for a brief period, but Carmen Zayas Bazán did not share her husband's revo-lutionary zest, and the couple separated.

José Martí died in battle at Dos Ríos, Ori-ente, in Cuba, on 19 May 1895, at the age of forty-two. The most important figure in Cuban history, he is revered by Cubans in his country and in diaspora not only as a man of letters but also as the apostle of Cuba's independence. When he walked the streets of New York City, this Latin American prophet with dark piercing eyes remained an uprooted foreigner, another face in the crowd. Today, a magnificent eques-trian statue of José Martí stands tall in the fringes of Central Park, as a tribute to the gentle man of letters slain in battle.

Uva de Aragón

REFERENCES

Calatayud, Antonio, ed. *Martí visto por sus contem-poráneos. Selección y prólogo: Antonio Calatayud* (Martí as seen by his contemporaries. Selections and prologue by Antonio Calatayud). Miami: Mnemosyne Publishing Co., 1976.

Martí, José. *The America of José Martí. Selected writings of José Martí*. Translated by Juan de Onís, with an Introduction by Federico de Onís. New York: Noonday Press, 1953.

———. *Martí on the USA*. Selected and translated, with an Introduction by Luis A. Baralt.

Carbondale and Edwardsville: Southern Illinois University Press, 1966.

Quesada y Miranda, Gonzalo de. *Martí, hombre* (Martí, the man). Miami: Editorial Cubana, 1998.

Ripoll, Carlos. *José Martí. Letras y huellas desconocidas* (José Martí. Unknown papers and traces). New York: Eliseo Torres & Sons, 1976.

———. *José Martí, the United States and the Marxist Interpretation of Cuban History.* New Brunswick, NJ: Transaction Books, 1984.

Sterling, Carlos Márquez. *Biografía de José Martí* (Biography of José Martí). Miami: La Moderna Poesía, 1997.

Martin, Xavier (1832–1897)
Immigrant leader and public official
Belgian

Xavier Martin, a native of Belgium, was an influential immigrant leader who achieved wide recognition for his contributions to the Belgian-American settlers in the Green Bay area of Wisconsin. He taught them English, educated them in the U.S. political system, and helped them assimilate.

Second son of Jean-Joseph Martin and Henriette Bassine, Xavier Martin was born on 11 January 1832 in Grez-Doiceau, a small town in Walloon Brabant, Belgium. Although by 1853 Martin was living in Brussels, he joined his parents when they and several other neighbor families immigrated to the United States. They were among the first Belgian settlers in Wisconsin, where they settled in Robinsonville (now Champion), near Green Bay. During the following decade, close to 15,000 Belgians followed in their pioneer footsteps.

At first, Martin did not accompany his countrymen to Wisconsin. He stayed in Philadelphia, where he studied law and, in 1855, married Rebecca Gray. Clearly, Martin was interested in assimilating into American life as quickly as possible. In 1857, however, upon repeated requests from his family in Wisconsin, he visited the Robinsonville colony. He was shocked by the destitution and needs of his compatriots and decided to stay and help organize Belgians in this area.

During the next decade, Martin became the principal leader and organizer of the Belgians in northeastern Wisconsin, not only around Green Bay but also in Kewaunee and Door Counties. He taught classes in English, educated the Belgians in the U.S. political system, and ensured Belgian participation in local elections. At his instigation, Belgians participated for the first time in the local elections of 1858. Subsequently, he instructed the newly appointed Belgian officials in their duties and he himself was elected justice of the peace, town clerk, and school superintendent. During subsequent years, he was instrumental in establishing school districts and obtaining funds for much-needed infrastructure in the area. He also became the first postmaster of Robinsonville.

In contrast to the large majority of the Belgian community living in Wisconsin in the early 1860s, Martin considered himself a freethinker and Protestant. While still in Belgium, at the age of fifteen, he had left the Catholic Church to join a small group of Protestant believers. It is generally believed that the first ten families who pioneered the emigration from Grez-Doiceau to Wisconsin were also followers of this Protestant "sect." Martin led his fellow Protestants in the founding of the French Presbyterian Church in Robinsonville in 1861 (now the Robinsonville Presbyterian Church).

Martin lived among the Belgians at Robinsonville from 1857 until 1862, when, as a newly elected register of deeds for Brown County, he moved to Green Bay. He continued his activities among the Belgians, although professionally he was known as a real estate insurance agent and broker, collection agent, and notary public. One further intense moment of involvement in the community occurred during the devastating fires of 8 and 9 October 1871, when he coordinated the relief efforts for the Belgian settlements. Martin died on 16 December 1897 in Wisconsin.

Kristine Smets

REFERENCES

De Smet, Antoine. "Antécédents et aspects peu connus de l'émigration belge dans le nord-est du Wisconsin" (Background and little known facts about the Belgian emigration to the Northeast of Wisconsin). *Wavriensia* 2 (1953): 17–39.

———. "La communauté belge du nord-est du Wisconsin" (The Belgian community in the Northeast of Wisconsin). *Wavriensia* 6 (1957): 65–129.

Defnet, Mary Ann, et al. *From Grez-Doiceau to Wisconsin.* Brussels: De Boeck-Wesmael, 1986.

Lempereur, Françoise. *Les Wallons d'Amérique du Nord.* Gembloux, Belgium: J. Duculot, 1976.

Martin, Xavier. "The Belgians of Northeast Wisconsin." *Wisconsin Historical Collections* 13 (1895): 375–396.

Tlachac, Math S. *The History of the Belgian Settlements in Door, Kewaunee and Brown Counties.* Brussels: Belgian-American Club, 1974.

Martínez, Elizabeth "Betita" (1925–)

Civil rights activist and author
Mexican-American

Elizabeth "Betita" Martínez has immersed herself in the struggles of several minorities in the United States, including African Americans, Chicanos, and Native Americans. Her many publications reflect the civil rights struggles of the past half century, and she continues to work for equal rights for all peoples.

Martínez was born in Washington, D.C., in 1925. Her early experiences with racial discrimination against blacks influenced and shaped her life. In the 1950s she worked as a staff member for the United Nations, then as an editor at Simon and Schuster. She became involved in the black Civil Rights movement in 1964 when she joined the New York chapter of the Student Nonviolent Coordinating Committee (SNCC) as a full-time staff member. In that year she participated in the Mississippi Summer Project, and SNCC placed her in charge of publicity and raising funds for activists in the South. Martínez helped publish *The Movement* (1964), a photo collection of the Civil Rights movement, and she edited *Letters from Mississippi* (1965), on SNCC activities in the South. After Freedom Summer, she was appointed coordinator of SNCC's New York office and was sent to California to speak in support of the United Farm Workers

of America, after which she wrote "Neither Black or White" (1966), an article concerning the inattention to Latinos within the Civil Rights movement. Martínez traveled to Cuba in 1967 as a SNCC representative, but her involvement with SNCC ended after that.

The following year, Martínez moved to New Mexico to support the land grant movement of Reies López Tijerina and the Alianza Federal de Pueblos Libres (National alliance of free pueblos). She soon started a newspaper, *El Grito del Norte* (The Cry of the North), and helped establish the Chicano Communications Center. She attended both the first Chicano Youth Liberation Conference in Denver, Colorado (1969), and the first national convention of El Partido de la Raza Unida (the United People's Party) in El Paso, Texas (1972). Martínez and other Chicanos even traveled to Wounded Knee, South Dakota, in early 1973 to help the American Indian Movement (AIM) draw attention to the plight of American Indians. In that same year, her anthology, *500 Years of Chicano History,* was published, along with the book *Chicanos,* coedited with Gilbert López y Rivas. These publications were followed with *Viva La Raza,* coauthored with Enrequeta Longeaux y Vasquez (1974).

In the 1980s Martínez was active in various causes, including the 1983 hearings in Madrid, Spain, against human rights violations in Guatemala; campaigning in 1994 against California's anti-immigration initiative, Proposition 187; and defending attacks on affirmative action programs. In 1996 she helped found the Institute for MultiRacial Justice, a resource center in San Francisco, California.

Martínez has received numerous honors for her work as a journalist, writer, and activist. She is a member of the Media Alliance, is on the editorial board of the journal *Social Justice,* and has taught ethnic studies and women's studies courses at various California universities. Her recent book, *De Colores Means All of Us,* appeared in 1998. She currently lives in San Francisco and has one daughter.

Zaragosa Vargas

REFERENCES

García, Alma. "The Development of Chicana Feminist Discourse, 1970–1980." In *Unequal Sisters: A Multicultural Reader,* edited by Vicki L. Ruiz and Ellen Carol DuBois, 531–544. New York: Routledge, 1994.

Gonzáles, Patrisia, and Roberto Rodríguez. "A Woman Warrior Recalls the Birth of a Movement. Interview with Elizabeth Martínez." *Latino Spectrum,* 19 February 1998, 4.

Hayakawa, Mana. "Elizabeth Martínez—Inimitable, Irrepressible, Indefatigable. Interview with Elizabeth Martínez." *Sister to Sister* 5.2/3 (Summer 1999). S2S Women of Color Research Center Homepage: www.coloredgirls.org/pub/pub_S2S.html (Accessed 20 December 2000.)

Muñoz, Carlos. *Youth, Identity, Power: The Chicano Movement.* New York: Verso Press, 1989.

Zinn, Howard. *SNCC: The New Abolitionists.* Boston: Beacon Press, 1964.

Massey, Raymond Hart (1896–1983)

Actor

Canadian

Raymond Massey was one of several outstanding Canadian performers who arrived on the American theater, film, and television scenes. They contributed significantly to twentieth-century arts and culture in the United States.

Born in Toronto into a wealthy family that had made its money in the manufacture of farm machinery, Massey grew up in a privileged life of servants and governesses. Yet, when World War I broke out, he volunteered for the Canadian army, where he became an officer in the field artillery. After considerable battle exposure, he returned home in 1916 with "shell shock" (battle fatigue) but, in 1918, joined a Canadian expeditionary force to Siberia.

In 1919 Massey enrolled in Balliol College, Oxford, leaving in 1921 without a degree. Bored with civilian life and the prospect of joining the family firm, he decided to become an actor and went to London in 1922. He gradually achieved considerable success there, thanks to his willingness to work to exhaustion on the management side of theatrical production (as stage manager) with such non–West End groups as the Everyman Theatre, while improving his on-stage technique. By the latter 1920s, Massey was much sought after as a director of works by the leading London playwrights of the day. He was also a substantial acting presence who played leading roles in many premieres.

Massey entered films in 1931, playing in *The Shape of Things to Come,* an important British production by Alexander Korda, based on the H. G. Wells novel. In 1937 he went to Hollywood to make *The Prisoner of Zenda* and then in 1938 premiered Robert Sherwood's *Abe Lincoln in Illinois* on Broadway. He settled in the United States in 1938 for the remainder of his life. Massey subsequently played Lincoln in the Hollywood film made from the play, joining fellow Canadian Walter Huston as one of the creators of the modern Lincoln mythology. At the time of Pearl Harbor, he wrote, "Although I was still a Canadian citizen, my wife was American, home was New York, and my professional future seemed to lie in the United States." Nonetheless, he ignored Humphrey Bogart's advice and became a major in the Royal Canadian Artillery of the Canadian army, serving for a year until returning to civilian life in 1943. He subsequently took Thornton Wilder's *Our Town* on tour to the U.S. troops in Europe for the American Theatre Wing.

By 1945 Massey was proving his versatility by performing in a weekly radio series, starring in a Broadway play, doing a Hollywood movie, and appearing on CBS television. He had a number of Broadway and Hollywood successes and a touring triumph with Stephen Benet's *John Brown's Body.* His last Broadway play was *J.B.* in 1958. A year later he moved to Beverly Hills and was soon appearing as Dr. Gillespie in the television series *Dr. Kildare* (until 1966). His last major theatrical performance was in Robert Anderson's *I Never Sang for My Father,* in London in 1970. Along with seventy movies, Massey's distinguished acting career included a number of Broadway revivals of George Bernard Shaw. Massey died in 1983.

J. M. Bumsted

REFERENCES

Massey, Raymond. *A Hundred Different Lives.* Toronto: McClelland and Stewart, 1979.

———. *When I Was Young.* Toronto: McClelland and Stewart, 1976.

"Massey, Hart." In *Dictionary of Canadian Biography,* vol. 12: 700–709. Toronto: University of Toronto Press, 1990.

Mattson, Hans (1832–1893)

Pioneer, soldier, journalist, and emigration agent
Swedish

Hans Mattson, a farmer's son from Skåne Province, Sweden, was, in his time, undoubtedly the most celebrated American born in Sweden, among his own people and among Americans at large. His achievements for the Union Army during the Civil War and, in particular, his extensive activities in promoting Swedish immigration to the United States—especially to Minnesota—earned him widespread recognition.

After obtaining some secondary schooling and serving briefly as cadet in a Swedish artillery regiment, Hans Mattson in 1851 sought wider opportunities in the United States, where he worked his way from New England to Moline, Illinois. Two years later, he moved with two comrades to the Minnesota Territory, establishing one of the earliest Swedish settlements, near Red Wing. There he farmed, ran a store, and read law. At the outbreak of the Civil War in 1861, Mattson was commissioned a captain and raised his own Scandinavian volunteer company. Through valor and skill, by 1864 he had advanced to colonel and regimental commander, the highest rank attained by a Swedish immigrant at the time.

In 1866, Mattson became the first editor of the Swedish-language newspaper *Svenska Amerikaren* in Chicago and, the following year, was appointed secretary of Minnesota's newly established Emigrant Bureau. In that capacity, as Minnesota's secretary of state for various periods after 1868, and as immigration agent from 1871 on for different railroads, he attracted large numbers of settlers to his state, particularly from his native Sweden. Drawing immigrants to localities where Swedes were already settled, he was notably more successful than his rivals. Between 1868 and 1876, Mattson spent much time in Sweden recruiting emigrants. He was also involved in banking and land transactions and even served as an emigration agent for Canada.

In 1877 Mattson helped found the newspaper *Svenska Tribunen* in Chicago. He published and edited *Minnesota Posten* in Minneapolis from 1878 to 1881. In the latter year he was appointed the U.S. consul general in Calcutta, where he served until 1883. Mattson is now remembered largely for his *Reminiscences: The Story of an Emigrant,* published in St. Paul in 1891, a classic immigrant autobiography. He became the symbol of the Swedish Americans' sacrifices during the Civil War, the "baptism of fire" through which, in their eyes, they had validated their rightful place in American society and no one played a more effective part in promoting Swedish immigration to the United States. If Minnesota is proverbially America's most "Swedish" state, that was surely above all his doing. After retiring to his large farm in the Red River valley, he died in 1893, at the age of sixty-one.

Mattson's many and varied accomplishments and honors provided inspiring proof of what an immigrant could aspire to in the New World. A staunch believer in the U.S. form of government and society, and thus often critical of Sweden, he remained nevertheless warmly attached to his immigrant countrymen and Swedish cultural heritage. His importance as a Swedish-American culture hero and role model can scarcely be overestimated.

H. Arnold Barton

REFERENCES

Barton, H. Arnold. *A Folk Divided.* Carbondale: Southern Illinois University Press, 1994.

Ljungmark, Lars. *For Sale—Minnesota: Organized Promotion of Scandinavian Immigration, 1866–1873.* Göteborg: Läromedelsförl. (Akad.-förl.), 1971; Chicago: n.p. 1971.

Mattson, Hans. *Reminiscences: The Story of an Emigrant.* St. Paul, MN: D. D. Merrill, 1891.

Maximovitch, John (1896–1966)
Church leader and saint
Russian

The life of John Maximovitch mirrors the lives of hundreds of thousands of Russians forced out of Russia by the civil war (1918–1921). He served many of those exiles as a bishop. Throughout his life, he practiced asceticism, going barefoot, depriving himself of sleep, and eating only one meal a day. After his death he was canonized as a saint.

Maximovitch was born in Kharkov Province in southern Russia (now Ukraine) in 1896. In 1918 he graduated with a degree in law from Kharkov Imperial University. In 1921 he immigrated with his parents and family to Belgrade, Yugoslavia. He continued his education there. Metropolitan Anthony of the Russian Orthodox Church Outside of Russia (ROCOR) tonsured him as a monk. In 1934 he was sent as a bishop to serve the Russian émigrés in Shanghai, China.

In 1946 Maximovitch was elevated to archbishop of all the Russian Orthodox in China. When the Communist government took over in China, the Russians were forced into a second exile. Maximovitch shepherded them to island refugee camps and then spent some time in Washington getting permission for thousands of them to come to the United States. In 1951 the archbishop was sent to Europe to serve as bishop in Paris and Brussels. He was also a member of the ruling church body, the Synod of Bishops of the Russian Orthodox Church Outside of Russia.

Disputes were dividing the Russian exiles who had settled in San Francisco, many of whom were his former constituents from China. The Synod of Bishops sent Archbishop John there in December 1962 as the bishop most likely to resolve the disputes. The San Francisco assignment proved to be a sad challenge. The previous bishop, Tikhon, had started to build a cathedral, but the construction had been halted by his temporary successor. When Maximovitch arrived, he ordered the construction to continue.

Apparently the faction that opposed Maximovitch had support from some bishops in leadership positions in the church, because the archbishop was recalled in six months. The majority that supported him, however, was able to have the recall decision reversed. The opposing faction then brought action against him and his church council in civil court. The civil court decided that the problem was an internal church dispute. The cathedral, Joy of All Who Sorrow, was finally finished, but the stress may have shortened the archbishop's life. He died in 1966.

The ROCOR, Maximovitch's organization, remains a very conservative body. It is not in communion with the Russian Patriarchate or its U.S. affiliate, the Orthodox Church in America. The church follows the Julian calendar, which in the twenty-first century is fourteen days behind the current calendar. In 1981 the ROCOR canonized the former Czar Nicholas II as a saint. When the Soviet Union collapsed, the ROCOR demanded that the Russian Patriarchate canonize him, too, as a condition for its reunification with the Moscow Patriarchate. It was the ROCOR that examined the ascetic life and miracles of John Maximovitch, archbishop of Shanghai and San Francisco, and canonized him as a saint in the summer of 1994.

Keith P. Dyrud

REFERENCES

Myers, Jacob, and Kenneth Beavers, compilers. *To the Glory of Saint and Wonderworker John Maximovitch*: the-internet-eye.com/stjohn/ (accessed 5 July 2000).

Perekrestov, Peter, compiler. *Man of God: Saint John of Shanghai and San Francisco*. Redding, CA: Nikodemos Orthodox Publication Society, 1994.

Rose, Seraphim, and Abbot Herman, compilers. *Blessed John the Wonderworker*. Platina, CA: St. Herman of Alaska Brotherhood, 1998.

Mayer, Louis B. (né Lazar Meir) (1885–1957)
Movie studio entrepreneur
Canadian-Jewish

Louis B. Mayer rose from rags to riches by recognizing the potential of the cinema. As the studio head of Metro-Goldwyn-Mayer, he contributed to the development of Hollywood's early studio system, which dominated the industry for several decades.

Born as Lazar Meir in 1885 in Dymer, Ukraine, he was brought to North America in the late 1880s and lived on Long Island, New York, before moving to St. John, New Brunswick, Canada, in 1892. His father, Jacob Mayer, became a Canadian citizen in 1895. After graduation from high school in 1902, young Louis (as he was then known) went to Boston in 1904, marrying Margaret Shenberg. After a few years peddling junk, he purchased an old burlesque theater in Haverhill, Massachusetts, and began a new career. His strengths were his abilities of persuasion and recognizing innovations that would prosper. With partners, he opened a grander theater in Haverhill in 1911. A year later, he became a U.S. citizen.

Mayer expanded quickly into motion picture distribution. By 1915 his Metro Pictures Corporation had made a small fortune on the New England distribution of *Birth of a Nation,* and Mayer was soon producing serials. He understood the need for a "name" performer and became associated with film star Anita Stewart. In a series of steps, Mayer moved first to New York and into the center of film distribution and production and, finally, in 1918 to California. He always had considerable ability to pick talented production people, including Fred Niblo, Irving Thalberg, and later Dore Schary, and to spot talented young actors and actresses before they became famous, notably fellow Canadian Norma Shearer.

In 1924 he merged with Goldwyn Pictures, which was under the command of Marcus Loew. Mayer would run the new studio, to be called Metro-Goldwyn-Mayer (MGM). He is usually credited with an appreciation of the star system and with the elaboration of what amounted to a studio stock company of stars and fledgling stars, providing a stable of well-known names to appear in all the films of MGM's golden era. Later, he was similarly credited with establishing the autonomous

producer within the studio system. MGM had weathered the shift from silent film to talkie extremely well and soon developed its specialty: the expensive musical.

In addition, Mayer had long been active in the Republican Party and by 1930 had become vice chairman of the California Republican State Central Committee. Throughout his life he remained involved with the party. Also, in 1939 he received an honorary degree from the University of New Brunswick and, in a luncheon address, spoke of the need for the world's democracies "to come to the rescue of Mother England." Although Mayer never quite suppressed his origins, he did not celebrate them either. Throughout his career, he was an ardent American, wrapping himself and his studio in the mantle of patriotism and celebrating mainstream American values in his films. During World War II, Mayer put the studio's resources at the service of the war effort at the same time that he ordered an emphasis on lavish escapist movies. Mayer's death in 1957 heralded the end of the golden days of Hollywood.

J. M. Bumsted

REFERENCES

Altman, Diana. *Hollywood East: Louis B. Mayer and the Origins of the Studio System.* New York: Carol Publishing Group, 1992.

Higham, Charles. *Merchant of Dreams: Louis B. Mayer, M.G.M., and the Secret Hollywood.* New York: Donald I. Fine, 1993.

Parish, James Robert, and Ronald L. Bowers. *The M.G.M. Stock Company.* New York: Bonanza, 1972.

Mazrui, Ali A. (1933–)

Political scientist, author, and humanist
Kenyan

Ali Mazrui, professor of politics, has been honored for his prolific writings, his activism in international ecumenical organizations, and for his efforts on behalf of human rights. He has taught in many universities worldwide.

Mazrui was born in Mombasa, Kenya, a British colony at the time. His Swahili culture is a mixture of African, Arabic, and Islamic elements. This triple heritage was the background in which Mazrui's early years were shaped. His father was chief *kadhi* for Kenya and one of the three major Islamic jurists in East Africa. He ran his own newspaper and espoused social reform, which influenced his son's aspirations and interests. However, Mazrui's education in British colonial schools resulted in his focus on secular intellectual interests rather than theological ones. He eventually received a B.A. from Manchester University, an M.A. from Columbia University, and a D.Phil. in political studies from Oxford University.

Mazrui's first job as a politics professor was at Makerere University, in Uganda, and he has taught in many other universities. An outspoken advocate for democracy, he left Uganda in 1972 after tyrant Idi Amin came to power in early 1971. As of the year 2001, he held several academic appointments, the main one as Albert Schweitzer Professor in the Humanities and director of the Institute of Global Cultural Studies at the State University of New York at Binghamton.

Although much of his life's work has been in the academic arena, Mazrui has been actively involved in promoting international causes. He has consulted on constitutional change in Nigeria, Uganda, and Sudan; on syllabus reviews for schools in New York State; on human rights, nuclear proliferation, and transnational corporations for the UN; and on development issues with the World Bank. He is chair of the board of the Center for the Study of Islam and Democracy and is on the board of the Center for Muslim-Christian Understanding.

Mazrui may be the most prolific African scholar in the world, having published more than twenty books and written hundreds of papers for journals, conferences, magazines, and newspapers. These range from nuclear nonproliferation, women's rights, and human rights in general to understanding Islam. Probably his work best known to the general public is the 1986 television series he wrote and narrated called *The Africans: A Triple Her-itage,* jointly produced by the BBC, PBS, and the Nigerian Television Authority. The main theme of the series was that Africa is the product of three interrelated civilizations: African, Western, and Islamic. In many respects, this triple heritage applies well to Mazrui himself in his background, work, and life.

Mazrui has been much honored for his academic work and service. For example, he has been awarded a Distinguished Service Award by the National University of Lesotho, an Icon of the Twentieth Century Award from Lincoln University, and the Du Bois-Garvey Award for Pan-African Unity from Morgan State University.

His personal life as well as public life is a tribute to multiculturalism and internationalism. In 1962, in London, Mazrui married Molly, a white, Christian, English woman, with whom he had three sons (one is a Kenyan; two are U.S. citizens). They divorced in 1982, and in 1991 he wed a Nigerian Christian woman, Pauline, with whom he has two sons, both U.S. citizens.

April Gordon

REFERENCES
Bemath, Abdul S., compiler. *The Mazruianna Collection.* Lawrenceville, NJ: Africa World Press, 1998.
Kokole, Omari H., ed. *The Global African: A Portrait of Ali A. Mazrui.* New Jersey: Africa World Press, 1998.
Mazrui, Ali A. "Growing Up in a Shrinking World: A Private Vantage Point." In *Autobiographical Reflections of Thirty-four Academic Travelers,* edited by Joseph Kruzel and James N. Rosenau, 469–487. Lexington, MA: Lexington Books, 1989.
Sawere, Chaly. 1993. "The Multiple Mazrui: Scholar, Ideologue, Philosopher, and Artist." Fact Sheet on Ali A. Mazrui. Society for the Study of Islamic Philosophy and Science. Binghamton, NY: SUNY Binghamton, 1999.

McClure, Samuel Sidney (1857–1949)
Editor and publisher
Scotch-Irish-American

Samuel Sidney McClure was an influential editor and publisher. His magazines informed Americans about important social and political issues during the Gilded Age and the Progressive Era.

McClure was born in County Antrim, now Northern Ireland, to Thomas McClure, a farmer and shipyard worker, and Elizabeth Gaston. When he was eight, his father was killed in a Glasgow shipyard accident, and the next year he immigrated with his mother and brothers to Indiana, where his mother married a farmer. A voracious reader, McClure enjoyed books and high school, but when his stepfather died, he was forced to quit school to work the farm. He entered Knox College in 1874 and there found his calling when he became editor of the *Knox Student* and established the Western College Associated Press. After graduation he moved to Boston to edit the *Wheelman,* a monthly cycling magazine. In 1884 he took a job at a printing firm in New York, worked for a while as an editor for *Century* magazine, and then decided to form his own literary syndicate. He was twenty-seven.

McClure traveled widely in search of publishable material from writers and editors and met with such success that by 1893 he had created his own magazine, *McClure's,* with which he intended to challenge other established publications. Initial prospects were not good because of the panic of 1893, but a breakthrough occurred when he hired Ida M. Tarbell to write a biography on Napoleon to be serialized in his magazine, followed by serialized installments of her biography of Lincoln. Within a few years *McClure's* was among the most successful of periodicals, carrying more advertising than any other magazine and featuring such famous authors as Bret Harte, Stephen Crane, Rudyard Kipling, Robert Louis Stevenson, Jack London, and Julia Ward Howe.

The secret to *McClure's* success was its subject matter. It focused on short biographies of fascinating people, articles on exploration, exotic animals, and scientific discoveries, and articles on the growing problems of the new urban and industrial American society: political corruption, the victimization of poor people, and the power and greed of big business.

Muckraking became one of the trademarks of *McClure's,* raising the consciousness of readers and helping to create support for reform legislation during the Progressive Era. At the turn of the century, circulation surpassed a third of a million, by 1907 about a half million.

McClure expanded his publishing empire to include books and financial services, but the 1907 panic caused problems, as did McClure's tendency to overreach himself and impose dictatorial decisions upon his staff and stockholders. His declining health added to his problems, and in 1911 he was forced sell his magazine and become a token editor. Yet, by joining Henry Ford's Peace Ship venture in 1915 to end the war in Europe, McClure kept a high profile, although he was suspected of being pro-German. During the 1920s he met Mussolini and seemed to be enthusiastic about the dictator.

McClure spent the remaining years of his life living off the charity of friends and relatives. He died in 1949 in relative obscurity.

William E. Van Vugt

REFERENCES
Lyon, Peter. *Success Story: The Life and Times of S. S. McClure.* Deland, FL: Everett Edwards, 1967.
McClure, Samuel S. (ghostwritten by Willa Cather). *My Autobiography.* New York: Frederick A. Stokes, 1914.
Mott, Frank Luther. *A History of American Magazines, 1886–1964.* Cambridge, MA: Harvard University Press, 1957.

McGarrity, Joseph (1874–1940)
Nationalist and political activist
Irish

Joseph McGarrity was possibly the most dedicated and uncompromising Irish nationalist of the late nineteenth and early twentieth century in the United States.

McGarrity was born in Carrickmore, County Tyrone, Ireland, on 28 March 1874, one of the eight children of John and Catherine Bigley McGarrity. His father was a small farmer and part-time tailor. County Tyrone had a long tradition of opposition to British rule and is a Republican stronghold to this day.

The McGarrity household encouraged lively discussions of politics. Young McGarrity came under the influence of a schoolteacher with a Republican philosophy, Master Marshall.

In January 1892, at the age of sixteen, McGarrity immigrated to the United States and settled in Philadelphia. There he worked as a general helper at a small hotel, a stonecutter's helper, locomotive worker, innkeeper, and tavern owner. He eventually made his mark in the wholesale wine and spirits trade. He wed Kathryn Hynes in 1911 and raised eight children.

McGarrity had not been long in the United States before he became involved in Irish nationalist activity. He was presented for initiation into the Ancient Order of Hibernians in 1893 but left the group because there was no mention of Irish freedom. He was initiated into the Clan Na Gael and in January 1904 was elected district officer for Philadelphia's Clan Na Gael camps. By 1918 he was a member of the national executive committee. He raised money for the Gaelic League, the Fianna Na h'Eireann, *Irish Freedom* (the monthly publication of the Irish Republican Brotherhood), and later the Irish Republican Army (IRA). He was responsible for financing the Howth gun importation prior to Easter Week. It is estimated that he helped raise $8.5 million for the Irish struggle, including over $100,000 of his own money.

Ideologically, McGarrity rejected all solutions that did not establish a thirty-two-county Irish Republic. He had little patience with those who would compromise on that goal. This stand caused him to break first with John Devoy in 1920 over the treaty. He reorganized the national Clan na Gael and ousted Devoy as secretary. In 1936, McGarrity also broke with his friend Eamon De Valera for good over this issue. In the 1930s he masterminded a bombing campaign in England that he hoped would cause chaos by crippling the electric power grid, factories, and communications. The campaign failed, ending only a few months before his death on 5 August 1950. In contrast, he assembled a library of over 10,000 volumes on Irish-American literature, which was donated to Villanova University.

When McGarrity died, condolences came from all over the world and from old enemies. On 7 August 1940, the Irish Press in Dublin announced on its front page, "Fighter for Irish Freedom Dead." Sean T. O'Kelly, the president of Ireland, said, "No man that I have met ever worked harder to win for Ireland her independence, or gave more generously of his substance as well as of his great talent in the service of his motherland."

Seamus P. Metress

REFERENCES
Cronin, Sean. *The McGarrity Papers.* Tralee, Ireland: Anvil Books, 1972.
Tarpey, Marie V. "Joseph McGarrity, Fighter for Irish Freedom." *Studia Hibernica* 11 (1971): 164–180.
———. *The Role of Joseph McGarrity in the Struggle for Irish Independence.* New York: Arno Press, 1976.

McKay, Claude (1889–1948)
Poet, novelist, and journalist
Jamaican

Claude McKay was born in central Jamaica and died in Chicago at the age of fifty-eight. A prolific author associated with the Harlem Renaissance, McKay produced four volumes of poetry, three novels, two sociological studies, an autobiography, a book of short stories, countless essays, and several unpublished works. McKay broke new and controversial ground by contending that Africans in the West should celebrate the black poor, the "down and out," the "noble savage." These ideas had their origins in his discovery that class and color influenced the way Jamaica's light-skinned civil servants treated the island's dark-skinned masses. A swarthy-complexioned grandson of slaves, young McKay was indignant at this hierarchy of inequality and reacted to it by writing poems in Creole, the popular dialect shunned by the local literati.

At the age of twenty-two, McKay left Jamaica, never to return. His objective was an American college degree, but before finishing his studies, he moved to New York to pursue a writing career. The city widened his horizons, introducing him to writers, artists, and political radicals. This exposure reinforced McKay's growing suspicion that communism was the answer to the injustices of race and class. A desire to embrace the British part of his heritage led him to London in 1919. There he learned that devotion to British culture afforded no protection from racism. A desire to increase his understanding of communism led him next to Russia, where he discovered that the Comintern subordinated individual initiative to the dictates of expediency. A desire to participate in the French literary scene brought him to Paris, where he learned that the French disdained blacks as much as the British. But unlike the British, the French denied their prejudice even to themselves. Disillusion followed disillusion. McKay moved again and again, taking up a variety of residences on the European and African sides of the Mediterranean.

In the works he wrote abroad, McKay attacked the established view that Africans in diaspora should embrace the "superior culture" of their French and British oppressors. To the contrary, McKay asserted that blacks could find salvation only by reclaiming and respecting their own ancestral roots. His first novel with this theme, *Home from Harlem* (1928), was financially successful, but the depression undermined sales of his most influential books, *Banjo* (1929) and *Banana Bottom* (1933). The insights in these novels contributed to the momentum of the anticolonial negritude movements in the French Caribbean and French West Africa as well as provided literary legitimation for the message "black is beautiful," which became popular during the civil rights era.

In 1934, McKay returned to the United States, hoping his earnings would improve. Unfortunately, his finances and health declined, although he continued to produce. In his later writings, McKay argued that strong all-black institutions offered the best chance to bring about racial equality. He arrived at this conclusion after having observed that North Africa's minorities prospered under segregation. But most African Americans disagreed, instead singing the praises of integration and assimilation. Paradoxically, at the age of fifty-five, McKay converted to Catholicism, a religion committed to integration and assimilation. When asked to justify this decision, he remarked that American blacks' greatest weakness was their acceptance of "the materialist Protestant God" as their own.

Claude McKay is a writer whose insights remain thought provoking today. Nonetheless, he also remains more appreciated abroad than in the United States, his adopted home.

Suzanne Model

REFERENCES

Cooper, Wayne F. *Claude McKay: Rebel Sojourner in the Harlem Renaissance.* Baton Rouge: Louisiana State University Press, 1987.

Fabre, Michael. *From Harlem to Paris, Black American Writers in France, 1840–1980.* Urbana: University of Illinois Press, 1991.

Tillery, Tyrone. *Claude McKay: A Black Poet's Struggle for Identity.* Amherst: University of Massachusetts Press, 1992.

Mehta, Ved Parkash (1934–)
Writer
Asian Indian

Ved Parkash Mehta, a native of India and longtime staff writer for the *New Yorker* magazine, has written more than a million words concerning the land of his childhood. Mehta, a highly esteemed Asian American, is widely respected for his written encounters with prominent intellectuals and political figures in India and the West as well as autobiographical accounts of his life in the United States and abroad.

Mehta was born in 1934 in Lahore, India. He became blind from spinal meningitis just before his fourth birthday. In Hindu society at that time, loss of sight had the stigma of punishment for sins in a previous incarnation and relegation to a life of begging—a verdict he and his family refused to accept. At the age of five, he was sent to Bombay, 1,300 miles from home, to what his father, a doctor, thought was the best school for the blind in India; it was an orphanage cum asylum that sent him home after three years. During this time, Mehta's father was trying to get him into a school in the West.

Their hopes of his studying abroad were dashed when, in 1947, India gained independence and Lahore was awarded to Pakistan. The Mehta family, like millions of others, became refugees, escaping with only their lives and the clothes on their back. Mehta had the good fortune of attending an institute for soldiers blinded in World War II. During the few months there he learned to touch-type. The result was a barrage of letters he wrote to schools for the blind in England and the United States. After numerous rejections he was accepted by the Arkansas School for the Blind and, at the age of fifteen, was on a plane to the United States, having experienced and suffered more than most people do in a lifetime.

Obtaining numerous scholarships, Mehta earned his B.A. from Pomona College in California, another from Balliol College, Oxford, and an M.A. from Harvard. While still a student, he started writing for the *New Yorker,* where he spent his career.

Mehta's first book, *Face to Face,* published when he was twenty-three, was autobiographical. Mehta was lauded for his simplicity, directness, and depth of thought that generally escapes writers of supposedly greater maturity. After *Walking the Indian Streets,* an account of his return to India, Mehta distinguished himself with *Fly in the Fly-Bottle,* which described his encounters with British intellectuals, and *The New Theologian,* dialogues with well-known contemporary theologians. Mehta's *Continents of Exile* series is composed of nine books, starting with biographies of his father and mother, followed by autobiographical accounts that focus on, but are not limited to, his life in the United States.

Mehta has been active in many causes regarding India and Asian Indians in the United States. He campaigned against abuses by In-

dira Gandhi as well as on behalf of fair treatment and just access to resources for Asian Indians in the United States. His representation of, and contributions to, the Asian Indian community have resulted in his receiving numerous honors, including being recognized by the mayor of New York City, the Statue of Liberty Foundation, and the Association of Indians in America for his contributions as a prominent Asian Indian in the United States.

Just before the start of the new millennium, Ved Mehta quit his position at the *New Yorker* after decades of productivity. He has left not only a superb body of literature but also another inspiring example of the contributions Asian Indians are making to the United States.

Arthur W. Helweg

REFERENCES
"Beinecke Library Acquires Papers of Author and Academic Ved Mehta." *Yale Bulletin and Calendar News Stories* 25.14 (25 November 1996–2 December 1996): www.yale.edu/opa/ybc/v25.n14.news.06.html (accessed 25 June 2000).
McKeown, Kristen. "Ved Mehta: Noted Author to Lecture on Crosscultural Experiences." *Bates Student* (Bates College, Maine), 1997.
Mehta, Ved. *Face to Face.* Boston and Toronto: Little, Brown, 1957.
———. "Sightless in a Sighted World." In *Encyclopedia Britannica, Medical and Health Annual,* 1985: www.vedmehta.com/biography.html (accessed 25 June 2000).
———. Personal papers. Yale University website http://www.library.yale.edu/beinecke/bloct96.htm (accessed 25 June 2000).
Sethi, Rumina. "Oxford, My Glittering World." *Spectrum, the Tribune,* 6 February 2000.

Melchior, Lauritz (Lebrecht Hommel) (1890–1973)
Opera and concert singer
Danish

Widely acclaimed as the greatest heroic tenor of his age, Lauritz Melchior won fame for his roles in the operas of Richard Wagner, particularly for his 223 performances as Tristan in *Tristan und Isolde.* He sang with New York's Metropolitan Opera from 1926 to

1950, starred in five American films, and made numerous radio, television, and concert appearances.

Melchior was born in Copenhagen in 1890, the son of Jorgen and Sofie Melchior. He attended a private school administered by his father, but perhaps the greatest influence on him came from Kristine Jensen, who became the family housekeeper when Sofie Melchior died after Lauritz's birth. Jensen encouraged the boy to become a singer and paid for his vocal lessons. Melchior sang in an English church choir as a boy soprano and, at eighteen, began voice studies as a baritone at Copenhagen's Royal Opera School. He debuted at the Danish Royal Opera in 1913 as Silvio, in Leoncavallo's *Pagliacci,* a baritone role. After hearing Melchior perform, Sarah Cahier, the American operatic contralto, convinced him that he was actually a tenor "with a lid on." After more than a year of training, he again debuted at the Royal Opera, this time in the Wagnerian tenor role of Tannhäuser.

Word soon spread in European musical circles about this young Dane with a powerful, yet lyrical, voice. The renowned British author Hugh Walpole became his friend and patron, securing many important engagements for him, culminating in an audition with Richard and Cosima Wagner, the composer's son and widow. They were seeking to revive the Wagnerian Bayreuth festival. In 1924 Melchior sang Siegmund in *Die Walkure* there, but New York beckoned. In 1926, he began a twenty-four-year career with the Metropolitan Opera, during which he gave 515 performances in Wagnerian operas.

Melchior married Inger Nathansen Holst-Rasmussen in 1915 and had two children. They divorced, and in 1925 he married Maria Hacker, a young film stunt woman whom he nicknamed Kleinchen because of her diminutive size. Kleinchen soon emerged as a shrewd manager and publicist and did much to make Melchior the most celebrated opera singer in the United States.

Melchior was blessed with a broad sense of humor, much evident in his five films: *Trill of*

a Romance (1945), *Two Sisters from Boston* (1946), *This Time for Keeps* (1947), *Luxury Liner* (1948), and *The Stars Are Singing* (1952). After retiring from the Metropolitan in 1950, he continued for fifteen years to appear on radio and television and give concerts.

The beginning of World War II forced Melchior to move from Germany to New York and later to a magnificent hilltop home in Beverly Hills that he named the Viking. It became a mecca for Danes and Danish Americans. Indeed, Melchior became a U.S. citizen in 1948 but joined or otherwise supported many Danish-American organizations in the United States. He developed a special friendship for Dana College, a small liberal arts college founded in Nebraska by Danish immigrants, and greatly enjoyed coming to the campus and singing with the college's choir. Melchior died in 1973.

Peter L. Petersen

REFERENCES
Emmons, Shirlee. *Tristanissimo: The Authorized Biography of Heroic Tenor Lauritz Melchior.* New York: Schirmer Books, 1990.
Rockwell, John. "The Heroes." *Opera News* 38 (23 March 1974): 12–15.
Schoenberg, Harold C. "The Heldentenor Species Died with Him." *New York Times,* 25 March 1973, B17.
Whitman, Alden. "Lauritz Melchio is Dead: Wagnerian Tenor Was 82." *New York Times* 20 March 1973, 41.

Mellon, Thomas (1813–1908)
Financier and jurist
Scotch-Irish-American

Thomas Mellon was one of the poor immigrants in the early nineteenth century who rose from rags to riches through banking, investments, and real estate, giving substance to an essential American myth that has attracted millions of immigrants. His sons would continue to expand the Mellon financial empire.

Mellon was born near Omagh, County Tyrone, Ireland. He was the son of Andrew and Rebecca Mellon, who were fairly prosperous on their twenty-three-acre farm. But because his father's parents and siblings were already in the United States, Andrew and Rebecca believed they could do better there and joined the family in 1818. The family proceeded to Franklin Township, twenty miles east of Pittsburgh, where his father bought a farm. To make ends meet during the depression of 1819, Thomas's father worked days as a farm laborer and nights as a flax spinner. In his autobiography, Mellon would attribute his values of hard work, self-sufficiency, and thrift to these early, difficult years.

Mellon was an intelligent lad; he loved to read so much that he would take the works of Shakespeare and Robert Burns to the fields. He assimilated quickly and considered himself fully American. Benjamin Franklin's *Autobiography* especially impressed upon him that in the United States a poor boy could rise to become successful and important. He would follow such a path, and nineteenth-century Pittsburgh was the ideal place to do it. Seeing Pittsburgh's growing iron and textiles industries and the fortunes of those who ran them, he decided against farming, went to school, and graduated from the Western University of Pennsylvania (which became the University of Pittsburgh) in 1837. He then studied law, passed the bar, and started his own practice in 1839.

Mellon rose quickly as a young lawyer but even more so as an investor in real estate and mortgages. He purchased ironworks and coal fields and increased his landholdings significantly when he married Sarah Jane Negley, the daughter of a local business magnate. Their five surviving sons would follow in their father's footsteps.

In 1859 Mellon ran successfully as a Republican for judge of the court of common pleas, a position he held for a decade. During and after the Civil War he benefited from the booming economy and brought his sons into his businesses. In 1870 he opened his most famous business, the banking house of T. Mellon and Sons, whose early customers included Henry Clay Frick, the coal magnate, who became Andrew Carnegie's partner. The Mellons continued to expand their other interests as well, particularly in transportation and real estate. The

corporations under their control included Alcoa, Gulf Oil, the Koppers Chemical Company, and the Mellon National Bank. The younger Mellons, in particular, became important philanthropists in the United States and Europe.

Mellon made a return trip to his native Ireland and then wrote his autobiography, *Thomas Mellon and His Times,* which was published in 1885. In the book he displayed his staunch conservatism. He spent his last years at his home in Pittsburgh and died there on his ninety-fifth birthday.

William E. Van Vugt

REFERENCES

Koskoff, David. *The Mellons: The Chronicle of America's Richest Family.* New York: Crowell, 1978.

Mellon, Thomas. *Thomas Mellon and His Times.* 1885. 2d ed. Edited by Mary Louise Briscoe. Preface by Paul Mellon. Pittsburgh: University of Pittsburgh Press, 1994.

Mikulski, Barbara Ann (1936–)
Social worker, U.S. House representative, and U.S. senator
Polish-American

The self-styled 1970s "Queen of the Ethnics," Barbara Mikulski has traveled the road from urban social worker and political activist to three-term U.S. senator from Maryland. She was the first Democratic woman elected to the Senate whose seat had not been previously held by her husband.

The oldest of the three daughters of William and Christine Eleanor (Kutz) Mikulski, Barbara Mikulski is the great-granddaughter of Polish immigrants who had a bakery. Her parents ran a grocery story in one of Baltimore's ethnic, working-class neighborhoods. She received a B.A. in sociology from Mount Saint Agnes College in 1958 and became a social worker for Catholic Charities and the City of Baltimore, earning her M.S.W. in 1965 from the University of Maryland School of Social Work.

Social work led to politics. Mikulski became involved in the Civil Rights movement and battles over housing desegregation. She recognized the rising tensions between black and white ethnic Americans. Confronting her own Polish and American identities, Mikulski defined herself as "a woman, a Polish American, and a Catholic," embracing urban ethnic coalition politics and the brief White Ethnic Renaissance of the 1960s and 1970s. Like Monsignor Gino Baroni and Michael Novak, she spoke for the "forgotten" ethnic residents of U.S. cities who "made a maximum contribution to the U.S.A., yet received minimal recognition," and she castigated liberals who labeled white ethnics as racists even though they had been the ones who "taught us the meaning of racism." Her political career began with the organization of a Polish, Italian, black, and Lumbee Indian coalition to stop construction of a highway through a Baltimore neighborhood of elderly and retired citizens. They succeeded, and Mikulski won a seat on the city council (1971–1977).

In 1973 Mikulski chaired the Commission on Delegate Selection and Party Structure of the Democratic National Committee, which voted to replace the system of delegate selection with a more flexible affirmative action rule to ensure more equitable and diverse representation. In 1976, she was elected to Congress. A liberal Democrat, Catholic, and member of the Polish Women's Alliance, Mikulski's genius has been her ability to couch her political approach in centrist terms, particularly on behalf of the elderly and the retired, women and children, the rights of working people, and jobs for Maryland; nevertheless, she is also a strong advocate of the right of abortion.

Mikulski was elected to the U.S. Senate in 1986, the first Democratic woman elected whose seat had not been previously held by her husband and the first Democratic woman to win a statewide office in Maryland. In 1994 she was the first woman to be elected to a Democratic Party leadership position in the Senate. In 2000 Mikulski was serving on the Labor and Human Resources and the Appropriations Committees and was the ranking member of the Subcommittees on Aging and on Veterans, Housing, and Independent Agencies.

Like the overwhelming majority of Polish Americans, the Mikulskis regarded 1945 Yalta Agreement as a betrayal for opening Eastern Europe to Soviet domination. Consequently, she strongly supported the vote to ratify the expansion of NATO to include Poland, the Czech Republic, and Hungary.

Stanislaus A. Blejwas

REFERENCES
Clancy, T. H. "The Ethnic American: An Interview with Barbara Mikulski." *America* 123 (26 December 1970): 558–559, 562–563.
Folkenflik, David. "Mikulski Likely Shoo-in for a Third Senate Term." *Baltimore Sun,* 18 November 1997.
Mikulski, Barbara. "Who Speaks for Ethnic Americans?" *New York Times,* 29 September 1970, 43.
"Mikulski, Barbara A(nn)." In *Current Biography Yearbook 1985,* 292–295. New York: H. W. Wilson, 1985.
"Mikulski: Queen of the Ethnics." *Newsweek* 84 (4 November 1974): 25.
"Sen. Barbara A. Mikulski (D)." In *CQ's Politics in America 2000. The 106th Congress,* edited by Philip D. Duncan and Brian Nutting, 604–606. Washington, DC: Congressional Quarterly, 1999.
Stineman, Esther. *American Political Women: Contemporary and Historical Profiles.* Littleton, CO: Libraries Unlimited, 1980, 109–111.

Minh-ha, Trinh T. (1952–)
Filmmaker, educator, writer, and composer
Vietnamese

The work of Trinh T. Minh-ha synthesizes visual art, philosophy, filmmaking, feminism, and cultural criticism. She enjoys international recognition as a leading filmmaker, theorist, and critic of Third World women.

Born in Vietnam, Minh-ha received her baccalaureate and completed a six-year music theory and history program at the National Conservatory of Music and Theater in Saigon prior to immigrating to the United States in 1970. Once in the country, Minh-ha attended undergraduate and graduate programs in Ohio and Illinois, earning two master's degrees in 1973, one in French literature and one in music composition, at the University of Illinois, Urbana. She then studied literature and music in France (University of Paris, Sorbonne, 1974–1975) before returning to Illinois and completing her Ph.D. in French literature in 1977. Minh-ha began her academic career teaching English in Paris (1974–1975), music and drama in Dakar, Senegal (1977–1980), and French, French civilization, and literature at University of Illinois (1973–1974 and 1975–1976).

Minh-ha's first documentary film, *Ressamblage* (1982), based upon her ethnographic research in Senegal, was a turning point in her career. It displayed her unique method of documentary filmmaking. Drawing from post-structuralism and Eastern philosophy, her films eschew deterministic narration. Instead, they utilize sound as nonsemantic musical language. Decried as a subverter of documentary filmmaking, she is also championed as a leading postcolonial artist. Her five documentary films have been screened at more than twenty film festivals in the United States, Asia, Europe, Africa, Australia, and New Zealand and have been reviewed by numerous U.S. and international publications. Three of her films (*Shoot for the Content; Surname Viet Given Nam; Naked Spaced—Living Is Round*) have received a total of nine international awards at the Sundance Film Festival (1992), Athens International Film Festival (1992), American International Festival (1987, 1990), Bombay International Film Festival (1990), and the Golden Athena Award for Best Feature Documentary at the 1986 Athens International Film Festival.

As a result of her acclaimed work, Minh-ha has become a well-known film educator. She has taught film at many universities, including Cornell (1991), Harvard (1993), Colgate (1994), San Francisco State (1993), Smith (1994), and the Chinese University of Hong Kong (1995). Presently, she is professor of women's studies, rhetoric, and film at the University of California, Berkeley.

Minh-ha is also the author, editor, and coeditor of eight books, including *Cinema Interval* (1999), *Drawn from African Dwellings* (with Jean-Paul Bourdier, 1996), *Framer*

Framed (1992), *When the Moon Waxes Red* (1991), and *Woman, Native, Other* (1989), as well as numerous articles and poems. Her work reflects her heritage, and her films, books, and articles have provided a body of knowledge for understanding the experiences of Vietnamese immigrants in the United States, the lives of women in the Third World, and the issues of identity, postcoloniality, and culture. Moreover, given the attention she receives in the ethnic media, she is well known and highly regarded by Vietnamese Americans. Minh-ha's ethnic background has no doubt contributed to her vision, influence, and success.

Hoan N. Bui

REFERENCES

Chen, Nancy. "Speaking Nearby." *Visual Anthropology Review* 8 (1992): 82–91.

Clough, Patricia T. *Feminist Thought.* Cambridge, MA: Blackwell, 1994.

Foster, Gwendolyn Audrey. *Women Filmmakers of the African and Asian Diaspora: Decolonizing the Gaze, Locating Subjectivity.* Carbondale: Southern Illinois University Press, 1997.

Kaplan, E. Ann. *Looking for the Other: Feminism, Film, and the Imperial Gaze.* London: Routledge, 1997.

Trinh, Minh-ha, and Jean-Paul Bourdier, *Framer Framed.* New York: Routledge, 1992.

Trong, Minh [pseud.]. "Trinh Thi Minh Ha." In *The Pride of the Vietnamese in the World,* edited by Trong Minh and R. Murphy, vol. 1., 73–80. Irvine, CA: Author, 1991.

Wheal, Nigel. *The Postmodern Arts.* London: Routledge, 1995.

Miyamura, Hiroshi "Hershey" (1925–)

War hero

Japanese-American

Hiroshi "Hershey" Miyamura was until recently the only living Japanese American to have been awarded the Congressional Medal of Honor, the nation's highest award for military valor. Consequently, he held an especially honored position in Japanese-American communities.

Miyamura was born in Gallup, New Mexico, on 6 October 1925, the son of Japanese immigrants who ran a restaurant. The fourth of six children, he enjoyed a typical small-town American childhood. A teacher unable to pronounce "Hiroshi" gave him the name Hershey. He graduated from high school in 1943 and worked for his uncle as an auto mechanic.

In 1945 he was drafted, but the war ended while he was bound for Italy, and he never saw combat in that war. Upon his discharge, he returned to Gallup, enlisted in the U.S. Army Reserve, worked again as a mechanic, and got married in 1949. Shortly thereafter, the United States entered the conflict in Korea, and Miyamura was recalled to active duty in Korea.

On 24 April 1951, in the hills near the village of Taejon-ni, in North Korea, Corporal Miyamura led a machine gun squad in Company H, Seventh Infantry Regiment, which came under attack by Chinese soldiers. Jumping from his trench, he killed at least ten enemy soldiers in hand-to-hand combat, then returned to his position to administer first aid. When another wave of enemy attacked, he fired his machine gun until all his ammunition was gone, then fought his way to a second machine gun and fired it until it jammed, providing cover for his men to escape and killing an estimated fifty enemy soldiers. He then used a grenade to destroy the machine gun and ran for safety. Encountering another enemy soldier, he bayoneted him, but not before being wounded by a grenade. Running on until he could continue no more, his hands and legs torn by barbed wire, he was taken prisoner by the Chinese.

Miyamura was held as a prisoner of war for more than two years. For the first year, his family had no idea he was alive. He was released on 20 August 1953 and returned to a hero's welcome in Gallup. On 27 October, 1953, he was one of seven men who received the Congressional Medal of Honor from President Eisenhower. Miyamura has lived in Gallup with his wife Tsuruko (Terry) ever since and has raised three children, operating a service station until retiring in 1984.

Given the important role Japanese-Ameri-can war veterans have played in the postwar Japanese-American community, Miyamura, as the only surviving Nisei Congressional Medal of Honor recipient until recently (in June 2000 President Clinton awarded this medal retroactively to twenty-one Nisei veterans of World War II), has been one of the most revered figures in the community, remaining highly visible and making numerous public appearances to educate schoolchildren and others about the role of Japanese-American soldiers. He has been honored numerous times by the community, most recently at the fiftieth anniversary Japanese-American–Korean War Veterans reunion in April 2000. He was also the subject of Jon Shirota's play *Honor, Duty, Country: The Hiroshi "Hershey" Miyamura Story,* which premiered in 1998.

Brian Niiya

REFERENCES

Doherty, Kieran. *Congressional Medal of Honor Recipients: Collective Biographies.* Springfield, NJ: Enslow Publishers, 1998.

"JA Korean War Veterans Reunion Slated." *Rafu Shimpo* (Los Angeles), 20 April 2000, 1.

Richter, Paul. "Twenty-one Asian Americans to Get Medal of Honor for WWII." *Los Angeles Times,* 13 May 2000, A16–17.

Miyasato, Albert H. (1925–)

Educator and community activist
Okinawan-American

An Okinawan living among Japanese in Hawai`i, Albert Hajime Miyasato, has devoted his professional career in education to overcoming group distrust and discrimination. He has worked to bridge the gaps between Japan and the United States, between Japan and Hawai`i, and especially between Okinawans and Japanese in Hawai`i.

Miyasato, the eldest of five children of Okinawan-immigrant parents, was born in Hilo, Hawai`i. His father, Shohei, and mother, Fumiko, moved the family to Honolulu, where they started a small business. In 1940, at the age of fourteen, Miyasato went to Japan to train to become a Buddhist priest. The outbreak of the Pacific war, however, profoundly altered the course of his life. In Japan, he was urged to cast his lot with the Japanese Empire, but he remained loyal to the United States, the country of his birth. After the war, he returned home to catch up with his former classmates, earning a bachelor of education from the University of Hawai`i and a doctorate in education (Ed.D.) at the University of Southern California in 1967.

Miyasato devoted his entire life to public education and public service. He held various teaching and administrative posts in Hawai`i and also spent several years in the field of education in Saudi Arabia. As administrative assistant (1976–1981) to George R. Ariyoshi, the first Japanese-American governor in the United States, he endeavored to promote closer relations between Japan and Hawai`i, whose economy was so heavily dependent on Japan. In addition, he assumed numerous key public and civil positions in Hawai`i and California and in these capacities was able to help the Japanese-American communities. Through the many different posts he held in the government, he was consistent in his goal of bringing Hawai`i and Japan closer—particularly Okinawa, Hawai`i, and the rest of the United States. The Okinawan community in Hawai`i was diffident about asserting itself, owing in part to some of its members' wartime experiences of being regarded as enemy aliens and being unsure of their identity. Miyasato was instrumental in bridging the gaps.

Miyasato was actively involved in dozens of projects and organizations, including the Japanese American National Museum, the Japanese Cultural Center of Hawaii, Japan-America Society of Hawaii, the United Japanese Society of Hawaii, Jikoen Honganji Temple Honpa Honganji Mission of Hawaii, Urasenke Tea Ceremony Hawaii Chapter, and the Hawaii United Okinawan Association.

From the standpoint of Okinawans, that Miyasato was elected as the president of the United Japanese Society of Hawaii for two terms, 1978–1980, with strong support from the Japanese, proved final acceptance by the Japanese. This was after more than a half century of persistent Japanese discrimination against Okinawans. Miyasato's outstanding work to better the life of Japanese overseas and to increase the affinity between the United States and Japan received due recognition when, in 1992, among a long list of honors and commendations from various organizations, he was awarded the Fourth Class Order of the Sacred Treasure from the government of Japan.

Mitsugu (Michael) Sakihara

REFERENCES
Hiura, Arnold T. "Dr. Albert Miyasato." *Hawaii Herald* (Honolulu), 17 March 1989, B12.
Knaefler, Tomi. "The Miyasato Story." In *Our House Divided: Seven Japanese Families in World War II*, 97–106. Honolulu: University of Hawaii Press, 1991.
Matsunaga, Katsuko. "Kyoiku itchokusen: Dr. Albert Hajime Miyasato" (In a straight line with the education; Dr. Albert Hajime Miyasato). *East-West Journal* (Honolulu), 15 October 1993–15 March 1994.
Miyasato, Albert. Interview by author, 23 November 1998.

Montejo, Victor Dionicio (1951–)
Anthropologist and community activist
Mayan-Guatemalan

Victor Montejo has dedicated his life to preserving Mayan history and to empowering Mayan Guatemalans through education. A prolific anthropologist, he has written, translated, and contributed to many books covering such issues as Mayan culture and folklore, indigenous literatures, and government repression in Guatemala. He has also helped established a library in Guatemala and archives in the United States in order to make history and literature written for and about indigenous peoples more accessible.

Montejo was born in Jacaltenango, a rural town of western Guatemala, in 1951. His first language is Popb'al ti' Maya, and he also speaks Q'anjob'al. He learned Spanish in Maryknoll schools and received his basic education at a Benedictine seminary. He later received a scholarship to train as a schoolteacher in Antigua, Guatemala. Montejo has lived in the United States since 1984. As his first book, *Testimony: Death of a Guatemalan Village*, depicts, Montejo fled Guatemala in 1982, having experienced political persecution in the village where he taught school.

Montejo initially spent time in Chiapas, Mexico, living in one of the refugee camps. Later, he returned there as an anthropologist to conduct a study for his book *Voices from Exile*. He obtained his M.A. in anthropology at the State University of New York, Albany, in 1989 and his Ph.D. at the University of Connecticut in 1993. Montejo studies the indigenous cultures of southern Mexico and Central America and has conducted ethnographic field research among the Maya in Guatemala, southern Mexico, and the United States. He is an associate professor in the Native American Studies and Anthropology Department at University of California (UC), Davis.

Montejo is involved in many educational projects that focus on the history and future of Mayan Guatemalans. For example, at UC Davis, he is one of the directors of the Native American Language Center Initiative, an archive under construction. The center promotes linguistic research on American Indian languages in the hopes of encouraging the intergenerational transfer of language knowledge. Montejo continues his ties to the Mayan community not only through his academic and literary work but also through his active involvement in Mayan education. He is the vice president of Yax Te' Foundation, a book-publishing group that has become a nonprofit organization committed to making accessible the materials by and about the contemporary Maya of Guatemala. He is also the president of the Foundation for Mayan Education, through which he oversees the Jacaltenango program. With this program, Montejo has begun a library, now under construction, La Casa de la Cultura, in his hometown. In 1993, together with 2,500 refugees, he took part in the first major organized return to Guatemala—his first time back since he had fled.

Montejo considers himself first a Jakaltek Maya and second a Guatemalan anthropolo-

gist. He feels that, as an *Ah Tz'Ib'* (writer), he has the responsibility to be one of the voices for the Mayan people and to educate others about their history and culture. Overall, he has involved himself with as many aspects of education as possible, teaching, writing, archiving, and speaking about the rich history and future of Mayan culture.

Leticia Hernández-Linares

REFERENCES
Montejo, Victor. *El Kanil: The Man of Lightning: A Legend of Jacaltenango.* Carrboro, NC: Signal Books, 1982, 1984.
———. "The Stones Will Speak Again: Dreams of an AH TZ'IB' (Writer) in the Maya Land." In *Speaking for the Generations: Native Writers on Writing,* edited by Simon J. Ortiz, 196–216. Tucson: University of Arizona Press, 1998.
———. *Testimony: Death of a Guatemalan Village.* Translated by Victor Perera. New York: Curbstone, 1987.
———. *Voices from Exile: Violence and Survival in Modern Maya History.* Norman: University of Oklahoma Press, 1999.
Montejo, Victor. Interview by author, 24 January 2000.
Thorn, Judith. *The Lived Horizon of My Being: The Substantiation of the Self and the Discourse of Resistance in Rigoberta Menchu, MM Bakhtin, and Victor Montejo.* Tucson: University of Arizona Press, 1999.

Moreno, Luisa (née Blanca Rosa Rodríguez López) (1906–1992)
Labor union and civil rights activist
Guatemalan

During the 1930s and 1940s, Luisa Moreno, who was strongly committed to justice for workers and immigrants, achieved many successes as a pioneering labor organizer and civil rights activist. These accomplishments were especially significant because she was a woman.

Born on 30 August 1906 in Guatemala and christened Blanca Rosa Rodríguez López, Moreno took the name Luisa Moreno when she began organizing in the United States in the early 1930s. As a teenager, she rejected the patrimony of her wealthy family and ventured to Mexico City. She found work as a journalist and pursued her talents as a poet. At the age of twenty-one, she published a critically acclaimed collection of poems, *El Venedor de Cocuyos* (Seller of fireflies). That same year she married an artist, and the couple immigrated to New York City, where she gave birth to her only child, a daughter, named Mytyl.

With the onset of the depression, Moreno, struggling to support her infant and unemployed husband, labored over a sewing machine in Spanish Harlem. She organized her compañeras into La Liga de Costureras, a Latina garment workers' union. In 1935 the American Federation of Labor hired her as a professional organizer. Leaving an abusive relationship, Moreno, with Mytyl in tow, boarded a bus for Florida. There, she would participate in the unionization of Latina and African American women cigar rollers. Within two years, she began to work for the Congress of Industrial Organizations (CIO) and, in 1938, became a representative of the United Cannery, Agricultural, Packing, and Allied Workers of America (UCAPAWA), which belonged to the CIO.

From 1938 to 1947, Moreno organized Mexican farm and food-processing workers throughout the Southwest. Her most notable success occurred among southern California cannery workers. Under UCAPAWA, cannery women secured higher wages and innovative benefits, including equal pay for equal work. During the 1940s Moreno became the first Latina vice president of a major U.S. trade union and the first Latina member of the California CIO Council. Moreno was also the driving force behind El Congreso de Pueblos de Habla Española (the Spanish-speaking-peoples' congress), the first national civil rights assembly among Latinos. Held in Los Angeles in April 1939, El Congreso crafted a comprehensive platform calling for an end to segregation in public facilities, housing, education, and employment. Representing more than 120 organizations, the delegates endorsed the right of immigrants to live in the United States without fear of capricious deportation and, although encouraging immigrants to become citizens, also emphasized the importance of preserving Latino cultures.

With UCAPAWA in decline and her marriage in 1947 to Gray Bemis, a colleague in the trade union movement, Moreno retired from public life. The next year she faced deportation proceedings. According to Moreno, she was offered citizenship in exchange for testifying against longshoremen leader Harry Bridges, but she refused to become "a free woman with a mortgaged soul." She left the United States in 1950 as a "voluntary departure under warrant of deportation" on the grounds that she had once belonged to the Communist Party. Luisa Moreno died in Guatemala on 4 November 1992.

Vicki L. Ruiz

REFERENCES

Camarillo, Albert. *Chicanos in California*. San Francisco: Boyd and Fraser, 1984.

García, Mario T. *Mexican Americans: Leadership, Ideology, and Identity, 1930–1960*. New Haven: Yale University Press, 1989.

Morena, Luisa. Interviews by author 1978, 1979, 1984, and by Albert Camarillo, 1977.

Ruiz, Vicki L. *Cannery Women, Cannery Lives: Mexican Women, Unionization, and the California Food Processing Industry, 1930–1950*. Albuquerque: University of New Mexico Press, 1987.

———. *From out of the Shadows: Mexican Women in Twentieth-Century America*. New York: Oxford University Press, 1998.

Morgan, Garrett Augustus (1877–1963)

Inventor and entrepreneur
African American

Garrett A. Morgan, who was largely unschooled, patented several inventions in the early twentieth century that have had a major impact on various fields of activity, including sewing machine attachments for garment manufacturing, the gas mask, and the automatic traffic signal light. In 1963 the U.S. Department of Transportation declared him the father of transportation safety technology.

Morgan, born in Paris, Kentucky, 4 March 1877, to former slaves Sidney and Elizabeth (Reed) Morgan, was the seventh of eleven children. An inventive genius, he had only six years of schooling in Kentucky. After working on his family farm, he moved to Ohio, first to Cincinnati (1895) and then Cleveland (1901). His initial invention was a belt fastener for a sewing machine, invented while he was working for a clothing manufacturer, followed by a zigzag-stitching attachment for manually operated sewing machines. These inventions enable him to open his own sewing machine business in 1907; later he started a clothes-manufacturing business that employed thirty-two people. Morgan also developed the first cream hair-straightener product for African Americans and established a company that made several products, including his Hair Refining Cream, hair-dying ointments, and the curved-tooth pressing comb.

In 1912 Morgan applied for a patent for his invention of the gas mask, also called a safety helmet. Two years later, when he received the patent, the invention won the Grand Prize at the Second International Exposition of Safety and Sanitation. Two years after that, he and his brother used the masks to rescue thirty-two workmen trapped in a toxic gas explosion that took place in a Cleveland water works tunnel under construction around 240 feet under Lake Erie; the explosion had killed twenty-one people. Morgan received both the Carnegie Medal and the Gold Medal for Bravery from the City of Cleveland. Eventually, the mask was widely used by fire and police departments throughout the United States and later the world. During World War I, it was used to protect combat soldiers from the chlorine gas employed by the Germans. It was also used in World War II, and modernized versions of it have been distributed in many subsequent military conflicts.

Garrett came up with his most famous invention, the automatic traffic signal, in response to the rise in the number of accidents taking place with the increasing use of the automobile. He was motivated after he had observed an accident between a horse-pulled buggy and an automobile at an intersection. In 1923, he received a U.S. patent for an electric, three-position traffic signal: Stop, Go, and All-direction Stop, the latter halting all traffic on both of the intersecting roads, thereby enabling pedestrians to cross safely. He subsequently sold his invention to the General Electric Company for $40,000.

A respected leader of the African American community, Morgan was founder (1920) and publisher of a newspaper, the *Cleveland Call,* and was also an active member of the NAACP. He died in 1963.

Juliet E. K. Walker

REFERENCES

Haber, Louis. *Black Pioneers of Science and Invention.* New York: Harcourt, Brace and World, 1970.

Hayden, Robert C. *Eight Black Inventors.* Reading, MA: Addison Wesley, 1972.

James, Portia. *The Real McCoy: African American Invention and Innovations, 1619–1930.* Washington, DC: Smithsonian Institution Press, 1989.

King, William M. "A Guardian of the Public Safety: Garrett A. Morgan and the Lake Erie Crib Disaster." *Journal of Negro History* 70.1–2 (Winter–Spring, 1985): 1–13.

McKinley, Burt, Jr. *Black Inventors of America.* Portland, OR: National Book Company, 1969.

U.S. Department of Energy. "Black Contributors to Science and Energy Technology." Washington, DC: Office of Public Affairs, 1979.

Williams, James C. *At Last Recognition in America: A Reference Handbook of Unknown Black Inventors and Their Contribution to America.* Chicago, IL: B.C.A. Publishing, 1978.

Mouton, Alexandre (1804–1885)
Planter, governor, and U.S. senator
Acadian

Alexandre Mouton exemplifies the diligence and determination of the descendants of an exiled people to adapt and prosper in a new home. As a prominent Louisiana politician and planter, he represents the remarkable ascendancy of the French Acadians (Cajuns) and their adoption of the cultural and political heritage of the antebellum South.

Alexandre Mouton was born on 19 November 1804 on Bayou Carenco, Attakapas County, in what is now Lafayette Parish, Louisiana. His parents, Jean Mouton and Marie Marthe Bordat, were descended from Acadian exiles. After graduating from Georgetown College, Washington, D.C., he read law in the offices of a St. Martinville, Louisiana, firm. Admitted to the bar, he briefly practiced law in Lafayette Parish before engaging in sugar cultivation. In addition, beginning a career in politics as a dedicated Jacksonian Democrat, Mouton served in the state legislature from 1826 to 1832 and 1836 to 1837. For two of those years, 1831–1832, he was speaker of the Louisiana House of Representatives. In 1837 Mouton was elected to the U.S. Senate, where he served until his election as governor in 1842.

When he took his oath of office in January 1843, Alexandre Mouton became the first Democratic governor of Louisiana. With a depression gripping the state, he instituted a policy of reducing state expenditures, limiting state borrowing, paying off the state debt, and balancing the state budget. In 1845 Louisiana Democrats, with Mouton's leadership, favored a new state constitution. During the constitutional convention the governor supported the direct election of local officials and the removal of property qualification for voting and holding office. Under Mouton and the Constitution of 1845, free white male suffrage came to Louisiana. However, despite the Jacksonian Democratic reforms, the constitution left the state firmly in the hands of the planter elite, of which Mouton, a sugar planter with hundreds of slaves, was a member. In addition to his political career and status as a sugar planter, however, Mouton was a railroad promoter in the 1850s, serving as vice president of a railroad and president of the Southwestern Railroad Convention, held in New Orleans.

Having earlier served as a Democratic presidential elector in 1828, 1832, and 1836, Mouton led the Louisiana delegation to the 1860 Democratic National Convention, where he joined in a walkout of southern Democrats. The next year, Mouton, being an immediate secessionist, served as president of the state secession convention, which took Louisiana out of the Union in January 1861. After failing to be elected to the Confederate Senate, Mouton returned to his plantation, Île Copal.

During the Civil War his home became headquarters for Union troops, who destroyed plantation property. His slaves were freed, but he retained his 1,900-acre plantation. However, he never recovered financially from his wartime losses. Nonetheless, whereas most Louisiana Cajuns had remained subsistence farmers and fishermen, Mouton represented the minority among them who had been able to join the Louisiana political and economic elite.

Mouton married twice, to Zelia Rousseau, a Creole, with whom he had five children, and to Emma Kitchell Gardner, with whom he had six. He died 12 February 1885.

Marietta LeBreton

REFERENCES

Baker, Vaughan. "The Acadians in Antebellum Louisiana: A Study in Acculturation." In *The Cajuns: Essays on Their History and Culture,* edited by Glenn R. Conrad, 115–128. Lafayette: Center for Louisiana Studies, University of Southwestern Louisiana, 1978.

Dormon, James H. *The People Called Cajuns: An Introduction to an Ethnohistory.* Lafayette: Center for Louisiana Studies, University of Southwestern Louisiana, 1983.

Gayarre, Charles. *The American Domination.* Vol. 4 of *History of Louisiana.* [1866.] 4th ed. 1903. Reprinted New Orleans: Pelican Publishing, 1965.

Gentry, Judith F. "Alexandre Mouton, Governor, 1843–1846." In *The Louisiana Governors from Iberville to Edwards,* edited by Joseph C. Dawson III, 118–122. Baton Rouge: Louisiana State University Press, 1990.

Schumacher, Elizabeth M. "The Political Career of Alexander Mouton." Master's thesis, Louisiana State University, 1935.

Muhlenberg, Henry Melchior (1711–1787)
Early leader of American Lutheranism
German

Henry Melchior Muhlenberg is considered to be the patriarch of American Lutheranism. Despite many hurdles in his path, his leadership and organizational skills enabled him to prevail in bringing Pennsylvania's Lutheran congregations together in the years before the American Revolution.

Muhlenberg was born in Einbeck, Principality of Hanover, Germany, in 1711. Having decided to join the ministry, he studied at the University of Göttingen and at Halle. After his ordination in 1739, he was a teacher, yet yearned to be a missionary in India. Reaching thirty and still awaiting his opportunity to travel to the Far East, Muhlenberg was encouraged by Hermann Francke, a prominent local theologian, to go to America and organize the many Lutheran congregations in Pennsylvania. Muhlenberg consented and departed in early 1742.

After an arduous eleven-month journey, he arrived in Philadelphia in November. Alone, in "culture shock," and immediately challenged by local pastors, Muhlenberg set about establishing his authority, brandishing his certificate of ordination, challenging opponents to debates on points of doctrine, and attempting to bring order to the chaos that was Lutheran Pennsylvania. An alarming attrition rate also plagued the local congregations. Nevertheless, Muhlenberg was pragmatic, energetic, and deeply committed to his calling; he accepted a "call" to lead three congregations. But his parishioners refused to pay him, insisting that he be compensated by his German sponsors. Thus, the thirty-four-year-old minister had to borrow money to live, a situation exacerbated when he married seventeen-year-old Anna Maria Weiser, daughter of Conrad Weiser. She would bear him eleven children and remain a devoted wife and partner for forty-two years. The couple bought land and built a house, which, many scholars believe, was the reason Muhlenberg remained.

Muhlenberg gradually established his authority and, in 1748, demonstrated his superb organizational skills and leadership by convening and successfully leading a meeting for the founding of "the Evangelical Lutheran Ministerium of Pennsylvania and the adjacent colonies." The Ministerium would be the first synod, or governing body, of the Lutheran Church in America.

Given his background and allegiance to the House of Hanover, the aging patriarch was uncertain as to how he and other Lutherans should respond to the approaching Revolution. Although he had praised the repeal of the Stamp Act and subsequently tried to remain neutral, in 1778 Muhlenberg finally felt compelled to take an oath of allegiance to the new government. He would, however, never become an activist, as would his sons: The Reverend John Peter Gabriel Muhlenberg served as a brigadier general in the Continental Army and the Reverend Frederick Augustus Conrad Muhlenberg became a member of the Continental Congress and the first speaker of the House of Representatives.

Muhlenberg certainly fulfilled his motto, *Ecclesia plantanda* (the church must be planted). His dogged and inspired leadership of the early Lutheran Church established a model for organizational structure and identity that continues to be followed today. His legacy also included three sons who became clergymen and secular leaders, a dynasty of ordained ministers, and a number of writings and journals that continue to inspire theologians and interest historians of colonial America.

Susanne M. Schick

REFERENCES

Baglyos, Paul. "Muhlenberg in the American Lutheran Imagination." *Lutheran Quarterly* 6 (1992): 35–50.

Doberstein, John, and Theodore Tappert, eds. *The Notebook of a Colonial Clergyman*. Minneapolis: Augsburg Fortress Press, n.d. [abridged version of Muhlenberg's journals].

Kleiner, John W., ed. *Henry Melchior Muhlenberg: The Roots of 250 Years of Organized Lutheranism in North America: Essays in Memory of Helmut T. Lehmann*. Lewiston, NY: Edwin Mellen Press, 1998.

Riforgiato, Leonard. *Missionary of Moderation: Henry Melchior Muhlenberg and the Lutheran Church in English America*. Lewisburg, PA: Bucknell University Press, 1980.

Rohrbough, Faith. "The Political Maturation of Henry Melchior Muhlenberg." *Lutheran Quarterly* 10 (1996): 384–405.

Strohmidel, Karl-Otto. "Henry Melchior Muhlenberg's European Heritage." *Lutheran Quarterly* 6 (1992): 5–34.

Wallace, Paul. *The Muhlenbergs of Pennsylvania*. Philadelphia: University of Pennsylvania Press, 1950.

Muir, John (1838–1914)
Naturalist and conservationist
Scottish

More than any other immigrant, John Muir was responsible for studying and popularizing the natural wonders of the American West and creating the environmental movement that resulted in the national parks of the United States.

Muir was born in Dunbar, Scotland, the son of Daniel Muir and Anne Gilrye, who were small farmers. At age eleven, together with his father and siblings, he immigrated to Wisconsin, where he worked hard on the new family farm. His mother followed later with the remaining children. His father was a strict disciplinarian, who frequently beat his son for punishment. John's escape was through his books, which he read secretly to avoid his father's wrath. His natural abilities to work with mechanical devices got him admitted to the University of Wisconsin in 1860, but there he turned his attention to botany and practical geology, even though those were not yet university-approved subjects. This study delighted Muir, as he hiked throughout Wisconsin and other states in the Old Northwest and Canada, gathering information on the local plant life and other forms of nature. He also hiked from Indiana to Florida, recording his observations on nature in a detailed diary that became the basis for his posthumously published book, *A Thousand-Mile Walk to the Gulf* (1916).

In 1868 Muir moved to California, a move that changed his life. Hiking from San Francisco east to the Sierra Nevada, he developed a lifelong love of the remarkable natural surroundings, especially the Yosemite valley. He lived in the valley for six years and made countless hikes to record what he saw in notes and sketches, which became the source of his later books. Muir was the first to suggest that the Yosemite valley had been formed by glaciers, a view contemptuously ridiculed by the state geologist and the U.S. Geological Survey but which turned out to be right.

Muir continued to explore the American West as well as Alaska, where today Muir Glacier testifies to its discoverer. Later, he made research trips to Asia and Europe, writing many articles for *Scribner's* and other popular magazines and numerous books on the West, most notably *The Mountains of California* (1894), *My First Summer in the Sierra* (1911), and *The Yosemite* (1912). But Muir is most remembered for his work to preserve the West from degradation and exploitation. He led the campaign for the establishment of Yosemite National Park (1890) and organized the Sierra Club in 1892, of which he was president until his death in 1914. He lobbied President Grover Cleveland to establish thirteen national forests. His remarkable energy and success also gained him the friendship and support of President Theodore Roosevelt, with whom he hiked and camped throughout Yosemite. This partnership between Muir and Roosevelt resulted in the establishment of more national forests and national parks, including Muir Woods National Monument, near San Francisco.

Muir's remarkable success and fame as a conservationist should not overshadow his importance as a naturalist and writer. He was truly a gift from Scotland to the United States for his invaluable efforts to understand and preserve the natural wonders of the American West.

William E. Van Vugt

REFERENCES

Clarke, James Mitchell. *The Life and Adventures of John Muir.* San Francisco: Sierra Club Books, 1979.

Millier, Sally. *John Muir, Life and Work.* Albuquerque: University of New Mexico Press, 1993.

Muir, John. *The Mountains of California.* 1894. Reprint, Garden City, NY: Doubleday, 1961.

———. *Our National Parks.* 1901. Reprint, foreword by Richard F. Fleck. Madison: University of Wisconsin Press, 1981.

Turner, Frederick W. *Rediscovering America: John Muir in His Time and Ours.* New York: Viking, 1985.

Wilkins, Thurman. *John Muir: Apostle of Nature.* Norman: University of Oklahoma Press, 1995.

Mukherjee, Bharati (1940–)
Writer
Asian Indian

Bharati Mukherjee, a native of India, is a novelist and short story writer. Her works reflect Indian culture, the immigrant experience, cultural clashes, and the intersection of gender issues.

Mukherjee was born in 1940 into a upper-middle-class Brahman family of Calcutta, India, the second of three daughters. Until she was eight, she lived near forty to fifty relatives. In 1951 her father obtained employment in England, and the family moved there. During their stay, Mukherjee developed her English-language skills and, after returning to India, entered the University of Calcutta, obtaining a B.A. with honors in 1959 and an M.A. in ancient Indian culture in 1961. She entered the prestigious Writer's Workshop at the University of Iowa, intent on returning with an M.F.A. and marrying a man chosen for her. However, after a two-week courtship in 1963, she impulsively married Clark Blaise, a Canadian writer. She finished her M.F.A. in 1963 and Ph.D. in English and comparative literature in 1969.

Immigrating to Canada in 1968 began the fourteen hardest years of her life. She was discriminated against as an immigrant and treated as a member of a "visible minority." Mukherjee taught at McGill University and wrote her first two novels, laying out her focus on cultural clashes and undercurrents of violence. Her first novel, *The Tiger's Daughter* (1971), chronicles a sheltered Indian woman jolted by immersion in American culture and shocked by her return to violent Calcutta. *Wife* (1975), her second novel, sets forth an Indian woman's descent into madness as she is trapped in New York City by her fears and passivity.

Fed up with Canada, in 1980 Mukherjee returned with her family to the United States, where she now resides and holds citizenship. She continued to write and, after holding several university positions, settled at the University of California, Berkeley, in 1989.

While in the United States, she has published *Darkness* (1985), a collection of short stories, many of which are indictments of Canadian racism and the traditional Indian view of women. *The Middleman and Other Stories* (1988) as well as *Jasmine* (1989), *The Holder of the World* (1993), *Wanting America: Selected Stories* (1995), and *Leave It to Me* (1997) feature Third World immigration to the United States. Based on her works, Mukherjee is described as a writer who has had a life of four phases: a colonial phase, as a national subject in India, as an exile in postcolonial Canada, and as immigrant and then citizen of the United States. She fuses these several backgrounds to create a new-immigrant literature.

In her contribution to the new-immigrant literature, Mukherjee focuses on the phenomenon of migration, the status of new immigrants, and the feelings of alienation often experienced by expatriates. She has also raised public awareness about the plight of Asian Indian women in North America as well as the degradation suffered by Indian women in general. Mukherjee is widely recognized for her work. She received the National Book Critics' Circle Award and a grant from the National Endowment for the Humanities in 1986. Her name appears regularly in the press as a reviewer or because her work is being reviewed. She is also a frequent lecturer on South Asian diaspora literature and women's issues.

Arthur W. Helweg

REFERENCES
Alam, Fakrul. *Bharati Mukherjee*. New York: Twayne Publishers, 1996.
Basbanes, Nicholas A. "Interview/Book Club: Bharati Mukherjee." *george jr. internet monthly*, Oct.–Nov. 1997: www.georgejr.com/oct97/mukerjee.html (accessed 19 June 2000).
Blaise, Clark. *Bharati Mukherjee. Days and Nights in Calcutta*. Garden City, NY: Doubleday, 1977.
Hussain, Azfar. Web site for Course 573: The Fiction of Postmodern America. Annotated Bibliography on Bharati Mukherjee and reviews of *The Holder of the World* (1993) (31 October 1996): www.wsu.edu:8080/~amerstu/573/mukherbib.html (accessed 19 June 2000).
"An Interview with Bharati Mukherjee." *MOSAIC,*

University of Pennsylvania web site (Spring 1994): dolphin.upenn.edu/~mosaic/spring94/page7.html (accessed 19 June 2000).

"Novelist Bharati Mukherjee Keynotes Indian Awareness Week" (February 1996): wupa.wustl.edu/record/archive/1996/02—22-96/6521.html (accessed 19 June 2000).

Swapan, Ashfaq. "People: Passage to America." Book Review of *Leave It to Me,* by Bharati Mukherjee. *Week* (India), 31 August 1997: www.the-week.com/97aug31/life5.htm (accessed 19 June 2000).

Musial, Stanley Frank (1920–)

Baseball player and then businessman
Polish-American

An outfielder and first baseman for the St. Louis Cardinals (1941–1944, [military service in 1945] 1946–1963), Stan Musial—nicknamed Stan the Man, Stash, and the Donora Greyhound—is on everyone's list of baseball's greatest players. The first player to hit five home runs in one day, he batted .331 lifetime and set National League records for the most .300 seasons (seventeen). Musial was named National League's Most Valuable Player (MVP) three times (1943, 1946, and 1948), won league batting titles seven times, and was inducted into the Baseball Hall of Fame in 1969.

Musial was born in Donora, Pennsylvania. His father, Łukasz Musial, a steelworker, came from the village of Mojstava, in Galicia, and his mother, Mary Lancos, a child of Czech parents, from New York City. Łukasz insisted that his children participate in Polish Falcon gymnastics. Musial cannot remember a time when he did not play ball. He pitched both for the Donora Zinc Works A.A., an industrial team, and for his high school, and he wanted to play professional ball. Eventually, his father relented and allowed him to sign a contract while still in high school. After pitching three seasons in the minors and marrying his childhood sweetheart, Lillian Labash, Musial suffered an injury in 1940 that ended his pitching career. He then debuted with the St. Louis Cardinals in September 1941, playing the outfield.

Musial established himself as a fearsome hitter. Dodger fans, awed by his prodigious hitting against Brooklyn pitching, christened him "Stan the Man" in 1946. Two years later, during a three-game series against Brooklyn, he hit .733 (eleven for fifteen). Musial was the first player in the National League to receive $100,000 a year from one team (Hank Greenberg had received that much the year before, but part was from the Pittsburgh Pirates and part from the Detroit Tigers). Ty Cobb said he was the "closest to being the most perfect in the game today." Musial, who played in four World Series and twenty-four All-Star games, retired in 1963. In 1967, he was general manager when the Cardinals won the World Series.

Like many other members of Catholic ethnic groups, Musial campaigned for John F. Kennedy in 1960. His activities have been quite varied since then. His business interests have included a popular St. Louis restaurant and hotels. Lyndon Johnson appointed him director of the President's Physical Fitness Program in 1964. In the 1970s, Musial visited Poland, was honored by the Polish Olympic Committee, and met his Polish relatives. He later accepted the honorary chairmanship of the Little League Poland Foundation's drive to construct a Little League European Leadership Training Center in Kutno, Poland. More recently, he met John Paul II and attended the 1999 Papal Mass in St. Louis.

The death of his father at fifty-eight reminded Musial that he would have liked to attend college, for if he had missed out in baseball, he could have ended up in Donora struggling with silicosis. Instead, although having come from a region where the Slavs were "hunkies," he had succeeded in getting enshrined in the Hall of Fame of the American national sport. Nevertheless, he is renowned for his modesty and respect for all people. His life and career exemplify the role of sports in integrating immigrants and, especially, the second generation, into American society.

Stanislaus A. Blejwas

REFERENCES

Broeg, Bob. *Stan Musial: "The Man's" Own Story, as told to Bob Broeg.* Garden City, NY: Doubleday, 1964.

Broeg, Moe. *The Man Stan: Stan Musial Then and Now.* St. Louis: Bethany Press, 1977.

Brosman, Jim. "Red and His Roomie—and the Pennant." *New York Times Magazine,* 17 September 1967.

Leggett, William. "Stanley, the General Manager." *Sports Illustrated* 26 (20 March 1967): 67–68.

Robinson, Ray. *Stan Musial: Baseball's Durable "Man."* New York: Putnam, 1963.

Schoor, Gene, with Henry Gilfond. *The Stan Musial Story.* New York: Julian Messner, 1955.

Muskie, Edmund Sixtus (1914–1996)
Lawyer, governor, and U.S. senator
Polish-American

Edmund Muskie, a second-generation Polish-American Catholic, broke tradition with his electoral successes in the predominantly Protestant state of Maine. He was elected to the U.S. Senate and nominated for vice president of the United States.

Edmund Muskie, the son of an immigrant tailor, Stephan Marciszewski, changed by an immigration officer on Ellis Island to Muskie, and his wife, Josephine (Czarnecka)—who was born in Buffalo's Polish community—was the second of six siblings, born in the paper-making town of Rumford, Maine. He graduated from Bates College in 1936 and from Cornell University Law School in 1939 and opened a small practice in Waterville, Maine. He served in the navy during World War II and in 1948 married Jane Gray. The couple had five children.

Muskie was elected to the Maine House of Representatives in 1946. In 1954 he became the first Polish-American elected governor of a U.S. state and the first Roman Catholic governor of then predominantly Protestant Maine. He revitalized Maine's Democratic Party and, in 1958, was the first Polish American elected to the U.S. Senate. A decade later, he was the unsuccessful Democratic candidate for vice president and then the leading contender for the 1972 Democratic presidential nomination. His campaign was sabotaged by Richard Nixon's dirty tricksters, compelling Muskie to withdraw from the race. In 1980,

President Jimmy Carter appointed him secretary of state, after which he joined a Washington law firm and subsequently served on the Tower Committee that investigated the Reagan administration's management of the Iran-Contra Affair.

Muskie was a direct, candid, pragmatic, and popular politician, with an explosive temper and Maine humor. A liberal Democrat in the Roosevelt New Deal tradition, he believed with deep conviction in the power of government to do good. He was a highly effective senator who believed that the public interest was advanced through mediation among conflicting interests. He evolved from a hawk to a dove on U.S. involvement in Vietnam, strongly supported civil rights legislation, school integration, federal spending for cities, Medicare and Medicaid, environmental protection, as well as arms control and a reduction in military spending. He chaired the Senate Subcommittee on Environmental Pollution and the Budget Committee.

Muskie was deeply marked by his immigrant father's values—integrity, self-discipline, self-reliance, self-respect, and respect for the individual and his rights. But Muskie also recalled encountering antiforeigner hostility as a youngster and being greeted at school as a "dumb Polack." Nevertheless, his view of the United States was broad, and he spoke directly to white ethnics about their fears concerning integration and the Civil Rights movement. In a 1968 address to the Polish American Congress, he invoked Tadeusz Kościuszko, reminding his audience, "You and I, having gained so much in this great land, should be in the forefront of those who want to help Americans who still suffer from discrimination—those who have not enjoyed the fruits of equal opportunity and equal participation in our society." When Muskie died in 1996, former president Jimmy Carter said that he had "never known any American leader more highly qualified to be president of the United States."

Stanislaus A. Blejwas

REFERENCES

Asbell, Bernard. *The Senate Nobody Knows.* Baltimore: John Hopkins University Press, 1981.

"Edmund S. Muskie." *New York Times,* 27 March 1996, D21.

"Edmund S. Muskie." *Washington Post,* 27 March 1996, A1, 4.

Lippman, Theo, Jr., and Donald C. Hansen. *Muskie.* New York: W. W. Norton, 1971.

Muskie, Edmund S. *Journeys.* Garden City, NY: Doubleday, 1972.

Nevin, David. *Muskie of Maine.* New York: Random House, 1972.

U.S. Congress. "Memorial Tributes Delivered in Congress: Edmund S. Muskie, 1914–1996, Late a Senator from Maine." Senate Document 104–107. Washington, DC: Government Printing Office, 1996.

Nader, Albert S. "Sam" (1919–)

Business executive and city mayor
Lebanese-American

Albert S. Nader is one of six children of Lebanese parents who immigrated to the United States in 1911. Like nearly two dozen other Lebanese-immigrant families, they went to Oneonta, New York, to work on the Delaware and Hudson Railroad. After growing up literally on the wrong side of the tracks, Nader was able to become a successful business executive and mayor of his hometown. As president and general manager of the Oneonta Yankees (Oneonta Tigers as of 1999), he has also achieved local and national recognition for his work in minor league baseball.

Born in 1919 and growing up in the "Lower Deck" area of Oneonta, near the railroad yards, Nader was taught by his parents, Elias and Rose, the importance of family, community, education, hard work, loyalty, and generosity. After serving in Europe during World War II, he returned to Oneonta and took a job at a nearby aerospace plant. He eventually rose to become purchasing director, retiring in 1982 after more than forty years with the company. He married Alice House, daughter of a local doctor and one of the town's founders. They raised three children in a house several doors from his parents and siblings.

Grateful for the opportunities it had been given, the family stressed the need to give back to the community. Nader launched a career in local politics in 1948, serving as alderman as well as assessor. However, he ran into local Republican Party Committee opposition when he decided to run for mayor in 1961. As he was a Roman Catholic Arab of modest background, there was some concern about finding a "real American" to run for mayor. Nader ran under his own party and on the Democratic ticket and won by fourteen votes. For his parents, their immigrant friends in Oneonta's informal Lebanese community, and his other supporters, it was a significant victory.

With Oneonta in decline economically and dispirited during the 1960s, Nader worked to promote urban renewal and expansion of the city's industrial base. He was responsible for construction of a city airport and a senior citizens' home (Nader Towers), extending water and sewer lines for the local colleges, increasing park facilities, and recodifying the city charter. He was also the moving force behind the campaign to bring minor league professional baseball to Oneonta (Yankees 1967–1998; Tigers since 1999). Nader left politics after two terms as mayor but continued to be active in several local organizations.

Often labeled a "dinosaur," he continues to stress the importance of family and community as president and chief executive officer (CEO) of the Oneonta Athletic Corporation. He has refused offers to buy the team, believing buyers would soon move the team. Maintaining the ballpark as a family environment, Nader has helped make Oneonta *the* place to find the true heart of the American pastime. Currently, he is the New York–Penn League representative on the board of trustees of the National Association of Professional Baseball Leagues. Both the Oneonta and the Otsego County Chambers of Commerce named him Man of the Year in 1999 in recognition of his years of community service.

Elizabeth Plantz

REFERENCES

Angell, Roger. "Dinosaur." *New Yorker* 68.26 (17 August 1992): 75–86.

Nader, Albert S. Interview by author, 17 October 1999.

Whittemore, Bob. *Baseball Town: A Place Where Yankees Grow.* Manchester Center, VT: Marshall Jones Co., 1995.

Nader, Ralph (1934–)
Consumer advocate, lawyer, and political activist
Lebanese-American

Ralph Nader, the leading consumer rights advocate in the United States, became a household name in the United States following the 1965 publication of his book *Unsafe at Any Speed,* documenting the dangerous design of General Motors' popular Corvair model. In 1968, he established the Center for Responsive Law in Washington, D.C., and a host of other consumer groups over the years. By 1971, a Harris Poll ranked him among the most popular public figures in the United States.

Nader was born in 1934 to Lebanese-immigrant parents, Nathra and Rose, in Winsted, Connecticut. Nader's parents instilled in him a deep appreciation for political discourse, education, Arabic and American cultures and speaking English and Arabic at home. He spent a year with his mother and grandparents in Zahle, Lebanon, before returning to attend elementary school. He was greatly influenced by his family's immigrant experience, political activism in their local community, and sense of social justice. Eventually, he developed an interest in law, obtaining his law degree from Harvard University in 1958. After leaving a private practice, he traveled, wrote for various publications, and, in 1964, went to work for Daniel Patrick Moynihan, then assistant secretary of labor.

In addition to his 1965 book and the Center for Responsive Law, Nader's other well-known efforts include his early call for automobile air bags, food safety, and stronger environmental legislation, his criticism of "corporate welfare," and his campaign to achieve compensation for airline passengers bumped from their flights because of over-booking. Working with sympathetic members of Congress and others, he campaigned for the creation of federal regulatory agencies, such as the Occupational Safety and Health Administration (OSHA).

During the 1980s Nader focused on state and local initiatives, for example, working with community groups to establish citizen utility boards that aim to make public utilities more accountable to consumers. In 1996, he received the Green Party nomination for president and spoke out on such issues as the need for campaign finance reform and the lack of ideological differences between the two major parties.

Nader remains distinguished among public figures for his modest lifestyle, consistency, and long working hours, even by Washington standards. In the wake of his revelations in *Unsafe at Any Speed,* GM executives hired a private detective to discredit him. They were unsuccessful, and Nader sued GM for $26 million. He settled for $280,000, using the funds to establish the Public Interest Research Group in 1970. A year later, he used a fundraiser to establish Public Citizen. Since then, he has relied heavily on college students and a cadre of dedicated young researchers and activists, known as "Nader's raiders."

Nader's success has stemmed in part from his ability to attract broad media attention for his efforts. Occasionally, he has experienced discrimination, such as when Federal Trade Commission (FTC) chairman Paul Rand Dixon used an ethnic slur to denounce him during a 1978 committee hearing. However, by then, his efforts had received considerable recognition, and he had become one of the most widely recognized Arab Americans in the United States. In 2000 he ran again as the Green Party's candidate for president, receiving 2.72 percent of the vote.

Deirdre M. Moloney

REFERENCES

Janofsky, Michael. "Green Party Selects Nader to Run as Its Presidential Nominee." *New York Times,* 26 June 2000, A14.

McCarry, Charles. *Citizen Nader.* New York: Saturday Review Press, 1972.

"Nader, Ralph." In *Current Biography Yearbook 1986,* 402–405. New York: H. W. Wilson, 1986.

Nieves, Evelyn. "This Time, Nader Promises, It's a Serious Run for President." *New York Times,* 7 March 2000.

Orfalea, Gregory. *Before the Flames: A Quest for the History of Arab Americans.* Austin: University of Texas Press, 1988.

"Ralph Nader for President": www.votenader.com (accessed 27 June 2000).

Rowe, Jonathan. "Ralph Nader Reconsidered." *Washington Monthly* 17.2 (1985): 12–21.

Nagy, Ferenc (1903–1979)
Prime minister of Hungary and
U.S. political activist
Hungarian

In his native Hungary, Ferenc Nagy rose to be prime minister shortly after World War II only to flee a Communist takeover. Immigrating to the United States, he provided for many years significant—although by no means uncontroversial—leadership to anti-Communist efforts among Magyar Americans.

In Hungarian history, the name of Ferenc Nagy provokes controversy. Some regard him as a true adherent to the democratic principles of the immediate postwar period; others consider him a traitor for leaving his post as prime minister and permitting the Communists to obtain absolute control. Born in 1903, in a small village, Bisse, in southern Hungary, Nagy grew up among the true peasantry; most inhabitants owned no more than four acres of land. He became a member of the Smallholders Party, supporting land reforms. He worked his way up in the party, becoming well known by the time of the outbreak of World War II. He opposed Regent Nicholas Horthy's cooperation with the Axis powers, and in March 1944, when the Germans occupied Hungary, he went into hiding. On 21 December, he reappeared on the political scene amidst the chaos of Germans fleeing the Russians. He helped reestablish his party and became the minister of reconstruction for the new government. In February 1946, he was named prime minister of Hungary.

The Communists had already surreptitiously infiltrated the high positions of the government, inciting purges and gradually eradicating opponents from the political arena. In May 1947, when Nagy went to Switzerland for a vacation, the Communists ousted his supporters. Informed of this, Nagy resigned and quickly immigrated to the United States. Many accused Nagy of planning the escape before leaving Hungary, but he would counter that if he had intended to quit, why would he have left his five-year-old son, Laszlo, in Hungary? Nevertheless, in June 1947, Laszlo and the rest of his family arrived in the United States.

In the United States, Nagy became a high committee member in the Hungarian National Council (HNC), a government-in-exile under the leadership of Tibor Eckhardt, a fellow member of the Smallholders Party and friend. Although they initially maintained good relations, a power struggle ensued, and one year later, Nagy severed his ties with the HNC and organized his own movement, the Hungarian Peasant Association (HPA). The HPA and other organizations continued to ask for assistance to free Hungary from the Communists, and since Nagy had been prime minister, the press frequently sought his opinions on Hungarian affairs, especially during the 1956 revolution. He also lobbied incessantly for the admission of Magyars into the United States during this period and thereafter, never stopping until his death in 1979.

Thus, Nagy attempted to transform the political establishment in Hungary while maintaining a high profile in Hungarian-American and even in U.S. political opinion. However, those in the United States were unable to influence the Kadar government in Hungary, and to the extent that their organizations survived, they concentrated on helping those who had been admitted after the 1956 revolution to adjust. In the final analysis, Nagy could not subdue the perpetual factionalism that undermined the activists' reputation with the U.S. government and created fragmentation in the community rather than a union to free Hungary from the Soviet satellite system.

Judith Fai-Podlipnik

REFERENCES

Hoensch, Jorg K. *A History of Modern Hungary, 1867–1986.* London: Longman, 1984.

"Magyar Demokratikus Szocialistak Szovetseg" (Hungarian Social Democratic Federation). Eckhardt Manuscripts, Hoover Institute, box 16.

Nagy, Ferenc. *The Struggle behind the Iron Curtain.* New York: Macmillan, 1948.

Sugar, Peter, Peter Hanak, and Tibor Frank, eds. *A History of Hungary.* Bloomington: Indiana University Press, 1990.

Szeplaki, Joseph, ed. *The Hungarians in America, 1583–1974: A Chronology and Fact Book.* Dobbs Ferry, NY: Oceana Publications, 1975.

U.S. Department of State. *Records of the Department of State Regarding the Internal Affairs of Hungary, 1933–1956.* Washington, DC: GPO, 1984.

Vardy, Stephen Bela. *The Hungarian Americans.* Boston: Twayne Publishers, 1985.

Naismith, James (1861–1939)

Educator (inventor of basketball)
physician, and chaplain
Canadian

Despite a long career as professor of physical education at the University of Kansas, it is for his development of basketball that James Naismith is best known. He was inducted posthumously into the Basketball Hall of Fame in 1959.

Born near Almonte, Ontario, Canada, Naismith and his two siblings were orphaned in 1870 and raised by their bachelor uncle. Naismith quit high school after his second year but returned when he was nineteen. His high school diploma was followed by a B.A. at McGill University, Montreal, and religious training at Montreal's Presbyterian College. During his years in Montreal, Naismith became interested in athletics. He came to believe that there was a connection between religion and athletics, and that he could do as much good with athletics as he could with preaching. In 1889, after playing on McGill's rugby team and the Montreal Shamrocks lacrosse team, he became the director of athletics at McGill. In 1890 he completed his theological training and moved to Springfield, Massachusetts, where he enrolled at the International Young Men's Christian Association's Training School. He taught athletics there as well.

It was in that school, in 1891, as a part of a class on the psychology of play, that he developed the game of basketball. That same year he also developed the first known head protection for football. He continued to teach at Springfield until 1895, when he moved to Denver, Colorado. While attending Gross Medical School, Naismith worked as director of physical education at the YMCA. In 1898, following graduation, he became director of the chapel at the University of Kansas, Lawrence. He also taught physical education, starting the school's basketball program. A few years earlier, in 1894, he married Maude Evelyn Sherman, and they had five children.

Ordained in 1916, Naismith served that year as chaplain to the First Regiment of the Kansas National Guard on the Texas–Mexico border. From 1917 to 1919 he served with the YMCA in France, tending to the spiritual needs of American soldiers there. He became a U.S. citizen in 1925.

It is said that Naismith's happiest moment was in 1936, when basketball was first played at the Berlin Olympics. Before the event began, he was honored with a parade of the athletes from twelve countries, including Canada.

Honored more after his death than while living, he was posthumously inducted into the Basketball Hall of Fame in 1959, sixty-eight years after he had developed the game. The building also bears his name—the Naismith Memorial Basketball Hall of Fame. His childhood home in Almonte, Ontario, is now a historic site, and a museum dedicated to his memory.

Gillian Leitch

REFERENCES

"Basketball's Roots in Canada." NBA official website: www.nba.com/canada/history.html (accessed 10 June 2000).

Devany, John. *The Story of Basketball.* New York: Random House, 1976.

"The History of Basketball." In *World Book Multimedia Encyclopedia*. New York: World Book Inc., 1996.

"Naismith, James." In *Who Was Who in America*, vol. 1, 1897–1942, 886. Chicago: A. N. Marquis Co., 1943.

Naismith, James. "Resume": www.hoophall.com/hoophistory/resume.cfm (accessed 10 June 2000).

"On a Wintery UMass Night, Basketball Was Born." *Union News* (Springfield, MA), 28 September 1997: http://www.hooptown.com/stories/history.html (accessed 10 June 2000).

Webb, Bernice Larson. *The Basketball Man*. Lawrence, KS: Kappelman's Historic Collections, 1973.

Navratilova, Martina (1956–)

Tennis player
Czech

After World War II, tennis became very competitive, with excellent young players entering the sport every year both in the United States and abroad. One of the best players tennis has ever produced is Martina Navratilova, whose place in the annals of women's professional tennis is assured.

Navratilova (Navrátilová in Czech) was born on 18 October 1956 in Prague, Czechoslovakia. Her interest in tennis was stimulated by her maternal grandmother, one of the top players in Czechoslovakia before World War II. Her stepfather also encouraged her, and she remembers practicing with a racket as early as the age of four and a half. At nine her game was so promising that she was being coached by a former Czechoslovak Davis Cup team member. All these efforts soon paid off: In 1968, before she was twelve, Martina won a junior tournament and by sixteen was the best female player in Czechoslovakia. After she had won the Czechoslovak championship in 1972 and an indoor tournament in England, the Czechoslovak Tennis Federation allowed her to compete in the United States.

Navratilova first came to the United States in 1973 at the age of sixteen to participate in an eight-week winter tournament circuit open to both amateur and professional players. The following year she was permitted to take part in a tournament tour that began in California, but by 1975 she had begun to have difficulty gaining permission from the Czechoslovak Tennis Federation to play in the United States. Its officials objected to her increasing "Americanization" and an extension of her stay in order to participate in a tournament in Florida. Fearing that she would not be allowed to play in the United States on a regular basis, she requested political asylum while competing in the 1975 U.S. Open at Forest Hills. In 1981 she became a U.S. citizen.

Before her retirement from singles competition in 1994, Navratilova had achieved an astonishing record: 167 singles and 164 doubles titles, including 2 French Open singles titles (1982 and 1984), 3 Australian Open singles titles (1981, 1983, and 1985), 9 singles titles at Wimbledon (between 1978 and 1990), and 4 U.S. Open singles titles (1983, 1984, 1986, and 1987). In 1984 she won the Grand Slam in women's doubles with Pam Shriver (that is, the two won all four major tournaments—the U.S. Open, Wimbledon, the French Open, and the Australian Open). As early as 1986, in Filderstadt, West Germany, she had become the second player in modern tennis history to win 1,000 professional matches, and in 1991 she held the record of 1,309 singles matches won. Navratilova received the Women's Sports Foundation Sportswoman of the Year Award for three years running (1982–1984), was named Female Athlete of the Decade (1980s), and was inducted into the Women's Sports Hall of Fame.

Navratilova has also distinguished herself in other ways. She is a talented photographer and a vigorous skier; she continues to be active in professional tennis affairs and has coauthored several mystery novels.

Zdenek Salzmann

REFERENCES

Collins, Bud, and Zander Hollander, eds. *Bud Collins' Modern Encyclopedia of Tennis*. Detroit: Gale Research., 1994.

Navratilova, Martina, with Mary Carillo. *Tennis My Way*. New York: Scribner's, 1983.

Navratilova, Martina, with George Vecsey. *Martina.* New York: Alfred A. Knopf, 1985.

"Navratilova, Martina." In *Encyclopedia of World Biography,* 2d ed., vol. 11: 325–326. Detroit: Gale Research, 1998.

Sherrow, Victoria. *Encyclopedia of Women and Sports.* Santa Barbara, CA: ABC-CLIO, 1996.

Zwerman, Gilda. *Martina Navratilova.* New York: Chelsea House Publishers, 1995.

Nelson, Knute (1842–1923)

U.S. House representative, governor, and U.S. senator

Norwegian-American

A trailblazing ethnic politician, Knute Nelson won election as the first Norwegian-born member of the U.S. House of Representatives in 1882 and went on to become the nation's first Scandinavian-born governor in 1892 and the first Scandinavian immigrant in the U.S. Senate in 1895. His electoral successes reflected the growing political clout of immigrant populations, the heavy settlement of Scandinavians in Minnesota at the time, and the credentials Nelson acquired that appealed to immigrants and old-stock Americans.

Born out of wedlock to the daughter of a small farmer in western Norway, Nelson arrived in the United States in 1849 with his mother. He was nine. His mother worked as a household servant in Chicago, sending off money to pay debts incurred in immigrating. Nelson later traced his determination of be free of debt and make his own way in life to these early years, when he also worked as a servant and sold newspapers on the streets of the city.

After his mother married, the family moved to a Norwegian-American community in Wisconsin. All his schooling was a balance of immigrant and Americanizing influences. Nelson first studied English in heavily Scandinavian northern Chicago and then with a Wisconsin teacher who was so impressed with the predominance of Norwegians in the area that she learned their tongue. He taught in a Norwegian-American district himself before completing studies at Albion Academy. In rural Wisconsin, he gained first-hand knowledge of the life of pioneer homesteaders, which later created a bond between him and the Scandinavians in rural Minnesota.

Returning from the Civil War as a wounded veteran who had endured a prisoner-of-war camp and had switched party allegiances while in service, Nelson won election to the Wisconsin State Assembly as a Republican. Relocating in Minnesota's western "upper country" in 1871, he established himself as a family farmer and completed his law studies. In 1874 he won election as state senator from the area. Known as a lawyer-politician who understood farmers' needs, he looked for mutual advantages for farmers and railroad developers in new train routes. He graduated to federal politics by running as a candidate in a new, mostly immigrant, congressional district, and he was elected in 1882, the first Norwegian-born congressman. In Congress, he sponsored bills that released Indian land for white settlement and resisted calls for immigration restriction.

Nelson's victories resulted in part from his facing a split opposition, caused by the defection of farmers to the Farmers' Alliance, the Populists, and the Nonpartisan League. Not supporting solutions proposed by these groups or conservative financial interests, he favored pragmatic approaches. Elected Minnesota governor in 1892, he increased the state's regulatory powers to protect farmers against rapacious middlemen. Elected U.S. senator just two years later, he sponsored the Nelson Bankruptcy Act, avoiding major financial changes but offering relief to rural debtors. Extolling the virtues of immigrants, he included southern and eastern European groups in his praise but supported a literacy test for newcomers. When he died in 1923, he was the Grand Old Man of Minnesota politics, his career testifying to the appeal of mainstream programs.

David C. Mauk

REFERENCES

Blegen, Theodore C. *Minnesota: A History of the State.* Minneapolis: University of Minnesota Press, 1963.

Chrislock, Carl. *The Progressive Era in Minnesota.* St. Paul: Minnesota Historical Society, 1971.

Gieske, Millard L., and Steven J. Keillor. *Norwegian Yankee: Knute Nelson and the Failure of American Politics, 1860–1923*. Northfield, MN: Norwegian American Historical Association, 1995.

Zeidel, Robert F. "Knute Nelson and the Immigration Question: A Political Dilemma." *Minnesota History,* Summer 1999, 328–344.

Nestor, Agnes (1880–1948)
Labor activist
Irish-American

Agnes Nestor had a long and illustrious career in the labor movement and in public service, organizing unions and holding various positions in them. She was the first woman elected president of an international union.

Nestor was born on 24 June 1880 in Grand Rapids, Michigan. Her father, Thomas, was an immigrant from County Galway, in Ireland. He was a machinist, tried the grocery business, and later entered local politics. Her mother, Anna McEwen Nestor, was an Irish American born in Tribes, New York. After some hard times, she moved to Grand Rapids, where she met Thomas. In 1897, he moved the family to Chicago.

At age seventeen, Agnes Nestor found a job in the Eisenrath Glove Factory, where she soon began challenging the management. She objected to the practice of charging workers "machine rent" and making them pay for their own needles, oil, and power. In 1898 she led the women glove makers out on a ten-day strike. The strike ended successfully, resulting in the formation of a local union of glove makers. In 1902 she helped found the International Glove Workers Union (IGWU) of America and led the women workers out of the all-male glove cutters union. Nestor became the president of the new women's local of the IGWU and served it in various official positions from 1902 to 1948. In 1913 she became the first woman ever to be elected to the presidency of an international union.

Nestor joined the Chicago Trade Union League in 1904 and was a member of the executive board of the National Women's Trade Union League (NWTUL) from 1907 to 1948. She was active in union issues for trades outside her own, including the stockyards, garment industry, mining, nursing, waitressing, and teaching and, over the years, worked with other women labor activists.

Nestor was a dedicated lobbyist. In 1909 she helped hammer out a compromise bill in the Illinois legislature for a ten-hour workday. However, she never quit agitating for an eight-hour-a-day bill, and when that was enacted in 1937, Nestor was credited with a victory. She also lobbied for the prohibition of child labor, minimum wages for women, maternal health programs, and high industrial standards. She was sought after for public service positions at both the state and national levels. During the Great Depression she served on the Illinois governor's Commission on Unemployment and Relief. She also joined the National Council of Catholic Women, chairing the Committee on Women in Industry.

Nestor was also a prolific writer and had numerous pieces in the *American Federationist* and *Life and Labor*. She wrote two books, one in 1942—*A Brief History of the International Glove Workers Union of America*—and *Woman's Labor Leader, an Autobiography,* which was released in 1954. In 1929, Nestor, who had only an eighth-grade education, was awarded an honorary doctorate of laws by Loyola University in Chicago. In addition, she continued to maintain her ties with the Irish community through the Church, her association with other activists, and her membership in the Daughters of Erin.

Throughout her life Nestor was a rather frail person and suffered from chronic fatigue and debilitating respiratory problems. On a number of occasions she needed sanitarium rest owing to complete exhaustion. She died on 28 December 1948.

Seamus P. Metress

REFERENCES

Conn, Sandra. "Three Talents: Robins, Nestor and Anderson of the Chicago Women's Trade Union League." *Chicago History* 9(4) (1980–1981): 234–244.

Mason, Karen M. "Testing the Boundaries: Women, Politics, and Gender Roles in Chicago, 1896–1930." Ph.D. diss., University of Michigan, 1991.

Nestor, Agnes. *A Brief History of the International Glove Workers Union of America.* Chicago: Research Department of the International Glove Workers Union of America, 1942.

———. *Woman's Labor Leader, an Autobiography.* Rockford, IL: Bellevue Books, 1954.

Nevelson, Louise (née Berliawsky) (1899–1988)

Sculptor

Russian-American

Louise Berliawsky Nevelson, who was born to Jewish parents in Kiev, Russia, in 1899 and immigrated to the United States at the age of five, became recognized as one of America's leading sculptors in the 1960s. Even in her later years, she continued to experiment with materials and received many prestigious awards.

In 1905 Berliawsky settled with her family in the small community of Rockland, Maine. By 1917 she had decided not to lead a "conventional" life and marry; she would be an artist. However, she married Charles Nevelson, one of four Russian-born brothers who owned a small shipping company. They agreed to have no children, so she could pursue an artistic career. Nevertheless, in 1922, she gave birth to a son, Myron, but continued her art classes and discovered modern art as represented by Picasso and others. Nevelson identified herself and her husband as Russians, but as an artist, she was critical of how the Russians in New York regarded creative people and, as with many artists, gradually shifted her identity from her ethnicity to her profession.

In 1931 she traveled to Germany to study cubism. During the depression years, Nevelson separated from her husband and went to work with the Federal Arts Project of the Works Progress Administration (WPA), studying and practicing various forms of sculpture with other artists, including a mural project with Diego Rivera. By the late 1930s, Nevelson should have been a recognized major modern art sculptor but had not received that recognition. She and other women artists felt that sexism on the part of the arbiters and collectors of art prevented shows of their works at the major galleries in New York. In 1941 Nevelson walked into Karl Nierendorf's showroom, one of the most prestigious in New York, and demanded a show. On seeing her work, he granted her space for a show, which was a critical success but produced no sales.

In 1958 Nevelson finally received acclaim and financial success for her *Sky Cathedral* at a one-woman exhibit, resulting in an exclusive contract that guaranteed her a good income. Four years later, she represented the United States at the Biennale Internazionale d' Arte exhibition in Venice, Italy. In 1964, she completed *Homage 6,000,000,* a black-painted wooden wall commemorating the Jews who died in the Holocaust. However, since she was a radical feminist, the *Homage* was probably inspired as much by her liberalism and radicalism as by her Russian-Jewish roots.

In 1977, Nevelson designed a white environment chapel in St. Peter's Lutheran Church in New York City and also created perhaps her greatest masterpiece, *Mrs. N's Palace,* a virtual room, a sculpture that the viewer entered. A German museum offered her $1 million for the sculpture, but determined that it stay in the United States, she donated it to the Metropolitan Museum of Art.

Nevelson continued to experiment with materials, such as aluminum plate, plexiglas and cor-ten steel, and, even before her death in 1988, had been recognized as a leading U.S. sculptor, receiving many major awards and recognitions in the United States and Europe. She was one of the first to receive the National Medal for the Arts; she also was given the Medal of Freedom by her beloved New York. Her sculptures grace urban and academic landscapes and museums from the Atlantic to the Pacific.

Keith P. Dyrud

REFERENCES

Cain, Michael. *Louise Nevelson.* New York: Chelsea House Publishers, 1989.

Glimcher, Arnold. *Louise Nevelson*. New York: E. P. Dutton, 1976.

Lisle, Laurie. *Louise Nevelson: A Passionate Life*. New York: Summit Books, 1990.

Nevelson, Louise, and Diana Mackown. *Dawns Plus Dusks*. New York: Scribner's, 1976.

Ng Poon Chew (1866–1931)
Minister, editor, author, and lecturer
Chinese

Ng Poon Chew (he used the traditional Chinese-name format; in Mandarin, Wu P'an-chao), in his role as Presbyterian minister, newspaper editor, and lecturer, spoke out against the racialized immigration laws and the injustices from which the Chinese community suffered. During an era when few of his coethnics had a good command of English or understood the laws of their adopted country, Ng served as a cultural broker.

Born on 14 March 1866 in Guangdong Province, China, young Ng came under the tutelage of a Daoist monk. Eschewing the priesthood, Ng was more enraptured by tales of wealth in *Gum Saan* ("Gold Mountain," or California). In 1879, his uncle returned from the United States laden with wealth, and two years later Ng left for California, only to find that the Gold Rush had passed its peak. Although working as a houseboy in San Jose, he attended school and quickly became receptive to American culture, cutting off his queue and donning Western clothing. A year later, he converted to Christianity and, in 1889, entered the San Francisco Theological Seminary. Following graduation he became pastor of the Presbyterian Church of Chinatown and soon after married Chun Fah.

Forced to supplement his income and aware that the community lacked a credible Chinese newspaper, he established a weekly one in Los Angeles in 1898. It soon failed, and in 1900 Ng moved to San Francisco and renamed his paper *Chung Sai Yat Bo* (*CSYP*; literally "Chinese-American daily newspaper"). It continued until the 1930s. In his editorials, Ng attacked the exclusion laws and urged China to limit its trade with the United States. He drew enough attention to garner support for the first of his many national speaking tours. He spoke on behalf of legislative reform and sought to convince Americans of the manifold contributions Chinese could make to society. On a second tour Ng met with President Theodore Roosevelt. Little changed, and when Congress passed new exclusion laws in 1902 and 1904, the resentful Chinese community—supported by Ng's newspaper and other ethnic organizations—organized a boycott of U.S. goods that did lead to some alterations of immigration procedures.

Ng realized that the image of the Chinese in the United States, and consequently their status, could improve only if social reform occurred in Chinatown. He viewed Christianity and modernization as a form of salvation and a way to end discrimination. Despite the ridicule of Ng by some Chinese (who viewed him as a traitor to Chinese heritage), the *CSYP* urged Chinese to oppose prostitution, foot binding, polygamy, arranged marriages, and the violence of secret societies.

Ng was appointed adviser to the Chinese consul general and, in 1913, vice-consul for China in San Francisco. Ng continued to be a leading lecturer on the Chautauqua and Lyceum circuits, using these opportunities to present a positive image of the Chinese. In 1913 the University of Pittsburgh, in recognition of his contributions, conferred upon him an honorary doctorate. Ng died in 1931 at the age of sixty-five, leaving behind a reputation of having succeeded to a certain extent in reducing the chasm between two seemingly irreconcilable cultures.

Benson Tong

REFERENCES

Hoexter, Corrine K. *From Canton to California: The Epic Chinese Immigration*. New York: Four Winds Press, 1976.

Woo, Wesley. "Chinese Protestants in the San Francisco Bay Area." In *Entry Denied: Exclusion and the Chinese Community in America, 1882–1943*, edited by Sucheng Chan, 213–245. Philadelphia: Temple University Press, 1991.

Novak, Michael John (1933–)
Writer, philosopher, and theologian
Slovak-American

Internationally known for his writings, Michael Novak initially gained recognition for helping fuel the ethnic revival of the 1970s. His publications and aggressive role as an advocate of the "new ethnicity" earned him widespread recognition in both mainstream and ethnic America.

A third-generation Slovak, Michael Novak was born in Johnstown, Pennsylvania, in 1933. Although his family maintained some festive customs, this grandson of four Slovak immigrants did not develop a strong ethnic identity during his childhood. Graduating with a B.A. from Stonehill College (1956), he went on to obtain a bachelor of theology degree from Gregorian University (Rome, 1958) and an M.A. from Harvard University (1966). A specialist in religious studies, Novak held academic or administrative positions at several institutions during the 1960s and early 1970s. From 1961 to 1971, he published two novels and twelve monographs on religion, American culture, and politics. Novak was also involved outside academia, especially as a journalist and political activist. He covered the 1970 and 1972 national elections for *Newsday* and was a speechwriter for the Democratic Party during the 1972 campaign.

National politics had a profound impact on Novak. He credited reports on voting patterns in the 1964 and 1968 presidential elections with arousing his own ethnic self-consciousness. Novak's newfound awareness, though, was accompanied by a resentment toward what he called the American superculture. This superculture, he argued, had suppressed ancestral heritages and stereotyped "white ethnics," a descriptive phrase meaning "white ethnic Catholics, especially from eastern and southern Europe." His convictions prompted him to write *The Rise of the Unmeltable Ethnics* (1972), a relentlessly scathing critique of American culture, politics, and capitalism. Calling for the promotion of ethnic diversity and a politics of cultural pluralism, this provocative work made Novak both a leading proponent and a defender of the "new ethnicity." Striking a responsive chord among "white ethnics," Novak became an aggressive voice not merely for Slovak Americans but also for the descendants of southern and eastern Europeans. He organized the Ethnic Millions Political Action Committee (EMPAC) and edited the short-lived organization's newsletter, *EMPAC!*

In 1976 Novak was a writer in residence for the *Washington Star;* he had a nationally syndicated column from 1976 to 1980. In 1978, he became a resident scholar in religion and public policy at the American Enterprise Institute (Washington, D.C.). By the early 1980s, Novak's political views had shifted dramatically, and he subsequently readjusted the thrust of his writings. Typically avoiding ethnic issues, he focused primarily on religion and capitalism. A prolific writer, he earned particular distinction for formulating theological defenses of capitalism. The recipient of a dozen awards, including the Ellis Island Medal of Honor (1986) and the prestigious Templeton Prize for Progress in Religion (1994), Novak also served on national and international commissions.

Novak's ethnic awakening helped launch a distinguished career marked by national and international prominence. Despite his changed focus during the 1980s and 1990s, championing the "new ethnicity" in the 1970s earned Novak long-term recognition among Slovak Americans as well as other "white ethnics."

June G. Alexander

REFERENCES

Novak, Michael. *Further Reflections on Ethnicity.* Middletown, PA: Jednota Press, 1977.

———. *The Rise of the Unmeltable Ethnics: The New Political Force of the Seventies.* New York: Macmillan, 1972; 2d ed. title: *Unmeltable Ethnics: Politics and Culture in American Life.* New Brunswick, NJ: Transaction Publishers, 1996.

"Novak, Michael." In *Who's Who in America, 2000,* 54th edition, 2: 3619. New Providence, NJ: Marquis Who's Who, 1999.

Novotná, Jarmila (1907–1994)
Opera singer
Czech

Not many singers earn from music critics such accolades as "lyrical grace," "intelligence," "regal bearing," and "finest musicianship." One who did was the world-renowned soprano and accomplished actress Jarmila Novotná.

Novotná was born in Prague on 23 September 1907. Her musical talent was recognized early, and she received voice lessons for several years before enrolling at the Prague Conservatory. There, she studied with the famous Czech soprano Emmy Destinn. In 1925 Novotná made her debut in Prague, singing the role of Mařenka in Smetana's comic opera *The Bartered Bride*. She was an instant success. Before her twentieth birthday she had become a star of the opera of the National Theater in Prague. Her beauty, exquisite voice, and superb acting soon gained her access to the major opera houses of the world—including those of Vienna, Berlin, Milan, Paris, London, and Salzburg.

She received an offer from the Metropolitan Opera in New York in 1928, but because she did not want to leave her future husband, she chose instead to go to the Kroll Oper in Berlin. There, she caught the eye of the great director Max Reinhardt, who cast her in a number of operas and—recognizing her dramatic abilities—attempted to persuade her to give up singing for the theater. In 1933 Novotná made her Vienna debut in Puccini's *Madama Butterfly* and was soon considered the finest lyric soprano in central Europe. Louis B. Mayer of MGM saw her and offered her a five-figure contract if she would give up opera for films. She preferred to continue with the Vienna State Opera.

Novotná came to the United States in 1939 to sing *Madama Butterfly* with the San Francisco Opera. The following year she made her debut at the Metropolitan Opera as Mimi in *La Bohème*. For the next sixteen years—until 1956—she was a treasured artist at the Met, appearing in 193 performances (142 in the house, 51 on tour). She sang such varied roles as Donna Elvira in *Don Giovanni*, Manon in *Manon*, Violetta in *La Traviata*, Antonia and Giulietta in *The Tales of Hoffmann*, Mélisande in *Pelléas et Mélisande*, Pamina in *The Magic Flute*, and Mařenka in *The Bartered Bride*.

Novotná's contributions to the world of music were not limited to opera. She also performed in operettas, such as Franz Lehár's *Merry Widow* and Johann Strauss's *Die Fledermaus;* gave recitals; appeared on Broadway in the title role of Erich W. Korngold's adaptation of *La Belle Hélène,* as well as in *Sherlock Holmes* (1953) and other musicals. She also appeared in a number of both American and European films, including *The Last Waltz, The Bartered Bride, The Search* (1948; a nonsinging role), and *The Great Caruso* (1951).

Novotná had married Baron George Daubek in 1931 and became the mother of two children. She received U.S. citizenship in 1946. After retiring from the Metropolitan Opera in 1956, she and her husband moved to Vienna, where she made her final appearances at the Volksoper in 1957. After her husband's death in 1981, she returned to New York to be near her children. She died at her Manhattan home on 9 February 1994.

Zdenek Salzmann

REFERENCES

"Novotná, Jarmila." In *Current Biography Yearbook 1994,* 655. New York: H. W. Wilson, 1994.

"Novotná, Jarmila." In *International Dictionary of Opera,* edited by C. Stephen LaRue, vol. 2: 946–947. Detroit: St. James Press, 1993.

Novotná, Jarmila. *Byla jsem šťastná.* Prague: Melantrich, 1991.

Price, Walter. "Jarmila Novotná, 1907–1994." *Opera News* 58.14 (2 April 1994): 43–44.

Rothstein, Edward. "Jarmila Novotna Is Dead at Eighty-six; Soprano of Aristocratic Bearing." *New York Times,* 10 February 1944, B10.

Oakar, Mary Rose (1940–)

U.S. House representative
Syrian-Lebanese-American

Mary Rose Oakar served as an Ohio congresswoman for eight terms, from 1977 to 1993, the first Arab-American woman elected to Congress. While there, she was particularly active with respect to women's and age-related issues.

Oakar was born in Cleveland to Syrian-Lebanese parents, Joseph (who had immigrated in 1920 at age sixteen) and Margaret Oakar (American-born). Her parents anglicized their name from Aucar to Oakar when her father was naturalized in the same year she was born, 1940. She attended Roman Catholic schools, receiving a B.A. from Ursuline College in 1962 and an M.A. from John Carroll College. Her career path was an unusual one for a politician. She taught English, speech, and drama at Cuyahoga Community College and worked as a telephone operator for the Ohio Bell Company from 1957 to 1962. After becoming active in the Democratic Party, she was elected to the Cleveland City Council, where she served from 1973 to 1976, and then was elected to Congress in 1976.

Although Oakar does not hold a law degree, she was able to capitalize on the fact that her solidly Democratic district was a heavily ethnic one, composed of Poles, Czechs, Germans, Italians, and other groups. She served in leadership positions, replacing Geraldine Ferraro as secretary of the House Democratic Caucus in 1984. Because of own her religious background and that of many of her constituents, Oakar opposed federal funding of abortions, distinguishing her from most other Democratic congresswomen. She was also an early advocate of increased funding for breast cancer research, of pay equity, and comparable worth initiatives. Oakar also promoted efforts to better recognize the 1.8 million female veterans who have served in the armed forces by cosponsoring legislation authorizing the building of the Women in Military Service for America Memorial, which was dedicated in 1997. She supported programs aimed at achieving an economic revival of the midwestern rustbelt and worked on behalf of a number of foreign policy issues, especially those pertaining to the Middle East. In 1982, she was part of a congressional delegation that traveled to the Middle East, where she met with various leaders, including Yasser Arafat of the Palestinian Liberation Organization (PLO).

Oakar has been outspoken about the bias faced by Arab Americans, from scrutiny over campaign contributions from Arab Americans to the negative portrayal of the ethnic group in American culture. "Somehow there's a stigma attached [to contributions from ethnic group members] when you're Arab American," she has noted. She was also active in efforts to establish a park in honor of the Arab-American writer Kahlil Gibran on federal land in Washington, D.C.

However, Oakar lost her reelection bid in 1992 as a result of her involvement in the congressional banking scandal; she later negotiated a plea bargain on related charges. After that she established a public relations and consulting firm in Cleveland and remains active in local charitable causes. She also served on the board of directors of the U.S.-Arab Chamber of Commerce. In 2000, she launched an effort to return to politics by winning the Democratic primary in the Ohio Thirteenth District State House of Representatives race.

Deirdre M. Moloney

REFERENCES

Duncan, Phil, ed. "Politics in America: The 100th Congress." *Congressional Quarterly,* 1987, 1215–1217.

Ehrenhalt, Alan, ed. "Politics in America, 1986." *Congressional Quarterly,* 1985, 1239–1241.

Haiek, Joseph, ed. *Arab-American Almanac.* Glendale, CA: News Circle Publishing, 1984.

"Oakar, Mary Rose." In *Who's Who in American Politics 1999–2000, 17th edition, 2:1742.* New Providence, NJ: Marquis Publishing, 1999.

Mehdi, Beverlee T., ed. *The Arabs in America, 1492–1977: A Chronology and Fact Book.* Dobbs Ferry, NY: Oceana Publications, 1978.

Shakir, Evelyn. *Bint Arab.* Westport, CT: Praeger, 1997.

Oh, Angela (1955–)

Attorney and community activist
Korean-American

Catapulted into the national spotlight in the wake of the 1992 Los Angeles uprising, attorney Angela Oh has been an articulate commentator and community activist on a number of issues, including race relations, the legal system, and women's issues. Oh has also served as cochair of California State Assembly's Special Commission on the Los Angeles Crisis, on Senator Barbara Boxer's judiciary advisory committee, and as a member of President Clinton's Initiative on Race.

Born in Los Angeles in 1955 to Korean-immigrant parents, Angela Oh grew up within the Korean-American community in southern California as it was transformed by the 1965 Immigration Act from a small group to a bustling population. Oh attended local public schools and the University of California, Los Angeles, graduating in 1977 with a degree in psychology. In 1981, after working on issues of women's health advocacy, Oh returned to UCLA to enter the doctoral program in public health. While in school, she founded the Los Angeles Committee of Occupational Safety and Health (LACOSH), a coalition of safety and health advocacy organizations. Through her experience with LACOSH, Oh realized that she could better advance her causes as an attorney. She enrolled in the University of Califor-

nia, Davis, Law School, earning a J.D. in 1986.

Oh then worked as a political consultant for the "No on Proposition 63" organization, which opposed the initiative making English the official language of California. She also worked as an attorney representing labor unions and, for a brief stint, represented law enforcement officers in official misconduct actions. Since the late 1980s, Oh has moved into criminal defense trial work with the law firm of Beck, De Corso, Barrera, and Oh. In addition to her career as a lawyer, Oh has been an active participant in civic and community affairs. She has been president of the Korean American Bar Association and the Women's Organization Reaching Koreans (WORK) and served on the board of the American Civil Liberties Union (ACLU).

The 1992 Los Angeles crisis gave Oh greater opportunities to serve her city and community by calling attention to the larger social, economic, and political issues and refusing to frame the situation in terms of a simplistic "Black-Korean conflict." Through her appearance in such shows as *Nightline* and *Donahue* and in her writings and speeches, Oh has struggled to find creative ways to surmount the barriers that divide Americans. In recognition of her efforts over the years, Oh was named by President Clinton to help oversee his ill-fated Initiative on Race. In that capacity and based on her own experience in California, Oh made a strong case that race in the United States must be seen beyond the black and white framework that has been so dominant. Because of her views, particularly on race and gender, Oh has not been without critics at large as well as within the Korean-American community. Nevertheless, she remains a committed and progressive voice on vital national issues. Oh continues to practice law and is a much-sought-after speaker on college campuses and before other organizations.

David Yoo

REFERENCES

Abelmann, Nancy, and John Lie. *Blue Dreams: Korean Americans and the Los Angeles Riots.* Cambridge, MA: Harvard University Press, 1995.

Abrams, Garry. "Out of Chaos, a New Voice." *Los Angeles Times,* 20 July 1992, E1–2.

Hicks, Joe, Antonio Villaraigosa, and Angela Oh. "Los Angeles after the Explosion: Rebellion and Beyond." *Against the Current* 40 (Summer 1992): 44–48.

"Oh, Angela." In *Notable Asian Americans,* edited by Helen Zia and Susan B. Gall, 294–296. Detroit, MI: Gale Research, 1995.

Olson, Floyd Björnsterne (1891–1936)

Attorney and governor
Norwegian-Swedish-American

From lumberyard worker and longshoreman, Floyd Olson rose to become governor of Minnesota. He was praised by Scandinavians for manifesting the best of their cultural heritage and by many Minnesotans as one of their most promising leaders.

The only child of a mother from Värmland, Sweden, and a father born in Trondheim, Norway, Olson was christened Floyd because his mother wanted an American name to assist his progress. In adding the middle name, his father showed pride in a Norwegian heritage that he perhaps hoped his son also would value: the free-thinking, liberal principles of the Norwegian poet-patriot, Bjørnstjerne Bjørnson. Olson was born and grew up in a working-class district of north Minneapolis, where he made friends among Scandinavians, Germans, east European Jews, and African Americans. Like many in his circumstances, he took odd jobs during the school year. Later, when he ran for elective office, what became the best-known of these tasks was his being paid to turn on the heat and to light candles for Orthodox Jews on the Sabbath. Among other jobs, he took lumberyard work with his father and farmwork in the countryside.

An indifferent high school student, Olson found his greatest stimulation in the debate society. After graduation, he attended the University of Minnesota for a year but dropped out. He sold farm machinery in Canada, wandered from the grain harvest there to gold prospecting in Alaska, and worked on the Seattle docks, where he joined the radical International Workers of the World before returning home in 1913.

He clerked in a Swedish American's law office while getting his law degree and then worked for a time as a trial lawyer in Minneapolis until being appointed Hennepin County's assistant attorney in 1919. When the county attorney was ousted, Olson won the position as a compromise nominee and held it for ten years, during which he won a reputation for prosecuting the Ku Klux Klan and political graft. He became Minnesota's governor in 1930 and was reelected three times but died suddenly of cancer in 1936, when he was a candidate for the U.S. Senate—having often been touted as a likely candidate for president.

In office prior to Roosevelt's presidency, Olson put forward proposals dealing with the depression that predated or exceeded the goals of much New Deal legislation. The governor proposed and signed such laws providing relief for the needy, employment through public works and conservation, tax and mortgage abatements for farmers, and protection legislation for unions that recognized their right to negotiate on an equal footing with employers.

Olson was remarkable for building and holding the diverse bipartisan support needed to be elected as the standard-bearer of the state's ultraliberal Farmer-Labor Party. Republicans broke rank to support him, and a disparate range of ethnic groups followed him loyally. Not least in importance among these was the Jewish community, from which he hired campaign and administrative staff. He was idolized by most Scandinavian Americans as embodying the best in their heritage, and they remained his most steadfast supporters. For them, his political principles and prowess provided a lasting political influence.

David C. Mauk

REFERENCES

Gieske, Millard L. *Minnesota Farmer-Laborism: The Third-Party Alternative.* Minneapolis: University of Minnesota Press, 1979.

Haynes, John Earl. *Dubious Alliance: The Making of Minnesota's DFL* [Democratic Farmer-Labor] *Party.* Minneapolis: University of Minnesota Press, 1984.

Mayer, George H. *The Political Career of Floyd B. Olson.* St. Paul: Minnesota Historical Society Press, 1951, 1987.

McGrath, John S., and James J. Delmont. *Floyd Björnsterne Olsen: Minnesota's Greatest Liberal Governor, a Memorial Volume. The Story of his Life and Many of his Greatest Speeches.* St. Paul, MN: Published by the authors, 1937.

O'Neill, Eugene G. (1888–1953)
Dramatist
Irish-American

One of the greatest playwrights of the twentieth century, Eugene O'Neill won three Pulitzer Prizes for his plays and, in 1936, the Nobel Prize in literature. His plays, rooted in his Irish heritage, touched on timeless themes of human struggle.

Born in New York City on 6 October 1888, O'Neill grew up in the world of drama and theater. His father, James, immigrated to the United States from Kilkenny, Ireland, during the Great Famine and gained fame and fortune for his nearly 6,000 performances as the lead in *The Count of Monte Cristo*. His mother, Ella (Quinlan), the daughter of Irish immigrants from Tipperary, was an unhappy woman who eventually became addicted to morphine. Most of O'Neill's early years were spent traveling while his father performed, and his career as a playwright clearly stemmed from this experience, just as the strained family relationships formed the basis for many of his plays.

O'Neill flunked out of Princeton in 1907 and spent the next five years living a precarious existence. His love of reading and theater (especially the works of Irish playwrights Yeats and Synge), however, prompted him to begin writing plays in 1913. His first break came in 1916, when the Provincetown Players performed his play *Bound East for Cardiff*. From that point on, O'Neill's fame soared. *Beyond the Horizon* won the Pulitzer Prize in 1920, *Anna Christie* did in 1922, and *Strange Interlude*

won in 1928. He produced eighteen plays in the 1920s.

O'Neill's output slowed in the 1930s (three plays). Yet he was named the Nobel laureate in literature in 1936. Indeed, he was actually most productive during the late 1930s and 1940s, writing his great masterpieces *Long Day's Journey into Night* (1941), *The Iceman Cometh* (1939), and *A Moon for the Misbegotten* (1943). He also wrote *A Touch of the Poet* (1935–1942), and *More Stately Mansions* (1935–1941). However, *Long Day's Journey into Night* was not published or produced during his lifetime (it was produced first, posthumously, in 1956); *The Iceman Cometh* (premiered in 1946) was not received well. *Moon for the Misbegotten* had an unproductive short run. A revival of his works began a few years after his death and has not waned.

Many of O'Neill's works—especially the later ones—reflected his Irish-Catholic background and his reverence for such great Irish playwrights as Yeats. "One thing that explains more than anything else about me," he said in 1946, "is the fact that I am Irish. . . . [I]t is something that all the writers who have attempted to explain me and my work have overlooked." Yet, that background provided the sources that enabled his works to present the timeless story of individuals struggling to find or maintain their faith in the face of life's challenges.

O'Neill married three times, to Kathleen Jenkins in 1909; in 1918 to Agnes Boulton (1893–1968) (their daughter Oona married Charles Chaplin); and in 1929 to the actress Carlotta Monterey (1888–1970), a marriage that lasted until his death. O'Neill spent the last decade of his life suffering from a palsy similar to Parkinson's disease. It left him unable to write. He died in Boston in 1953.

Edward T. O'Donnell

REFERENCES

Black, Stephen A. *Eugene O'Neill: Beyond Tragedy and Mourning.* New Haven, CT: Yale University Press, 1999.

Gelb, Arthur, and Barbara Gelb. *O'Neill.* Rev. ed. New York: Harper & Row, 1973.

O'Neill, Eugene. *The Complete Plays.* 3 vols. Edited
by Travis Bogard. New York: Viking Press, 1988.

Ranald, Margaret Loftus. *The Eugene O'Neill
Companion.* Westport, CT: Greenwood Press,
1984.

O'Reilly, Leonora (1870–1927)

Labor activist and teacher
Irish-American

Leonora O'Reilly was one of the true pioneers of women's rights in the workplace. She was long active in suffrage, labor, and political organizations.

O'Reilly was born in New York City of Irish-immigrant parents on 16 February 1870. Her father, John, was a printer, and her mother, Winifred Rooney O'Reilly, was a garment worker. The O'Reillys had fled Ireland to escape starvation and sociopolitical repression. In 1871 Leonora's father and younger brother died. Her mother, left destitute in a tenement on the east side of Manhattan, worked long hours in a shirt factory. Leonora, when she was eleven years old, began to work in a collar factory as a piece worker, growing up under conditions of intense poverty and the horrible conditions of factory work. Her mother was an active trade unionist and introduced Leonora to radical labor politics at an early age.

In 1886, O'Reilly joined a Knights of Labor local. She helped found the Working Women's Society, an organization that led to the first factory inspection laws. She also worked ten hours a day in a factory on New York's Third Avenue, eventually rising to forewoman. In 1897 she and Mary Kenny O'Sullivan organized a women's local of the United Garment Workers of America. In addition, O'Reilly directed a garment workers' cooperative, the Henry Street Settlement.

She attracted the attention and financial support of some wealthier social reformers, who encouraged her to attend the Pratt Institute in Brooklyn. In 1900, she graduated in domestic arts, which qualified her to train teachers for secondary school. Between 1899 and 1902, she served as the head of the workers at Asacog House in Brooklyn. From 1902 to 1909, she was supervisor of the machine-operating department at the Manhattan Trade Schools for Girls, encouraging women to acquire vocational skills.

O'Reilly was appointed to the executive board of the Women's Trade Union League (WTUL) in 1903. Six years later, she became vice president and was heavily involved in the 1909–1910 strike of garment workers in New York City. She remained with the WTUL until 1914. After the Triangle Shirtwaist Company fire in 1911, which killed 146 women, she investigated the circumstances, published a preliminary report on job safety and building codes, and testified on health and safety violations in the garment industry.

O'Reilly cofounded the Wage Earners Suffrage League in 1911 and then joined the New York Women's Suffrage Party, believing that the right to vote could give working women more power to alter poor work conditions. She was a participant in a number of other social movements as well as an active member of the Socialist Party, a founding member of the NAACP in 1909, and a supporter of the Russian Revolution. She also continued to live among the Irish in New York, actively supported the independence movement, and raised funds for the Irish nationalists.

O'Reilly never married, a not uncommon outcome among Irish-American women of the day. She finally withdrew from public life because of heart disease, dying in Brooklyn at the age of fifty-seven, on 3 April 1927.

Seamus P. Metress

REFERENCES

Bularzik, Mary J. "The Bonds of Belonging:
Leonora O'Reilly and Social Reform." *Labor
History* 24(1) (1983): 60–83.

Howe, Frances H. "Leonora O'Reilly, Socialist and
Reformer." Honors Thesis, Radcliff College,
1952.

Sandquist, Eric L. "Leonora O'Reilly and the
Progressive Movement." Honors Thesis, Harvard
University, 1966.

Otero, Miguel, Jr. (1859–1944)
Territorial governor, public official,
and business owner
Mexican-American

Miguel Otero, Jr., gained national prominence in entrepreneurial and political pursuits in the New Mexico Territory, eventually becoming its governor. Because of his considerable economic and political influence, he represented the territory both as a Republican and as a Democrat over a nearly four decade period.

Otero was born in October 1859. He was the son of Miguel Antonio Otero, Sr., a prominent businessman and politician who was then serving as the Democratic delegate from the New Mexico Territory to the U.S. Congress. The early education of Otero, Jr., was sporadic, limited to that available in the railroad towns in Missouri, Kansas, and the Colorado and New Mexico Territories. He gained much experience from his father's numerous business pursuits in the merchant firm Otero, Seller, and Company, representing the Union Pacific; the Atchison, Topeka, and Santa Fe; and the Southern Pacific Railroads. He did attend St. Louis University, the U.S. Naval Academy, and Notre Dame University, with the presidential nomination to attend the U.S. Naval Academy no doubt stemming from his father's standing in the U.S. Congress. However, periodic illness resulted in Otero's not receiving a degree. Instead, he drew on his business experience and the acumen as cashier, bookkeeper, and manager that he had acquired while working in his father's businesses.

Upon his father's unexpected death in 1882, Otero, Jr., inherited the family's mercantile business interest and the former Otero, Seller, and Company—reorganized as the Las Vegas firm of Gross, Blackwell, and Company. He likely profited from his father's investments in mining, banking (the San Miguel National Bank in Las Vegas), a hot springs resort, and a telephone company, in addition to his own sheep ranching and real estate interests. However, Otero, Jr., achieved more prominence from his father's political reputation and connections gained through the commercial and industrial development of the New Mexico Territory.

Otero, Jr., was city treasurer of Las Vegas, New Mexico (1883–1884), served as probate court clerk (1886–1887), county clerk (1889–1890), and district court clerk (1890–1893). In 1888 he was the New Mexico delegate to the Republican National Convention, where he befriended William McKinley. In 1894, Otero was a candidate for the vice presidential nomination on the Republican ticket, and in 1898, President McKinley appointed him governor of the New Mexico Territory. He proved an apt leader. In keeping with the territory's patronage tradition, he developed and led an effective Spanish-speaking political organization. During his second term as governor, he supported statehood for New Mexico. His career as governor ended when President Theodore Roosevelt did not reappoint him, a result of his opposing the president's national forest policy. Subsequently, President William Taft did appoint Otero treasurer of the New Mexico Territory in 1909. In 1912, having become a Democrat, he served as president of the New Mexico Parole Board and as U.S. marshal of the Panama Canal Zone. He headed Canal Zone delegations to the Democratic National Convention in 1920 and 1924. Miguel Otero, Jr., died at age eighty-four in 1944.

Zaragosa Vargas

REFERENCES

Brown, John Henry, ed. *The Encyclopedia of the New West*. Marshall, TX: United States Bibliographical Publishing Co., 1881.

Lamar, Howard. *The Readers' Encyclopedia of the American West*. New York: Crowell, 1977.

Otero, Miguel A., II. *My Life on the Frontier, 1864–1882*. New York: Press of the Pioneers, 1935.

———. *My Life on the Frontier, 1882–1897*. Albuquerque: University of New Mexico Press, 1939.

———. *My Nine Years as Governor of the Territory of New Mexico, 1897–1906*. Albuquerque: University of New Mexico Press, 1940.

Twitchell, Ralph Emerson. *The Leading Facts of New Mexican History*. 5 vols. Cedar Rapids, IA: Torch Press, 1911–1917.

Othman, Talat Mohamad (1936–)
Banker, corporate executive, and community activist
Palestinian

Talat M. Othman is a highly respected Chicago-area businessman, specializing in U.S.–Middle East business and finance. Without the benefit of a college education, he succeeded through hard work and a reputation for honesty and integrity. A leader in his community, he is well known for his commitments to interethnic understanding and religious tolerance. By bringing people of different backgrounds together, he has helped build a better future for Arab and Muslim Americans.

Born in Betunia, Palestine, on 27 April 1936, Othman came to Chicago with his family in 1947 and became a citizen in 1954. Active in the small Arab Muslim community on Chicago's South Side, his family helped to found the area's first mosque. In 1956 Othman went to work for Harris Trust and Savings Bank, where he worked his way his way up to vice president and administrator of the International Money Management Division, which he had helped create. A nationally recognized expert in currency and international money matters, Othman subsequently served on the boards of numerous companies and went on to manage several companies, including the Saudi Investment Group of Jeddah, Saudi Arabia, and Dearborn Financial of Arlington Heights, Illinois. Currently, he is chairman and CEO of Grove Financial, Long Grove, Illinois.

Believing that it is his duty as an Arab and a Muslim to be active in his community and to help others, Othman has been involved in a number of Arab-American business groups, political organizations, and educational initiatives. Founder and president of both the Mid-America Arab Chamber of Commerce and the Arab-American Business and Professional Association of Illinois, he also served as president of the Arab Bankers Association of North America. Seeking to empower the community, Othman has been active in local and regional politics and has pushed to get Arabs and Muslims appointed to various commissions and boards in order to increase their visibility and influence.

Othman also served on a select committee of Arab Americans consulting with the Bush administration during the Persian Gulf war. Other civic commitments include serving on the boards of St. Jude Children's Research Hospital, the Center for Excellence in Education, the Greater Middle East Studies Center at RAND Corporation (California), and the Middle East Policy Council, as well as the Dean's Council of Advisers of Harvard's Kennedy School of Government and the University of Chicago's Center for Middle Eastern Studies. In 1997 he received an award from Yasser Arafat, chair of the Palestine Authority (PA), for his contributions in support of the Palestinian people.

Othman's leadership has been particularly important for the Chicago-area Islamic community. A founding member of the Islamic Cultural Center (ICC) of Greater Chicago, he has helped lead the ICC through many years of expansion and growth, serving Muslims from Bosnia, the Middle East, Pakistan, and other regions of the world. As president of the ICC board, he is dedicated to keeping the community together and open to Muslims of all backgrounds and has been instrumental in maintaining a vital and united center. Othman was honored by the ICC in both 1994 and 1997, and Governor Jim Edgar proclaimed 1 November 1997 as Talat M. Othman Day in Illinois.

Elizabeth Plantz

REFERENCES

"Othman, Talat M." In *Who's Who in Finance and Industry 1989–1990,* 26th ed., 585. Chicago: Marquis Who's Who, 1989.

"Othman, Talat M." In *Who's Who in the Midwest 1990–1991,* 22d ed., 486. Chicago: Marquis Who's Who, 1990.

"Othman, Talat M." In *Who's Who in the World 1999,* 16th ed., 218. Chicago: Marquis Who's Who, 1998.

Othman, Talat M. Interview by author, 27 March 2000.

"Spotlight on People (Talat M. Othman); History of ICC from Islamic Cultural Center of Greater Chicago web site": www.icc-chicago.org/history/h10.html (accessed 14 June 2000).

"Talat Othman, Successful Chicago Businessman, Honored by Islamic Cultural Center." *Arab American News*. 10.486 (23 December 1994): 5.

Ottendorfer, Anna Behr Uhl (1815–1884)

Newspaper publisher and philanthropist
German

Anna Uhl Ottendorfer, the wife of a struggling printer, rose to become the publisher of the largest German-language newspaper in the United States. She was one of the most successful businesswomen of the nineteenth century.

Born in Bavaria in 1815, Anna Behr immigrated to New York in 1837. In 1839 she married a New York City printer, Jakob Uhl, also from Bavaria. In 1844 he purchased the printing establishment that handled the printing of the New York *Staats-Zeitung,* the city's principal German-language Democratic newspaper. The next year the Uhls took over the newspaper itself. While raising six children, Anna Uhl joined in the active management and development of the newspaper, changing it from a weekly to a daily as the flow of German immigrants grew. Upon the death of Jakob Uhl in 1852, she became the sole publisher of the newspaper. Anticipating the rising fortunes of the German-language press in the United States, she rejected offers to purchase the newspaper and determined to continue it on her own.

Before Uhl's death, the newspaper had hired Oswald Ottendorfer, a refugee from the revolution of 1848 in Austria. Uhl made him her principal assistant in the editing of the paper. They married in 1859. Thereafter, he handled editorial affairs and played an active role in New York Democratic Party politics, while she continued to manage the paper's business affairs. The newspaper prospered under her management, occupying an imposing building on Park Row and commanding social and political influence that rivaled that of the city's principal English-language newspapers. By the time of Anna Ottendorfer's death, the *Staats-Zeitung* could claim to be the sixth-largest daily in the United States.

The success and considerable profitability of the newspaper allowed Anna Ottendorfer to turn increasingly to philanthropy. Her charitable benefactions were directed toward German-American cultural preservation and women's welfare. Her first important contribution was for a home for elderly German women in Astoria, New York. She lent her support to the German Hospital on East Seventy-seventh Street, contributing to its expansion and the construction of a women's pavilion. Closely tied to the German Hospital was the German Dispensary at Second Avenue and Ninth Street, for which the Ottendorfers contributed the land and building.

Many of Ottendorfer's charities were directed to German-American schools and to the preservation of the German language in the United States. She supported various German-language schools in the New York City area and the German-American Teachers' Seminary in Milwaukee. She and her husband endowed the Ottendorfer Library, a branch of the New York Free Circulating Library, on land adjacent to the German Dispensary. Dedicated a few months after her death in 1884, the library, which had both German-language and English-language materials, served what was then a heavily German working-class neighborhood.

Never a campaigner for women's political rights, Ottendorfer wielded her considerable influence within the social and cultural limitations of her era. Nevertheless, she took a leading place among the many women activists who championed the emerging urban welfare system at a time when it still remained in the hands of voluntary agencies.

James M. Bergquist

REFERENCES

Arndt, Karl J. R., and May E. Olson. *German-American Press of the Americas*. Vol. 1, *History and Bibliography, 1732 to 1955*. 3d rev. ed. Heidelberg: Quelle and Meyer, 1976.

Lemke, Theodor. *Geschichte des Deutschthums von New York von 1848 bis auf die Gegenwart* (History of the German element of New York from 1848 to the present). New York: T. Lemke, 1891.

Rattermann, Heinrich A. "Eine deutsch-amerikanische Philanthropin: Frau Anna Ottendorfer" (A German-American philanthropist: Mrs. Anna Ottendorfer). *Deutsche Pionier* 16 (November 1884): 293–301.

Sonntagsblatt der New Yorker Staats-Zeitung (Sunday edition of the New York *Staats-Zeitung*). 6 April 1884 (obituaries and memorials).

Zur Erinnerung an Anna Ottendorfer (In remembrance of Anna Ottendorfer). New York: Staats-Zeitung, 1884.

Owen, Robert Dale (1801–1877)
Social reformer, U.S. House representative, and diplomat
Scottish

Robert Dale Owen was one of the most influential nineteenth-century Scottish immigrants, advocating the rights of industrial workers, women, and African Americans. He held a variety of public positions, and his life reveals much about nineteenth-century reform movements.

Owen was born in Glasgow, son of the famous industrialist and utopian socialist, Robert Owen, and Ann Caroline Dale. Owen spent much of his youth in New Lanark, Scotland, where his father managed the family's textile mills and organized them to improve the condition of the workers, an experiment that gave hope that industrialism would not have to be brutal. Thus, from an early age Robert Dale developed a concern for child labor and social reform. He was convinced that education was the key to solving social division and industrial poverty. His ideas were developed further in Switzerland, where he attended a progressive school from age eighteen to twenty-two. Upon his return to New Lanark, he taught the children of the workers and wrote *An Outline of the System of Education at New Lanark* (1824), the first of his many books that promoted social reform.

When Owen's father founded the experimental utopian-socialist community in New Harmony, Indiana, in 1825, the younger Owen accompanied him to teach and write. Within two years the New Harmony experiment collapsed, but Robert Dale Owen continued to live in the United States and promote his ideals for social reform and freethinking. With Frances Wright, another Scottish reformer who immigrated to the United States, Owen founded another community in Nashoba, Tennessee, which was devoted to teaching freed slaves and preparing them to be resettled in Africa. His attitude toward blacks became more enlightened with time, and his concern continued for the rest of his life. In 1829 Owen and Wright moved to New York City, where Owen edited the *Free Enquirer*, a freethinkers' newspaper that challenged organized religion and promoted various reform movements, especially those in support of industrial workers and women. Owen married Mary Jane Robinson in 1832, and together they had six children.

After an extended trip to Europe, Owen returned to New Harmony in 1833 and, in 1836, ran for the Indiana state house, served three terms, and in 1843 was elected as a Democrat to the U.S. House of Representatives. He ran several times for the U.S. Senate but was defeated. Yet Owen continued to have influence in the United States. For example, he kept up his crusade to improve the position of women, in particular concerning their property rights, fairer divorce laws, and women's suffrage. He also maintained his support for public education, served as a trustee for Indiana University, and introduced the bill that established the Smithsonian Institution. At the same time, he supported America's Manifest Destiny policy to expand west and spread its democratic institutions, and in 1853 President Franklin Pierce made him a chargé d'affaires and minister to the Kingdom of the Two Sicilies, in Naples.

Throughout the rest of his life, Owen continued to write on a wide range of topics, most of which promoted social reform and some spiritualism. He died in 1877.

William E. Van Vugt

REFERENCES

Bestor, Arthur. *Backwoods Utopias: The Sectarian Origins and the Owenite Phase of Communitarianism in America, 1663–1829.* Rev. ed. Philadelphia: University of Pennsylvania Press, 1970.

Leopold, Richard. *Robert Dale Owen: A Biography.*
  1940. Reprint, New York: Octagon Books,
  1969.
Woodrow, Amanda. "Robert Dale Owen: Social
Reformer." McLeansboro website.
http://www.mcleansboro.com/features/
harmony_temp.htm. (Accessed 20 December
2000.)

Paine, Thomas (1737–1809)

Pamphleteer and political philosopher
English

Thomas Paine was one of the most important political philosophers during the Age of Reason. His writings influenced both the American and the French Revolutions.

Paine was born in Thetford, Norfolk, son of Joseph Paine, a corset maker, and Francis Cocke. Thomas was educated at the local grammar school, was apprenticed, and served briefly on a ship before moving to London. There, he attended scientific lectures and became convinced that all human inquiry and institutions should be based on reason—an intellectual standard Paine would apply to British rule in America, hereditary rule in general, and the political system of France. The results profoundly influenced the modern world.

Losing his job as an excise officer in 1774, Paine was desperate until a friend introduced him to Benjamin Franklin. Franklin was impressed enough to write a letter of introduction for Paine to take with him to Philadelphia. Immigrating later that year, Paine obtained the position of editor of the *Pennsylvania* magazine. By late 1775, he was associating with John Adams, Benjamin Rush, and others who were foreseeing American independence. Paine was asked to write a pamphlet calling for independence, and the result was *Common Sense.*

In *Common Sense* Paine used reason and an engaging literary style to convey a democratic message that hereditary rule, and in particular the rule of the American continent by the small island of Great Britain, clearly violated the laws of nature. An immediate best-seller, the pamphlet crystallized the thinking of Americans, moving them from fighting for English liberties to fighting for independence. As he also said, the cause of America was the cause of all mankind, for it would provide a model of freedom. Paine gave the profits from his writings to the American cause, served in the Continental Army, and, during one of the most difficult times—the "times that try men souls"—wrote *The American Crisis,* a series of essays that uplifted the soldiers' morale.

After the war, Paine returned to Europe and became involved with the revolutionary fervor engulfing France. In response to Edmund Burke's *Reflections on the Revolution in France,* Paine wrote his famous *Rights of Man,* calling for a radical break from the past, a call that was condemned in England. In France, Paine was elected to the National Convention and voted for the abolition of the French monarchy; he was later arrested under the more radical Jacobins. In prison, Paine wrote *The Age of Reason* (1794), a vicious attack on organized Christianity that earned him the hatred of many of his U.S. compatriots.

When he returned to the United States in 1802, he was shunned for his anti-Christian views as well as for his conviction that the United States was not as democratic as he had envisioned. In 1809 he died in Greenwich Village, New York, largely forgotten. Six persons attended his funeral. Only later would Americans recognize that no other immigrant had had more influence on the creation of the United States as independent republic.

William E. Van Vugt

REFERENCES

Claeys, Gregory. *Thomas Paine: Social and Political Thought.* Boston: Unwin Hyman, 1989.

Foner, Eric. *Tom Paine and Revolutionary America.* Oxford: Oxford University Press, 1976.

Fruchtman, Jack, Jr. *Thomas Paine: Apostle of Freedom.* New York: Four Walls Eight Windows, 1994.

Keane, John. *Tom Paine: A Political Life.* London: Bloomsbury, 1995.

Palance, Jack (né Volodymyr John Palahniuk) (1920–)

Actor
Ukrainian-American

Jack Palance, the son of Ukrainian immigrants, has carved out a career in film and television (appearing in nearly 100 movies), receiving some of the top awards for his performances. His activities in the Ukrainian community have likewise brought him renown.

Palance was born on 18 February 1920, in Lattimer Mines, Pennsylvania. In high school, he excelled in athletics and appeared in school plays. At the University of North Carolina he was a star fullback and then turned to professional boxing. During World War II, the B-24 bomber he was piloting crashed, and he was severely burned. Plastic surgery produced the taut, menacing look on his face. Nevertheless, he was determined to escape the rigors of a coal miner's life, for he had been a high school honor student with a passion for reading, poetry, and painting. He returned to school under the GI Bill and studied acting and journalism at Stanford University.

It was Palance's assignment as an understudy to Marlon Brando in the New York production of *A Streetcar Named Desire,* directed by Elia Kazan, that gave him his major break. Kazan brought Palance to Hollywood in 1950 for his initial film role, in *Panic in the Streets.* At first, he was cast exclusively as a sinister heavy, only later revealing an anguished, soulful side. In 1952, he earned an Academy Award nomination for best supporting actor for his performance in *Sudden Fear* and, in 1953, for his role in *Shane,* one of Palance's most acclaimed works. More than three decades later, he won an Oscar as best supporting actor for his portrayal of a tough trail boss named Curly, in the film *City Slickers* (1991). In the sequel, *City Slickers II* (1994), he showed an unexpected flair for comedy. Among his other films are *Arrowhead* (1953), *The Big Knife* (1955), *The Professionals* (1966), *Mission: Rommel* (1970), and *Oklahoma Crude* (1973). In addition, by 1968 Palance had also done seventeen television shows, including the Emmy-winning role he created of a has-been prizefighter in the 1956 *Playhouse 90* production *Requiem for a Heavyweight.* The six-foot-four actor also starred in the title roles of *Dracula* and *Dr. Jekyll and Mr. Hyde* and as Jabberwock in *Alice Through the Looking Glass.*

Palance's delivery has been compared to that of Richard Burton and has provided him with many narrative roles in documentaries. His voice is particularly familiar to Ukrainian audiences in the documentary film *Helm of Destiny,* depicting the achievements of Ukrainian Americans. Indeed, he has often appeared at Ukrainian festivals and other events throughout North America, still speaks Ukrainian, expounds on his ethnic heritage, and regards his roots with respect and admiration. When he was honored in New York as Ukrainian of the Year 1986 by the Ukrainian Institute of America, he accepted the commendation and recalled Ukraine's national poet-hero, pointing out: "Taras Shevchenko wrote about freedom. Freedom should be the primary concern of everyone in the world." Palance himself is also a Ukrainian-American poet, and his own book of poetry, *The Forest of Love,* illustrated with many of his own paintings and sketches, appeared in 1996.

Roman Sawycky, Jr.

REFERENCES
Gregorovich, Andrew. "Jack Palance Hosts 'Ripley's Believe It or Not.'" *Forum: A Ukrainian Review* (Scranton, PA), 56 (Fall 1983).
"Jack Palance." http://us.imdb.com/name?Palance%2c+Jack. (Accessed 20 December 2000).
Katz, Ephrain. *The Film Encyclopedia.* New York: Harper & Row, 1990.
Kuropas, Myron B. *The Ukrainians in America.* Minneapolis: Lerner, 1972.
Pauser, J. R. *Actors' Television Credits, 1950–1972.* Metuchen, NJ: Scarecrow Press, 1973.

Pantoja, Antonia (1921–)

Educator and community activist
Puerto Rican

Antonia Pantoja has played a major role in the development of key organizations within New York City's Puerto Rican community.

She has spearheaded important changes particularly with respect to the education and training of its children.

Pantoja was born San Juan, Puerto Rico, on 13 September 1921. She had four siblings. She came to New York City in 1944 with a normal-school diploma (two years at the University of Puerto Rico) and experience as a rural schoolteacher. She earned a B.A. at Hunter College, a master's in social work from the School of Social Work, Columbia University, and a doctorate in sociology from the Union Graduate School. While teaching at Columbia University, Pantoja served as a member of the 1967 New York State Constitutional Convention and as a member of the Bundy Panel overseeing the decentralization of New York City Public Schools. She understood the impact of racism on her community and its children and the need to restore their sense of well-being and to improve their skills in order to survive and thrive in New York.

In keeping with her concerns, she organized the Puerto Rican Forum, an institution-building organization. Its first was ASPIRA (Aspire), which was committed to helping Latino/a youths develop their intellectual and leadership potential in order to improve the quality of life in their communities. She also founded the Puerto Rican Association for Community Affairs (PRACA). These two organizations became the most influential in the community. PRACA and the Puerto Rican Forum functioned as antipoverty programs during the 1960s. ASPIRA concentrated on preparing this young community for the workplace and political arena.

In 1961, at its founding, ASPIRA's proponents argued that one of its goals was to foster social change by bridging the gap between parents and children regarding education and the factors affecting the achievement of success. In 1968, the focus of ASPIRA was on the decentralization of the city's public school system and community control of the schools. Under the leadership of Pantoja, significant changes began to take place. An aggressive and controversial agenda for reform was spearheaded by ASPIRA, with Puerto Ricans claiming their right to access higher education, calling for open enrollment at the City University of New York, and demanding relevant academic programs and curricula. In 1974, ASPIRA initiated a lawsuit that led to the Supreme Court's imposing on New York's public schools a consent decree for bilingual education. Over time, ASPIRA has provided career and college counseling, scholarship and financial assistance, and other assistance. It has developed affiliates in New Jersey, Pennsylvania, Chicago, Connecticut, Florida, and Puerto Rico, and it has established a central office in Washington, D.C., as an advocate, research, and fund-raising arm.

Pantoja was honored by the Thousand Points of Light Foundation and was awarded the prestigious Lenore and George Romney Citizen Volunteer Award. At the time, the award presenter stated: "ASPIRA means to aspire and through the years Dr. Pantoja and ASPIRA have helped change the lives of millions of Hispanic men and women. She is truly an inspiration to all of us." On 9 September 1996, President Bill Clinton awarded her the Presidential Medal of Freedom, the highest honor bestowed on civilians.

Linda Delgado

REFERENCES

"The ASPIRA Story, 1961–1991." Washington, DC: ASPIRA Corp., 1991.

Korrol, Virginia Sánchez. *From Colonia to Community: The History of Puerto Ricans in New York City.* Westport, CT: Greenwood Press, 1983; reprint, with new introduction, Berkeley: University of California Press, 1994.

La Prensa, San Diego press release, 11 June 1999.

Pantoja, Antonia. Interview by author, 26–27 June 2000.

Papanicolaou, George Nicholas (1883–1962)

Physician and medical researcher
Greek

George Papanicolaou, an anatomist and oncologist, was the research scientist and doctor who developed the Pap smear screening test for the detection of cervical cancer. That test has saved the lives of thousands of women.

Papanicolaou was born in Kyme, Evia, Greece, in 1883. He was the son of Nicholas Papanicolaou, a physician, and Mary Critsutas. He attended a gymnasium in Athens and studied medicine at the University of Athens, receiving his medical degree in 1904. Following mandatory military service, he joined his father's practice for a year and then left for Germany for further studies, receiving a Ph.D. in zoology in 1910 at the University of Munich.

He returned to Greece to marry Mary Andromache Mavrogeni in September 1910 (they had no children). Papanicolaou, who was doing research in Monaco, was drawn back to Greece, like thousands of Greek men who had recently immigrated to the United States, to fight the Ottoman Turks in the Balkan Wars of 1912–1913, serving in the army medical corps. Afterward, he and his wife (his lifelong research associate) immigrated to the United States, where he acquired citizenship in 1927. He was soon appointed as a research assistant at Cornell University and worked his way up to full professor of clinical anatomy in 1947.

Papanicolaou's name is associated with the discovery of a screening technique for the early detection of cancerous and precancerous cells that cause the deadly cervical cancer in women. His discovery bears his name, the Pap smear test. He first described his technique in 1928. He established himself as an outstanding researcher, particularly in collaboration with Herbert F. Traut, of Cornell's Department of Obstetrics and Gynecology. In 1941, they jointly authored "Diagnostic Value of Vaginal Smears in Carcinoma of the Uterus," which generated much interest and support. Two years later, they coauthored *The Diagnosis of Uterine Cancer by the Vaginal Smear.* Quite soon, the Pap smear test became widely used, for at that time more than 26,000 women were dying each year from cancer of the cervix.

In 1950, Papanicolaou was appointed director of the Papanicolaou Research Laboratory of Cornell Medical School; he was consultant to many other institutions. When he retired in 1961, he became the director of the Papanicolaou Cancer Research Institute in Miami, Florida, but died shortly afterward of a heart attack at age seventy-nine. Over all, he published more than 100 medical and scientific articles, but his main contribution to public health remains the Pap test.

Papanicolaou received many honors and awards, including the Borden Award of the Association of American Medical Colleges (1948); the Amory Prize of the American Academy of Arts and Sciences (1948); and the Honor Medal of the American Cancer Society (1952). He was also honored by Greece with the Royal Order of George I (1951) and the Cross of the Grand Commander of the Royal Order of the Phoenix (1953). In Thessaloniki, the Papanicolaou Research Hospital was named in his honor. Greeks consider him to be one of the most outstanding Greek medical researchers of the twentieth century. However, although he was a Greek Orthodox Christian, his research was primary to him, and he was not very active in the Greek community.

George A. Kourvetaris

REFERENCES

American Society of Clinical Pathologists. "George Papanicolaou, M.D.": www.ascp.org/general/about/pioneers/Papanicolaou.asp (accessed 15 June 2000).

Fuchsman, Charles. "Papanicolaou, George N." In *American National Biography.* Vol. 16, edited by John A. Garraty and Mark C. Caimes, 969–970. New York: Oxford University Press, 1999.

Michalakis, Dimitri C. "Dr. George Papanicolaou," *National Herald* (New York), 1–2 January 2000.

"Papanicolaou, George N." In *Cambridge Biographical Dictionary,* edited by Magnus Magnusson, 1123. New York: Cambridge University Press, 1990.

Women's Health Forum (OBGYN.Net). "Discussions in Pap Smear Screening, pt. 2" (1997): www.obgyn.net/women/features/whfv11_b.htm (accessed 15 June 2000).

Paul, William Lewis, Sr. (1885–1977)
Lawyer and community activist
Alaska Native (Tlingit)

In 1971, William L. Paul, Sr., spoke before the Alaska Federation of Natives (AFN) regarding Native land claims. A longtime advocate of Native rights, the elderly Paul minced no words in opposing the settlement of land claims. "We own the land. It is our land," he thundered before the AFN delegates. A lifelong advocate on behalf of his fellow Alaska Natives, Paul did not believe in compromise when it came to civil, sovereign, or land rights, and he achieved many changes that secured more equal rights for Natives in Alaska.

Paul was born in 1885 to mixed-blood Tlingit parents in the southeastern Alaskan village of Tongass. As a child, he attended Sheldon Jackson's Presbyterian mission school in Sitka; he later traveled thousands of miles to the Carlisle Indian Boarding School in Pennsylvania. After Carlisle, Paul studied in Philadelphia and Spokane before completing a law degree through the LaSalle University extension program. Although his life seemed to exemplify the success of contemporary Indian assimilation policies, he remained first, last, and always a Tlingit Indian man who valued his heritage.

Returning to Alaska in 1920, William Paul quickly moved into politics. That year he assumed a leadership role in the Alaskan Native Brotherhood (ANB), an early civil rights organization. He and the ANB membership fought against segregated schools for Alaska Natives and "Jim Crow" style voting restrictions that limited their suffrage. Over the next decade, they organized Natives in support of suffrage and equal access to schools. These efforts eventually landed him a seat in the Alaskan Territorial Legislature in 1924. From that power base, Paul worked to end discrimination against Alaska Natives. He and the ANB successfully boycotted movie theaters that segregated patrons during the 1920s. Later, his advocacy led the territorial legislature to pass a landmark antidiscrimination law in 1945. Paul's efforts also extended into the economic arena. In the *Alaska Fishermen,* a newspaper devoted to Native issues that he edited from 1923 to 1932, he opposed the destruction of salmon fisheries by non-Indians using nets and encouraged the formation of a union for Natives working in the canneries.

Segregation, salmon, and suffrage notwithstanding, Paul's most ardent advocacy work came on behalf of Alaska Native land claims cases. Between 1929 and 1965, he led the successful fight for adequate compensation for the Haida and Tlingit for lands taken by the U.S. government for the creation of the Tongass National Forest. In the late 1960s, Paul spoke out against the proposed Alaska Native Claims Settlement Act (ANCSA). He repeatedly reminded Native supporters of that legislation that non-Natives had never challenged the sovereignty of their lands until there were resources deemed valuable. Paul warned federal officials, "This land is our own land even under your own rules." In the end, however, Paul lost, and ANCSA became law in 1971.

In 1977, six years after this bitter defeat, Paul died at the age of ninety-two. With his death, Alaska Natives lost one of their most determined and effective advocates.

Lisa E. Emmerich

REFERENCES

Haycox, Stephen. "William Paul, Sr., and the Alaskan Voters' Literacy Act of 1925." *Alaskan History* 2 (1986): 17–38.

James, Beverly. "The *Alaskan Fisherman* and the Paradox of Assimilation: Progress, Power, and the Preservation of Culture." *Native Press Research Journal* 5 (1987): 2–25.

Metcalfe, Peter M. *The Central Council of the Tlingit and the Haida Tribes of Alaska: An Historical and Organizational Profile.* Juneau, AK: CCTHITA, 1981.

Paul, William L., Sr. "We Own the Land: Statement by William L. Paul, Sr., to the AFN Board of Directors, Alaska Federation of Natives' Convention, Fairbanks, Alaska, October, 1971." *Alaska Native News Magazine,* August 1984, 18.

Skinner, Ramona Ellen. *Alaska Native Policy in the Twentieth Century.* New York: Garland Publishing, 1997.

Payán, Ilka Tanya (1943–1996)
Actress and community activist
Dominican

Ilka Tanya Payán, one of the very few prominent theater personalities in the Dominican-American community, achieved considerable visibility as an actress and community activist. By the time of her death in 1996 she had also become a powerful voice on behalf of AIDS victims.

Born in Santo Domingo in 1943, Payán came to North America in 1956. She began acting in 1969, performing mostly in Spanish-language theaters in New York City, but her dramatic work also took her to Spain, Puerto Rico, and the Dominican Republic. She played a leading role in *Angélica, mi vida,* the first Spanish-language television soap opera to air nationally in the United States, broadcast via the Spanish-language network. She also played parts in some Anglophone American film and television productions, most notably in HBO's *Florida Straits,* in which she costarred with the late Raul Julia.

Payán acquired a law degree in 1980 because she feared she would not be able support herself solely on her acting career. But her legal services "drew her increasingly into public affairs." She developed an immigration law practice beginning in 1984 and wrote a column on immigration issues for the New York Hispanic newspaper *El Diario/La Prensa* and for the New York edition of the Dominican daily *El Nacional.* In addition, as a volunteer with many direct-service community organizations, such as Catholic Charities and the Center for Immigrants, she became associated with the Gay Men's Health Crisis, first as a volunteer and subsequently as supervisor of the organization's Legal Services Department. Linking her interest in legal affairs with her love of the theater, she often donated her work as a counsel for theater groups like the Actors' Fund and for such cultural institutions as the Association of Hispanic Arts.

Payán had become so prominent in the defense of human rights for immigrants and for people with HIV in Hispanic political and civic circles that in 1992 Mayor David N. Dinkins appointed her to the City of New York's Commission on Human Rights. Consequently, her startling announcement—at a press conference on 14 October 1993—that she had contracted the HIV virus propelled her to a broad national stage. Her declaration was saluted the following day by *El Diario/La Prensa* with front-page coverage and an editorial. The paper celebrated Payán for giving "us all a lesson in personal courage" and shared her hope that her confession would educate the Latino community. She subsequently became the object of much news coverage, including the spotlight on 1 December 1993, during a United Nations forum on World AIDS.

After her death in April 1996, Payán drew much homage and many tributes, including a lengthy obituary in the *New York Times.* Her public confession and its consequences showed that she had the mettle to confront the drama of human existence with bold determination and to put an end to thirteen years of fearful silence after she learned that she had become infected. To honor her memory, the Manhattan-based Dominican Women's Caucus instituted a yearly Ilka Tanya Payán Leadership Award for young women.

Silvio Torres-Saillant

REFERENCES

Navarro, Mireya. "An Actress Openly Faces AIDS and Receives an Audience's Ovation." *New York Times,* 5 December 1993.

Thomas, Robert Mag, Jr. "Ilka Tanya Payán, Fifty-three, Dies: Champion for Anti-AIDS Cause." *New York Times,* 8 April 1996, B12.

Torres-Saillant, Silvio, and Ramona Hernández. *The Dominican Americans.* Westport, CT: Greenwood Press, 1998.

Pei, I. M. (Ieoh Ming) (1917–)
Architect
Chinese

The son of Tsuyee Pei and Lien Kwun, an upper-middle-class couple in southern China, I. M. Pei cultivated a keen aesthetic sensibility that contributed to his becoming a world-renowned architect. His numerous accolades stem from his bold reinterpretation of the uses of modernism for commercial buildings, large urban schemes, and public spaces.

Born on 26 April 1917 in Guangzhou (Canton), China, Pei was given a personal name, Ieoh Ming, that means "to inscribe brightly," notwithstanding that dark era of local wars and socioeconomic chaos. The family retreat in Suzhou introduced young Pei to the harmonious blend of built-up spaces and nature, framed vistas, and the interplay of light and shadow that would figure prominently in his architectural work.

Pei's father convinced him to pursue advanced education abroad, and in 1935, Pei attended the Massachusetts Institute of Technology (MIT) and, in 1942, the Harvard Graduate School of Design. Two Harvard professors, Walter Gropius and Marcel Breuer, further molded Pei's imagination. Graduating in 1946, Pei found himself unable to return to China because of the civil war there. He would make his life and career in the United States. In 1948, Pei signed on with Webb and Knapp as director of the architectural division, during the next seven years overseeing large-scale public housing projects and other urban developments that exposed him to the challenges of devising grand plans for the urban United States.

Constrained by commercial-oriented projects, in 1955 Pei formed his own firm, I. M. Pei and Associates (later Pei, Cobb, Freed, and Partners). Through innovative collaboration with professionals, Pei began making his mark in architecture, such as with the National Center for Atmospheric Research (NCAR) complex in Boulder, Colorado. Completed in 1967, it is a highly ordered arrangement of sculptural shapes that blends in with the mountainous site.

Over the years Pei gained recognition for his abstract designs, which emerge as monumental minimalist structures, including the visually arresting Dallas Municipal Administration Center (1977), the rigorously geometric East Building of the National Gallery of Art in Washington, D.C. (1978), and the atrium-defined John F. Kennedy Memorial Library at Boston Harbor (1979). Among the 100 other Pei works is the Bank of China in Hong Kong, one of Asia's tallest structures. For Pei, this was a personal reconciliation with his birthplace: His father had worked for that bank until the fall of the Nationalist government in 1949.

But Pei has had his share of critics. Most of them lambasted overblown budgets, the absence of a social conscience in urban planning, a penchant for high-visibility works, and a supposedly callous disregard for traditions, such as his glass pyramid (1989) that serves as the new entrance for the restored Louvre Museum in Paris. Aside from having been initially hostile to the modern architecture, the French public found it difficult to accept a non-Frenchman restoring a national treasure.

Pei has received numerous awards for his achievements, but perhaps the highest honor was the Medal of Liberty, bestowed in 1986 at the centennial of the Statue of Liberty. On that occasion Pei said that sometimes in the past he felt like "an outsider" but that the medal represented his acceptance by mainstream U.S. society.

Benson Tong

REFERENCES

Starbuck, James C. *The Buildings of I. M. Pei and His Firm.* Monticello, IL: Vance Bibliographies, 1978.

Wiseman, Carter. *I. M. Pei: A Profile in American Architecture.* New York: Harry N. Abrams, 1990.

Penn, William (1644–1718)
Quaker leader and founder of Pennsylvania
English

Although William Penn was a temporary immigrant to the colonies, he shaped American colonial history profoundly by his novel efforts to colonize lands granted to him and by the steps he took to build a new, peaceful society. He remains the only immigrant with a state named in his honor.

William Penn was born in London, the son of Admiral Sir William Penn and Margaret Vanderschuren, daughter of a wealthy Dutch merchant. Penn's privileged background brought him to Christ Church College, Oxford, but he was expelled in 1662 for criticizing the Church of England. He studied law at Lincoln's Inn and then assisted in his father's business and military work. Penn's exposure to the English court led to connections that would result in the huge land grant that became Pennsylvania.

While in Ireland in 1667 Penn became a Quaker and, upon his return to England, eventually became the Society of Friends' leading advocate, calling for greater religious toleration and social equality. His denial of the trinity and his continual preaching without a license got him imprisoned several times, but with his considerable resources and connections, he always managed to get released and continue his work. In the early 1670s he preached in Holland, Germany, and southern England.

Upon inheriting his father's estate, Penn became involved in schemes to colonize North America. He started his project in 1680 to establish a colony that would serve as both a haven for fellow Quakers and a source of financial security. His solution was to exchange a debt that King Charles II had owed Penn's father for a land grant. In 1681, he was granted a charter for Pennsylvania.

Penn had much personal control over organizing the colony, constituting its government, and distributing the land. He recruited settlers through his extensive Quaker network and by writing promotional tracts. The colony's constitution reflected Quaker morality—prohibiting dice, cards, cockfights, plays, and the like—and voting and office holding were restricted to devout Christians. Penn's years in the colony during the early 1680s were the best of his life, for he successfully mediated disputes with the Delaware Indians, consolidated his holdings along the Delaware River, and by late 1682 had sold 620,000 acres of land to more than 500 settlers. However, the colony proved unprofitable, and the ideal society he envisioned never materialized.

Penn returned to England in 1684. Because of his relationship with King James II, he was charged with treason, and in 1692, the new king, William III, took control of Pennsylvania's government. Penn had to defend his proprietorship of the colony. In 1699 he remigrated to Pennsylvania and returned to England two years later. He fell into debt, was sued in 1707, and spent nine months in prison. Indeed, the remainder of his life was dominated by his attempts to resolve his financial and proprietary problems. Financial disputes and defaults led him to conclude that his "holy experiment" was a failure, but he did take pleasure in his marriage in 1696, to Hannah Callowhill, and in their seven children. He died in 1718.

William E. Van Vugt

REFERENCES

Bronner, Edwin B. *William Penn's Holy Experiment: The Founding of Pennsylvania, 1681–1701.* New York: Temple University Publications/Columbia University Press, 1962.

Dunn, Mary Maples. *William Penn: Politics and Conscience.* Princeton, NJ: Princeton University Press, 1967.

Dunn, Mary Maples, and Richard S. Dunn, et al. *The Papers of William Penn.* 5 vols. Philadelphia: University of Pennsylvania Press, 1981–1987.

Peare, Catherine Owens. *William Penn.* Philadelphia: J. B. Lippincott, 1956.

Perales, Alonso S. (1898–1960)

Lawyer and diplomat
Mexican-American

Alonso Perales was a lawyer and diplomat. He gained national prominence as one of the founders of the League of United Latin American Citizens and for his civil rights work from the 1920s to the 1950s.

Perales was born on 17 October 1898 to Susana Sandoval Perales and Nicolas Perales, in Alice, Texas, but was orphaned at age six. Perales completed his public school education in Alice and later graduated from Draughn's Business College in Corpus Christi, Texas. He served in the U.S. Army during World War I and, upon his discharge, moved to Washington, D.C., where he worked for a year and a half as a staff member with the U.S. Commerce Department. After attending several schools in the Washington area and earning a B.A., he went on to acquire a law degree in 1926. He also married Marta Pérez, a bookstore owner, and they adopted a daughter and two sons.

In the 1920s and 1930s Perales served in the diplomatic corps in the Dominican Republic, Cuba, Nicaragua, Mexico, Chile, and the West Indies and, in 1945, was legal counsel to the Nicaraguan delegation at a United Nations conference. In addition, he served under both the Truman and Eisenhower administrations.

Perales was one of the founders in 1929 of the important civil rights organization, the League of United Latin American Citizens (LULAC). Along with José Tomás Canales and Eduardo Idar, he wrote the LULAC constitution. He then served as LULAC's second president, during which time he helped establish twenty-four new LULAC councils. In 1930, he testified before a U.S. congressional hearing in Washington on Mexican immigration. His testimony helped defeat the Box immigration bill, which would have placed a quota on Mexican immigrants to the United States. In addition, through LULAC Perales helped in the desegregation of hundreds of public facilities throughout Texas. In 1930 he brought the first class–action lawsuit against the segregation of Mexicans in Texas public schools—*Salvatierra v. Del Rio Independent School District*—which ended the designation in Texas of "Mexican schools." He also campaigned for better education for Mexican Americans, including the formation of the Liga Defensa Pro-Escolar (School improvement league) and he advocated that the Bureau of the Census reclassify people of Mexican descent from "Mexican" to "White."

In the 1940s he and other LULAC members, including fellow attorney Manuel Gonzáles, fought job discrimination against Mexican Americans, the dominant minority group in the Southwest. This effort focused on the creation of defense-related jobs for Mexican Americans, particularly in the state of Texas. Thus, he helped introduce a bill in the Texas state legislature prohibiting discrimination based on race. Perales also wrote about civil rights and racial discrimination in Texas. His books include the two-volume *En Defensa de Mi Raza*. He was, in addition, a columnist for *La Prensa* and other Spanish-language newspapers.

Besides being active in the Democratic Party in Texas, he continued to struggle at the national level in the 1950s for an end to racial discrimination and segregation against Mexican Americans. Perales died on 21 October 1960. A park and a statue were created in Alice, Texas, to honor him.

Zaragosa Vargas

REFERENCES

Gómez-Quiñones, Juan. *Roots of Chicano Politics, 1600–1940.* Albuquerque: University of New Mexico Press, 1994.

Gutiérrez, David G. *Walls and Mirrors: Mexican Americans and Mexican Immigrants, and the Politics of Ethnicity.* Berkeley: University of California Press, 1995.

Limon, Jose E. "Stereotyping and Chicano Resistance: An Historical Dimension." *Aztlán* 4.2 (Fall 1973): 257–270.

Orozco, Cynthia E. "The Origins of the League of United Latin American Citizens (LULAC) and the Mexican American Civil Rights Movement in Texas with an Analysis of Women's Political Participation in a Gendered Context, 1910–1929." Ph.D. diss., University of California, Los Angeles, 1992.

"Perales, Alfonso S." The Handbook of Texas Online. http://www.tsha.utexas.edu/handbook/online/articles/view/P/fpe56.htm. (Accessed 20 December 2000).

Vento, Adela Sloss. *Alonso S. Perales.* San Antonio: Artes Gráficas, 1977.

Vigil, Maurilio. *Chicano Politics.* Washington, DC: University Press of America, 1978.

Perpich, Rudolph "Rudy" George (1928–1995)

Governor and foreign policy adviser
Croatian-American

Rudolph "Rudy" George Perpich achieved recognition in the United States and Croatia as lieutenant governor and governor of the state of Minnesota. He was also foreign policy adviser to Croatian president Franjo Tudjman during Croatia's struggle for independence in 1991 and 1992.

Perpich was born of Croatian parentage in Carson Lake, near Hibbing, Minnesota, on 27 June 1928. His father was a native of Senj, Croatia, and his American-born mother was also of Croatian descent. After high school, Perpich went into the U.S. Army in 1946, serving until 1948. He attended dental school at Marquette University and worked as a dentist in Hibbing. In 1954 Perpich married Delores Lola Simich, also of Croatian descent.

He started his political career in 1955, when he was elected to the Hibbing School Board. As a board member he successfully proposed one of the first equity plans to assure women equal pay. In 1962 Perpich was elected to the Minnesota State Senate on the Democratic-Farmer-Labor ticket and was reelected in 1966. In 1970 he was elected lieutenant governor and was reelected in 1974. Following Walter Mondale's 1976 election to the U.S. vice presidency and Wendell Anderson's resignation as governor, Perpich became governor of Minnesota and appointed Anderson to the U.S. Senate to replace Mondale.

Perpich's inaugural celebration included a polka mass in downtown St. Paul, an event characteristic of Catholic Slavic Americans. Similarly, during his first term, he donated his $25,000 raise to promote the bowling game of bocce ball (popular in northern Minnesota). Although he lost the 1978 election to former congressman Albert Quie, he won reelection four years later, the first Minnesota governor to hold nonconsecutive terms. His running mate, Marlene Johnson, became the first female lieutenant governor in Minnesota history.

In 1984 Perpich toured seventeen nations to promote Minnesota. He was passionate about the idea of turning the Twin Cities into the Paris of the United States. He enthusiastically promoted the proposal of the Ghermezian brothers to build a gigantic indoor shopping mall, including an amusement park. Contrary to the expectations of skeptics, the successful Mall of America is today the largest

shopping and entertainment mall under one roof in the nation. In 1986 Perpich won reelection as governor and, the next year, saw one of his pet projects materialize, the opening of a World Trade Center in St. Paul. Three years later, Perpich hosted Soviet president Mikhail Gorbachev and his wife, Raisa, and that same year also hosted Croatian president Franjo Tudjman, when Croatia was in transition from being a federated republic of Yugoslavia to a sovereign republic with a free market economy.

In 1990 Perpich again lost the gubernatorial election and, the following year, moved to Zagreb, Croatia, as a consultant on foreign policy to Tudjman's government. However, the U.S. State Department denied his request to take dual Croatian citizenship, and therefore he did not serve as Croatian foreign minister. Perpich died in Minneapolis in 1995.

Matjaž Klemenčič

REFERENCES

Coffman, Jack B. "Minnesota Loses a Legend, Passing Stuns Friends and Colleagues." *St. Paul Pioneer Press,* 22 September 1995, 1, 13.

Luketich, Bernard M. "Umro je bivsi guverner drzave Minnesote brat Rudy Perpich" (Brother Rudy Perpich, former governor of the State of Minnesota, died). *Zajedničar* (Pittsburgh) 90 (40) (4 October 1995): 16, 22.

Whereatt, Robert, and Patricia Lopez. "Minnesota Loses a Leader Both Brilliant and Baffling, Perpich a Man of Vision, Former Governor Dies of Cancer at Age of Sixty-seven." *Star Tribune* (Minneapolis), 22 September 1995, 1A.

Peterson, Esther Eggertsen (1906–1997)

Educator, labor and consumer activist, women's advocate, and public official
Danish-American

Frequently described as the "mother of the consumer movement," Esther Peterson spent much of her life fighting for better working conditions, rights for women and minorities, and informed decision making by consumers. In 1981 she received the Presidential Medal of Freedom, the nation's highest civilian honor for public service. Twelve years later she was among thirty-six women inducted into the National Women's Hall of Fame at Seneca Falls, New York. At the ceremony she was characterized as "one of the nation's most effective and beloved catalysts for change."

The daughter and granddaughter of Danish Mormons who immigrated to Utah (her mother had been born in Denmark, as were her father's parents), Esther Eggertsen was born in Provo in 1906 to Lars and Annie Eggertsen. Her father was superintendent of schools, and Esther decided to become a teacher. She graduated from Brigham Young University, went in 1930 to Teachers College of Columbia University in New York City, and met and married Oliver Peterson, a Lutheran of Norwegian ancestry and socialist sympathies.

She taught at a girls' college-preparatory school and volunteered at the Young Women's Christian Association (YWCA) to teach "current events" to working-class women, which, along with teaching at the experimental Bryn Mawr Summer School for Industrial Workers, drew her into the trade union movement. She worked as an organizer for the Amalgamated Clothing Workers of America in New York during World War II and helped break down the color barrier in several shops. In 1944, she went to Washington as a labor lobbyist and, after the war, campaigned for an increase in the minimum wage.

In late 1948 the Petersons and their four children moved to Sweden, where Oliver was the labor attaché at the United States Embassy in Stockholm. When the family returned in 1957, Esther resumed her career as a lobbyist but soon joined John F. Kennedy's presidential campaign. After winning, Kennedy asked her what she wanted. She chose to head the Women's Bureau in the Department of Labor. With Peterson's encouragement, Kennedy established the Presidential Commission on the Status of Women and appointed her executive chair. The commission's report, *American Women: An Invitation to Action,* called for equal pay for equal work. In 1963 she became assistant secretary of labor, the highest-ranking woman in the Kennedy administration. President Lyndon Johnson named her the first special assistant to the president for consumer affairs, a position she would also occupy in the Carter administration.

In 1970 she became vice president for consumer affairs at Giant Foods, a large supermarket chain. She fought for clearer product labeling, unit pricing, and open dating of perishable products. She won many converts among food wholesalers and retailers and considered those years among "the most productive and useful" of her life. During the 1980s she assisted the United Nations in developing a set of international consumer guidelines. She later served as consumer adviser of the National Association of Professional Insurance Agents, concerning herself primarily with needs of older people, women in particular. In the 1990s she briefly served as a member of the U.S. Delegation to the United Nations. Peterson died in 1997.

Peter L. Petersen

REFERENCES

Molotsky, Irving. "Esther Peterson Dies at 91; Worked to Help Consumers." *New York Times,* 22 December 1997.

Peterson, Esther, with Winifred Conkling. *Restless: The Memoirs of Labor and Consumer Activist Esther Peterson.* Washington, DC: Caring Publishers, 1995.

Petrescu, Paul (1921–)

Writer and academician
Romanian

Paul Petrescu—one of Romania's primary authors, researchers, and academicians—established his career against great odds in the Communist era in his homeland. He defected in 1987 and reestablished himself as a writer and commentator in the United States.

Born to an upper-middle-class family in 1921, in Cetatea Alba, Romania (now Ukraine), Petrescu, hoping to become a diplomat, earned his first Ph.D. in political science from the University of Bucharest in 1947. This degree was soon considered by the Communist authorities as tainted by bourgeois and capitalist influences. Consequently, Petrescu started over and earned a second doctorate, this time in architectural history, from the Romanian Academy in 1969. He was a professor at the Institute of Fine Arts, head of the Folk Art Department, scientific secretary of the Institute of Art History, and a member of the editorial board of two influential journals, *Revue Roumaine d'Historie de L'Art* and *Revista de Etnografie si Folclor*. During his homeland career Petrescu was awarded a German Academic Exchange Service Award and a Fulbright Lectureship to the University of Utah. He wrote more than 100 journal articles and fifteen books in Romanian, French, and Russian, many of which were also translated into English and Spanish, on Romanian folk architecture, handicrafts, and textiles, the most famous of which is *Romanian Vernacular Architecture* (Bucharest, 1958).

Increasing restrictions on his personal and professional life in Romania under the Ceausescu dictatorship compelled Petrescu to defect to the West while at a scientific meeting in Switzerland in 1987. He ended his Romanian career as head of the Ethnological Department of the Institute of Ethnography and Dialectology and editor in chief of the *Ethnographic Atlas of Romania*.

He remained in limbo in a refugee camp in Germany for two years until he finally received permission to immigrate to the United States. Settling in Stockbridge, Massachusetts, Petrescu has continued to write and comment about folk art and architecture in central and eastern Europe and about politics in the post-Communist era, offering his insights to North American audiences. Because of his pioneering work with the Open Air Museum in Bucharest, he has been a consultant to museums of art and architecture in Hungary, Denmark, and the United States. His most recent scholarly publication is the entry on central Europe in the *Encyclopedia of Vernacular Architecture of the World* (Cambridge, 1998).

Petrescu is married and the father of an adult son; his wife and son both reside in Stockbridge. Called a savant by some for his insightful works, Petrescu continues his transnational career at age seventy-eight, with publications in the United States, Romania, and Western Europe in English, Romanian, French, and German. He is often invited to international scholarly conferences.

Petrescu is a member of the Romanian Orthodox Church in Hartford, Connecticut and is also a frequent participant in Romanian-American events in Boston. He recently was consultant to a Romanian theater production in Stockbridge, his adopted town.

G. James Patterson

REFERENCES

Bobango, Gerald. *The Romanian Orthodox Episcopate of America: The First Half Century, 1929–1979.* Jackson, MI: Romanian American Heritage Center, 1979.

Bock, Joanne. *Ethnic Vision: A Romanian American Inheritance.* Niwot, CO: University Press of Colorado, 1997.

Galitzi, Christine A. *A Study of Assimilation among the Roumanians of the United States.* New York: Columbia University Press, 1929.

Patterson, G. James. "Greek and Romanian Immigrants as Hyphenated Americans: Towards a Theory of White Ethnicity." In *New Directions in Greek American Studies,* edited by Dan Georgakas and Charles C. Moskos, 153–160. New York: Pella Publishing, 1991.

———. "Romanians." In *Encyclopedia of Canada's Peoples,* edited by Paul Robert Magocsi, 1092–1100. Ottawa: University of Toronto Press, 1999.

Petrescu, Paul. "Central Europe." In *Encyclopedia of Vernacular Architecture of the World,* edited by Paul Oliver. Cambridge: Cambridge University Press, 1997.

———. Interviews by author numerous times, 1970–present.

Piasecki, Frank Nicholas (1919–)

Aeronautical and mechanical engineer, pilot, and business executive
Polish-American

Aviation and helicopter pioneer Frank Piasecki was the first person in the United States to hold a commercial helicopter license. He and his firm have designed some of the most important helicopters used in the United States since the end of World War II.

Piasecki was born in Philadelphia, Pennsylvania, to Nikodem and Emilia (Lotocka) Piasecki. His father, a tailor, had emigrated from Poland. Early exposure as a teenager to autogyros prepared Piasecki for his later career. He received a degree in mechanical engineering from the University of Pennsylvania in 1939 and in aeronautical engineering from New York University in 1940. After working for two companies for several years, he—along with several other engineering students from the University of Pennsylvania—founded the research group, P-V Engineering Forum, which was incorporated in 1943 and became the Piasecki Helicopter Corporation in 1946. The firm's employees grew from 200 at the end of World War II to around 2,000 by the time of the Korean war. After the Boeing Airplane Company purchased the firm, Piasecki organized another firm in 1955.

During World War II, Piasecki was the designer and builder of the PV-2 helicopter, which demonstrated the advanced concepts of vertical take-off/landing (VTOL). The maiden flight, piloted by Piasecki, on 11 April 1943, marked only the second time a helicopter had been successfully flown in the United States. P-V Engineering Forum was offered a navy contract for a tandem rotor helicopter, and the PV-3 Dogship, the "Flying Banana," flew successfully in March 1945. The H-21 model (1949) was considered the first heavy-lift helicopter and was used as a utility and rescue craft in the Korean war, whereas the Flying Banana proved valuable for minesweeping, amphibious assault, and heavy-load transport. Piasecki subsequently was the codesigner of numerous other models to meet the needs of the armed services, including the YH-16, the largest helicopter in the world. He holds twenty-three patents on helicopter development.

In December 1958 Piasecki married Vivian O'Gara Weyerhauser, with whom he had five sons and two daughters. Voted one of the Ten Outstanding Young Men of the Year by the U.S. Junior Chamber of Congress in 1952, Piasecki is the recipient of honorary degrees and numerous awards. He is a founding member of the American Institute of Aeronautics and Astronautics, a member of the Army Aviation Hall of Fame since 1974 and, among other awards, the recipient of the Philip H. Ward, Jr., Gold Medal of the Franklin Institute, awarded to individuals who contribute the most to U.S. industrial welfare and progress. President Ronald Reagan presented Piasecki with the National Medal of Technology in 1986.

Piasecki also belongs to Polish-American organizations. He served as a trustee of the Kościuszko Foundation, is a member of the Polish Institute of Arts and Sciences in America, the Polish American Congress, the American Council of Polish Culture, the Polish American Citizens league, and many others. President Lech Wałęsa decorated Piasecki in 1994 with the Medal of Merit of the Republic of Poland.

Stanislaus A. Blejwas

REFERENCES

Holt, W. J., Jr. "He Likes to Fly Straight Up." *Saturday Evening Post,* 11 August 1951, 32–33, 61–65.

Kolmer, Susan E. "Frank Piasecki." In *Notable Twentieth-Century Scientists,* 4 vols., edited by Emily J. McMurray, 3: 1579–1581. Detroit, MI: Gale Research, 1995.

"Piasecki, Frank Nicholas," In *Who's Who in Polish America,* edited by Bolesław Wierzbiański, 353. New York: Bicentennial Publishing Corp., 1996.

"Piasecki: Getting Set for Mass Transportation." *Business Week,* 26 September 1953: 144–152.

"Piasecki H-21B Workhorse," Web site description, March Field Air Museum: www.marchfield.org/uh21.htm (accessed 20 May 2000).

Pickford, Mary (née Gladys Louise Smith) (1892–1979)

Actress and movie producer
Canadian

Mary Pickford was one of the earliest "stars" of the emerging motion picture industry. Her performances over more than a decade of the silent film era made her "America's Sweetheart."

Born in Toronto, Canada, as Gladys Louise Smith on April 8, 1892—she always maintained that she was born in 1893—Pickford made her first appearance on stage at the age of six. She loved the theater, went on tour in 1901, and was living in New York with her family by 1902, for Canadians in the entertainment business found greater opportunities in the United States. After an apprenticeship in touring companies, Gladys auditioned in 1906 for the impresario David Belasco. He hired her, changed her name to Mary Pickford, and cast her as a child in *The Warrens of Virginia*. In 1909 she successfully auditioned for D. W. Griffith, of the Biograph Company, quickly becoming a rising film actress.

Pickford was soon starring in films for Adolph Zukor's Famous Players Studio. Her first hit was *Tess of the Storm Country* in 1914. By 1915 she was receiving 500 fan letters daily and her screen persona (a working-class waif constantly being exploited by various forces and villains) was internationally famous. In her most popular roles she always played the waif, as in *The Poor Little Rich Girl* (1917), *Rebecca of Sunnybrook Farm* (1917), *Pollyanna* (1920), and *Little Annie Rooney* (1925).

After 1915, Pickford produced her own pictures, retained control over her own affairs, and became a major Hollywood entrepreneur. Known as "America's Sweetheart," she signed a contract in 1918 giving her full control over her films. A year later, she, Douglas Fairbanks, Charlie Chaplin, and D. W. Griffith created United Artists (UA). *Pollyanna* was Pickford's first release for UA. It grossed over $1 million internationally, astounding for the era. Pickford divorced her husband, Owen Moore (they had wed in 1911), and married Fairbanks in March 1920. The couple soon began developing a twenty-two-room mansion on eighteen acres in Beverly Hills, "Pickfair," the social and artistic center of 1920s Hollywood.

Although Pickford won an Oscar for her first talking film, *Coquette* (1929), and made a series of talkie successes from 1929 to 1933, her screen presence did not long survive beyond the silent film era. With her high piping voice and the new cinema acting styles calling for more naturalistic techniques, her earlier screen persona did not work well. She retired

from the screen in 1933 but continued to produce pictures for several years. In fact, she remained active in United Artists until she and Charlie Chaplin sold it in 1953. In 1934 she visited Toronto and was greeted by larger crowds than had gathered to see the Prince of Wales (later Edward VIII). That same year Fairbanks was listed as co-respondent in a divorce suit; Pickford and he divorced in 1936, and she married screen actor Charles "Buddy" Rogers the following year.

Pickford received an honorary Oscar at the 1976 Academy Awards. The Canadian government considered giving her the Order of Canada but determined she had left when young and infrequently returned. Canada did, however, renew her citizenship. Yet she had become a virtual recluse, spending most of her last years confined to bed, a maple leaf prominently displayed on the wall of her bedroom. She died on May 29, 1979.

J. M. Bumsted

REFERENCES

Balio, Tino. *United Artists: The Company Built by the Stars.* Madison: University of Wisconsin Press, 1976.

Brownlow, Kevin. *Hollywood: The Pioneers.* London: William Collins Sons, 1979.

Carey, Gary. *Doug and Mary: A Biography of Douglas Fairbanks and Mary Pickford.* New York: E. P. Dutton, 1977.

Eyman, Scott. *Mary Pickford.* London: Robson Books, 1992.

Herndon, Booton. *Mary Pickford and Douglas Fairbanks.* New York: W. W Norton, 1977.

Niver, Kemp. *Mary Pickford, Comedienne.* Los Angeles: Locare Research Group, 1969.

Pickford, Mary. *Sunshine and Shadow.* New York: Doubleday, 1955.

Whitfield, Eileen. *Pickford: The Woman Who Made Hollywood.* Lexington: University Press of Kentucky, 1997.

Windeler, Robert. *Sweetheart: The Story of Mary Pickford.* New York: Praeger, 1974.

Pierre, Frantz Marie (1957–)
Educator and community activist
Haitian

Even before arriving in the United States, Frantz Marie Pierre knew that he would go on in life to become an educator and a purveyor of empowerment. As a teacher specializing in secondary education, special education, and instructional technology, he has had an impact on both his own ethnic community and society at large.

Born and raised in Gonaïves, Haiti, Pierre was surrounded by a family of teachers. His parents, aunts, and uncles instilled in him the importance of acquiring and sharing knowledge. He immigrated to the United States at the age of fourteen and earned a bachelor's degree from Adelphi University and two master's degrees at the University of Miami in Miami, Florida, focusing on special education and foreign-language education.

Pierre began his career in education by serving Cuban and Haitian refugees as an employability-skills instructor at Miami-Dade Community College. He then added the roles of adult education teacher and English speakers of other languages (ESOL) and French instructor. He also coordinated the Martinique/Guadeloupe ESOL Summer Language Institute and facilitated cross-cultural studies for a number of students.

While working with students at the North Dade Center for Modern Languages, Pierre realized that his students' progress could be greatly enhanced by the inclusion of technology in the curriculum. He coauthored and was awarded a Technology Incentive Grant in 1994. As a result of his work, he was named Technology Teacher of the Year in 1994 and 1995.

In 1995, Pierre moved on to Horace Mann Middle School as an exceptional education teacher. He continued to motivate and encourage students, culminating in his being named a finalist for Teacher of the Year in 1997–1998 for Miami–Dade County public schools. Other examples of Pierre's contributions to education include a variety of leadership positions with student and parent groups, training programs, and numerous conference presentations.

Pierre's efforts have gone beyond the schools; he has reached out to the community, especially by working with the Haitian-American community. He served as a volunteer translator for the Haitian Refugee Center, assisting incarcerated refugees. As the adviser of the Haitian Ibo Club at Miami-Dade Community College for four consecutive years, he coordinated Konbit Kreyol, the Haitian Cultural Fair. The proceeds were used to establish the Toussaint L'Ouverture scholarship for needy Haitian students. He also successfully encouraged the members of the Haitian Ibo Club to tutor other members of the Miami Haitian community. At Horace Mann Middle School he worked with the Haitians with a Positive Attitude Club, where he redirected the energy of students from gang activity to community development. In addition, he assisted the Haitian Mission Baptist Church in La Romana, Dominican Republic. In order to better serve the people working with underprivileged Haitian children there, he provided teacher training and aided with school construction.

Pierre's philosophy of empowerment is evident in the impact he has had on his students and his community. Believing that all students have the capacity to learn, he has gone on a humble crusade to ensure that every student he touches is aware that they have the power within them to succeed.

Nancy C. Lespérance

REFERENCES

Pierre, Frantz Marie. Interview by author, 5 May 2000.

———. Resume and professional biography, 1999.

Poitier, Sidney (1927–)

Actor

Bahamian-American

Sidney Poitier defied stereotypical typecasting of African American performers and built an acting career in which his roles have represented a new level of dignity for black actors and actresses. He is ranked among the greatest screen legends.

Born in Miami, where his Bahamian parents had come to sell their tomato crop, Poitier spent his formative years on a small Caribbean island. When he was ten, the family moved to Nassau, Bahamas, where he went to school for two years. After a minor run-in with the law, he was shipped to an older brother in Miami.

In his late teens, Poitier decided to become an actor. His first film was *No Way Out* (1950). Eight year later, the New York Film Critics' Circle named him best actor for his role in *The Defiant Ones.* In 1963 he won an Academy Award as best actor for *Lilies of the Field. In the Heat of the Night,* a film in which he costarred, won the Oscar for best picture in 1967. Poitier's performance as Walter in the stage and the screen versions of *A Raisin in the Sun* also drew praise. More recently, Nelson Mandela requested that Poitier portray him in the television movie *Mandela and de Klerk* (1997).

Much can be learned about Poitier from his autobiographies: *This Life* (1980) and *The Measure of a Man* (1999). These candid memoirs describe the grinding poverty yet self-respect of the family that Poitier credits for his success. Raised where blacks were the majority, Poitier refused to believe that the color of his skin limited what he could accomplish. He aspired to become the best actor he could, even unlearning his native sing-song accent. Nevertheless, in the 1950s, there were few scripts with meaningful roles for blacks.

In a 1968 article in the *New York Times,* journalist Clifford Mason accused Poitier of being an "Uncle Tom" because he so often portrayed nonthreatening, middle-class blacks. Evidently, Mason discounted the fact that Poitier had refused to sign a loyalty oath repudiating leftist black actors or that Poitier had revised the script of *In the Heat of the Night* to protect the integrity of its black lead or that he and his friend Harry Belafonte had delivered bail money to civil rights workers in Mississippi.

In the early 1970s, Poitier became part of a film production company dedicated to improving the position of blacks in the industry. After two decades of producing and directing, he returned to acting, appearing in a spate of television films, such as the Emmy Award–winner *Separate But Equal* (1991). Twice mar-

ried and the father of six daughters, Poitier indirectly made headlines when impostor David Hampton wheedled his way into the lives of wealthy Americans by claiming to be the actor's son, a story that became the basis for the successful stage and screen drama, *Six Degrees of Separation.*

Poitier, who has been knighted by Queen Elizabeth, ranks twenty-second in the American Film Institute's listing of the fifty greatest "screen legends." In 1993, he and Belafonte were jointly awarded the Thurgood Marshall Lifetime Achievement Award. In May 2000 Poitier received the Screen Actors' Guild Lifetime Achievement Award. A citizen of both the United States and the Bahamas, Poitier is currently that island nation's ambassador to Japan.

Suzanne Model

REFERENCES

Keyser, Lester J., and Andre H. Ruszkowksi. *The Cinema of Sidney Poitier.* San Diego: A. S. Barnes, 1980.

Poitier, Sidney. *This Life.* New York: Alfred A. Knopf, 1980.

"Welcome to the Golden Years: Sidney Poitier": www.geocities.com/Hollywood/9766/poitier.html (accessed 27 June 2000).

Popé (c. 1630–1690)
Healer and resistance leader
Native American (Pueblo)

A Tewa medicine man from the San Juan pueblo, Popé devoted his life to the preservation of indigenous cultural practices in the face of Spanish encroachment. He led the Pueblo Revolt of 1680, the most successful Native American uprising in American history.

By 1680 there were nearly forty pueblos, containing approximately 16,000 people, spread along the Rio Grande river valley in present-day New Mexico. Failing to find any wealth, the Spanish sought to extract goods and services through forced labor and tribute, and intensive efforts were being made by Franciscan friars to stamp out native religious practices and convert the people to Christianity through coercion.

When disease, famine, drought, and Apache attacks exacerbated these conditions, religious leaders like Popé ascribed the situation to the people's failure to adhere to traditional ways. He called for resistance to Spanish authority and Christianity, initiating a cultural revitalization movement that would unite the factionalized Pueblos and restore balance and harmony to Pueblo life.

Popé, his allies, and his family suffered for their outspokenness. His brother was enslaved, and Popé was arrested and flogged. More than forty other leaders were whipped or jailed; three were hung. In the kivas, traditional places of ceremonies and instruction, secret forums were held that organized a resistance movement. Popé knew that although their worst enemy was the Spanish, the failure of previous attempted revolts was due mainly to informers. He ruthlessly weeded out any internal enemies, including his son-in-law. As his organization solidified, early in summer 1680 he had a prophetic dream calling on him and his people to rid their lands of the Spanish Christian oppressors with fire. Mocking Christian symbols, he told his followers that Spanish power was weak and sent out a knotted cord to each pueblo. On the day the last knot was released, all the pueblos were to rise up.

On 11 August 1680, the rebellion erupted with ferocity, overwhelming the 2,500 Spanish in New Mexico. The insurgents killed more than 400 priests and colonists, burned every mission and church, and drove the retreating survivors out of New Mexico. Popé ordered converted Pueblo people to renounce their Christianized names, the Spanish language, and Christianity by washing away the holy water from their baptized bodies with yucca suds. However, although he was a great leader of the rebellion, he was ill suited to lead the Pueblos in peacetime. His autocratic ways alienated most of his followers, and he was removed from power.

No longer powerful or popular, Pope died in 1690, two years before the Spanish reconquest. But as a result of his efforts, the Spaniards had learned some painful lessons. They moderated their ways and dared not reinstitute the labor tribute system or coercive forms of evangelization. The effects were intercultural accommodation, exchange, and intermarriage, which created the distinct cultural fusion that exists in New Mexico today. Another long-term consequence of Popé's leadership and the Pueblo Revolt of 1680 is that to this day the Pueblos continue to practice their cultural and religious practices free from outside interference. Pueblo resistance preserved their religious freedom.

John M. Shaw

REFERENCES
Dozier, Edward P. "The Pueblo Indians of the Southwest." *Current Anthropology* 5.2 (April 1964): 79–97.
Gutierrez, Ramon A. *When Jesus Came the Corn Mothers Went Away: Marriage, Sexuality, and Power in New Mexico, 1500–1846.* Palo Alto, CA: Stanford University Press, 1991.
Josephy, Alvin M. *The Patriot Chiefs: A Chronicle of American Indian Resistance.* New York: Penguin Books, 1958.
Knaut, Andrew L. *The Pueblo Revolt: Conquest and Resistance in Seventeenth-Century New Mexico.* Norman: University of Oklahoma Press, 1995.
Ortiz, Alfonso. "San Juan Pueblo." *Handbook of North American Indians.* Vol. 9. *The Southwest,* 278–295. Washington, DC: Smithsonian Institution, 1979.
Spicer, Edward H. *Cycles of Conquest: The Impact of Spain, Mexico, and the United States on the Indians of the Southwest, 1533–1960.* Tucson: University of Arizona Press, 1962.
Weber, David J., ed. *What Caused the Pueblo Revolt of 1680?* New York: Bedford/St. Martin's Press, 1999.

Pothier, Aram Jules (1854–1928)
Banker, mayor, and governor
French Canadian

Born in the Province of Quebec, Aram Pothier arrived with his family in Woonsocket, Rhode Island, at the age of sixteen, in 1870. He started out as a grocery store clerk, but his talents quickly opened doors for him, first in the field of banking and later in politics, where he rose to the governorship of Rhode Island.

Five years after his arrival in the United States, Pothier obtained a position at the Woonsocket Institution for Savings, becoming its president in 1912. He was later elected to the presidency of the Union Trust Company of Providence, at that time one of the three largest financial institutions in the state. Woonsocket's large French Canadian population relied greatly on his dedication to his fellow immigrants and his ability to conduct business in their mother tongue, thereby helping them acquire homes and start small businesses.

In 1885, he successfully ran for a position on Woonsocket's school committee. Two years later, as a Republican, he was elected to the state general assembly and reelected the next year. He was elected mayor in 1894 and, again, the following year—the first person of French Canadian descent to be elected mayor. Pothier then moved to the state level, being elected lieutenant governor in 1897. In 1899 and 1900, President William McKinley named him commissioner from the State of Rhode Island to the Paris Universal Exposition. While there, he convinced a number of French textile barons to establish factories in Woonsocket, bringing large infusions of foreign capital to the city and transforming it into an international textile center.

In 1908, the Republican Party nominated Pothier for governor. Elected that year and the next, he held the position for six consecutive years. In the end, he was to serve seven terms for a total of ten years: 1908–1914 and 1924–1928, dying in office during the last year of his governorship. His accomplishments as governor included reorganizing the state's financial structure; reducing the workweek to fifty-four hours; establishing a state police force; passing an antilobbying law; revising the state constitution allowing for an executive veto, biennial gubernatorial and cabinet elections; the reapportionment of the general assembly; and revamping the port of Providence and promoting the economic development of Narragansett Bay.

Through the efforts of Aram J. Pothier, French Canadian immigrants to the United States earned recognition as an industrious, conscientious group, capable of reaching the pinnacle of local and state power. Pothier was deeply respected in both financial and political circles for his integrity and for not forgetting the "little people" of his state of adoption, among whom could be counted a large number of his fellow French Canadian immigrants—around 500,000 of whom came into New England between 1850 and 1900. In 1920, the Société des Artisans Canadiens-Français, a mutual benefit society that was headquartered in Montreal but that counted many French Canadian immigrants to New England among its members, bestowed on Aram J. Pothier the title of honorary president "as an expression of their esteem for him and in recognition of the respect that he has earned for his people."

Claire Quintal

REFERENCES
"Aram Pothier." Woonsocket: My Home Town on the Web.
    http://www.geocities.com/athens/parthenon/9105/pothier.html. (Accessed 20 December 2000).
Bonier, Marie Louise. *The Beginnings of the Franco-American Colony in Woonsocket, Rhode Island.* Translated, edited, and revised by Claire Quintal. Worcester, MA: Institut français, Collège de l'Assomption, 1997.
———. *Les Débuts de la Colonie Franco-Américaine à Woonsocket, Rhode Island.* Framingham, MA: Lakeview Press, 1920.
Veader, John Robert. "Aram Jules Pothier as Governor of Rhode Island." Master's thesis, University of Rhode Island, 1966. Reprinted in part in *Je me souviens* 14.1 (Autumn 1991): 5–106.

Powell, Colin (1937–)
Soldier, chair of the joint chiefs of staff, and U.S. secretary of state
Jamaican-American

Chairman of the Joint Chiefs of Staff from 1989 to 1993, Colin Powell played a key role in the allied offensive to oust Iraq from Kuwait, known as Operation Desert Storm. Powell's thirty-five-year career included two tours of duty in Vietnam, and a wealth of administrative positions in Washington. Retiring from the army as a four-star general in 1993, Powell led America's Promise, a nonprofit organization devoted to assisting child welfare agencies, prior to being appointed U.S. secretary of state by President George W. Bush.

Colin Powell, born in 1937, was the second child of Jamaican immigrants who settled in New York. His father was a shipping clerk, his mother a seamstress. Powell spent his childhood in the South Bronx, then a solidly working-class neighborhood. An unremarkable student, he entered the City College of New York in 1954. There, he discovered the Reserve Officers' Training Corps (ROTC) and soon decided on a military career.

In 1968, after his first Vietnam assignment, the once-mediocre student graduated second in his class at the U.S. Army Command and General Staff College; four years later, following a short second tour of duty in Vietnam (he was wounded), Powell was selected as a White House fellow. He was known as an officer who "takes care of his people" and "puts himself last." But Powell's rise also reflected his diligence, organizational talent, excellent memory, and "ebullient charm." In 1989, President Bush named him chairman of the Joint Chiefs of Staff.

Politically, Powell's opinions represent a centrist position. He has endorsed affirmative action, the right to abortion, and the death penalty. In his best-selling autobiography, *My American Journey,* Powell wrote that "government should not interfere with the demonstrated success of the free marketplace, beyond controls to protect public safety and to prevent distortions of competition by either labor or industry." Despite his enormous appeal, ultimately, Powell declined to run for president, citing the desire to devote more time to his family.

After leaving the army, Powell accepted paid and unpaid posts. His main source of income was public speaking. An appearance earned him in excess of $50,000. Powell, a charismatic speaker, never tired of praising the United States and exhorting his listeners to take advantage of the opportunity it offers.

Powell's primary unpaid job was as chairman of America's Promise. This organization solicits funds for child welfare agencies from private donors, many of them corporations. In addition, Powell served on the board of directors of such organizations as the United Negro College Fund, the Boys and Girls Clubs of America, and Howard University.

Until the year 2000, his most important legacy, however, was in the realm of military policy. The Powell Doctrine holds that the United States should intervene militarily only when its vital interests are at stake, only with decisive force, and only when there is a clear goal and defined strategy for getting out. These views led Powell to condemn U.S. military action in Somalia as well as in Yugoslavia. Although it is too soon to judge the wisdom of this advice, the fact that Powell once had the authority to counsel presidents and was chosen by President George W. Bush to be the U.S. secretary of state beginning in 2001 may give him an opportunity to implement his own doctrine.

Suzanne Model

REFERENCES

Gates, Henry Louis. "Powell and the Black Elite." *New Yorker* 71 (25 September 1995): 64–74.

Powell, Colin, with Joseph E. Persico. *My American Journey.* New York: Random House, 1995.

Prisland, Marie (1891–1980)

Writer and community activist
Slovene

Marie Prisland was an ethnic activist, the first woman to become vice president of the Grand Carnolian Slovenian Catholic Union (KSKJ) and the founder and first president of the Slovenian Women's Union (SWU). She was also an author who achieved recognition in her homeland and within the Slovene community in the United States.

Prisland was born in 1891, in Rečica pri Savinji, Province of Carniola, then part of Austria-Hungary, today in the Republic of Slovenia. In 1896, her parents left for Brazil in search of fortune, leaving her behind to be raised by her maternal grandmother. At fifteen, she immigrated to the United States and settled in Sheboygan, Wisconsin. There, she found her first job in a chair factory, learned the English language by attending night school, and after three years became an accountant. She married another Slovene immigrant and had three children. She also joined the local KSKJ lodge and actively promoted the equality of women within the organization on the national level. At the 1923 convention of KSKJ in Cleveland, the first at which women as well as men were delegates, she was elected second vice president.

In 1926 she founded the Slovene Women's Union (SWU). Its goals were to unite Slovene-American women; provide assistance; and promote education, ideas about the United States, Slovene consciousness among Slovene Americans, and active participation of Slovene-American women in public affairs. SWU lodges were organized in all major Slovene settlements in the United States. Prisland served as president for twenty years, after which she became honorary president. During her tenure as president, she published and edited a book, *Ameriška Slovenka* (Slovene-American woman, 1928); founded the monthly review *Zarja—The Dawn* (1929), which is still published; and began the young women's division of the Slovene Women's Union.

At a meeting of the Slovene National Congress in December 1942, she was elected vice president of the Slovene American National Council, an umbrella group of all Slovene-American organizations created to promote political action to help Slovenes in the homeland during the war. In May 1943, she was also elected second assistant secretary of the United Committee of South Slavic Americans, an organization of Americans with origins in Bulgaria and Yugoslavia who wanted to provide political and material aid to their homelands, which were being devastated by World War II. However, she resigned from both positions in 1944 over a dispute about Slovene-Americans' support for the Communist-led partisans who were fighting the Germans and the Italians and their allies in Slovenia and Yugoslavia.

After Prisland became honorary president in 1946, she served on different committees of the KSKJ and did a great deal of writing. She wrote *From Slovenia to America* (1968), which presents a mixture of autobiographical sketches and some aspects of Slovene-American history, culture, and organizational life, as well as a segment on the lives of her successors as presidents of SWU, Antonija Turek and Albina Novak. She also contributed numerous articles to *Zarja—The Dawn* and other Slovene-American newspapers and almanacs. Prisland died in 1980.

Matjaž Klemenčič

REFERENCES
Klemenčič, Matjaž. *Ameriški Slovenci in NOB v Jugoslaviji: naseljevanje zemljepisna razprostranjenost in odnos ameriških Slovencev do stare domovine od sredine 19. stoletja da konca druge svetovne vojne* (American Slovenes and the national liberation struggle in Yugoslavia. The process of settlement, geographical distribution and the relation of the Slovene Americans toward their homeland from the mid–nineteenth century until the end of World War II). Maribor: Založba Obzorja, 1987.
Prisland, Marie. *From Slovenia to America*. Chicago: Slovenian Women's Union of America, 1968.
Žitnik, Janja, and Helga Glušič, eds. *Slovenska izseljenska književnost 2, Severna Amerika* (Slovene emigrant literature in North America, vol. 2). Ljubljana: ZRC SAZU, Založba Rokus, 1999.

Pritsak, Omelian (Omeljan) (1919–)
Historian
Ukrainian

Omelian Pritsak has excelled as a historian. He was responsible for promoting programs in Ukrainian studies at Harvard University and, in particular, the Ukrainian Harvard Research Institute. He has been honored in the United States and Ukraine.

Pritsak was born in Luka-Ozerne, in western Ukraine. In 1940, he graduated from the University of Lviv. Three years later, faced with the threat of another Soviet occupation, he and thousands of other Ukrainians fled to the West. He subsequently earned a doctorate in 1948 at the University of Göettingen, Germany, with a specialization in Oriental studies.

Primarily, he was interested in incorporating Arabic, Turkish, and Persian sources into Ukrainian historiography.

Pritsak taught at the University of Hamburg, Germany, before accepting a position at the University of Washington, Seattle, in 1961, and permanently moving to the United States. An outstanding scholar and an expert in the rather esoteric field of Turkology, he was soon offered a position at Harvard University and remained there from 1964 until his retirement in 1989. Although he is an author of numerous scholarly articles and books, it was the six-volume project on the origins of Kievan Rus, the first volume of which is *Old Scandinavian Sources Other Than the Sagas* (1981), that marked his lifelong scholarly labor.

Pritsak came to Harvard at the time when Ukrainian university student clubs were actively seeking funds for the creation of an endowed chair in Ukrainian studies at an American university. Although new to the academic community at Harvard, he successfully undertook the negotiations. The first chair, in 1968, was in Ukrainian history, which he was the first to hold. Two other chairs, in Ukrainian literature and Ukrainian linguistics, were established in 1973. At his initiative, the Ukrainian Harvard Research Institute was founded in 1973, and he became its director. He was also editor of a scholarly quarterly, *Harvard Ukrainian Studies,* which the institute started publishing in 1977.

In 1988, Pritsak organized a major international conference, in Ravenna, Italy, on the millennium of Christianity in Ukraine and also edited its proceedings. He was elected a member of the Turkish Language Academy (1957), the Finno-Ugric Science Academy (1958), and the American Academy of Science (1971). When glasnost began to sweep away the "iron curtain," Pritsak took the opportunity to establish friendly contacts within the academic community in Ukraine. He became the first Ukrainian from the Ukrainian diaspora in the West to be elected a member of the Academy of Sciences of Ukraine (1990). Moreover, in Kyiv he established the acad-

emy's Institute of Oriental Studies and became its director.

Although Ukrainian studies at Harvard University were strictly academic, for the Ukrainian community, they were also politically important. At the time when the Soviet Union had implemented an intense process of Russification in Ukraine, Ukrainian studies at Harvard counteracted the falsifications made by the Soviet government. Another benefit was the summer courses in Ukrainian studies that provided an opportunity for serious students to broaden their knowledge of their ethnic heritage. In recognition of Pritsak's contributions, the Harvard Institute of Ukrainian Studies published two festschrifts in his honor (1979–1980 and 1990).

Daria Markus

REFERENCES
"O. Pritsak Obranyi Chlenom AN USSR, Pershyi Inozemnyi Chlen" (O. Pritsak elected member of the Academy of Sciences of the Ukrainian SSR, the first foreign member). *Svoboda,* 11 July 1990.
"Omelja Pritsak." *Harvard Ukrainian Research Institute Newsletter,* no. 8, February 1988.
"Prof. Dr. Omelian Pritsak Naimenovanyi na Profesora dlia Harvards'koii Katedry Istorii Ukrainy" (Prof. Dr. Omalian Pritsak was named the first professor of the Harvard Ukrainian history chair). *Svoboda,* 29 January 1975.

Puente, Ernesto "Tito" Anthony, Jr. (1923–2000)

Musician and composer
Puerto Rican

Tito Puente, a five-time Grammy Award winner, was known as the "King of Latin Music." His recordings and arrangements extend from classics in Latin American music to popular rock. Puente, who received honorary doctorates from Hunter College and SUNY Old Westbury, also helped young artists through the Tito Puente Scholarship Fund. He was named the Latino Ambassador of Good Will, receiving numerous keys to cities around the world.

Puente was born in New York City on 20 April 1923, eldest son of Ercilia Ortiz and

Ernesto Puente, Sr. His father worked for a razor blade manufacturer. His mother was responsible for shortening his nickname, Ernestito, to Tito. She enrolled him in piano lessons when he was seven, and by age ten he was a child prodigy in Spanish Harlem. During the 1930s, Puente performed with local and society bands, playing regularly at the Park Plaza Hotel in New York, sometimes with his younger sister, Ana. At age sixteen, he appeared in his first U.S. orchestral tour. Three years later, he was drafted into the U.S. Navy, discharged in 1945, and then completed his education under the GI Bill, graduating from New York's Julliard School of Music, where he studied conducting, orchestration, and theory.

By 1948, he was the most sought after young arranger of the time. He formed his own ten-piece band *(conjunto),* called the Picadilly Boys. The following year Piccadilly recorded its first hit, "Abaniquito" (the fan). When Cuban artists were asked to return home in 1957 to celebrate fifty years of Cuban music, Puente was the only Puerto Rican invited by the government, in recognition of his contributions to the arts. He then collaborated with Cuban artists for a string of hits and, in 1963, recorded his classic "Oye Cómo Vaz," later rerecorded by Carlos Santana.

Puente performed at the Metropolitan Opera and hosted a Spanish-language TV show, *The World of Tito Puente,* in 1968. In the 1970s he was responsible for bringing a new kind of music to the next generation. His album *Abraxas* introduced salsa to a new audience. In the late 1970s, he won his first Grammy; in February 2000, he earned his fifth. He received eight other nominations, more than any other artist in the field of Latin music.

In terms of official recognitions, besides his two honorary degrees, Puente served as grand marshal of the Puerto Rican Day Parade in New York City and, in 1969, received the keys to New York City from Mayor John Lindsay. In 1990, he received the Eubie Blake Award from the National Academy of Arts and Science and the next year launched his 100th album, *El Numero Cien.* He was then cited in the *Congressional Record* and received the Smithsonian Medal. More recently, in September 1999, he received the Hispanic Heritage Award from President Bill Clinton. In addition, Puente has earned the title "El Rey del Timbales" for working continuously since 1937. Meanwhile, since 1980, when he created the Tito Puente Scholarship Foundation, Puente has been contributing money to benefit talented children.

In April 2000, English-language radio stations announced that the seventy-seven-year-old Puente was busily planning his next concert, but heart problems forced him to cancel his concerts. On 1 June, he died in New York. His talent and spirit bridged racial, cultural, and generation gaps, and the Puerto Rican government declared three official days of mourning in San Juan.

Linda Delgado

REFERENCES

Forero, Juan. "Tito Puente, Famed Master of Latin Music, Is Dead at Seventy-seven." *New York Times,* 2 June 2000, 1.

Puente, Tito. Interview by author, 7 May 1999.

Varona, Frank de. *Latino Literacy.* New York: Owl Books, Henry Holt, 1996.

Pukui, Mary Kawena (1895–1986)
Linguist, author, and scholar
Hawaiian

Scholar, author, chanter, composer, linguist, storyteller, genealogist, translator, and lifelong teacher, Mary Kawena Pukui was the intellect of Hawai`i who made possible the Hawaiian cultural renaissance that began in the late 1960s and is in full flower today. She never attended college and never left the Hawaiian Islands, yet she received two honorary doctorates and was nominated for the Nobel Prize in literature for her work in bringing Hawaiian culture and traditions into a Western scholarly format that could be shared worldwide.

Pukui was born in 1895 in the small town of Na`alehu, on the southern slopes of Mauna Loa Volcano, Hawai`i Island. She was the daughter of Henry Nathaniel Wiggen, of Salem, Massachusetts, and Mary Pa'ahana

Kanaka'ole, a pure Hawaiian. Shortly after her birth Pukui was given in the Hawaiian manner to be raised by her maternal grandmother, Nali`ipo`aimoku Kanaka`ole, a kahuna from a long line of priests of the Pele (goddess of volcanoes) tradition. Her grandmother named the girl "Mary Abigail Kawena-`ula-o-kalani-a-Hi`iaka-i-ka-poli-o-Pele-ka-wahine-`ai honua Na-lei-lehua-a-Pele Wiggen," meaning "The rosy glow in the sky made by [the goddess] Hi`iaka in the bosom of Pele, the earth-consuming woman, the crimson lehua [flower] wreaths of Pele." From her grandmother, Kawena was steeped in the language and traditions of Hawai`i.

When her grandmother died, Kawena returned to her parents in Honolulu. She attended eight different schools, but her formal education was interrupted at age fifteen. By that time she had begun collecting Hawaiian proverbs and sayings and translating and editing articles. At eighteen she married Napoleon Kaloli`i Pukui. (They adopted two daughters, both of Japanese ancestry, before Pukui, at the age of thirty-six, had her only biological child.) A decade later she returned to the Hawaiian Mission Academy to complete high school.

She then began teaching Hawaiian culture and language and completed her first book of Hawaiian sayings and proverbs for children. Kawena's reputation as a competent young Hawaiian-language expert came to the attention of Vassar professor Martha Beckwith and anthropologist E. S. Craighill Handy, which led to the debut, around 1928, of Kawena's long career with the Bishop Museum staff. With them, Pukui began interviewing Hawaiians throughout the archipelago, beginning a lifetime of recording "landscape stories." She quickly adapted the tape recorder in her documenting of Hawaiian traditions, translating carefully and using diacritical marks to preserve meaning.

Working with linguist Samuel H. Elbert, Kawena produced a Hawaiian dictionary in 1957. Elbert noted that Pukui was "way ahead of her times" in incorporating references to

legends, sayings, and proverbs in their dictionary. She would write or cowrite 52 books and articles and more than 150 songs and chants. Her other major works include the ethnological study *The Polynesian Family System in Ka`u Hawai`i,* the two-volume *Nana I ke Kumu* (Look to the source) study on Hawaiian thinking patterns, and `Olelo No`eau on Hawaiian proverbs and poetical sayings, published just before her death at ninety-one.

Kawena gave us a lei of knowledge bridging two worlds, affirming the values of Hawaiian tradition and thought and preserving those values for the world. She was fond of saying, "Knowledge to me is life."

David W. Shideler

REFERENCES
Cooke, Mary. "Mary Pukui Dies at 91." *Honolulu Advertiser* (May 22, 1986): A-1.
Handy, Edward Smith Craighill, and Mary Kawena Pukui. *The Polynesian Family System in Ka-'U, Hawai'i.* Wellington, NZ: Polynesian Society, 1958; Rutland, VT: Tuttle, 1972.
"*He Lei Hulu.*" Videotape. Honolulu, HI: AluLike O`ahu Island Productions, 1984.
"*Legacy of Light.*" Videotape by Martha H. Noyes and Elizabeth Lindsay for KITV (Honolulu, 1993).
"Mary Pukui Dies at 91." *Honolulu Star Bulletin* (May 26, 1986): C-8.
Pukui, Mary K. `Olelo No`eau: Hawaiian Proverbs and Poetical Sayings. Honolulu, HI: Bishop Museum Press, 1983.
Pukui, Mary Kawena, E. W. Haertig, and Catherine A. Lee. *Nana i ke kumu* (Look to the source). 2 vols. Honolulu, HI: Hui Hanai, 1972–1979.

Pupin, Michael (Mihajlo) Idvorski (1854–1935)

Professor, inventor, author, and Pulitzer Prize winner
Serbian

Mihajlo Idvorski Pupin, Columbia University professor, inventor, and author, achieved worldwide recognition in the field of transmission of electric waves. He was also author of a Pulitzer Prize–winning autobiography, *From Immigrant to Inventor* (1923).

Pupin was born in the village of Idvor, in what is today Vojvodina, a province of Serbia.

When he received his secondary education, he came into contact with a strong Serbian democratic and progressive national movement that would influence him for his entire life. Because of his participation in Serbian anti-Austrian demonstrations, he had to continue his education in Prague. He left for the United States in 1874.

During the 1874–1879 period he earned his living as a laborer. After that, he studied at Columbia University, continued in Cambridge and Berlin, and was granted his doctorate in 1889. He returned to Columbia University, where he taught electrical engineering until he retired. Pupin's research extended to several different topics. He worked on components of alternating current causing magnetism in iron and patented a device for multiple telegraphy, which is still used in city telephone networks. Pupin also did pioneer work in the field of X-rays, discovering, for example, a method of quick photography in medicine. In all, he received twenty-four U.S. patents.

Both his period in Prague and his period in the United States were characterized by his struggle for national identity. In his autobiography he reported his answer when asked if he intended to become an American: "No . . . I shall run away . . . if I am expected to drop my Serbian notions and become an American. . . . [O]ne might as well expect me to give up the breath of my life as to give up my Serbian notions." However, Pupin was not actively involved in politics until 1908, when he became president of the National Committee of the South Slavs. In 1908, he participated in founding the Slavic Immigrant Union, organized to help immigrants from Slavic countries on their arrival in the United States.

Pupin also helped organize a relief organization by American Serbs and Montenegrins during the Balkan Wars of 1912–1913. He served as honorary consul general of Serbia in New York and, during World War I, spoke in favor of the creation of Yugoslavia. During that period he served as president of the Union of the United Serbs, "Sloga," and as honorary president of Serbian National Defense in America.

Pupin became involved in attempts to find favorable solutions to the border questions of the newly emerged Yugoslavia. He supported the opposition to secretly arranged Italian claims to Dalmatia and the western parts of what is today the Republic of Slovenia. The head of the Yugoslav delegation at the Paris Peace Conference (1919–1920) asked Pupin to come and help explain the Yugoslav claims with regard to the Italian-Yugoslav border. Pupin's influence and explanations helped Yugoslavia gain Dalmatia and the northwestern and eastern parts of what is today the Republic of Slovenia.

Matjaž Klemenčič

REFERENCES

Klemenčič, Vladimir, ed. *Mihajlo I Pupin, znanstvenik, politik, gospodarstvenik* (Michael I. Pupin, scientist, politician, economist). Ljubljana: University of Ljubljana, 1980.

Koca, Joncic, ed. *Život i delo Mihajla Idvorskog Pupina, Zbornik radova naučnog skupa Novi Sad—Idvor, 4–7 oktobar 1979* (Life and work of Michael Idvorski Pupin. Papers from the International Scholarly Meeting, Novi Sad—Idvor, 4–7 October 1979). Novi Sad: Pokrajinska konferencija SSRN Vojvodine (Provincial Conference of Socialist Alliance of Vojvodina), 1985.

Pupin, Michael I. *From Immigrant to Inventor.* New York and London: Scribner's, 1925.

Quill, Michael (1905–1966)
Union leader
Irish

Mike Quill was one of the most important labor leaders of modern time. He was the colorful and controversial founder of the Transport Workers Union (TWU).

Michael Quill was born on a small farm near Kilgarvin, County Kerry, Ireland, on 18 September 1905. His father, John Quill, was a student of Irish history and culture, an advocate of the forcible overthrow of British rule in Ireland, and a member of the South Kerry Irish Republican Army (IRA) volunteers. Quill was raised with a strong dose of Irish Republicanism. He became involved in Ireland's fight for freedom, but with the end of the Irish Civil War, there was no place in the Irish Free State for antitreaty IRA people like Quill. He emigrated, arriving at Ellis Island on 16 March 1926. He sought out various jobs, including one on the construction of the Independent Subway in New York City.

After the stock market crash, jobs became scarce. Quill and his younger brother, John, found work with the Interborough Rapid Transit (IRT) as toll takers, working twelve hours a night, seven nights a week for thirty-three cents an hour. During the late evening hours, Quill studied works on industrial unionism and concluded that unionism would help subway workers. In 1933, he joined the Irish Workers' Club, a secret group committed to the formation of an industrial union. The group also included old IRA men who worked in the subway. Quill and others worked to organize the Transport Workers Union (TWU). By 1934, they had won over about 400 members of the IRT Brotherhood, a company union. The TWU was born, and the passage of the Wagner Act in 1935 legalized their organizing actions. In January 1937, the TWU carried out its first successful sit-down strike and, later that year, it gained further stature by joining the new Congress of Industrial Organizations.

In 1937, Quill was elected on the American Labor Party ticket to the city council from the South Bronx. Though reelected three times, he never considered himself a politician. However, as a teenager, Quill had been outraged with the Catholic Church's condemnation of the IRA and he felt that the Church was antilabor. He retained a strong feeling against the Catholic Church, continued his support for a united Ireland, and in the United States joined the revolutionary Clan na Gael. After World War II, he also fought to end segregation in the armed forces, abolish the poll tax, end Jim Crowism in major league baseball, outlaw the Ku Klux Klan (KKK), terminate government contracts with discriminatory business firms, and revoke tax exemptions from colleges denying entrance to minorities. In addition, he encouraged women in the TWU to take on leadership roles.

In January 1966, a TWU strike shut down the New York City transit system for ten days. Despite an injunction, Quill refused to call off the strike and was arrested. The strike was settled, but his heart condition worsened and he died on 28 January 1966. His Irish roots had remained important to him and had consistently influenced his career in the labor movement.

Seamus P. Metress

REFERENCES

Freeman, Joshua B. *In Transit: The Transport Workers Union in New York City, 1933–1966.* New York: Oxford University Press, 1989.

———. "Irish Workers in the Twentieth Century United States: The Case of the Transport Workers Union." *Saothar* 8 (1982): 34–46.

O'Reilly, Gerald. *The Birth and Growth of the Transport Workers Union.* Enterprise, AL: Printing Press, 1988.

Quill, Shirley. *Mike Quill—Himself: A Memoir.* Greenwich, CT: Devin-Adair, 1985.

Whittemore, Louis H. *The Man Who Ran the Subways: The Story of Mike Quill.* New York: Holt, Rinehart & Winston, 1968.

Quintal, Claire (1930–)

Teacher and scholar
Franco-American

An internationally recognized scholar, Claire Quintal is perhaps best known for her creation (1979) of the Institut français (French institute) at Assumption College, Worcester, Massachusetts. The institute is a major research center for scholars in the various fields of Franco-American studies.

Born in Rhode Island, Quintal is a fourth-generation Franco-American. She received her doctorate from the Université de Paris (1961), after which she spent ten years in Paris doing research in comparative literature and medieval history. She then began a long, distinguished career, first teaching at the American College in Paris (1965–1968) and then at Assumption College and elsewhere. In addition to teaching French, she also taught courses on ethnicity and cultural identity; literature of the Francophone countries; the civilizations of France and French Canada; and Franco-American social and cultural history.

Always at the cutting edge in those areas of study, she has written and edited a lengthy list of books, articles, and lectures. Among her most noteworthy works are *The First Biography of Joan of Arc* (1964), *The Letters of Joan of Arc* (1969); and *Steeples and Smokestacks: A Collection of Essays on the Franco-American Experience in New England* (1996), a selection of essays initially presented at the annual colloquia on Franco-Americans organized by Claire Quintal and sponsored by the Institut français, which she created and developed. The high quality of the essays in *Steeples and Smokestacks* and their scope make that voluminous opus (681 pages) a sine qua non for anyone working in these areas of study. Another major work is her translation, editing, and updating of *The Beginnings of the Franco-American Colony in Woonsocket, Rhode Island* (1997), a model of what the French call *édition critique.* She has also edited and cotranslated *The Franco-Americans of New England: A History,* by Armand Chartier (1999). In addition to her publications, she participates in cultural and community activities and organizes academic colloquia and workshops.

Her achievements have been recognized by the governments of several states, by several professional organizations, and by Assumption and other colleges. Her most prestigious honors have come from France, whose government elevated her to the rank of Chevalier de la Légion d'Honneur (1991), an honor seldom bestowed on non-French citizens. Also noteworthy are her nomination to the rank of Chevalier de l'Ordre national du Mérite de France (1974) and her promotion to *officier* in that same order (1997). Furthermore, the government of Quebec has bestowed on her one of its highest honors, the Ordre des Francophones d'Amérique (1980). Given her achievements, it was no surprise that she received the congressionally sponsored Ellis Island Medal of Honor (1986) as a representative of the Franco-American community in the United States.

In retrospect, Quintal's farthest-reaching achievements are clearly the institute's colloquia and subsequent publications, through which she has raised the area of French New England studies to an academically sanctioned field of research. In 2000 Quintal continued to be director emerita of the institute as well as professor emerita at Assumption College.

Armand Chartier

REFERENCES

Quintal, Claire. Resume.

Quintal, Claire, and family members. Interviews by author, periodically, 1975–2000.

Quintal, Claire, ed. *The Little Canadas of New England: Third Annual Conference of the French Institute/Assumption College, Worcester, Massachusetts, March 13, 1982.* Worcester, MA: French Institute/Assumption College, 1983.

———. *Steeples and Smokestacks: A Collection of Essays on the Franco-American Experience in New England.* Worcester, MA: Institut français, Assumption College, 1996.

Qureshey, Safi Urrehman (1951–)
Computer engineer, entrepreneur, and philanthropist
Pakistani

With technical skills acquired in Pakistan and the United States, Safi Qureshey—along with two colleagues—entered the personal computer market early, becoming the sixth-largest manufacturer by the mid-1990s. Qureshey has been honored by the Muslim community for his public service efforts and his devotion to improving educational conditions in his homeland.

Safi Qureshey was born on 15 February 1951 in Karachi, Pakistan. With a B.Sc. in physics from the University of Karachi, Qureshey came to the University of Texas, Arlington, in 1971, for an electrical engineering degree. He and two colleagues, Albert Wong and Tom Yuen, formed AST Research Inc. in 1980, using the first letters of their names for the company name. Based in Irvine, California, the company moved from communications consulting services to manufacturing multifunction option boards for IBM to manufacturing its own complete personal computer (PC) systems. AST shipped its first PC in 1986 and in 1995 its PC broke the $1,000 barrier, the first to do so. AST ultimately had more than forty-five offices and six manufacturing facilities and became the leading PC vendor in China.

Chair or cochair of AST's board from 1988 through 1996, Qureshey remained when the other founders, first Wong and then Yuen, left. AST became a Fortune 500 company in 1992, the fourth-largest computer manufacturer in the United States and the sixth-largest in the world by 1995. Samsung Electronics acquired the company in 1997. Qureshey is involved with several start-up companies as adviser, board member, and seed investor, and he works particularly closely with The Indus Entrepreneurs (TIE).

As a member of President Clinton's Export Council, Qureshey traveled with delegations to such emerging markets as China, Indonesia, Thailand, and India, accompanying successive secretaries of commerce Ron Brown, Robert Mosbacher, and William Daley. A founding member of the California Business–Higher Education Forum and its chairman for 1994–1995, he has been Regent's Professor at the Graduate School of Management, University of California, Irvine. Qureshey has been named Distinguished Alumnus, University of Texas, Arlington; International Entrepreneur of the Year, University of Illinois, Carbondale; and has received the UCI Medal, the highest honor of the University of California, Irvine, for university service. In 1998 the Muslim Public Affairs Council awarded him its American Muslim Achievement Award.

Qureshey and his wife, Anita, have been visible by helping to fund Muslim organizational events, and they play major roles in business and philanthropic circles not only in the United States but also in Pakistan. One of their objectives has been to use television and new media to fight illiteracy; in Pakistan, Qureshey founded Active Learning Initiative Facility (ALIF), which orchestrated the local-language adaptation of Sesame Street for Pakistani viewers. By advocating an innovative public-private partnership in a major national educational movement, he hopes to reverse declining literacy trends, particularly for women, in his homeland. He has established a reputation in both the United States and Pakistan as a dedicated professional who works tirelessly for his business ventures and socially to uplift others.

Karen Leonard

REFERENCES
"Conference on Status of Education in Pakistan Held by ALIF." *Pakistan Link*, 28 April 2000, 14.
Fields, Robin, and P. J. Huffstutter. "Ex-AST Exec to Sell Portable MP3 Player." *Los Angeles Times*, 7 February 2000, C1.
"Growth Minded AST." *Los Angeles Times*, 5 February 1993, Orange County edition, D5.

Kesmodel, David. "South Asian Entrepreneurs and Mentors Form a Tie That Binds." *Los Angeles Times,* 3 July 2000, C1, 4.

Lee, Christina. "Commerce Chief, CEOs Head for Asia." *Los Angeles Times*, 28 July 1990, D5.

Miller, Greg. "Beleaguered Qureshey Stepping Down at AST." *Los Angeles Times*, 3 November 1995, Orange County edition, A1.

———. "Samsung Raises Its Stake in Orange County's AST to Almost 50%." *Los Angeles Times*, 29 June, 1996, D1.

Takahashi, Deen. "Safi U. Qureshey, President and Chief Executive, AST Research Inc." *Los Angeles Times*, 10 August 1992, Orange County edition, D 4.

Rahman, Fazlur (1919–1988)
Modernist scholar of Islam
Pakistani

The leading modernist scholar of Islam of his generation, Fazlur Rahman, redefined Islam for the contemporary world. Through his publications and the students he trained, his work has had an impact on Muslims, from the United States to Indonesia.

Fazlur Rahman was born in Seraisaleh, Punjab, in what is now Pakistan, on 21 September 1919. He earned B.A. and M.A. degrees from the University of Punjab in Lahore in 1940 and 1942, respectively, and he went on to Oxford University, where he received his Ph.D. in 1949 for a thesis on the medieval philosopher Ibn Sina. He taught for several years at the University of Durham, England, and at the Institute of Islamic Studies, McGill University, in Montreal, Canada. Called back to Pakistan to the Islamic Research Institute in Karachi in 1961, he then became director of the Islamic Research Institute in Islamabad (1962–1968). However, he was placed in personal danger in the late 1960s by religious fanatics in Pakistan who found his modernist positions offensive, and he came to the University of California, Los Angeles, for the 1968–1969 academic year. He then moved to the University of Chicago as professor of Islamic thought, where he stayed from 1969 on. He was the first Muslim to be appointed to the University of Chicago's Divinity School, and he was honored by the university in 1986 with his appointment as the Harold H. Swift Distinguished Service Professor. He was also awarded the prestigious Girogio Levi Della Vida Medal for the study of Islamic civilization by UCLA's Gustave E. Von Grunebaum Center for Near Eastern Studies.

Rahman's scholarship falls into three areas: his early work on classical Islamic philosophy and theology, his work on Islamic morals and ethics, and his work on religious or communal themes. In his Chicago years, all three dimensions were fully integrated in a mature and Qur'anically grounded vision of an authentic Islam for the contemporary world. He believed strongly that medieval scholars had misconstrued the Qur'an (Allah's revelation to Muhammad, the Prophet) and Hadith (traditions of the Prophet) to produce a rigid and inflexible set of teachings, and he urged that changing times and contexts must be taken into consideration to constitute a modern system of jurisprudence and interpretation. He hoped to liberate the Qur'an from medieval structures of tradition and interpretation to make it a reliable and dynamic guide for modern life.

Rahman's rigorous scholarly writings and the students he trained, Muslim and non-Muslim, continue to have a significant impact on the development of contemporary Muslim discourse and practice. Students who came from Muslim countries to the United States for higher education have carried his ideas back home, and Muslims in the United States find Rahman's emphasis on the commonalities among Judaism, Christianity, and Islam helpful for promoting interfaith understanding and activism.

After his international scholarly reputation was firmly established, his homeland, Pakistan, called him back and honored him. Throughout his life, Rahman spoke out against what he considered to be fundamentalist obscurantisms. In his person, he embodied activist, modernist Muslim discourse and practice. Rahman died in Chicago, Illinois, on 26 July 1988.

Karen Leonard

REFERENCES

Bijlefeld, Willem A. "In Memoriam, Dr. Fazlur Rahman." *Muslim World* 79 (1989): 80–81.

Cragg, Kenneth. "Fazlur Rahman of Karachi and Chicago." In *The Pen and the Faith: Eight Modern Muslim Writers and the Qur'an,* edited by Kenneth Cragg, 91–108. London: Allen & Unwin, 1985.

Denny, Frederick M. "The Legacy of Fazlur Rahman." In *The Muslims of America,* edited by Yvonne Yazbeck Haddad, 96–108. New York: Oxford University Press, 1991.

Rahman, Fazlur. *Islam.* 2d ed. London and New York: Holt, Rinehart & Winston, 1966; Chicago: University of Chicago Press, 1979.

——. *Islam and Modernity: Transformation of an Intellectual Tradition.* Chicago: University of Chicago Press, 1982.

——. *Major Themes of the Qur'an.* Minneapolis and Chicago: Bibliotheca Islamica, 1980.

Ramos, Leda G. (1961–)

Visual artist and educator
Salvadoran-American

Visual artist Leda Ramos is the director of technology and education at the Central American Resource Center in Los Angeles. Through this expansive program and her site-specific, community-focused installations, Ramos plays a major role in the documentation and empowerment of Salvadorans in the United States. Ramos was born in 1961 and raised in the Echo Park neighborhood of Los Angeles. She studied at the University of California, Santa Barbara, where she received a B.A. in sociology. She also holds an M.F.A. from Rutgers University.

In 1984, while in Santa Barbara, she organized an exhibit of artists protesting the war in El Salvador at La Casa de la Raza, and she has continued to design important exhibits that recognize overlooked voices and art forms. She returned to Los Angeles and began to apply her training and artistic talent in community-focused projects in 1995. When CARECEN began to restructure its education department, Ramos was hired as a consultant and soon became the director of technology and education. She reorganized the department and implemented new interdisci-plinary web-based programs, poetry workshops, youth community design with visiting architects, literacy building, and youth leadership opportunities.

Poetry writing workshops are an important part of the education program at CARECEN. Ramos has published books of poetry written by youth participants in the workshops offered by visiting poets. She also started the Memoria Histórica Community Archive with the goal of preserving Central American cultural heritage and documenting Central American–immigrant experiences. The archive contains thousands of photographs, film and videos, Central American literature books, and ephemera from the solidarity movement in Central America. The archive is to be a resource for the community, educational institutions, artists, and youth. Ramos is also the guest editor of the book *Izote Vos,* a collaboration between young Salvadoran-American artists and writers in San Francisco and Los Angeles. Concurrent with the publication of *Izote Vos,* Ramos coorganized Foro 2000, a historic cultural exchange between Salvadoran and Salvadoran-American writers, artists, students, and community activists in February 2000. One of the resolutions of the cultural delegation was the continued building of a network among Salvadoran and Salvadoran-American communities.

Ramos's creative focus is to document and represent the Central American and Latina/o cultural landscape. As a college art association fellow at the Getty Museum, she designed a prototype exhibition that represented less-visible community archives and collections. She has also worked with Artists and Designers Opening the Border Edge (ADOBE) in Los Angeles, a group of Latina/o artists, architects, and designers that raises awareness about Latina/o contributions to the urban landscape. She taught seminars and collaborated on public art projects until she formed her own partnership with artist Alessandra Moctezuma. Together with Moctezuma, she has designed installations that include the participation of students, community groups, street vendors, and garment workers and union members. Ramos views her art as architectural intervention, dialogue, and documentation. Ultimately, her many activities intersect and make her an important force in the representation and empowerment of Central Americans in the United States.

Leticia Hernández-Linares

REFERENCES

Davis, Mike. "Huellas Fronterizas: Retranslating the Urban Text in Los Angeles and Tijuana." *Grand Street* (Los Angeles), 56 (Spring): 1996.

Kim, Katherine Cowy, Leda Ramos, and Alfonso Serrano, eds. *Izote Vos: A Collection of Salvadoran American Writing and Visual Art.* Coproduced by CARECEN-LA and Pacific News Service. San Francisco: Pacific News Service, 2000.

Moctezuma, Alessandra, and Leda Ramos. "Hidden Economies in Los Angeles: An Emerging Latino Metropolis." In *Space, Site, Intervention: Situating Installation Art,* edited by Erika Suderberg, 143–157. Minneapolis: University of Minnesota, 2000.

Ramos, Leda, and Angela Sanbrano. "Cronología de Carecen: Historia en Movimiento, 1983–1998" (Chronology of Carecen: History of the movement, 1983–1998). Los Angeles: CARECEN, 1999: www.carecen-la.org/Internet/index.html (accessed 14 June 2000).

Ramsey, Meserak "Mimi" (1953–)

Community activist and leader
Ethiopian

Meserak "Mimi" Ramsey was born in Addis Ababa, Ethiopia, in 1953. She is the executive director of Forward USA, which she founded in 1996. Forward USA is a nonprofit organization based in San Jose (California) that is devoted to eliminating the practice of female circumcision, commonly known as female genital mutilation (FGM). Mimi Ramsey has dedicated herself to a crusade to end it and to persuade Americans to address FGM as a serious health and human rights issue. Ramsey has been at the forefront of the campaign to pass legislation banning female genital mutilation at both the state and the national levels.

Mimi Ramsey arrived in the United States in 1973, accompanying her husband, who came for educational purposes. She attended nursing school. In addition to her activism,

Ramsey has a part-time job at a California psychiatric facility, where she works as a nurse. Her educational experience in nursing school opened her eyes to the lifelong health problems caused by female circumcision. She realized that in her own case circumcision had led to the severe complications she experienced in the birth of her child. In 1993, when visiting the home of a friend from Ethiopia, she noticed a little girl stooped in the corner. She was told that the eighteen-month-old child was recovering from the circumcision procedure that had been performed in Washington, D.C. Ramsey was enraged that the practice had followed her to her adopted country.

Ramsey broke the taboo that kept victims of female circumcision silent about this tradition. She vowed to campaign to outlaw FGM in California and the United States. She has given numerous interviews on radio and in various printed publications and has appeared on television in order to increase awareness of the negative consequences of female circumcision. Ramsey lectures to students in nursing, social work, human sexuality, and other educational programs and has addressed many national and international meetings on the many harmful effects of FGM. As a result, she has endured ostracism, insults, and even death threats for speaking publicly about FGM and about her own suffering from FGM at the age of six, which left her physically and emotionally scarred. However, Ramsey was ultimately instrumental in obtaining the passage of 1995 federal legislation that criminalized the practice in the United States.

Ramsey has worked diligently in immigrant communities, supporting victims of FGM and their families. She has held workshops aimed at raising the awareness of immigrant communities about the dangers of FGM and in favor of legislation making it a crime. In addition, she has acted as consultant and adviser to doctors, health care personnel, teachers, and other professionals and community leaders who work closely with African-immigrant communities. Ramsey's efforts in African-immigrant communities have resulted in saving many little girls from circumcision. Through her efforts many older girls and young women victims of severe forms of female circumcision called infibulations (the use of a ring, clasp, or stitches to fasten the labia majora of the vagina to prevent sexual intercourse) have been successfully de-infibulated. As recognition of her dedication to this human rights issue, Mimi Ramsey was one of the honorees at the 100 Heroines reception and dinner held in Rochester, New York, in October 1998.

Tekle M. Woldemikael

REFERENCES

Burstyn, Linda. "Female Circumcision Comes to America." *Atlantic Monthly,* October 1995, 28–35.

Crossette, Barbara. "Female Genital Mutilation by Immigrants Is Becoming Cause for Concern in the U.S." *New York Times,* 10 December 1995, Y11.

Forward USA. *Leading the Fight against FGM (Female Genital Mutilation). Providing support for girls and women violated by FGM* 1999: www.forwardusa.org/ (accessed 13 June 2000).

Ramsey, Meserak "Mimi." "Cruel Tradition" (1999): www.fgm.org/CruelTrad.html (accessed 13 June 2000).

———. "Rising Daughters Aware: The Stories" (19 March 1999): www.fgm.org/TheStories.html (accessed 13 June 2000).

Vanzi, Max. "Ethiopian Led Campaign to Ban Female Mutilations." *Los Angeles Times,* 24 September 1996, A22.

Randolph, A. (Asa) Philip (1889–1979)

Labor leader and civil rights activist
African American

A. Philip Randolph, socialist, organizer of the first African American union, labor and civil rights activist, pressured leaders to end segregation and improve economic conditions for African American workers. Known for his innovative, confrontational, nonviolent protest strategies and his unflagging commitment to racial and economic justice, Randolph made crucial contributions to the political struggles of his time and was an inspiration to later activists.

Randolph was born in April 1889 in Crescent City, Florida. His family was poor, but as a minister, his father encouraged education. Randolph read extensively and was deeply influenced by W. E. B. Du Bois and Karl Marx. In 1911, he moved to New York to work and study at City College. There, he met Lucille Campbell Green, whom he married in 1914. He also met Chandler Owen, a law student who shared Randolph's socialist leanings. They became soapbox orators in Harlem, organized an employment bureau for black southern migrants, and began editing a magazine for a society of black waiters, *The Hotel Messenger.* But their often radical discussions prompted the waiters to end their relationship.

Randolph continued the magazine as *The Messenger,* first with Owen and later with African American journalist George Schuyler. The U.S. Justice Department considered Randolph dangerously militant because he argued against U.S. involvement in World War I. He also urged African Americans to arm themselves against white mob violence, though he opposed Marcus Garvey's black separatism. In 1925, Randolph was invited to organize the Pullman Railroad Company's sleeping-car porters; it took ten years to win union recognition. Buoyed by this success, Randolph organized the Negro American Labor Council to encourage other African Americans to unionize, for he saw unionization as black labor's best hope for improved opportunities and working conditions. Given his stature, in 1936 the National Negro Congress, a new progressive civil rights organization, invited him to be its president. Four years later he resigned, believing the organization dominated by Communists.

His commitment to African American civil rights and labor struggles came to a head when he called for a national march on Washington to protest segregation in war industries and the armed forces. President Roosevelt, fearful of wartime disunity, signed Executive Order 8802 in July 1941 to forestall the march. The order prohibited segregation in defense industries but neither provided much enforcement nor desegregated the armed forces. Although some black leaders criticized Randolph as too conciliatory because he canceled the march, he continued his fight for black equality. In 1948 he urged young Americans to resist the draft until the armed forces were desegregated. President Truman did so that year. Committed to interracial organizing and to working from within institutional structures in order to achieve change, Randolph continued to be active in the labor movement. After the AFL and CIO merged in 1955, he became its first African American vice president.

The March on Washington that Randolph had called for during World War II finally took place on 28 August 1963, when more than 200,000 rallied for civil rights. Younger activists acknowledged his contributions to the movement, and he, in turn, understood their frustration and anger, though remaining a pacifist. He died in May 1979.

Cheryl Greenberg

REFERENCES

Anderson, Jervis. *A. Philip Randolph*. New York: Harcourt Brace Jovanovich, 1973.

Hanley, Sally. *A. Philip Randolph*. New York: Chelsea House, 1989.

Harris, William. *Keeping the Faith: A. Philip Randolph, Milton P. Webster, and the Brotherhood of Sleeping Car Porters, 1925–37*. Urbana: University of Illinois, 1977.

Pfeffer, Paula. *A. Philip Randolph, Pioneer of the Civil Rights Movement*. Baton Rouge: Louisiana State University Press, 1990.

Santino, Jack. *Miles of Smiles, Years of Struggle: Stories of Black Pullman Porters*. Urbana: University of Illinois Press, 1991.

Wintz, Cary, ed. *African American Political Thought 1890–1930: Washington, Du Bois, Garvey, Randolph*. Armonk, NY: M. E. Sharpe, 1996.

Red Cloud (1822–1906)
Warrior and tribal chief
Native American (Oglala Sioux)

Until his death in 1906, Red Cloud played a prominent role in Oglala Sioux society and in relations between the United States and the Sioux Nation. As post–Civil War U.S. expan-

sion strained the increasingly volatile situation across the West, Red Cloud first gained recognition as an Oglala "shirt wearer," because of his ambition and military skill in campaigns against the Pawnees, Crows, and Shoshonis. Later, he would evolve from a brilliant warrior into a reflective diplomat seeking to quell tensions on the northern plains.

Red Cloud and other Oglala Sioux lived in the Powder River country, on the western plains between the Black Hills and the Big Horn Mountains. In the mid-1860s he and his people encountered migrating settlers, gold seekers, and soldiers traveling the Bozeman Trail into Montana. Hoping to secure a peace treaty and access to regional resources, officials proposed a meeting at Fort Laramie in June 1866. In response to the construction of forts along the trail, Red Cloud denounced the treaty commission and promised attacks on the trail.

In December, Red Cloud helped orchestrate the Fetterman Massacre near Fort Philip Kearny, in northern Wyoming. He and several Sioux leaders lured nearly 80 soldiers out of the fort and over a ridge, where approximately 1,500 warriors attacked them. The event made national headlines and exacerbated the debate over U.S.-Indian relations. The ensuing attacks on surveying parties and gold seekers between 1866 and 1868 became known as Red Cloud's War. These conflicts, coupled with a new railway line into Montana, caused the federal government to abandon the Bozeman Trail.

In 1870, Red Cloud met President Ulysses Grant to discuss settling the Sioux on a reservation in the northern plains. In view of Red Cloud's previous defiance, this discussion surprised officials, who hoped to calm the tumultuous plains. The stay in Washington taught Red Cloud about negotiations with white officials and introduced him to the vastness of the eastern population and its industry. The visit increased his political stature and sharpened his diplomatic acumen but also convinced Red Cloud that negotiations were preferable to outright resistance. Indeed, he won an increase in trade for his tribe as well as for the Red Cloud Agency in northwestern Nebraska, on the outskirts of the Great Sioux Reservation.

After the Red Cloud Agency was moved to southwestern Dakota and renamed Pine Ridge, Red Cloud's relationship with Indian Agent Valentine T. McGillycuddy illustrated the former's diplomatic skill. Pine Ridge witnessed the ongoing conflict between McGilly-cuddy and Red Cloud, which repeatedly brought the reservation to the brink of vio-lence, with Red Cloud pushing an issue but ultimately accepting a compromise. Although that tactic lost him support among some younger Oglala men, it nonetheless demon-strated his desire to improve his people's qual-ity of life. During the rest of his life, he served as an important mediator between officials and his people. It was this combination of strong leader, intelligent diplomat, and savvy politi-cian that made him one of the most important Indian figures of the late 1800s.

Jeffrey P. Shepherd

REFERENCES

Allen, Charles Wesley. *Autobiography of Red Cloud: War Leader of the Oglalas.* Edited by R. Eli Paul. Helena: Montana Historical Society Press, 1997.

Hyde, George E. *Red Cloud's Folk: A History of the Oglala Sioux Indians.* Norman: University of Oklahoma Press, 1976.

Land of Red Cloud: Home of the Lakota Oglala. Pine Ridge, SD: Oglala Sioux Indian Tribe, 1983.

Larson, Robert W. *Red Cloud: Warrior-Statesman of the Lakota Sioux.* Norman: University of Oklahoma Press, 1997.

Olson, James C. *Red Cloud and the Sioux Problem.* Lincoln: University of Nebraska Press, 1965.

Utley, Robert. *The Indian Frontier of the American West, 1846–1890.* Albuquerque: University of New Mexico Press, 1984.

Zimmerman, Karen P. "Red Cloud." In *Notable Native Americans,* edited by Sharon Malinowski, 353–355. New York: Gale Research, 1995.

Reuther, Walter Philip (1907–1970)
Autoworker and union leader
German-American

Walter Reuther was one of the leading fig-ures in the twentieth-century labor move-ment. He secured important gains for au-toworkers and guided the United Auto Work-ers (UAW) for a quarter century.

Reuther was born on September 1, 1907, in Wheeling, West Virginia. The son of Ger-man-immigrant parents, he was reared on a diet of activism, for both parents were ardent Socialists and supporters of the trade union movement. At the age of nineteen, Reuther traveled to Detroit to find work in the auto-mobile industry. In 1932 he was promoted to shop foreman and almost immediately fired for his political views. A trip abroad with his brother, Victor, was highlighted by a stint in a car factory in the Soviet Union, which would lead him to publicly decry the lack of free-dom in Stalin's Russia.

After returning to Detroit, Reuther in-volved himself in organizing the autoworkers in the Ford plant. He was chosen president of his local UAW branch in 1936, just in time to participate in violent sit-down strikes. A union branch was not established in that plant until 1941, owing to the rancor between strikers and management. However, World War II offered Reuther an opportunity to serve his country. Franklin Roosevelt recog-nized Reuther's contributions and asked him repeatedly to serve in an official capacity. Loy-alty to the UAW prevented him from leaving his post, but he did advise the president on an informal basis for the duration of the conflict.

At war's end, Reuther again promoted the UAW's agenda. In 1945, he led a strike against General Motors Corporation, seeking a 30 percent wage increase and a public account-ing of the company's finances. The success of this strike allowed him to articulate his vision for a new, sympathetic, socially aware corpo-rate culture. The following year he became president of the UAW and won sweeping gains for his members. Workers acquired un-employment benefits, vacation time, and pen-sions in addition to monetary gains. Reuther helped arrange the CIO's merger with the AFL in 1955, and George Meany, president of the AFL, assumed the leadership of the AFL-CIO. But relations between Meany and

Reuther became prickly because of Reuther's perception of Meany's lukewarm, if not reactionary, views on the emerging Civil Rights movement. Reuther secured the withdrawal of the UAW from the AFL-CIO.

Reuther once again turned his attention to reforming and improving his country, establishing close ties with the postwar presidents and allying with Martin Luther King, Jr. Advocating legislation to help the downtrodden and unrepresented, Reuther participated in marches and demonstrations and was very enthusiastic about Johnson's War on Poverty. However, Reuther's advocacy of labor and social issues made him a target of venomous words and violent acts. Indeed, a shotgun-wielding assailant wounded him in the arm, leaving him with chronic pain. Yet, these dangers did not distract him from his goals.

On May 9, 1970, he and his wife, May, died in a plane crash in rural Michigan. For his contributions Reuther received many honors, including the Presidential Medal of Freedom in 1995 and inclusion in *Time* magazine's list of the 100 Most Influential People of the Century.

Susanne M. Schick

REFERENCES

Barnard, John. *Walter Reuther and the Rise of the Auto Workers.* Boston: Little, Brown, 1983.

Bluestone, Irving. "Working Class Hero: Walter Reuther." *Time 100*: www.time.com/time/time100/builder/profile/reuther.html (accessed 30 June 2000).

Carew, Anthony. *Walter Reuther.* New York: Manchester University Press, 1993.

Dickmeyer, Elisabeth Reuther. *Reuther: A Daughter Strikes.* Detroit: Wayne State University Press, 1989.

Lichtenstein, Nelson. *The Most Dangerous Man in Detroit: Walter Reuther and the Fate of American Labor.* New York: Basic Books, 1995.

Reuther, Victor. *The Brothers Reuther and the Story of the UAW: A Memoir.* Boston: Houghton Mifflin, 1976.

Tyler, Robert. *Walter Reuther.* Grand Rapids, MI: Eerdmans, 1973.

Revere, Paul (1735–1818)
Silversmith, engraver,
manufacturer, community activist,
Revolutionary War hero and officer
Franco-American

Paul Revere is one of the popular heroes of the American Revolution, owing largely to Henry Wadsworth Longfellow's poem "Paul Revere's Ride." Revere's own life was lived to its fullest in the service of Massachusetts, the American revolutionary army, and in the political, social, and industrial worlds of his times.

Revere was born in Boston on January 1, 1735 to Apollo Rivoire (later Paul Revere, Sr.), a French Huguenot, and Deborah Hichborn, of Boston. His father, born near Bordeaux, France, had come to America in 1715 and learned the goldsmith trade in Boston. Revere studied smithing under his father but also taught himself copperplate engraving, which he employed to draw political cartoons, illustrations, advertisements, and paper money. In 1757, Revere married Sara Orne, who was from Boston, but she died in 1773, shortly after the birth of their eighth child; five months later, he married Rachel Walker.

In addition to joining the Freemasons, Revere had become active in the Sons of Liberty and participated in the Boston Tea Party, 16 December 1773. He became a messenger between Boston and the Massachusetts delegates to the Continental Congress in Philadelphia, but his most famous ride took place during the night of 18–19 April 1775, when he alerted fellow colonists that British troops were proceeding by land to Lexington. The message was relayed by lanterns in the bell towers of churches. A year later, Revere was commissioned a major in the militia, then transferred to an artillery regiment, and, in late 1776, promoted to lieutenant colonel. His regiment participated in the Rhode Island Expedition in 1777–1778. Although compelled to resign in order to answer accusations by fellow officers, he was vindicated in a 1782 court-martial.

Following American Independence, Revere gradually moved from artisan to businessman, engraving the plates for printing

Massachusetts's paper money and expanding his silversmith enterprise by patterning his products so that his employees could manufacture them. In 1788, he started a new career as a copper founder and roller (he was apparently the first in the nation to roll copper into sheets in 1800) as well as a cannon and bell founder. Meanwhile, his status as a businessman contributed to his greater role as a community leader. In 1795, he was chosen president of the Massachusetts Charitable Mechanic Association (reelected until 1799), and he was a co-founder of the Massachusetts Mutual Fire Insurance Company in 1798. His Freemason activities also continued, further solidifying his status in Boston society. Moreover, as a strong New England Federalist, Revere was dismayed when Thomas Jefferson became president of the United States in 1801.

A decade later, in 1811, after Paul's son, Joseph Warren Revere, had taken over the foundry, Revere retired from both the city's political squabbles and the daily care of his business, although he did participate at a dinner honoring the Marquis de Lafayette's visit to Boston in 1815. On May 10, 1818, five years after the death of his wife, Rachel, Revere died in Boston.

André J. M. Prévos

REFERENCES

Goss, Elbridge Henry. *The Life of Colonel Paul Revere*. 2 vols. 2d ed. Boston: Howard W. Spurr, 1898.

Revere, Paul. *Paul Revere's Three Accounts of His Famous Ride*. Introduction by Edmund S. Morgan. Boston: Massachusetts Historical Society, 1961.

Triber, Jayne E. *A True Republican: The Life of Paul Revere*. Amherst: University of Massachusetts Press, 1998.

Rhee, Syngman (1875–1965)

Political activist and president of South Korea
Korean

As the first president of the Republic of Korea (South Korea), Syngman Rhee gained international prominence, serving as the head of state during a tumultuous period (1948–1960) in which Korea emerged from World War II, engaged in civil war, and developed as a divided nation. His leadership culminated a long political career, including more than forty years spent in the United States as a student and leader within the Korean-American community.

The life of Rhee, who was born in northern Korea in 1875, paralleled the opening of Korea to foreign influence in the late nineteenth century. He was educated by American Protestant missionaries and eventually joined the Independence Club, a political organization whose members argued for democratic reforms in Korea. His political views and activities were not popular with the monarchy, and he was imprisoned in 1898. Granted amnesty several years later, he left for the United States and attended George Washington University (for a B.A.), Harvard University (for an M.A.), and Princeton University (for a Ph.D. in political science). He then took a post with the American YMCA in Korea, but his opposition to the Japanese annexation of Korea in 1910 soon prompted his return to the United States.

Rhee settled in Honolulu, where he worked with the Methodist denomination as an educator of Korean immigrants. He also served as an important—if controversial—leader in the independence movement, championing the cause of freeing Korea from Japanese domination. When a provisional Korean government-in-exile was established in Shanghai in 1919, Rhee, in the United States, presented himself to others as president, an act that dismayed many of his compatriots in China. Although he was well educated and recognized as an important figure, Rhee's strong personality and authoritarian manner polarized Korean Americans in Hawai'i and on the mainland into pro- and anti-Rhee forces.

For many years, Rhee carried on a campaign in Washington, D.C., to cultivate U.S. support for Korean independence. Despite their tenuous financial situation, Korean immigrants raised funds that enabled him and others to carry on their work. Caught within the web of international politics, Korea's fate was sealed as the United States refused to intervene—recognizing Japan's imperial claim on Korea just as Japan reciprocated by acknowledging U.S. colonization of the Philippines.

Rhee's long association with the United States and his strong anti-Communist stance marked him as a likely candidate for U.S. support at the close of World War II, even though he drew strong opposition from many whom he represented. Elected president of South Korea in 1948, Rhee held a vision of a unified Korea that was not to be, as the Korean War and its ensuing stalemate left the country divided. His quest for power resulted in an increasingly repressive government. Charges of fraud in the 1960 election fueled growing unrest, and student protests led to his exile.

Ironically, Rhee spent the last years of his life in Hawai`i among fellow independence leaders, whom he had denied visitation to Korea during his presidency because they had disagreed with him. Rhee died in July 1965.

David Yoo

REFERENCES

Allen, Richard C. *Korea's Syngman Rhee: An Unauthorized Portrait.* Rutland, VT: Tuttle, 1960.

Jung, Byron. "Rhee, Syngman." In *Asian American Encyclopedia,* edited by Franklin Ng, vol. 5, 1274–1278. New York: Marshall Cavendish, 1995.

Robert T. Oliver, *Syngman Rhee: The Man behind the Myth.* New York: Dodd, Mead, 1960.

Rhees (né Rhys), Morgan John (1760–1806)

Baptist minister and pioneer
Welsh

Morgan Rhees came to the United States as a preacher and revolutionary thinker, espousing many civil and religious liberties. He envisioned a Welsh national home in America and, although his frontier community was short-lived, his efforts exemplified the spirit of the revolutionary era.

Born in Glamorgan, Wales, in 1760, into the small-holding family of John and Eliza-

beth Rhys, Morgan John Rhees showed an early interest in education. After studying at Bristol College in 1776–1777, he opened a school and taught for two years, published handbooks on administering Sunday schools, and preached for three years. After further study, he became an ordained Baptist minister in 1787. Attracted to revolutionary ideas, he joined the antislavery movement, supported the cause of religious liberty, and traveled to Paris in 1790 as a missionary for rational religion at the outset of the French Revolution. Active in founding political societies upon his return to the United Kingdom, he became acquainted with the Welsh intellectuals in London. He helped plan an expedition to the American frontier to contact a tribe of "Welsh" Indians on the Missouri River, supposedly the descendants of Prince Madoc, a legendary twelfth-century Welsh explorer. The visionaries also hoped to establish a Welsh-speaking colony in the American West.

In 1793, Rhys published *Cylchgrawn,* the first Welsh-language political periodical. The following year, fearing arrest for sedition, he hastily departed from Liverpool on a ship to New York. Assisted by the network of Welsh Baptists in Pennsylvania, Rhys (who began spelling his name "Rhees") engaged in a preaching tour that took him through most of the Atlantic states. He was critical of the institution of slavery in the South and, in Savannah, planned to develop a church and schools for blacks. Resuming his quest for a site for a Welsh settlement, he trekked to the frontier in Ohio, where he spoke against injustices to Native Americans in the West, much as he had against slavery in the South. Returning to New England, in 1796 Rhees married Ann Loxley, daughter of a prominent Philadelphia family.

Rhees helped revive the Philadelphia Welsh Society just in time to welcome a fresh wave of immigrants escaping the agricultural crisis in Wales. He preached in his native language to these newcomers, mainly small farmers and artisans, who were self-consciously Welsh. To provide a Welsh colony for the immigrants, Pennsylvanians founded the

Cambrian Company in 1796, with Rhees as its president. When it proved impossible to acquire the land that Rhees had identified in Ohio, he secured an alternative area of 17,400 acres in central Pennsylvania. Becoming a U.S. citizen in 1797, Rhees busily organized the immigrants bound for the Cambrian Company land and Beulah, an embryonic settlement with a biblical name. The land, however, was rocky and unsuited to agriculture, and Welsh immigrants were soon bypassing Beulah for a superior location at Paddy's Run, Ohio.

Rhees died of pleurisy before the ultimate failure of the town that he had founded. A man of many causes, he exemplified the revolutionary spirit of his age and did much to foster the welfare of the early Welsh community in the United States.

D. Douglas Caulkins and Lorna W. Caulkins

REFERENCES

Allison, William Henry. "Rhees, Morgan John." *Dictionary of American Biography*. Vol. 11, Supplement 1: 624–625. New York: Scribner's, 1944.

Williams, Gwyn A. *Madoc: Making of a Myth*. Eyre Meuthen: London, 1979.

———. *The Search for Beulah Land*. New York: Holmes & Meier, 1980.

Rhode, Paweł Piotr (1871–1945)

Roman Catholic priest and bishop
Polish-American

Paweł Piotr Rhode, auxiliary bishop of Chicago, was the first Pole appointed to the Roman Catholic hierarchy in the United States. For Polish nationalists, Rhode's elevation was the achievement of ethnic respectability, and for Polish religionists, recognition of their nationality by American Catholicism.

Rhode was born in Wejherowo, Poland, the son of August and Krystyna (Kirschbaum) Rhode. He came to the United States in 1880 with his widowed mother and attended Saint Stanislaus Kostka School in Chicago. He studied at Saint Mary's College in Kentucky, and Saint Ignatius College, in Chicago; completed his degree work at Saint Francis Seminary, in Wisconsin; and was ordained on 16 June 1894.

In 1895, Rhode was appointed pastor of Saint Adalbert Parish in Chicago. He then established Saints Peter and Paul Church and, from 1897 to 1915, was pastor in another Chicago parish, Saint Michael the Archangel, to which many steelworkers belonged. He was a talented administrator and built a new church and convent. Modest and quiet, Rhode was popular among his confreres, and when Archbishop James M. Quigley asked his diocesan Polish priests to nominate a candidate for auxiliary bishop, they chose Rhode.

At the time, Polish immigrants were approximately 8 percent of the Roman Catholics in the United States, but there was no Pole in this Catholic hierarchy. Nationalist leaders felt that the Irish-dominated hierarchy discriminated against Poles and wanted to Americanize them and denationalize their community. Reverend Wacław Kruszka pleaded the Polish case in Rome, urging "equality"—the appointment of Poles as bishops. The establishment of the schismatic Polish National Catholic church in 1904 added urgency to the matter.

Rhode's consecration as bishop on 28 July 1908 was a landmark in Polish-American history, best expressed by the headline in *Dziennik Chicagoski* (Chicago daily), *Habemus Episcopum* (We have a bishop). An estimated 200,000 people celebrated the event. The Poles were joined by archbishops and bishops and by Poles from throughout the United States and representatives of other nationalities.

As auxiliary bishop, Rhode mobilized the Polish clergy to raise contributions for an orphanage, a hospital, and a home for the aged and, in 1912, helped organize the Union of Polish Clergy in America. Nonetheless, Rhode considered himself the leader of all Polish Catholics in the United States, and the Bishop Wanderer traveled widely. Poles who had abandoned Rome often returned after Rhode's appearance. Faith and Polishness were integral for Rhode, whose support for Polish independence lessened tensions between immigrant nationalists and religionists. He helped lay the organizational foundation for support for the Polish cause during World War I. He also traveled to Rome *ad limina* in 1919 (the obligatory journey that bishops make to Rome every five years), encouraged Pope Benedict XV to name more Polish bishops in the United States, and then traveled to Poland to visit his native home. Independent Poland decorated Rhode with the Polonia Restituta medal. In 1915 Rhode became the ordinary (head bishop) of Green Bay, Wisconsin, and led the diocese for thirty years, until his death in 1945.

Stanislaus A. Blejwas

REFERENCES

Green, Victor. *For God and Country. The Rise of Polish and Lithuanian Ethnic Consciousness in America,* Madison: State Historical Society of Wisconsin, 1957.

Haiman, Mieczysław. "J. E. Ks. Biskup Paweł P. Rhode, Jego Życie i Czyny" (His Excellency Reverend Bishop Paweł P. Rhode, His Life and Activity). *Przegląd Katolicki* (The Catholic Review) 9 (March–April 1934): 11, 14, 16, 18–27.

Kruszka, X. Wacław. *Siedem Siedmiolecie czyli pół wieku życia* (Seventy-Seven years, or Half a Century of Life). Poznań: Drukarnia Św. Wojciecha, 2 vols., 1924.

Kuzniewski, Anthony J. *Faith and Fatherland. The Polish Church War in Wisconsin, 1896–1918,* Notre Dame, IN: University of Notre Dame Press, 1980.

"Odszedł Wódz Polonii Amerykańskiej po nagrodę wieczną" (The Leader of American Polonia Has Gone to His Eternal Reward). *Naród Polski* (Polish Nation), 15 March 1945.

Parot, Joseph John. *Polish Catholics in Chicago, 1850–1920.* De Kalb: Northern Illinois University Press, 1981.

"Rhode, Paul Peter." In *Who's Who in Polish America,* edited by the Reverend Francis Bolek, 375. New York: Harbinger House, 1943.

Riis, Jacob August (1849–1914)
Urban reformer, author, photographer, and lecturer
Danish

No individual in American history did more than Jacob Riis to expose the wretched living conditions of the poor in the nation's cities in the late nineteenth and early twentieth centuries. *How the Other Half Lives* (1890) is still widely read, and his use of photographs to record the blight of tenement life is recognized today as a pioneering step in the evolution of photojournalism.

Riis was born in the ancient Danish town of Ribe, the third of Carolina and Niels Riis's fourteen children. His father, a poor but respectable schoolteacher, hoped that Jacob would seek a literary education, but instead he chose to become a carpenter. Depressed economic conditions and a rejected marriage proposal led to Riis's decision in 1870 to leave for the United States.

For three years he wandered across the eastern part of the country, working at menial jobs and often without money, food, or lodging. Eventually, he found employment as a newspaper reporter. With some measure of financial security, he wrote to Elisabeth Nielsen, who had spurned him, and asked her to marry him. She accepted, and they were married in 1876. After writing for several New York papers, he was hired as a police reporter first for the *Tribune* (1877–1888) and then the *Evening Sun* (1888–1899). Riis was assigned to a press office just across the street from police headquarters on Mulberry Street, but it was in the surrounding tenement district of New York's Lower East Side that, as he wrote, "I was to find my lifework."

For the next two decades he wrote and lectured about the life of the urban poor, constantly reminding his largely middle-class audiences that their squalid conditions contradicted the American vision of progress, prosperity, and justice. In an effort to expose the miserable existence of many slum dwellers, Riis used photography, especially the "flash gun," to record life inside dark tenements and alleyways. A lengthy article with nineteen photos in the influential magazine *Scribner's* led to publication of *How the Other Half Lives* in 1890. The book was an instant success and went through several printings, making Riis a national figure. Many illustrated books and lectures followed, as did a growing friendship with a young politician named Theodore Roosevelt. Although Roosevelt, as

New York City police commissioner, governor of New York, and then president of the United States, offered Riis many appointments, Riis was content to use his pen, camera, and voice in the struggle to improve the lot of the other half. His work helped spark crusades for tenement reform, child labor laws, public parks, better schools, and humane treatment of the disadvantaged by the police and others.

Riis also maintained his ties with Denmark, frequently visiting his hometown of Ribe and even writing a history of it. Nevertheless, he became a U.S. citizen in 1895 and was widely praised as an "ideal" American. His autobiography, *The Making of an American* (1901), went through several editions. At the time of Riis's death a reporter described him as "the finest immigrant that we have ever known."

Peter L. Petersen

REFERENCES

Alland, Alexander, Sr. *Jacob A. Riis: Photographer and Citizen.* Millerston, NY: Aperture, 1974.

Fried, Lewis, and John Fierst. *Jacob A. Riis: A Reference Guide.* Boston: G. K. Hall, 1977.

Lane, James B. *Jacob A. Riis and the American City.* Port Washington, NY: Kennikat Press, 1974.

Meyer, Edith Patterson. *"Not Charity But Justice": The Story of Jacob A. Riis.* New York: Vanguard Press, 1974.

Riis, Jacob A. *How the Other Half Lives.* Edited with an introduction by David Leviatin. Boston: Bedford Books, 1996.

———. *The Making of an American.* Edited with an introduction by Roy Lubove. New York: Harper & Row, 1966.

Ware, Louise. *Jacob A. Riis: Police Reporter and Useful Citizen.* New York: Appleton-Century, 1938.

Robel, John M. "Jolly Jack" (1903–1968)

Musician and band leader
Slovak-American

A well-known band leader, "Jolly Jack" Robel, helped make polka music part of the U.S. national culture in the 1930s and 1940s. Credited with arranging the extraordinarily popular version of "Beer Barrel Polka," Robel enjoyed recognition in both mainstream and ethnic America. Between 1936 and 1941, his orchestra recorded forty-nine tunes for Decca Recording Company.

Born in 1903 in Austria of Slovak parentage, Robel immigrated to the United States at a young age with his family. They settled in Bethlehem, Pennsylvania. He lived there until the mid-1920s, when he moved to Shenandoah, a Pennsylvania coal-mining town, and became a clerk in a music store, a job that apparently energized his interest in music. Robel learned the clarinet and started his musical career with local bands. When he laughed off a "friendly scuffle" with a fellow musician, his adversary allegedly described Robel as a "jolly fellow," a remark that created his lasting identity as "Jolly Jack."

In the early 1930s Robel formed his own band and played regularly scheduled "hours" on local radio. Performing a mix of American and ethnic tunes, especially polkas, his band quickly gained popularity. By 1936 the band had caught the attention of Decca, which invited Robel to record on its label. Seven of the eleven recordings made at the first session were polkas, melodies that reflected Robel's ethnic heritage and that had nurtured the band's appeal among audiences in eastern Pennsylvania. A 1939 set by the Jolly Jack Orchestra included "Beer Barrel Polka," a melody that brought the orchestra widespread fame.

Even though the orchestra and its leader gained national recognition, they remained in eastern Pennsylvania. In 1937 the group began performing in regional ballrooms and, over the next two decades, continually attracted large crowds. Assisting government endeavors to bolster morale during World War II, Robel's orchestra went on tour, playing in locales with concentrations of military personnel. Robel also coproduced a popular polka radio series distributed to U.S. forces overseas.

The broad appeal of the orchestra's polka melodies accounted for its regional and national successes, but "Jolly Jack's" joviality and "good humor in front of the band" were signature characteristics contributing to its popularity. In 1950, the Universal Motion Picture

Company put national attention on Robel, the jocular band leader. Promoting its new release, *Harvey,* the studio sought a real-life person who exemplified the movie's central character, a performer who enjoyed spreading happiness. It selected Robel to receive the Harvey Happiness Award. Robel continued playing ballrooms in eastern Pennsylvania and on local radio until he retired in the late 1950s. He died in 1968 and, in 1987, was inducted into the Polka Music Hall of Fame.

Although he served one year (1931) as president of the Shenandoah branch of a Slovak Catholic fraternal, there is scant information concerning Robel's ethnic consciousness or involvement in the Slovak community. His music, however, was an outgrowth of his ethnic heritage and of the Slavic culture where he lived. It was this heritage that ultimately led to "Jolly Jack" Robel's success in ethnic and mainstream America.

June G. Alexander

REFERENCES

Greene, Victor. Interview by author, December 30, 1999.

———. *A Passion for Polka: Old-Time Ethnic Music in America.* Berkeley: University of California Press, 1992.

Jednota (The union). March 1930–April 1932.

"'Jolly Jack' Provided Plenty of Fodder for the Newspaper." *Evening Herald* (Shenandoah), 4 July 1987.

"'Jolly Jack' Robel to be Feted." *Evening Herald* (Shenandoah), 4 July 1987.

Spottswood, Richard K. *Ethnic Music on Records: A Discography of Ethnic Recordings.* Vol. 5. Urbana: University of Illinois Press, 1990.

Robert, Adolphe (né Louis-Adolphe) (1886–1966), and Robert, Gérald-Jacques (1910–1999)

Journalist and community activist; journalist, musician, and community activist French Canadian and Franco-American, respectively

As officers of the Association Canado-Américaine (ACA), a New England and Quebec-wide fraternal life insurance society, and as editors of its publication, *Le Canado-Américain,*

Adolphe Robert and his son Gérald Robert worked toward the financial protection of French-speaking families throughout their region of North America. The various other activities of father and son similarly contributed to the linguistic and cultural advancement of their compatriots.

The son of a farming family, Louis-Adolphe Robert was born on 26 August 1886 in the village of Sainte-Elisabeth, Joliette County, Quebec. His distaste for farmwork led him to pursue a classical education at the Collège de Joliette, where he engaged in his passion for reading and writing. Immediately after his graduation in 1907, he followed the wave of migration to New England's industrial centers. In Woonsocket, Rhode Island, he obtained a position as sales representative and eventually a reporter for the French-language daily *La Tribune.* The following year an offer from the ACA to assume the editorship of *Le Canado-Américain* led him to Manchester, New Hampshire. He did, however, return to Woonsocket in 1909 to marry Azélie Asselin, whom he had known in his youth and with whom he subsequently had three children.

With the exception of the years 1913 through 1916, during which he worked for two other publications, Adolphe Robert would spend the rest of his life in Manchester as editor of *Le Canado-Américain.* Over the years, he gradually broadened the scope of the newspaper by including, in addition to news items that pertained to the ACA and its members, historical and contemporary articles, cultural features, poetry, and other writings by authors from New England, Quebec, and elsewhere that informed and entertained the region's French-speaking population.

Besides his newspaper work, Robert also became more involved with the insurance side of the ACA. In 1920, he was elected secretary-general and, in 1936, succeeded Elphège J. Daignault, becoming the ACA's fourth president. He occupied the post for the next twenty years and continued to promote the economic, social, and cultural well-being of the ACA's members through his writings and speeches. When the ACA celebrated its fiftieth anniversary in 1946, he wrote a history of the society. During his tenure, his reputation as a defender of the French language in North America won him honorary doctorates from l'Université Laval in Quebec City and l'Université de Montréal. Foreign governments recognized his achievements in various ways, including France's making him a Chevalier of the Légion d'Honneur (1937) and *officier* (1951). In 1956, Robert retired from the presidency of the ACA but continued to edit *Le Canado-Américain,* which, in 1958, he transformed into a cultural magazine upon which he worked until his death. In his final year, the Vatican inducted him into the Order of the Knights of St. Gregory, and the Conseil de la Vie française en Amérique, in Quebec City, awarded him its Prix Samuel de Champlain for his autobiography, *Souvenirs et portraits.* Adolphe Robert died on 9 May 1966.

The eldest of Adolphe Robert's three children, Gérald-Jacques, was born in Manchester, New Hampshire, on 28 July 1910. Early on, he developed a love of music. After his graduation from his father's alma mater, the Collège de Joliette, he studied piano, organ, and voice at the Conservatoire national de Montréal, followed by courses in conducting choirs and symphonies at the New England Conservatory of Music in Boston and private lessons in Gregorian chant. For several decades, beginning in 1929, the younger Robert served alternately as organist, choir member, or choir master in several of Manchester's French-language parishes and founded and directed a variety of vocal and instrumental groups, a few of which performed in French-speaking areas throughout New England and French Canada. Likewise, for around thirty years, beginning in the 1940s, he entertained French-speaking radio audiences, first as host of the musical portion of *L'Heure française* on WFEA and later as host of his own classical music and discussion program, *Radio-Franco,* on WMUR/WGIR.

Through his contacts in the musical world, Gérald met and in 1943 married Alice Long-

val, an organist, pianist, and singer and, the year after her death in 1954, wed her sister, Rachel Longval. Both women worked actively throughout New England in Franco-American women's organizations. Neither had any children.

Gérald Robert followed in his father's footsteps as both journalist and mutualist. From 1937 to 1943, he worked as a reporter for Manchester's daily, *L'Avenir National.* When it ceased publication in 1949, he occasionally contributed pieces to its successor, the weekly *L'Action,* until its demise in 1971. However, from 1943 until his retirement, Robert devoted most of his time and energy to the ACA, working his way up to secretary-general by 1956. In 1965, he became the society's seventh president. Upon the death of his father the following year, he succeeded him as editor of *Le Canado-Américain.* Similarly, when the ACA celebrated its seventy-fifth anniversary, he compiled a sequel to his father's history, *Mémorial II des Actes de l'Association Canado-Américaine, 1946–1971.* Upon his retirement from both the ACA presidency and the editorship of *Le Canado-Américain* in 1980, Robert spent his final years engaging in his two passions, music and writing, as well as cofounding a choral group that performed in New England and researching a history of the nation's oldest credit union, La Caisse Populaire Sainte-Marie, founded in Manchester in 1908 and for which he had served as secretary of the board for twenty-five years. Gérald Robert died on 1 March 1999, at the age of eighty-eight.

Both Adolphe Robert and Gérald Robert were highly respected in the New England Franco-American community, though, as sometimes happens, the father outshone his son. Adolphe received numerous awards and was a much-sought-after public speaker and writer, and his son struggled to follow in his father's footsteps. Although a born musician, he pursued music as an avocation rather than as a career. Those who knew and admired him believe that had he regarded his music as a full-time profession, he would have made a far greater contribution toward the advancement of Franco-American culture.

Robert B. Perreault

REFERENCES

"Adolphe Robert." In *Littérature franco-américaine de la Nouvelle-Angleterre: Anthologie* (Franco-American literature of New England: Anthology), vol. 8, edited by Richard Santerre, 292–341. Manchester: National Materials Development Center for French and Creole, 1981.

Belleau, Massue. "Les Francos." *Le Magazine Maclean* (Montréal), 4 (February 1964): 19–21, 32–36.

Dion-Lévesque, Rosaire. "M. Adolphe Robert." In *Silhouettes franco-américaines,* 768–775. Manchester, NH: Publications de Association Canado-Américaine, 1957.

———. "Gérald-Jacques Robert." In *Silhouettes franco-américaines,* 775–778. Manchester, NH: Publications de Association Canado-Américaine, 1957.

Le Canado-Américain 4.10 (April-June, 1966): 2–8 (Special commemorative section on Adolphe Robert).

Le Canado-Américain 25.3 (Summer 1999): 6–7 (Special commemorative section on Gérald Robert).

Perreault, Robert B. "Présidents ACA—ACA Presidents—Portraits: Adolphe Robert 1886–1966." *Le Canado-Américain* 7.4 (October-December 1981): 14, 25 (Bilingual).

Robert, Adolphe. *Le Canado-Américain,* 1908–1913; 1916–66. Includes articles signed "Adolphe Robert," "A.R.," and "Le Mohican."

Robert, Adolphe, ed. *Les Franco-Américains peints par eux-mêmes* (Self-Portraits of Franco-Americans). Montréal: Editions Albert Lévesque, 1936.

———. *Mémorial des Actes de l'Association Canado-Américaine.* Manchester, NH: L'Avenir National, 1946.

Robert, Gérald-Jacques, *Le Canado-Américain,* 1966–1980.

———. *Mémorial II des Actes de l'Association Canado-Américaine 1946–1971.* Manchester, NH: Ballard Bros., 1975.

Roberts, Margaret E. (née Margaret Evans) (1833–c. 1911)

Lecturer, writer, and temperance activist
Welsh

From lowly origins, Margaret Evans Roberts rose to literary and intellectual eminence among her ethnic peers and successfully over-came prevailing gender assumptions regarding the place of women in society. She was widely regarded as one of the most gifted Welsh writers in the United States and Wales of her time.

Roberts (whose maiden name was Evans) was born in Carmarthenshire, South Wales, in 1833. Early on, she developed a love of reading and soon earned a reputation as a dedicated member of her Calvinistic Methodist Nonconformist church. In 1853, she married William Roberts, a local man, and after running a business for eight years, they immigrated to the United States. For twenty years they farmed at Old Man's Creek, Iowa. Then, because of her husband's ill health, they moved to Iowa City and then to Scranton, Pennsylvania, in 1881, where she established a successful bookstore. In 1907, widowed, she returned to Iowa but lived for periods in Wales and Scranton. She had no children.

Despite receiving barely any education when young, from her thirties on, Roberts became a devoted, self-taught student of new theories in philosophy and science. She embraced the theory of evolution, adapting her religious beliefs accordingly. In Iowa City she attended university lectures and, in 1882, was awarded the diploma of the American Institute of Phrenology. Roberts would thereafter lecture widely on these subjects in Iowa, Pennsylvania, and Wales and taught very popular phrenology classes.

Roberts became most widely known as a prodigious and extremely lucid and cogent writer. Up to 1911 she wrote literally hundreds of Welsh-language articles, especially for the premier Welsh-language Welsh-American newspaper, *Y Drych* (The mirror). The range of subjects she wrote on is dazzling, including religion, geology, astronomy, current affairs, and travel. In addition, in 1875 she had joined the Women's Christian Temperance Union and, throughout her life, she was a dedicated contributor of articles in support of temperance. Also close to her heart was feminism. "The role of defending the rights of the female sex among the Welsh in this country has been left almost exclusively to me. I choose to magnify this privilege," she wrote in 1894. Her campaigning for, and defense of, the rights of women sometimes earned her derision and criticism in the pages of *Y Drych*. However, her formidable debating skills, in print and on the platform, usually ensured that she got the better of her opponents.

In early 1911, her eyesight having failed, she returned to Wales, but so complete was her subsequent disappearance from public life that neither the date nor the place of her death is known. Yet in her time she was regarded as the most eminent female writer in the Welsh language in the United States, lauded by fellow writers, and her visits and tours were regularly reported in *Y Drych*. It was also believed that her writings were admired by thousands, especially for her dedicated service to her ethnic group and, above all, her bravery in challenging entrenched orthodoxies and promoting new ideas in the fields of feminism and science.

Bill Jones

REFERENCES

Jones, W. R. "Swyddogaeth Dynes" (The role of women). *Y Drych* [The mirror], *The American Organ of the Welsh People*, 4 January 1894, 1.

"Mrs. Margaret E. Roberts, Scranton Pa." *Cambrian* (Utica, NY), 22.12 (December 1902): 419–421.

"Mrs. Margaret E. Roberts." *Y Drych* [The mirror]: *The American Organ of the Welsh People*, 24 October 1907, 1.

Roberts, Margaret E. "Llith o Hirwaun, De Cymru" (Letter from Hirwaun, South Wales). *Y Drych* [The mirror], *The American Organ of the Welsh People*, 2 March 1911, 6.

———. "Merched yn y Pwlpud" (Women in the pulpit). *Y Drych* [The mirror], *The American Organ of the Welsh People*, 4 January 1894, 2.

Robeson, Paul (1898–1976)
Athlete, scholar, actor, and singer
African American

A prize-winning athlete, scholar, singer, and actor, Paul Robeson was one of the most versatile figures of the twentieth century. Having achieved great renown, he paid dearly for his willingness to speak forthrightly on political and racial issues.

Robeson was born on 9 April 1898 in Princeton, New Jersey. His mother, a teacher, died when he was six. His father, a minister and ex-slave who later completed degrees in theology, was an outspoken civil rights advocate forced out of his position and compelled to moved as he sought jobs at various churches. Finally, the family settled in Somerville, New Jersey. In 1915, Robeson won a four-year scholarship to Rutgers University. An excellent student, he was also a football All-American, eventually winning fifteen varsity letters. In 1919, he was valedictorian of his class.

Robeson entered Columbia University Law School in 1920, financing his education by tutoring Latin and playing professional football. That year he met and married Eslanda Goode. She convinced him to accept the lead role in a Harlem YMCA production, launching his acting career. Completing his law degree, he was hired by a prestigious law firm, only to resign after his secretary refused to take dictation. He turned full-time to acting, appearing in Eugene O'Neill's *All God's Chillun Got Wings* and in *The Emperor Jones*. His singing voice was first heard publicly in a concert in 1924, and shortly afterward he became more famous as a singer than as an actor.

By 1928, Robeson had become an established performer in both theater and music. That year he played Joe in the musical *Showboat,* singing "Old Man River." He tackled the lead role in Shakespeare's *Othello* and tried motion pictures in 1933, with the movie version of *The Emperor Jones.*

In the meantime, Robeson's political views were maturing. After a trip to the Soviet Union in 1936, he began to reject stereotyped roles and to devote himself to projecting positive images of blacks. Supporting African self-rule and opposing the spread of fascism in Spain, he paid a heavy price when, in 1941, the Federal Bureau of Investigation (FBI) placed him under surveillance. FBI investigations increased as he led protests and demonstrations against lynching, supported a strike by autoworkers, and advocated aid for the Soviet Union and China against German and Japanese invaders. Later, with the Cold War on, Robeson became a major target of the House Un-American Activities Committee (HUAC). His passport was revoked, and he faced a steep decline in concert dates.

The 1950s were years of political and, eventually, physical exile. His travel was restricted, and recording companies blacklisted him. In 1956, Robeson castigated the HUAC as "the true un-Americans." Restrictions on his travel were lifted in 1958, but years of strain had affected his health. He suffered a series of breakdowns but continued his performances and activism until the early 1960s.

Finally, in 1966, Robeson's failing health and the death of his wife brought him back to the United States from England, where he had been living. Honors and awards for his service and courage had come from nations around the globe, and his death on January 23, 1976, generated numerous eulogies. Nevertheless, his name had been removed from the College Football Hall of Fame and has not been restored.

Emory Tolbert

REFERENCES

Robeson, Paul. *Here I Stand.* New Introduction by Sterling Stuckey. London: D. Dobson, 1958; Boston: Beacon Press, 1988.

———. *Paul Robeson: Here I Stand.* A coproduction of Thirteen/WNET and Menair Media International. New York: WinStar Home Entertainment; Fox Lorber Home Video, 1999.

———. *Paul Robeson Speaks: Writings, Speeches, Interviews, 1918–1974.* Edited by Philip S. Foner. New York: Brunner/Mazel, 1978.

Rock, Howard (Siqvoan Weyahok) (1911–1976)

Artist, journalist, and community activist
Alaska Native (Inupiaq)

At Point Hope, a village in northeastern Alaska, Inupiaq people follow lifeways shaped by the currents of the Chukchi Sea. There, Howard Rock (Siqvoan Weyahok) learned that the preservation of Native lands and cultures called for the best efforts of all members of the community. He used his talents as an artist, activist, and journalist in service to all Alaska Natives.

Rock was born in 1911. Following Inupiaq traditions, his father, Weyahok, hunted and his mother, Keshorna (Emma Rock), managed the family of eight children. Rock learned to hunt and work with dog teams in the Point Hope region. He also learned the songs and stories of his people from village elders. After a few years at an Episcopalian mission school, he moved on to a Bureau of Indian Affairs vocational school, discovering his artistic talents. He honed them at the University of Washington in the 1930s.

Rock stayed in Seattle during the 1940s and 1950s, returning after a stint in North Africa with the air force during World War II and resuming his career as a sculptor and jewelry designer. But in the early 1960s he decided to return to Alaska. He arrived just in time, for the Inupiaq were fighting federal attempts to "help" them by using atomic bombs to blast a deep-water harbor there. Characterized as a peacetime use of atomic power, Project Chariot threatened the environmental integrity of the region and jeopardized Inupiaq culture. The Point Hope elders formed Inupiaq Paitot, the People's Heritage, to oppose this plan and quickly drafted Rock to write the organization's newsletter.

The Inupiaq won the battle, in large part owing to Rock's journalistic skills. In 1962, the small community newsletter expanded into the *Tundra Times,* the first statewide Alaska Native publication and a pioneer in mass communications among the state's Native population. With it, Rock organized opposition to the flooding of Athabaskan hunting lands with the Rampart Dam, fought the state's claim to Alaska Native lands, and exposed the exploitation of Native seal hunters working for the U.S. government.

Using the newspaper as a political springboard, Rock helped organize the Alaska Federation of Natives (AFN) in 1966. He and the AFN pushed aggressively for a resolution of pending land claims cases. A staunch supporter of the Alaska Native Claims Settlement Act (ANCSA), he believed that the controversial act offered Natives a unique opportunity to strengthen their self-determination and protect self-government. He frequently wrote editorials reminding Native leaders that the passage of the act in 1971 gave them the chance to "do more for the good of the people today and of those of tomorrow."

Until his death in 1976, Rock continued to edit the *Tundra Times,* tirelessly working on behalf of Alaska Natives. After his death, the Anchorage Museum of History and Art claimed his Royal Standard typewriter for permanent display. It is a small, but fitting, monument to a man of great and lasting influence.

Lisa E. Emmerich

REFERENCES

Coates, Peter, 1989. "Project Chariot: Alaskan Roots of Environmentalism." *Alaska History Magazine* 4.2 (Fall 1989).

Fogarino, Shirley. "Rock, Howard (Siqvoan Weyahok)." In *Biographical Dictionary of American Journalism,* edited by Joseph P. McKerns, 599–600. New York: Greenwood Press, 1989.

"Howard Rock." In *The Native North American Almanac,* edited by Duane Champagne, 1146–1147. Detroit: Gale Research, 1994.

Magraw, Katherine. "Teller and the 'Clean Bomb' Episode." *Bulletin of the Atomic Scientists* 44 (May 1988): 32–37.

Morgan, Lael. *Art and Eskimo Power: The Life and Times of Alaskan Howard Rock.* Fairbanks, AK: Epicenter Press, 1992.

O'Neill, Dan. "Project Chariot: How Alaska Escaped Nuclear Excavation." *Bulletin of the Atomic Scientists* 45 (December 1989): 28–37.

Skinner, Ramona Ellen. *Alaska Native Policy in the Twentieth Century.* New York: Garland Publishing, 1997.

"Voice of Native Alaska Speaks Again." *Anchorage Daily News,* 21 January 1993.

Roebling, John Augustus (1806–1869)

Engineer and bridge builder
German

John A. Roebling is most famous as the designer of the Brooklyn Bridge. Having brought his engineering skills from his native Germany, he became one of the pioneers of the engineering profession in the United States.

Born in Saxony of middle-class background, Roebling studied engineering at the Royal Polytechnic Institute in Berlin. His studies in architecture, bridge building, and hydraulics proved to be of great importance to his career in the United States. In 1831 he emigrated as leader of a group from his native town of Mühlhausen. The group was bent upon establishing an agricultural community near Pittsburgh; they named the community Saxonburg.

Tiring of agricultural life, Roebling found employment with the State of Pennsylvania as surveyor and engineer. He soon became involved with the expanding canal network. Having read in a German engineering journal of the possibilities of cables made from twisted wire, he introduced their use on the canal system to replace the heavy hemp ropes used to pull canal boats over inclined planes. He first used them in 1841–1842 on the Allegheny Portage Railroad, connecting the canal systems of eastern and western Pennsylvania by way of an inclined plane over the mountains.

In 1842 he established his own company, John A. Roebling and Sons, to make the wire cable; in 1848 he relocated the company to Trenton, New Jersey. In 1844 he designed his first suspension bridge, an aqueduct that carried a canal over the Allegheny River. Having proved the feasibility of the technique, he built many wire-suspended canal aqueducts in the late 1840s.

The versatility and capabilities of the twisted-wire cables led Roebling to innovations in the designs of other suspension bridges. In 1851 he began construction of a bridge across the Niagara River, below Niagara Falls, introducing a stiffening truss below the roadway to minimize swaying and vibration, allowing the bridge to carry both carriage and railroad traffic. This success led to bridges across the Allegheny River at Pittsburgh and across the Ohio River at Cincinnati. When the Cincinnati bridge opened in 1867, it was the longest suspension span in the world.

In 1867 the New York legislature issued a

company charter to build a bridge across the East River, connecting Manhattan and Brooklyn. Roebling, who was famous for his bridge-building expertise, was hired to design and build the bridge. His daring plan was for a main span 1,595 feet in length, a new world record, suspended by cables from towers 273 feet high, which would be the tallest structures in the United States. The bridge towers were to be sunk into bedrock and steel-wire cables would replace the conventional iron in his design.

However, in the summer of 1869, while Roebling was on the site of one of his bridge towers, a ferryboat struck the dock where he was standing and crushed his foot between two timbers. He died of tetanus two weeks later. His son Washington Roebling supervised the bridge construction until its opening in 1883.

John A. Roebling had come to the United States in an era of technological revolution and helped to shape that development by applying knowledge brought from the engineering profession in Germany. The many German Americans in the engineering profession recognized him as foremost among them, and their pride was shared by German Americans in general.

James M. Bergquist

REFERENCES

Brown, Frances Williamson. "When They Built the Big Bridge." *American Heritage* 7.2 (1956): 68–73, 110–112.

John A. Roebling's Sons Company On-Line History Archive: www.inventionfactory.com/history/main.html (accessed 27 June 2000).

McCullough, David. *The Great Bridge.* New York: Simon & Schuster, 1972.

Steinman, D. B. *The Builders of the Bridge: The Story of John Roebling and His Son.* New York: Harcourt, Brace, 1945.

Trachtenberg, Alan. *Brooklyn Bridge: Fact and Symbol.* New York: Oxford University Press, 1965.

Rogers, Will (1879–1935)

Film star and entertainer
Native American (Cherokee)

William "Will" Penn Adair Rogers, the Cherokee performer who "never met a man he didn't like," brought a uniquely Western presence to American popular culture. Until his untimely death in 1935, Rogers personified the amiable cowboy who could spin a humorous yarn as quickly as he could spin his lasso.

Born 4 November 1879, in Oolagah, Indian Territory, Rogers was one of eight children of Clement Vann Rogers and Mary America Schrimsher. His father, a former Confederate Army officer, was a rancher prominent in Oklahoma tribal politics. Will Rogers felt great pride in his Cherokee heritage, boasting, "My people didn't come on the *Mayflower* but they met the boat."

Rogers was a restless scholar who bounced from school to school before leaving formal education behind in his late teens. While managing his father's ranch, he began to perfect his fancy roping techniques. His remarkable ability served him well, for it got him out of Oklahoma and into an entertainment career. He left the United States in 1901 and wound up performing as the "Cherokee Kid" in South Africa. This stage name, and the reputation that he could "lasso the tail off a blowfly," stayed with him for the rest of his career.

Rogers returned home in 1903 and moved to New York City. In 1905, he broke into vaudeville at Hammerstein's Roof Garden. During the next decade, his act was successful enough that he could marry his childhood sweetheart, Betty Blake, and begin a family. It was Betty Blake Rogers who inspired her husband to add some commentary on the events of the day to his rope tricks. A brief series of anecdotes, always preceded by the line "Well, all I know is what I read in the papers," ultimately blossomed into a syndicated newspaper column, a syndicated radio broadcast, and a string of books with such engaging titles as *The Illiterate Digest.*

Rogers and his family left New York in the early 1920s for Hollywood. There, he appeared in seventeen motion pictures and became one of the highest paid actors of his era. Rogers's folksy, engaging style and gently barbed wit made him America's favorite movie star cum pundit. Prior to the 1928 election, *Life,* a humor magazine, talked him into running for president as the Anti-Bunk Party's nominee. Rogers's party platform was succinct: "Whatever the other fellow don't do, we will."

For all his fame and wealth, Will Rogers had a keen understanding of the plight of those in need, especially farmers and the unemployed. At the start of his career, he was a generous supporter of the American Red Cross. In later years, he regularly performed benefits for relief and charitable organizations. Charity was one of the constants in his life.

Another constant was his love of travel and airplanes. In 1935, he joined world-renowned aviator Wiley Post for a "vacation" to the Soviet Union. Their plane crashed off Point Barrow, Alaska, on 15 August 1935, killing both. Rogers was fifty-six years old. One of his favorite sayings was: "Everybody is ignorant. Only on different subjects."

Lisa E. Emmerich

REFERENCES
Alworth, E. Paul. *Will Rogers.* Boston: Twayne Publishers, 1974.
Robinson, Ray. *American Original: A Life of Will Rogers.* New York: Oxford University Press, 1996.
Sterling, Bryan B. *Will Rogers and Wiley Post: Death at Barrow.* New York: M. Evans & Co., 1993.
———. *The Will Rogers Scrapbook.* New York: Grosset & Dunlap, 1976.
Yagoda, Ben. *Will Rogers: A Biography.* New York: Alfred A. Knopf, 1993.

Rohani, Shardad (1954–)

Conductor, composer, and writer
Iranian

Shardad Rohani has achieved renown as a composer and conductor. He performs in Asia, Europe, and the United States.

Rohani was born in Tehran to a musical family; his father played the violin and his mother the tar, a Persian lute. Like his brothers, he started playing the piano when he was six and, at age ten, took up the violin also. By sixteen, he was ready for his conducting debut. In 1974, he graduated from the Tehran Conservatory and received a full scholarship

to study composition and conducting at the Vienna Music Academy and Conservatory. He received many awards and scholarships, such as a scholarship in 1981 given by th Austrian society for composers and authors. The following year, he graduated from the Vienna Academy.

In 1984, Rohani moved to Los Angeles to study the art of film music at UCLA and once again received many prestigious awards, including the Jerry Fielding Award for film composers. In 1987, he became the music director and conductor for the Committee of the Arts (COTA) Symphony Orchestra in Los Angeles, a position he held until 1991. He has conducted as well as had his works performed by symphony orchestras in Europe and the United States and has also guest conducted with many world-class ensembles, among them the London Royal Philharmonic Orchestra. Given his considerable traditional classical talent, Rohani has been commissioned to record classical masterpieces by the Viennese label Koch Discover International, under the title "Musica per Tutti." He also conducted an open-air concert with the London Philharmonic Orchestra at the Parthenon, in Athens, Greece, one of the most widely viewed programs on U.S. public television.

A U.S. citizen since 1994, Rohani continues to compose and arrange music interspersed with Middle Eastern melodies, Persian tribal and instrumental rhythms, as well as classical, contemporary, and jazz modes. His albums *Eternity* and *Beauty of Love* provide listeners a showcase of his multiple talents and creativity. He says: "Middle Eastern music is in my blood. I really didn't need to study it, but I did of course." To many, he is best known for his collaboration with Yanni. He supplemented Yanni's keyboard compositions with arrangements for a sixty-piece orchestra and also arranged, conducted, and played violin on all but two tracks of Yanni's top-ten performance album *Live at the Acropolis.*

In December 1998, Rohani was commissioned by the government of Thailand and the committee of the Thirteenth Asian Olympic

Games to compose the music for the opening ceremony. His composition was one of the most successful and popular songs of the games. He continues to be active in the international sphere and hopes to create more connections among Iranian musicians and composers of Iranian ancestry. Rohani currently resides in Los Angeles with his family and has been frequently interviewed on Iranian press and television there. He emphasizes in particular the impact of both Persian and Western classical music on his conducting, encourages young Iranians to learn their musical heritage as well as that of the West, and points out how together the two have enabled him to create music that is representative of both cultural experiences.

Arlene Dallalfar

REFERENCES

Grimes, P. J. "Man behind Yanni's Success Steps into the Limelight." *Beach News,* 2 June 1994.

Heckman, Don. "Yanni Gets Large Sound from Happy Band." *Los Angeles Times,* 23 May 1994.

"Music and Books." *Whole Life Times,* August 1994.

Rohani, Shardad. Interview by author, 10 December 1999.

Sultan, Jana. "Composer Conductor Performer Arranger Shardad Rohani." *Beirut Times,* 7–14 July 1994.

Rølvaag, Ole Edvart (1876–1931)

Professor and author
Norwegian

Ole Rølvaag wrote significant and riveting works depicting the struggles of newcomers in the United States. He was inspired by his immigrant experiences in the Upper Midwest.

The third of seven children born to Peder and Ellerine Rølvaag, Ole Edvart grew up in a fishing family near the Arctic Circle on an island that faces the sea and has towering mountains at its back. Finding Ole more fitted for the fisheries than schooling, his father ended his education when he was fourteen and made him a sailor and commercial fisherman. But his son dreamed of something more, and when a terrible storm at sea almost ended his life, he decided to wait no longer to

achieve his goals. Turning down the offer of his own boat and the hand of a local woman in 1896, he immigrated to South Dakota with money borrowed from an uncle there.

After three years' work as a farmhand, he had acquired enough English and funds to resume his education. He graduated first from a nearby Norwegian-American preparatory school, then from St. Olaf College, and finally from advanced studies at the University of Oslo. Along the way, he spent summers working as a country salesman and writing his first novel, *Nils and Astri,* about Norwegian-American life in the Upper Midwest.

On returning from Oslo, Rølvaag took a position as an instructor of Norwegian and natural sciences at St. Olaf College in 1906. Two years later, he acquired U.S. citizenship and married Jennie Berdahl, the daughter of a South Dakota pioneer family. After ten years at the college, he became the chair of its Norwegian Department, a position he kept until shortly before his death. His dedication to teaching resulted in the publication of several textbooks and fabled courses in Norwegian and Norwegian-American cultural history.

His literary career developed simultaneously. First came two novels in Norwegian under the pseudonym Paal Mørk, which means Paul Dark, and then two novels under his own name, *To Tullinger* (Two fools) in 1920, a critique of materialistic immigrants, and *Længselens Båt* (The boat of longing) in 1921, a portrait of the departure from northern Norway and of immigrant quarters and squandered human potential in south Minneapolis. A year later, Rølvaag published *Omkring Fædrearven* (Concerning our heritage), his culled and collected nonfiction pieces of the previous twenty years. They forcefully presented his conviction that only by preserving their ancestral heritage in the United States could Norwegian Americans both retain self-knowledge and enrich American culture. However, none of these first five books were published in Norway.

He then embarked on a trilogy. The first of his novels accepted for publication in Norway,

Giants in the Earth, had appeared there in 1924–1925 as *I De Dage* (In those days) and won high praise. Although two sequels to *Giants in the Earth* (U.S. publication, 1927) were translated as *Peder Victorious* (1929) and *Their Father's Gold* (1931) before Rølvaag's death, they never received the attention or critical praise in Norway or the United States that greeted the opening volume of the trilogy. *Giants,* the epic of homesteading on the frontier, became a classic of American literature, making Rølvaag one of the most famous of immigrant writers.

David C. Mauk

REFERENCES

Haugen, Einar. *Ole Edvart Rølvaag.* Boston: Twayne Publishers, 1983.

Øverland, Ørm. *The Western Home: A Literary History of Norwegian America.* Northfield, MN: Norwegian-American Historical Association, 1996.

Reigstad, Paul. *Rølvaag: His Life and Art.* Lincoln: University of Nebraska Press, 1972.

Thorson, Gerald, ed. *Ole Rølvaag: Artist and Cultural Leader.* Northfield, MN: Norwegian-American Historical Association, 1974.

Romagoza, Juan José (1951–)
Physician and community activist
Salvadoran

For more than a dozen years Juan Romagoza, a refugee from El Salvador, has run La Clinica del Pueblo (the people's clinic) in Washington, D.C., an organization that provides preventive and general health care to a predominantly Latina/o population. Previously, he had been a founding member and leader of the Sanctuary movement for Central American Refugees in San Francisco.

Born in August 1951, Romagoza is from Usulutan, El Salvador. In 1977, he was finishing his residency in medicine at the National University of El Salvador and had become involved with the Catholic church. He participated in priest-led missions to provide basic health care for the rural population. The war had not officially started, but Romagaza was shot, imprisoned, and tortured for his "suspicious" aid efforts. He left the country to es-

cape persecution, fleeing to Mexico, where he recovered from his wounds and helped establish a refugee clinic for Guatemalan and Salvadoran refugees in Cuernavaca. He arrived in Los Angeles in 1983.

In San Francisco he met other Central Americans with stories similar to his. When a group of refugees came together for resources and food at Holy Redeemer Church, an important component of the Sanctuary movement in San Francisco began, a solidarity movement of diverse peoples combining their resources to help refugees enter the United States. Romagoza gradually assumed leadership of the effort to organize the Central American refugees, holding meetings and helping establish an organization for the San Francisco chapter of the Committee of Central American Refugees (CRECE). As CRECE grew, it offered information about housing and community resources, legal referrals, and emotional support to refugees.

After overcoming his fear of deportation and political persecution, Romagoza became active in educating U.S. communities about the war in El Salvador. He gave public testimonials about his experiences and encouraged others to share their stories and speak out against war crimes in their countries. Romagoza also joined caravans traveling throughout the United States in order to drop off representatives of the Sanctuary movement in different cities. In 1986, many members of CRECE worked with other groups to form the San Francisco CARECEN (Central American Resource Center), as well as official places of Sanctuary in universities and Bay Area cities.

Romagoza traveled to Washington, D.C., initially to help with Sanctuary work there, then began volunteering at La Clinica del Pueblo. In San Francisco, he started a clinic modeled after the one in Washington. When he learned that the D.C. clinic was in danger of closing, he moved to Washington and, despite his training, supported himself through blue-collar jobs until 1989, when he was able at last to reestablish the clinic. At that point, he officially became the director, a salaried position. It presently has a staff of forty and offers a broad range of medical services.

Romagoza has received numerous awards in recognition of his work in preventive health care to the Latino community, including the La Raza Maclovio Baraza Leadership Award given by the National Council of La Raza, the Washington Hispanic Ringo Humanitarian Award, and the Carlos Rosario Public Service Award. He travels frequently to El Salvador in order not to neglect those who remained.

Leticia Hernández-Linares

REFERENCES

Acosta, Andrea. "Homenaje al Dr. Juan Romagoza." *El Pregonero,* 6 August 1996.

Barth, Dianne. "El Salvador Appeal: Refugees Bring Protest March through Town." *Lodi News-Sentinel,* 20 March 1986.

Constable, Pamela. "Health Worries Rising for D.C. Latinos." *Washington Post,* 14 October 1997.

Kirby, Brendan. "Survivor: Salvadoran Refugee will Spend Award on Clinic He Directed." *Rock Creek Current* 5.22 (29 May–11 June 1996).

Madden, Mike. "Ten Health-Care Pioneers Take a Bow." *USA Today,* 29 May 1996.

Penchaszadeh, Nicolas. "Refugee Center Assists Changing Latino Community." *American Observer* 2.13 (27 February 1997).

Romagoza, Juan, Dr. "En peligro el presupuesto de salud para los latinos del área Metropolitana" (Health proposal for Latinos in the metropolitan area is in danger). *La Nación,* 3 October 1997.

———. Interview by author, 17 January 2000.

Suro, Roberto. *Strangers among Us: Latino Lives in Changing America.* New York: Vintage, 1998.

Ross, John (1790–1866)
Diplomat, tribal chief, and merchant planter
Native American (Cherokee)

The three most important aims of the Cherokee Nation under the chieftainship of John Ross were to reassert their treaty-based sovereign status, preserve their tribal autonomy, and protect their tribal lands. The objectives of self-determination remained Ross's paramount concern throughout his tenure as principal chief (1828–1866).

Ross was descended from Scots traders and British loyalists allied with the Cherokee during and after the American Revolution. Since his great-grandmother was Cherokee, Ross was only one-eighth Cherokee, but kinship—not blood quantum—secured Cherokee identity. As a young man, Ross received a formal education, learned about the trading post business, and fought with Andrew Jackson in the War of 1812. Afterward he became a merchant, slave-owning planter, and operator of a ferry landing.

The United States pressed the Cherokee for more land. Trusting the protection of their treaties, Ross drafted the Cherokee National Constitution in 1827. The following year he was elected principal chief. At the same time, gold was discovered on Cherokee lands, Georgia was demanding sovereignty over all Indian land claims, and President Jackson introduced the Indian Removal Bill. One Cherokee political faction led by Major Ridge urged the tribe to accept Jackson's treaty terms. Ross believed that Cherokee territory and sovereignty were protected. The Cherokee did win recognition as being a distinct political community (1832), yet Ridge had been correct that Jackson would not abide by the U.S. Supreme Court decision affirming the Cherokee community. Ridge and his followers signed the Treaty of New Echota in 1835, agreeing to the removal of the Cherokee to Indian Territory (Oklahoma).

After the infamous "Trail of Tears," Ross and other leaders were faced with reconstituting the tribe, and Ross believed that new political strategies were needed in the face of changing policies and white land pressures. Ridge, his son, and his nephew were killed by followers of Ross, and a vicious cycle of murder and revenge took place from 1840 to 1846. Both factions claimed to be the legitimate government. Ross and the vast majority of the Cherokee believed that preserving their communal integrity was the key to Cherokee survival, and Ross was able to begin the process of reunification by drafting a new constitution, which lasted from 1839 until termination in 1898.

The period from 1846 to 1860 was an era of peace and relative prosperity, and Ross and other tribal leaders focused on economic, educational, and institutional measures to strengthen the nation. Unfortunately, the American Civil War broke out in 1861, and Cherokee tribal unity was victimized by the competing sovereignties. Ross, a slaveholder, wanted to remain neutral, but the council was forced to sign a treaty with the Confederacy. The majority of the Cherokee rallied to the Union cause, and Lincoln later assured Ross that the treaty would not be held against the Cherokee Nation. However, neither Ross nor Lincoln survived, and the Cherokees were again divided, and again splitting up was rejected by the dying Ross. Nevertheless, the Cherokee were forced to sign a new treaty eroding their sovereignty and opening their territory to railroads. The fact that the Cherokee were able to surmount so many crises and still prevail is a tribute to the persistence of Cherokee culture and the resilience of Chief John Ross.

John M. Shaw

REFERENCES

Anderson, William L., ed. *Cherokee Removal, Before and After.* Athens: University of Georgia Press, 1991.

King, Duane H. *The Cherokee Indian Nation: A Troubled History.* Knoxville: University of Tennessee Press, 1979.

McLoughlin, William G. *After the Trail of Tears: The Cherokees Struggle for Sovereignty, 1840–1880.* Chapel Hill: University of North Carolina Press, 1993.

———. *Cherokee Renascence in the New Republic.* Princeton, NJ: Princeton University Press, 1986.

Moulton, Gary E. *John Ross: Cherokee Chief.* Athens: University of Georgia Press, 1978.

Wahrhaftig, Albert L. "Renaissance and Repression: The Oklahoma Cherokee." *Trans-Action* 6.4 (1969): 42–48.

Woodward, Grace Steele. *The Cherokees.* Norman: University of Oklahoma Press, 1963.

Rossides, Eugene Telemachus (1927–)

Lawyer, government official, and community activist
Cypriot-American

Eugene Rossides, a second-generation Cypriot American, has, throughout his long and distinguished career as a lawyer, held a variety of official positions in New York City, New York State, and Washington, D.C. He has been extremely active in the promotion of Cypriot and Hellenic causes in the United States and has played a prominent role in a number of major Greek and Cypriot organizations.

Rossides was born in 1927 in New York City. His father, Telemachus Rossides, had emigrated in 1920 from the town of Keryneia, in northern Cyprus, and his mother, Anna Maravelias, had emigrated in 1910 from the Peloponnisos, in southern Greece.

Rossides received both his B.A. and his J.D. degrees from Columbia University in 1949 and 1952, respectively. As an undergraduate, he had received All-American honors in football. Upon graduating, he served as criminal law investigator in the office of the district attorney in New York City in 1952. From 1952 to 1956, he was employed as an associate in the international law firm of Rogers and Wells. For two periods, 1966 to 1969 and 1973 to 1992, he worked there as a partner; he has been a senior counsel in the firm since 1993.

Earlier in his career, from 1956 to 1958, Rossides also served as assistant attorney general for the State of New York in New York City. For the next three years, he was assistant to the undersecretary of the Treasury Department, in Washington, D.C. As assistant secretary in the Treasury Department from 1969 to 1973, he supervised several government agencies. During that same period, he was also U.S. representative to the International Criminal Police Organization (INTERPOL) and from 1969 to 1971 one of its three vice presidents. From 1982 to 1984, Rossides served as a member of the executive committee of the Grace Commission, the president's private-sector survey on cost-control in the federal government.

Rossides has, in addition, an extensive publication record that covers the areas of law as it pertains to import regulations and practices and issues pertaining to Cyprus and Greece. Central to Rossides's writings are issues concerning the rule of law in U.S. foreign policy toward Cyprus and the Truman Doctrine and its role in the containment of communism in Greece. He has also written on conducting business in Greece.

Moreover, Rossides founded and served as president of the American Hellenic Institute (AHI) and its filial organizations, the American Hellenic Institute Public Affairs Committee (AHIPAC) and the American Hellenic Institute Foundation (AHIF). In that capacity he organized and addressed several legislative conferences on issues of U.S. foreign policy toward Greece, Turkey, and Cyprus. Indeed, his membership in several professional and ethnic organizations illustrates the breadth of his activities: He is a member of the Greek Orthodox church and the Order of AHEPA (American Hellenic Educational Progressive Association), and he is a trustee of Anatolia College. His active involvement in Hellenic-American organizations for the promotion of Cypriot and Hellenic causes in the United States has proven invaluable. His wife, Aphrodite Macotsin, is Greek-American.

Stavros T. Constantinou

REFERENCES

Rossides, Eugene T. "Cyprus and the Rule of Law." *Syracuse Journal of International Law and Commerce* 17.1 (Spring 1991): 22–90.

———. Interviews by author, 1998, 1999.

———. "The Rule of Law and Conditions on Foreign Aid to Turkey." In *The Rule of Law and Conditions on Foreign Aid to Turkey,* AHI Conference Proceedings 2, 28 January 1989. Washington, DC: American Hellenic Institute, 1989.

———. "The Truman Doctrine and the Value in Developing a Special Relationship with Greece." In *The Truman Doctrine Aid to Greece: A Fifty Year Retrospective,* 179–182. New York: Academy of Political Sciences; Washington, DC: American Hellenic Institute, 1998.

"Rossides, Eugene Telemachus." In *Who's Who in America 1997,* 51st ed., 2:3660. New Providence, NJ: Marquis Who's Who, 1996.

Roybal, Edward R. (1916–)

Community activist, city councilor, and U.S. House representative Mexican-American

Edward Roybal's political career spanned more than forty-three years, beginning in 1949, when he became the first Mexican American since 1881 to win a seat on the Los Angeles City Council. In 1962, he was elected to the U.S. House of Representatives from California's Twenty-fifth District (Los Angeles) and held that office for thirty years.

The first of eight children of Eloisa and Baudilio Roybal, Edward Roybal was born in 1916 in Albuquerque, New Mexico, where his father worked for the railroad. In 1920, the family moved to the Boyle Heights area of Los Angeles, a growing working-class Mexican community. Although his family stressed the importance of education, the Great Depression prevented Roybal from continuing his studies, and he joined the Civilian Conservation Corps (CCC), a New Deal program to reduce unemployment among young men.

After leaving the CCC, Roybal enrolled at the University of California, Los Angeles. Following graduation, he went to work for Twentieth Century Fox studios. He also began participating in community affairs and became aware of the high incidence of tuberculosis within the Mexican-American community. Public health care became an issue for him, and he volunteered to work with the California Tuberculosis Association, which eventually hired him (1942–1944). After one year's army service in World War II, he returned and was appointed director of public health education for the Los Angeles County Tuberculosis and Health Association. In the process, he became a well-known and respected figure in the Mexican-American community.

In 1947 Roybal ran for a seat on the Los Angeles City Council and lost by only a small percentage of votes. He continued his community activism and began working with longtime community organizer Fred Ross and his Community Service Organization (CSO). With the CSO's support and a large community following, Roybal won the 1949 race, becoming the first Mexican American to sit on the council since 1881. He continued to serve until 1962, winning twice with no opposition. In 1962, he ran for the U.S. House of Representative in California's Twenty-fifth District and won, a major breakthrough for Mexican Americans.

Roybal's distinguished work as a congressman spans the period from 1963 until his retirement in January 1993. His political concerns always centered on issues critical to all his constituencies, but he specifically addressed issues confronting the Mexican-American community. He introduced legislative reforms on health care and aging and served on major committees, including the Subcommittee on Inter-American Affairs, the Appropriations Committee, and the Subcommittee on Education and Training. In 1967, he introduced a bill that would have long-lasting consequences: the federal bilingual education act.

Roybal was one of a handful of Mexican-American political figures with a national reputation. He championed increased citizen participation in the political arena and helped found the National Association of Latino Elected and Appointed Officials (NALEO) in 1975 and the Congressional Hispanic Caucus two years later. As caucus chair, Roybal led the initial struggles against the Simpson-Rodino Immigration Reform and Control Act (IRCA) of 1986. Roybal's unwavering commitment to public life earned him numerous prestigious awards, including the Joshua Award for his advocacy of Jewish-Latino relations.

Alma M. Garcia

REFERENCES

"Edward Roybal." Hispanic Americans in Congress, 1822–1995. http://lcweb.loc.gov/rr/hispanic/congress/roybal.html. (Accessed 21 December 2000).

Martinez, Al. *Rising Voices: Profiles of Hispano-American Lives.* New York: New American Library, 1974.

Morey, Janet, and Wendy Dunn. *Famous Mexican Americans.* New York: E. P. Dutton, 1989.

Rosales, R. Arturo. *Chicano: The History of the Mexican American Civil Rights Movement.* Houston: Arte Publico Press, 1996.

"Roybal, Edward Ross." Biographical entry. U.S. Congress web site: bioguide.congress.gov/scripts/biodisplay.pl?index=R000485 (accessed 21 June 2000).

Saarinen, Eero (1910–1961)

Architect

Finnish

Eero Saarinen was one of the most important American architects in the post–World War II era, and one of the most creative. The son of Eliel Saarinen, also a prominent architect, he worked with the father yet also staked out a distinctive career, creating an architecture that resonated with the industrial age.

Born in Kirkkonummi, Finland, on 20 August 1910, Saarinen was something of a child prodigy, winning design competitions while still a teenager. With his family, he immigrated to the United States in 1923 and took up residence at the Cranbrook Academy of Art in Bloomfield Hills, Michigan, where his father served as a teacher and administrator. After a year of study in Paris in 1929–1930, Saarinen returned to the United States to attend Yale, earning a bachelor of fine arts degree in three years and a prestigious fellowship. He returned to Finland in 1935, where he joined an architectural firm and became acquainted with the work of the famous Finnish architect Alvar Alto.

He remained in Finland for only about a year, joining his father's business in 1937 and teaching at Cranbrook. The two gained several commissions in the following decade, including the Berkshire Music Center in Tanglewood, Massachusetts, and the Smithsonian Institution Art Gallery. Although they worked well together, their approaches began to diverge as the younger Saarinen forged a distinctive style. His ideas were shaped by such diverse influences as the International style and by such modern architects as Le Corbusier, Walter Gropius, and Frank Lloyd Wright.

In 1948, father and son submitted independent entries to the competition for the Jefferson Expansion Memorial in St. Louis (later known as the Gateway to the West), and Eero won with his soaring steel archway. The memorial was completed in 1964, three years after Eero's death, but his selection for this project marked the beginning of a highly productive period. During the thirteen years following 1948, he experimented with new approaches. His first major commission was to design the General Motors Technical Center, a sprawling complex in Warren, Michigan. After Saarinen completed a successful chapel and auditorium at the Massachusetts Institute of Technology, numerous colleges and universities contracted with him to design buildings, including the University of Chicago, the University of Pennsylvania, Drake University, and his alma mater, Yale, where he designed both Samuel Morse and Ezra Stiles Colleges and the Ingalls Hockey Rink.

Numerous corporate clients also contracted for his services, including IBM, Bell Telephone, and John Deere. In addition, Saarinen designed a number of governmental buildings. Among his most important government designs were the U.S. embassies in London and Oslo. One of his most successful projects was the TWA Terminal at New York's Kennedy International Airport. When he died, he was working on what some architectural critics considered his most ambitious and most important project, the Dulles International Airport Terminal Building outside of Washington, D.C.

Although Saarinen was not active in the Finnish-American community, his achievements were lauded by them as examples of Finnish creativity. However, his career was cut tragically short when he died during brain surgery at the age of fifty-one.

Peter Kivisto

REFERENCES

Kuhner, Robert. *Eero Saarinen: His Life, His Work.* Monticello, IL: Council of Planning Librarians, 1975.

Saarinen, Aline, ed. *Eero Saarinen on His Work.* New Haven, CT: Yale University Press, 1963.

Spade, Rupert. *Eero Saarinen.* New York: Simon & Schuster, 1971.

Temko, Allan. *Eero Saarinen.* New York: Brazillier, 1962.

Saarinen, Eliel (1873–1950)

Architect
Finnish

Eliel Saarinen was one of the most important Scandinavian architects of the first half of the twentieth century, establishing a successful career in Finland and later in the United States. Like Frank Lloyd Wright, Saarinen was intent on creating structures that were integrated into their environments.

Gottlieb Eliel Saarinen was born on 20 August 1873 in Rantasalmi, Finland. His father was a Lutheran pastor who served congregations in Finland and the Finnish population in the vicinity of St. Petersburg, Russia. It was in this latter setting that young Saarinen developed an interests in the arts. He set out to pursue art, later moving to the Polytechnical Institute in Helsinki, where his studies in architecture commenced.

In 1896, his architectural career began in a firm created with former classmates, Armas Lindgren and Herman Gesellius. The group made its mark with its plan for the Finnish Pavilion at the 1900 Paris Exposition, followed with the contract to design the National Museum in Helsinki. However, it was the design of the Helsinki Railroad Station, essentially Saarinen's alone, that catapulted him into the ranks of the most successful architects in Europe. During his early career he was one of the foremost exponents of National Romanticism, his designs weaving together the influences of Finnish medieval architecture, Art Nouveau, and the Arts and Crafts style. But he made a partial shift, and modernist influences, including those from the United States, began to be reflected in his designs. The Helsinki Railroad Station, with its cleaner lines and a more abstract modernist style, marked his break from romanticism. He then received commissions in a number of European countries and also turned his attention to urban planning in Finland and in such cities as Tallinn, Estonia, and Canberra, Australia.

In 1922, Saarinen entered a competition to design the Chicago Tribune Building. His second-place entry was received with enthusiastic acclaim and would prove to influence skyscraper design for years to come. Because of his entry, he became well known in the United States. Encouraged by the response to his design and concerned about the Finnish economy in the wake of the nation's recent civil war, Saarinen immigrated with his family the following year. He settled in at the Cranbrook Academy of Art in the Detroit suburb of Bloomfield Hills, where he served as director of the Departments of Architecture and City Planning. He then engaged in an ambitious series of projects, including designing the School for Boys, the Kingwood School for Girls, the Academy of Art, the Institute of Sciences, and the Museum and Library, all in Bloomfield Hills.

In 1937, he entered into a partnership with his son, Eero, completing a number of important commissions, including the Berkshire Music Center at Tanglewood, Massachusetts; the Crow Island School in Winnetka, Illinois; and the First Christian Church in Columbus, Indiana.

His stature in the profession resulted in his receiving numerous honorary doctorates and design awards. He was honored with the Gold Medal of the American Institute of Architects, and his native country recognized his career by making him a commander first class of the White Rose Order. In addition, although he was not involved with the Finnish-American community, that community embraced his achievements as examples of the contributions Finns have made in the United States. Saarinen died July 1, 1950, in Bloomfield Hills.

Peter Kivisto

REFERENCES

Christ-Janer, Albert. *Eliel Saarinen: Finnish-American Architect and Educator.* Chicago: University of Chicago Press, 1984.

Doumato, Lamia. *Eliel Saarinen, 1873–1980.* Monticello, IL: Vance Bibliographies, 1980.

Hausen, Marika. *Eliel Saarinen: Projects, 1896–1923.* Cambridge, MA: MIT Press, 1990.

Saarinen, Eliel. *The Search for Form: A Fundamental Approach to Art.* New York: Reinhold Publishing Corp., 1948.

Sandburg, Carl (1878–1967)
Poet and biographer
Swedish-American

One of the leading American poetic voices of his era, Carl Sandburg was born in largely Swedish-American Galesburg, Illinois, the son of an immigrant blacksmith. He would achieve great renown, becoming, in effect, America's poet laureate. He is still very popular.

Born 6 January 1878, Carl Sandburg left school at age thirteen and worked at various odd jobs before he drifted west, riding boxcars, following the harvests, and taking whatever work he could find. He joined the army and served in Puerto Rico during the Spanish-American War. After being mustered out, he went to Lombard (now Knox) College in Galesburg, where he graduated in 1902. He then worked in Milwaukee as a newspaperman and in 1910–1912 as secretary to the city's Socialist mayor. In 1908 Sandburg married photographer Edward Steichen's sister, Lillian. Four years later, they moved to Chicago, where he continued his journalistic career. In 1918–1919 he served as a correspondent for the *Chicago Daily News* in Sweden.

Sandburg had brought out privately his first small selection of poems in 1904. In Chicago he began publishing his verse in Harriet Monroe's influential literary journal, *Poetry,* which disseminated the work of the younger midwestern writers. By 1914 he had gained wide recognition. Sandburg's *Chicago Poems* appeared in 1916, followed by *Cornhuskers* (1918), *Smoke and Steel* (1920), *Slabs of the Sunburnt West* (1922), *Good Morning, America* (1928), and *The People, Yes* (1936). Sandburg's poetry celebrates, in vigorous blank verse, the United States of his time—above all, common people and common things, the great open spaces, the restless tempo of the big city, youthful strength and energy, and the Americans' underlying idealism—all of it with a love and undaunted optimism reminiscent of Walt Whitman.

His most ambitious work was his epic, Pulitzer Prize–winning biography of Abraham Lincoln, *The Prairie Years* (two volumes, 1926) and *The War Years* (four volumes, 1939), in which Lincoln symbolizes all that was sound in American life. Sandburg also wrote, among other things, four collections of children's tales, *Rootabaga Stories* (1922–1930); two anthologies of folksongs, *The American Songbag* (1927) and *The New American Songbag* (1950); a novel, *Remembrance Rock* (1948), spanning the sweep of U.S. history; and an account of his youth, *Always the Young Strangers* (1950). He was, meanwhile, well known for public readings from his works and singing folksongs to his own guitar.

In a period when many American writers expatriated themselves to find new inspiration, Sandburg remained staunchly and quintessentially American, with strong roots in his native Midwest. North Callahan has called him the "Lincoln of our literature." He was also warmly attached to his Swedish heritage. His reminiscences fondly recall his Swedish-American childhood in Galesburg, as he likewise did for more than two spellbinding hours as featured speaker in 1948 at the great Swedish Pioneer Centennial celebration in Chicago. The Swedish Pioneer (now the Swedish-American) Historical Society evolved out of the centennial that fall, and Sandburg took great pride in being elected its honorary chairman. His birthplace in Galesburg is an Illinois State Historic Site. His later home, Connemara, in North Carolina, is a national park. Sandburg died 22 July 1967.

H. Arnold Barton

REFERENCES
Golden, Harry. *Carl Sandburg.* Cleveland: World Publishing Co., 1962.

Callahan, North. *Carl Sandburg.* University Park: Pennsylvania State University Press, 1986.

Niven, Penelope. *Carl Sandburg.* New York: Scribner's, 1991.

Sandburg, Carl. *Always the Young Strangers.* New York: Harcourt, Brace, 1950.

Sandoz, Mari (1896–1966)
Historian and novelist
Swiss-American

Mari Sandoz, a child of homesteaders, became a "story catcher of the Plains." Her works expressed both the white and the Indian perspectives.

Sandoz was born on the frontier of northwestern Nebraska, just south of the Pine Ridge Reservation. She was the first child of homesteaders Jules Ami Sandoz (from French-speaking Switzerland) and Marie Elizabeth Fehr (from German-speaking Switzerland). Until the age of nine Sandoz spoke only Swiss German, yet she moved in a multicultural world of American Indians as well as Euro-Americans, whom she keenly observed. Although attending school only irregularly, she learned English well and was determined to become a writer.

In 1914 she married the neighboring rancher Wray Macumber, divorced him in 1918, and moved to Lincoln, Nebraska's capital, where, despite the lack of a high school diploma, she attended the university. Poor, at times suffering from malnutrition, and for years without success—but inspired by such writers as Joseph Conrad and Thomas Hardy as well as by her professors and others—Sandoz devoted all her free time to writing. She based her writings on a passion for accuracy and on a belief in "nemesis," which she understood as the inescapability of fate. The dialogue that she invented in her historical works was derived from a painstakingly informed understanding of the protagonists and their unique historical situations and given surroundings. Their words, therefore, became in her view "truer than any documented record."

She probed, first, the world of white settlers shaped by competing interest groups, such as homesteaders, cattlemen, and sheepherders, especially in the biography of her father *Old Jules* (1935), her first prize-winning work among more than twenty books. Second, Sandoz understood the world of white arrivals in North America increasingly as the creation of empire on the ruins of vibrant and culturally complex indigenous worlds. She explored this theme from the white perspective in such works as *The Beaver Men* (1964), *The Buffalo Hunters* (1954), *The Cattlemen* (1958), and *The Battle of Little Bighorn* (1966), and from the indigenous perspective in the biography *Crazy Horse* (1942), in *Cheyenne Autumn* (1953), and in the cultural portrait *These Were the Sioux* (1961). Like John G. Neihardt's *Black Elk Speaks* (1932) or Joseph E. Brown's *The Sacred Pipe* (1953), Sandoz's works also replaced the dominant interpretation of a savage Indian world with a keen appreciation of its profound difference as well as genuine equivalence to that of whites. Third, deeply affected by the brutality of totalitarian regimes, Mari Sandoz probed, especially in such novels as *Slogum House* (1937), *Capital City* (1939), and *The Tom-Walker* (1947), the nature of human violence as revealed by events in her world of origin.

In 1940 Sandoz moved to Denver, Colorado, and in 1943 to New York City, where she continued to publish until her death from cancer. Although her novels have received less praise than her historical works, several of the latter have remained unsurpassed in their attention to documented detail, their masterful re-creation of past events, and their portrayal of cultural difference. As a daughter of immigrants, Sandoz probed their world as well as the Indians' with engaging skill and unique understanding.

Leo Schelbert

REFERENCES

Sandoz, Mari. *Cheyenne Autumn.* New York: McGraw-Hill, 1953.

———. *Crazy Horse, the Strange Man of the Oglalas.* New York: Alfred A. Knopf, 1942.

———. *Old Jules.* Boston: Little, Brown, 1935.

Stauffer, Helen Winter. *Mari Sandoz, Story Catcher of the Plains.* Lincoln: University of Nebraska Press, 1982.

Stauffer, Helen Winter, ed. *Letters of Mari Sandoz.* Lincoln: University of Nebraska Press, 1992.

Villiger, Laura. *Mari Sandoz. A Study in Post-Colonial Discourse.* New York: Peter Lang, 1994.

Sarafa, Margarett George
(1930–1998)

Community leader
Chaldean

Margarett Sarafa was one of the founding members of the Chaldean American Ladies of Charity (CALC), an organization of women associated with the Chaldean Catholic church in Detroit, Michigan. She served as its first vice president and as president on six different occasions, for a total of ten years. In recognition of her services to her community, the CALC awarded her its first Guardian Angel Award in October 1997.

Sarafa was born on 10 July 1930 in Detroit. She was the daughter of Tobia and Naima (Shammami) George (also known as the Lossia family in their village). Tobia and Naima were recent immigrants from the town of Telkaif, in the northern portion of what is now Iraq. Sarafa's parents, like nearly all residents of Telkaif, were Chaldeans, members of one of the Eastern Rites of the Roman Catholic church. Most early members of Detroit's community of Chaldeans made their living in the grocery business. Sarafa and her four siblings, like other Chaldean children in the 1930s and 1940s, were expected to help in the family store and deliver groceries.

In 1953, Margarett George wed Salim Sarafa, an immigrant also from Telkaif. He was a teacher and later was in the grocery business and real estate. They had five children. Yet Sarafa was not content to devote herself solely to family matters. She played an active role in the establishment of the Chaldean American Ladies of Charity, which began informally to assist community members who were ill, old, or had suffered from fires or other disasters. Sarafa particularly devoted her attention to the needs of the elderly and children. As one of the few women in her community who had completed high school and spoke fluent English, she worked for many years with the teachers at St. Michael's Catholic School, even after her children had graduated, to help the teachers understand the needs of Chaldean children and to help the the teachers adapt to the American school system.

As concerned as she was for children, however, Sarafa was even more devoted to the needs of the elderly. She recognized that Chaldean elderly were often lonely and had difficulties getting to their church or meeting their Chaldean friends. Visiting the old people was a project that she carried out throughout her life. In 1990–1991, she served as community liaison to a needs assessment of Chaldean and Arab elders sponsored by the Michigan State Office of Services to the Aging. At her constant urging, CALC undertook the development of a senior citizens' home, a project that finally became a reality when the Chaldean Diocese opened the home in January 1999.

Sarafa exemplified the important role that women play in a largely male-dominated community. Her father and, later, her brothers and her husband's family were prominent members of the Chaldean community. She used her influence with her family and with her family's connections within the community to obtain support for the many projects that the Chaldean American Ladies of Charity conducts. Sarafa died on 5 January 1998 from breast cancer.

Mary Cay Sengstock

REFERENCES

Chaldean American Ladies of Charity. "Millionaire Party Program." Southfield, MI: Chaldean American Ladies of Charity, 1997.

Sengstock, Mary C. *Chaldean-Americans: Changing Conceptions of Ethnic Identity.* New York: Center for Migration Studies, 1999.

———. "Telkaif, Baghdad, Detroit—Chaldeans Blend Three Cultures." *Michigan History,* Winter 1970, 293–310.

Sarbanes, Paul (1933–)

U.S. House representative and U.S. senator
Greek-American

Paul Sarbanes, a second-generation Greek American, was elected to the Maryland House of Delegates. He followed that with three terms as a Democratic congressman from Maryland and, then, four successive terms in the U.S. Senate, winning a fifth term in the 2000 election with 63 percent of the vote. He is regarded as the dean of Greek-American politicians.

Sarbanes was born in Salisbury, Maryland, on 3 February 1933. He was the son of Spyros and Matina Sarbanes, both of whom immigrated to the United States from Laconia, a southern province in the Peloponnisos, Greece. His father, who had come to the United States in 1908, had opened a restaurant after World War I called the Mayflower Grill. Sarbanes went to local schools and received his bachelor of arts degree in 1954 magna cum laude from the Woodrow Wilson School of Public and International Affairs at Princeton University. He was a Rhodes Scholar at Balliol College, Oxford University, 1954–1957, earning an honors degree in philosophy, politics, and economics. In 1960 he received a law degree cum laude at Harvard Law School.

Following graduation, he was a law clerk to Judge Morris A. Soper, U.S. Court of Appeals for the Fourth Circuit (1960–1961). Then, as a member of the Maryland State Bar Association, he was an associate of two different law firms in Baltimore (1961–1962, 1965–1970). In between those two periods, he began his career in public service, working as an administrative assistant to Walter W. Heller, chairman of President Kennedy's Council of Economic Advisers (1962–1963), and then as director of Baltimore's Charter Revision Commission (1963–1964).

Sarbanes has had a spectacular career in public service. In 1970, following four years in the Maryland House of Delegates (where he had several important committee assignments), he was elected to the Ninety-second Congress and served three-terms as a member of the U.S. House of Representatives. While there, he was a member of the House Judiciary Committee, Merchant Marine and Fisheries Committee, and the Select Committee on House Reorganization. In November 1976, he was first elected U.S. senator and reelected four times. In that capacity he has been on the Joint Economic Committee (Chair, 100th and 101st Congresses); Foreign Relations Committee; Senate Committee on the Budget; and as ranking member of the Senate Committee on Banking, Housing, and Urban Affairs. He was also chairman of the Maryland congressional delegation.

Sarbanes is also a member of the Greek Orthodox Cathedral of the Annunciation, Baltimore, is active in the Greek community, and involved in Greek-American affairs, receives the support of Greek voters from both parties, and has been one of the strongest voices in the Senate on behalf of the Greeks in Cyprus. He is considered the dean of Greek-American politicians.

In June 1960 Sarbanes married Christine Dunbar, of Brighton, England, an Oxford graduate, who has been teaching in a private school since 1978. He and his wife have three children and two grandchildren.

George A. Kourvetaris

REFERENCES

Almanac of American Politics 2000. Washington, DC: National Journal Group, 1999.

"Biography of the Honorable Paul Spyros Sarbanes, United States Senator from Maryland": www.senate.gov/~sarbanes/biography.html (accessed 15 May 2000).

Moskos, Charles C. *Greek Americans,* 2d ed. New Brunswick, NJ: Transaction Publishers, 1990.

"Paul Spyros Sarbanes, United State Senator from Maryland (Democrat)." United States Senate (September 8, 1998): www.mdarchives.state.md.us/msa/mdmanual/39fed/html/msa02169.html (accessed 15 June 2000).

Rossides, Eugene. *American Hellenic Who's Who.* Washington, DC: American Hellenic Institute, 1990.

"Sarbanes, Paul Spyros." *Who's Who in American Politics 1997–1998,* 16th ed. Vol. 1, Alabama-Montana. New York: R. R. Bowker, 1997.

Sarkisian, Cherilyn "Cher" (1946–)
Entertainer and actress
Armenian-American

Cherilyn Sarkisian, better known to her millions of fans worldwide as Cher, has achieved remarkable success as a singer, performer, and award-winning actress. At the same time, in her philanthropic efforts, she has demonstrated her attachment to her ethnic roots.

Cher was born in El Centro, California, on 20 May 1946. Her father, John Sarkisian, was an Armenian-American farmer, and her mother was the former Georgia Holt. It was in 1962 that Cher met her future husband and mentor, Sonny Bono, in Hollywood. Two years later, she started her phenomenal entertainment career when she sang back up as well as duets with Sonny and they married informally in Tijuana, Mexico.

In 1965, the Sonny and Cher record, *I Got You Babe,* was their first million seller. The next year, Cher put out her first solo million seller, *Bang Bang.* In 1969 they made their first movie, *Chastity*—and Cher gave birth to their daughter, Chastity. In 1971, Sonny and Cher's CBS-TV show, the *Sonny and Cher Comedy Hour,* debuted and quickly achieved top audience ratings. It was there that Cher proved to be a versatile performer, and her second solo gold record, *Gypsies Tramps and Thieves,* came out. In 1975, Cher and Bono were divorced and Cher married rock star Greg Allman. Her television show became a solo effort, *Cher,* a weekly variety show. The next year she gave birth to Elijah Blue Allman, but in 1977 she and Allman divorced.

At this point, Cher seriously pursued an film acting career, receiving a Golden Globe nomination in 1982 for *Come Back to the Five and Dime, Jimmy Dean, Jimmy Dean;* winning one in 1983 for *Silkwood* as well as a best supporting actress Academy Award; and the next year earning the best actress award at the Cannes Film Festival for *Mask.* In 1987 she appeared in *Witches of Eastwick, Suspect,* and *Moonstruck* and received the Academy Award for best actress for her role in *Moonstruck.* At that time, she began to have more successful albums and sold-out singing tours, followed by several more films, including *Mermaid, Faithful,* and *Tea with Mussolini,* and award-winning albums. Her single, "Believe," became the biggest-selling record in England by a female recording artist. Her live performances, extravaganzas of costumes and dancers, continue to sell out all over the world.

Given her successes, Cher did not find her ethnic roots until middle age, when she began to reevaluate her life and career and engaged in relief work in Armenia during the dire years of that country's blockade. Her visits to Armenia not only raised the morale of those in Armenia but also set an inspiring example to the Armenian-American community, for they, like most ethnic groups, find inspiration in the successes of their compatriots, especially those acknowledging their ethnic roots. In 1993, she endeared herself to millions of Armenians when she accompanied airlift supplies to war-torn and earthquake-devastated Armenia, bringing beneficial public attention to a nation in need of help. She has also silently figured in charitable donations. Cher's "coming home" has inspired a generation of young Armenian Americans.

Dennis R. Papazian

REFERENCES
Cher, with Nigel Goodall. *Cher in Her Own Words.* London: Omnibus Press, 1992.
Cher, with Jeff Coplon. *The First Time.* Rev. ed. New York: Simon & Schuster, 1998; London: Warner, 2000.
Svetkey, Benjamin. "Hip to Be Cher." *Entertainment Weekly,* 23 April 1999, 16–21.
Russell, Lisa, and Danelle Morton. "Cher." *People Weekly,* 15–22 March 1999, 190–192.
Udovitch, Mim. "Q&A: Cher." *Rolling Stone,* 15 April 1999, 45ff.

Sarnoff, David (1891–1971)
Radio and television entrepreneur
Jewish-American

America's three major television networks were all founded by second-generation American Jews: William Paley of CBS, David Sarnoff of NBC, and Leonard Goldenson of the American Broadcasting Companies

(ABC). Of the three, Sarnoff played the most critical part in the development of American radio and television.

Sarnoff was born in 1891 in the Russian-Jewish shtetl (town) of Uzlian. His family arrived in New York's Lower East Side in 1900. He was nine, the eldest of five children. To help the family, he left school before the ninth grade and found work as a newsboy. As a messenger for the Commercial Cable Company, he developed an interest in long-distance communication. Taking courses in telegraphy at the Educational Alliance, the leading settlement house of the Jewish East Side, Sarnoff soon developed enough expertise to be hired by the Marconi Wireless Company. He spent his free time reading manuals on mathematics, science, and telecommunications. At eighteen, he was appointed chief wireless operator of the Marconi organization.

Staffing a wireless station in New York, Sarnoff was the first radio operator to pick up confirmation of the sinking of the *Titanic* on 15 April 1912. The news frenzy convinced him of the power of mass communications. He envisioned the potential of wireless radio transmission as a medium of news and mass entertainment, coining the term "radio music box." Moreover, he saw the potential profit from sales of the "radio music box" and from advertising for sponsors. In 1919, American Marconi and General Electric jointly established an independent company, the Radio Corporation of America (RCA)—with Sarnoff as its commercial manager and de facto chairman. During the 1920s, RCA acquired at least 2,000 patents, covering all the basics of an integrated radio-transmission system. With interest exploding in the early 1920s, RCA began to manufacture its "radio music boxes." With his RCA stocks, Sarnoff became one of the wealthiest men in the United States.

In 1926 he launched a "network" of RCA-affiliate stations, called the National Broadcasting Company, which would become the incubator of television. In 1929, he hired Vladimir Zworykin, a Russian scientist who led the way in developing the cathode-ray tube at the heart of the television receiver, and backed his research during the 1930s. By 1939 the basic technology was available. When World War II intervened, Sarnoff converted RCA to defense production and volunteered his services. He was appointed General Eisenhower's chief of communications and rapidly organized all radio communications for the western front, eventually being promoted to brigadier general. He thereafter insisted on being called General Sarnoff.

After the war, Sarnoff poured his resources into the development of television. In 1945 the first sets went into production and sales soon multiplied exponentially. He also insisted on the development of affordable color television. Sarnoff thus had built RCA into the world's leading electronics company by the 1960s and NBC into America's pioneering television network.

As a son of the Jewish ghetto, Sarnoff also donated his time and influence to a number of Jewish institutions, and dearest to his heart, undoubtedly, was the Educational Alliance. He died at age eighty, universally acclaimed.

David E. Kaufman

REFERENCES
Bilby, Kenneth. *The General: David Sarnoff and the Rise of the Communications Industry.* Harper & Row, 1986.
Dreher, Carl. *Sarnoff: An American Success.* New York: Quadrangle Books, 1977.
Lewis, Tom. *Empire of the Air: The Men Who Made Radio.* New York: Burlingame Books, 1991.

Saroyan, William (1908–1981)
Writer
Armenian-American

William Saroyan became a celebrated American dramatist, short story writer, novelist, autobiographer, scriptwriter, essayist, and songwriter, and his popularity reached hero worship in Armenia itself. In the United States, he became a symbol of those born of immigrant parents who succeeded and, in so doing, added brilliance to the patchwork of American cultures.

Saroyan was born on August 31, 1908, in Fresno, California, of Armenian parents who had emigrated from Bitlis, Armenia. His father, a Presbyterian minister, died while Saroyan was a youngster. Saroyan began selling newspapers on the streets when eight years old, later working at a variety of jobs while still in school. He began to write at thirteen, and his works were first published in the *Hairenik* (Fatherland), an Armenian-American newspaper. His work became widely known in 1934, when *Story* magazine published "The Daring Young Man on the Flying Trapeze." By the late 1930s, he had gained a national reputation as a short story writer and had turned his attention to playwriting. He was awarded the Pulitzer Prize in drama in 1940 for *The Time of Your Life* but refused to accept it because he did not believe in critical or commercial sanctions for art.

Saroyan had a rare talent that led him to success in many literary fields—for example, as dramatist and novelist, *The Human Comedy* (1943); as humorist, *My Name Is Aram* (1940); as short story writer, *The Daring Young Man on the Flying Trapeze and Other Stories* (1934); as playwright, *The Time of Your Life* (1939); and as songwriter, "Come On a My House" a 1950s number that he cowrote. Among other works were screenplays, too: *The Human Comedy,* starring Mickey Rooney, and *The Time of Your Life,* starring James Cagney.

Saroyan never hid his roots, always maintaining his status as not just an American writer but an Armenian-American writer. He wrote of the lighter side of the immigrant experience, emphasizing family life and humor. His works, which were mostly set in the United States, reveal his appreciation of the American Dream and the strengths and weaknesses of U.S. society. He captured the general immigrant experience of the period and immortalized the Fresno experience of the Armenians. He became a hero as well to Armenian people, who, having fled the genocide by the Ottoman Turks, were scattered in diaspora.

A key may be that Saroyan never seemed to quit believing in the innate goodness of man and the humor that tempered the passing of time and personal isolation and suffering. His facile optimism led later critics to view his works as simplistic and superficial, but that criticism was a temporary aberration, and Saroyan's work aroused new respect. Since his death on May 18, 1981, Saroyan festivals, college classes, symposia, and books have kept his memory and works fresh. There is a statue of him in Fresno, where a society continuously publishes his works, and in San Francisco, where there is a Saroyan museum in the house in which he wrote. In Armenia, too, he still inspires awe and respect. In 1981, Saroyan's ashes were buried in his beloved Fresno and in Armenia.

Dennis R. Papazian

REFERENCES
Balakian, Nona. *The World of William Saroyan.* Canbury, NJ: Associated University Presses, 1998.
Darwent, Brian, ed. *Saroyan Memoirs.* London: Minerva Press, 1994.
Ford, Elizabeth. *William Saroyan: A Reference Guide.* Boston: G. K. Hall, 1989.
Foster, Edward Halsey. *William Saroyan: A Study of the Short Fiction.* New York: Twayne Publishers, 1991.
Keyishian, Harry, ed. *Critical Essays on William Saroyan.* New York: G. K. Hall, 1995.
Lee, Lawrence, and Barry Gifford. *Saroyan: A Biography.* New York: Paragon House, 1988.
Whitmore, Jon. *William Saroyan: A Research and Production Sourcebook.* Westport, CT: Greenwood Press, 1994.

Saund, Dalip Singh (1899–1973)

U.S. House representative and political activist
Asian Indian

Dalip Singh Saund immigrated to the United States and soon challenged the laws denying him the right to U.S. citizenship (and denaturalizing his wife). The laws were changed, and he became a citizen and succeeded in getting elected as the first Asian Indian congressman.

Saund was born on 20 September 1899 into a poor community near Amritsar, India. Educated primarily in boarding schools and then at the University of Punjab, he received his bachelor's degree in 1919. In 1920 he studied at the University of California, Berkeley, earning master's and doctorate degrees in mathematics. In 1928, he married Marian Kosa.

Saund entered American society when there was considerable anti-immigrant sentiment and anti-immigrant action by the federal government, particularly the immigration quota acts of 1921 and 1924, the 1922 Cable Act—which continued the revocation of the citizenship of U.S.-born women who married foreigners ineligible for citizenship—and the 1923 U.S. Supreme Court ruling in *United States v. Bhagat Singh Thind* that Asian Indians were "aliens ineligible for citizenship" because although "Caucasian," they were not "white" as commonly understood. As a result, Saund's wife lost her citizenship when they married in 1928, regaining it only when the law was changed in 1931.

Like many other Punjabis at the time, Saund settled in the Imperial Valley in California and, unable to secure a job with his advanced degrees, became a lettuce farmer and distributor of chemical fertilizers from 1930 to 1953. He was also active in Asian Indian affairs. He researched and wrote *My Mother India,* which countered Katharine Mayo's scathing depiction of Indian society and culture in her *Mother India.* He formed the Indian Association of America to secure an amendment to the immigration laws that would make Asian Indians eligible for citizenship. His efforts, in conjunction with those of J. J. Singh's Indian League of America and Mubarak Ali Khan's India Welfare League, met success in 1946, when President Harry S. Truman signed the Luce-Celler Act, which conferred the right of citizenship on Asian Indians as well as Filipinos.

After becoming a citizen in 1949, Saund became active in mainstream organizations, such as the Democratic Party and the March of Dimes. He was a delegate to the Democratic National Convention in 1952, 1956, and 1960. In 1950, he ran for a judgeship in the town of Westmoreland and won, only to be denied the position because he had not

been a citizen a full year before his election. He ran in 1952, won again, and served until his election to Congress in 1956. Saund served three terms in Congress, falling ill late in his last term. His election in a California district with almost no Asian Indians during an era still marked by considerable racial discrimination was an impressive achievement. He died in April 1973.

Dalip Singh Saund's phenomenal achievements are not recognized as they should be, possibly because his upbeat and optimistic tone, coupled with lack of anger in his autobiography, *Congressman from India,* counters the mode of protest and challenge to the established system more current among Asian Americans. In addition to his belief—that "there is no room in the United States for second-class citizenship"—he maintained that his "guideposts were two of the most beloved men in history, Abraham Lincoln and Mahatma Gandhi."

Arthur W. Helweg

REFERENCES
Kamath, M.V. *The United States and India, 1776–1976.* Washington, DC: Embassy of India, 1976.
Nash, Phil Tajitsu. "Dalip Singh Saund: An Asian American Pioneer." *AsianWeek* 21.4 (16 September 1999).
Saund, Dalip Singh. *Congressman from India.* New York: E. P. Dutton, 1960.

Schaff, Philip (1819–1893)
Church historian and theologian
Swiss

For nearly half of the nineteenth century, Philip Schaff was an outstanding theologian, prolific writer, teacher, and ardent promoter of interdenominational dialogue. In an autobiographical sketch, Schaff observed, "I am a Swiss by birth, a German by education, and an American by choice."

Schaff was born on January 1, 1819, "in poverty and obscurity" in Chur, an episcopal see since Roman times and the capital of the Romansh- and German-speaking Swiss canton Graubünden. He lost his father as an infant, and when his mother, Anna Schindler, married a widower and moved, Philip was left behind in an orphanage. He developed into a gifted student and in 1833, with the help of a benefactor, attended the academy in Kronthal, Württemberg, in Germany. He enrolled in a gymnasium in Stuttgart in preparation for university studies, which he pursued in Tübingen, Halle, and Berlin, and there he absorbed an evolutionist view of Christianity, influenced by such philosophers as Georg Hegel and Friedrich Schleiermacher.

Driven by a sense of mission, in 1844 he accepted a professorship in church history and biblical literature at the seminary of the Reformed church in Mercersburg, Pennsylvania. He and John W. Nevin (1803–1886) developed the so-called Mercersburg Theology, which viewed Christianity, although unchangeable in its basics, as evolving its rich potential in the context of the vagaries of human history. Schaff's *The Principle of Protestantism*, translated by Nevin and published in 1845, led to a heresy trial that both men weathered undamaged. Because of the Civil War, the seminary closed in 1863. Schaff, an outspoken opponent of slavery, then became secretary of the New York Sabbath Committee, dedicated to saving Sunday from being "crucified between Irish whiskey . . . and German beer." In 1870 he became professor at Union Theological Seminary and emerged as a leading American church historian and theologian.

Besides being engaged in teaching, Schaff published around fifty-five books and contributed to numerous other theological works. He also edited the *American Church History* series (twenty-eight volumes) and the first edition of the *Schaff-Herzog Encyclopedia* (1882–1884), a work still valued today. He served as the U.S. representative on the contentious committee for the revision of the English Bible that was begun in 1870 in Great Britain. A fervent promoter of the Evangelical Alliance, which was dedicated to interdenominational dialogue, he successfully organized its sixth session, in New York in 1873, with international attendees. Schaff also cofounded the Council of Reformed Churches, which met for the first time in 1877, in Edinburgh, Scotland. He traveled to Europe often, meeting with leaders of diverse denominations, attending several Evangelical Alliance meetings, and visiting his mother and friends. He viewed himself as a bridge builder between religious groups and mapped a course between narrow-minded sectarianism and scientific rationalism.

Although too ill to deliver his speech in person, he attended in 1893 the World Parliament of Religions in Chicago; he died shortly after his return to New York. An inscription in Latin at the entrance of Union Theological Seminary aptly defines Schaff's outlook: "I am a Christian, and nothing Christian I view as alien to me." He died October 20, 1893, in New York City.

Leo Schelbert

REFERENCES

Pranger, Gary K. *Philip Schaff (1819–1893). Portrait of an Immigrant Theologian.* New York: Peter Lang, 1997.

Schaff, David. *The Life of Philip Schaff.* New York: Scribner's, 1897.

Schaff, Philip. *America: A Sketch of Its Political, Social and Religious Character.* Edited by Perry Miller. 1885. Cambridge, MA: Belknap Press of Harvard University, 1961.

———. *English Language: Heterogeneous in Formation, Homogeneous in Character, Universal in Destination for the Spread of Christian Civilization.* Nashville, TN: Cumberland Presbyterian Publishing House, 1887.

———. *History of the Christian Church.* 8 vols. [1894.] Grand Rapids, MI: William B. Eerdman's Publishing Co., 1950.

Shriver, George. *Philip Schaff: Christian Scholar and Ecumenical Prophet.* Macon, GA: Mercer University Press, 1987.

Schmemann, Serge (1945–)

Journalist
Russian-American

Serge Schmemann was born in Paris to Russian émigré parents and brought to the United States as a young child. A professional journalist, he won the Pulitzer Prize in 1991.

Schmemann's parents were prominent

people. His father, Alexander, was educated as a theologian at the Orthodox Theological Institute of St. Sergius in Paris, where he also taught church history until 1951. Then he joined the faculty of St. Vladimir's Theological Seminary in Crestwood, New York, becoming one of America's leading Orthodox theologians. Schmemann's mother, Juliana Osorgin, was descended from a landowning family south of Moscow and was a direct descendant of St. Juliana, who died in 1605. The legacy of both parents figures in his later life.

Schmemann was six years old when his family came to the United States, so his education was almost entirely American. He received his B.A from Harvard University in 1967 and an M.A. from Columbia University in 1971. In 1972, he joined the Associated Press, spending some years as a South African correspondent. In 1980 he was appointed Moscow Bureau Chief for the *New York Times (NYT)*. Later, he served as its bureau chief in Bonn, Germany, winning a Pulitzer Prize in 1991 for his reporting of the reunification of that country. Four years later, he was appointed *NYT* bureau chief in Jerusalem.

When Schmemann taught a seminar at Princeton University in Spring 1999, he discussed, among other topics, "the powers and limits of foreign reporting in shaping American public opinion." As *NYT* bureau chief, Schmemann has been placed at the center of world-changing events. He has reported on those events at the same time that U.S. public opinion was being formed concerning the rebuilding of Russia, the reunification of Germany, and the peace process in the Middle East.

In 1997 Schmemann published *Echos of a Native Land,* a 200-year history of his mother's family estate, with its tragic end. It is an especially good documentation of a rural community south of Moscow before and after the revolution. The next year, he was reminded of his father's role as one of the leading theologians in the United States. In June 1998, a bishop from the conservative faction of the Orthodox church in Russia burned theological books written by Alexander

Schmemann and John Meyendorff. When contacted by a reporter for the *Moscow Times,* Schmemann expressed "dismay and anger" that a Russian bishop should choose to express his freedom in such a way.

Serge Schmemann's life expresses an unusual continuity in the transition of several generations from Russia as a homeland to the United States as a homeland. Schmemann concluded *Echos of a Native Land* by telling of his turning down a request that he repurchase a portion of his mother's estate. He observed: "I hoped it would end up in good hands. But . . . my life was elsewhere." However, he concluded, "I had claimed my rightful place on this Sergiyevskoye soil, and it did not require a Soviet or a Russian [property] deed."

Keith P. Dyrud

REFERENCES
Schmemann, Serge. *Echos of a Native Land: Two Centuries of a Russian Village.* New York: Alfred A. Knopf, 1997.
"Winners of the 1991 Pulitzer Prizes in Arts and Journalism." *New York Times,* 10 April 1991, A21.
Zolotov, Andrei, Jr. "Patriarchate Denies Report of Book Burning. Orthodox Book Burning." Russia Intercessory Prayer Network News Release, 3 June 1998: www.ripnet.org/beseiged denies. htm (accessed 28 June 2000).

Schurz, Carl (1829–1906)
Politician, U.S. senator, and secretary of the interior
German

Carl Schurz was the most famous of the German refugees who came to the United States after the revolution of 1848. He was the "forty-eighter" who most successfully climbed the ladder of U.S. politics.

Born of middle-class background near Cologne on 2 March 1829, Schurz was a university student at Bonn when the revolution of 1848 began. Under the influence of the liberal nationalist professor Gottfried Kinkel, Schurz readily followed him in republican revolutionary activism. When the revolution failed, Schurz helped free Kinkel from prison, and both fled to England.

Schurz married Margarethe Meyer in London. In light of the failure of the revolution in Germany, Schurz and his wife came to the United States in 1852. He first resided in Philadelphia but in 1856 moved to Wisconsin, where the substantial German population offered an opportunity for him to enter American politics. He joined the new Republican Party, agreeing with its antislavery inclinations. However, efforts to convert German Americans to the party were always hampered by their fears of the Republicans' nativism. Nevertheless, Schurz remained steadfast in the party and in 1860 campaigned widely for Lincoln among the Germans. Lincoln rewarded him by appointing him ambassador to Spain.

Schurz returned to the United States in 1862 and accepted a commission as brigadier general in the Union forces, but his efforts as a commander were not successful. Following Lincoln's assassination, Schurz found himself at odds with President Andrew Johnson over Reconstruction policies, and Schurz aligned himself with the Radical Republicans. In 1867 he moved to St. Louis, became editor of the German-language *Westliche Post,* and was active in Missouri Republican politics. He was elected to the U.S. Senate in 1868. However, disillusioned with the Radical Republican policies, Schurz began to advocate a more conciliatory policy toward the South and, by 1872, was identified with the Liberal Republican movement. Eventually, at odds with both parties in his own state of Missouri, he chose not to seek reelection in 1874.

By now Schurz was developing a reputation as a political reformer, advocating civil service reform and opposing the widespread political corruption. He supported Rutherford B. Hayes for the presidency in 1876, and Hayes appointed him secretary of the interior. He applied his reform efforts to the Bureau of Indian Affairs with some success, resigning at the end of Hayes's term in 1881 and becoming the editor of the *New York Post,* a paper known for its advocacy of reform. Two years later, he resigned from the *Post* and got involved in political activity and lecturing on

behalf of reform. Thereafter, he supported candidates of both major parties at various times, depending on their positions on reform: William McKinley in 1896 and William Jennings Bryan in 1900.

Schurz had begun his political life in the United States as a potential leader of Germans but never managed to unite them. Nonetheless, all German Americans, despite their disagreements, had to acknowledge his reputation as foremost among them in public life. His larger influences were among the general American public, where he served for many years as a conscience in politics. He died in New York City 14 May 1906.

James M. Bergquist

REFERENCES
Easum, Chester V. *The Americanization of Carl Schurz*. Chicago: University of Chicago Press, 1929.
Schurz, Carl. *Intimate Letters of Carl Schurz, 1841–1869*. Edited and translated by Joseph Schafer. Madison: State Historical Society of Wisconsin, 1928.
———. *Reminiscences of Carl Schurz*. 3 vols. New York: McClure, 1907–1908.
———. *Speeches, Correspondence and Political Papers of Carl Schurz*. Edited by Frederic Bancroft. 6 vols. New York: Putnam, 1913.
Trefousse, Hans L. *Carl Schurz: A Biography*. Knoxville: University of Tennessee Press, 1982.

Scorsese, Martin (1942–)
Director, producer, and filmmaker
Italian-American

Martin Scorsese is regarded as one of the greatest directors of his generation. He is best known for films inspired by his social and cultural heritage. Martin Scorsese is a daring artist whose Catholic and Italian-American sensibilities have helped shape the consciousness of his films.

Scorsese was born on 17 November 1942 in Flushing, New York, to Charles and Catherine (Cappa) Scorsese. After several years, the Scorseses returned to their former home in New York City's Lower East Side, where Martin grew up amid the flavor and rhythm of life in Little Italy. Raised a devout

Roman Catholic and intent on becoming a priest, Scorsese found in filmmaking what he called his "true vocation." As a student at New York University (NYU), he turned out films that won national awards. While subsequently teaching in NYU's film department in 1968, he wrote and directed his first feature film, *Who's That Knocking at My Door?* about the struggle of a young Italian male attempting to reconcile his rigid Catholic mores with the actualities of life in Little Italy.

Scorsese's Italian-American and Catholic heritage, notably the rituals of the Catholic mass and the notions of sin and redemption, have had a major impact on his films. This "Catholic sensibility," combined with themes of ethnicity, social class, and family dynamics, defines many of his films. In 1973, he filmed *Mean Streets,* about a young Italian American trying to get ahead in the Mafia. It was lauded as "a triumph of personal filmmaking." In other films of that genre—*GoodFellas* (1990) and *Casino* (1995)—Scorsese explores the world of organized crime, blood imagery, and its Catholic intonations—associating blood-shed with redemption.

Although several of his early films deal with Mafia themes, viewed with disdain by the Italian-American public, Scorsese re-deemed himself with his compatriots in the 1973 documentary of an after-dinner conver-sation with his parents. His affectionate por-trait of family life in *Italian American* (1974) is realized through family reminiscences and a demonstration of his mother making spaghetti sauce. His ability to capture the cen-tral role of the mother in Italian family life and the Italian love of food and cooking brought tears of recognition to Italian-Amer-ican viewers.

Taking his camera outside of Little Italy, Scorsese has explored themes of patriarchy, morals, social norms, and religion in *Alice Doesn't Live Here Anymore* (1975), *The King of Comedy* (1982), *The Last Temptation of Christ* (1986), *The Grifters* (1990), *Cape Fear* (1991), *The Age of Innocence* (1993), and *Kundun* (1997). As a moralist and artist examining the world in which he lives, Scorsese has used his films to arouse and disturb his audience as few other filmmakers have been able to do. In the process, he has received numerous honors for his works, including being named best direc-tor by the National Society of Film Critics for *Taxi Driver* in 1976 and *Raging Bull* in 1980. In 1986 he was named best director at the Cannes Film Festival.

Diane C. Vecchio

REFERENCES
Blake, Richard A. "Redeemed in Blood: The Sacramental Universe of Martin Scorsese." *Journal of Popular Film and Television* 24.1 (Spring 1996): 2–8.
Bliss, Michael. *The Word Made Flesh. Catholicism and Conflict in the Films of Martin Scorsese.* Lanham, MD: Scarecrow Press, 1995.
Ehrenstein, David. *The Scorsese Picture: The Art and Life of Martin Scorsese.* New York: Birch Lane, 1992.
Kelly, Mary Pat. *Martin Scorsese: A Journey.* New York: Thunder's Mouth Press, 1991.
Lourdeaux, Lee. *Italian and Irish Filmmakers in America, Ford, Capra, Coppola and Scorsese.* Philadelphia: Temple University Press, 1990.
Thompson, David, and Ian Christie, eds. *Scorsese on Scorsese.* Boston: Faber and Faber, 1989.

Seckar, Alvena V. (1916–)
Painter, writer, and social activist
Slovak-American

Alvena Seckar, an artist recognized prima-rily for paintings expressing social and politi-cal commentary, also wrote children's books featuring Slovak-immigrant families. For overcoming a physical disability in order to continue her career, Seckar was designated by *Newsweek* in 1986 as one of its "100 New American Heroes."

Born in 1916 in McMechen, West Virginia, a coal-mining town, Seckar was the daughter of Slovak immigrants, Zuzana and Valentín Seckar. She was eight when Zuzana left her alcoholic husband, took her children, and ul-timately moved to Allentown, Pennsylvania. There, a teacher, discovering young Alvena's artistic abilities, helped arrange a scholarship to art school. From age twelve through high school, she attended weekly art classes. She won competitions and a scholarship to the Moore Institute of Art but accepted one to the University of Pennsylvania. Then the rise of fascism and the Spanish Civil War turned Seckar into an activist. Along with various protest activities, she drew posters depicting anti-Hitler themes and supporting American volunteers fighting General Francisco Franco in Spain. In her third year, these activities played a role in her transferring to New York University, and she graduated from NYU with a B.A. in 1939. Winning a fellowship, she attended the Institute of Art and Archeology in Paris the same year; in 1949 she received an M.A. from New York University.

During World War II, while working in the signal corps, Seckar continued painting. In 1944, a New York gallery granted her a one-woman exhibition; two years later, the Pittsburgh Art and Crafts Center did the same. Starkly depicting the physical environment endured by coal-mining families in towns where Seckar had grown up, the paintings reflected the realism and acerbic commentary that would characterize her lifelong work. She produced serene landscapes, but the works that she calls "socially conscious paintings" earned the widest attention.

In the 1950s, Seckar published three children's novels, all inspired by her childhood experiences as a second-generation Slovak. Set in coal-mining towns, the stories sensitively portrayed Slovak culture and family life. The *New York Times* selected *Zuzka of the Burning Hills* as one of the "hundred best books published for children" in 1952. Painting, however, remained Seckar's passion, and when stricken in 1963 by multiple sclerosis, which paralyzed her right side, she taught herself to paint with her left hand. Her triumph prompted the 1986 *Newsweek* citation.

Seckar has earned the recognition of activists and art galleries, especially in the Northeast, where she has lived most of the time. Although her achievements have not been explicitly classified as those of a Slovak American, she has maintained her ethnic identity. Her paintings include Slovak folk costumes, and her children's books reveal a strong ethnic identity. Moreover, although it was only as an adult that she took Slovak-language courses, she still emphasized, in a piece for a 1990 Slovak publication, that she "was the product of a proud [Slovak] heritage." In 1988, her parent's homeland honored this Slovak American with an exhibition of her paintings in Bratislava, the capitol of modern-day Slovakia. Nevertheless, the combination of her achieving recognition principally in the arts and her controversial politics have prevented Seckar from gaining significant notice among Slovak Americans. She continues painting, exhibiting, and receiving awards.

June G. Alexander

REFERENCES

Seckar, Alvena. Clipping File. Provided to author by Alvena Seckar, November 1999.

———. *Exhibit of Paintings: December 14, 1946, through January 1945, Arts and Crafts Center, Pittsburgh, Pennsylvania.* Pittsburgh: Arts and Crafts Center, 1946.

———. Interview by author, 9 November 1999.

———. "My Slovak Heritage." In *National Slovak Society of the USA. Kalendàr—Almanac for the Year of 1990,* 72–73. Pittsburgh: Slavia Printing Co., 1990.

Sennett, Mack (né Michael Sinnott) (1880–1960)

Movie producer
Irish-Canadian

Mack Sennett made at least 1,000 movies during his fifty-year career. He was one of the great pioneering directors during the silent movie era.

Sennett was born Michael Sinnott in Richmond, Quebec, on 17 January 1880. He was the son of John Francis Sinnott, an Irish Catholic farmer, and Catherine Foy Sinnott, who moved to East Berlin, Connecticut, in 1897 and later to Northampton, Massachusetts. Working as a boilermaker, Mack Sennett (his stage name) was introduced to Marie Dressler, a Canadian actress, who encouraged the aspiring entertainer to consult Broadway producer David Belasco about work on the Broadway stage.

By 1899 Sennett was a chorus boy and bit player in burlesque theaters in New York City. Drawn to the Biograph Company silent movie productions in New York, Sennett had found minor roles by 1909. Another unknown Irish-Canadian Catholic actor, Mary Pickford, encouraged him to submit movie scripts to Biograph's leading director-producer, D. W. Griffith. Although Sennett avoided being typecast as an ethnic performer, he infused his silent movie comedies with a satirical view of authority rooted in an Irish sense of life as absurd and heartbreaking. By 1910 he moved to Los Angeles, directing short two-reel silent comedies for Griffith, whom Sennett later called "my university." In 1912 Sennett established his own Keystone Company in a small town east of Los Angeles.

Sennett's first movies were often impromptu, using film of real parades, fires, and automobile accidents together with studio scenes and close-ups to tie the motion picture together. Borrowing from French comedies, Sennett was best known for slapstick humor, risky stunts performed by leading actors, pie-in-the-face scenes, and kick-in-the-pants pratfalls. His Keystone Kops were inspired by filming the Los Angeles Police Department at a city parade, and the mustachioed Irish-American cop became a staple of his movies.

Sennett employed many fledgling movie stars, writers, and directors. Among his discoveries were Roscoe "Fatty" Arbuckle, Frank Capra, Charles Chaplin, Chester Conklin, Bing Crosby, Minta Duffee, W. C. Fields, Harry Langdon, Carole Lombard, Mabel Normand, Gloria Swanson, Ben Turpin, and Darryl F. Zanuck. His assembly-line production and long hours yielded at least one movie a week, popular and profitable two-reel comedies. In 1914 alone he made thirty-five movies with an unknown English comic, Charles Chaplin. One of these may have been Sennett's best film, *Tillie's Punctured Romance* (1914), starring Chaplin, Normand, and Marie Dressler.

In 1915 Sennett joined Thomas Ince and D. W. Griffith to establish the Triangle Film Corporation; when it dissolved in 1917, he formed the Mack Sennett Studios, where he amassed a fortune he estimated at $15,000,000 before the 1929 stock market crash wiped him out. He retired in 1935 but returned to receive an Oscar in 1938.

Sennett wrote his autobiography in 1954; he died on 15 November 1960 in Woodland Hills, California. His tombstone reads "King of Comedy." The Mack Sennett Keystone Custard College is remembered today as Hollywood's first school of film studies, promoting an American commedia dell'arte before the era of the big movie studios.

Peter C. Holloran

REFERENCES

Lahue, Kalton C. *Mack Sennett's Keystone: The Man, the Myth, and the Comedies.* South Brunswick, NJ: A. S. Barnes, 1971.

Sennett, Mack. *King of Comedy.* Garden City, NY: Doubleday, 1954.

Sherk, Warren M., ed. *The Films of Mack Sennett.* Lanham, MD: Scarecrow Press, 1998.

Shalala, Donna (1941–)

Educational administrator and U.S. secretary of health and human services
Lebanese-American

Donna Shalala, secretary of health and human services in the Clinton administration was the first Arab American to serve in a cabinet-level position. Before that, she was the first female head of a "Big Ten" university.

A third-generation Lebanese American, Shalala was born in Cleveland, Ohio, to James and Edna Shalala. She credits her success in part to their inculcating her with "an immigrant's zeal to succeed." Her father, a leader in Cleveland's Syrian-Lebanese community, ran grocery stores and sold real estate. Her mother, while raising twin daughters, earned a law degree and continued to practice into her eighties. After graduating from college in 1962, Shalala served in the newly created Peace Corps in Iran before returning to Syracuse University, where she obtained an M.A. and, in 1970, a Ph.D.

Shalala served as an assistant secretary of

housing and urban development during the Carter administration. Among her initiatives was increasing the number of mortgages held by women. The author of several books and articles on state and urban politics, Shalala taught political science at Baruch College, Columbia University's Teachers College, and Hunter College. From 1975 to 1977 she served as director and treasurer of the Municipal Assistance Corporation (MAC) for the City of New York during that city's fiscal crisis. Afterward, she was appointed president of Hunter College and, subsequently, chancellor of the University of Wisconsin (1988–1993). There, she supported several racial- and ethnic-diversity initiatives, placed greater emphasis on undergraduate education, and significantly increased the university's endowment. She has also served on the boards of numerous corporations and foundations. Shalala is well known for her tremendous energy and for her extensive networks in education, politics, and journalism.

As secretary of health and human services, Shalala was one of several female cabinet members appointed by President Clinton as part of his pledge to bring greater gender and racial diversity to his administration. She oversaw an agency with a budget of $590 billion, larger than that of any other cabinet member. She administered the significant changes resulting from the Welfare Reform Act of 1996, and she played a significant role in Clinton's health care task force, charged with reforming the nation's health care system. Shalala has been particularly active on behalf of several women's and children's issues: lowering teen pregnancy rates, funding breast cancer research, and expanding immunization rates. But she came under criticism for the administration's decision not to provide funding for needle exchange as a means of addressing the AIDS crisis.

As a cabinet member, Shalala traveled to the Middle East in 1998, making a goodwill trip to Lebanon to support the peace process and visiting Egypt to discuss public health issues. In both countries, she spoke of the importance of her Lebanese heritage, even as a third-generation American, for although not overly emphasizing her ethnic roots, she has acknowledged them as one source of her success. Perhaps of more importance is that she is still identified by Arab Americans and their organizations as a "prominent" Arab American, the first cabinet-level Arab American. In June 2001, she became the president of The University of Miami. Given her diverse achievements, she is, for this growing population of Arab Americans, a model ethnic American success story.

Deirdre M. Moloney

REFERENCES

"ArabicNews.com" (4 December 1998): www.arabicnews.com/ansub/Daily/Day/981204/FP.html (accessed 15 June 2000).

Bernstein, Alison, and Shirley Mow. "On Changing Academic Culture from the Inside: An Interview with Donna Shalala." *Change,* January/February 1989, 20–29.

"Donna E. Shalala, Secretary of Health and Human Services." U.S. Department of Health and Human Services website. http://www.os.dhhs.gov/about/bios/dhhssec.html. (Accessed 21 December 2000).

"Donna Shalala in Lebanon on Mission" (7 December 1998): www.lebanon-online.com/news/dec7.html (accessed 15 June 2000).

Kasem, Casey. "Arab Americans: Making a Difference" (n.d.): www.arabmedia.com/achievers.html (accessed 15 June 2000).

Schultz, Jeffrey D., and Laura van Assendelft, eds. *Encyclopedia of Women in Politics.* Phoenix: Oryx Press, 1999.

"Shalala, Donna." In *Current Biography Yearbook 1991,* edited by Charles Moritz, 514–518. New York: H. W. Wilson, 1991.

Toobin, Jeffrey. "The Shalala Strategy." *New Yorker,* 26 April 1993, 53–62.

Shea, Suzanne Strempek (1958–)

Journalist and novelist
Polish-American

Suzanne Strempek Shea writes about the experiences of a coming-of-age female "in a blue-collar ethnic community in North America." Her novels have portrayed Polish Americans with honesty and humor and have been embraced by critics and readers both within and outside the Polish-American community.

The grandchild of Polish immigrants, Strempek was born, raised, and resides near the "Polka Capital of New England," Palmer, Massachusetts. She is the daughter of Edward Frank and Julia (Milewski) Strempek. Her writing talents emerged at age ten, when she published her own hand-lettered *Nutty News.* In 1976, she participated in the Summer School of Polish Language and Culture at the Jagiellonian University, Kraków, Poland, and also studied the accordion. She has worked for the *Springfield Union-News* (Massachusetts) and the *Providence Journal* (Rhode Island) and has contributed to several other publications.

Shea is the author of three acclaimed novels that critics praised for opening a window into the warmth and humor of Polish-American life: *Selling the Lite of Heaven* (1994); *Hoopi Shoopi Donna* (1996); and *Lily of the Valley* (1999). She has been compared to such ethnic writers as Amy Tan (Chinese), Isaac Bashevis Singer (Jewish), Jimmy Breslin (Irish), Mario Puzo (Italian), and Terry McMillan (African American). In each novel the Polish-American community of Western Massachusetts is the backdrop and the source of the novel's heroes and heroines. *Selling the Lite of Heaven* tells the story of a woman left not *at* the altar but *for* the altar. After a vision, pious Eddie Balicki breaks his engagement so that he can enter the priesthood. His fiancée is left with the engagement ring, which she attempts to sell through a classified ad. In the process, she meets a variety of individuals and learns about herself. *Hoopi Shoopi Donna* tells the story of Donna Milewski, who organizes an all-girl polka band and discovers that music is the key to healing her estrangement from her father. Lily Wilk, in *Lily of the Valley,* is a commercial artist whose painting of a family portrait for supermarket-owner Mary Ziemba becomes a journey of self-discovery.

Academic discourse classifies Shea's fiction as both ethnic women's writing and American romance fiction. Shea's comfort with her ethnicity and her femininity both worries and attracts feminist literary theorists. Her novels' Polish-American women are nonactivist and apolitical, not a part of an earlier tradition of liberal, urban working-class activists. One heroine, for example, does not reject but refashions ethnicity and ethnic identity to preserve herself as a woman who is more individualistic and autonomous in mother- daughter relations and in matters of the heart. For Polish critics, Shea's novels are an entrée into American culture, mediated through a specific Polish-American world.

Shea is a skilled, acutely observant author with an ear for unaffected dialogue. She writes about Polish Americans with warmth, deadpan humor, and sensitivity. Her novels reconstruct a changing immigrant ethnic world and have struck responsive chords among people of various ethnic backgrounds, most especially among Polish Americans. The novels "had good things to say about the Polish" and are humorous but not "at the expense of making fun of someone."

Stanislaus A. Blejwas

REFERENCES

Kowalik, Barbara. "Nie wszystko na sprzedaż" (Not everything for sale). *Akcent* 2.68 (1997): 68–73.

Napierkowski, Thomas. "A Stepchild of America: My Polish American Literary Odyssey." *Forkroads* 1.2 (Winter 1995): 57–68.

Shea, Suzanne Strempek. *Hoopi Shoopi Donna.* New York: Pocket Books, 1996.

———. *Lily of the Valley.* New York: Pocket Books, 1999.

———. *Selling the Lite of Heaven.* New York: Pocket Books, 1994.

Tempska, Urszula. "From (Ethnic) Mama's Girl to Her Own (New Ethnic) Woman: Gender and Ethnicity in Suzanne Strempek Shea's *Selling the Lite of Heaven.*" In *Something of My Very Own to Say,* edited by Thomas S. and Rita H. Gladsky, 297–304. Boulder, CO: East European Monographs, 1998.

Shumeyko, Stepan (1908–1962)
Lawyer, editor, and community leader
Ukrainian-American

Stephan Shumeyko, the son of immigrants, became one of the foremost leaders of the

Ukrainian-American community. He represents the second generation's efforts both to preserve Ukrainian ethnicity and to campaign for the independence of Ukraine.

Shumeyko, who was born on 17 January 1908 in Newark, New Jersey, belongs to the first American-educated generation that matured at the time when old immigrants leaders were reaching retirement age and, owing to immigration laws, few new ones were arriving. It was this "third chapter," as they referred to themselves, that became a crucial link for the community's continuation.

Shumeyko graduated from New Jersey Law School in 1931 and went to work for the Ukrainian newspaper *Svoboda* with the objective of starting an English-language supplement for the American-born younger generation. He became the first editor of the *Ukrainian Weekly,* a post he held until 1959. The newspaper, including his articles on current events and his translations of Ukrainian literature, became a source of information on the life of Ukrainians in the United States and about Ukraine. He had significant influence on the younger generation.

It was in the midst of the depression, 1933, that this younger generation defined itself in the context of an ethnic-American community. The Ukrainian Pavilion at the World Exhibit in Chicago provided the opportunity for extensive gatherings of Ukrainians, and that led to the birth of new organizations, among them the Ukrainian Youth League of North America—with Shumeyko its first president—and the Ukrainian Professional Association, in which he held various executive positions.

Freedom for Ukraine was always a central theme of community activism. World War II renewed old hopes for Ukraine's independence, and to that end a representative body of all Ukrainian organizations in the United States was established, the Ukrainian Congress Committee of America. It had a shaky start, but by 1944 a new and successful attempt was made to make it viable, with Shumeyko as its president from 1944 to 1949. In that capacity he went to the founding conference of the United Nations

in 1945 to promote the cause of Ukraine's independence and he represented Ukrainian Americans at the Paris Peace Conference in 1946. To strengthen the political influence of Ukrainians, another umbrella organization, the Pan-American Ukrainian conference, was founded. It represented Ukrainians from North and South American countries, and Shumeyko served as its secretary-general.

For three decades Shumeyko played a determining role in the activities of the Ukrainian-American community. He defined the role of the American-born generation vis-à-vis its community and the larger society. He believed that by cultivating the positive values of Ukrainian culture, one brings new riches to the whole society as well as into one's individual life. The political aspect of his activism sprang from his deep belief in democratic values and the right of every human being and every nation to enjoy freedom.

Shumeyko's first wife, Mary Sawicky, was Ukrainian American; his second wife, Maria Bodruk, was a Canadian-born Ukrainian. He died in New York on 12 August 1962.

Daria Markus

REFERENCES

Lew, Khristiine. "The Editors of the Ukrainian Weekly: Youth at Work." *Ukrainian Weekly,* 10 October 1993.

"Stepan Shumeiko, pershyi i dovholitnii redaktor 'Ukrainskoho Tyzhnevyka'" (Stephen Shumeyko: First and long-term editor of the "Ukrainian Weekly"). *Svoboda,* 14 August 1962.

"Stephen Shumeyko: Energetic Builder of Ukrainian American Life." *Ukrainian Weekly,* 23 October 1983.

Sikorsky, Igor I. (1889–1972)
Aircraft designer and inventor
Ukrainian

Igor Sikorsky remains known for inventions that reshaped passenger and cargo-carrying aircraft. But it was his development of the helicopter that is his greatest legacy.

Sikorsky was born on 25 May 1889 in Kyiv, Ukraine, the youngest of four children. His father, Ivan, a distinguished professor of medicine and psychology, introduced him to physics, astronomy, and chemistry. His mother, also a doctor, was fascinated by Leonardo da Vinci and inspired her son with tales of da Vinci's attempts to design a flying machine. They, along with Jules Verne's stories, instilled in him a lifelong interest in science. At about the age of twelve, he succeeded in making a flying model of a helicopter, rubber-band powered.

After trying different schools in St. Petersburg, Paris, and Kyiv, Sikorsky grew impatient with theoretical studies that had no practical applications for building flying machines and decided to work on his own. Unlike other pioneers at that time, Sikorsky believed that vertical lift-off was possible. In 1909, he attempted to construct a helicopter but was unsuccessful and turned to fixed-wing models. Two years later, Sikorsky constructed the S-5 (S for Sikorsky) model, which remained airborne for more than an hour, attaining an altitude of 1,500 feet and earning him International Pilot's License no. 64. In 1913, he constructed "Le Grand," the first four-engine airplane designed to carry heavy loads. It also had the first enclosed cabin for pilots and passengers. The next year he tested the new machine on a long haul, flying the "Iliya Muromets" from St. Petersburg to Kyiv.

War and revolution then disrupted his life, and in March 1918, he fled to Russia, staying for short periods in England and France en route. A year later, in March 1919, Sikorsky landed in New York, an impoverished immigrant. After a few years of hardship, he started his own company, Sikorsky Aero Engineering Corporation, on a farm near Roosevelt Field, on Long Island, New York. Meantime, he married a fellow immigrant, Elizabeth Semionova, in 1924 and, in 1928, became a U.S. citizen. The Sikorskys had five children.

In his newly adopted country, Sikorsky had the opportunity to perfect projects conceived back in Kyiv. In 1931, model S-40, the "American Clipper," became the flagship of Pan American World Airways, a pioneer on the Caribbean and South American routes

and later routes across the Atlantic and Pacific Oceans. In the late 1930s he returned to his early love—the helicopter. On 14 September 1939, Sikorsky tested the vertical liftoff capability of his new flying machine, VS-300. The helicopter finally became a reality, firmly establishing Sikorsky's legacy.

During his career, Sikorsky established many aviation records and received many awards and honorary degrees, in both the United States and Europe. After retiring as engineering manager of his company in 1957, he worked as a consultant. And although he always remained a "proud son of Kyiv," Sikorsky was also "deeply thankful to this great country of unequaled opportunities which enabled me to resume my life's work. . . . I doubt if this could have taken place anywhere else in the world." Sikorsky died on 26 October 1972, in Easton, Connecticut. His archives are at the factory in Stratford, Connecticut, in the U.S. Library of Congress, and with his family.

Daria Markus

REFERENCES

Cochrane, Dorothy, and Russell Lee von Hardesty. *The Aviation Careers of Igor Sikorsky.* Seattle: University of Washington Press, 1989.

Hunt, William E. *Helicopter: Pioneering with Igor Sikorsky.* Shrewsbury, England: Airlife Pub., 1998; Swan Hill Press, 1999.

Sikorsky, Igor. *The Story of the Winged-S: An Autobiography.* New York: Dodd, Mead, 1941.

Taylor, John W. R., ed. *Images of America: Sikorsky.* Stroud, Gloucestershire, UK: Tempus Publishing, 1998.

Šimutis, Leonardas (1892–1975)
Journalist, editor, and community activist
Lithuanian

A native of Lithuania, Leonardas Šimutis towered among the laity for his intense lifetime devotion to his Roman Catholic faith, interwoven with passion for his ethnic heritage. He combined extensive journalistic and writing endeavors with intensive involvement in many Lithuanian organizations, especially those concerned with the Church and his homeland.

Born on 6 November 1892, one of eight children, in the village of Šerikai, County of Tauragė, Šimutis completed secondary school in Kaunas in 1912 and immigrated the following year to Chicago. After briefly considering the priesthood, he studied at De Paul and Loyola Universities in Chicago (English literature, journalism, and law) and later at Fordham University in New York (sociology).

In his youth he had already shown patriotic fervor by belonging to secret cells during the budding nationalist movement. During his distinguished career in the United States, he was a member and held office in all major Lithuanian societies, including the Lithuanian Catholic Moksleiviai Alliance (college-level students) and the Knights of Lithuania. He organized Knights of Lithuania councils and choruses, provided youth courses, and directed plays. Active in reinvigorating the Catholic Federation, he became general secretary from 1932 to 1952 and then president. During World War I, he was elected one of the directors of the Lithuanian Fund, becoming its secretary and fund-raiser. Within a year he had collected over $350,000. In 1918 he worked for the Lithuanian Roman Catholic Alliance, eventually becoming its president from 1934 to 1962.

In 1926 he went to Lithuania, where he was elected to the Third Seimas (parliament) as a Christian Democrat. When the parliament was suspended in 1927, he returned to the United States. After the Soviets invaded his homeland in 1940, Šimutis organized a meeting of nationalists in Pittsburgh on 9 August 1940. With even Socialists agreeing to participate, they formed the American Lithuanian Council (ALT), and Šimutis was chosen president, 1940 to 1965, leading delegations to meet with U.S. presidents (five times) and other high officials. In addition, in 1943, when the United Lithuanian Relief Fund (BALF) was started, he was among the founders as well as one of its directors.

Šimutis managed to blend his activism with his writing talents. His writing career began with contributions to *Vienybė* (Unity) in 1913.

Soon he began editing *Katalikas* (The Catholic) in Chicago, aided in launching the Knights of Lithuania journal, *Vytis* (The Knight), and (in 1916) lent a hand editing the almanac *Metraštis* (Yearbook). He became editor in chief of *Garsas* (Clarion) (1918 to 1926), the voice of the Lithuanian Roman Catholic Alliance, and then editor in chief of the daily Chicago newspaper, *Draugas* (Friend) (1927 to 1952)—continuing as contributing editor until his retirement in 1968. In addition to poetry, novels, and an operetta, he also published a 500-page history of the ALT in 1971.

For his homeland devotion, the Lithuanian government granted him the Order of Gediminas in 1937, and Pope Pius XII added the Pro Ecclesia et Pontifice (For church and pontiff) Medal in 1952. Šimutis died on 17 April 1975.

William Wolkovich-Valkavičius

REFERENCES

Laučka, J. B. "L. Šimučio 80 m. sukaktį minint" (Remembering the eightieth birthday of L. Šimutis). *Aidai* (Echoes), vol. 8, 1972.

"Simitus, Leonardus." *Lietuviškoji enciklopedija* (Lithuanian encyclopedia), Vol. 29, edited by J. Girnius, 541. Boston: Lithuanian Encyclopedia Press, 1963.

Šimutis, Leonard, Jr. Letter to the author, 16 February 1999.

Šimutis, Leonardas. *Lietuvą aplankius: Pirmo Pasaulio Lietuvių Kongreso Įspudžiai* (Visit to Lithuania: Impressions of the First Lithuanian World Congress). Chicago: Lietuviškos Knygos Klubas, 1995.

"Šimutis, Leonardas." In *Encyclopedia Lituanica,* edited by Simas Sužiedelis and Antanas Kučas, vol. 5: 179–180. Boston: Juozas Kapočius Publisher, 1975–1978).

Singstad, Ole (1882–1969)
Civil engineer
Norwegian

A professional civil engineer, Ole Singstad sought opportunities in the United States greater than those he could find in his native Norway. His engineering skills and innovations led to major breakthroughs in the construction of tunnels and bridges in New York City and elsewhere.

Singstad departed from his birthplace, Leksvik, Norway, in 1905 after graduating from the College of Technology in Trondheim, having been trained as a civil engineer. At the age of twenty-three, he left a homeland with few suitable jobs and settled in the United States, then offering the most job opportunities and highest wages for engineers. Singstad later said he came to the United States to "get experience, see the world, and find opportunity." And he did.

His skills and creative imagination were in great demand at a time of transportation revolutions in U.S. cities, and railroad companies immediately offered Singstad work. At first, he designed railroad lines in New Jersey. He then took a position with the Virginian Railway in rail and bridge construction but left that job for more varied work and better pay in railway, subway tunnel, and bridge engineering for the Hudson-Manhattan Railroad. During these years, he accumulated experience, became familiar with diverse American professional environments, and won a reputation for brilliantly original engineering solutions. In 1919 he accepted the challenge of designing a tunnel under the Hudson River from lower Manhattan, a project that had twice earlier ended in failure. Singstad's plans were innovative. The two vehicular tubes he designed were larger than any previous underwater tunnels, and with his unique ventilation system, he made the automobile tunnel a practical construction for the first time. His engineering solutions for the Holland Tunnel became the model for such projects across the country and abroad. Singstad served for thirty-five years as chief consulting engineer for tunnels for the Port Authority of New York, then the largest transportation authority in the United States, and his designs became the basis for all the city's vehicular tunnels, including the Lincoln, the Queens Midtown, and Brooklyn-Battery Tunnels.

Thus it was that he became acclaimed in his own lifetime as one of a handful of the most eminent engineers in the world, in his case as one of the people who had made possible the relatively rapid movement of massive motor traffic that people now expect and depend upon in large urban areas. Moreover, expanding beyond his specialty in tunnel design, Singstad became an authority on foundation engineering for large structures, including multilevel bridges such as the George Washington Bridge, which spans the Hudson River between New Jersey and Manhattan. Before he retired in 1945, Harvard University hired him to lecture on this subject, and New York University and Stevens Institute of Technology recognized the significance of his career by bestowing honorary doctoral degrees on him.

Singstad's career was among the most admired success stories for Norwegian immigrants and their descendants on the East Coast. Relatively affluent, he and his wife lived in a fine suburban home that typified the material goals of many other Norwegian-American families. He was active member and speaker for the New York chapter of the Norwegian-American Technical Society, an association organized into a national network to assist engineers arriving from Norway and publicize members' progress.

David C. Mauk

REFERENCES

Bjork, Kenneth. *Saga in Steel and Concrete: Norwegian Engineers in America.* Northfield, MN: Norwegian-American Historical Association, 1947.

Myhre, Liv Irene, ed. *Norwegians in New York, 1825–2000: Builders of City, Community and Culture.* "Biographical Supplement." New York: Norwegian Immigration Association, 2000.

Skinner, Frank W. "The Holland Vehicular Tunnel, under the Hudson River." *Engineering* 11 (London), 25 November and 9 December 1927.

Skouras, Spyros P. (Panagiotes) (1893–1971)
Corporate leader and film industry entrepreneur
Greek

Spyros P. Skouras was a Greek immigrant who personified the American Dream. In 1942 he became the president of the Twentieth Century Fox film corporation. His ownership and management, along with his two brothers, of 563 theaters were rated as "one of the outstandingly successful theater operations in the country."

Skouras was born in Skourohorion, a village in the Province of Elia, Greece. His father, Panagiotes Skouras, was a sheepherder, with five sons and five daughters. When Spyros was fifteen he began to study for the priesthood, earning a living as a journalist while managing also to study English and bookkeeping. The brothers saved their money to send Charles, the eldest, to the United States. He sailed in 1907 and, three years later, sent for Spyros and, eventually, two others (the youngest soon died). Skouras was naturalized in 1913.

For a time the brothers worked as busboys in a hotel in St. Louis, Missouri. By 1915 they had saved enough money to buy a local theater, which they renamed the "Olympia." In 1919, after serving in the army air force, Spyros Skouras returned to St. Louis and began to expand his theater interests, closely studying motion picture finance, real estate values, and theater operation. By 1926, he controlled (along with Paramount) thirty-seven theaters in St. Louis and a large number in Kansas City and Indianapolis. Warner Brothers bought the Skouras holdings and retained him as general manager.

In 1931, he left Warner in order to assume the presidency of a subsidiary operating all Paramount theaters in seven eastern states. In 1932, he became the head of the Fox Metropolitan Theaters as well. The brothers continued to acquire theater chains and, by 1942, were operating 563 theaters. By 1938, Skouras —with a salary of $254,000—was the fifth-highest-salaried cinema executive. After the president of Twentieth Century Fox died, Skouras, on 9 April 1942, became its president, a post he held until 1962. Among the outstanding films made during his tenure as president were *The Oxbow Incident* (1943), *Winged Victory* (1944), *State Fair* (1945), *Miracle on 34th Street* (1947), *All About Eve* (1950), *Twelve O'-Clock High* (1950), *Gentlemen Prefer Blondes*

(1953), *Carousel* (1956), *South Pacific* (1958), *The Diary of Anne Frank* (1959), and *The Hustler* (1961).

Skouras had a rich record of involvement in civic and patriotic affairs, and he and his brothers remained active in the Greek-American community. He organized and conducted the National War Heroes Parade in June 1942; was the director of Freedom House; and was elected head of the Greek War Relief Association, formed to assist Greek people during the German and Italian occupation between 1941 and 1944. He helped raise $9,700,000. Skouras was also a member of the Greek Orthodox church and was on the board of the New York Greek Cathedral. Later, he and his brothers contributed to build St. Sophia's Cathedral in Los Angeles.

Spyros Skouras was married in 1920 in St. Louis to the former Saroula Bruiglia. They had three daughters, Daphne, Diana, and Dionysia, and two sons, Spyros and Plato.

George A. Kourvetaris

REFERENCES

Moskos, Charles, C. *Greek Americans: Struggle and Success*. 2d ed. New Brunswick, NJ: Transaction Publishers, 1989.

"Skouras, Spyros." In *Current Biography 1943*, 702–704. New York: H. W. Wilson, 1943.

"Skouras, Spyros." In *Webster's American Biographies*, edited by Charles Van Doren, 955–956. Springfield, MA: Merriam Co., 1974.

Slater, Samuel (1768–1835)

Cotton manufacturer and entrepreneur
English

More than any other immigrant, Samuel Slater was responsible for the rapid development of America's early textile industry. He also established the industry's initial managerial practices, crucial in an emerging industrial economy.

Samuel Slater was born on June 9, 1768, in Belper, Derbyshire, the son of William Slater, a farmer and merchant, and Elizabeth Fox. The first water-powered textile mills were built in Derbyshire, and Slater, after receiving a common (elementary) school education, worked for his father's friend, Jedediah Strutt, a former partner of Richard Arkwright, the inventor of the first water-powered spinning frame. In 1783 Slater signed a six-year apprenticeship with Strutt in a new local mill. He rose to become overseer and, eventually, supervisor. During these years Slater absorbed the complete design of the Arkwright spinning system, which he would bring to the United States and with which the new nation would enter the industrial revolution.

Slater was attracted to the United States by the advertisements for skilled mechanics that state legislatures were publishing in English newspapers. Because England had banned the emigration of textile mechanics in an effort to preserve its lead in industrial technology, Slater simply declared himself an apprentice when he sailed from London, arriving in November 1789. He soon went to Rhode Island, where he knew manufacturers were eager to hire mechanics who could replicate Arkwright's machines. In 1790 Slater signed a contract with William Almy and Smith Brown to build a water-powered cotton-spinning mill according to Arkwright's designs. In return, Slater would receive fully one-half of the net profits and retain one-half ownership of the machinery.

Slater successfully replicated Arkwright's revolutionary machines. By the end of 1790 he and his partners were operating three carding machines and two spinning frames with seventy-two spindles. In 1793 the company moved to a new, larger building that became known as the Old Slater Mill. By this time he had married Hannah Wilkinson, and with his new in-laws he formed Samuel Slater and Company, with a second factory in Rehoboth, Massachusetts. (Hannah is credited with discovering that cotton thread was superior to the linen thread used for sewing at the time.)

Slater was also instrumental in overcoming the horrible reputation of English factories by using a family system of labor, which integrated some of the aspects of Arkwright's management system but employed new approaches. Children tended the machines, and

their fathers worked in the same factory, performing more traditional tasks, and supervised their children. By 1807, Slater's brother, John—who had knowledge of a new Derbyshire spinning mule and had who had come to the United States in 1803—had joined the partners and set up three new mills in a Rhode Island town soon called Slatersville. The War of 1812 stimulated the U.S. textile industry, much to Slater's benefit. And because of his diversification and leadership in American textiles, he was able to survive the postwar glut when cheap English imports flooded the market. In 1827 he built one of the first steam-powered cotton mills in the United States. By the year of his death in 1835 he was involved with thirteen textile mills.

William E. Van Vugt

REFERENCES

Cameron, Edward Hugh. *Samuel Slater, Father of American Manufactures.* Freeport, ME: B. Wheelright Co., 1960.

Tucker, Barbara M. *Samuel Slater and the Origins of the American Textile Industry, 1790–1860.* Ithaca, NY: Cornell University Press, 1984.

Smith, Alfred "Al" E. (1873–1944)
Alderman, assembly member, sheriff, and governor
Irish-American

Alfred E. Smith was the son of a teamster and factory worker. His father, Alfred E. Smith, Sr., was of Italian and German ethnicity. His Irish roots come from his mother, Katherine Mulverhill. Even though of multiethnic background, Smith always thought of himself, as did the public, primarily as Irish.

Smith grew up in the Lower East Side of New York City. Although surrounded by abject poverty, the Smiths lived in respectable, working-class comfort. He served as an altar boy and attended parochial school. He joined the school's drama club, where he developed the poise and oratorical skills invaluable in politics.

His father died when Smith was thirteen, a tragedy that forced him to quit school and work to help support his family. Work and socializing brought him into contact with the city's Irish-dominated political machine, Tammany Hall. He soon joined the organization and developed a reputation as a skilled campaign worker and effective speaker. By the time he married Catherine "Katie" Dunn in 1900, Smith's political connections had helped him get a job as a city inspector of jurors. In 1903 he won election to the state assembly.

Smith represented a new era for Tammany Hall machine politics. Previously, Tammany garnered the votes of the working class by using money obtained through graft or kickbacks to pay people's rent, pass out Christmas turkeys and bags of coal, and buy rounds of beer at the local saloon. At the turn of the century, however, Progressive Era politicians like Smith recognized the need to deliver social legislation. As a result, Smith steered Tammany toward support for child labor laws, worker's compensation, tenement reform, and women's suffrage. His reformer credentials were confirmed in 1911 when, in the wake of the horrific Triangle Shirtwaist Company fire that killed 146 garment workers, he cochaired the investigative committee on factory safety.

Smith left the state assembly in 1915 and, after serving as sheriff of New York County and president of the board of aldermen, was elected governor of the state in 1918. In this and three subsequent terms Smith furthered his reputation as a reformer, signing into law numerous measures regarding rent control, public transportation, the rights of workers, and social welfare benefits. Many historians credit Smith's initiatives with laying the groundwork for Franklin D. Roosevelt's New Deal.

After an unsuccessful try in 1924, Smith won the Democratic nomination for president in 1928. He proved popular among urban ethnics, especially Irish Catholics, but in the Midwest and South, evangelical Protestants, Prohibitionists, nativists, anti-Catholics, and members of a rejuvenated Ku Klux Klan viewed him as the representative of big city corruption and immorality. For Irish Catholics, many of whom viewed Smith as a symbol of their own rising aspirations, his loss to Herbert Hoover was a bitter experience.

Out of office, Smith took an active role in various charities and hoped to win the Democratic nomination in 1932. When his successor as governor of New York State, Franklin Roosevelt, won the nomination and the general election, Smith hoped for an appointment to head a New Deal initiative. When that failed to materialize, he let his bitterness get the best of him and turned against Roosevelt and the New Deal, becoming a leading spokesman for the conservative Liberty League. That was a bizarre and unfortunate end to a brilliant career. However, he did become president of Empire State, Inc. which operated the Empire State Building. Smith died in New York City on October 4, 1944.

Edward T. O'Donnell

REFERENCES

Eldot, Paula. *Governor Alfred E. Smith: The Politician as Reformer.* New York: Garland Publishing, 1983.

Handlin, Oscar. *Al Smith and His America.* Boston: Little, Brown, 1958.

Josephson, Matthew. *Al Smith, Hero of the Cities: A Political Portrait Drawing on the Papers of Frances Perkins.* Boston: Houghton Mifflin, 1969.

Moore, Edmund Arthur. *A Catholic Runs for President: The Campaign of 1928.* New York: Ronald Press, 1956.

O'Connor, Richard. *The First Hurrah: A Biography of Alfred E. Smith.* New York: Putnam, 1970.

Snow, Clarence Eugene "Hank" (1914–1999)

Entertainer
Canadian

Hank Snow parleyed his Canadian background, early experience, and careful imitation of American models into a successful American career. He was a yodeling country western–style singer and he ultimately sold 70 million records.

Snow was born in Brooklyn, Nova Scotia, the son of George Lewis Snow and Marie Alice Boutlier, who separated when he was young. He was brought up by grandparents, rejoining his mother at age twelve. Working sporadically in fish-processing plants and on fishing boats—when not unemployed and practicing his guitar and singing—Snow got his first break performing at radio station CHNS Halifax in 1934, about the same time he married Minnie "Min" Blanche Aalders, who was his wife for six decades.

Despite his mother's musical background and Nova Scotia's music heritage, Snow insisted that the chief influence on his music making was American music, particularly the recordings of Jimmie Rodgers. Snow was advertised on the radio as the "Cowboy Blue Yodeler" and then as "Hank, the Yodeling Ranger." In April 1935, RCA Victor Records invited him to audition but insisted on original numbers. Snow wrote two songs in the cowboy tradition the night before the audition. One that he recorded for RCA in November 1937—"The Blue Velvet Band"—became a best-seller.

Snow gradually completed his apprenticeship in the music business by going on tour in Atlantic Canada and Quebec, while continuing to record for RCA as "Hank, the Yodeling Ranger." Rejected for Canadian military service for medical reasons, he recorded more cowboy songs before getting a job in 1945 as announcer and performer on WWVA, a powerful American radio station in Wheeling, West Virginia. He immigrated to the United States that year.

Snow moved steadily ahead in the United States as a country music performer, complete with horse and fancy cowboy outfits. In January 1950, he began a long association with the Grand Old Opry on station WSM, introduced as "The Singing Ranger, Hank Snow" and becoming well known for his flashy Cadillacs and gaudy rhinestone suits. In 1950, his song "I'm Movin' On" remained for twenty-nine weeks at the top of national (country music) charts. A number of his subsequent compositions also achieved Billboard's hit status, around eighty-five recorded by him and additional ones by others. Snow became a U.S. citizen in 1958 and regarded his performances for American troops overseas as the highlight of his career.

Snow sold 70 million records (most of them singles) over a career that was at its peak from 1950 to 1965 but continued on until 1996, despite early ill health and a hard-living lifestyle of women and drink. In 1979 he was inducted into the Country Music Hall of Fame in Nashville. Later that same year he was inducted into the Canadian Academy of Recording Arts and Sciences Hall of Fame. Snow's recorded legacy consists of 833 commercial sides, 98 recorded in Montreal for RCA Canadian, and more than 100 albums. He died December 20, 1999.

J. M. Bumsted

REFERENCE
Snow, Hank, with Jack Ownbey and Bob Burris. *The Hank Snow Story*. 1994.

Snowe, Olympia (née Olympia Jean Bouchles) (1947–)

State and U.S. House representative and U.S. senator
Greek-American

Daughter of a Greek-immigrant man and a Greek-American woman, Olympia Snowe was the first Greek-American woman elected to Congress and the second woman senator to represent Maine—as well as only the fourth woman to be elected to both houses of Congress. She has also won more federal elections in Maine than any other person since World War II.

Snowe was born Olympia Jean Bouchles, on 27 February 1947, in Augusta, Maine. She is the daughter of George Bouchles, a native of Mytilene, a Greek island in the eastern Aegean. Her mother was Georgia Goranites Bouchles, an American-born woman whose parents had immigrated to the United States from Sparta. Following the death of her parents, Snowe was raised by her aunt and uncle in Auburn, Maine. She attended St. Basil's Academy in Garrison, New York, which served as a Greek Orthodox orphanage. Graduating in 1962, she returned to Auburn to attend high school and then went to the University of Maine at Orono, receiving a degree in political science in 1969.

Before Snowe's election to the U.S. Congress, she was elected to both the Maine State House of Representatives and the Maine State Senate. She was first elected to the state house in 1973, taking the seat vacated by the death that year of her first husband, Peter Snowe. She was reelected in 1974 and in 1976 was elected to the Maine Senate. There, she was particularly recognized for her leadership role on health care issues.

Snowe was first elected to Congress in 1978, at the age of thirty-one, the youngest Republican woman; she represented Maine's Second Congressional District for sixteen years. During her eight terms, she earned respect for her leadership as a cochair of the Congressional Caucus for Women's Issues; she served on the Foreign Affairs Committee and the Select Committee on Aging. In November 1994, she was elected U.S. senator from Maine, replacing George Mitchell.

As U.S. senator, Snowe is known nationally for her work on budget-deficit reduction, fiscal issues, and foreign affairs. She has carved out a reputation as a leading moderate Republican and she has been a member of many committees, including the Senate Budget Committee, where she was instrumental in establishing education as a priority. She has also been on the Armed Services and Small Business Committees. Among her key legislative concerns have been prescription drug coverage, student loan funding, access to high-tech telecommunication technology and the internet in schools, and campaign finance reform. She was one of the few Republicans who voted with her Democratic colleagues against the removal of President Clinton from office in the 1999.

Snowe is married to former Maine governor, John R. McKernan, Jr. She is a member of the Holy Trinity Greek Orthodox Church of Lewiston-Auburn and has been an active member in a number of community organizations. The larger Greek-American community has taken great pride in Snowe's record in Congress and her enthusiastic support of issues important to Greek Americans, especially concerning Cyprus and the Aegean.

George A. Kourvetaris

REFERENCES

Moskos, Charles, C. *Greek Americans: Struggle and Success,* 2d ed. New Brunswick, NJ: Transaction Publishers, 1989.

Rossides, Eugene, ed. *American Hellenic Who's Who, 1994–1995.* Washington, DC: American Hellenic Institute, 1994.

"Olympia J. Snowe, United States Senator—Maine. Biography": www.senate.gov/~snowe/bio.htm (accessed 15 June 2000).

Soros, George (1930–)
Investor and philanthropist
Hungarian

George Soros is known around the world. He is one of the greatest investment entrepreneurs and philanthropists of the late twentieth century.

Born in Budapest, Hungary, into an assimilated Jewish family, Soros learned to survive and succeed early in life. In 1944 Soros faced the terror of the Holocaust. He stated, however, that he never internalized the probability of his death—he was just a teenager whose father was quite effective in keeping his family safe—yet, he did profess that the experience had a profound impact on his life: "I was facing extermination at the age of fourteen because I was Jewish. . . . This was when the problem came to the forefront of my consciousness, but . . . [it] took the better part of my life to come to terms with it." (He would later acknowledge his Jewish roots but, because of his early experiences, he would not emphasize that identity.) Following the war, Soros left his war-torn homeland and went to England. In London, he did menial-labor while studying at the London School of Economics. In 1953 he received his economics degree and afterward worked in various firms as a trainee in different business fields, from sales to the stock market.

In 1956, already well known within the European business community, Soros moved to New York to seek greater fortune, immediately obtaining a position as an arbitrageur for a New York firm buying securities in one country and selling them in another. Most Americans were ignorant about the European market, giving Soros a decided advantage.

During the next decade and a half, Soros moved to two different companies, maintaining his specialty as a European arbitrageur and gaining a notable reputation within the international business community.

In 1973, Soros established the Soros Fund Management Foundation. With $12 million invested in this new foundation, Soros and Jimmy Rogers, his partner, cultivated it into one of the most prosperous corporations in the world, worth, by the end of 1981, about $381 million. Soros and Rogers parted, and the former changed the name of the business to the Quantum Fund. He continued to expand the business, dealing with everything from commodities to electronic warfare equipment. This corporation proved so successful that for twenty-six years the shareholders received almost 35 percent in annual returns.

Having established the Open Society Fund in 1979, Soros began philanthropic ventures in 1980 to encourage open societies for nations that were under repressive regimes. He first created scholarships for South Africans to attend Cape Town University. Thereafter, he offered financial aid for the Solidarity Movement, Charter 77, the Sakharov Movement, and many educational institutes throughout Eastern Europe. In his native country he founded the Central European University and the Open Society Archives. He attempted to make changes in China and the Soviet Union, the former proving futile, whereas the latter is in progress. Following California voters' approval of the nativist Proposition 187 in 1994, he also established through the Open Society Institute a $50 million Emma Lazarus Fund to promote citizenship among foreigners in the United States. Soros still manages the Quantum Fund and grants millions of dollars to aid those nations that are in the process of establishing democracy, or hoping to do so. For example, between 1994 and 1996, The Open Society Fund and the Open Society Institute spent more than $1.1 billion on programs in more than thirty countries, mostly in Central and Eastern Europe.

Judith Fai-Podlipnik

REFERENCES

"George Soros: A Short Biography." Open Society Institute website. http://www.osi.hm/soros.html. (Accessed 21 December 2000.)

Lindsey, Lawrence. *Economic Puppetmasters: Lessons from the Halls of Power.* Washington, DC: AEI Press, 1999.

Slater, Robert. *Invest First, Investigate Later: And Twenty-three Other Trading Secrets of George Soros, the Legendary Investor.* New York: John Wiley, 1999.

———. *Soros: The Life, Times, and Trading Secrets of the World's Greatest Investor.* Burr Ridge, IL.: Irwin Professional Publishing, 1996.

Soros, George. *George Soros Speaks: Insight from the World's Greatest Financier.* New York: John Wiley, 1999.

———. *Underwriting Democracy.* New York: Free Press, 1991.

Spanos, Alex G. (1923–)
Entrepreneur and philanthropist
Greek-American

One of the major real estate developers and philanthropists in the Unites States, Alex Spanos is the founder of ten companies bearing his name, an entrepreneur epitomizing the American Dream. His life exemplifies the American and Greek values of faith, philanthropy, and entrepreneurship, three areas in which he has been recognized as one of the most successful Greek Americans of the latter half of the twentieth century.

Alex G. Spanos was born in Stockton, California, on 28 September 1923, to Greek-immigrant parents from the city of Kalamata, in the southern Peloponnisos. An air force veteran, after World War II he attended California State University at San Luis Obispo and the College of the Pacific in Stockton, California. In 1951, he borrowed $800, purchased a truck, and started a business catering sandwiches to migrant farmworkers in the San Joaquin Valley. By the age of thirty-two, he had made his first million dollars and by forty had built a construction empire spanning fifteen states and making the Spanos Corporation one of the top-ten building giants in the United States. By the late 1990s, his companies were employing more than 500 people nationwide.

As a churchman, Spanos has been an active member and supporter of the Greek Orthodox Church in the United States and the Orthodox Ecumenical Patriarchate in Istanbul, Turkey. Among his many philanthropic activities, he is a frequent contributor to local Greek Orthodox churches and the major contributor of over $500,000 to Patriarch Athenagoras Orthodox Institute at the University of California, Berkeley, an inter-Orthodox religious research and learning center. He has been president of the Archdiocesan Council of the Greek Orthodox Archdiocese in the United States, a group appointed by the archbishop to help him administer church programs. For his devotion and support of his Orthodox faith, Spanos was made an archon of the patriarchate in 1972, an honorary title given by the patriarch to those who have shown their devotion and support of the Orthodox Christian faith.

Spanos is also known as a great philanthropist in nonreligious matters and has been associated with many charities. He has contributed to the victims of physical disasters, such as the earthquake in his father's hometown of Kalamata, Greece, and he donated $1 million to the American Red Cross for California flood victims in 1997. Spanos is the benefactor of the United Service Organization (USO), the YMCA, and several children's institutions, including St. John's School for Boys, which is under the Greek Orthodox jurisdiction in Whitewater, California. He has also supported the Children's Hospital and Health Center in San Diego.

Over the years Spanos has received many honors and awards for his numerous philanthropic and philhellenic contributions, his support of his church, and his entrepreneurial activities, including the Ellis Island Medal of Honor; the Horatio Alger Award, sponsored by the American Hellenic Educational Progressive Association (AHEPA); two honorary doctoral degrees; and the National Distinguished Community Service Award from the Anti-Defamation League of B'nai Brith. Married to Faye Faklis (they have four children), Spanos has successfully combined his entrepreneurial success with his philanthropic, religious, and philhellenic sentiments.

George A. Kourvetaris

REFERENCES

American Red Cross Disaster Relief News. "American Red Cross Receives One Million Dollar Gift from Alex G. Spanos for Flood Victims" (January 10, 1997): www.redcross.org/news/disaster/97/01–10–7a.html (accessed 15 June 2000).

GOAL—Greek Orthodox American Leaders—"Voithia." "Alex G. Spanos, Man and Mason," reprinted from Scottish Rite Journal and the Supreme Council, 33degree, Southern Jurisdiction, USA, 12 August 1998: www.voithia.org/content/qmpdp081298171.html (accessed 15 June 2000).

Greek Orthodox Archdiocese of America. "Alex G. Spanos: Churchman, Philanthropist, Entrepreneur" (1977): www.goarch.org/goa/observer/1997_march/Spanos.html (accessed 15 June 2000).

Rossides, Eugene. *American Hellenic Who's Who in 1990.* Washington, DC: American Hellenic Institute, 1990.

Stevenson, Robert Louis (1850–1894)
Writer
Scottish

Robert Louis Stevenson was one of the most popular and important writers of the late nineteenth century. His work bridged two worlds—the Victorian and the modern.

Stevenson was born in 1850 in Edinburgh, Scotland, the son of Thomas Stevenson, a civil engineer and lighthouse builder, and Margaret Balfour. As a chronically ill child, Stevenson was influenced by his nurse, Alison Cunningham, whose stories filled him with a love of folklore. Another source of inspiration was the island of Earraid, off Mull, where his father supervised the construction of a lighthouse and Stevenson spent time as a young man. The island later appeared in several of Stevenson's novels, including *Kidnapped* (1886). To please his father, Stevenson studied law and passed the bar in 1875, although he never did practice law. He was destined to become a writer.

Stevenson was a voracious reader who was fluent in several languages and traveled extensively throughout Europe. In France in 1876 he met the American painter Fanny Osbourne, with whom he fell in love, though she was married with two children. Three years later, Stevenson—with limited funds—traveled by steerage compartment to the United States to be with her. He crossed the continent as part of an emigrant "train," an experience that furnished him with material for his writings, including *The Amateur Emigrant* (1883), a vivid account of the young nation as seen by a traveler. Stevenson and Osbourne wed in San Francisco in 1880, and Stevenson quickly assimilated fully into American life. He was influenced by some of the great American writers, especially Walt Whitman and Nathaniel Hawthorne. In the public mind he had become an American, though he was first and last a Scotsman.

In 1880 Stevenson returned to France and England for a four-year period that proved fruitful. After publishing his most famous works, *Treasure Island* (1883), *Kidnapped* (1886), and *The Strange Case of Dr. Jekyll and Mr. Hyde* (1886), he became famous. In 1887, he moved to New York, where his publishing career continued to flourish. There, Stevenson was persuaded to write twelve monthly articles for *Scribner's* magazine, some of which were to be among his best-loved essays. Then, Samuel Sidney McClure, a Scotch-Irish immigrant who had become a powerful newspaper publisher, offered Stevenson $10,000 to write a series of "letters" from the South Seas. Stevenson relished the experience as he sailed through the Pacific, traveled to Tahiti, Hawai`i (where he became a friend of the royal family), and eventually settled (and built a home) on the island of Samoa. Some of his best work came from this period, including *The Ebb-Tide* (1894) and the posthumously published *In the South Seas* (1896).

In 1894, Stevenson died in his South Sea home of a cerebral hemorrhage, having become a legend in his own time. He was sculpted and painted by some of the greatest artists of his day, including John Singer Sargent and Augustus Saint-Gaudens. His many writings were and are loved for their artistic and philosophical brilliance, for their vivid attention to detail, but perhaps most of all because they contain wonderful stories.

William E. Van Vugt

REFERENCES

Balfour, Graham. *The Life of Robert Louis Stevenson.* New York: Scribner's, 1901.

Furnas, Joseph. *The Voyage to Windward.* New York: Sloane, 1951.

McLynn, Frank. *Robert Louis Stevenson: A Biography.* London: Pimlico, 1993.

Menikoff, Barry. *Robert Louis Stevenson: Tales from the Prince of Storytellers.* Evanston, IL: Northwestern University Press, 1993.

Stewart (née Kostyra), Martha Helen (1941–)
Multimedia entrepreneur and author
Polish-American

Martha Helen Stewart has created a multi-million-dollar, multinational multimedia empire devoted to providing women with ideas, models, and products concerning many aspects of home life. This third-generation American woman of Polish origin is so successful that she has become an arbiter of American cultural tastes and a cultural icon.

Born in 1941 in Jersey City, New Jersey, Stewart was the second of the six children of Martha (Ruszkowski) and Edward Kostyra, a schoolteacher and a pharmaceutical salesman. She learned cooking, baking, canning, and sewing from her mother, and her father introduced her to gardening. She married Andrew Stewart in 1961 (they divorced in 1990) and graduated from Barnard College in 1964. The Stewarts had a daughter, Alexis, born in 1965. Initially a stockbroker (1967–1973), in 1976 Stewart started a catering business in Westport, Connecticut, which became a million-dollar-a-year enterprise, and she opened a specialty food retail store.

Stewart has since contributed articles to the *New York Times,* been an editor and columnist for *House Beautiful,* and appeared on various television programs. Her first book, *Entertaining* (1982), cowritten with Elizabeth Hawes, was an immediate success and became an influential U.S. lifestyle book. She has published more than a dozen lavishly illustrated books on home decorating, weddings, and entertaining and launched her own magazine, *Martha Stewart Living* (November 1990), syndicated television program (1993), and daily radio show. Now, she sells her wares on the internet. Stewart's merchandizing empire is called Martha Stewart Living Omnimedia, a corporate entity that in 1997 generated over $200 million in sales. Omnimedia president Sharon Patrick declared that Martha Stewart will become "the world's first true multimedia brand [name]."

"Explaining Martha" is a new cottage industry for cultural commentators and academicians. Yet, notwithstanding the parodies and academic discussions of the "Martha Stewart phenomenon," her glorification of domestic tasks has attracted ordinary women who identify with their roles as mothers, wives, and homemakers. She provides order and responds to a desire for ritual and tradition. In so doing, she has celebrated the American world and built an empire that packages a distinctive American style.

Detractors have noted with malicious glee that she is not a WASP but a Pole. Although she does not feature her ethnicity, she does not deny it. Her mother and family members have appeared on her television programs making *chruszczyki* (intertwined strips of dough, baked and sprinkled with powdered sugar), and various "Martha's Calendars" in *Martha Stewart Living* have included a Good Friday entry to "make pierogi," "bake babka for Easter breakfast," and "go to Poland for Andrzej Dudzinski's fiftieth birthday." Her ethnicity is a discrete but integral part of her public persona, particularly evident when she discusses family values acquired during her upbringing.

In June 1996, *Time* named Stewart one of "America's Twenty-five Most Influential People," and, in October 1998, *Fortune* proclaimed her one of the "Fifty Most Powerful Women." In 1998, too, she was inducted into the National Sales and Marketing Hall of Fame and elected a member of the Polish Institute of Arts and Sciences in the United States. Despite the accolades, it has apparently grated on some who have held on to the "Polack" stereotype to witness a third-generation woman of Polish origin become an arbiter of American tastes.

Stanislaus A. Blejwas

REFERENCES

"About Martha—Biography": www.marthastewart.com/about_martha/index.asp (accessed 20 May 2000).

Dugan, I. Jeanne. "Someone's in the Kitchen with Martha." *Business Week,* 17 July 1997.

Green, Michelle. "The Best Revenge." *People Weekly,* 2 October 1995: 100–110.

Lippert, Barbara. "Our Martha, Ourselves." *New York,* 15 May 1995, 28–35.

Oppenheimer, Jerry. *Martha Stewart—Just Deserts: The Unauthorized Biography.* New York: Morrow, 1997.

Stewart, Martha. *Entertaining.* New York: Clarkson Potter, 1982.

Stravinsky, Igor (1882–1971)
Composer and conductor
Russian

Igor Stravinsky was one of the world's foremost twentieth-century composers. He is identified with several schools of music composition, including Russian, neoclassical, and serialism, having placed his signature on each of those schools.

Stravinsky was born near St. Petersburg, Russia, in 1882. Although his father, Fyodor, was the leading bass singer in the Imperial Opera in St. Petersburg, Igor was encouraged to study law, but he enjoyed music and was allowed to take some music classes and study privately. In 1902, he met Vladimir Rimsky-Korsakov and became his informal student. Rimsky-Korsakov thought Stravinsky's earliest works demonstrated only promise; however, he was pleased with drafts of Stravinsky's *Symphony in E Flat* (1907).

Stravinsky married his cousin, Catherine Nossenko, in 1906, and they made their home in Volhynia, currently part of western Ukraine. However, his association with Serge Diaghilev's Ballets Russes, for which he composed *The Firebird* (1910), provided Stravinsky with the opportunity to spend most of the next thirty years in western Europe, primarily in France. Thus, the extreme disruptions that occurred in his homeland as a result of World War I and the Russian Revolution were somewhat distant from his experience but not in their impact on him. During that period Stravinsky composed many musical scores for ballet (*Apollo,* 1928), orchestra (*Symphonies of Wind Instruments,* 1920), and voice (*Persephone,* 1934).

Stravinsky's oldest daughter, wife, and mother died in 1938 and 1939, and he decided to move to the United States, accepting a one-year appointment at Harvard University. In 1940 he married Vera Sudeikina, and they settled in West Hollywood, California, which was to be their home until 1969. At first, many of his guests were other Russian émigrés, but as his English improved, his circle of friends became more diverse, including, among others, Aldous Huxley. Stravinsky became a U.S. citizen in 1945.

The war years provided few financial opportunities for Stravinsky. He completed the *Symphony in C* (1940), commissioned by the Chicago Symphony Orchestra, and the *Circus Polka* (1942), commissioned by the Barnum and Bailey Circus. He also wrote music for jazz bands and small ballet scores for Broadway and Hollywood. His most important postwar work was the opera *The Rake's Progress* (1947). It was one of the few pieces Stravinsky wrote without a commission.

In 1949, Stravinsky invited the young musician Robert Craft to become his assistant. Craft introduced him to "serialism," music based on a twelve-note chromatic scale, with the melody being a series of pitches. His last major composition, *Requiem Canticles* (1966), is an example of this shift to "serialism," a change that was gradual but unpopular with his traditional audience. He had met and admired John Kennedy and mourned his death

with an *Elegy for J. F. K.* (1964). In 1968, he scored his last work.

Stravinsky also enjoyed traveling. In 1962 (he was eighty), he conducted orchestras in North America, South America, Africa, the Middle East, and Europe and spent a month in Russia. When he died nine years later, Russian Orthodox funerals were held for him in New York and in an Orthodox church in Venice, where the service incorporated his *Requiem Canticles.*

Keith P. Dyrud

REFERENCES

Craft, Robert. *Stravinsky, Chronicle of a Friendship.* Nashville and London: Vanderbilt University Press, 1994.

Griffiths, Paul. *Stravinsky.* New York: Schirmer Books, 1992.

Oliver, Michael. *Igor Stravinsky.* London: Phaidon Press, 1995.

Stravinsky, Igor. *An Autobiography.* 1936. Reprint, New York and London: W. W. Norton, 1962.

Stukas, Jack J. (1924–1994) and Stukas, Loretta (1932–)

Community activists
Lithuanian-Americans

Jack J. Stukas and his wife, Loretta, stand out among members of second-generation Lithuanians for their unsurpassed love of their heritage. On his part, Jack Stukas epitomized an uncommon combination of an academic career mingled with constant activism as an economist, businessman, radio producer, and ethnic organization leader. Loretta Stukas combined her background in mathematics with an enthusiasm that matched her husband's, likewise participating in an extensive number of Lithuanian organizations, both religious and secular.

Jack Stukas was born on 8 October 1924 in Newark, New Jersey. He acquired his undergraduate degree in 1949 at New York University, his master's degree at Columbia University's Graduate School of Business in 1951, and his doctorate in 1965 from the Graduate School of New York University. Stukas's dissertation, *Awakening Lithuania* (which was published), was a study of the rise of modern nationalism.

As a precocious adolescent, age sixteen, he began airing his own Lithuanian radio program, *Memories of Lithuania,* persuading WBNX in New York City to provide air time. Then, as a staff member of the U.S. Information Agency from 1951 to 1954, Stukas served as radio director and producer for the Voice of America in the North Europe section that included the Baltics. His broadcasting career lasted from 1941 to 1963 on stations WEVD and later WGYN-FM. From 1963 until his death in 1994, he hosted an English-language radio hour of Lithuanian culture through a station at Seton Hall University, South Orange, New Jersey, where he was a professor of marketing and international business. Stukas wisely recruited guest participants from the storehouse of talent in the New York metropolitan area and, by 1966, had already produced more than 1,000 broadcasts. He also prepared a half dozen television programs for Channel 13 (WATV) in New York City. In 1983 the Lithuanian Community (Bendruomenë) singled out Stukas with the Lithuanian equivalent of a Nobel Prize in the category of radio.

The versatile Stukas lent his expertise to the presentation of Lithuanian Days at the World's Fair of 1964 in New York and aided in the erection of a permanent wayside memorial at the exhibit grounds. He frequently lectured on the ethnic circuit and was a board member of most nationwide Lithuanian associations. Among his positions was vice president of the Supreme Lithuanian Liberation Committee and president of the New Jersey Lithuanian Council. He was also director and later president for more than a decade at the Schuyler Savings Bank, Kearney, New Jersey, whose board always consisted of Lithuanians. But he is best remembered for his longtime role in the Knights of Lithuania, where he was president from 1968 to 1972 and chair of Lithuanian Affairs up until his death. He also organized a knights' pilgrimage to Rome in 1972 for the blessing of the Lithuanian chapel in St. Peter's Basilica.

Loretta Stukas (née Kaselytë) was born on 19 December 1932, in Cicero, Illinois. Having won a four-year scholarship, she obtained her undergraduate degree at Xavier College, Chicago. In 1964 she acquired her master's degree in mathematics at De Paul University, Chicago. On 10 October 1964, she married Jack Stukas, settling in New Jersey. In her professional career, Loretta held positions at Argonne National Laboratory, 1954–1964; Bell Laboratories, 1964–1984; and Bell Communications Research, from 1984 to her retirement in 1988.

Stukas's command of Lithuanian has allowed her to provide translation services for the Counterpoint Language Services and the Lithuanian Alliance of America, for which she has been national treasurer from 1994 to the present. In 1952, she joined the Knights of Lithuania, to which she has dedicated much of her lifetime. She edited *Vytis,* the Knights of Lithuania magazine, 1961–1963 and 1970–1981, and always held national office, including an unprecedented four successive annual terms as president, beginning in 1981. In her travels, she revived councils of knights and inaugurated new ones in such places as Kansas and Texas. In addition, she organized choruses, sextets, and other ensembles, participating in all of them. She was a regular announcer and assistant writer for her husband's radio hours in both Lithuanian and English. As a member of the nationwide Executive Committee for the 600th Jubilee of renewed Lithuanian Christianity, Loretta made presentations to President Ronald Reagan and Pope John Paul II.

Since 1986, Stukas has served as Lithuanian representative on the New Jersey Ethnic Advisory Council. With her husband, she directed the Deborah Foundation Lithuanian Children's Fund, collecting over $60,000 for travel for fifty-one medical personnel to and from Lithuania, along with medical equipment and supplies and surgery for nineteen children—all during 1992–1994. (Since 1994 a parallel fund as a memorial for Jack Stukas has continued aid to Lithuanian children with medical and educational needs.) Loretta Stukas's accomplishments in religious and ethnic circles won her the papal medal—*Pro Ecclesia et Pontifice* (For church and pontiff)—in 1985 (when her husband became a papal knight of St. Sylvester), the Woman of the Year Award in 1988 from the Baltic Youth Congress, and the Order of Gedmenas from the Lithuanian government on July 6, 2000.

William Wolkovich-Valkavičius

REFERENCES

Budreckas, Algirdas M. "Jack Stukas." *Lietuvių dienos* (Lithuanian days), May 1982: 4–7 [Cover story].

Stukas, Jack J. *Awakening Lithuania*. 2d ed. Madison, NJ: Florham Park Press, [1966], 1991.

"Stukas, Jack J." In *Lietuvių enciklopedija* (Lithuanian encyclopedia), vol. 29: 80–81; vol. 36: 496; vol. 37: 558. Boston: Lithuanian Encyclopedia Press, 1953–1969, 1985.

"Stukas, Jack J." In *Encyclopedia Lituanica,* edited by Simas Sužiedelis and Antanas Kučas, vol. 5: 313–314. Boston: Juozas Kapočius Publisher, 1975–1978.

Wolkovich-Valkavičius, William. *Lithuanian Fraternalism: Seventy-five Years of U.S. Knights of Lithuania*. Brooklyn, NY: 1988.

Stuyvesant, Peter (Petrus) (1610–1672)

Governor of New Amsterdam
Dutch

Peter Stuyvesant was the last Dutch governor of New (Nieu) Amsterdam. Although his eminence rested neither on any popular endearment nor, ultimately, on his capacity to deter the British takeover of the colony, he did strive to stabilize the colony and place it on a sound moral, economic, and even political basis.

Stuyvesant was born in 1610 in Scherpinzeel, Friesland, the Netherlands (older sources claimed his birth year as 1592). The son of a Calvinist minister, Balthazar Johannes Stuyvesant, he trained for the military and excelled as a soldier. He rose in the service of the Dutch West India Company and, by 1643, was governor of Curaçao and other islands under Dutch rule. In 1644 he led an attack against the Portuguese on St. Martin, losing a leg.

When it did not heal properly, Stuyvesant returned to the Netherlands. His peg leg, decorated with silver bands and nails, earned him the nickname Old Silver Nails.

In 1646, Stuyvesant was named director-general (governor) of Dutch possessions in America. He arrived in New Amsterdam (present-day New York) late that year with his family, finding the colony in some disorder. The previous government had been lenient on vice and had antagonized neighboring Native American tribes through shady trading deals. Stuyvesant quickly took control, closing down the taverns and brothels and negotiating at least temporary peace with the tribes. His iron-fisted, no-nonsense manner was useful in restoring order.

Unfortunately, he verged on the tyrannical, a character flaw that would eventually undermine his reign. For example, a strict Calvinist, Stuyvesant persecuted all who did not conform to the Reformed church, even his fellow Dutchmen. He was especially antagonistic toward Lutherans, Catholics, and Quakers. In one case he deported a Dutch Lutheran minister back to the Netherlands and, in another, had a Quaker whipped and imprisoned for practicing his faith.

In matters of government, Stuyvesant was patriarchal and autocratic. He opposed giving the people a voice in government affairs, and when they finally won an independent city government in 1653, he felt his power significantly diminished. However, he did much to establish and strengthen the economic and commercial base of New Amsterdam, yet it was wracked with problems. In the mid-1660s the peaceful relations he had negotiated with the Native Americans gave way to more skirmishes, including a 1663 massacre at nearby Esopus. Outbreaks of smallpox weakened the populace, and crops were ruined in a Hudson River flood precipitated by an earthquake. Ultimately, however, Stuyvesant's undoing resulted from his alienating nearly all his potential supporters.

In 1664, Britain, which had long coveted the strategic seaport, moved to invade.

Stuyvesant stood firm to defend the city against invasion, but the people were ready for a new ruler, of whatever nationality. They refused to resist the British, and Stuyvesant was forced to surrender. Without bloodshed, New Amsterdam became New York. Stuyvesant retired to his farm, the Bouwerie, where New York's Bowery district is now located. He died in New York in February 1672. Although Stuyvesant's personality may have been repellent, his intelligence and strength of will did much to lay the foundation for one of the world's largest and most cosmopolitan cities.

Jennifer Leo

REFERENCES

Goodwin, Maud Wilder. *Dutch and English on the Hudson.* New Haven, CT: Yale University Press, 1919.

Kammen, Michael. *Colonial New York: A History.* White Plains, NY: KTO Press, 1987.

Rink, Oliver A. *Holland on the Hudson: An Economic and Social History of Dutch New York.* Ithaca, NY: Cornell University Press, 1986.

Suleri Goodyear, Sara (1953–)

Scholar and writer
Pakistani

Sara Suleri Goodyear has made her mark as a writer and scholar of postcolonial literature and cultural studies in the United States. She is professor of English Literature at Yale University.

Suleri, born in Lahore, Punjab, Pakistan, in 1953, was educated in Pakistan at Lahore's Kinnaird College for Women and Punjab University and then in the United States at Indiana University. She now resides in New Haven, Connecticut, where she is a professor of English literature at Yale University. She has recently married an American.

Suleri's finely nuanced studies of the impact of English and colonial rule in India have established her reputation as a leading scholar (most of her work was published under her maiden name, Suleri). However, it is her compellingly written and highly personal account of growing up in Pakistan, in *Meatless Days* (1989), that has brought her a wide audience

in the United States, particularly in women's studies and cultural studies circles.

"Excellent Things in Women," the first chapter of *Meatless Days,* won the 1987 Pushcart Prize and has attracted critical attention for its final, enigmatic line, "There are no women in the third world." Yet that chapter, in fact all of *Meatless Days,* brings women in Pakistan vividly to life, as Suleri relates her own family's idiosyncratic history. (Her mother was Welsh and taught English literature; her father was a leading political journalist in Pakistan.) She interweaves Pakistan's traumatic political history with that of her own family, achieving an extraordinarily memorable account of the troubled years of her own adolescence and of Pakistan's history. Suleri is a very personal and intimate writer but she also knows that private lives intersect with public life and that writing is a public act. The portraits she draws of deaths and losses in her homeland pull readers into the complexities of politics and gender in Pakistan in a way few other books have been able to do.

Her second book, *The Rhetoric of English India,* deals with the speeches of Edmund Burke, the novels of Rudyard Kipling and E. M. Forster, travel accounts by British women, and the writings of V. S. Naipaul and Salman Rushdie. A study of such diverse topics, she states, "obviously seeks to make an issue of cultural migrancy in order to situate the language of the colonizer within the precarious discourse of the immigrant," and to "confirm the precariousness of power." Her work pushes English literary history away from its Eurocentric past to its increasingly postcolonial and transnational ramifications, arousing controversy as well as intense interest as it does so.

In women's studies programs in the United States, she is frequently compared to Maxine Hong Kingston, who achieved similarly stunning evocations of the gendered self; of mothers, grandmothers, and sisters; and of the intersections between personal and political histories. Thus, Suleri Goodyear stands as an eminent postcolonial and transnational scholar, writer of a classic memoir and text in the new academic canon, and as thoughtful producer of influential and highly original books and articles in her scholarly field.

Karen Leonard

REFERENCES

Bizzini, Silvia Caporale. "Sara Suleri's *Meatless Days* and Maxine Hong Kingston's *The Woman Warrior*: Writing, History and the Self after Foucault." *Women: A Cultural Review* 7.1 (Spring 1996): 55–65.

Kanga, Firdaus. "Slices of Bread and Bhutto." London *Sunday Times,* 15 July 1990, Features.

MacMillan, Margaret. "What It Means to Be a Woman in Traditional Islam Society: *Meatless Days*." *Toronto Star Magazine,* 3 June 1989, M10.

Suleri, Sara. *Meatless Days.* Chicago: University of Chicago Press, 1989.

———. *The Rhetoric of English India.* Chicago: University of Chicago Press, 1992.

Sullivan, John (1740–1795)

Major general, governor,
and U.S. district court judge
Irish-American

General John Sullivan's military and political contributions to colonial America during the revolutionary period are legendary. He also later served as governor of New Hampshire and was the first judge of the U.S. District Court of New Hampshire.

John Sullivan was born in Somersworth, New Hampshire. His mother was Margery Brown, who had emigrated from Ireland to Maine. She married John O'Sullivan, who was born in Limerick in 1690 and had immigrated in 1723 (at which time he dropped the "o" in his name). Sullivan's military skills might be linked to an Irish military heritage that included a grandfather, Major Philip O'Sullivan, who fought against William and Mary in 1690. Sullivan's intellectual pursuits were no doubt shaped by his father, a classical scholar fluent in Latin, who was the schoolmaster and also prepared his community's legal documents.

John Sullivan developed a legal practice, which he expanded in 1763 to Durham, New Hampshire, where there was no lawyer because the residents refused to have one. Overcoming the hostility of an unruly mob with the help of his younger brother, James (1744–1808), who later became governor of Massachusetts, Sullivan had a very successful career, acquiring £40,000 by 1775, all of which he had lost by 1777 after joining the rebellious Boston patriots. He often supported the families of his soldiers who had not been paid by the Continental Congress.

As the first rebel in New Hampshire, John was the target of several unsuccessful attempts to regain his loyalty to King George. Ironically, in 1774 Sullivan captured Fort William and Mary in New Hampshire, ending all hopes of a reconciliation with Britain. George Washington admired Sullivan, who crossed the Delaware with the general for the Battles of Trenton and Princeton. Washington ordered Sullivan to New York in 1779 for the attack on the British and their Indian allies among the Iroquois at the Battle of Newtown and neighboring areas. Crops and houses were destroyed, particularly those of the Seneca and Cayuga, and many warriors and British soldiers were killed. The total desolation wrought by Sullivan's forces prevented any further attacks upon the Continental Army and settlers in the region.

After the New York campaign, Sullivan resigned from the army in 1779, and Washington wrote to him, expressing his unequivocal judgment, "You are the saviour of this country, and to your fortitude, bravery and steady performance do we owe the independence and freedom we enjoy." Subsequently, Sullivan was elected governor of New Hampshire in 1786 and reelected in 1788. Indeed, New Hampshire, under Sullivan's leadership, became the ninth state to ratify the new U.S. Constitution in 1788. President Washington then appointed Sullivan the first judge of the United States District Court of New Hampshire, a position he held until his death in 1795, six months before the death of his 105-year-old father, John O'Sullivan.

Sullivan Counties in New York and New Hampshire are named in his honor, and in

1912, New York State erected a monument at Newtown, in the Chemung valley, to commemorate his service to the cause of liberty.

Eileen A. Sullivan

REFERENCES

Clarke, Joseph I. C. "Unveiling the Sullivan Monument." *Journal of the American Irish Society* 12 (1913): 217–237.

General John Sullivan's [Account of His] Expedition against the Iroquois, 1779: home. ptd.net/~revwar/tocong.html (accessed 1 May 2000).

Lyne, Gerald. "The Irish Family Background of Major General John Sullivan." Paper presented at the O'Sullivan/Sullivan Seminar, Tallahassee, FL, 1993.

Whittemore, Charles. *A General of the Revolution, John Sullivan of New Hampshire.* New York: Columbia University Press, 1961.

Tallchief, Maria (née Elizabeth Marie Tall Chief) (1925–)

Ballet dancer
Native American (Osage)

Maria Tallchief, America's first prima ballerina, was born on the Osage Indian Reservation in Oklahoma in 1925. When she attended school in Los Angeles as a child, her surname was Anglicized into Tallchief. A self-described "typical Indian girl—shy, docile, introverted"—she achieved international stardom at the age of twenty-four with her extraordinary performance in George Balanchine's *Firebird*. Although long retired from the stage, Maria Tallchief remains active in the arts and continues her support for American Indian issues.

Maria Tallchief's ascendance to the rank of prima ballerina followed an unlikely path. The daughter of Osage leader Alexander J. Tall Chief and his Scotch-Irish wife, Ruth Porter, Maria (Elizabeth Marie) spent her childhood playing in the rolling countryside near her hometown of Fairfax, Oklahoma, and spending time with her Osage grandmother. Thanks to the oil boom on Oklahoma Indian lands, the Tall Chief family lived in relative prosperity. Maria Tallchief's parents could afford private schooling, dance, and music lessons for her and her sister Marjorie. Ruth Porter Tall Chief believed that her daughters should pursue artistic careers and encouraged that goal by persuading her husband to relocate the entire family to Los Angeles, California, in the 1930s.

Once there, Maria Tallchief began lessons with the renowned dancer-choreographer Bronislava Nijinska. The move to California also led, ironically, to her first exposure to discrimination as an American Indian. Fellow high school students ridiculed Tallchief's last name, teased her by making war whoops, and asked if her father took scalps. Public dance recitals at country fairs found Tallchief and her sister Marjorie performing in buckskin, beads, and feathers for audiences who expected "Indian" dancing.

An audition for the famed Ballet Russe de Monte Carlo beckoned Tallchief to New York City in 1942. As a member of that permanent company, she won prominent roles in ballets as diverse as *Rodeo, Les Sylphides,* and *Chopin Concerto.* Reviewers admired her budding virtuosity and her distinctive appearance and predicted an exceptional career. Tallchief realized those prophecies over the next two decades in leading roles choreographed by the premier American ballet master, George Balanchine. As Balanchine's wife (1946–1952) and artistic muse, she appeared in *Swan Lake, The Nutcracker,* and her signature ballet, *Firebird*. Although these professional successes took her far from Oklahoma, Tallchief's Osage roots remained important to her. In 1953, the tribe and the State of Oklahoma honored her for her fidelity to tribal tradition and her artistry. The Osage Tribal Council named her "Wa-Xthe-Thonba," or Woman of Two Worlds, to acknowledge her melding of Osage and American cultures.

Since her retirement in 1965, Tallchief has remained involved in both American ballet and American Indian issues. She served as artistic director of the Chicago Lyric Opera Ballet and the Chicago City Ballet in the 1970s and 1980s. She also joined Americans for Indian Opportunity in the 1960s and promoted the participation of American Indians in the arts. Additional recognition for her remarkable achievements came in 1996, when she received the prestigious Kennedy Center Honors. With that award, Americans acknowledged Maria

Tallchief for her accomplishments as a Woman of Two Worlds.

Lisa E. Emmerich

REFERENCES

Gruen, John. "Tallchief and Mejia's Chicago City Ballet." *Dance,* December 1984: HC 25–27.

Livingston, Lili Cockerville. *American Indian Ballerinas.* Norman: University of Oklahoma Press, 1997.

Tallchief, Maria, with Larry Kaplan. *Maria Tallchief: America's Prima Ballerina.* New York: Henry Holt, 1997.

Taper, Bernard. *Balanchine: A Biography.* 2d ed., paperback. 1984. Berkeley: University of California Press, 1996.

TallMountain, Mary D. (Demoski) (1918–1994)
Poet
Alaska Native (Athabaskan)

Mary Demoski TallMountain was born in an Athabaskan village just south of the Arctic Circle. She fashioned her childhood memories of life close by the Yukon River into prize-winning poetry.

The daughter of Mary Joe Demoski, a mixed-blood Athabaskan-Russian woman, and Clem Stroupe, a Scotch-Irish soldier, Tall-Mountain spent her early childhood living in the Koyukon village of Nulato, Alaska. Tuberculosis, epidemic there, ultimately killed her mother and her brother. Adopted by her mother's physician, a Dr. Randle, she moved with him and Mrs. Randle to Oregon at age six, but they moved back to Alaska before finally settling in California. Isolation and alienation became painfully familiar to Tall-Mountain during those years.

TallMountain's adult life in the "lower forty-eight" was no easier than her childhood. Two marriages failed. Alone after the deaths of her adopted parents, she worked as a legal secretary first in Reno, Nevada, and later in San Francisco, California. During this period of emotional upheaval, she became an alcoholic. Her struggle against the disease of alcoholism ironically foreshadowed later battles with cancer and heart disease.

This lifelong pattern of turmoil and loss shaped TallMountain's voice as a writer. Her poetry blended Roman Catholic and Athabaskan spirituality with a Native cultural orientation. The Friars Press published her early poems in the 1960s. An apprenticeship during the 1970s with the Laguna writer Paula Gunn Allen honed her skills as a writer and encouraged her to continue publishing. TallMountain's poem "Ashes unto Eden" took a second-place award from the Catholic Press Association in 1970. The Friars Press continued to publish her works throughout the 1970s and 1980s. In 1982, the Blue Cloud Quarterly Press published TallMountain's book, *There Is No Word for Goodbye;* and the title poem won that year's Pushcart Prize. Soon after, her work was anthologized in *That's What She Said: Contemporary Poetry and Fiction by Native American Women* (1984) and *The Harper's Anthology of Twentieth-Century Native American Literature* (1988). Bill Moyers interviewed her and had TallMountain read some of her poems for his PBS series *The Power of the Word* in 1989.

TallMountain's professional successes led to opportunities to revisit her birthplace and reestablish ties with her birth father. In 1976, she returned to her home village, Nulato, where she rekindled her connections to her people and the Alaskan countryside. Later that year, she found her father, Clem Stroupe, in Phoenix, Arizona, and lived with him until his death in 1978, spending hours talking about her family history. Those conversations taught her "how to forgive, how to sharpen [her] perceptions of human beings, to love." From those conversations, as well as her own memories and voluminous notes taken during her 1976 trip to Alaska, she began an autobiographical novel, *Doyon.*

TallMountain died in 1994 at the age of seventy-six. By that time, she had made peace with the losses of her childhood and youth. She said she had gained the knowledge that "Alaska is my talisman, my strength, my spirit's home. . . . You *can* go home again."

Lisa E. Emmerich

REFERENCES

Bruchac, Joseph. "We Are the Inbetweens: An Interview with Mary TallMountain." *Studies in American Indian Literature* 1 (Summer 1989): 13–21.

Green, Rayna, ed. *That's What She Said: Contemporary Poetry and Fiction by Native American Women.* Bloomington: Indiana University Press, 1984.

TallMountain, Mary. *Matrilineal Cycle.* Oakland, CA: Black Star Red Rose Printing, 1990.

——. *There is No Word for Goodbye.* Marvin, SD: Blue Cloud Press, 1982.

——. "You Can Go Home Again: A Sequence." In *I Tell You Now: Autobiographical Essays by Native American Writers,* edited by Bryan Swan and Arnold Krupat, 1–13. Lincoln: University of Nebraska Press, 1987.

Tecumseh (1768?–1813)

Pan-Indian tribal leader
Native American (Shawnee)

Tecumseh, the Shawnee political leader who created a pan-Indian confederation among tribes from the Canadian border to the Gulf of Mexico, lived during a pivotal era for American Indians. With settlers flooding into the Northwest Territory after the American Revolution, Indian nations found themselves battered by a human tide that had little regard for their territorial rights. Tecumseh dedicated his life to developing a political message and movement that could help disparate tribes oppose American expansionism.

Tecumseh, or Shooting Star, was born in approximately 1768 in Shawnee homelands, in present-day western Ohio. One of a family of four children, he was the son of Puckeshinwa, a Shawnee military leader, and Methoataske, a mixed-blood Creek and Cherokee woman. Tecumseh's childhood was greatly affected by the increasing violence between the Indians and settlers in the trans-Appalachian west. His father died fighting the British in 1774. Tecumseh's beloved elder brother and mentor, Chicksika, died in 1788 in a battle with the Americans. Death and loss became familiar companions for the young Shawnee. So, too, did the desire to build a coalition of Indian nations that would be strong enough to resist American encroachments.

Tecumseh's emerging pan-Indian consciousness was symbolized in his refusal to participate in the negotiations for the 1795 Treaty of Greenville, a compact that surrendered Native land in most of Ohio and parts of Indiana. He rejected out-of-hand the idea that any one tribe had the right to relinquish any part of its title, believing that Indians held tribal lands in common. Tecumseh began to spread a message of unity among tribes like the Miami, the Wyandot, the Ottawa, and the Kickapoo. A battle-tested young warrior with a powerful intellect and a genius for public speaking, he was the perfect messenger for a pan-Indian confederation.

In the early 1800s, Tecumseh joined forces with his brother, Tenskwatawa, to promote intertribal unity. Tenskwatawa had become the prophet of a new pan-Indian movement that stressed the revitalization of religious traditions. Together, the brothers attracted the attention of many Indians and territorial governor William Henry Harrison. For years, Tecumseh's reputation as a humane warrior and honest negotiator had been a part of western legend. But in the early 1800s the Americans began to distrust the powerful politician who threatened westward movement with his Indian federation. This long-simmering political crisis erupted in 1811, when Harrison and nearly a thousand troops engaged the followers of Tecumseh and Tenskwatawa at the Battle of Tippecanoe. Tecumseh, away recruiting allies in the South, returned to find his community destroyed and his followers scattered.

Fleeing the Americans, Tecumseh moved north and allied himself with the British during the War of 1812. Hopeful that a British victory would result in protection for Indian communities, he rallied tribes to the British side. Once again, however, William Henry Harrison intervened. At the Battle of the Thames, on 15 October 1813, Tecumseh was killed. His death ended one of the most successful pan-Indian movements in American Indian history.

Lisa E. Emmerich

REFERENCES

Dowd, Gregory E. *A Spirited Resistance: The North American Indian Struggle for Unity, 1745–1815*. Baltimore: Johns Hopkins University Press, 1992.

Edmunds, R. David. *The Shawnee Prophet*. Lincoln: University of Nebraska Press, 1983.

———. *Tecumseh and the Quest for Indian Leadership*. Boston: Little, Brown, 1984.

Sugden, John. *Tecumseh: A Life*. New York: Henry Holt, 1998.

———. *Tecumseh's Last Stand*. Norman: University of Oklahoma Press, 1985.

Teller, Edward (1908–)
Nuclear physicist and Cold War political activist
Hungarian

Edward Teller, the "Father of the Hydrogen Bomb" and a Cold War political activist, was among the most brilliant and controversial physicists of the twentieth century. He is one of many great scientists to come out of Hungary.

Born in Budapest into a wealthy Jewish family on 15 January 1908, Teller displayed his talent for mathematics at a young age. He pursued a degree in chemical engineering at the University of Munich and then, having lost a foot in a streetcar accident, he transferred to the University of Leipzig, changing his focus to physics. In 1930, at the age of twenty-two, Teller received his doctorate in theoretical physics. Six years later, several universities in the United States offered him positions in their departments. In 1936 he and his wife, Mici, immigrated, and he began to work at George Washington University.

After World War II began, news circulated that the Germans had already discovered nuclear fission. Scientists feared that Hitler would benefit from this breakthough and reported the matter to President Franklin Roosevelt, who approved the official establishment of a scientific defense group. The Manhattan Project, as they called it, included Albert Einstein, J. Robert Oppenheimer, Teller, and several other physicists, including some from Hungary. Their goal was to develop the atomic bomb before the Germans, and they demonstrated their success at Hiroshima and Nagasaki.

During the Cold War, Teller continued to promote the augmentation of the nation's defense program, whereas some of his other colleagues, after witnessing the tragic outcome of the bombs dropped in Japan, began retracting their support of nuclear technology. In addition, during the McCarthy era, when the government accused Oppenheimer of past leftist affiliations, Teller, although not condemning his colleague as a Communist, did not refute the accusation, which caused a great rift between Teller and other scientists. Yet, for the most part, Teller and the other Hungarian physicists, especially Leó Szilárd, remained very close, for most of them abhorred communism because of their negative experiences during the Béla Kun Communist coup in 1919 in Hungary. Teller, however, focused his attentions almost exclusively on his scientific pursuits and never really became formally involved with the large number of Hungarian-American political organizations, although they recognized him with pride as a significant Hungarian immigrant.

Teller proceeded to develop an even more volatile and destructive weapon against the Soviet Union, even though other scientists questioned not only its destructiveness but also the feasibility of creating a greater fusion weapon. In 1952, Teller produced the first hydrogen bomb, further validating his scientific genius. Thereafter, as a lobbyist in Congress and an adviser to the Atomic Energy Commission, he continued advocating the need for further research. A director of the Livermore Laboratory in California, he led the team that developed the X-ray laser. During the Reagan years, Teller was the predominant force in the Star Wars project, which many people dubbed a wild goose chase costing billions of dollars. However, in spite of the negative press and obstacles during his career, Teller is considered one of the most influential scientists of the twentieth century, and he has yet to back down from his work and convictions.

Judith Fai-Podlipnik

REFERENCES

Blumberg, Stanley A. *Edward Teller: Giant of the Golden Age of Physics: A Biography.* New York: Scribner's, 1990.

Broad, William J. *Teller's War.* New York: Simon & Schuster, 1992.

Moss, Norman. *Men Who Play God: The Story of the H-Bomb and How the World Came to Live with It.* New York: Harper & Row, 1968.

O'Neill, Dan. *The Firecracker Boys.* New York: St. Martin's Press, 1994.

Simmons, John G. *The Scientific 100: A Ranking of the Most Influential Scientists, Past and Present.* Secaucus, NJ: Carol Publishing Group, 1996.

Teller, Edward, and Albert Latter. *Our Nuclear Future.* New York: Criterion, 1958.

Teller, Edward, and Allen Brown. *The Legacy of Hiroshima.* Garden City, NY: Doubleday, 1962.

York, Herbert F. *The Advisors: Oppenheimer, Teller and the Superbomb.* Stanford, CA.: Stanford University Press, 1989.

Tenayuca, Emma (1916–1999)

Community organizer, teacher, and author
Mexican-American

Emma Tenayuca gained national prominence for labor and civil rights activities, union organizing, and as a radical author during the 1930s. In particular, her role in the famous pecan shellers' strike of 1938 remains memorable.

Tenayuca was born in San Antonio, Texas, in 1916 and was raised by her maternal grandparents in a devout Catholic household. Her grandfather exposed her to a range of ideas and the everyday experiences of the Mexican worker. Her first labor-organizing experience was in 1933, at age sixteen, during the Fink Cigar Company strike. She was jailed with the strikers the second time police arrested them. The following year she helped organize garment workers at the Dorothy Frocks Company.

In 1935, as secretary of the West Side Unemployed Council, Tenayuca held mass meetings to protest the elimination of Mexican families from the city's relief roles. The next year, she set up chapters of the Workers' Alliance; with a membership of 3,000, it was one of the strongest in the country. In 1937,

she was appointed to the National Executive Committee of the Workers' Alliance, continued to stage protests against relief conditions and the abuse of Mexican-born workers, and joined the Communist Party. She also married fellow Communist Homer Brooks.

The following year, Tenayuca led over 10,000 pecan shellers out on strike, the largest in San Antonio history and the biggest community-based strike by Mexican Americans in the 1930s. The police arrested her and several organizers from the United Cannery, Agricultural, Packing, and Allied Workers of America (UCAPAWA) on charges of Communist agitation. Upon her release, she resumed her strike work. However, the CIO had taken an interest in the strike and its organizers took charge, insisting, however, that their support was conditional on Tenayuca's not participating further, for too much attention had been focused on her open ties to communism. The Texas Industrial Commission began public hearings on the strikers' grievances, but the strike gains eroded within a few months when the pecan industry mechanized.

In 1938, the Texas Communist Party nominated Tenayuca as its candidate for the U.S. Congress from San Antonio. In 1939, she formulated and coauthored with her husband a treatise on Mexicans and the question of nationalism, "The Mexican Question in the Southwest," printed in the *Communist*. In the same year, the Texas Communist Party was to hold its state convention in San Antonio, but a riot at the Municipal Auditorium prevented it from meeting. In any event, Tenayuca's remaining credibility as a community organizer was destroyed by the announcement that the Soviet Union and Nazi Germany had signed a nonaggression pact, the prelude to Germany's invasion of Poland and the start of World War II. Ostracized and unable to find work in San Antonio, she worked briefly as a secretary and bookkeeper for a garment manufacturer before moving to Houston.

Tenayuca spent the war years in San Francisco, California, graduating from San Francisco State College. After the war, she returned to San Antonio and taught in the local elementary schools. She died in 1999 at age eighty-three.

Zaragosa Vargas

REFERENCES

Blackwelder, Julia Kirk. *Women of the Depression: Caste and Culture in San Antonio, 1929–1939.* College Station: Texas A&M University Press, 1984.

Calderón, Roberto, and Emilio Zamora. *Chicana Voices: Intersections of Race, Class, and Gender.* Austin: University of Texas Press, 1986.

Filewood, David Lewis. "Tejano Revolt: The Significance of the 1938 Pecan Shellers' Strike." Master's thesis, University of Texas, Arlington, 1994.

García, Mario T. *Mexican Americans: Leadership, Ideology, and Identity, 1930–1960.* New Haven, CT: Yale University Press, 1989.

Nelson-Cisneros, Victor. "UCAPAWA Organizing Activities in Texas, 1930–1950." *Aztlán,* Spring, Summer, Fall 1978, 7–84.

Ramos, Raúl. "Así Fue: La Huelga de los Nueceros de San Antonio, Texas, Febrero 1938" (It Happened This Way: The San Antonio Pecan Shellers' Strike). Senior thesis, Princeton University, 1989.

Vargas, Zaragosa. "Tejana Radical: Emma Tenayuca and the San Antonio Labor Movement." *Pacific Historical Review* 66 (November 1997): 553–580.

Terrell, Mary Church (1863–1954)
Activist, educator, and women's club founder
African American

Lecturer, educator, and activist, Mary Church Terrell devoted her life to improving political and social conditions for African Americans, especially African American women. She challenged segregation and lynching, worked for women's suffrage, and helped found two important political organizations to advance these causes, the National Association for the Advancement of Colored People (NAACP) and the National Association of Colored Women (NACW).

Church was born in Memphis, Tennessee, in 1863. Both her parents had been enslaved and sought for their children the educational opportunities that they had been denied. Sent to Yellow Springs, Ohio, at age six to attend school, Church eventually graduated from Oberlin College in 1884, took a teaching position at Wilberforce College, in Ohio, and pursued a master's degree at Oberlin. She moved to Washington, D.C., to teach high school. There she met Robert Terrell, whom she married in 1891. (He eventually became a municipal court judge in Washington and died in 1925.)

The Terrells had a daughter, Phyllis, in 1898, and adopted a niece, Terrell Church, in 1905. Although Mary stopped teaching when she married, she became increasingly politically active. In 1892, a friend in Memphis was lynched by white men jealous of his business success, spurring her to mount an antilynching campaign that took her to the White House to meet with President Benjamin Harrison (who refused to condemn racial violence publicly).

Such activism brought home women's political powerlessness, and Terrell threw herself into the fight for women's suffrage. At the same time, she understood the particular burdens of black women and organized a local black women's club called the Colored Women's League. In 1896 it merged with others around the country, forming the National Association of Colored Women. The NACW embraced social reform issues, including women's suffrage, child care, civil rights, and decent working conditions for black women. Terrell was elected the NACW's first president and served three terms. She was then named honorary president for life.

All that catapulted her into a professional career of lecturing, politicking, and writing on African American and women's issues in the United States and Europe. She was the first black woman to be elected to the Washington, D.C., Board of Education and was invited by W. E. B. Du Bois to become a founding member of the NAACP. She became active in Republican Party politics as well. In 1940 she completed her autobiography, *A Colored Woman in a White World.*

Subsequently, Terrell concentrated on ending public segregation in Washington and in

1949 became chairwoman of the Coordinating Committee for the Enforcement of District of Columbia Anti-Discrimination Laws. Almost ninety years old, she led public demonstrations and joined a discrimination suit against a local restaurant. That case, *District of Columbia v. John Thompson,* was ultimately heard by the U.S. Supreme Court, which ruled in favor of equal accommodations in 1953. A year later, on 24 July 1954, Terrell died, just after the historic *Brown v. Board of Education of Topeka* decision extended her desegregation victory to all public education.

Cheryl Greenberg

REFERENCES

Giddings, Paula. *When and Where I Enter: The Impact of Black Women on Race and Sex in America.* New York: Morrow, 1984.

Jones, Beverly Washington. *Quest for Equality: The Life and Writings of Mary Church Terrell.* Brooklyn, NY: Carlson Publishing, 1990.

Terrell, Mary Church. *A Colored Woman in a White World.* Washington, DC, Ransdell, 1940; New York: Arno Press, 1980.

Wesley, Charles. *A History of the National Association of Colored Women's Clubs, Inc.: A Legacy of Service.* Washington, DC: National Association of Colored Women's Clubs, 1984.

Tesla, Nikola (1856–1943)
Scientist and inventor
Serbian

Nikola Tesla was a scientist and inventor who pioneered in radio and invented the alternating current motor and a system that made possible the universal transmission and distribution of electricity. He also worked on torpedoes and radio-guided ships. He achieved worldwide recognition.

Tesla was born in 1856 in Smiljan, near Gospič, a Serbian-populated part of the Hungarian region of Austria-Hungary in what is today the republic of Croatia. His father was a Serbian Orthodox clergyman, and his mother an expert needleworker and inventor of home implements. Tesla attended the polytechnic school in Graz and the university in Prague before joining the newly founded telephone company in Budapest in 1881. The following year he started working for the Continental Edison Company in Paris, but unable to interest Europeans in his new alternating current motor, he immigrated to the United States in 1884. He worked for Thomas Edison in New York City, redesigning dynamos, until differences with Edison on the future of electrical technology prompted Tesla to leave the Edison Company in 1885. Two years later, he established his own laboratory. He became a U.S. citizen in 1891.

Tesla's inventions during the 1890s (several of them patented) had to do with electric power transmission and radio and wireless power, which he had predicted as early as 1893. He invented the rotating magnetic field and adapted it for the generation, transmission, and distribution of electric power, providing for the first time a practical means for generating large quantities of electricity in one place and transmitting it economically over long distances. By 1903, the first large power plant was built on his model at Niagara Falls. At the same time, he developed the Tesla coil, an air core transformer and, for operation at high voltages, gas-filled tubular lights without filaments, the precursors of fluorescent lights. Among other things, on his international lecture tour, 1891–1893, Tesla had described his high-frequency currents, which became known as Tesla currents, and by 1900 virtually every university laboratory in the world had acquired a Tesla coil to demonstrate them. In 1898, anticipating radio-guided missiles and aircraft, Tesla developed torpedoes and ships guided by radio and, by 1917, had accurately forecast the invention of radar. As early as 1900 Tesla had also proposed a "world wireless" plant that would provide many other services in addition to sending ordinary messages, including transmitting facsimiles of pictures.

As he was one of the most famous living Serbian Americans in the late 1930s, Tesla's accomplishments did not pass unnoticed by his fellow Serbian Americans. During World War II, he was made honorary president of the Serb National Federation but resigned in 1942 because he opposed Serbian-American actions against the wartime unity of Yugoslav Americans. Shortly before his death he wrote a letter called "To My Brothers in America," in which he asked all Serbian, Croatian, and Slovene Americans to remain united in the fight against the forces of fascism. He also asked Serbs, Croats, and Slovenes at home to fight together against the German and Italian Fascists occupying Yugoslavia. His letter was published by all the Yugoslav ethnic newspapers in the United States. However, in January 1943, before President Roosevelt could acknowledge his work, Tesla died.

Matjaž Klemenčič

REFERENCES

Klemenčič, Matjaž. "Stiki Tesle in Adamiča v zadnjem letu Teslovega življenja" (Connections between Tesla and Adamic during the last year of Tesla's life"). *Naši Razgledi* (Ljubljana), 11 March 1983: 132–133.

Swezey, Kenneth M. "Nikola Tesla." Science 127 (16 May 1958): 1147–1159.

Tesla, Nikola. *My Inventions. The Autobiography of Nikola Tesla*. Edited by Ben Johnston. Willston, VT: Hart Brothers, 1982.

Thao, Xoua ("Shua") (1963–)
Medical doctor, lawyer, and community activist
Hmong

Xoua Thao is the founder of Xoua Thao medical center and cofounder of both the Hmong Minnesota Bar Association and the St. Paul Hmong Chamber of Commerce. He is the former president of Hmong National Development, a nationwide Hmong organization. He was the first Hmong to attend Brown University, the Dartmouth Program in Medicine, and Harvard University, and he remains as of the year 2001 the only Hmong with three graduate degrees (M.D., J.D., and M.P.H.). He is also the only Hmong medical doctor and lawyer who is actively involved in Hmong traditional cultural activities, such as wedding rites. He represents the value many Hmong Americans cherish: preserving the best of Hmong cultural heritage and learning the most from what the United States has to offer.

Thao was the seventh child in a family of eight. All of his brothers and sisters are in Minnesota, his oldest brother having worked in many capacities in the Secret War in Laos from the early 1960s to 1975. Only his two older brothers had a formal high school education before the family left Laos to go to Thailand in 1975.

After a year in a refugee camp in Thailand, Thao's family was resettled in Providence, Rhode Island, in April 1976. Thao started school in the ninth grade and worked his way through college (B.A. in biology, Brown University), Brown Medical School (the Brown-Dartmouth Program in Medicine), Harvard School of Public Health, and law school. He earned a master's of public health (M.P.H.) in 1989, the same year that he received his M.D. In 1995 he moved to St. Paul, Minnesota, and completed a J.D. degree two years later, making him the first Hmong to have earned joint degrees in medicine and law. By 1999 Thao had almost completed his M.B.A. He is currently the principal family physician in the Xoua Thao Medical Center—probably the only medical center in the state of Minnesota where Hmong language and culture are used in providing medical services to Hmong patients. For the Hmong, Thao's educational achievements represent a major achievement, for the Hmong did not have their own written language until the early 1950s. And Thao is not alone in his achievements: His three brothers have both bachelor's and master's degrees, and his wife is one of only a few Hmong Minnesota attorneys-at-law.

Thao is also a student of Hmong culture. He has managed to learn many aspects of Hmong culture—including the procedures, flowery language, and chants of the rites of the Hmong wedding ceremony—and he practices them. He has been involved as the go-between for families during Hmong traditional wedding ceremonies. Gifted in Hmong oral language and Hmong etiquette, Thao is thus a modern Hmong man in both worlds, Hmong and American.

In Hmong traditional values, a household

of more than two generations is a symbol of harmony, strength, prosperity, and family continuity. Thao also preserves this Hmong value, for his parents live with him, his wife, and his two young sons.

Kou Yang

REFERENCES

Chagnon, Jacquelyn, and R. Rumpf. "Decades of Division for the Lao Hmong." *Southeast Asia Chronicle* 91 (1983): 10–15.

Cooper, Robert. *The Hmong.* Bangkok: Artasia, 1991.

Mottin, Jean. *History of the Hmong.* Bangkok: Odeon Book Store, 1980.

Thao, Xoua. Interview by author, 15, 16 January 1999.

Yang, Dao. *Hmong at the Turning Point.* Minneapolis: World Bridge Associates, 1993.

Yang, Kou. "The Hmong Are Not Mongols." *Hmong Forum,* 1996.

———. *The Hmong in Fresno: A Study of Welfare Participation and Self-Sufficiency.* Ann Arbor, MI: University Microfilm International , 1995.

Thind, Bhagat Singh (1892–1967)

Author and community activist
Asian Indian

Bhagat Singh Thind, a native of India, fought for Asian Indian rights in the United States. He was also a spiritual leader and founder of metaphysical groups in North America.

Thind was from India's Punjab region, a high-caste Hindu Aryan born in 1892. He was a member of a small Jat (agricultural) clan that incorporated Brahmin and Muslim rituals. He would later be considered a holy man, a seeker after God, who borrowed from Sikhism but did not claim to be exclusively Sikh. Such religious and caste distinctions were far less sharply defined in the early 1900s.

Thind entered the United States in 1913 and began studying at the University of California, Berkeley. Although he was on friendly terms with Ram Chandra and others connected with Ghadr Party, a group advocating the overthrow of British rule in India, Thind himself was a pacifist and very religious. He advocated the principle of India for Indians but not armed rebellion. However, he was

drafted, served in the U.S. Army for six months during World War I (and wore his turban), and was honorably discharged. In 1920, he was refused naturalization on the grounds that the 1917 Immigration Act had created the Asiatic barred zone.

With little financial or emotional backing, Thind began a two-year taxing legal process to get the decision reversed. He correctly argued that he, like the other people of North India, was an Aryan, a descendent from the same nomadic people that Germanic races claimed as their forebears. Being an Aryan, he maintained, he was not Asian but Caucasian and therefore white within the meaning of U.S. naturalization law.

The case reached the U.S. Supreme Court, and in 1923 *United States v. Bhagat Singh Thind* was heard. Thind lost. Justice Jabez T. Sutherland stated that the "words of the statute are to be interpreted in accordance with the understanding of the common man from whose vocabulary they were taken." In other words, those who were from north India were not white as commonly understood, regardless of their racial origins. Thus, although the court accepted the arguments of social scientists that Indians were Aryans and hence Caucasian, they were not perceived as white and therefore were ineligible for citizenship. This consequently put the Constitution at the disposal of a legal fiction called "the common man" and legitimized a contrived distinction between Caucasian and white.

That was a major setback for the Asian Indians in the United States. The government denaturalized forty-five Asian Indians, and many were forced off their land in California, for California laws at that time only allowed persons eligible for citizenship to own land. Clerks in California also began to refuse marriage licenses to Asian Indians applying to marry white women. Some in California erroneously argued that the ruling should be a basis for denaturalizing Asian Indian children born in the United States. Eventually, the ruling in the Thind case was reversed with the passage of the Luce-Celler bill in 1946, granting Asian Indians and Filipinos the right to citizenship.

In addition to his legal battles, Thind was also a spiritual leader in North America. During the 1920s and 1930s he wrote more than twenty books and conducted classes throughout the country on metaphysics. Until his death in 1967, he claimed that his inspiration came from the Sikh religion. The Thind home, where he lived with his wife, who was French, was in Hollywood, California, and it was always open to Asian Indian students studying at UCLA, Pomona College, or elsewhere in the area. Students and others of that era still speak about the Thind family's love and hospitality.

Arthur W. Helweg

REFERENCES

Jensen, Joan M. *Passage from India: Asian Indian Immigration to North America.* New Haven, CT: Yale University Press, 1988.

Kamath, M.V. *The United States and India, 1776–1976,* Washington, DC: Embassy of India, 1976.

"Pioneer Asian Indian Immigration to the Pacific Coast: Historical Photographs." University of California, Davis (6 March 2000): www. lib.ucdavis.edu/punjab/t_usphot.html (accessed 25 June 2000).

Thind, Bhagat Singh. *Divine Wisdom.* Omana, NE: H. E. Ledyard, 1925.

———. *Radiant Road to Reality: Tested Science of Religion.* Los Angeles: Wetzel, 1947.

United States v. Bhagat Singh Thind. Argued 11, 12 January 1923. Decided 19 February 1923. 261 U.S. 204 (1923) 67 L.Ed.616. www.multiracial. com/government/third.html (accessed 12 February 2001).

Thomas, David (1794–1882)

Ironmaster and industrial innovator
Welsh

One of the great ironmasters of the world, David Thomas developed the first commercially successful use of anthracite coal in the making of iron, opening up both the Swansea valley in Wales and the Lehigh valley in Pennsylvania to the production of high-quality iron. He is regarded as the father of the American anthracite coal industry.

Born in 1794 in the parish of Cadoxtan, Glamorganshire, South Wales, the only son of David and Jane Thomas, young David proved to be an apt pupil and was given a broader education than most farmers' sons. He worked on the farm until age seventeen, when he began working in the machine shop at Neath Abbey Iron Works, making parts for blast furnaces. During his five years there, his abilities were recognized, and in 1817 he was offered the superintendency of the Ynyscedwyn Iron Works, where he worked for the next twenty-two years. There, he began experiments as early as 1820 using the abundant anthracite coal of the region in the smelting of iron. After several failures using cold blast furnaces, he heard of experiments with a hot blast furnace in Glasgow, Scotland. After viewing it, Thomas built a similar one at Ynyscedwyn under license. The combination of anthracite and the hot, or preheated, blast was successful, and by 1837 Thomas knew he had solved the problem of commercial production of anthracite iron. The anthracite-rich Swansea valley could become a major iron producer using local raw materials.

Learning of this success, the Lehigh Coal and Navigation Company of Pennsylvania sent a representative to Wales in 1838 to confirm the applicability of the process and to persuade Thomas to come to the United States and build a hot blast furnace. Situated in an abundant anthracite region, the Lehigh firm had faced disappointments in commercially exploiting this resource. Although reluctant to leave, Thomas contracted to the Lehigh Crane Iron Company for five years, left Wales in 1839 with his wife, Elizabeth, and five children, and by July 1840 had the first hot blast furnace in operation in Catasauqua, Pennsylvania. The Lehigh Crane Iron Company, which was created by the owners of Lehigh Coal and to which Thomas added "Crane" in honor of his employer in Wales, became very successful. In 1854 he organized the Thomas Iron Company, turning over the management of the Crane Iron Company to his son John the following year.

Thomas developed an interest in many other industrial enterprises in the area, including collieries and the railroads, but also contributed to his community as a trustee of St. Luke's Hospital and Lafayette College and, in 1840, by establishing the Presbyterian Church in Catasauqua. With conditions in Wales encouraging emigration, the news of Thomas's success spurred many of his acquaintances to follow his example. A Welsh settlement developed rapidly in Catasauqua (originally settled by Irish and Germans), followed by a Welsh Baptist chapel and Sunday school and a Congregational Church that used Welsh. Thomas was deeply involved in every aspect of the early development of the community and was much honored by his fellow citizens when he died of pneumonia in 1882, at the age of eighty-eight.

D. Douglas Caulkins and Lorna W. Caulkins

REFERENCES

Perry, Hobart S. "Thomas, David." In *Dictionary of American Biography,* vol. 13: 427–428. New York: Scribner's, 1936.

Roberts, E. D. "David Thomas: The Father of the Anthracite Iron Trade." In *The Red Dragon,* edited by Charles Wickins, vol. 4. Cardiff: Daniel Owen & Co., 1883.

Williams, Peter N. *David Thomas, Iron Man from Wales: The Story of an Immigrant and of the Country He Left Behind.* Trucksville, PA: National Welsh-American Foundation, 1995.

Thomas, Thomas L. (Llyfnwy) (1911–1983)

Concert singer
Welsh

Through his concert appearances and radio and television broadcasts, Thomas Llyfnwy Thomas became one of the best-known and most popular singers in mid-twentieth-century America and acquired an international reputation. His renown brought his ethnicity to the attention of a wider audience and reinforced mainstream U.S. society's identification of Welshness with music and singing.

Thomas was born in the coalmining town of Maesteg, South Wales, into a mining family rich in musical talent. In 1923, the family immigrated to Scranton, Pennsylvania, whose large Welsh contingent and flourishing Welsh cultural life sustained the Thomases' ethnic identity and interest in music. Young Thomas first trained as a technical draftsman but, at the age of twenty-two, decided to take up singing full-time.

Over the next thirty years Thomas's mellow yet haunting baritone voice would be heard by millions, and it rewarded him with great wealth. Level-headed as well as naturally talented, he cultivated a relaxed, easygoing rapport with his audiences. He therefore had the qualities to maximize the opportunities available on the booming concert circuit and expanding radio network in the United States. In 1933, on the advice of Nelson Eddy, he moved to New York and began to appear on radio broadcasts and in concerts. His breakthrough came in 1936, when, at the age of twenty-five, he became the youngest winner ever—and the first Welsh winner—of the New York Metropolitan Opera competition.

Although Thomas made his debut at the Met the following year, it was through concerts, radio, and television, not opera, that his became a household name. In 1942 he joined the *Voice of Firestone* radio program and later sang on its television premiere. Indeed, many would remember him primarily as the *Voice of Firestone,* so frequent were his appearances over a nearly twenty-year period. There were also regular appearances on other programs and solo concerts with major symphony orchestras throughout the United States, Canada, Australia, and the British Isles. In the 1950s, when his career was at its zenith and he was averaging sixty concerts a year, he was one of the highest-paid concert artists in the United States and was regarded as one of the top concert soloists in the world. However, during the 1960s he withdrew from public performances but still taught in several colleges and universities in Arizona and at his private studio in Scottsdale, where, after years of constant travel, he had finally settled down with his wife.

Throughout his life, Thomas's Welshness remained important to him. He continued to speak his native language and regularly took advantage of his public platforms to publicize his love of Wales. Apparently, he never gave a concert without including a selection of Welsh songs and always sang in Welsh during his appearances on television and radio on 1 March, St. David's Day (Wales's patron saint's day). The acclaim he earned in his adopted country was matched by the recognition he had in his homeland. Fittingly, his last public appearance was in a film marking the inauguration of the Welsh-language television channel in Wales in November 1982. He died five months later.

Bill Jones

REFERENCES
"Famed Singer Dies." *Y Drych* [The mirror], *The American Organ of the Welsh People,* May 1983, 4.
"A Great Voice is Silent." *Ninnau* [Ourselves], *The North American Welsh Newspaper,* 1 May 1983, 3.
Jones, William D. *Wales in America: Scranton and the Welsh 1860–1920.* Cardiff, Wales, and Scranton, PA: University of Wales Press/University of Scranton Press, 1993.
"A Singer Talks." *Y Drych* [The mirror], *The American Organ of the Welsh People,* 15 December 1956, 5.
Thomas, Edward and Barbara. "Thomas Llyfnwy Thomas (1911–1983): Portrait of a Professional." *Welsh Music* 8.3 (Autumn 1986): 7–12; and 8.4 (Winter 1987): 28–39.
Thomas, Thomas L., Collection. Welsh Music Information Centre, Cardiff, Wales.
Wilson, Maggie. "Baritone Thomas Voices Love for World of Song." *Arizona Republic,* 26 December 1971.

Thompson, Nainoa (1952–)

Seafaring navigator
Hawaiian

Nainoa Thompson, senior navigator with the Polynesian Voyaging Society, is a legend and inspiration to the people of Hawai`i. The youngest of three children of a prominent and affluent Hawaiian family, Thompson practically lived on the water while growing up in Honolulu, surfing, fishing, and paddling outrigger canoes. In 1974, he was contacted by the fledgling Polynesian Voyaging Society, which was looking for paddlers for a new project of long-distance sailing using only traditional navigational techniques.

When Thompson heard of the Hokulea project (named for the zenith star over Hawai`i, known as the Star of Gladness), he thought, "It was the most romantic thing, . . . an exercise in experimental archaeology to replicate (using modern materials) a craft by the voyaging Polynesians millennia ago." Successful voyaging—relying on celestial navigation and using long-forgotten techniques—would prove that the Polynesians' crossing the Pacific Ocean and settling over long distances had not been the result of chance. For the first voyage to Tahiti in 1976, Mau Piailug, a navigator from Satawal, in the Caroline Islands, was at the helm. When Thompson sailed on the return voyage to Hawai`i, he decided to learn to navigate, like Piailug, without instruments.

He took astronomy courses, graduating in 1986 in ocean science at the University of Hawaii. He spent nights on the ocean, lying in the bottom of a small skiff, studying the turning vault of the sky. He read all he could find regarding Polynesian navigation techniques. Working with the Bishop Museum Planetarium in Honolulu, he spent countless hours learning star patterns and observing changes across latitudes and seasons. He developed a system using pairs of stars that rise simultaneously at a given latitude. In addition, he lived with Mau Piailug to improve his daytime navigational skills. In 1980 he was the first Hawaiian in a thousand years to navigate to Tahiti.

In 1986 and 1987, Thompson guided the Hokule`a voyaging canoe from Hawai`i to Tahiti, the Cook Islands, New Zealand, Tonga, and Samoa and back. The navigator must stay awake for practically the entire voyage, studying the clouds and swells and tracking the canoe on a mental map of the ocean. In 1999, he attempted his most difficult challenge, setting off for tiny Rapa Nui, or Easter Island, a thousand miles away and against prevailing winds and currents, which no Polynesian had done for 1,500 years. Making the voyage in eighteen days, half the anticipated time, a euphoric Nainoa Thompson, master navigator, was mobbed by a cheering crowd of Rapa Nui residents.

Thompson emphasizes that the activities of the Polynesian Voyaging Society are for Hawai'i's children, to teach them the values of their ancestors and the importance of preserving their islands and the ocean surrounding them. Because of the huge commitment of time and energy required to learn noninstrument navigation, he is reluctant to urge others to follow his path, for, he observes, they should be learning the essential values associated with navigation—direction, dedication, study, perseverance, confidence, and leadership. Thompson hopes to instill those values in future generations of Hawaiians.

David W. Shideler

REFERENCES

"Nainoa Thompson and the Lost Art of Polynesian Navigation." *Oceans* 21.4 (August 1988), and numerous newspaper accounts.

Tran, Kim (1941–)
Restaurant owner and community leader
Vietnamese

Turning personal tragedy into productive concern for others is a defining characteristic of Kim Tran. As a Vietnamese refugee and active entrepreneur, she has devoted her own resources and time to helping those less fortunate than herself. Today, as cofounder of the Vietnamese Association of Missouri, an organization committed to the education and social betterment of new Americans, she has translated her early experiences into a continued family tradition of community service.

Tran grew up near Hanoi, in what became North Vietnam, where her father was mayor. When the Communists took over, her family fled to South Vietnam. To protect the family, her parents sent their older daughters to France. Kim, who was sixteen years old, refused to leave. After years of hardship, where she worked in a factory at night and studied during the day, she finished her education and became a teacher. In spite of the years of struggle in Vietnam, she noted that her father always stood as a model of community involvement, honesty, and hard work. She, in turn, tried to live up to the standards he set. At the fall of Vietnam in 1975, she fled the country. Her husband, Kinh T. Tran, a South Vietnamese military officer, was also able to escape. Although they had no money and no home, she felt that she was lucky because she and her family were alive. Once in the United States, she and her husband both worked. She took a job as a waitress, learning about the restaurant business through observation. Within a short time she felt confident enough to open a small restaurant herself. Having her own business gave her flexibility to take care of her young sons while making an income. Her hours were long, but her family was together.

Tran was among the first Vietnamese to settle in St. Louis. After a time, as she saw others coming into the area, she felt a need to help the newly arrived fellow Vietnamese. Drawing on her own family's limited income, she began buying clothing, blankets, and other items for the newcomers, continuing a pattern of personal and familial community commitment. In 1982 she and her husband started the Vietnamese Association of Missouri. Eventually, with influx into the St. Louis area of refugees from other areas of the world, Tran decided to open the center's doors to the multiethnic array of newcomers. Today, the association has a community center that, besides social service and cultural activities, offers Vietnamese- and English-language classes as well as civics training for people seeking to become U.S. citizens.

Many young people, graduate students at local universities, inspired by her commitment and dedication, volunteer to work in the community center. In this way, she is training others in the value of community service. As her father did before her, Tran worked for the financial stability of her family but also felt a strong commitment to help those less fortunate than herself. Working with the support of her husband, she continues to run the Vietnamese Association and its community center as an educational and social service organization for new Americans.

Pamela A. DeVoe

REFERENCES

O'Neil, Tim. "Asian Groups Prepare for New Year's Festivities." *St. Louis Post-Dispatch*, 4 February 2000, B1.

———. "A Distinctive Regional Culture Was Built with Influences from Foreign Places." *St. Louis Post Dispatch*, 3 October 1999, B1.

Tran, Kim. Interview with author, 25 April 1999.

VandeWater, Judith. "'Asiatown' Emerges on South Side." *St. Louis Post-Dispatch*, 24 July 1989, Business, 1.

Tran, Kim Huy (1963–)

Engineer

Vietnamese

Entering the United States as a teenage refugee, Kim Huy Tran overcame numerous obstacles associated with her origins and gender to become a leading aerospace engineer. Her administrative effectiveness and designs for heat shield materials have been essential to numerous National Aeronautics and Space Administration (NASA) missions.

The third of ten children, Tran started life in 1963 in Ho Phong, a small village in the Mekong Delta of Vietnam. In 1979, Tran, her parents, and her nine siblings escaped from Vietnam by sea. Reaching Malaysia, they stayed for several months in the notorious Pulau Bidong refugee camp before arriving in the United States in 1980. Initially sponsored by a Lutheran congregation in South Dakota, the family soon moved to San Jose, California, where they joined a growing Vietnamese community. Tran graduated from Sunnyvale High School in 1981 and went on to San Jose State University, where she studied materials engineering. Splitting her time between classes and part-time employment, Tran earned a bachelor's degree in materials engineering in 1987 and a master's degree in mechanical engineering in 1990.

In order to explore her interests in material research and space technology, during her second year in college Tran applied for an internship at the NASA Ames Research Center (Moffit Field, California). Accepted into the program, she thrived and became a regular staff member upon completing her bachelor's degree. In 1994, she began working on the development of heat shield materials to protect the Mars Pathfinder spacecraft during reentry into the earth's atmosphere. After less than a year on the job, Tran had invented an entirely new heat shield material that would replace a previous technology that had been in use for decades—ever since the Apollo and Viking space programs.

Recognized as an expert in materials research and an authority in the development of heat shield materials, Tran was appointed as the leader of a group of top-flight engineers and scientists who would oversee the planning and coordination of technical efforts for Mars exploration. By 1998, Tran and her team had created many new thermal protective materials that would prove their worth on numerous Mars missions.

Outside the laboratory, Tran, who is married to Mark Sullivan and has two sons, has actively disseminated scientific and technological knowledge. She has been awarded two patents and has written twenty-five technical papers for publication and presentation at professional conferences across the country. In recognition of her achievements, Tran has received numerous awards, including the NASA Exceptional Engineering Achievement Medal, and she has won the Ames Technical Paper Contest for Women. Although Tran has not been especially active within the Vietnamese community, as a result of her outstanding career achievements, she is viewed by the ethnic media as the pride of the Vietnamese community and as an inspiration for Vietnamese women pursuing careers in science and technology. She is presented as a role model in Trong Minh's series (*The Pride of Vietnamese in the World*) and on the Vietspace website because she was the first Vietnamese-American woman—and the first among the Vietnamese refugees—to attain such high achievements in the field of aerospace technology.

Hoan N. Bui

REFERENCES

Burton, Kathleen. "Ames Researchers Support Mars Robotic Exploration." *Astrogram,* 15 January 1999: george.arc.nasa.gov/dx/astrogram/astrostories/011599/Marsrobo.html (accessed 21 May 2000).

Farrar, Diane. "Ames Scientists Share in Pathfinder's Perfect Success." *Astrogram,* 11 July 1997: george.arc.nasa.gov/dx/basket/Astrogram/pathfinder.html (accessed 21 May 2000).

Khoa Hoc Gia Tran Kim Huy: kicon.com/events/activities/trongminh/ (accessed 21 May 2000).

Minh, Trong [pseud.]. "Tran Kim Huy." In *The Pride of Vietnamese in the World,* edited by Trong Minh and R. Murphy, vol. 4: 88–95. Irvine, CA: Author, 1999.

Tran, K. Huy. E-mail communication to author, 15 September 1999.

Treutlen, John (né Johann) Adam (1733–1782)

Revolutionary leader, planter, and governor
Austrian

Johann Adam Treutlen played a major role in transforming British Georgia into a state of the Union. His most important roles were as delegate to the Provincial Congress and later governor of Georgia.

Although the origin of the Treutlens remains uncertain, Johann Treutlen was shaped by the Pietist faith of the Lutherans of Georgia, who had been expelled from Austria by the Catholic archbishop, Firmian, of Salzburg. The family left for Pennsylvania in 1743, but their ship was captured by privateers and brought to Bilboa, Spain, where several passengers died, among them Treutlen's father. Redeemed by the English and brought to England, Anna Clara Treutlen in 1745 accepted for herself and two sons an indenture—four years of service for free passage—offered by the Georgia Trustees. In August the Treutlens boarded the boat *Judith,* yet ship fever killed many on the voyage, including the captain, but a Swiss named Zuberbühler, skilled in geometry, was able to steer the boat safely to Frederica, Georgia.

Young Treutlen was indentured to Michael Burckhalter, of Vernonburg, but was allowed to enroll at school in Ebenezer, dominated by the Reverend Boltzius, the Salzburgers' leader. To Boltzius's delight, the boy became steeped in Lutheran piety, fluent in English, and familiar with English law. Grown up, he taught at Ebenezer, but to Boltzius's dismay, Treutlen preferred commerce, gradually amassed wealth in land and slaves, and became one of the most prominent men in Ebenezer. In 1760 he served in the provincial legislature, championing the cause of yeoman farmers and small planters. He was also an influential parish deacon, and in the conflict between early settlers and newcomers in the parish, the aged Reverend Henry Mühlenberg was sent from Pennsylvania to adjudicate. Treutlen impressed the minister by his skillful support of the Whiggish Reverend Rabenhorst and by his sharp critique of the recently arrived authoritarian Reverend Triebner, later a committed Tory.

Supporting the emerging independence movement, Treutlen was elected on 4 July 1775 to the Provincial Congress and served on its Council of Safety. He had a major hand in writing Georgia's first constitution, which is noteworthy for its democratic thrust. Chosen governor in 1777, Treutlen promoted military preparedness and gained desperately needed monetary support from the Continental Congress. He also warded off a move by South Carolina, led by William H. Drayton, to absorb Georgia into its domain. As "Captain-General, Governor, and Commander-in-Chief," Treutlen issued a proclamation, ending with "God save the Congress," that offered a big reward for Drayton's capture. When the British reoccupied Savannah, Treutlen moved to the vicinity of Orangeburg, South Carolina. On 1 July 1780, the British disbarred him from holding any "office of trust, honor or profit," yet with independence assured, Treutlen was elected to the state assembly that would convene in Augusta.

Before he could take his seat, however, he

was murdered in spring 1782 by unknown hands. His career highlights the transformation of an immigrant boy, educated by the Austrian Salzburgers, into a man of wealth and political activism dedicated to gaining Georgia's independence from Great Britain.

Leo Schelbert

REFERENCES

Cook, James F. *The Governors of Georgia, 1754–1995.* Rev. ed. Macon, GA: Mercer University Press, 1995.

Jones, George Fenwick. *The Georgia Dutch. From the Rhine and Danube to the Savannah, 1733–1783.* Athens: University of Georgia Press, 1992.

———. "John Adam Treutlen's Origin and Rise to Prominence." In *Forty Years of Diversity: Essays on Colonial Georgia,* edited by Harvey Jackson and Phinizy Spalding, 217–232. Athens: University of Georgia Press, 1984.

Trunk, Rev. George (Jurij) (1870–1973)

Catholic priest and author
Slovene

The Reverend George Trunk was a Catholic priest, the author of five books, and a journalist. A frequent contributor to Slovene ethnic newspapers in the United States and his native Carinthia, he achieved wide recognition in his homeland and among the Slovene ethnic community in the United States.

Trunk was born in Faak/Bače, in the Austrian province of Carinthia, in 1870. He finished his theological studies in Klagenfurt/Celovec in 1891. A Slovene- and German-speaking ethnically mixed population lives in southern Carinthia, and Trunk was a Slovene political activist in this environment.

During World War I, Trunk was known to the Austrian police as being pro-Yugoslav. At the end of the war, he actively participated in the struggle to unite southern Carinthia with Slovenia and Yugoslavia, even serving as an adviser to the Yugoslav delegation at the Paris Peace Conference. Following a plebiscite in southern Carinthia, which determined that Carinthia would remain part of Austria, he worked as coeditor of *Glas Pravice* (Voice of Justice), a Carinthian Slovene newspaper, and remained one of their political leaders. However, conflicts with the Austrian authorities forced him to retire from the Austrian priesthood at age fifty.

In 1906, he had made a trip to the Holy Land and afterward wrote his first book, *Na Jutrovem* (On the Orient), a journal of his travels. Between 1909 and 1913, he visited the United States four times and wrote *Amerika in Amerikanci* (America and American-Slovenes), covering history, politics, and geography and containing the first published descriptions of Slovene-American communities. Copies can be still found in private homes of descendants of Slovene immigrants and in Slovene national homes and priests' houses in every Slovene settlement.

In 1921, Trunk immigrated permanently to the United States. He served from 1921 to 1924 in Fulda, North Dakota, in a parish populated by Germans who had emigrated from Russia and, from 1924 to 1946, in the Slovene parish in Leadville, Colorado. There, Trunk continued his efforts on behalf of the Slovenes, holding Mass in Slovene and encouraging the Slovenes to preserve their ethnic identity. He decorated the church with paintings of the holy cross, adding captions in English and Slovene.

During this second half of his life, Trunk remained in close contact with Slovene immigrants and their organizations, writing more than two thousand articles for the Slovene ethnic press (the monthly *Ave Maria,* the weekly *Glasilo K.S.K.J.,* and the dailies *Edinost* [Unity] and *Amerikanski Slovenec* [American-Slovenes]). He served as coeditor of *Novi svet,* a semischolarly journal of the Slovene Americans, wherein very useful information could be found on the history of many Slovene settlements in the United States up to the 1940s. In his own column, which he wrote for *Amerikanski Slovenec,* he commented on the situation in Europe. In Slovenia, in 1950, Trunk published *Spomini* (Memoirs). He also left an unpublished sequel to his book *Amerika in Amerikanci.* At the age of 76, Trunk retired from his Leadville parish and moved to San Francisco, where he served as guest priest in a Slavic parish, dying in 1973 at the age of 103.

Matjaž Klemenčič

REFERENCES

Drnovšek, Marjan. "Odmevnost Trunkove knjige *Amerika in Amerikanci v letih 1912–1913*" (The echoes of Trunk's book *Amerika in Amerikanci* during the years 1912 and 1913). *Zgodovinski časopis* (Historical journal) 43.4 (1999): 606–609. (Ljubljana: Zveza zgodovinskih društev Slovenije—Federation of Historical Societies of Slovenia).

"Fr. Trunk Notes Golden Jubilee, Was Great Leader in Europe." *Denver Catholic Register,* 16 July 1945.

Klemenčič, Matjaž. *Jurij Trunk med Koroško in Združenimi državami Amerike ter zgodovina slovenskih naselbin v Leadvillu, Kolorado, in v San Francisco, Kalifornija* (Jurij Trunk between Carinthia and the United States and the history of Slovene settlements in Leadville, Colorado, and San Francisco, California). Klagenfurt/Celovec: Mohorjeva družba, 1999.

Trunk, Jurij. *Spomini* (Memoirs). Celje: Mohorjeva družba, 1950.

Truong, Thanh Nguyen (1961–)
Scientist and educator
Vietnamese

For Thanh N. Truong, ambition, hard work, diligence, and scholarship are the pathway to success. Now a leading academic scientist, Truong grew up in an impoverished rural family in Vietnam and entered the United States among the Vietnamese boat people in the 1980s, speaking no English and with scarcely any education.

Born in 1961 in Binh Dinh Province, Central Vietnam, Thanh Truong was the third of nine children. When Thanh was eleven, his father became disabled. Moving to a small town on the outskirts of Saigon, Truong worked with his mother, peddling cigarettes at a bus station to support his family. His need to work meant he could attend school only in the afternoon. Despite these limitations, he loved learning and developed a passion for mathematics, often solving math problems while selling cigarettes. Later, the family moved to the countryside, where Truong assisted in subsistence farming and raising and tutoring his six younger siblings.

In 1981, Troung, along with almost two hundred other refugees, including a younger brother, fled Vietnam by sea. After losing power and drifting for days, the boat was rescued by the U.S. Navy. He was admitted into the United States under the sponsorship of a Minnesota farmer. Knowing no English upon arrival, Truong found his high school years in Minnesota to be truly an ordeal. However, with a great deal of effort, he finished high school and attended the University of North Dakota. In 1985 he earned a B.S. in chemistry, with minors in math, computer science, physics, and statistics. Five years later, he received a Ph.D. in theoretical chemistry from the University of Minnesota. In 1992, after completing a postdoctoral fellowship at the University of Houston, Truong was hired as an assistant professor of chemistry at the University of Utah. The following year, Truong became the first Vietnamese American to win the prestigious National Science Foundation's Young Investigator Award in chemistry for his supercomputer-based research in molecular chemistry.

Despite his demanding career and family life (he is married to Ayumi Ueno, who is Japanese), Truong still finds time to organize and participate in ethnic community activities. As part of his effort to preserve Vietnamese traditional culture, he helps with preparations for the community's annual celebration of Tet, the Vietnamese New Year. At the same time, as cofounder of the Vietnamese Association of Utah, he is especially committed to aiding Vietnamese youth in their adjustment to the United States. In particular, believing that culture shock and language barriers foster pessimism among young immigrants, he has supported the efforts of the Vietnamese Youth Group in Salt Lake City to teach its members English and to help them integrate into American society. In these ways he is viewed by local leaders as an important role model. Thus, besides numerous awards for his academic achievement, including the American Institute of Chemists Award, he has also received the Outstanding Community Services Award from the Asian Association of Utah for his contributions to the community.

Hoan N. Bui

REFERENCES

Minh, Trong [pseud.]. "Truong Nguyen Thanh." In *The Pride of Vietnamese in the World,* edited by Trong Minh and R. Murphy, vol. 3: 154–161. Irvine, CA: Author, 1996.

Truong, Thanh N. website: truong.hec.utah.edu/ (accessed 21 May 2000).

Ure, Jon. "U. Chemist Who Fled Vietnam Wins Science Award, $500,000 Grant." *Salt Lake Tribune,* 9 June 1993, B1.

———. "Vietnamese Mark Lunar New Year with Celebration." *Salt Lake Tribune,* 24 January 1993, B3.

Truth, Sojourner (née Isabella Baumfree) (1799–1883)

Evangelist, abolitionist, and women's rights activist
African American

Sojourner Truth was one of the two most prominent African American women before the Civil War (the other was Harriet Tubman), challenging the forces of oppression in the United States, especially in the fight against slavery. A dynamic, charismatic woman, with a commanding presence, Truth also spoke out for the rights of both women and blacks—the first American woman to underscore the intersection of race, class, and gender and one of the nation's first feminists.

Truth was born a slave in a Dutch community in Ulster County, New York. She was originally named Isabella Baumfree, the second youngest of the eleven or twelve children of her slave parents, James and Elizabeth (called Mau-Mau Bett). All the children were sold, Sojourner four times—beginning at age nine. Able to speak only low Dutch, she was whipped for failing to understand orders in English. During her slavery, she had five children, one by a white slave owner. Her experiences as a six-foot-tall slave woman, including

whippings, sexual assaults, and forced hard labor, would subsequently provide the poignancy for her powerful speeches in support of abolitionism of slavery and for women's rights.

Truth escaped in 1826 and settled in New York City, working as a domestic. A strongly religious woman, she began preaching at camp meetings and was involved in several white religious and utopian social reform groups. In 1843, she claimed a religious vision, changed her name, and embarked on a mission to speak out against oppression. She became Sojourner Truth and joined a Massachusetts utopian reform group that emphasized cooperation over competition, women's rights, and the abolition of slavery. There, she met Frederick Douglass and William Lloyd Garrison.

A powerful, eloquent, and compelling speaker, with a commanding mystical presence, Truth took up her life as an itinerant preacher and social reformer, denouncing slavery and the subordinate status of women and emphasizing the need to aid the poor. Whites particularly embraced her in a way that they did not embrace her educated black female contemporaries. Thus, in Akron, Ohio, at the second National Woman's Suffrage Convention in 1852, she gave her most famous address, "Ain't I a Woman," and in a speech delivered in 1858, at Silver Lake, Indiana, she bared her breasts when white men in the audience claimed that the tall, gaunt Truth was not a woman.

During the Civil War, she met with President Lincoln and worked, from 1864 to 1868, to assist freed slaves who had fled in search of freedom. In the 1870s, concerned for the impoverished conditions of the freedmen, she embarked on a speaking tour to collect signatures for a petition demanding that the federal government provide land in the West to former slaves as reparation for their unpaid slave labor.

Sojourner Truth died in 1883 in her home. She said: "I'm Sojourner Truth. I fought for the rights of women as well as Negroes." A U.S. postage stamp was issued in Sojourner

Truth's honor in 1986, and she has been named to National Women's Hall of Fame.

Juliet E. K. Walker

REFERENCES

Bernard, Jacqueline. *Journey Toward Freedom: The Story of Sojourner Truth.* New York: Feminist Press, 1990.

Mabee, Carleton. *Sojourner Truth: Slave, Prophet, Legend.* New York: New York University Press, 1993.

Ortiz, Victoria. *Sojourner Truth: Self-Made Woman.* New York: Lippincott-Raven Publishers, 1987.

Painter, Nell. *Sojourner Truth: A Life, A Symbol.* New York: W. W. Norton, 1996.

Washington, Margaret, ed. *Narrative of Sojourner Truth.* New York: David McKay, 1993.

Tubman, Harriet (née Arminata Ross) (c. 1821–1913)

Antislavery activist
African American

Harriet Tubman is the best-known "conductor" of the Underground Railroad, a secret network of abolitionists who spirited many African Americans out of antebellum slavery. Tubman's exploits earned her the nickname Moses among those who followed her from the captivity of the South to the "Promised Land" of the North.

Tubman was born Arminata Ross around 1821, in Dorchester County, Maryland, one of eleven children to slave parents. She was given her mother's first name, Harriet, when she was about ten. Young Harriet endured a brutal childhood. In one incident, a slave owner hit her on the head with an iron for refusing to help detain a runaway. The blow caused permanent neurological damage; throughout her adult life she suffered from periodic losses of consciousness.

In 1844, she married freeman John Tubman, and five years later escaped north. (Her husband refused to flee with her and later remarried.) Tubman settled initially in Philadelphia, where she met William Still, a "stationmaster" of the Underground Railroad, who introduced her to its workings. Tubman returned to Maryland numerous times, first to rescue members of her family and then later,

other slaves. She undertook at least nineteen missions to the South between 1850 and 1860. In all, she helped 300 people escape to the northern United States and Canada. Southern plantation owners placed a $40,000 bounty on her head, and the State of Maryland offered a $12,000 reward for her capture.

Tubman was famed for her quick thinking, personal calm, and many disguises. She was just as infamous for carrying a pistol, which she threatened to use on any escaped slave attempting to turn back. She developed close ties to abolitionists and sympathizers, such as Frederick Douglass, Garrett Smith, and William Seward. She is reported to have missed John Brown's 1859 raid on Harper's Ferry, Virginia, only because she fell ill.

In 1861, after living in Canada (the 1850 Fugitive Slave Law, allowing slave owners to retrieve runaway slaves in the North, jeopardized her freedom in the North), Tubman returned to the United States to aid the Union in the Civil War. She served as a scout for the federal army, and as a nurse, she cared for wounded and sick "contraband" slaves. She organized many of these slaves to spy behind Confederate lines. Tubman was recognized for her wartime services but never paid.

After the Civil War, she returned to a residence in Auburn, New York, where she married Nelson Davis, a Union war veteran. (He died in 1890.) She became an avid supporter of women's suffrage, in addition to raising money to assist former slaves with food, education, and housing. In 1908, she built a home to care for the black elderly and indigent and for a period received care herself at this institution. Tubman, who died on 10 March 1913, received a burial with military honors. In the 1970s, the U.S. Department of the Interior designated her home in Auburn as a national historic landmark. She was later commemorated on a U.S. postal stamp.

Clarence Lang

REFERENCES

Bradford, Sarah H. *Scenes in the Life of Harriet Tubman.* 1869. Reprint, New York: Corinth Books, 1961.

McClard, Megan. *Harriet Tubman: Slavery and the Underground Railroad.* Englewood Cliffs, NJ: Silver Burdett Press, 1990.

Sterling, Philip, and Rayford Logan. *Four Took Freedom: The Lives of Harriet Tubman, Frederick Douglass, Robert Smalls, and Blanche K. Bruce.* Garden City, NY: Doubleday, 1967.

Yee, Shirley J. *Black Women Abolitionists: A Study in Activism, 1828–1860.* Knoxville: University of Tennessee Press, 1992.

Turkevich, Leonid (Metropolitan Leonty) (1876–1965)

Educator, journalist, and
Orthodox church leader
Russian

Leonid Turkevich came to the United States from Russia in 1906 as a missionary priest in the Russian Orthodox Mission in North America. Until his death in 1965, he was a leader in the religious lives of Carpatho-Rusyn immigrants from the Austro-Hungarian Empire. As Metropolitan Leonty, beginning in 1950, he was the undisputed leader in the Americanization of the Orthodox church in the United States, transforming an ethnic church into an American church.

Turkevich was born in 1876 in Kremenets, Volhynia, which at that time was in western Russia. He received an ecclesiastical education, a Kiev Theological Seminary degree, and ordination in 1905, following his marriage to Anna Chervinsky. The next year, Bishop Tikhon, of the North American Mission, asked Turkevich to come to the United States to be the rector of the new Orthodox seminary in Minneapolis. After the Carpatho-Rusyns there had converted to Orthodoxy, they generally identified themselves as Russians, accepting the leadership of Russian priests.

From 1914–1930, Turkevich was the editor of the *Russian American Orthodox Messenger,* giving him extensive exposure among the Russian Orthodox in the United States. During World War I, he was one of the U.S. delegates to the Russian Orthodox church convention *(sobor),* where he had the honor of nominating Metropolitan Tikhon as the Russian church's first patriarch in 200 years.

Returning home after the Bolshevik Revolution, Turkevich was one of the chief architects guiding the development of a Russian Orthodox church in America that was not dependent on the muzzled Russian patriarchate but also not too closely identified with the anti-Communist, pro-czarist Russian Orthodox Church Outside of Russia. In 1933 the widower Turkevich, who had become a U.S. citizen, was consecrated bishop of Chicago, taking the name Leonty. He remained committed to two ideals from his mentor, Patriarch Tikhon: First, Christian unity meant that various ethnic Orthodox churches in the United States must unite to form a single American Orthodox church, reaching out to the non-Orthodox in the United States. Second, *sobornost,* a Russian word meaning conciliarity (unity within multiplicity), implied that there should be a "balance between hierarchical authority and democratic equality." The church councils should include lay people, and lay people, including women, should be an essential part of the Church's decision-making structure.

In 1950 Leonty was elected metropolitan of the Russian Orthodox Church in North America, called the Metropolia, which in practice was an autonomous church. Leonty's dream of Christian unity was being implemented. The Metropolia joined the National Council of Churches in 1950 and the World Council of Churches in 1954. In 1960 Leonty was one of the principal founders of the Standing Conference of Canonical Orthodox Bishops in America (SCOBA).

From 1950 until his death in 1965, Metropolitan Leonty was the undisputed leader in the Americanization of the Orthodox church in America, creating an American priesthood, English-language churches, and a multiethnic identity. When autocephaly (independence) was granted in 1970, the church immediately changed its official name from the Russian Orthodox Greek Catholic Church in America to the Orthodox Church in America.

Leonid Turkovich led Carpatho-Rusyns and Russians in the United States from an ethnic church into an American church.

Keith P. Dyrud

REFERENCES

Dyrud, Keith P. *The Quest for the Rusyn Soul: The Politics of Religion and Culture in Eastern Europe and in America, 1890–World War I.* Philadelphia: Balch Institute Press, 1992.

Fitzgerald, Thomas E. *The Orthodox Church.* Westport, CN: Greenwood Press, 1995.

Garklavs, Alexander. "The Orthodox Church in America and the Russian Orthodox Church." *St. Vladimir's Theological Quarterly* 36.1–2 (1992): 131–140.

Grigorieff, Dmitry. "The Orthodox Church in America from the Alaska Mission to Autocephaly." *St. Vladimir's Theological Quarterly* 14.4 (1970): 196–218.

Stokoe, Mark, and Leonid Kishkovsky. *Orthodox Christians in North America, 1794–1994.* Syosset, NY: Orthodox Christian Publications Center (OCPC), 1995.

Tarasar, Constance J., ed. *Orthodox America, 1794–1976: The Development of the Orthodox Church in America.* Syosset, NY: Orthodox Church in America, 1975.

To make a living, Van de Poele started a furniture business, specializing in church furniture. The business soon flourished, and a year later he was employing more than 200 men. In 1870, he married Adamina Van Hoogstraten, daughter of a Dutch immigrant. He also continued to study science and electricity and, on Christmas 1875, on the main altar of Holy Trinity Church, he lit the first electric lamp in Detroit. After his parents joined him in the United States, his father took over the business, leaving his son with the time to devote to electrical experimentation.

From then on, Van de Poele's inventions followed rapidly, resulting in close to 250 U.S. patents by the time he died in 1892. His innovations involved the application of electric power, used as a source for lighting or driving, to power suction motors or rock drills for mine works, or to generate heating and cooling. In 1880, he established the Van de Poele Electric Light Company in Detroit but moved it to Chicago, where he found greater financial support. During the 1880s he was especially active with respect to electric railways. In 1883, he constructed the first electric trolley car and, a year later, at the Toronto Exposition, demonstrated electric rail tracks with an underground conduit. Within a few years his electric streetcar systems were installed in several U.S. cities. In 1888 he sold his trolley patents to the Thomson-Houston Electric Company (later to become General Electric Company) and became the manager of the trolley business.

Though he moved away from the Flemish-immigrant community in Detroit, Van de Poele remained in close contact with his fellow countrymen, both through visits and contacts with his family as well as through generous charitable contributions. In 1885 he reportedly donated the main altar and a substantial sum of money to the first Belgian church in Detroit, Our Lady of Sorrows. On 18 March 1892, Charles Van de Poele died from a lung infection. He was forty-six.

Kristine Smets

V

Van Andel, Jay
See **De Vos, Richard, and Van Andel, Jay**

Van de Poele, Charles Joseph (1846–1892)
Entrepreneur, scientist, and inventor
Belgian

Charles Van de Poele, a native of Belgium, is known best for his inventions that helped create the first electric trolley. During his lifetime, he was recognized as a great man, both by his fellow countrymen in Detroit and by the American business and scientific communities.

Born in Lichtervelde, a town in East Flanders, Belgium, Van de Poele was the only son of Pieter Van de Poele, a carpenter working on the first railroad between Brugge and Poperinge. Fascinated, his son watched the growth of the railroad and its companion, the telegraph. The youth began studying and experimenting with electricity. Legend has it that he produced his first electric light at age fifteen, using about forty battery cells. However, the family moved to Lille, France, in 1864, where he was sent to learn the carpentry and woodcarving trades. He hid his nightly experimentations with electricity from his father.

By 1868, Van de Poele had had enough of the carpentry business and family pressures. He left home and sailed for the United States, settling in Detroit, a town with about 200 Flemish immigrants. It would become the largest Flemish community in the United States on the eve of World War I.

REFERENCES

"Van Depoele, Charles Joseph." In *Webster's American Biographies,* edited by Charles Van Doren, 1068–1069. Springfield, MA: Merriam Co., 1974.

Goddeeris, John, and Robert Houthaeve. *Flandria Americana: Een studie van Vlaamse emigranten naar het Amerikaanse continent.* (Flandria Americana: A study of Flemish emigrants to the American continent). Kortemark-Handzame, Belgium: Familia et Patria, 1983.

Houthaeve, Robert. *Camille Cools en zijn Gazette van Detroit: Beroemde Vlamingen in Noord-Amerika* (Camille Cools and his *Gazette van Detroit:* Famous Flemish in North America). Moorslede, Belgium: R. Houthaeve, 1989.

"Van de Poele, Charles Joseph." In *National Cyclopedia of American Biography,* vol. 13: 246–247. New York: James T. White & Co., 1906.

Sabbe, Philemon D., and Leon Buyse. *Belgians in America.* Tielt, Belgium: Lannoo, 1960.

"Van de Poele, Charles Joseph." In *Who Was Who in America: Historical Volume 1607–1896,* rev. ed., 618. Chicago: Marquis Who's Who, 1967.

Verth'e, Arthur. *One Hundred Fifty Years of Flemish in Detroit.* Tielt, Belgium: Lannoo, 1983.

Van Loon, Hendrik Willem (1882–1944)

Author
Dutch

Hendrik Van Loon was a prolific author, journalist, illustrator, and teacher. He was perhaps best known for his nonfiction books popularizing scholarly subjects, including *The Story of Mankind* (1921).

Van Loon was born on 14 January 1882, in Rotterdam. His father, a jeweler, was a cold disciplinarian, and an oppressive, Calvinist-influenced atmosphere of hard work and harsh discipline pervaded the home. At age thirteen, Van Loon was sent to boarding school and then to an upper-class Dutch prep school. Although he did well in the humanities, the rigid discipline of home and school influenced him to resist conformity and to speak out against tyranny for the rest of his life. When he was twenty, his mother died, his father remarried, and Van Loon inherited some money, which enabled him to immigrate to the United States. On the advice of a family friend, he enrolled at Cornell University, receiving a B.A. there in 1905.

After college Van Loon became a journalist with the Associated Press (AP), a job that allowed him to travel while developing his writing skills. His ability to draw out the human interest side of a story earned him a growing readership. While covering Europe, he earned a Ph.D. at the University of Munich; he served as a war correspondent in Belgium and Russia during World War I. After the war, Van Loon, a witty and personable speaker, was frequently invited to lecture. He delighted audiences by illustrating talks with his own sketches and doodles. His career as a college professor, however, was short-lived, as his unorthodox (but highly entertaining) methods proved more popular with students than with administrators and fellow faculty members.

Van Loon's agility at interpreting history and the arts for a popular audience contributed to his success as an author. He wrote and illustrated more than forty books, nearly a book a year, including popularized treatments of the Bible, geography, art, music, and philosophy. Although criticized by the academic community for a lack of rigorous scholarship, his books nonetheless opened a world of culture and learning to the common reader.

He did not have much contact with other Dutch immigrants in the United States, save his membership in the Netherlands Club in New York City, where he met "early New York" Dutch, such as the Knickerbockers and DeLancys. However, his ties to his homeland remained strong. At the height of his career he bought a house in the Netherlands, where he lived part of the year. In World War II he supported the cause of Dutch freedom, organizing a shortwave radio program for the Netherlands from WRUL-Boston. In recognition of this work, he was knighted by Queen Wilhelmina of the Netherlands in 1942. Heartbroken when his hometown of Rotterdam was bombed, Van Loon hoped to return there after the war, but he died on 12 March 1944.

Many prominent Dutch attended Van Loon's funeral, including Dutch diplomats and New York City Mayor Fiorello La Guardia. The Dutch ambassador called Van Loon a "friend of his native country who . . . has well earned the deepest gratitude of all Netherlanders."

Jennifer Leo

REFERENCES

"Hendrik Van Loon Dies at Home at Sixty-two." *New York Times,* 12 March 1944, 37.

"Milestones." [obituary]. *Time,* 20 March 1944, 75.

Mulder, Arnold. *Americans from Holland.* New York: J. B. Lippincott, 1947.

"Roosevelt Saddened by Van Loon's Death." *New York Times,* 14 March 1944, 19.

"Transitions." [obituary]. *Newsweek,* 20 March 1944, 8.

"Van Loon Buried in Old Greenwich." *New York Times,* 15 March 1944, 19.

Van Loon, Gerard Willem. *The Story of Hendrik Willem Van Loon.* New York: J. B. Lippincott, 1972.

"Van Loon, Hendrik Willem." In *Concise Dictionary of American Biography,* 5th ed., 1341. New York: Scribner/American Council of Learned Societies, 1997.

Van Raalte, Albertus Christiaan (1811–1876)

Religious leader and founder of Holland, Michigan

Dutch

Albertus Christiaan Van Raalte was a pioneer religious leader. He led a group of Dutch followers to the United States and established a community that has endured to the present time.

Van Raalte of Wanneperveen, the Netherlands, was born in 1811. He studied theology at the University of Leiden in preparation for a career in the ministry of the Reformed church. At that time, the Reformed church was undergoing great change in response to evangelistic and Pietistic influences arising in reaction to the Enlightenment. These changes included the singing of hymns and the relaxation of dogmatic rules that conservative adherents held dear.

In 1832 Van Raalte underwent a personal religious experience during a cholera epidemic. It led him to embrace the "old" standards of the Reformed church and to reject the new influences. With some university friends (including Hendrik Scholte, founder of Pella, Iowa), he formed a group of people who wanted to keep the Reformed church close to its Calvinist roots, igniting what would become known as the Secession of 1834. Reformed church authorities, and ultimately the Dutch king, clamped down on the separatists, denying them freedom of worship and forbidding them to meet. The group met in secrecy and endured persecution, including fines, imprisonment, abuse from the townspeople, threats of violence, and job loss. In addition, an economic depression—and the same potato famine that would soon decimate Ireland and other parts of Europe—swept the country in the 1830s.

By 1845, Van Raalte had had enough. Hearing of the success of Dutch who had immigrated to the United States, he organized a group of followers, approximately sixty of them, who, in light of the reports of economic opportunity and religious freedom there, were persuaded to book passage with Van Raalte. Van Raalte raised funds to purchase land and establish a colony treasury. In 1846 he sailed for the New World with his wife, five children, and a maid. He received a warm welcome from Reformed pastors in New York but set out immediately for the Midwest. He thought he would establish his settlement in Wisconsin. However, owing to the onset of winter, he was unable to cross Lake Michigan; he ultimately settled in Michigan's Black Lake region in early 1847.

The Black Lake region turned out to be a propitious choice, as there were major trade routes nearby and plenty of timber. Living in log cabins in quite primitive conditions, members of the young settlement were plagued by epidemics brought on by stagnant water and unsanitary conditions. Relations with neighboring Native American tribes were generally peaceful, although cultural misunderstandings were common. Eventually, the tribes sold off their land to the settlers and abandoned the area, which became Holland, Michigan.

Van Raalte was a natural leader, an energetic fund-raiser, and an outgoing "booster," who formed cordial relationships with influential people, including those in Michigan's government. Under Van Raalte's leadership Holland flourished as a commercial center and as a primary entry point for new immigrants. He also encouraged his followers to participate in American life while not forgetting their Dutch origins. He died on 7 November 1876.

Jennifer Leo

REFERENCES

DeJong, Gerald F. *The Dutch in America, 1609–1974.* Boston: Twayne Publishers, 1975.

Hyma, Albert. *Albertus C. Van Raalte and His Dutch Settlements in the United States.* Grand Rapids, Eerdmans, 1947.

Jacobson, Jeanne M., et al. *Albertus Christian Van Raalte: Dutch Leader and American Patriot.* Holland, MI: Van Raalte Institute, 1999.

Lucas, Henry S. *Netherlanders in America: Dutch Immigration to the United States and Canada, 1789–1950.* Ann Arbor: University of Michigan Press, 1955.

Smit, Pamela, and J. W. Smit. *The Dutch in America, 1609–1970.* Dobbs Ferry, NY: Oceana Publications, 1972.

Van Raalte, Albertus C. *Dutch Leader and American Patriot.* Holland, MI: Hope College, 1996.

Varela y Morales, Félix (1788–1853)

Priest and community activist
Cuban

Felix Varela y Morales, a Cuban priest who sought refuge in New York City, was a leading defender of the Catholic Church in the 1830s and 1840s and, in his pastoral work, an ardent advocate of the needs of the poor. He was also a proponent of Cuban independence.

Born in Havana on 20 November 1788, Félix Varela y Morales had, by age six, lost both his parents and was under the tutelage of his maternal grandfather, a military officer stationed in the Spanish colony of St. Augustine, Florida. Although his father had also been in the military, Varela rejected that career, announcing, "I wish to be a soldier of Jesus Christ." He was sent to Havana to complete his education, receiving his bachelor of theology degree at the Seminary of San Carlos, where he started teaching. He was ordained in December 1811. This energetic and revolutionary professor soon became Cuba's foremost philosopher and educator. In 1821 he was elected deputy to the Cortes (the Spanish parliament), where he spoke out for civil rights and the gradual abolition of slavery. Amid the mounting tensions between King Ferdinand VII and the deputies, the Cortes was dissolved, and Varela was forced into exile.

On 15 December 1823, Varela arrived in New York, where he began as assistant pastor of St. Peter's Church. The building of the Transfiguration Church—in the midst of today's Chinatown—was brought about through his efforts. The church became the largest, and probably the poorest, parish in New York City. From 1837 until his death, Varela held the position of vicar general for New York.

During the early years of his exile, Varela founded the Spanish-language newspaper *El Habanero* and became a prophet of Cuba's independence. His three decades in the United States, however, were dedicated mainly to the Catholic Church, including the establishment of a nursery school for the children of working widows and a coeducational bilingual school. He devoted boundless energy to fight against alcoholism, and his concern for the poor likewise became legendary—even giving his own coat to a poor man to protect him from the cold New York winter. At the same time, between 1830 and 1860, violent clashes between Protestants and Catholics turned doctrinal controversies into vicious debates. Varela penned hundreds of articles to clarify the principles of the Catholic Church and soon became the leading Catholic polemicist in the country—but always addressing his adversaries with decorum and respect. A life of self-denial eventually took its toll on Varela's health, and he sought refuge in the milder climate of St. Augustine, his childhood home, dying there on 25 February 1853, less than a month after José Martí, the most important figure of Cuban independence, was born in Havana.

Cubans cherish Padre Félix Varela "as the man who taught us how to think." His face—slight, drawn, elongated, with dark, bespectacled eyes—appears today on a U.S. Postal Service stamp as homage to his missionary work. The Vatican is considering a petition to recognize him as a saint. He lived true to his youthful wish to become a soldier of Christ.

Uva de Aragón

REFERENCES

Hernández Travieso, Antonio. *El Padre Varela. Biografía del forjador de la conciencia cubana* (Father Varela: Biography of the forger of the Cuban conscience). La Habana, Cuba: Montero, 1949.

Lasaga, José Ignacio. "A Nineteenth Century Priest One Hundred Years ahead of His Times." *Vidas cubanas: Página de la historia de Cuba* (Cuban lives: Pages from the history of Cuba), edited by José I. Lasaga, translated by Nelson Durán, vol I, 157–180. Miami: Revista Ideal, 1984–1988.

Martínez-Ramos, Alberto. "Father Félix Varela: Cuban Catholic Apologist in the United States." M.A. thesis, University of Miami, 1979.

McCadden, Joseph and Helen M. McCadden. *Felix Varela. The Torch Bearer from Cuba.* San Juan, Puerto Rico: Ramallo Brothers Printing, 1984.

"Varela y Morales, Felix." In *Dictionary of American Biography,* vol. 10. New York: Scribner's, 1936.

Vega, Bernardo (1885–1965)

Writer and political activist
Puerto Rican

Bernardo Vega is an important figure in the early history of the Puerto Rican community in New York City not only because he wrote about it but also because he helped to shape it. His book *Memoirs* is still considered the most detailed and politically coherent accounting of Puerto Rican life from 1916 until after World War II.

Vega participated in the formation of Puerto Rico's first large-scale working-class organization in 1899. By 1915, he had become a charter member of the Partido Socialista, which was founded in his hometown. He arrived in New York City in 1916 and provided a link to an earlier cohort of activists already living there. At that time *la colonia* was made up mostly of *tabaqueros* (cigar makers) and their families. Vega was a *tabaquero* when he arrived, and it was through this connection that he navigated his way through the city and found work. The strong sense of brotherhood provided a network for finding a place to live and work.

Although his love of his home culture can never be doubted, it was the global perspective and keen sense of history of this self-educated "card-carrying Socialist" that has made him one of the most prominent figures in Puerto Rican history. In his *Memoirs,* which Vega began writing in the 1940s, he vividly described the story of migration, of the Puerto Rican worker, and of camaraderie in the community, portraying national identity as a modality through which working-class identity was experienced. As a Socialist, he also maintained that the class struggle should not be directed at the colonial elite alone but at the whole system of imperial exploitation that was based in the United States.

In the late 1930s, as the depression deepened, his network became a source of survival. Cigars had become an expensive luxury, and the cigar makers found themselves scraping tar off ships, washing dishes, or working in munitions factories. But those were not easy jobs, especially for men who saw themselves as the elite of their craft. The Socialist Party, the Cigar Makers Union, and the Seamen's Union were the only groups openly defending the rights of immigrant workers. Vega depicted the struggles to find gainful, though not necessarily meaningful, employment within the context of that teeming, competitive, urban immigrant mecca.

Vega wanted to put into print this story of Puerto Ricans in New York City, highlighting not only their struggles but also their contributions to its growth and prosperity. In doing so, he also provided a framework and guidelines for the early independence movement against the United States. Indeed, in the 1950s, Vega was openly protesting HUAC's investigations of the Puerto Rican community and further helping to consolidate El Movemiento por Independencia (MPI), the base for an important proindependence movement after World War II.

Vega died in San Juan in 1965. His legacy can be found in his writings, which are often cited to refute the notion that Puerto Ricans are "newcomers" to the U.S. shores, thus contributing to the continuing political and ideological debates about the status of Puerto Ricans.

Linda Delgado

REFERENCES

Torres, Andrés, and José E. Velázquez, eds. *The Puerto Rican Movement: Voices from the Diaspora.* Philadelphia: Temple University Press, 1998.

Vega, Bernardo. *Memoirs of Bernardo Vega. A Contribution to the History of the Puerto Rican Community in New York.* Edited by César Andreu Iglesias and translated by Juan Flores. New York: Monthly Review Press, 1984.

Velázquez, Baldemar (1947–)
Civil rights activist and union organizer
Mexican-American

Baldemar Velásquez is founder and president of the Farm Labor Organizing Committee (FLOC) in the Midwest and the founder of the Farm Worker Network for Economic and Environmental Justice. Since the 1970s, he has been leading successful strikes and boycotts on behalf of farmworkers.

Velásquez was born in 1947 in Pharr, Texas. He began working in the fields with his parents at age four. In 1953, his family settled in Gilboa, Ohio. He enrolled in 1965 at Pan American University, in Harlingen, Texas, but two years later, he transferred to Bluffton College, a Mennonite school in Bluffton, Ohio. While there, he did farmwork to pay for college; the next year he and other farmworkers formed the Farm Labor Organizing Committee. Meanwhile, in 1969, Velázquez graduated with a B.A. in sociology and married Sara Templin, the daughter of a Bluffton College professor. They have four children.

In 1978, Velásquez organized a strike by FLOC against the Campbell Soup Company and launched an eight-year consumer boycott of the company's products. The campaign had widespread support among the public, religious organizations, political groups, and labor unions. In 1979, FLOC was formally organized as an AFL-CIO affiliate union, and four years later Velásquez led farmworkers on a 600-mile march, from Toledo, Ohio, to Campbell Soup headquarters in Camden, New Jersey. The resulting national attention led to a collective bargaining agreement between farmworkers and tomato growers.

Velázquez expanded FLOC membership and focused on education, food and fuel cooperatives, and legal services for farmworkers. He formed the Donlop Commission and another independent commission in Mexico to negotiate collective bargaining rights for farmworkers. The latter culminated in the nation's first tripartite contracts—between farmworkers, farmers, and produce corporations. In February 1986, FLOC signed three-year labor contracts with the Campbell Soup Company and its subsidiary, Vlasic Pickles, gaining wage increases and benefits for 800 workers on twenty-eight farms in Ohio and Michigan. Sixteen months later, FLOC signed a three-year contract with H. J. Heinz Company. By 1991, more than 7,000 farmworkers were working under FLOC contracts.

In 1993, Velásquez formed the Farm Worker Network to increase collaboration among U.S. and international farmworker organizations. Then, in 1998, as the first step toward building a farmworker-labor movement in the South, he organized a national boycott of the North Carolina–based Mt. Olive Pickle Company, the South's largest pickle company. His goal was another tripartite contract. He succeeded, and FLOC has expanded its activities into Georgia and North Carolina.

Besides his labor struggles, Velásquez continued to study. He earned an advanced degree in practical theology from Florida International Seminary in 1991 and was ordained a minister by Rapha Ministries. He has lectured and published widely on conditions of migrant farmworkers. He has received numerous honors for his life's work to improve the working and living conditions of migrant farmworkers and their families, including a John D. and Catherine T. MacArthur Fellowship in 1989 and the Aguila Azteca Medal in 1994, the highest award Mexico bestows to noncitizens. He was also awarded honorary doctorates from Bowling Green State University in 1996 and Bluffton College in 1998.

Zaragosa Vargas

REFERENCES

Acuña, Rodolfo. *Occupied America: A History of Chicanos.* 2d ed. New York: Harper & Row, 1983.

Barger, W. K., and Ernesto M. Reza. *The Farm Labor Movement in the Midwest: Social Change and Adaptation among Migrant Farmworkers.* Austin: University of Texas Press, 1994.

———. "Views of Midwestern Farmworkers Concerning the Farm Labor Movement." *La Red* 78 (1984): 2–7.

O'Neill, Patrick. "Union Leader Brings Organizing Campaign to Cucumber Pickers." *National Catholic Reporter* 33.33 (4 July 1997): 12–14.

Sowash, Rick. *Heroes of Ohio: Twenty-three True Tales of Courage and Character.* Bowling Green, OH: Gabriel's Horn Publishing Co., 1998.

Vera Cruz, Philip (1904–1994)
Labor leader
Filipino

Already in his sixties in 1965, Philip Vera Cruz helped spark the strike of 1,000 Filipino agricultural workers in Delano, California, which led to the emergence of the United Farm Workers of America, under César Chavez. Vera Cruz served as the union's second vice president until 1977.

Like many Filipino old-timers in the United States, Vera Cruz hailed from the impoverished Ilocos Provinces of Northern Luzon, Philippines. Between his arrival in Seattle in 1926 and the early 1930s he worked in a box factory, thinned sugar beets in North Dakota, and did hotel and restaurant work in Spokane and Minneapolis, graduating from high school and managing a year of college at Gonzaga University in Spokane. Unable to continue in college, he drifted to Chicago for almost another decade of restaurant work. He moved to California in 1942, returning to the fields, where he picked cantaloupe, lettuce, grapes, and asparagus.

Vera Cruz's life reflects the experience of a generation of Filipinos who immigrated to the United States in the 1920s and 1930s in search of educational and economic opportunities. Denied U.S. citizenship during the American colonial era (1900–1946), these old-timers faced major obstacles on the West Coast, particularly economic discrimination, which confined many to seasonal migratory labor, and antimiscegenation laws that consigned many men in a mostly male cohort to lifelong bachelorhood.

Vera Cruz read widely, including *The Jungle* and "some Marxist literature," saved money, bought land, and became a U.S. citizen when the law changed after World War II. "It was only after the war when I seriously realized that this was really becoming my home and that if I wanted to stay here I had better start exercising my rights," he recalled. "I got my citizenship, not because I embraced the capitalist system but more because of my belief in a working democracy." In 1949, he headed the Delano local of the National Farm Labor Union and, in 1960, helped found the Agricultural Workers Organizing Committee, composed mostly of Filipino Americans, which later merged into Chavez's United Farm Workers.

The old-timers had a difficult encounter as a minority in a union led by Mexican Americans, most of whom had worked fewer years. Some locals conducted meetings in Spanish. Growers, in turn, rewarded Filipinos who jumped to the rival Teamsters Union by giving them seniority. Vera Cruz's main project with the United Farm Workers (UFW) was the Paolo Agbayani Village retirement center, which opened in 1975 and became embroiled in controversies over finances and control. Vera Cruz disagreed with UFW leaders over support for undocumented workers (he backed them) and Chavez's trip to the Philippines as guest of then-president Ferdinand

Marcos, the incident that led to Vera Cruz's resignation in 1977.

Vera Cruz lived on as a hero to California radicals. His autobiography, taped in the 1970s at the UCLA Labor Center, appeared in 1992. Though he had sent remittances to the Philippines since the 1920s, putting a brother through law school, he first returned to the islands in 1987 to receive the Ninoy Aquino Movement Lifetime Achievement Award from President Corazon Aquino.

Roland L. Guyotte

REFERENCES
Bacdayan, Albert. "Remembering Philip Vera Cruz." *Heritage,* September 1994, 9.
"Chavez Visit Stirs Controversy." *Philippine News,* 22–28 October 1977, 1–2.
"Philip Vera Cruz, Eighty-nine, Helped to Found Farm Worker Union." *New York Times,* 16 June 1994, B9.
Scharlin, Craig, and Lilia V. Villanueva, eds. *Philip Vera Cruz: A Personal History of Filipino Immigrants and the Farmworkers Movement.* Los Angeles: UCLA Labor Center, 1992.

Vig, Peter Sorensen (1854–1929)
Theologian and historian
Danish

More than seventy years after his death, Peter Sorensen Vig is still widely recognized as one of the most influential Danish-American religious leaders. He was also the pioneering historian of the Danish-American experience.

Born near Egtved, Denmark, Vig was the eldest of twelve children in a poor farm family. Influenced by his pious mother, he decided early on to be a minister. But lack of money and connections frustrated his dream, and at age twenty-five, he immigrated to the United States. For three years he worked in Chicago, saving his money. Vig decided that his future ministry would be among the Danes who had immigrated to the United States. Returning to Denmark in 1882, he enrolled in a special two-year theological program, after which he returned to the United States and was ordained in the Danish Lutheran Church in America. He taught briefly at the Danish folk high school in Elk Horn, Iowa, while serving a nearby congregation, but in 1887 joined the faculty of the Danish Lutheran Theological Seminary in West Denmark, Wisconsin.

Soon, however, conflicts within the Church of Denmark between followers of Bishop N. F. S. Grundtvig and a Pietistic group, the Inner Mission, spread to the United States, compelling the seminary to close and creating a schism among Danish-American Lutherans. Vig sided with the Inner Mission and was eventually elected professor of theology and president of Trinity Seminary, Blair, Nebraska, the theological school of the newly formed United Danish Evangelical Lutheran church. By the time of his retirement in 1921, 132 students had received their education under Vig. A majority were ordained in the United church, carrying on Vig's ideas. More than any other person, he set the spiritual tone for what became the largest Danish Lutheran denomination in the United States and Canada.

Vig's second important legacy developed out of his interest in the history of Danish Americans. Between 1889 and 1921, he published six books on the Danish-immigrant experience in the United States and wrote or coauthored more than 400 pages of text for the first volume of *Danske i Amerika* (Danes in America). He also wrote several shorter works. Historians have acknowledged Vig's pioneering role. In the 1980s, Erik Helmer Pedersen asserted that Vig did "more than any other person to preserve the historical inheritance of Danish immigrants."

Given Vig's ethnic loyalty, he was deeply hurt when Governor William Lloyd Harding questioned the loyalty of Iowa's Danish speakers during World War I. A public exchange of angry letters between Vig and the some of the governor's supporters followed. Ironically, Vig was a moderate who believed that for his church to grow and prosper, it would have to make the transition from Danish to English. Nevertheless, he found Harding's remarks insulting and said so.

In 1921, the year of his retirement, Vig received two of his greatest honors. King Christian X of Denmark made Vig a knight of Dannebrog. A few months later, Luther Theological Seminary, of St. Paul, Minnesota, bestowed upon him an honorary doctor of divinity degree. It was a remarkable journey for a poor Danish farm boy. Vig died in 1929.

Peter L. Petersen

REFERENCES

Beck, Theo. P. *The Professor: P. S. Vig.* Blair, NE: Lutheran Publishing House, 1930.

Petersen, Peter L., and John Mark Nielsen. "Peter Sorensen Vig and the Americanization Issue During World War I." *Bridge* 11.1 (1979): 57–61.

———. "Peter Sorensen Vig: Danish-American Historian." In *Danish Emigration to the U.S.A.*, edited by Birgit Flemming Larsen and Henning Bender, 124–141. Aalborg, Denmark: Danes Worldwide Archives and the Danish Society for Emigration History, 1992.

———. *A Place Called Dana: The Centennial History of Trinity Seminary and Dana College.* Blair, NE: Dana College, 1984.

Voliansky, Ivan (1857–1926)

First Ukrainian Catholic priest
Ukrainian

In the history of Ukrainian Americans no other individual has shaped the development of the community to the extent that Ivan Voliansky did. Nevertheless, he spent only four years in the United States.

The first Ukrainian immigrants in the 1870s, predominantly from the western regions of Ukraine—then under Austro-Hungarian rule—were impoverished, largely illiterate peasants, whose ethnic identity hinged on language and religion. They belonged to the Uniate, that is, the Eastern (often called Greek or Byzantine) church that retained Eastern liturgical rites, the Old Slavonic language, and a married clergy. Under foreign domination, the church had become a surrogate national authority and the clergy its leading class. Prominent leaders sought to abandon the historical (easily confused with Russian) names—Rus', and its people, Rusyny (Ruthenians)—in favor of a name from the Cossack period: Ukraine (Ukraina) and Ukrainians (Ukraintsi).

Voliansky, who had been born on 1 August 1826, in Yabloniv, Ukraine, was a married Uniate priest who was in the avant-garde of this Ukrainian movement. Thus, when in 1884 a group of Ukrainian immigrants in Shenandoah, Pennsylvania, asked for a priest of their rite, Voliansky volunteered. Educated at the Universities of Vienna and Lviv, a linguist who knew—besides Ukrainian, Greek, and Latin—German, French, and English (and, later, Portuguese), Voliansky was energetic and enthusiastically committed to his flock. In December 1884, he arrived in New York with his wife, who proved herself his equal in pioneering work. Denied recognition by the Roman Catholic hierarchy because he was married, Voliansky nevertheless celebrated the first Ukrainian liturgy in North America in Shenandoah, on 22 December 1884. In January, he founded the first organization, Brotherhood of Saint Nicholas, to help build a church and to maintain a fund in case of the illness or death of its members. By 1889 there were at least twenty-four brotherhoods in different localities, mainly in Pennsylvania.

The church was completed in Fall 1886, and Ukrainians came to Shenandoah from Baltimore, New York, and other areas to be married. Besides organizing parishes—the last one in Minneapolis, Minnesota, in 1889—Voliansky brought over more priests and tried to entice educated laymen to participate. Under his guidance, schools for illiterate adults, reading rooms, orchestras, choirs, dance, and dramatic ensembles as well as cooperative grocery stores were established. In August 1886, he started a Ukrainian biweekly (later weekly) newspaper, *Ameryka*. Knowing English and keeping himself well informed, he was probably the first Catholic priest to join a labor union and to encourage his parishioners to support the labor movement.

But despite his prolific achievements, Voliansky was under pressure from the Roman Catholic hierarchy and was recalled to Ukraine. After his departure, things started to disintegrate and he was sent back for a short visit in 1890 to set them straight. Then, in 1896, he went to work with Ukrainian immigrants in Brazil. His wife died there of yellow fever, and he returned to Ukraine and served his church there until his death on 1 August 1926.

His legacy to the Ukrainian-American community is the organizational foundation that is still vital. And more than that, his charisma and vision laid the foundation of the ethnonational identity of Ukrainian immigrants.

Daria Markus

REFERENCES
Bachynsky, Yulian. *Ukrainska Immihratsiia v Spoluchenykh Shtatakh Ameryky* (Ukrainian immigrants in the United States of America). 2d ed. Kyiv: Ukrainian Diapora Library, 1995.
Krawcheniuk, Osyp. *Stezhkamy otsia Ivana Volianskoho v Amerytsi* (On the pathways of Father Ivan Voliansky in America). Yorkton, Sask., Canada: Eastern Rite Redemptionist Fathers, 1981.
Kuropas, Myron. "Nashi perspektyvy" (Our perspectives). *Svoboda,* 6 June 1989.

von Braun, Wernher (1912–1977)
Rocket scientist
German

Wernher von Braun first achieved distinction for his contributions to Germany's war effort during World War II. It was, however, his many achievements on behalf of the U.S. rocket program and space exploration that firmly established his importance for the United States.

Born in Wirsitz (currently in Poland), von Braun showed an early aptitude for things scientific and enjoyed experimenting with explosives and rockets. He would complete his B.S. from Berlin Technological Institute in 1932 and finish his doctorate in 1934, at age twenty-two. While a graduate student at the University of Berlin in the early 1930s, von Braun assisted his professor in seminal research on the design and construction of liquid-fuel rockets.

Von Braun was chosen as technical director at the German Rocket Research center on the Baltic coast, Peenemuende, serving from 1937 to 1945. There he would do research and teach for the duration of the war. As the leader of a group of scientists, von Braun made invaluable contributions to the German war effort. The V-2 liquid-fuel rocket, with a range of more than 200 miles and velocities of 3,500 miles per hour (mph), was his most important invention. The rockets were first employed in Fall 1944, and the British found them devastating.

Despite his contribution to Nazi Germany, von Braun was not punished by the Allies. In 1945, he (and much of his team) was brought to the United States to continue the work. For five years the von Braun team labored at two sites: the White Sands Proving Grounds in New Mexico and at Fort Bliss, Texas. With the early Cold War years creating a sense of urgency, von Braun continued his work at Huntsville, Alabama, from 1950 to 1960 as chief of the Guided Missile Development Division. At the Redstone Arsenal and the Army Missile Ballistic Agency, progress was made in the area of intercontinental ballistic missiles and spacecraft. Amid all this, von Braun became a U.S. citizen in 1955.

In 1970, von Braun's interest in space exploration was rewarded with his appointment as deputy associate administrator of the National Aeronautics and Space Administration (NASA). His major contribution to space flight was the Saturn V launch vehicle, which proved critical in the success of the Apollo moon program. Von Braun was an ebullient proponent of space exploration and never lost his enthusiasm for speaking and writing about the topic. He fostered the public excitement about space through such publications as: *Across the Space Frontier* (1952), *The Exploration of Mars* (1956), and *First Men on the Moon* (1960).

The glowing reports of von Braun's accomplishments, however, must include some discussion of his connection with Nazism and the collaboration of the U.S. government in saving him from punishment. Recently declassified documents reveal that the German scientist had not been simply a disinterested scientist during the 1930s and 1940s and that von Braun's story is much more complicated, for the U.S. Army covered up his tainted past.

Such revelations have led to a reassessment of him and his work for the space program. Von Braun, who died in 1977, has proved to be a brilliant, yet complex and contradictory figure.

Susanne M. Schick

REFERENCES

Gimbel, John. "U.S. Policy and German Scientists: The Early Cold War." *Political Science Quarterly* 101 (1986): 433–451.

Hickman, Homer. "Coming to America." *Air and Space/Smithsonian* 9 (1994): 78–88.

Mack, Joanna, and Steve Humphries. *London at War: The Making of Modern London, 1939–1945.* London: Sidgwick & Jackson, 1985.

Piszkiewicz, Dennis. *Wernher von Braun: The Man Who Sold the Moon.* Westport, CT: Greenwood Publishing Group, 1999.

Stuhlinger, Ernst. "German Rocketeers Find a New Home in Huntsville." *Yearbook for German-American Studies* 31 (1996): 157–166.

Stuhlinger, Ernst, and Frederick Ira Ordway. *Wernher von Braun: Crusader for Space.* Malabar, FL: Krieger Publishing Co., 1996.

Tarter, Donald. "Peenemuende and Los Alamos: Two Studies." *History of Technology* (Great Britain) 14 (1992): 150–170.

Vuksic, Nelly Perez (1938–)

Music director and voice teacher
Argentinean

Nelly Perez Vuksic has earned a reputation over the past quarter century as an important conductor of choral groups in the United States. In particular, she has used her many appearances and teaching position to disseminate Latin American music and thereby familiarize Americans with both classical and contemporary Latin American composers.

Vuksic was born on 19 August 1938, into a musical family in Tortoras, Santa Fe, a rural Argentinean town. Her father, Emilio Perez, played guitar, and her mother, Lydia, organized musical evenings with the whole family. Vuksic was taught to play the piano. She had additional early music education in the Catholic Church, where she performed on the harmonium, an instrument similar to the organ, and learned how to sing in a group and sing Gregorian chants. For financial reasons, Vuksic did not complete secondary education until her early twenties. She then attended Rosario University, devoting herself to conducting youth and adult choruses.

In 1969, Nelly married pianist Cesar Vuksic, and they had one son, Alejandro. She accompanied her husband to Ball State University, in Muncie, Indiana, where both were offered scholarships. Vuksic did her doctoral study and conducted a women's chorus and concert choir there, too. In both 1976 and 1977, she received Ball State's Music Concerto Night Award. Vuksic then went with her husband to Western Michigan University, where she conducted the choir and several chamber orchestras and taught piano.

When the couple traveled to Columbia University, where she was a conductor, their music interests broadened. They brought their new interests to New York City. Vuksic formed the choral group, which became the Americas Vocal Ensemble in 1982. She remains the musical director of this group, whose mission it is to foster understanding among the people of the Americas and to preserve the musical and cultural richness of the diverse countries of North and South America.

With the ensemble, she is able to introduce people to a variety of music; the repertoire spans four centuries and encompasses a wide range of styles, including folk arrangements by distinguished Latin American composers. Vuksic's professional mission is to expand and disseminate Latin American music. She unites classical and contemporary music from Latin America and the United States to create an enjoyable musical experience that is also educational. The ensemble has also premiered more than 100 contemporary works. In addition to live performances and recordings, the ensemble has been presented on National Public Radio and Voice of America.

Besides her work with the ensemble in New York, Vuksic was a bilingual teacher of music at the Bloomingdale House of Music and taught all grade levels at the Friends Seminary and at Columbia University's program for gifted children. She also has worked with individuals. Vuksic, who has received several national and international awards, is also musical director of the United Nations Singers and has been a regular guest conductor at the New York Chorale since 1988. She performs regularly with her husband, pianist Cesar Vuksic.

Kathleen Paparchontis

REFERENCES

American Composers Orchestra. "Argentine Composers and Performers Biographies (March 1998)": www.americancomposers.org/sa98bios.htm (accessed 30 June 2000).

Jeffrey James Arts Consulting. "The Americas Vocal Ensemble": www.jamesarts.com/AVEFLYER.htm (accessed 30 June 2000).

———. "Tangos y Zambas: Performance and Instruction": www.jamesarts.com/AVETGOZBA.htm (accessed 30 June 2000).

Telgen, Dianne, and Jim Kamp, eds. *Notable Hispanic American Women.* Detroit: Gale Research, 1993.

"Vuksic, Nelly Perez." In *Who's Who among Hispanic Americans, 1994–1995,* edited by Amy L. Unterburger and Jane L. Delgado, 3d ed. Detroit: Gale Research, 1996.

W

Wagner, Robert F. (1877–1953)

State assembly member, state senator, jurist, and U.S. senator

German-American

Robert F. Wagner entered U.S. politics as a representative of a neighborhood of German immigrants. Nevertheless, he became a powerful advocate of the entire working class in the eras of Progressivism and the New Deal.

Born in the Rhineland, Robert Wagner immigrated to New York City with his family at the age of nine. When his parents returned to Germany in 1896, he remained behind as a student at the City College of New York. He graduated in 1898 and studied law at the New York Law School. In 1900 he entered law practice and quickly became involved in Democratic Party politics. He married an Irish Catholic, Margaret McTague, in 1908. She died in 1919, leaving him to raise their only son (who eventually became mayor of New York City).

Wagner was first elected to the New York State Assembly in 1904, representing the heavily German district of Yorkville on the Upper East Side of Manhattan. He became increasingly identified with the rising Progressive wing in the state's Democratic Party and in 1908 was elected to the state senate. During the next decade he became known for promoting legislation for the causes of working people, including workmen's compensation, workplace safety laws, and regulation of the labor of women and children. In 1918 he was elected a judge of the New York State Supreme Court, where he also became known for his support of the rights of workers. At his party's behest he ran for the U.S. Senate in 1926, winning decisively. He served there continuously from 1927 to 1949.

When the Great Depression struck during the administration of Herbert Hoover, Wagner became known among the Democratic minority as a leader for the causes of working people and the unemployed, advocating relief measures and public works employment. He consistently argued for the need to increase employment, even at the cost of deficit spending, in order to restore purchasing power to the common man and thereby revive the economy. When Franklin D. Roosevelt was elected president in 1932, Wagner was among the chief congressional architects of New Deal programs and the chief supporter of the causes of labor. His greatest achievement was drafting the National Labor Relations Act (1935), which was known thereafter as the Wagner Act. The act, whose provisions were originally embodied in the failed National Industrial Recovery Act (1933), gave organized labor a charter of liberties, with federal government protection for the process of unionization and the obligation of employers to recognize unions formed under the act. Wagner was also one of the principal sponsors of the Social Security Act of 1935 and an advocate of the Fair Labor Standards Act of 1938, which established minimum-wage regulation. In the years around World War II he promoted other social welfare legislation for federal support of housing and urban renewal. He resigned from the Senate for health reasons in 1949. Wagner can be seen as an ethnic politician who rose to political leadership, but the key to his success was in broadening his political base beyond immigrants to the entire working class.

James M. Bergquist

REFERENCES

Huthmacher, J. Joseph. *Senator Robert F. Wagner and the Rise of Urban Liberalism.* New York: Atheneum, 1968.

Schlesinger, Arthur M., Jr. *The Age of Roosevelt.* 3 vols. Boston: Houghton Mifflin, 1957–1960.

Tomlins, Christopher L. *The State and the Unions: Labor Relations, Law and the Organized Labor Movement in America, 1880–1960.* New York: Cambridge University Press, 1985.

Wesser, Robert. *A Response to Progressivism: The Democratic Party and New York Politics, 1902–1918.* New York: New York University Press, 1986.

Yellowitz, Irwin. *Labor and the Progressive Movement in New York State, 1897–1916.* Ithaca, NY: Cornell University Press, 1965.

Wald, Lillian (1867–1940)

Public health nurse and community activist German-Jewish-American

Lilian Wald was best known for her achievements in creating the Settlement House movement (specifically, the Henry Street Settlement in New York City) and for launching the career of the "public health nurse." She also came to personify many of the concerns of the Progressive Era and the changing goals of middle-class, educated women.

Wald was born to German-Jewish immigrant parents, Max and Minnie Wald, in Cincinnati. They had fled Germany after the abortive 1848 revolution. The Walds prospered in Cincinnati, but the family moved to Rochester, New York, and Wald was enrolled in a rigorous boarding school. Whereas other young girls were dreaming of marriage, she felt her life must take a different course. Deciding on nursing, she enrolled at the New York Training School.

Wald finally discovered her "purpose" when she encountered impoverished immigrant women on New York's Lower East Side. The crumbling and squalid tenements left her heartsick. She determined to spend her life serving this immigrant community. A successful fundraising effort enabled Wald to purchase a home that would henceforth be known as the Henry Street Settlement House. Her ambitious plans were to improve the lives of the women and children of the slums with programs for playgrounds, park facilities, educational opportunities, and provisions catering to children's special needs, including free lunches, school nurses, and special assistance for those with physical or mental handicaps. The local board of education began to implement her ideas. Meanwhile, Wald continued to expand the services offered at Henry Street—among them a savings bank, numerous clubs, health clinics, job training, and a lending library. Public health nurses began to set up branches throughout the city, following the Henry Street model.

Wald was an inveterate "joiner," lending her name and considerable energies to organizations that she believed would help her constituency—specifically to improve conditions for women and children workers, new immigrants, African Americans, and her own fellow nurses. These organizations included the Women's Trade Union League, the New York Immigration Commission, the Nursing Insurance Partnership, the NAACP, and the Federal Children's Bureau.

Along with her commitment to women's suffrage, Wald was horrified by the prospect of a world war and participated in a women's peace parade. Her outspokenness would affect Henry Street's funding. However, when the United States entered the war in 1917, Wald focused on improving both nursing training and nursing care for victims of the influenza epidemic and for the war wounded and establishing clinics throughout the city.

Her visibility, however, left Wald open to charges of radicalism. Indeed, she was labeled as a dangerous, pro-Bolshevik agitator, but she did not stop her association with radical activists and causes. As the leading public health nurse in the country, she traveled extensively, speaking to audiences about her dreams for children, women's rights, health care, and pacifism. However, as she aged, Wald became increasingly introspective, and in her memoirs, *Windows on Henry Street*, she analyzes several decades in the life of the Settlement House neighborhood. Like many educated, professional women of her time, she eschewed marriage and family life in favor of serving her community. When she died in 1940, thousands gathered to pay their respects.

Susanne M. Schick

REFERENCES

Carson, Mina. *Settlement Folk: The Evolution of Social Welfare Ideology in the American Settlement Movement, 1883–1930.* Chicago: University of Chicago Press, 1990.

Cook, Blanche Wiesen. "Female Support Networks and Political Activism: Lillian Wald, Crystal Eastman, and Emma Goldman." *Crysalis* 1 (1977): 43–61.

Hirsch, Arnold. "Unsettling Settlements." *Reviews in American History* 22 (1994): 480–485.

Lasch-Quinn, Elisabeth. *Black Neighbors: Race and the Limits of Reform in the American Settlement House Movement, 1890–1945.* Chapel Hill: University of North Carolina Press, 1993.

Spratt, Margaret. "Beyond Hull House: New Interpretations of the Settlement House Movement in America." *Journal of Urban History* 23 (1997): 770–776.

Wald, Lillian. *Lillian Wald Papers.* Microfilm. 37 reels. New York: New York Public Library, 1983.

———. *Windows on Henry Street.* Boston: Little, Brown, 1934.

Walker, Madame C. J. (McWilliams) (née Sarah Breedlove) (1867–1919)
Inventor, entrepreneur, and business leader
African American

Madame C. J. Walker, along with Annie Minerva Turnbo-Malone, has the distinction of being a member of a small group of American women in the early twentieth century who developed enterprises with sales in the millions. She is considered among the first African American millionaires. In 1998, a Madam C. J. Walker commemorative stamp was issued by the U.S. Postal Service.

Walker was born Sarah Breedlove on 23 December 1867, on a cotton plantation in Delta, Louisiana. Her parents, Owen and Minerva Breedlove, were former slaves and then impoverished sharecroppers. Walker had no formal education, and her parents died when she was only eight. When she was fourteen, she married Moses McWilliams (the father of her daughter Lelia), but he died. In 1887 she moved to St. Louis, where she was a laundress for eighteen years, saving enough to send her daughter to college.

To supplement her income, Walker worked briefly as an agent selling black hair-care products for Annie Turnbo-Malone. Most urban black women then were laundresses, who came in constant contact with chemicals that were damaging their hair. Because of stress, poor diet, and the hair-care methods used at that time, many black women were suffering from premature baldness. Walker decided to develop her own line of hair products for black women. What was unique about her products was that she combined them with the use of a hair-straightening comb, unlike Turnbo-Malone's plain curlers and "hair pullers" that stretched and straightened the hair. The comb revolutionized the care and styling of black women's hair.

In 1906, having moved to Denver, she married newspaper salesmen Charles Joseph Walker and assumed the name Madame C. J. Walker. Walker and her husband soon began to travel to promote the hair-care products as well as to train sales agents in what became known as the Walker system. The system included other items that Walker also marketed through mail orders. In 1908, she opened a training school in Pittsburgh and, in 1910, built the Mme. C. J. Walker Manufacturing Company in Indianapolis. In 1916, she founded the National Beauty Culturists and Benevolent Association of Mme. C. J. Walker Agents, soon changed to the Madam C. J. Walker Hair Culturists Union of America. Her Walker method opened up a new field of employment, and by 1919 more than 20,000 women worked as sales agents. Her accomplishments demonstrated the extent to which a market existed for black hair products and facial creams.

Walker's success as one of leading African American entrepreneurs gave her prestige and standing in the African American community and nationwide. She was active in the National Negro Business League and spoke out against racism, discrimination, and lynching. She was also known for her generous philanthropy to black colleges and organizations. Walker died at the age of fifty-one, having achieved millionaire status in the thirteen years from the time she first developed her business. In 1976, Walker's New York home, Villa Lewaro, was listed on the National Register of Historic Places. The Madam Walker Building, completed in 1927, is a national historic landmark.

Juliet E. K. Walker

REFERENCES

Bundles, A'Lelia Perry. *Madame C. J. Walker—Entrepreneur.* New York: Chelsea House, 1991.

———. *On Her Own Ground: The Life and Times of Madam C. J. Walker.* New York: Scribner, 2001.

———. "Walker, Madam C. J. (Sarah Breedlove)." In *Encyclopedia of African American Culture and History,* edited by Jack Salzman, David L. Smith, and Cornel West, 5: 2765–2766. New York: Macmillan Library Reference, 1996.

Omoiele, M. Tambura. "Sarah Breedlove [Madam C. J.] Walker." In *Encyclopedia of African American Business History,* edited by Juliet E. K Walker, 581–585. Westport, CT: Greenwood Press, 1999.

Walker, Juliet E. K. *The History of Black Business in America: Capitalism, Race, Entrepreneurship.* New York and London: Macmillan/Prentice Hall International, 1998.

"Walker, Madame C. J. (Sarah Breedlove)." In *Black Women in America,* edited by Darlene Clark Hine et al., 1209–1214. New York: Carlson Publishing, 1993.

Wallace, Lila Bell Acheson (1887–1984)

Social services administrator, entrepreneur, and philanthropist
Canadian

Lila Acheson Wallace was a successful social services administrator when she and her husband launched *Reader's Digest.* That turned out to be one of the most successful publishing ventures in the twentieth century.

Acheson was born in Virden, Manitoba, on Christmas Day 1887. Her father, Thomas David Acheson, an Irish-Canadian Presbyterian minister, would later move constantly across the northern tier of the United States, finally settling in Tacoma, Washington, where he became vice president of Whitworth College. Lila Acheson graduated from Lewiston High School, Lewiston, Illinois, in 1907, attended Ward-Belmont College in Nashville,

Tennessee, and graduated with a degree in social work from the University of Oregon in 1917. Following graduation, she began as a rural schoolteacher on an island in Puget Sound, successfully organizing a summer YWCA camp there.

Acheson had joined the national YWCA when the United States entered World War I. She administered a large social service program for women at a munitions plant in Pompton Lakes, New Jersey, and subsequently a social work program in New Orleans. In 1920 she joined the Presbyterian Board of Home Missions as national secretary of its social service department. She was sent to Minneapolis–St. Paul to open an industrial YWCA branch for working women and met her brother's friend DeWitt Wallace.

The couple soon became engaged and began working on his plan for a magazine that would offer condensed versions of articles in leading journals of the day. They moved to New York in 1921 and wed. Early in 1922 they formed the Reader's Digest Association, Inc., with DeWitt holding 52 percent of the stock and Lila 48 percent. The new publication was an instant success and it moved from New York City to Pleasantville, New York. Lila Wallace soon left editorial control to her husband, though she retained a voice in major managerial decisions. As the magazine's circulation grew, the Wallaces, who had no children, decided to devote themselves to their employees. *Reader's Digest* became one of the great paternalistic success stories of modern corporate America.

In 1936, Lila began construction of a large mansion called High Winds on 110 hilly acres in Mount Kisco; her husband always called it Lila's place. When the magazine ran out of office space in the mid-1930s, it was Lila Wallace who decided not to return to New York City. *Reader's Digest* expanded internationally after World War II. It began a condensed fiction branch in 1949, later expanding into recordings. The Reader's Digest Sweepstakes also proved a brilliant marketing ploy, and in 1955 the Wallaces further startled the publishing world by announcing they would accept advertising. However, by the later 1950s they had lost most of their control over executive decisions. Meanwhile, in 1954 Lila Wallace had become a director of the New York Central Railroad, the first woman to serve as a railway director in the United States.

In 1970, Wallace announced that she and her husband had composed a new one-sentence will: "Being of sound mind and body, we are giving it all away." Their philanthropy was often spontaneous. However, by 1979 both she and her husband were no longer capable of making major decisions, and they lived out their lives in isolation while their empire was being fought over. Lila Wallace's involvement in most of the later philanthropy carried out in her name is questionable. She died May 8, 1984, in Mt. Kisco, New York.

J. M. Bumsted

REFERENCES

Canning, Peter. *American Dreamers: The Wallaces and* Reader's Digest: *An Insider's Story*. New York: Simon and Schuster, 1996.

Heidenry, John, and Charles Murphy. *Theirs Was the Kingdom: Lila and DeWitt Wallace and the Story of the* Reader's Digest. New York: W. W. Norton, 1993.

Sutherland, Fraser. *The Monthly Epic: A History of Canadian Magazines, 1789–1989*. Toronto: Fitzhenry & Whiteside, 1989.

Walz, Maggie (née Margareeta Johanna Kontraa Niranen) (1861–1927)

Feminist, entrepreneur, and temperance crusader
Finnish

An independent spirit, Margareeta Johanna Kontraa Niranen immigrated to the United States alone at age twenty and shortly thereafter changed her name to the more American-sounding Maggie Walz. For the remainder of her life in the United States, she was involved in a variety of business enterprises in which she worked with immigrants seeking to find a niche in their new environment. She spent some time as a labor broker. She was also

a journalist and an activist in the temperance movement, and her participation in the suffrage movement made her one of the pioneer feminists in the ethnic community.

Walz's parents were religious followers of the sectarian revivalist Lars Laestadius. The imprint of their beliefs would shape her throughout her life as an immigrant. Like others in her generation, she caught the American "fever" and departed for the United States alone. Many single Finnish women first found employment as a domestic, and she was no exception. She was intent on making it in the United States and, to that end, worked hard to learn English and in other ways fit into her new homeland. Within a short time, she was running an employment agency that found work for newly arrived women in circumstances similar to her own. The business thrived, providing her with the resources to study business for a year at Valparaiso College. Afterward, she not only resumed her earlier work but also expanded her business, running a money exchange and selling steamship tickets, among other ventures.

At the same time, Walz became involved in what was one of the major institutions of the Finnish-immigrant community: temperance societies. She was one of the founders and leaders of the Northern Star Temperance Society. In 1894 she helped to found the Finnish Women's Society in Calumet, Michigan, an organization devoted to improving the status of women. She used money from her business ventures to help support both of these activities.

In 1903 she combined her business skills with her reformist views when she became the U.S. government land agent for Drummond Island, in Lake Huron, where she attempted to create a utopian society founded on Christianity and temperance ideals. The effort was a failure, and many people who lost money in the attempt thought Walz had swindled them.

In the final decade of her life, she began to link her reform activities within the immigrant community to parallel organizations run by native-born Americans. Thus, she worked with the Women's Christian Temperance Union, serving as an American delegate to an international conference in Scotland. Likewise, she served as a delegate from Michigan to the Women's Suffrage Convention. She continued in these activities and in her business ventures until her death in 1927. Among Finnish Americans, she is remembered as a colorful and somewhat controversial figure.

Peter Kivisto

REFERENCES

Niemi, Clemens. *The Americanization of the Finnish People of Houghton County.* Duluth, MN: Paivalehti Publishing, 1921.

Walz, Maggie. File. Finnish American Historical Archives at Suomi College, Hancock, MI.

Wargelin Brown, Marianne. "Maggie Walz: Entrepreneur and Temperance Crusader." In *Women Who Dared: The History of Finnish American Women,* edited by Carl Ross and K. Marianne Wargelin Brown, 151–157. St. Paul, MN: Immigration History Research Center, 1986.

Ward, Nancy (Nan-ye'hi) (1738–1822)

Warrior, political leader, and peacemaker
Native American (Cherokee)

Because of her distinguished lineage and bravery in battle when she took up her slain husband's weapons and led the Cherokee to victory over their Creek rivals in the Battle of Taliwa (1755), Nancy Ward was honored with the Cherokee Nation's highest position for a woman. She became the *Ghigau,* or Beloved Woman, of the Cherokee. This made her head of the Women's Council, which had veto power over wars, war parties, and the fate of prisoners. As the Beloved Woman, she was an influential spokesperson in the chief's councils.

Ward's powerful role in Cherokee politics derived from the matrilineal clan system of the Cherokee: Women held the property. Thus, as part of her share of the war prizes after Taliwa, Ward was given an African slave. As a war priestess, one of her primary responsibilities involved maintaining diplomatic relations with other tribes and with Euro-Americans. Many traders gained access and

influence by marrying Cherokee women. An Irishman, Bryan Ward, married Nan-ye'hi shortly before the American Revolution.

Prior to the Revolution, American colonists aggressively defied British policy and began illegally occupying Cherokee lands. The "war" chief Dragging Canoe declared that there would be no more land cessions. But he had exceeded his authority to make such a declaration, and his unilateral decision to attack nearby settlements brought about the retaliatory destruction of many Cherokee towns. As Beloved Woman and a "war" chief (or priestess), Nancy Ward had the authority to start or stop a war. She was opposed to war and Dragging Canoe's actions but was unable to stop them. Because of her regard for many Euro-American neighbors, she decided to warn the settlers, saving many American lives but causing heavy Cherokee losses.

The American Revolution was a disaster for the Cherokee. The results were a severe factional political breach in Cherokee governance, the end of the Women's Council as a political institution, and the transformation to a more centralized, male-dominated political structure along Euro-American lines, leaving no room for Cherokee women's formal political power. Within this context Ward became a "cultural broker," shrewdly realizing that the Cherokee needed to acculturate to retain their lands and gain respect for their tribal sovereignty. Although no longer having a formal position, she participated in the negotiations over the Treaty of Hopewell in 1785, the first official treaty between the Cherokee and the new United States.

But in the aftermath of the War of 1812, despite the fact that the Cherokee had become one of the "civilized" tribes and had helped General Andrew Jackson win victories over the Creeks and the British, the United States once again pressed the Cherokee for more land. An old woman, Ward was unable to attend a tribal council in 1817. But she sent them a most remarkable document. She reiterated her strong stand against land cessions and additional treaties and forcefully spoke out against any removal from their sacred homeland. As the final Beloved Woman, Ward, who died in 1822, was the last major Cherokee female political leader until Wilma Mankiller became the first elected woman tribal chief in 1987.

John M. Shaw

References

Holm, Tom. "Politics Came First: A Reflection on Robert K. Thomas and Cherokee History." In *A Good Cherokee, A Good Anthropologist: Papers in Honor of Robert K. Thomas,* edited by Steve Pavlik, 41–56. Los Angeles: UCLA American Indian Studies Center, 1998.

Mankiller, Wilma, and Michael Wallis. *Mankiller: A Chief and Her People.* St. Martin's Press, 1993.

Perdue, Theda. *Cherokee Women.* Lincoln: University of Nebraska Press, 1998.

Tucker, Norma. "Nancy Ward, Ghighau of the Cherokees." *Georgia Historical Quarterly* 53.2 (June 1969): 192–200.

Woodward, Grace Steele. *The Cherokees.* Norman: University of Oklahoma Press, 1963.

Wargelin, John (1881–1967)
Religious leader
Finnish

John Wargelin served as a pastor at many parishes in the Suomi Synod—the common American name for the Finnish Evangelical Lutheran Church—as president of the synod's Suomi College, and as president of the synod during the era when the second and third generations came of age. He was instrumental in facilitating the transition from an essentially immigrant institution to an ethnic one and he worked to promote Americanization while simultaneously preserving core elements of the immigrant heritage.

Born to Pietistic Lutherans in Finland, Wargelin, along with his mother and siblings, immigrated to the United States in 1890 to join his father, who had found employment in the iron-mining industry in Michigan's Upper Peninsula three years earlier. Wargelin entered the first class at Suomi College and upon graduation entered the school's seminary. The seminary was the educational institution of the newly formed Finnish Evangel-

ical Lutheran Church in America. Wargelin was, thus, a part of the first generation of American-trained church leaders.

Upon ordination, he entered into parish ministry, beginning with a church in Sault Ste. Marie, Michigan. He served several parishes in Michigan, Minnesota, and Illinois, as well as in Ontario, Canada, operating in every locale in an ethnic community split between Socialists, or "red Finns," and more conservative "church Finns." Moreover, he sought to find a place for a church body with ties to the state church in Finland in an environment with numerous other religious institutions, including the more conservative Finnish National Lutheran Church and the sectarian Laestadians.

Wargelin was called to assume the presidency of the Suomi college after the sudden death of J. K. Nikander during the influenza epidemic of 1919. During this period, he did graduate work at the University of Michigan under the direction of Charles Horton Cooley. Out of his encounter with sociology, he produced *The Americanization of the Finns,* which argued that assimilation was an inevitable process in the U.S. context. Seeing himself as a "progressive conservative," Wargelin urged the synod to prepare for the Americanization of the younger generations. This position generated considerable controversy—as did his harsh stance toward the political Left—alienating him from segments in the Finnish-American community. Ultimately, he resigned his position in 1927 to return to the parish.

He was called back in 1930 to lead the college a second time and remained in that position until 1937. Then Wargelin once again returned to parish ministry, where he stayed until 1950, when he was chosen as president of the synod. He served in this capacity for five years, during which merger plans with other Lutheran religious bodies entered the final stages of negotiations. Wargelin, though sensitive to the Finnish heritage, was an important spokesperson for the merger. He retired shortly thereafter—with his son, Raymond, subsequently becoming head of the synod—but he did live to see the Suomi Synod merge with other Scandinavian Lutheran bodies to form the Lutheran Church in America in 1963.

Peter Kivisto

REFERENCES

Jalkanen, Ralph. "Suomi College." In *Old Friends— Strong Ties,* edited by Vilho Niitemaa, 175–179. Turku, Finland: Institute for Migration, 1976.

Ollila, Douglas. "The Formative Period of the Finnish Evangelical Lutheran Church in America or Suomi Synod." Th.D. diss., Boston University, 1963.

Wargelin, John. *The Americanization of the Finns.* Hancock, MI: Finnish Lutheran Book Concern, 1924.

———. *A Highway to America.* Hancock, MI: Book Concern, 1967.

Warhol, Andy (né Andrew Warhola) (1928–1987)

Painter, filmmaker, and publisher
Carpatho-Rusyn-American

Andy Warhol is universally recognized as one of the leading figures in pop art. Because of his lifestyle, witty aphorisms, interest in celebrities, and self-promotion, he became and remains a symbol of American culture in the rapidly changing 1960s and 1970s.

Warhol was born Andrew Warhola, in Pittsburgh, Pennsylvania. Both his parents immigrated to the United States from a small mountain village called Miková, in the eastern part of present-day Slovakia. The village was inhabited by Carpatho-Rusyns, or Ruthenians, a small Slavic people who had never had their own state and were little known to the outside world—and, thus, were already marginalized in their own homeland. In the United States, too, Andy's immigrant parents' religion, which was passed on to Warhol and his two older brothers, was outside the mainstream, for they were Catholics but of the Greek, or Byzantine Ruthenian, rite. Warhol was a devout Christian his entire life, and his funeral was celebrated in the same Byzantine Ruthenian Catholic church, located in the so-called Rusyn valley *(Ruska dolyna)* of Pittsburgh, where he had been baptized.

After studying commercial art and fashion illustration at the Carnegie Institute of Technology in Pittsburgh, Warhol moved in 1949 to New York City to begin a career as a designer for department store window displays. His fascination with the commercial world and with common objects that surround all of us prompted him to choose those subjects for his paintings. Such works as "Green Coca Cola Bottles" (1962), "One Hundred Campbell Soup Cans" (1962), and "Brillo Boxes" (1964) quickly became among the most famous examples of pop art. During this period, he made a series of portraits of famous people (including Marilyn Monroe, Elvis Presley, and Jackie Kennedy), using a silk-screen technique that allowed for multiple images reproduced as if on a strip of film. Warhol caught these personalities at their most beautiful and idealized moment. As with the timeless icons in the Eastern Christian churches, Warhol created in his silk-screen portraits new icons for the twentieth century. In the mid-1960s he turned to cinema. All his films, including *Eat* (1963), *Sleep* (1963), *My Hustler* (1965), *Trash* (1971), and *Sex* (1971), were experimental in nature.

Warhol never played any role in Rusyn-American community life, and he said, "I never like to give my background and, anyway, I make it all up different every time I'm asked." Since his death, however, Warhol's fame has been used by Rusyn activists in the United States and Europe to help raise awareness about Carpatho-Rusyns as a distinct people. An annual Carpatho-Rusyn Day is held at the Warhol Museum in Pittsburgh, and the Warhol Foundation in New York City helped to fund the Warhol Family Museum of Modern Art, established in 1991 near his parent's birthplace in Slovakia. Local Rusyns have set up Andy Warhol clubs in Slovakia and Hungary, and recent literary works written in the Rusyn language have been inspired by the persona of the American artist. The relationship of the Warhol legacy to the post-1989 Rusyn national revival has been recorded in a documentary film by the Danish anthropologist Tom Trier and entitled *The Warhol Nation* (1997).

Paul Robert Magocsi

REFERENCES
Bokris, Viktor. *Warhol*. London: Frederick Muller/Century Hutchinson, 1989.
Bourdon, David. *Warhol*. New York: Harry N. Abrams, 1989.
Colacello, Bob. *Holy Terror: Andy Warhol Close Up*. New York: HarperCollins, 1990.
Herbenick, Raymond. *Andy Warhol's Religious and Ethnic Roots: The Carpatho-Rusyn Influence on His Art*. Lewiston, NY: Edward Mellon, 1997.

Washington, Booker T. (Taliaferro) (1856–1915)

Educator, black business promoter, and community leader
African American

Booker Taliaferro Washington, founder of the Tuskegee Institute, was the foremost black American during the period from 1895 to 1915 (called the era of Booker T. Washington) and one of the most prominent figures in U.S. history. He had a major but controversial influence on southern race relations and the lives of African Americans.

Washington was born a slave on 5 April 1856 in Hales Ford, Virginia; his father was white. After the Civil War, his family moved to Malden, West Virginia, where he worked in coal mines and salt furnaces. In 1872 he left to attend Hampton Institute, a black industrial school in Hampton, Virginia. He then attended a seminary but soon left to become a teacher at Hampton. In 1881 Washington founded Tuskegee Normal and Industrial Institute (later renamed Tuskegee Institute, now Tuskegee University). He was the first principal and later president. Although Tuskegee trained teachers, the curriculum emphasized trades for men and domestic arts for women.

The first two of Washington's three wives were Hampton graduates; they died, leaving him with three children. He then wed Margaret Murray Washington (1861–1925), a Fisk University graduate who was the principal for women at Tuskegee and a leader in the black women's club movement.

Washington spent a great deal of time fundraising, but it was not until his 1895 "Atlanta Compromise" speech that he achieved national recognition and that Tuskegee Institute became the recipient of extensive white philanthropy. The address shocked black Americans, for he urged them to give up temporarily the quest for political equality and to earn whites' respect by their economic achievements. He also appealed to southern whites to continue using black labor rather than hiring the new wave of immigrants. At the time Washington made his speech, around 90 percent of American blacks lived in the South, with 85 percent working in agriculture and many in debt peonage. Violence against blacks had intensified, and under new southern state constitutions, blacks were losing most of the rights they had gained during Reconstruction.

With the speech urging black subordination, Washington was anointed the leader of black America by white America. Ironically, however, he did have the support of many blacks and was widely admired. In 1900, he founded the National Negro Business League, with branches in most states and several African countries. In 1901, invited by President Theodore Roosevelt, Washington became the first black to dine at the White House. Both Roosevelt and President Taft consulted with him on race relations and black political appointments, giving him substantial control over patronage and philanthropic funding for black America.

Nonetheless, the crafts taught at Tuskegee were outdated, black liberal arts colleges were seriously underfunded, and Washington's accommodationist philosophy was based on an anticipated white reciprocity—which did not happen. Although Washington was secretly funding legal cases that challenged Jim Crowism, his influence among blacks began to decline (especially with the rise of the NAACP). He began to publicly question the practicality of his strategy and, by 1912, had become more outspoken against racial injustice. He died 14 November 1915.

Juliet E. K. Walker

REFERENCES
Harlan, Louis R. *Booker T. Washington: The Making of a Black Leader, 1856–1901*. Urbana: University of Illinois Press, 1972.

————. *Booker T. Washington: The Wizard of Tuskegee, 1901–1915.* Urbana: University of Illinois Press, 1983.

Hawkins, Hugh. *Booker T. Washington and His Critics: The Problem of Negro Leadership.* 2d ed. Lexington, MA: D. C. Heath, 1974.

Marable, W. Manning. "Booker T. Washington and African Nationalism." *Phylon* 35 (1974): 398–406.

Meier, August. *Negro Thought in America: Racial Ideologies in the Age of Accommodation, 1880– 1915.* Ann Arbor: University of Michigan Press, 1963.

Thornbrough, Emma L. "Booker T. Washington as Seen by His White Contemporaries." *Journal of Negro History* 53 (1968): 161–182.

Washington, Booker Taliaferro. "Atlanta Exposition Address, September 18, 1895." In *The Booker T. Washington Papers,* edited by Louis R. Harlan et al., vol. 3: 584–587. Urbana: University of Illinois Press, 1974.

Watumull, Ellen Jensen (1897–1964) and Watumull, Gobindram Jhamandas "G. J." (1891–1959)

Community activist and philanthropist; entrepreneur, community activist, and philanthropist, respectively
Danish-American and Asian Indian, respectively

Gobindram Jhamandas Watumull, a native of India and prominent businessman, and his wife, Ellen Jensen Watumull, provided community leadership and financial support for Asian Indians to study in universities. They also promoted better understanding between India and the United States and fought discrimination against Asian Americans in the United States.

Gobindram Watumull, known as G. J., was born in Hyderabad, Sind, India (now Pakistan) on 26 June 1891. A wealthy landlord paid for part of his early schooling, but it was his mother who pawned her last jewels to send Watumull to Karachi University, where he earned a degree in engineering. After working as an engineer in India for several years, he immigrated to Honolulu, Hawai`i, in 1917 to manage his older brother's business. The brother having subsequently left to handle other businesses, Watumull developed the shop into a small bazaar and, eventually, into a major department store that was, among other things, the first to sell all-silk Hawaiian aloha shirts on the islands. The newly constructed Watumull building became headquarters for Watumull Brothers enterprises, which, by 1947, were grossing $2.6 million annually and continuing to grow.

When Watumull applied for citizenship, his application was rejected as a result of the 1923 U.S. Supreme Court ruling in *United States v. Bhagat Singh Thind* that Asian Indians were not "free white persons" and therefore were ineligible for U.S. citizenship. Moreover, his wife, although native-born, lost her citizenship, too, because the Cable Act of 1922 had provided for the revocation of the citizenship of American-born women who had married foreign-born men ineligible for citizenship. Thus, several dozen people in the Asian Indian community lost their U.S. citizenship. Ellen Watumull worked with the League of Women Voters and many others to get the 1922 legislation amended so that American-born women would retain their U.S. citizenship regardless of their husbands' nationality. The amendment was enacted 3 March 1931, and Ellen Watumull was the first woman to regain her citizenship under the revised law. Her husband participated in the continuing struggle to make Asian Indians eligible for citizenship, and victory was realized with the enactment of the Luce-Celler Act of 2 July 1946. Watumull acquired his citizenship almost immediately.

Meanwhile, Watumull maintained his love for India and worked to help his land of birth become free. Starting in 1942, he was active in the Committee for India's Freedom. He financed the movement, traveled to Washington many times, and supported such publicists as Syed Hussain, Anup Singh, and Krishnalal Shridharani, who were working to popularize India's case for independence. In addition, in 1942, he set up the Watumull Foundation. Its threefold mission was to increase India's national efficiency, promote better understanding between India and the United States, and support educational, philanthropic, and cultural work in Hawai`i.

To fulfill the first goal, the foundation placed books in libraries in India, gave technical equipment to hospitals, installed wells, and promoted birth control, among other things. In fact, Ellen Watumull worked with Margaret Sanger and helped hold the first International Planned Parenthood Conference ever in Bombay, India, in 1952. The foundation also supported such organizations the Cooperative for American Relief to Everywhere (CARE) to provide famine relief. To promote better understanding between India and the United States, the foundation sponsored exchange professorships between universities and enabled professors in India to visit and study at U.S. colleges and universities. It gave funds for U.S. libraries to buy books on India and offered biennial awards through the American Historical Association to authors of the best books written on India. In order to achieve the third objective, the foundation supported the University of Hawaii, especially the East-West Center. It also supported such local organizations as the Boy Scouts, YMCA and YWCA, and various private schools and projects. To educated and professional persons and to Asian Indians, "Watumull" was a household word. When he died in 1959, the *Honolulu Star Bulletin* quoted the *Reader's Digest,* saying, "G. J. shows that East and West can meet."

In his various activities Watumull had the full support of his wife, Ellen Jensen Watumull, a second-generation Danish American from Portland, Oregon. Born on 26 June 1897, she attended Reed College, moved to Hawai`i in 1922, and married Watumull in 1923. After her husband's death, Ellen Watumull continued her own involvement in the Asian Indian community and civic affairs in general. Until her own death in 1964, she was intensely active in a wide variety of organizations, along with the Watumull Foundation. In addition to being closely associated with the International Planned Parenthood Federation and serving on its governing body, she was a member of the Western Hemisphere Regional Council, the U.S. board of the Vellore Christian Medical College and Hospital, and vice-chair of the Honolulu Chapter of World Brotherhood. Watumull was also the first woman member of the board of governors of the Pacific and Asian Affairs Council and received its citation for "Outstanding Contribution to U.S.-Asian Relations by a citizen of Hawaii"—along with many other awards.

Today, under the next generation of Watumulls, the business is still strong and the foundation continues to support the education of Asian Indians, Asian Indian causes, and travel, research, conferences, and scholarships, as well as a wide variety of other issues.

Arthur W. Helweg

REFERENCES
Clark, Blake. "G. J. Shows That East and West Can Meet," *St. Louis Press Dispatch,* 19 October 1947, condensed in *Reader's Digest* 51 (December 1947): 73–77.
Kamath, M.V. *The United States and India, 1776–1976.* Washington, DC: Embassy of India, 1976.
"Watumull, G. J. (Gobrindram Jhamandas)." In *The Asian American Encyclopedia,* edited by Franklin Ng, vol. 6, 1652–1655. New York: Marshall Cavendish, 1995.
"Watumull, Ellen Jensen." In *Who's Who of American Women 1964–65,* 3d ed, 2: 1069. Chicago: Marquis Who's Who, 1963.

Weiser, Conrad (1696–1760)
Farmer, businessman, and colonial ambassador to the Iroquois
German

Conrad Weiser lived a full life on the frontier of New York and in eastern Pennsylvania. His contributions to his fellow colonists and to the Native Americans whom he encountered had a major impact on eastern Pennsylvania and the preservation of peace. His skills as a diplomat, interpreter, linguist, judge, lay minister, and farmer (just to name a few) qualify him for the appellation Renaissance Man.

John Conrad Weiser welcomed the birth of his son Conrad on 2 November 1696. The elder Weiser was eager to leave Württemberg and immigrate to the British colonies, but it was not until 1709 that the family traveled to the rural Hudson valley in New York. Sixteen-year-old Conrad chose to live with a group of nearby Mohawks in 1713, becoming fluent in their language. In addition, he strove to learn everything about the Six Nations of the Iroquois Confederacy and thus became one of the few whites to understand the heritage and languages of the group.

By the early 1720s, members of the German community known as Palatines immigrated to southeastern Pennsylvania, Tulpehocken valley, today Berks and Lebanon Counties. Weiser married Anna Eve in 1729 and purchased approximately 200 acres in Womelsdorf. (Today the Conrad Weiser Homestead is a national historic landmark.) The next several decades saw Weiser prosper as a farmer, businessman, and family patriarch. He and his wife were blessed with fourteen children (seven would survive until adulthood). At the time of his death in 1760, Weiser would own thousands of acres, a farm, and two businesses.

Weiser, however, was not satisfied with his bucolic existence. His name began to circulate in Philadelphia because of his knowledge of Indian life and culture. Specifically, government leaders hoped to negotiate a treaty with the Iroquois. Weiser was hired as a representative to the local Iroquois and instructed to develop a policy guaranteeing English hegemony over the Lenni Lenape tribes, thereby ensuring peace and safety along the Pennsylvania frontier. Weiser would spend twenty years negotiating, renegotiating, traveling, and buying the surrounding land from the Iroquois, thus helping to avert bloodshed.

Tensions between England and France during the 1750s and 1760s jeopardized Weiser's work. He supported the British colonies by joining the First Pennsylvania Regiment as a lieutenant colonel. Afterward, he helped found Berks County and the town of Reading and worked as a judge. However, after eight years of spiritual searching and living monastically at the Ephrata Cloister of Conrad Beissel, a radical separatist Protestant, Weiser became disillusioned, returned to his family, rejoined the Lutheran church, and founded a parish near his home. The marriage of his daughter Anna Maria to Henry Melchior Muhlenberg, the father of organized Lutheranism in the colonies, further cemented his ties with the church.

Weiser's greatest accomplishment was establishing and maintaining cordial relations with the Iroquois Confederacy. He achieved his goal while treating the Native Americans with respect and speaking to them in their own languages. His enlightened attitudes and abilities as a peacemaker and diplomat earned him great renown, especially in that region of Pennsylvania.

Susanne M. Shick

REFERENCES

Doblin, Helga, and William A. Starna, eds. *The Journals of Christian Daniel Claus and Conrad Weiser: A Journey to Onondaga, 1750.* Philadelphia: American Philosophical Society, 1993.

Frantz, John. "Franklin and the Pennsylvania Germans." *Pennsylvania History* 65 (1998): 21–34.

Hagedorn, Nancy. "Brokers of Understanding: Interpreters as Agents of Cultural Exchange in Colonial New York." *New York History* 76 (1995): 379–408.

Pendleton, Philip. "Finding a Light in the Forest: Conrad Weiser Homestead." *Pennsylvania Heritage* 22 (1996): 12–19.

Walton, Joseph. *Conrad Weiser and the Indian Policy of Colonial Pennsylvania.* Philadelphia: Ayer Company Pub., 1900.

Wells–Barnett, Ida B. (Bell) (1862–1931)

Journalist, lecturer, and community activist
African American

Ida Bell Wells-Barnett, born a slave, became editor of her own newspaper and was active in numerous women's and civil rights organizations. A courageous crusader against lynching, segregation, and economic injustice, she maintained her commitment and determination in the face of great personal danger, although her unwillingness to compromise also led to struggles with colleagues.

Wells was born to enslaved parents in Mississippi in July 1862. Her father, an educator and politician during Reconstruction, died along with his wife and youngest child in the 1878 yellow fever epidemic. To support the remaining family members, Wells obtained a teaching job. She and two sisters then moved to Memphis, Tennessee, where she taught school and studied at Fisk University.

Her engagement with civil rights issues began when she was physically thrown off a train in 1884 for refusing to move to the black car. She sued the railroad and won, but the state supreme court reversed the decision. Wells began to write political essays about her experiences and racial conditions across the South and was elected secretary of the Colored Press Association in 1889. In 1889, she purchased a one-third stake in the *Memphis Free Speech and Headlight* and soon became its editor. She wrote powerful editorials denouncing segregation and unequal treatment of African Americans. For exposing the poor quality of segregated schools, she lost her teaching post. But it was the 1892 lynching of three African American grocery store managers and the escalation of racial violence that prompted her most furious outbursts. Her editorials both denouncing the canard that black men's sexual attacks on white women justified lynching and suggesting that white women felt attracted to black men so infuriated whites that a mob destroyed the press and threatened her life.

Wells moved to New York and began writing a series on lynching for the *New York Age.* She confirmed earlier observations that accusations of rape were a pretext for lynching and urged African Americans to arm themselves in self-defense. An international lecture tour followed, and she helped establish antilynching groups wherever she went. Settling in Chicago, she organized black women's clubs that engaged in civil rights activity and in improving services for black women and children. Although she married Ferdinand Barnett, a lawyer and editor, in 1895 and had four children, she did not cease her political activities. In 1896 the clubs merged with others to form the National Association of Colored Women

(NACW). She established the Negro Fellowship League to aid black migrants to Chicago and remained active in antilynching, women's suffrage, and Republican Party politics. Never a conciliator, she found herself in frequent conflict with Booker T. Washington, which led her to join in forming the NAACP in 1909. She also embraced both Marcus Garvey's nationalism and T. Thomas Fortune's immediatist programs for racial and economic justice.

Although her insistence on unremitting agitation kept her from leadership positions in many of the organizations she had helped found, Wells-Barnett remained active until the end of her life. She died in March 1931, leaving a legacy of activism and a powerful body of writings.

Cheryl Greenberg

REFERENCES

Dunster, Alfreda, ed. *Crusade for Justice: The Autobiography of Ida B. Wells.* Chicago: University of Chicago Press, 1970.

Holt, Thomas. "The Lonely Warrior: Ida B. Wells-Barnett and the Struggle for Black Leadership." In *Black Leaders of the Twentieth Century,* edited by John Hope Franklin and August Meier, 39–61. Urbana: University of Illinois Press, 1982.

McMurry, Linda. *To Keep the Waters Troubled: The Life of Ida B. Wells.* New York: Oxford University Press, 1998.

Royster, Jacqueline. *Southern Horrors and Other Writings: The Anti-Lynching Campaigns of Ida B. Wells.* Boston: Bedford Books, 1997.

Thompson, Mildred. *Ida B. Wells-Barnett: An Exploratory Study of An American Black Woman, 1893–1930.* Brooklyn, NY: Carlson Publishing, 1990.

Townes, Emilie. *Womanist Justice, Womanist Hope.* Atlanta, GA: Scholars Press, 1993.

Wells-Barnett, Ida B. *Selected Works of Ida B. Wells-Barnett.* New York: Oxford University Press, 1991.

Wergeland, Agnes Mahilde (1857–1914)
Historian, essayist, and poet
Norwegian

Agnes Wergeland had to overcome many of the obstacles that women intellectuals have encountered in their quest for self-expression.

In her final years she and her writings began to receive the recognition they deserved.

Unable to support his wife and six children in Oslo, Sverre Nicolai Wergeland, Agnes's father, tried his luck in the United States in the mid-1800s but came back empty-handed. In the meantime, his wife took a housekeeper's position at a sanitarium to support their five children, and lodgings were provided for her and her children but not for her husband. Only Agnes and her brother, Oscar, who was thirteen years older, survived childhood; they were brought up by their mother. Their father returned to the United States, and contact was never reestablished between him and his family. While their mother devoted her meager savings to Oscar's and then Agnes's education, she discouraged her daughter's extraordinary talents for art and poetry, providing only irregular hours of general education with private teachers. Finally, contributions from friends paid Wergeland's tuition at a school for governesses, where poor girls studied for a vocation suited to conventional expectations at the time for women who had to work.

Wergeland continued to draw and write poems, however, and convinced her mother to pay for piano lessons, which she had for nearly eighteen months with none other than Edvard Grieg. She also cultivated relations with the illustrious branch of the Wergeland family, which included two of the country's most admired authors, Henrik Wergeland and his sister Camilla Collette. Nonetheless, when she finished her schooling in 1878, Norwegian universities remained closed to women, and during the next four years she found only a few hours' income as a private teacher. Her mother and friends rescued her from poverty by paying for graduate studies in Munich and Zurich, where in 1890 she became the first Norwegian woman to earn a doctorate. She then successfully applied for postdoctoral study at Bryn Mawr, one of the most admired colleges for women in the United States. After a second year there, as an instructor, she moved to Chicago, where she sought academic positions in vain while working part-

time at the University of Chicago and improving her academic credentials by publishing articles on legal history in such journals as the *Dial* and the *Journal of Political Economy.*

Finally, in 1902 the University of Wyoming at Laramie offered her a professorship in history and French, which she held until her death in 1914. She became chair of the History Department and published in English, German, French, and Norwegian on a variety of subjects, including the legal origins of slavery in Europe, the causes of emigration from Norway, and Norwegian-American literature. In her final years, she found an intellectual home among members of the Norwegian-American intelligentsia. She became a regular correspondent with them, reviewing their work and publishing her collected poems in Norwegian, *Amerika og andre digte* (America and other poems, 1912), in her ethnic group's premier newspaper, *Decorah-Posten.* At her death in 1914 Wergeland was both an admired Norwegian-American scholar-poet and a model for the ethnic group of what a gifted woman could accomplish in the United States.

David C. Mauk

REFERENCES

Løken, Lisa B. "Dr. Agnes Mathilde Wergeland—Historian, Poet, and American University Professor." Master's thesis, University of Oslo, 1995.

Michelet, Maren. *Glimpses from Agnes Mathilde Wergeland's Life.* Minneapolis, MN: Folkebladet Publishing Co., 1916.

Øverland, Ørm. *The Western Home: A Literary History of Norwegian America.* Northfield, MN: Norwegian-American Historical Association, 1996.

Semmingsen, Ingrid. "A Pioneer: Agnes Mathilde Wergeland, 1857–1914." In *Makers of an Immigrant Legacy: Essays in Honor of Kenneth O. Bjork,* edited by Odd Lovoll. Northfield, MN: Norwegian-American Historical Association, 1980.

Whitefield, George (1714–1770)
Methodist preacher and evangelist
English

George Whitefield was perhaps the most influential religious orator of the eighteenth century. He was the primary leader of the Great Awakening, making dissent respectable and an important force behind the American Revolution.

Whitefield was born in Gloucester, son of innkeepers Thomas Whitefield and Elizabeth Edwards. At Oxford University the young George Whitefield was persuaded by John and Charles Wesley to go to Georgia after his graduation to become a missionary. He arrived in the colony in 1738 and quickly earned the reputation of promoting piety and establishing orphanages, a cause that he held dear for the rest of his life and for which he made numerous trips to England to raise the necessary funds. Back in England Whitefield realized his gift as a preacher, though he angered many other Anglican clergymen after he criticized them for not preaching the truths of the Bible.

In 1739 Whitefield traveled to Philadelphia, where he attracted large crowds and sparked the religious revival that became known as the Great Awakening. Then, he traveled throughout the American colonies, preaching and unifying the spiritual awakening that had been spread by other, lesser preachers. In South Carolina he was accused by a representative of the bishop of London of violating the canons of Anglican orthodoxy and ordered not to preach. Whitefield ignored the order and took the liberty of preaching as he pleased. He always claimed to be a Calvinist and frequently preached on the cardinal doctrines of original sin, election, and justification by faith alone. However, his Calvinism was at best a modified version: Although professing his belief in election, he always called on his audience to choose salvation.

Such theological contradictions did not bother Whitefield or the many thousands who heard his highly dramatic sermons, which were more emotional than intellectual in content. Although not all found Whitefield's charismatic revivals to their liking, those who did and split off from their existing congregations were called New Lights, whereas those who did not and remained with their existing churches were called Old Lights. This split soon affected Yale University, where disen-

chanted New Lights decided to establish universities more in line with their Whitefieldian beliefs: the College of New Jersey (Princeton), the College of Rhode Island (Brown), and Dartmouth. Such was the impact of the revival led by George Whitefield.

During, but especially after, the Great Awakening, Whitefield made numerous trips back and forth between England and the colonies and other parts of the British Empire, calling sinners to repent as well as raising funds for his orphanage in Georgia, "Bethesda," which became colonial Georgia's best school as well. Although he had wed Elizabeth Burnell James in 1741 (their one child died in infancy), it is clear his life was devoted to his preaching. He died in Newburyport, Massachusetts, and, at his request, was buried there, in the cemetery of the First Presbyterian Church. More than any other itinerant preacher, Whitefield spread religious revival in the American colonies. In addition to the need for repentance, he preached an attitude of dissent and personal choice, which many scholars believe were crucial for preparing the American colonies for the fight for independence.

William E. Van Vugt

REFERENCES

Belden, Albert David. *George Whitefield, the Awakener: A Modern Study of the Evangelical Revival.* New York: Macmillan, 1953.

Henry, Stuart Clark. *George Whitefield: Wayfaring Witness.* New York: Abingdon Press, 1957.

Pollock, John C. *George Whitefield and the Great Awakening.* Garden City, NY: Doubleday, 1992.

Stout, Harry S. *The Divine Dramatist: George Whitefield and the Rise of Modern Evangelicalism.* Grand Rapids, MI: Eerdmans, 1991.

Winfrey, Oprah Gail (1954–)

Television talk show host, actress, entrepreneur, and philanthropist
African American

Undoubtedly, Oprah Winfrey, the wealthiest African American, will become the nation's first black billionaire. She strategically maneuvered her outstanding abilities with her television talk show to emerge as a leading entrepreneur in the television and communications industries. She is one of only three American women in the television and movie industry to establish and own a production studio. She has also contributed millions to various philanthropic causes. In 1998, she was named one of the "100 Most Influential People of the Twentieth Century" by *Time* magazine.

Winfrey was born on 29 January 1954 in Kosciusko, Mississippi. Her mother, Vernita Lee, and father, Vernon Winfrey, never married, and for six years, she was raised by her grandmother. While very young, Winfrey was able to memorize speeches and she delivered them with great oratorical skill, which won her recognition in the community. Because of her intellectual abilities, when living either with her mother in Milwaukee or with her father in Nashville, she was placed in integrated schools. At historically black Tennessee State University, she majored in speech and drama and then media studies and was selected Miss Black Tennessee.

Her career in television began when she was nineteen, working as an anchor and coanchor for television stations in Nashville, Baltimore, and Chicago. In 1984, Winfrey moved to Chicago to host "A.M. Chicago," which was an immediate success and soon renamed the "Oprah Winfrey Show." It went into national syndication in 1986 and was eventually seen by 15–20 million viewers a day in 132 countries. The show has won thirty-two Emmy Awards—including seven for Winfrey herself. Her influence could be seen in the impact of her on-air book-reading club, for each book selected has become an instant best-seller, averaging 1 million copies in sales. *Newsweek* named her in 1997 its Most Important Person in Books and Media.

In addition to her show, Winfrey also starred in or has had cameo appearances in a number of films, including: *The Color Purple* (1985), for which she received an Oscar nomination; *Native Son* (1986); *Women of Brewster Place* (1989); *Lincoln* (1992); *There Are No Children Here* (1993); and *Beloved* (1998), in which

she starred with Danny Glover. In 1999, Winfrey partnered with Oxygen Media, a cable and Internet programming venture for women, and in 2000 her Harpo Entertainment Group launched *O, the Oprah Magazine*.

Winfrey's success was achieved despite the dysfunctional family life she had, for, from age nine to thirteen, males in her mother's family and their friends sexually abused her, and at fourteen she gave birth to a premature baby that died. Using her power and prestige, Winfrey has worked assiduously to empower women and children not only through her charitable and philanthropic contributions but also through political activism. In 1991, she initiated the Oprah Bill, which became the 1993 National Child Protection Act. She also founded the Family for Better Lives Foundation and the Angel Network, which includes volunteering with Habitat to Humanity to build homes. She has, in addition, given millions for college scholarships and to historically black colleges and universities.

Juliet E. K. Walker

REFERENCES

Brand, H. W. *Masters of Enterprise: Giants of American Business from John Jacob Astor and J. P. Morgan to Bill Gates and Oprah Winfrey.* New York: Free Press, 1999.

Caldwell, Oluwatoyin. "Winfrey, Oprah." In *Encyclopedia of African American Business History,* edited by Juliet E. K. Walker, 595–597. Westport, CT: Greenwood Press, 1999.

Greene, Robert, and Winfrey, Oprah. *Make the Connection: Ten Steps to a Better Body and a Better Life.* New York: Hyperion, 1996.

Mair, George. *Oprah Winfrey: The Real Story.* Secaucus, NY: Carol Publishing Group, 1998.

Walker, Juliet E. K. "Oprah Winfrey, The Tycoon: Contextualizing the Economics of Race, Class, Gender in Black Business in Post-Civil Rights America." In *African American Entrepreneurship,* edited by Alusine Jalloh. Rochester: Rochester University Press, forthcoming.

———. *The History of Black Business in America: Capitalism, Race, Entrepreneurship.* New York/ London: Macmillan/Prentice Hall International, 1998.

Winthrop, John (1588–1649)
Colonial governor
English

John Winthrop was the preeminent leader in early New England. He was the man most responsible for ensuring the survival of the Massachusetts Bay Colony and forming its initial institutions.

Winthrop was born in Edwardstone, Suffolk, England, the son of Adam Winthrop, who was the lord of Groton Manor, and Anne Browne. He studied at Trinity College, Cambridge, and became lord of the manor in 1618. He also became a lawyer at Gray's Inn, a county justice at age twenty-eight, and the author of bills drafted for Parliament—all of which prepared him well for his future roles in early Massachusetts. Three of his four wives died before him, but he fathered sixteen children, eight of whom died young. One son, John Jr., became governor of Connecticut.

Winthrop's Puritanism profoundly shaped his life and the colony he would govern. His economic problems and the intolerance of Archbishop William Laud led him to see America both as refuge and as an opportunity to do God's work, particularly spreading the faith among the Indians and countering the spread of Catholicism by the Spanish and French. In 1629 Winthrop agreed with the officers of the Massachusetts Bay Company to establish a colony. He would serve as governor. In 1630 Winthrop boarded the ship *Arbella* and, with three other ships and 700 other emigrants, sailed to the New World. On the journey he composed one of the most famous sermons in America, "A Model of Christian Charity," remembered especially for the words "we shall be as a City upon a Hill . . . the eyes of all people are upon us."

Winthrop was elected governor of the colony twelve times between 1629 and 1649. Although he did make many decisions unilaterally, they were generally for the colony's benefit and held it together during the difficult early years when hundreds died of disease and starvation. He provided newcomers with food and shelter, often at his own expense. He also shepherded the colony from corporation to commonwealth, involving a broadening of the electorate and a two-house legislature.

He was important for other activities, too. He built Massachusetts's first ship, operated a windmill, and invested in and extended the lands of the colony. During the tensions of England's Civil War, he withstood the pressure to surrender the company's patent and control to Parliament or the Crown. He also wrote the first history of New England, an invaluable source for understanding the times in which he lived.

Nevertheless, Winthrop did experience considerable controversy. He was tried and acquitted by the General Court for exceeding his authority. He led the attack on Anne Hutchinson, whose Antinomian beliefs—that good works were not evidence of one's salvation and that the church magistrates did not have the authority they claimed—were seen by Winthrop and others as dangerous heresy that threatened social and religious order. Winthrop presided over the court that banished her to Rhode Island. Although he also urged the banishment of Anabaptists, his pursuit of conformity was not so harsh as that of many of the other magistrates of the colony. He died in 1649 while still governor of the Massachusetts Commonwealth.

William E. Van Vugt

REFERENCES

Morgan, Edmund S. *The Puritan Dilemma: The Story of John Winthrop.* Boston: Little, Brown, 1958.

Moseley, James G. *John Winthrop's World.* Madison: University of Wisconsin Press, 1992.

Rutman, Darrett B. *Winthrop's Boston: Portrait of a Puritan Town.* Chapel Hill: University of North Carolina Press, 1965.

Witherspoon, John (1723–1794)
Clergy, college president, and patriot
Scottish

John Witherspoon was an American Founder who played an important role in establishing America's independence. He also helped shape American Presbyterianism and intellectual life.

Witherspoon was born in Gifford, about twenty miles east of Edinburgh, the son of James Witherspoon, a preacher in the Church of Scotland, and Anne Walker. At age thirteen he entered the University of Edinburgh and earned a master's degree at age sixteen. He then studied theology and in 1745 accepted a call to preach for the Church of Scotland in Ayrshire. The next year he helped resist the invasion of Charles Stuart, "Bonny Prince Charlie," who had invaded from France. After being captured, Witherspoon spent a short time in prison, where he suffered permanent damage to his nervous system but developed a strong commitment to liberty.

As a minister within the Church of Scotland, Witherspoon made his mark supporting the Popular Party, which favored the right of congregations to select their own ministers, as opposed to the Moderates, who favored patronage and a more liberal theology. His satirical attack on the Moderates, titled *Ecclesiastical Characteristics,* was published in fifteen editions and earned him considerable fame. That brought him to the attention of American Presbyterians at the College of New Jersey (Princeton University), who were looking for a new president who could end a feud that had developed over the issue of the enthusiastic religious revivals that were becoming common at the time. After being persuaded to take the job by Benjamin Rush, who was studying medicine at Edinburgh at the time, John Witherspoon, his wife, Elizabeth, and five children arrived in Princeton in 1768.

Witherspoon brought unity to Princeton and reorganized its instruction around lectures. Moreover, he was responsible for contributing to the growth in America of Scottish "common sense realism," which held that ordinary people's perceptions, or common sense, was a good basis for science and politics as well as ethics. He also contributed to the linking of Christian theology and republican ideology, which became an important idea during the 1770s. Witherspoon led the New Jersey patriots as they began to organize in 1774, and he was selected to be their representative at the Continental Congress in Philadelphia in 1776. There, he contributed ideas to the Declaration of Independence and was the only clergyman to sign it. He continued to serve in the congress through 1782 and was prominent for his committee work, his handling of foreign nations, and his contributions to the Articles of Confederation. After independence, he served in the New Jersey legislature and, as a member of the New Jersey convention, voted to approve the U.S. Constitution.

As a leading Protestant and intellectual, John Witherspoon was important for showing that reason and science did not contradict revelation and that there could be harmony between religion and science and between Christian tradition and new ideas about liberty. He thus contributed much to the religious and political culture of the new United States.

William E. Van Vugt

REFERENCES
Collins, Varnum Lansing. *President Witherspoon.* 2 vols. 1925; reprinted as 1 vol., Princeton, NJ: Princeton University Press, 1969.
Noll, Mark A. *Princeton and the Republic, 1768–1822.* Princeton: Princeton University Press, 1989.
Sloan, Douglas. *The Scottish Enlightenment and the American College Ideal.* New York: Teachers College Press, Columbia University, 1971.

Wollner, Norma (1929–)
Medical doctor and pediatrics specialist
Brazilian

Norma Wollner, a native of Brazil, is professor of pediatrics at Cornell Medical School and founder of the Pediatric Day Hospital at Memorial Sloan-Kettering Cancer Center. She has achieved wide recognition both in her homeland and in the United States.

Wollner was born in São Paulo in 1929, her parents having immigrated to Brazil from Yugoslavia. When she was nine, her father died, leaving her mother to raise her and her brother on a seamstress's income. At age eighteen, she announced her intention to become a doctor, but her mother disapproved, fearing that such an educated woman would not find a husband. In medical school, where she was one of fifteen women in a class of eighty, Wollner was a rebel, helping to organize women medical students and protesting the excessively theoretical training they received.

After finishing medical school in 1955, and a one-year residency in oncology in São Paulo, Wollner won a fellowship to the United States to learn medical research techniques. In January 1958 she traveled to New York to what is today Memorial Sloan-Kettering Hospital. Although all of her previous work had been with adults, the hospital needed a pediatrician, and she switched to pediatric oncology. She "fell in love" with her young patients, she says, because "death doesn't exist for them." Yet at that time, most children with cancer died.

When Wollner first became a member of the house staff at Memorial Sloan-Kettering in 1966, its pediatric clinic was "a dungeon." She developed the country's first pediatric day hospital, in which young cancer patients received treatment during the day and, if not too ill, returned home to be with their families at night. Today, the Pediatric Day Hospital, which Dr. Wollner directs, sees 75 to 100 patients daily and has become a widely copied model for treating children with cancer and other serious illnesses. Dr. Wollner is also recognized for her medical research. She developed a protocol for non-Hodgkin's lymphoma in children, which has seen the survival rate from this disease rise from 10 percent in the 1970s to over 85 percent today. Author or coauthor of more than 130 scientific papers, book chapters, reviews, and abstracts, she is recognized as a pioneer in pediatric oncology.

Despite her many years in New York and her naturalization as a U.S. citizen, Dr. Wollner has never forgotten her homeland. She initiated a program that brings Brazilian children stricken with cancer to New York for treatment, has helped raise money to assist families during their stays in New York, and was instrumental in organizing local Brazilian volunteers to serve as interpreters and to advise such families on adapting to New York City. Furthermore, she has aided in the establishment of the Brazilian Children's Fund Observerships, a program that brings Brazilian medical personnel to New York for training.

Although married to a distinguished research pathologist and the mother of two daughters, Wollner has retained her maiden name to "honor" her father. In addition, despite the fact that she was forced to renounce her Brazilian citizenship in 1987 when she became a U.S. citizen, Wollner still "feels Brazilian in every way," remains proud of the country of her birth and the warmth of its people, and loves Brazilian food and music.

Maxine L. Margolis

REFERENCES
"Cover Tribute to Dr. Norma Wollner." *Cancer Research: A Journal of the American Association of Cancer Research* 57.11 (1 June 1997).
Margolis, Maxine L. *An Invisible Minority: Brazilians in New York City.* Boston: Allyn & Bacon, 1998.
———. *Little Brazil: An Ethnography of Brazilian Immigrants in New York City.* Princeton: Princeton University Press, 1994.
Sales, Teresa. "Constructing an Ethnic Identity: Brazilian Immigrants in Boston, Mass." *Migration World* 26.5 (1998): 15–21.
Wollner, Norma. Interview with author, summer 1998.

Wong, Anna May (1907–1961)
Actress
Chinese-American

Born in 1907 in Los Angeles, California, Anna May Wong starred in more than 100 films during a nearly forty-year career, the first popular Chinese-American movie star. Usually cast as the deceitful "Oriental" woman with deadly charms, Wong had the dubious distinction of having been the first Asian American woman to play cinematic roles that reflected the specter of "yellow peril." Yet, she was also the only Asian American performer to capture the limelight prior to the 1960s.

Her family, like many other Chinese, ran a struggling laundry, and Wong found her escape at the local nickelodeon. Her interest in silent films soon turned into a strong desire to act. At twelve she made her debut as one of several hundred Chinese extras in *The Red Lantern* (1919). Knowing her parents would not approve—traditional Chinese believed only "loose" women were drawn to the arts—she kept her career a secret until offered a role with screen credit in *Bits of Life* (1921). Following a generational and cultural family conflict, her parents finally relented, with the condition that her father chaperon her on the film sets.

At seventeen, Wong played her first—and one of her very few—romantic lead roles in *Toll of the Sea* (1923). Her character, Lotus Flower, was the selfless "Oriental" female who was sexually available but committed suicide so as to underscore the doomed nature of miscegenation. Wong was often the diabolical Oriental female villain, and her Dragon Lady image took off when she played the exotic slave girl who resorted to treachery to help an unscrupulous Mongol prince attain his love interest in *The Thief of Bagdad* (1924).

Tired of being marginalized and typecast, Wong fled to Europe in 1928, learned German and French, dabbled in theater, and starred in several foreign-language films. Returning to the United States in 1931, she was soon cast in the thriller *Shanghai Express* (1932). Although receiving critical praise, she returned to Europe, having found it less racially hostile. When she was denied the highly sought after leading role in *The Good Earth* (1936), she became even more disillusioned with Hollywood. She then visited China and, realizing that Hollywood would never consider her an American actress, explored the Chinese stage—only to discover that she was viewed as too Westernized. This identity dilemma, one shared by countless acculturated Chinese Americans, did not stifle her creative energies. She was featured in several other films before World War II but by 1942 she was unwilling to tolerate the Hollywood system any longer and announced her retirement at age thirty-five. She would return

to film several times and, in the 1950s, even starred in her own television series, *Mme. Liu Tsong,* yet never recaptured the earlier attention she had received.

Wong died in 1961. Although she had performed alongside such actors as Douglas Fairbanks, Laurence Olivier, and Lana Turner, her full potential was never realized because of racial discrimination and typecasting. Nevertheless, though second generation, she retained her ethnic identity, and her films influenced both the representation of Asians and Asian Americans and how non-Asians perceived them, including notions of Asian beauty.

Benson Tong

REFERENCES
"Anna May Wong: Combination of East and West." *New York Herald Tribune,* 9 November 1930.
Chu, Judy. "Anna May Wong." In *Counterpoint: Perspectives on Asian America,* edited by Emma Gee, 284–288. Los Angeles: Asian American Studies Center, University of California, 1976.
Davis, Mac. "Fled from Fame for Five Years." *New York Enquirer,* 18 February 1957.
Okrent, Neil. "Right Place, Wrong Time: Why Hollywood's First Asian Star, Ana May Wong, Died a Thousand Movie Deaths." *Los Angeles Magazine,* May 1990, 84–96.

Woods, Granville T.   (1856–1910)
Inventor and engineer
African American

Granville T. Woods's electrical inventions were in the communications and transportation industries, and many of his patents were sold to American Bell Telephone Company, General Electric, and Westinghouse. Woods had more than sixty patents by the time of his death in 1910, many of them still in use today, notably the "third rail" in mass-transit subway systems. His contemporaries called him the Black Thomas Edison.

Woods was born in Ohio in 1856. Although he left school when he was ten to go to work, his varied work experience, first as an apprentice in a machine shop that repaired railroad equipment and then as a railroad train engineer, provided basic mechanical knowledge. He also increased his knowledge through self-education, getting white friends to check out library books for him. Then, attending an eastern college from 1876 to 1878, he took mechanical and electrical engineering courses. Although he worked as an engineer on a British steamer and as a train engineer—and had impressive engineering skills—racism prevented his advancement in those companies. In 1880, he therefore established his own shop in Cincinnati and, in 1885, in New York City, where he continued to manufacture and sell telephone, telegraph, and electrical instruments.

Wood's first patent in 1884 was for an improved steam boiler furnace. The following year, he patented a telephone transmitter, which was bought by Bell Telephone. Subsequent patents were in electricity, including an efficient light dimmer used on the theater stage and fifteen appliances for electric railways. One of his most important inventions, patented in 1887, was the Synchronous Multiplex Railway Telegraph System, which allowed for communications between train stations and moving trains. Before that, there was no way for trains to communicate with either railroad stations or other moving trains. With Woods's invention, railroad dispatchers were able to note the location of running trains and relay information.

In 1888, Woods developed and patented a system for overhead electric-conducting lines for railroads. A complete electric railway system, based on that format, was operated at Coney Island, New York, in 1892. Ever diverse, Woods in 1900 received a patent for an electrical egg incubator that allowed 50,000 eggs to be incubated at one time. He then received patents for several devices involving air brakes, an automatic safety cut-out for electric circuits—a circuit breaker for high-tension lines—a galvanic battery, a zinc-carbon battery, a telephone transmitter, which was an early version of the diaphragm microphone, and a telephone system and apparatus that reduced induction interference from other power lines.

Nevertheless, from the beginning of his work as an inventor, Woods was involved in court suits, for large corporations attempted to steal his inventions or infringe on his patents. Several companies, including Edison's, tried to claim credit for Woods's Synchronous Multiplex Railway Telegraph System. He won his case against Edison but, at the same time, had to finance development of new inventions by selling off patent rights to his previous ones. In 1910, Woods died in poverty, a result of his numerous lawsuits to protect his patent rights.

Juliet E. K. Walker

REFERENCES

Baker, Henry E. *The Colored Inventor.* New York: Arno Press, 1969.

Carwell, Hattie. *Blacks in Science: Astrophysicist to Zoologist.* Hicksville, NY: Exposition Press, 1977.

Haber, Louis. *Black Pioneers of Science and Invention.* New York: Harcourt, Brace and World, 1970.

Hayden, Robert C. "The Inventive Genius of Granville T. Woods." *Journal of the National Technical Association,* Summer 1900.

McKinley, Burt, Jr. *Black Inventors of America.* Portland, OR: National Book Co., 1969.

U.S. Department of Energy. *Black Contributors to Science and Energy Technology.* Washington, DC: Office of Public Affairs, 1979.

Williams, James C. *At Last Recognition in America: A Reference Handbook of Unknown Black Inventors and Their Contributions to America.* Chicago, IL: BCA Publishing Co., 1978.

Wright, Frances "Fanny" (1795–1852)

Social reformer and writer
Scottish

Fanny Wright was a controversial woman who was loved and hated by many Americans. She challenged them to live up to their ideals of liberty and equality for all.

Wright was born in Dundee, the daughter of a linen merchant, James Wright, and Camilla Campbell. James Wright was an enthusiast for the radical ideas of Thomas Paine, and although Frances was not yet three years old when her father and mother died, she developed the same ideas and would live her life according to them. Raised by relatives in England, Wright was appalled by the vast poverty and opulent wealth of London and was revolted by the enclosure movement that mercilessly ejected laborers from the land. These injustices, and the role model of her uncle, a professor at the University of Glasgow who opposed the slave trade, left a lasting impression on Wright and inspired her to commit her life to the cause of liberty and greater social equality. At the same time, she developed her talents as a writer and wrote two plays.

In 1818, at age twenty-three, Wright immigrated to the United States with her sister and fell in love with it because of the greater equality there. Following a two-year stay in New York, she traveled throughout the northeastern United States to record her observations, which were published in *Views of Society and Manners in America* (1821). This attracted the attention of Jeremy Bentham and the Marquis de Lafayette, with whom Wright developed a close, possibly sexual, relationship when she returned to England for a visit in 1821 and when the two traveled together back to the United States in 1824.

By this time Wright had become obsessed with the curse of American slavery. Inspired by Robert Owen's utopian community in New Harmony, Indiana, she established a community in Tennessee she called Nashoba. There, she hoped to prove slavery unprofitable through an experiment by which slaves would be freed after five years as an incentive for them to work harder and render the plantation more profitable than ones with slaves. By 1818 the project was abandoned, owing to economic troubles, mismanagement, and an erosion of support in reaction to Wright's challenges to organized religion.

Wright then developed a partnership with Robert Dale Owen, with whom she edited the *New Harmony Gazette*. She also traveled throughout the country, delivering speeches against organized religion, the subjection of women, slavery, and capital punishment, and speeches that promoted gender equality, tolerance, free public education, and the use of birth control. Occasionally, her speeches incited mob violence. She also promoted the pro-labor Workingman's Party. After a return

trip to Europe in 1830, Wright married a French physician and returned to the United States to resume her lecturing career. She joined the Democratic Party but became disillusioned by the public's declining interest in her and her proposals for reform. She divorced her husband in 1850 and died in Cincinnati. Probably no immigrant did more to challenge social conventions and push the boundaries of gender inequality than did Fanny Wright.

William E. Van Vugt

REFERENCES

Bartlett, Elizabeth Ann. *Liberty, Equality, Sorority: The Origins and Interpretation of American Feminist Thought: Frances Wright, Sarah Grimke, and Margaret Fuller.* Brooklyn, NY: Carlson Publishing, 1994.

Eckhardt, Celia Morris. *Fanny Wright: Rebel in America.* Cambridge, MA: Harvard University Press, 1984.

Wright, Frank Lloyd (1869–1959)
Architect
Welsh-American

Frank Lloyd Wright stands as a giant in the history of architecture. He is known above all for his designs of residential buildings and his single-minded pursuit of his aesthetic ideals, often against difficult odds.

Wright's maternal grandfather, Richard Jones, a hatter and Unitarian preacher in Wales, emigrated with his wife, Mary Lloyd, and seven children. They settled in rural Wisconsin, in a landscape that would shape Wright's vision of nature and his approach to architecture. Of English heritage, Wright's father, William, inspired in his son a lifelong love of music but left the family when Wright was in high school. His mother, Anna, imbued with a passion for education and the ideal of beauty, was the greatest early influence in Wright's life, intending even before his birth that he become an architect.

Wright began his career with the eminent Chicago architect Louis Sullivan. Going independent in 1893, he evolved his concept of "organic architecture," buildings that harmonize with their environment and their purpose. By the early 1900s he was well known for the "prairie house," a style that was to have enormous influence. His career thrived, but scandal in his personal life proved costly and drove him to create a retreat in Spring Green, Wisconsin. There, he found himself alienated from Welsh relatives and neighbors, who could not accept his unconventional views on marriage. There, too, he built his home, Taliesin, or "shining brow" in Welsh, as the house was built into the crest of a hill and designed to merge with its environment. But the name had dual significance for Wright, referring also to the legendary Welsh poet and druid-bard, from whom Wright claimed artistic inspiration. Heavily damaged twice by fire and rebuilt each time, Taliesin remains one of the most important expressions of Wright's genius.

Wright's innovations were not limited to residential architecture. Commercial buildings designed by him introduced such features as mechanical ventilation, steel furnishings, and the lightweight walls of glass and metal that were to become common in tall buildings. In 1922 he completed the Imperial Hotel in Tokyo, which, because of its resilient jointed structure and cushion foundations, was the only large building to survive the earthquake of 1923.

The most fulfilling portion of his career began when Wright was in his late sixties. He designed one of the world's best-known houses, Fallingwater, in Bear Run, Pennsylvania, in 1936. Taliesin West, his winter retreat, was built in 1938 near Phoenix, Arizona. During this time he founded the Taliesin Fellowship, a training program for architectural apprentices. In his final years he articulated a philosophy of architecture, produced plans for numerous private residences, and designed some of his most daring commercial and public buildings, including the widely acclaimed Guggenheim Museum in New York City.

Wright was always conscious and proud of his Welsh heritage. Although his aesthetic vision was inspired by the American landscape, he embraced the drama, passion, and independence of his mother's family, which he associated with the Welsh character. An honorary degree from the University of Bangor in Wales gave him special pleasure. He died in 1959.

D. Douglas Caulkins and Lorna W. Caulkins

REFERENCES

Frank Lloyd Wright. A film by Ken Burns and Lynn Novick. The American Lives Film Project, Inc., 1997.

Frank Lloyd Wright Foundation: www.franklloydwright.org/ (accessed May 21, 2000).

Larkin, David, and Bruce Brooks Pfeiffer, eds. *Frank Lloyd Wright: The Masterworks.* New York: Rizzoli and the Frank Lloyd Wright Foundation, 1993.

Twombly, Robert C. *Frank Lloyd Wright: His Life and His Architecture.* New York: John Wiley, 1979.

Wright, Frank Lloyd. *An Autobiography.* 1943. New York: Horizon Press, 1977.

Wright, Olgivanna Lloyd. *Frank Lloyd Wright: His Life, His Work, His Words.* New York: Horizon Press, 1966.

Yamamoto, Hisaye (1921–)
Writer

Japanese-American

Hisaye Yamamoto was one of the first Japanese-American writers to gain national prominence after World War II. Her deceptively simple, often autobiographical short stories reveal frequently hidden aspects of Japanese-American life and culture.

Yamamoto was born in Redondo Beach, California, the daughter of Japanese immigrants. Her father farmed strawberries along the coast, halfway between Los Angeles and San Diego, and she grew up in the sort of rural setting that is the backdrop for many of her stories. An avid reader as a child, she studied languages in high school and at junior college.

With the Japanese attack on Pearl Harbor in December 1941, she and her family were removed from their homes and sent to the Poston internment camp in Arizona. There, she wrote for the camp newspaper, the *Poston Chronicle,* on everything from camp life to a serialized mystery story. Yamamoto left camp early for points east, in her case Springfield, Massachusetts, but returned to Poston following the death of her brother in Italy, a member of the famed 442d Regimental Combat Team.

At the conclusion of the war, Yamamoto moved to Los Angeles and worked for three years for the *Los Angeles Tribune,* an African American newspaper. In 1948, she left the paper, planning to return to college. Then, the publication of her story "The High-Heeled Shoes" in *Partisan Review* and a John Hay Whitney Foundation Opportunity Fellowship in 1949 encouraged her to pursue her writing seriously. In addition, there was a new baby in the family who needed care, and Yamamoto eventually adopted him. Despite the rigors of single motherhood, she wrote and published extensively in the next few years, including her most famous works, "Seventeen Syllables (1949), "The Legend of Miss Sasagawara" (1950), and "Yoneko's Earthquake" (1951). Four of her stories were included in Martha Foley's Annual List of Distinctive Short Stories, and the last was selected for Foley's 1952 edition of *Best American Short Stories.*

In 1952, she turned down a Stanford Writing Fellowship and journeyed across country with her five-year-old son to join Dorothy Day's famed *Catholic Worker* colony in New York. After two years, she returned to Los Angeles, married Anthony DeSoto, and had four more children over the next seven years. Though family life was her preoccupation for the next twenty years, she did continue to write, publishing annual stories in the English language sections of Japanese-American newspapers, to which she had been contributing since the 1930s.

In the 1970s and 1980s, Yamamoto was rediscovered by a new generation. Her stories were anthologized in many new compilations of Asian American literature and a new generation of literary critics reevaluated her work. In 1986, she received the American Book Award for lifetime achievement from the Before Columbus Foundation. Two years later the first anthology of her work was published, *Seventeen Syllables and Other Stories* (1988). In 1991, her stories "Seventeen Syllables" and "Yoneko's Earthquake" were made into a dramatic film entitled *Hot Summer Winds,* which was shown nationally on PBS. She resides today in Eagle Rock, California, and continues to write.

Brian Niiya

REFERENCES

Cheung, King-kok. *Articulate Silences: Hisaye Yamamoto, Maxine Hong Kingston, Joy Kogawa.* Ithaca, NY: Cornell University Press, 1993.

Crow, Charles L. "A MELUS Interview: Hisaye
    Yamamoto." *MELUS* 14.1 (Spring 1987):
    73–84.
Kim, Elaine H. *Asian American Literature: An
    Introduction to the Writings and Their Social
    Context.* Philadelphia: Temple University Press,
    1982.
McDonald, Dorothy Ritsuko, and Katharine
    Newman. "Relocation and Dislocation: The
    Writings of Hisaye Yamamoto and Wakako
    Yamauchi." *MELUS* 7.3 (Fall 1980): 116–125.
Osborn, William P., and Sylvia A. Watanabe. "A
    Conversation with Hisaye Yamamoto." *Chicago
    Review* 39.3-4 (Summer-Fall 1993): 34ff.
Trudeau, Lawrence J., ed. *Asian American Literature:
    Reviews and Criticism of Works by American Writers
    of Asian Descent.* Detroit: Gale Research, 1999.
Yogi, Stanley Stuart. "Rebels and Heroines:
    Subversive Narratives in the Stories of Wakako
    Yamauchi and Hisaye Yamamoto." In *Reading the
    Literatures of Asian America,* edited by Shirley
    Geok-lin Lim and Amy Ling, 131–150.
    Philadelphia: Temple University Press, 1992.

Ybor, Vicente Martínez (1818–1897)

Cigar manufacturer and founder of Ybor City
Spanish

Vicente Martínez Ybor was born on 17
September 1818 in Valencia, Spain. Following
a pattern typical of young men of his generation, when he reached fourteen he was sent to
Cuba by his parents to avoid military service
in the Spanish army. At seventeen, he worked
as a broker in the booming cigar industry on
the island and, a few years later, started his
own cigar factory, marketing his cigars under
the brand name "El Príncipe de Gales." As international demand for high-quality Havana
cigars grew during the 1840s and 1850s, Ybor
became one of the wealthiest and best-known
cigar manufacturers in Cuba.

By the 1860s the oppressive economic
policies of Spain toward Cuba convinced
Ybor of the need to support the incipient
separatist movement. Shortly after the beginning of the Ten Years' War (1868–1878) between Spain and Cuba, Spanish officials ordered his arrest. In 1869, he fled Cuba for Key
West, Florida, remaining there for five years.
In 1875, he moved to New York City and
opened a factory there, but labor strife and the

end of the war in Cuba prompted him to return to Key West three years later. In 1878 he
established a tobacco leaf distributorship in
New York, selling tobacco leaf to other manufacturers and traveling widely between the
United States and Cuba. In the 1880s, growing labor unrest and anti-Spanish sentiment
among the Cuban-immigrant community in
Key West prompted him to move away. A
chance encounter with two fellow Spaniards
convinced him to visit Tampa.

Ybor arrived in Tampa in July 1885, purchased a forty-acre tract of land northeast of
the town, and, in October, started to build the
first cigar factories and homes for the cigar
workers. The new community, now called
Ybor City, was so successful that in 1892 a
similar company town was established on the
other side of the Hillsborough River: West
Tampa. Within a few years, the two communities were bursting with hundreds of cigar
factories and thousands of immigrants from
Cuba, Spain, and Italy. In less than ten years
Tampa went from being a village of fewer
than 1,000 people to the third-largest city in
the state and the U.S. capital of the Clear Havana Cigar industry.

As the quintessential nineteenth-century
patron, Ybor maintained a close relationship
with his workers, many of whom he knew by
name. When he moved into a brand-new
brick factory, he donated the first wooden factory to the workers as a social center. His support for Cuban independence made him particularly popular among his Cuban workers.
Although he never learned to speak English,
Ybor remained involved in the development
of Tampa until his death on 14 December
1896. Ybor City still maintains its distinct
"Latin" flavor today and boasts the publication
of the only trilingual (English, Spanish, Italian)
newspaper in the United States.

Ana M. Varela-Lago

REFERENCES
Long, Durward. "The Historical Beginnings of
    Ybor City and Modern Tampa." *Florida Historical
    Quarterly* 45.1 (1966): 31–44.
Mormino, Gary R., and George E. Pozzetta. *The*

Immigrant World of Ybor City. Italians and Their Latin Neighbors in Tampa, 1885–1985. Urbana: University of Illinois Press, 1987.

Westfall, L. Glenn. Don Vicente Martinez Ybor, the Man and His Empire: Development of the Clear Havana Industry in Cuba and Florida in the Nineteenth Century. New York: Garland Publishing, 1987.

Yezierska, Anzia (1881?–1970)
Author
Jewish

Anzia Yezierska, a noted immigrant Jewish writer, is best known for her depictions of Jewish immigrant lives and her ability to capture both the opportunity and the oppression of immigrant life in the new country. In her writing career, which spanned nearly fifty years, she produced six novels and collections of short stories, a long autobiographical memoir, and numerous other works.

Yezierska was born in 1881 (or 1885) in the village of Plotsk, in Russian Poland. At the age of ten, she immigrated to New York City with her family, where she worked in factories, sweatshops, and domestic service, clashing frequently with her pious father, who was not gainfully employed. After leaving her parents' home, she began to pursue her ambition for education with a single-minded determination. She attended Columbia University's Teachers College on scholarship from 1901 to 1905, teaching in high school for a brief period. Following a brief marriage to Jacob Gordon and five years after her marriage to Arnold Levitas, a teacher, Yezierska moved to San Francisco with her daughter, Louise. In 1916 they moved to New York, and the following year Yezierska met the poet John Dewey, who was to be the great romance of her life and her mentor as well as the prototype of the genteel Gentile man in many of her stories.

Yezierska's first novel, *Hungry Hearts* (1920), was a dazzling success. *Hungry Hearts* and her subsequent novel, *Salome of the Tenements* (1922), were made into silent films. But Yezierska turned her back on the sudden wealth and success Hollywood offered her and returned to New York, back to the culture she knew. In the early 1930s she worked for the federal government's WPA Writers' Project, cataloging trees in Central Park. In 1950, she published her autobiographical memoir, *Red Ribbon on a White Horse,* and during the last decade of her life, she wrote about old age, the diminution of one's faculties, and the loss of dignity and respect. She died in 1970.

The themes that inspired her own struggles with her pious father and her two failed marriages to Jewish men inspired her fiction as well, notably her novel *Bread Givers* (1925). The motifs of the rebellious immigrant daughter, struggling against the old sexism of traditional patriarchal culture and of the woman writer struggling against the new sexism of the American Gentile world find expression in her work and make her the object of a renewed critical and academic interest. The ability to use a new language to convey the cultural subtleties of a different ethnic experience and the ability to paint this ethnic world as both repulsive and alluring are considered among Yezierska's most abiding assets.

Though recognized early on as an authentic voice of the tenements, capable of describing the poverty and economic struggles of immigrants driven by the desire to acculturate, Yezierska had fallen into obscurity in the 1950s and 1960s. Mainstream critics had perceived her as "too Jewish," and Jews saw her exposure of the gains and losses in assimilation as too offensive. However, with ethnic studies and feminist studies programs, the situation changed in the 1980s, and she became the subject of renewed interest by scholars and students in several disciplines.

Esther Fuchs

REFERENCES

Hyman, Paula E., and Deborah Dash Moore. *Jewish Women in America: An Historical Encyclopedia.* New York and London: Routledge, 1997.

Wexler, Laura. "Looking at Yezierska." In *Women of the Word,* edited by Judith R. Baskin, 153–181. Detroit: Wayne State University Press, 1994.

Yezierska, Anzia. *Bread Givers: A Struggle between a Father of the Old World and a Daughter of the New.* New York: Doubleday, 1925.

———. *Children of Loneliness: Stories of Immigrant Life in America.* New York and London: Funk and Wagnalls, 1923.

Yglesias, José (1919–1995)
Writer, journalist, and playwright
Spanish-American

José Yglesias, of Spanish and Cuban ancestry, achieved renown as a novelist and writer, particularly for his works focusing on life in his native Ybor City, the Latin-immigrant community in Tampa, Florida. (In Tampa, the term "Latin" was used to describe the mixed ethnic backgrounds of the immigrant enclaves of Ybor City and West Tampa, which included Spanish, Cuban, and Italian immigrants and their descendants.)

Yglesias was born in West Tampa, Florida, on 29 November 1919, but grew up in nearby Ybor City, Tampa's immigrant enclave. His father had emigrated from Galicia (Spain), and his mother was a second-generation Cuban American. Yglesias's parents worked as cigar makers in one of the numerous factories in Tampa. In these immigrant communities, Spaniards, Cubans, and Italians (mostly Sicilians) developed a common culture based on labor militancy and mutual aid, which Yglesias's family experienced when his father suffered a crippling illness and returned to Spain, where he died. Yglesias, only six years old then, recounted this story in *The Goodbye Land* (1967).

After graduating from high school in 1937, Yglesias left for New York, the destination of unemployed Tampa Latins. He soon participated in demonstrations organized by Spanish immigrants and sympathizers in favor of the Spanish Republic, then under attack by General Francisco Franco. After serving in the U.S. Navy during World War II, Yglesias took advantage of the GI Bill and entered Black Mountain College in North Carolina, where he developed his literary skills and published his first short story, an autobiographical piece set in Ybor City. In 1946, he returned to New York and was a film critic for the *Daily Worker* from

1948 to 1950. The Cold War climate made it difficult for Yglesias to find a writing job.

In 1962, he achieved recognition with his translations of two Spanish writers into English. The following year he published his first, autobiographical, novel: *A Wake in Ybor City*. A year later, he traveled to his father's home region, Galicia, and found a family he did not know existed. He wrote about that experience in his second novel, *The Goodbye Land*. He returned to Spain a decade later to write about life under Franco, but Franco died while Yglesias was there. Consequently, *The Franco Years* offered a fresh account of the dictatorship and the first stages of Spain's transition to democracy. Yglesias also felt an intimate connection to Cuba, visiting it in 1967 and living in the countryside, where he wrote *In the Fist of the Revolution: Life in a Cuban Country Town*.

During the 1960s and 1970s, following his literary successes, his articles appeared in the *New York Times, New Yorker,* and *Esquire,* and elsewhere. He wrote several plays centered around the Latin-immigrant community of Ybor City. As he once said, "In all my work as a writer I tried to make American readers aware of Ybor City and its Latin cigar makers." In recognition of his contribution to the study of Tampa's immigrant heritage, the University of South Florida awarded him an honorary doctorate in 1989. During the 1990s, he continued to work with the university giving lectures and attending conferences and to write books. Overall, he produced thirteen books, four plays, and numerous articles, reviews, and short stories. He died in November 1995 and was buried in Tampa's Cemetery of the Centro Asturiano, a mutual aid society founded by Spanish immigrants in 1902.

Ana M. Varela-Lago

REFERENCES

Garza, José Marcelo. "Deaths I Have Known: The Literary Radicalism of José Yglesias." Iowa City: Ph.D. dissertation, University of Iowa, 1986.

"José Yglesias." *Tampa Bay History* 18(1) (Spring/Summer 1996): entire issue.

Terkel, Studs. *Hard Times: An Oral History of the Great Depression.* New York: Pantheon, 1970.

Yorke, Peter C. (1864–1925)
Priest, writer, and labor activist
Irish

Peter Yorke was one of the key leaders of the Irish nationalist community in the United States in the early twentieth century. He was a Catholic priest.

Yorke was born in Galway, Ireland, to Brigid and Captain Gregory Yorke, on 15 August 1864. He studied theology, and in 1886 the diocese of San Francisco recruited him. He was ordained in December 1887 and was named assistant pastor at St. Mary's Cathedral in San Francisco.

Yorke became a controversial public figure, defending the Catholic faith against the lies and misconceptions of the anti-Catholic American Protective Association (APA). As editor of the *Monitor,* the official newspaper of his archdiocese, Yorke fiercely counterattacked the criticisms by the anti-Catholic groups. He founded the Catholic Truth Society and the Women's Liberal League to defend the religious liberty of Catholics against nativism. Using basic principles of Pope Leo XIII's 1891 encyclical *Rerum Novarum,* he defended collective bargaining. In 1901, he supported the teamsters' right to strike and attacked city officials for their bias in favor of the employers' association. His intervention eventually led to the recognition of bargaining rights for union labor.

In 1902, Yorke founded and edited a weekly newspaper, the *Leader,* which defended both the rights of labor and Irish nationalism. He sided with the Union Labor Party during the prosecution of corrupt city officials. He was also involved in many other social issues at a time when many did not understand the implications of *Rerum Novarum.* He tried to persuade the capitalists of his day that they had social responsibilities. He was also a strong advocate of temperance, founded the League of Cross to advance its cause, established a home for working girls, Innisfael, and worked tirelessly for victims of the 1906 San Francisco earthquake.

In addition, education was a major priority for Yorke. He became the vice president of the National Catholic Educational Association and he served as a regent of the University of California at Berkeley. He wrote eight books, including *The Roman Liturgy* (1903), *The Ghosts of Bigotry* (1913), and *The Mass* (1921).

Father Yorke is remembered most for his Irish nationalist activities. In 1902 he established the California branch of the Gaelic League and, in 1905, raised $20,000 for the Gaelic-language revival in Ireland. He was also, until his death in 1925, the main spokesperson for Irish Republicanism in California. However, the postponement of Irish Home Rule in September 1914 convinced Yorke that there was a need to raise money for the militant Irish Volunteers Fund. In March 1916, he helped organize the Friends of Irish Freedom (FOIF), a major support group for Irish revolutionaries, and he became the vice president for Sinn Fein in the United States. During the 1919 De Valera tour, the California FOIF raised $500,000 in Sinn Fein bonds.

Yorke lived his life as he believed it, contending that persecution, sectarianism, and oppression should be fought frontally and aggressively. He died on Palm Sunday, 5 April 1925. San Francisco United Irish Societies continue to hold a memorial service for Father Yorke every Palm Sunday.

Seamus P. Metress

REFERENCES

Brusher, Joseph C. *Consecrated Thunderbolt: A Life of Father Peter C. Yorke of San Francisco.* Hawthorne, NJ: J. F. Wagner, 1973.

Cronin, Bernard C. *Father Yorke and the Labor Movement in San Francisco, 1900–1910.* Washington, DC: Catholic University of America Press, 1944.

Herlihy, Dennis J. "Battle against Bigotry: Father Peter C. Yorke and the American Protective Association in San Francisco, 1893–1897." *Records of the American Catholic Historical Society of Philadelphia* 42 (1951): 95–120.

Sarbaugh, Timothy J. "Ireland of the West: The Development of Irish Republicanism in California, 1900–1916." *Pacific Historian* 28 (1985): 43–51.

Walsh, James P., and Timothy P. Foley. "Father Peter C. Yorke: Irish-American Leader." Studia Hibernica 14 (1974): 90–103.

Zapata, Carmen Margarita (1927–)

Actress, producer, and community activist
Mexican-Argentinean-American

Carmen Zapata achieved renown on stage and television and was long involved in promoting the employment of Latino performers. She also developed programs to bring Latino culture to children of all ages through bilingual shows.

Zapata was born in New York City on 15 July 1927. Her father, Julio, was a Mexican immigrant, and her mother, Ramona Roca, came from Argentina. Zapata grew up in New York's Spanish Harlem with three sisters. Though Spanish was the only language spoken at home, she was not, as a child, well informed about Mexican culture. Although disapproving of her desires for a show business career, her mother sacrificed much to give her dancing and music lessons. She also studied at the Actors Studio.

In 1946, Zapata made her Broadway debut with *Oklahoma*. She also appeared in *Stop the World, I Want to Get Off; Bells Are Ringing;* and *Guys and Dolls.* For twenty years, she performed in stage musicals and worked in night clubs, singing and doing comedy acts. In 1967, after the sudden closing of a show she was in and the end of her five-year marriage to comedy writer Roy Freedman, she moved to California. Though Zapata enjoyed visibility and high earnings, she was almost always stereotyped as either a maid or a mother.

Zapata's disappointment in the roles that many Hispanics were given provided the impetus to form the first minority committee of the Screen Actors' Guild. She was also one of the original members of the Hispanic actors' organization, Nosotros, begun by Ricardo Montablan. In 1970, she was cofounder of the Bilingual Foundation of the Arts (BFA) and, until her retirement in 1993, remained its president and managing producer. Since its inception, this Los Angeles–based performing arts organization has brought the Hispanic experience and culture to audiences through bilingual theater. For example, the Teen Theater Project (Teatro para los Jovenes), an innovative theater-in-education program, was designed to meet the needs of junior high and high school students identified as "at risk." The program presents performances with ethnically diverse professional actors, followed by audience discussions. It was modeled after BFA's successful program for elementary students. The endeavor has served almost 1 million children since its inception in 1985. Zapata received much acclaim from the community and critics for her organization's productions.

Zapata has appeared in numerous television programs, her favorite being her nine-year role as Doña Luz on PBS's *Villa Allegre.* She has received many awards—including three Emmy nominations, the Mexican-American Foundation Award, and recognition as 1985 Woman of the Year from the Hispanic Women's Council. Zapata is referred to as the First Lady of the Hispanic Theater.

In addition to acting, she has translated Spanish literature and plays into English and has been involved in community work, serving on the board of the Mexican-American Opportunity Foundation and as a member of the California Arts Council's Ethnic Advisory Minority Panel. Since 1993, she has been a commissioner of the Cultural Affairs Department of Los Angeles. In 1991 Zapata was knighted by the king of Spain, Juan Carlos I.

Kathleen Paparchontis

REFERENCES

Telgin, Diane, and Jim Kamp, eds. *Latinas! Women of Achievement.* Detroit: Visible Ink, 1996.

———. *Notable Hispanic American Women.* Detroit: Gale Research, 1993.

"Zapata, Carmen." *Notable Latino Americans: A Biographical Dictionary,* edited by Matt S. Meier with Conchita Franco Serri and Richard A. Garcia, 409–411. Westport, CT: Greenwood Press, 1997.

Žebris, Juozas (1860–1915)

*Priest-activist, parish organizer,
social worker, and writer*
Lithuanian

Juozas Žebris ranks as the premier luminary among all Lithuanian Roman Catholic clergy in the United States. He earned this distinction by being a parish builder, cooperative movement founder, and journalist.

Žebris's birth in the village of Palaukiai, Lithuania, occurred on 16 February 1860, the day that would later become his homeland's Independence Day, as restored in 1918. He attended the famed secondary school (equivalent to high school and junior college) at Šiauliai from 1874 to 1881, where he became friends with the future priest-activist, Aleksandras Burba. He then entered the Samogitian seminary at Kaunas, completing four years of training in three, while also being a member of a secret cell in the nascent nationalist movement. He became a priest in November 1884.

His only homeland assignment, from 1884 to 1893, was in the parish at Akmenė, near the Latvian border. There, he engaged in extensive landscaping of the church grounds; forged a bond with the pastor at nearby Laižuva, the priest-bard Antanas Vienožinskis; and, most significantly, promoted the distribution of Lithuanian literature despite a czarist ban. However, the pressure of surveillance by czarist officials and the urgent need for priests in the United States prompted Žebris to accept Burba's invitation to go to Pennsylvania in mid-1893.

During his travels to all known Lithuanian enclaves in Pennsylvania, he wrote numerous articles for the leading newspaper, *Vienybė Lietuvninkų* (Unity of Lithuanians). In his talks, he urged the formation of chapters of the Lithuanian Alliance of America and encouraged plans for separate Lithuanian parishes. A burgeoning colony in Connecticut needed a pastor, and in March 1894, Žebris was assigned to establish St. Joseph Parish in Waterbury. He quickly set up a bakery, farm, and weekly newspaper, *Rytas.* Though loosely called parish ventures, they were almost entirely solo undertakings. The bakery gave loaves to the poor at reduced rates or even gratis, and the farm provided jobs and housing. The newspaper became the priest's pulpit beyond his parish, and he wrote essays on temperance, hygiene, and agriculture and culled national and international news on religion and politics, including reports on Lithuanian enclaves. *Rytas* also became the voice of the Lithuanian cooperative movement founded by Žebris.

The priest traveled constantly to other Lithuanian settlements to hear confessions and promote mutual-benefit societies, and he was partly responsible for the founding of at least fifteen Lithuanian parishes in the Northeast. He also envisioned a high school, seminary, orphanage, and an academy of agriculture but found little support. At the national level, he held posts in the Lithuanian Alliance, although at a meeting in 1901 this network split into Catholic and nationalist branches; Žebris left the hall with the nationalist protesters. But his influence subsequently waned, and he soon sold his newspaper, gave up the bakery and farm, and concentrated on pastoral duties.

Ironically, his short-lived enterprises and pastoral visitations came back to haunt him, for most likely he had received generous donations. Although he lived a nearly ascetic life, he created the aura of opulence, and on 8 February 1915, Lithuanian thugs robbed and killed him. Žebris was quickly erased from public memory, yet he furnished an example of extraordinary zeal for both his faith and his ethnic heritage.

William Wolkovich-Valkavičius

REFERENCES

Wolkovich-Valkavičius, William. *Lithuanian Pioneer Priest of New England: The Life, Struggles and Tragic Death of Fr. Juozas Žebris.* Brooklyn, NY: Franciscan Press, 1980.

"Žebris, Juozas." In *Encyclopedia Lituanica,* edited by Simas Sužiedelis and Antanas Kučas, vol. 6: 303–304. Boston: Juozas Kapočius Publisher, 1975–1978.

"Žebris, Juozas." In *Lietuvių enciklopedija* (Encyclopedia Lituanica), edited by J. Girnius, vol. 35: 185–186. Boston: Lithuanian Encyclopedia Press, 1963.

Zenger, John Peter (1697–1746)
Printer and journalist
German

Although his name is associated with the notion of freedom of the press, John Peter Zenger was truly a self-made man. He made a brave decision to stand on his principles as a journalist and spent time in jail on a charge of libel.

After living thirteen years in his native Bavaria, Zenger immigrated to the British colony of New York, becoming an indentured servant in order to repay his debt. Fortunately, he was apprenticed to a prominent printer, William Bradford, and was able to satisfy his financial responsibilities and learn a trade. For eight years Zenger toiled under Bradford's tutelage. He was able to start his own publishing house in 1726. Although he struggled with the English language, Zenger was determined not to publish a German-language newspaper. Soon after the founding of Zenger's publishing house, the *New York Weekly Journal* made its debut. Critical articles about the activities of Governor William Cosby began appearing in 1734. Cosby was not a likable character, having become embroiled in controversial financial scandals and dubious prosecutions and harassment of a political opponent. The articles in question were, as was the custom, written anonymously, and Zenger, as publisher, accepted responsibility for the contents of his journal.

Zenger's principled stand landed him in jail on a charge of seditious libel against Governor Cosby. The immigrant publisher could not raise bail and had to languish in jail for nine months as he awaited his day in court. (His wife, Anna Zenger, continued to publish the newspaper while he remained in jail.) Zenger was defended by Andrew Hamilton, a well-respected attorney from Philadelphia. Hamilton, who was then speaker of the Pennsylvania Assembly, was—like Zenger—a self-made man, having come to Pennsylvania as an indentured servant.

Zenger's trial during fall 1735 was followed closely by New Yorkers. Hamilton's strategy was incendiary and risky. He readily admitted that Zenger was responsible for the offending articles in his newspapers! However, he asked that he be given the opportunity to prove that the articles were true. In other words, Hamilton wanted to make the case that libel that is true is not criminal. The judges denied that line of defense. Not dissuaded, Hamilton turned to the jury and asked them to acquit his client because he had been morally obligated to tell the truth as a member of the press. Zenger's duty was to print the truth. Newspaper articles should not be considered libelous unless they were false.

According to contemporary reports, the jury spent a mere ten minutes debating Zenger's fate. To the dismay of the judges and the irate governor, a verdict of not guilty was announced. Amid great rejoicing by the masses and members of the press, Zenger returned home. He would continue to work as a journalist for the remaining eleven years of his life.

The Zenger case set a precedent for freedom of the press and speech and ultimately provided a basis for the First Amendment of the Bill of Rights. In addition, it is considered to be one of the most important events in the history of American journalism.

Susanne M. Schick

REFERENCES

Buranelli, Vincent. *The Trial of Peter Zenger.* New York: New York University Press, 1957.

Covert, Cathy. "'Passion Is Ye Prevailing Motive': The Feud behind the Zenger Case." *Journalism Quarterly* 50 (Spring 1973): 3–10.

Eldridge, Larry. "Before Zenger: Truth and Seditious Speech in Colonial America, 1607–1700." *American Journal of Legal History* 39 (1995): 337–358.

Finkelman, Paul, ed. *A Brief Narrative of the Case and Tryal of John Peter Zenger: Printer of the New York Weekly Journal.* St. James, NY: Brandywine Press, 1997.

Huxford, Gary. "The English Libertarian Tradition in the Colonial Newspaper." *Journalism Quarterly* 45 (1968): 677–686.

Robbins, Peggy. "The Trial of John Peter Zenger." *American History Illustrated* 11 (1976): 8–17.

Smith, Jeffrey. *Printers and Press Freedom: The Ideology of Early American Journalism.* New York: Oxford University Press. 1988.

Zworykin, Vladimir K. (1889–1982)
Co-inventor of television; Russian

Vladimir Kosma Zworykin applied for a patent for television in 1923 and continued to direct the development of that technology until television became a commercial success. His many awards attest to the impact he had on this technology.

Zworykin was born in Murom, Russia, which is on the Oka River, where his father operated river boats. The young man was more interested in the electrical equipment on the boats than in the boats themselves. He enrolled in the Imperial Institute of Technology in St. Petersburg, where he worked under Boris Rosing, who was trying to develop a method of sending pictures by wire using a cathode-ray tube as a receiver.

In 1912 Zworykin went to Paris to work with Paul Langevin, who was studying X-rays. When World War I started, Zworykin returned to Russia to work on radio communications for the military. Leaving the turmoil caused by the end of the war and the Bolshevik Revolution, he came to the United States in 1919 and joined the research staff at Westinghouse. While there he registered a number of patents for television cameras—among them the iconoscope—and for television receivers, including his kinescope.

In 1929 Westinghouse was reluctant to fund further research on the development of the primitive television, so Zworykin accepted an invitation from David Sarnoff to set up a television research laboratory for RCA. At that time the technology for making television commercially viable was rapidly being developed. Although not all the inventions were Zworykin's, RCA did hold the patent on the orthicon camera tube that replaced Zworykin's iconoscope and became the standard. Other innovations were adapted from a system patented by Philo Farnsworth, who worked in his own laboratory in California.

If there was any intrigue connected to the development of television technology, it centers on Zworykin's competition with Farnsworth. When Zworykin was hired by RCA, Sarnoff instructed him to visit Farnsworth's Laboratory as an "interested researcher." Zworykin saw that Farnsworth's system produced better pictures than his own did. The RCA laboratory then incorporated parts of Farnsworth's technology but was required to pay technology license fees to Farnsworth. It was Zworykin's RCA laboratory that developed commercially successful television systems. Commercial television, however, was not used in a manner that pleased Zworykin. In his later years, he felt that U.S. television, with programming to satisfy popular interests, led the industry to produce poor programs, which produced a negative image of the United States abroad.

By the mid-1950s, when television was already commercially successful, Zworykin shifted his research interest to other fields, especially medical technology. He founded and was the first president of the International Federation of Medical Electronics. Zworykin received many honors in later life, including the Faraday Medal from Great Britain in 1965; the U.S. Presidential Medal of Science in 1966; and the National Medal of Science, awarded by the National Academy of Sciences in 1967. In 1977 he was elected to the U.S. National Hall of Fame. He died in 1982.

Keith P. Dyrud

REFERENCES

Abramson, Albert. *Zworykin, Pioneer of Television.* Urbana: University of Illinois Press, 1995.

———. *The History of Television, 1880 to 1941.* Jefferson, NC: McFarland & Co., 1987.

Fisher, David E., and Marshal Jon Fisher. *Tube: The Invention of Television.* Washington, DC: Counterpoint, 1996.

Heyer, Mark, and Al Pinsky. "Interview with Vladimir Zworykin," 4 July 1975: www.ieee.org/organizations/history_center/ oral_histories/transcripts/zworykin21.html (accessed 21 June 2000).

ACRONYMS

AATC	Asian American Theatre Company	APA	American Protective Association
AATW	Asian American Theatre Workshop	BALF	United Lithuanian Relief Fund
AAVC	Asian American Voters Coalition	BBC	British Broadcasting Corporation
ABC	American Broadcasting Companies	BFA	Bilingual Foundation of the Arts
ACA	Association Canado-Américaine	BIA	Bureau of Indian Affairs
ACCESS	Arab Community Center for Economic and Social Services	CALC	Chaldean American Ladies of Charity
ACLU	American Civil Liberties Union	CARE	Cooperative for American Relief to Everywhere
ADOBE	Artists and Designers Opening the Border Edge	CARECEN	Central American Resource Center
AFL	American Federation of Labor	CBS	Columbia Broadcasting System
AFL-CIO	American Federation of Labor and Congress of Industrial Organizations	CCC	Civilian Conservation Corps
		CCNY	City College of New York
		CEO	chief executive officer
AFN	Alaska Federation of Natives	CFU	Croatian Fraternal Union
AGBU	Armenian General Benevolent Union	CIA	Central Intelligence Agency
		CIO	Congress of Industrial Organizations
AHEPA	American Hellenic Educational Progressive Association	CMIU	Cigar Makers' International Union
AHI	American Hellenic Institute	CNN	Cable News Network
AHIF	American Hellenic Institute Foundation	COO	chief operating officer
		COPRODH	Committee for Development in Honduras
AHIPAC	American Hellenic Institute Public Affairs Committee	COTA	Committee of the Arts
AIFPE	American Indian Forum for Political Education	CRECE	Committee of Central American Refugees
AIM	American Indian Movement	CSO	Community Service Organization
AIPRC	American Indian Policy Review Commission	CSYP	Chung Sai Yat Bo
		CUNY	City University of New York
AIWA-NJ/NY	Armenian International Women's Association of New Jersey/New York	CUSPEA	China–United States Physics Examination and Application
		DEA	Drug Enforcement Agency
AJC	American Jewish Committee	DP	displaced person
ALT	American Lithuanian Council	DPPA	Demonstration Project for Asian Americans
ANB	Alaskan Native Brotherhood		
ANCSA	Alaska Native Claims Settlement Act	DRUMS	Determination of Rights and Unity for Menominee Shareholders
AP	Associated Press		

EEOC	Equal Employment Opportunity Commission	MAC	Municipal Assistance Corporation
EMA	Eritrean Medical Association	MAYO	Mexican American Youth Organization
EMPAC	Ethnic Millions Political Action Committee	MGM	Metro-Goldwyn-Mayer
ESL	English as a second language	MIT	Massachusetts Institute of Techonology
ESOL	English speakers of other languages	MPI	El Movemiento Por Independencia
FANHS	Filipino American National Historical Society	MUGAMA	Mujeres Garinagu en Marcha
		MVP	Most Valuable Player
FBI	Federal Bureau of Investigation	NAACP	National Association for the Advancement of Colored People
FGM	female genital mutilation	NACARA	Nicaragua Adjustment and Central American Act
FHM	Free Hungary Movement		
FLOC	Farm Labor Organizing Committee	NACW	National Association of Colored Women
FOIF	Friends of Irish Freedom	NAHA	Norwegian American Historical Association
FTC	Federal Trade Commission		
FYA	Filipino Youth Activities	NALEO	National Association of Latino Elected and Appointed Officials
GED	General equivalency degree		
GM	General Motors	NASA	National Aeronautics and Space Administration
HNC	Hungarian National Council		
HPA	Hungarian Peasant Association	NATO	North Atlantic Treaty Organization
HUAC	House Un-American Activities Committee		
		NBC	National Broadcasting Company
ICC	Islamic Cultural Center	NCAI	National Congress of American Indians
IGWU	International Glove Workers Union		
		NCAR	National Center for Atmospheric Research
ILGWU	International Ladies' Garment Workers' Union		
		NCJW	National Council of Jewish Women
INS	Immigration and Naturalization Service		
		NCS	National Croatian Society
INTERPOL	International Criminal Police Organization	NDAC	National Defense Advisory Council
IRA	Irish Republican Army	NFL	National Football League
IRB	Irish Republican Brotherhood	NGO	nongovernmental organization
IRCA	Immigration Reform and Control Act	NOI	Nation of Islam
		NWTUL	National Women's Trade Union League
IRT	Interborough Rapid Transit		
IWO	International Workers' Order	*NYT*	*New York Times*
IWW	Industrial Workers of the World	NYU	New York University
KKK	Ku Klux Klan	OAAU	Organization of Afro-American Unity
KSKJ	Grand Carnolian Slovenian Catholic Union		
		OPM	Office of Production Management
LACOSH	Los Angeles Committee of Occupational Safety and Health	OSA	Salvadoran American Organization
LAPD	Los Angeles Poverty Department	OSHA	Occupational Safety and Health Administration
LCLAA	Labor Council for Latin American Advancement		
		OSS	Office of Strategic Services
LHJ	*Ladies' Home Journal*	PA	Palestine Authority
LRUP	La Raza Unida Party	PAC	Political action committee
LULAC	League of United Latin American Citizens	PBS	Public Broadcasting Service
		PC	personal computer

PLO	Palestinian Liberation Organization	UCSF	University of California, San Francisco
PRACA	Puerto Rican Association for Community Affairs	UFW	United Farm Workers
		UMWA	United Mine Workers of America
PSEKA	International Coordinating Committee of Justice for Cyprus	UN	United Nations
		UNESCO	United Nations Economic, Scientific, and Cultural Organization
RCA	Radio Corporation of America		
ROCOR	Russian Orthodox Church Outside of Russia	UNIA	Universal Negro Improvement Association
ROTC	Reserve Officers' Training Corps		
SALEF	Salvadoran American Leadership and Education Fund	UNICEF	United Nations International Children's Emergency Fund
SCLC	Southern Christian Leadership Conference	UNITE	Union of Needle Trade Industrial and Textile Employees
SCOBA	Standing Conference of Canonical Orthodox Bishops in America	USC	University of Southern California
		USO	United Service Organization
SANAD	Social Services Assisting Neighborhood Arab-American Development	VIP	Very Important Pinoy/Pinay
		VTOL	vertical take-off/landing
		WAHL	Women's Association of Hmong and Lao
SNCC	Student Nonviolent Coordinating Committee	WCTU	Woman's Christian Temperance Union
SWU	Slovenian Women's Union		
TIE	The Indus Entrepreneurs	WORK	Women's Organization Reaching Koreans
TWU	Transport Workers Union		
UA	United Artists	WPA	Works Progress Administration
UAF	United Armenian Fund	WTPA	Woman's Temperance Publishing Association
UAW	United Auto Workers		
UC	University of California	WTUL	Women's Trade Union League
UCAPAWA	United Cannery, Agricultural, Packing, and Allied Workers of America	YMCA	Young Men's Christian Association
UCLA	University of California, Los Angeles	YWCA	Young Women's Christian Association

EDITOR AND CONTRIBUTORS

Elliott Robert Barkan edited this volume and wrote the Introduction. He is a professor of history and ethnic studies at California State University, San Bernardino. His principal fields of teaching and research are immigration, race relations, and the multidisciplinary, multiethnic, comparative approaches to these subjects. His latest books are *U.S. Immigration and Naturalization Laws and Issues: A Documentary History* (coedited, 1999); *A Nation of Peoples: A Sourcebook on America's Multicultural Heritage* (edited, 1999); and *And Still They Come: Immigrants and American Society, 1920 to the 1990s* (1996). Recently elected vice president and president-elect of the Immigration and Ethnic History Society, he is now completing a study of immigrants and the American West in the twentieth century.

June G. Alexander, who wrote the entries on Slovaks, is an adjunct assistant professor (Russian and East European studies) in the History Department of the University of Cincinnati. An authority on American Slovaks, she is completing a monograph on ethnicity and American culture between the world wars.

Uva de Aragón wrote the Cubans' biographies. Born in Cuba and living in the United States since 1959, she is assistant director of the Cuban Research Institute at Florida International University and associate editor of the academic journal *Cuban Studies*. She has published nine books of poetry, short stories, and essays and has received several literary awards. She also contributes a weekly Op-Ed column to *Diario Los América*.

Barbara Aswad, who did one of the Arab entries, is a professor in the Department of Anthropology at Wayne State University, Detroit, Michigan. She has conducted research in Arab villages and in Arab-American communities, with her three books reflecting that research and family and gender among American Muslims. She is past president of the Middle East Studies Association.

H. Arnold Barton did the Swedish biographies. He is a professor emeritus of history, Southern Illinois University at Carbondale. He has written several works on Swedish migration in the nineteenth and early twentieth centuries and relations between Swedes in Sweden and in the United States. He was editor of the *Swedish-American Historical Journal* from 1974 to 1990.

James M. Bergquist wrote several of the German entries. A professor of history at Villanova University, Villanova, Pennsylvania, he has been there since 1963. His books and articles focus on German Americans, in particular nativism, German-American political history, and the German-American press. He edits the newsletter of the Immigration and Ethnic History Society.

Stanislaus A. Blejwas, who wrote the biographies on Poles, is a CSU University professor of history at Central Connecticut State University, New Britain, and holds the endowed chair of Polish and Polish-American studies. He has published numerous articles and books in Poland and in the United States on Polish and Polish-American issues and is currently working on a study of relations between Communist Poland and Polish Americans, 1945–1989.

Hoan N. Bui, who wrote most of the Vietnamese entries, is a doctoral candidate at the School of Criminal Justice, Michigan State University. Her research interests include race and ethnicity, class, gender and crime, domestic violence, and immigrants in the criminal justice system. She has done research on spousal abuse among Vietnamese-Americans and in Mexican-descent families as well as domestic violence victims' experiences with the criminal justice system.

J. M. Bumsted wrote several of the entries on Anglo-Canadians. He has been a professor in the Institute for the Humanities, University of Manitoba, in Winnipeg, since 1980. He has written, edited, and coedited numerous books and journal articles on early America as well as the peopling of Canada. His two-volume study of the Canadian peoples since the 1860s reflects his expertise in this area.

D. Douglas Caulkins and Lorna W. Caulkins contributed half of the Welsh biographies. Douglas Caulkins is a professor of anthropology at Grinnell College, Grinnell, Iowa, and has written extensively on Welsh and Welsh-American identity as well as on voluntary associations in Norway and economic development in peripheral regions of the United Kingdom. Lorena Caulkins is director of the Stewart Public Library in Grinnell, a member of the Iowa Welsh Society, and a collaborator with her husband on many anthropological projects.

Armand Chartier wrote several of the French Canadian entries. He is a professor emeritus of French in the Department of Languages, University of Rhode Island, in Kingston, where he taught 1971–2000. His specialties are Quebec and Franco-American studies and he recently published a history of Franco-Americans in New England.

Stavros T. Constantinou contributed the Cypriot biographies. He is an associate professor of geography at Ohio State University, in Mansfield. His research interests focus on migration and ethnicity, particularly the model-

ing of ethnicity and its application to Greek Americans in Ohio and the dynamics of international migration and their validity with respect to Greece and Cyprus. His has written numerous articles on Greeks and Cypriots.

John F. Crossen wrote entries on persons involved in the movie industry. He is an assistant professor of Spanish at Mansfield University of Pennsylvania. His research interests include colonial Spanish-American writers and eighteenth-century exiled Jesuit writers from Latin America, and he has published essays on these topics. He also has a strong interest in the history of the horror film and is associate editor of the *Journal of Dracula.*

Arlene Dallalfar writes on the Middle East and contributed entries on Iranians. Born in Iran, she is an assistant professor in the Sociology Department of Lesley College, Cambridge, Massachusetts. She is completing a study of Iranian immigrants, particularly gender and family dynamics among them.

Linda Delgado, who specializes in Puerto Rican subjects, wrote the pieces on Puerto Ricans. She was the director of the Latino/a Student Cultural Center at Northeastern University, in Boston, Massachusetts 1996–2000. She is now completing her dissertation, a study of Jesús Colón. For many years, prior to her current position, she was involved with the Office of Educational Opportunity at the State University of New York, New Paltz, where she also taught as an adjunct lecturer.

Barlow Der Mugrdechian contributed half of the Armenian entries. He has been a lecturer in the Armenian Studies Program at California State University, Fresno, for more than fifteen years, having graduated from UCLA's program in Armenian language and literature. He publishes articles on various topics concerning Armenia and Armenians.

Pamela A. DeVoe contributed the most diverse set of biographies—on a Sudanese, a Thai, a Vietnamese, and a Bosnian. A graduate of the University of Arizona, she has been researching and publishing studies of refugees and immigrants in the Midwest for more than two decades, focusing on economic, educa-

tional, health, acculturation, and religious issues. She is a research specialist at St. Louis
Community College, in Meramec, Missouri.

William A. Duna, himself a Romani,
wrote the Roma biography. He has been
teaching in the Department of Music at the
University of St. Thomas, in St. Paul, Minnesota, for a dozen years. In 1987, he was the
first Romani person appointed to the United
States Holocaust Council by President
Ronald Reagan, and he has served on it for
more than twelve years.

Keith P. Dyrud wrote the Russian entries. He received his Ph.D. from the University of Minnesota and taught at Concordia
College, in St. Paul. He writes on Russians
and East Slavs in Europe and the United
States. A recent book of his was on the politics of religion and culture in Eastern Europe
and the United States in the late nineteenth
and early twentieth centuries. He is currently
researching legal issues in the U.S. Russian
Orthodox church following the Russian
Revolution.

Jeronima Echeverria, who is the daughter of Basque immigrants, wrote the Basque
biographies. A professor of history, she is also
the associate provost at California State University, Fresno. She has recently published several major studies of Basques in the United
States, particularly two on Basque boarding-
houses and one, coedited with Richard Etulain, on Basques in the New World. In addition, she is editor of the *Journal of the Society for
Basque Studies.*

Lisa E. Emmerich, who wrote most of
the Native Americans' biographies, is a professor of history and coordinator of the American Indian Studies Program at California State
University, Chico. She has written extensively
on American Indian women and assimilation
programs in the nineteenth and twentieth
centuries. Her current projects include Indian
gaming in California and the field-matron
program.

Judith Fai-Podlipnik wrote the biographies on Hungarians. She is an assistant professor of modern European history, with spe-

cialization in Eastern Europe, in particular
Hungary, at Southeastern Louisiana University, in Hammond. She has presented papers at
conferences as well as published numerous articles and essays on Hungarian immigration
and migration during the post–World War II
era for encyclopedias, journals, and books.

Esther Fuchs contributed entries on several Jewish women. She is a professor in Judaic
Studies at the University of Arizona, Tucson.
Her particular interest centers on Judaism and
feminist issues. She is the author of works on
Israeli authors, women in contemporary Hebrew fiction, women and the Holocaust, and,
forthcoming, *Sexual Politics: Reading the Hebrew Bible like a Woman.* She recently joined
the editorial board of *Shofar: An Interdisci-
plinary Journal of Jewish Studies.*

Alma M. Garcia wrote several of the entries on Mexicans. She is a professor of sociology, Santa Clara University, Santa Clara, California. She has served on the editorial board
of several journals, including *Gender and Society* and *Race, Gender and Class.* She has published an anthology of Chicana feminist writings and is currently writing a book on
Mexican-American women in higher education and one on Mexican immigration.

Steven J. Gold wrote the Israeli biographies. He is a professor and associate chair of
sociology at Michigan State University, in East
Lansing. His extensive publications (and
photo essays) have concentrated on Soviet
Jews and Israelis in the United States as well as
on qualitative research methods with respect
to immigration, ethnic economies, and ethnic
community development. He is currently
working on a study of the Israeli diaspora.

April Gordon, who contributed most of
the Africans' entries, teaches in the department of sociology, Winthrop University, in
Rock Hill, South Carolina, and is coordinator
of its Women's Studies Program. She has published two books on Africa, *Understanding
Contemporary Africa* and *Transforming Capitalism and Patriarchy,* and numerous articles on
development issues in Africa and on African
immigration to the United States.

Cheryl Greenberg wrote several of the African American biographies. She is a professor in the Department of History, Trinity College, Hartford, Connecticut, teaching African American and twentieth-century history. Her books focus on Harlem in the Great Depression and the Student Nonviolent Coordinating Committee during the 1960s. She is currently completing a history of political relations between African Americans and Jewish Americans.

Roland L. Guyotte contributed several of the pieces on Filipinos. He is a professor of history and vice-chair of the Division of the Social Sciences at the University of Minnesota, Morris. A recipient of the all-university Horace T. Morse Award for Contributions to Undergraduate Education, he has written about twentieth-century U.S. history, especially the history of immigration and the history of higher education.

Arthur W. Helweg wrote the biographies on Asian Indians. He is a professor of sociology at Western Michigan University, in Kalamazoo. He has written, coauthored, or edited six books and more than 100 articles. His book *An Immigrant Success Story* won the Theodore Saloutos Award of the Immigration History Society for the best book written on immigration in 1990.

Leticia Hernández-Linares wrote the biographies on various Central Americans. A U.S.-born Salvadoran and currently a Ph.D. student at the University of Pennsylvania, Philadelphia, she now lives in San Francisco and teaches art and creative writing to youth. Her dissertation will be on the relationship between violence and identity in Latina/o narratives. Her poetry appears in *Frontiers, Puerto Del Sol,* and *Izote Vos: A Collection of Salvadoran American Writing and Visual Art.*

Peter C. Holloran contributed to the Irish pieces. He is an assistant professor of history at Worcester State College, in Massachusetts, and is executive secretary of the Northeast Popular Culture/American Culture Association.

Rhys James, who provided one of the West Indian biographies, is of Haitian descent and is a graduate student in sociology at the University of Massachusetts, Amherst. Her M.A. degree is in multicultural education and her areas of interest are race, equality, the Caribbean, crime, and law. She has visited several parts of the Caribbean and has lived in Puerto Rico, Costa Rica, and Mexico.

Bill Jones wrote half of the Welsh pieces. He has been lecturer in modern Welsh history at the School of History and Archaeology, Cardiff University, Wales, since 1994. Previously, he was assistant keeper at the National Museum of Wales. He wrote a study of the Welsh and Welsh press in Scranton, Pennsylvania, and various articles on Welsh emigration and Welsh communities. He is presently coauthoring the official history of the Welsh-American newspaper *Y Drych* [The Mirror].

David E. Kaufman provided an entry on Jews. He is an assistant professor in contemporary Jewish studies at Hebrew Union College–Jewish Institute of Religion, in Los Angeles. His published works have focused on the social and architectural history of the American synagogue.

Peter Kivisto wrote the entries on Finns. He is professor and chair of sociology at Augustana College, Rock Island, Illinois. His books include studies of immigrant socialists, immigrants and their children, and a sociological-historical analysis of the American ethnic experience. He is presently working on the role of ethnic festivals in the Finnish-American community.

Matjaž Klemenčič provided nearly all the biographies of people from the former Yugoslavia—Bosnian, Slovene, Croatian, Serbian, and Macedonian. He is a professor and chair of history at the University of Maribor, in Maribor, Slovenia, and the University of Ljubljana. He teaches courses on world history, Slovenes, and Yugoslav history and has published numerous articles on the history of Slovene and Yugoslav immigration to the United States and on the disintegration of Yugoslavia.

George A. Kourvetaris wrote the Greek biographies. Educated in both Greece and the

United States, he is currently a professor of sociology at Northern Illinois University. His major interests include political sociology, intergroup relations, and social theory. He has published alone and with others twelve books and seventy articles in various professional journals. His books include *Studies on Modern Greek Society and Politics* (1999) and *Studies on Greek Americans* (1997).

Clarence Lang, a graduate student in the Department of History, University of Illinois, Urbana, wrote one of the African American biographies. He has published several articles on Louis Farrakhan, black political ideologies, and black youth as well as entries in the recent *Encyclopedia of African American Business History.*

Marietta LeBreton, who teaches history in the Social Sciences Department of Northwestern State University of Louisiana, in Natchitoches, wrote the Acadian biography. Her research interest is Louisiana history, and she has written several other pieces on Acadians and Louisiana history.

Gillian Leitch contributed half of the Anglo-Canadian biographies. She is a graduate student in the Département d'Histoire, Université de Montréal, Quebec. The focus of her dissertation and research interests is the British population in the nineteenth century in Montreal and the nature of their ethnicity in relation to their social organization.

Jennifer Leo, who wrote the Dutch biographies, has an M.A. in communications and is the marketing manager for a book publisher in Illinois. She recently coauthored a history of Hanover Township in Illinois.

Karen Leonard wrote the Pakistani biographies. She is a historian and anthropologist working on South Asia and Asian America, teaching at the University of California, Irvine. She has published three major books: on an Indian caste (1978), on California's unique Punjabi Mexican Americans (1992), and a survey of South Asian Americans (1997), as well as numerous articles. She looks at issues of migration and identity, focusing on class, caste, gender, language, and generational changes.

Nancy C. Lespérance contributed the Haitian biographies. Haitian-American herself, she has recently completed her master's in international and intercultural development education at Florida International University, Miami. She currently resides in Washington, D.C., and is pursuing a career in international education.

Bernard Maegi, who provided the Estonian biography, is the son of an Estonian father and German mother. He is completing his dissertation on U.S. immigration and labor history in the Department of History, University of Minnesota, Minneapolis.

Paul Robert Magocsi wrote the Carpatho-Rusyn piece. He is chair of Ukrainian studies at the University of Toronto, in Ontario. Among his many published works, he was the principal editor of the mammoth *Encyclopedia of Canada's Peoples.*

Maxine L. Margolis wrote the Brazilian biography. She is a professor of anthropology at the University of Florida, Gainesville. She is author or coeditor of six books, most recently, *An Invisible Minority: Brazilian Immigrants in New York City* (1998).

Daria Markus wrote the Ukrainian biographies. Born in Ukraine and an immigrant to Canada, Markus earned a Ph.D. in history and philosophy of education, Loyola University, Chicago. She has published several articles on Ukrainians in the United States and Europe, edited a volume on Ukrainians in Illinois, and is currently the associate editor of the American volume of the *Encyclopedia of Ukrainian Diaspora.* Her special interest is multiculturalism in a democratic society.

David C. Mauk, who wrote the Norwegian biographies, is a professor in the English Institute of the Norwegian University of Science and Technology, in Trondheim. He recently published a book on the Norwegian community in Brooklyn, New York, *The Colony That Rose from the Sea,* supervised a multiyear project preparing a history of Norwegians in the Twin Cities, Minneapolis–St. Paul, and has edited several volumes of essays ·for the Norwegian-American Historical Association in Norway.

Seamus P. Metress wrote most of the Irish biographies. He has been a professor of anthropology and Irish studies at the University of Toledo, Ohio, since 1969, where he has received a number of teaching awards. For more than two decades he has been publishing works on the Irish in Ireland and in North America, most recently *The Irish in North America* (1999). His current project is on the American Irish, "From the Frontier to the White House."

Suzanne Model contributed most of British West Indian biographies. She is a professor of sociology, University of Massachusetts, Amherst. Of Haitian descent, her academic interests include issues of race, equality, the Caribbean (particularly Haiti and the Dominican Republic), crime, law, and, most recently, cross-national comparisons of the socioeconomic attainment of immigrants in North America and Europe. The group she has studied in greatest depth is black Caribbeans.

Deirdre M. Moloney provided a variety of biographies on persons from the Middle East. She is an assistant professor of history at St. Francis College, in Loretto, Pennsylvania. She has published journal articles and is now revising for publication her dissertation on lay groups in the American Roman Catholic Church, 1880–1925. Her articles have dealt with the Catholic temperance movement and with Irish women immigrants in Boston.

Nizar A. Motani wrote the biography of the Pakistani-Burmese. Born in Kampala, Uganda, Motani received his Ph.D. from the School of Oriental and African Studies, University of London. Following eight years teaching at Bowdoin College and Western Michigan University, he worked for two years at the Institute of Ismaili Studies in London. For the past two decades he has been working as a consultant in Atlanta, Georgia. He recently authored an essay on Ismailis.

Michael L. Murray wrote one of the Irish biographies. He teaches in the Center for Folklore and Ethnography, University of Pennsylvania, in Philadelphia.

George R. Nielsen wrote the biography of the Wend (Sorb). He is a professor emeritus of history at Concordia University, River Forest, Illinois. His publications are principally on ethnic history, including a volume on Danish Americans and his work on Wends.

Brian Niiya provided the biographies of the Japanese and Japanese Americans. He is a writer, editor, and curator who specializes in Japanese-American history and culture and is a columnist for the *Pacific Citizen, Rafu Shimpo,* and *Nikkei West.* He just edited the revised edition of *Japanese American History, an A-Z Reference, 1868 to the Present,* and the companion volume to the Los Angeles exhibition *More Than a Game: Sport in the Japanese American Community* (2000).

Edward T. O'Donnell contributed to the Irish biographies. Having received his Ph.D. in 1995 from Columbia University, he is presently an associate professor of history at Hunter College, City University of New York. He has three books forthcoming: a history of the United States (coauthored), a social biography of Henry George in New York City, and *1001 Things Everyone Should Know about Irish American History.*

Kathleen Paparchontis wrote the biographies on South Americans. She is currently working on her master's thesis in public history at California State University, Sacramento. She is a freelance indexer and editor for scholarly texts.

Dennis R. Papazian, who contributed half of the Armenian entries, directs the Armenian Research Center at the University of Michigan–Dearborn and is a professor of history there. He is also president of the Society for Armenian Studies, editor of the *Journal of the Society for Armenian Studies,* and one of the founders of the Armenian Assembly of America, a public interest group, based in Washington, D.C.

G. James Patterson wrote the Romanian biographies. He is a professor emeritus of anthropology at Eastern Oregon University, Corvallis. Two of his three Fulbright fellowships were to Romania. He is the author of three books and the entry on Romanians in the new *Encyclopedia of Canada's Peoples.*

Robert B. Perreault wrote several of the French Canadian entries. He has done oral histories in Manchester, New Hampshire, been the librarian-archivist for the Association Canado-Américaine, and written more than 140 articles and several books, fiction and nonfiction. Since 1988 he has taught French in the Native Speakers' Program at St. Anselm College, Manchester, New Hampshire.

Peter L. Petersen, who contributed the Danish biographies, is the regents professor emeritus of history at West Texas A&M University, in Canyon, having retired after thirty-three years as a member of the History Department. He has published extensively on the history of Danish and Norwegian immigrants in North America. He currently serves on the board of directors of the Danish American Heritage Society and as book review editor for that organization's journal, *The Bridge.*

Elizabeth Plantz wrote many of the entries on the Middle Easterners. She is the Africana cataloger in the Northwestern University Library, Evanston, Illinois. She holds an M.A. in library science and a second in Middle Eastern studies, both from the University of Chicago. She worked for two years with the Kuwait University Library Task Force and is strongly interested in projects promoting diversity, tolerance, and an understanding of Islam in America.

Barbara M. Posadas wrote half of the Filipino biographies. The daughter of a Filipino father and a Polish-American mother, and born and raised in Chicago, she is a professor of history at Northern Illinois University, in De Kalb, and president of the Illinois State Historical Society. She recently published *The Filipino Americans* (1999).

André J. M. Prévos provided biographies on French and Franco-Americans. He is an associate professor of French and Spanish on the Worthington Scranton campus of Pennsylvania State University, in Dunmore. His doctorate from the University of Paris was in the study of North American civilization. His publications have been on the French in the United States, French culture in America, and aspects of American culture in France.

Claire Quintal, who wrote several of the French Canadian entries, is a professor emerita of French and Francophone culture and civilization and director emerita of the Institut Français, Assumption College, Worcester, Massachusetts. Under her direction the institute has published fourteen books, two of them by her and, most recently, her revision and translation of Armand Chartier's history of New England Franco-Americans.

Vicki L. Ruiz wrote one of the Central American biographies. She is a professor of history and chair of the Department of the Chicana/Chicano Studies, Arizona State University, Tempe. Her recent book, *From out of the Shadows,* was named a *Choice* Outstanding Academic Book of 1998. Ruiz and Ellen Carol DuBois recently published the third edition of *Unequal Sisters* (1999) and she and Virginia Sánchez Korrol will be coediting *Latinas in the United States: A Historical Encyclopedia.*

Ernesto Sagás contributed several of the Dominican biographies. He is a professor in the Department of Puerto Rican and Hispanic Caribbean Studies, at Rutgers University, in New Brunswick, New Jersey. He has published articles on Haitian-Dominican relations, Dominican migration, and elections in the Dominican Republic. In addition to his book on Dominican politics, he is now coediting a volume on Dominican transnational migration.

Mitsugu (Michael) Sakihara wrote the Okinawan biography. Born in Okinawa, he was, for twenty-five years, a professor of Okinawan history at the University of Hawaii, Manoa, where he had earned his doctorate. Since July 1995 he has been president of Hawaii International College, Honolulu.

Zdenek Salzmann provided the biographies on the Czechs. Born and raised in Prague, Czechoslovakia, he immigrated to the United States in 1947 and became a professor of anthropology at the University of Massachusetts, Amherst, specializing in linguistic anthropology, Native Americans, and Czech language and culture. In addition to being a visiting professor at various universities, he is currently an adjunct professor at Northern Arizona University, Flagstaff.

Paul Sando wrote the Latvian biographies. He is an assistant professor of geography at West Texas A&M University, Canyon, with interests in Eastern Europe and the Baltic states. His dissertation was on Latvian agriculture after communism. Born in Latvia, he retains close ties with family and colleagues in Latvia.

Roman Sawycky, Jr., who wrote one of the Ukrainian biographies, is a media specialist, musicologist, and music editor, working for the *Encyclopedia of Ukrainian Diaspora.* His "Ukrainian Film Guide" lists contributions to international film and television by actors, directors, and technicians of Ukrainian descent.

Kenneth Scambray contributed an Italian biography. He is a professor of English at the University of La Verne, in La Verne, California, where he teaches film and literature and a course on North American Italian literature. He has published several books on that topic and has been book critic for two decades for *L'Italo-Americano,* a West Coast newspaper established in 1908.

Leo Schelbert wrote the Austrian and Swiss entries. He has been a professor of history at the University of Illinois, Chicago, since 1971, specializing in immigration to the British mainland colonies, especially of German-speaking peoples. Besides many articles, his books include one on Switzerland and the United States and eighteenth- and nineteenth-century Swiss-immigrant accounts in America. He is past president of the Swiss American Historical Society and editor of its *Review.*

Susanne M. Schick wrote two-thirds of the German biographies. She is an assistant professor of history at Messiah College, in Grantham, Pennsylvania. She received her Ph.D. in 1993 from the University of Illinois at Urbana-Champaign and is currently revising her dissertation for publication: "'For God, Mac, and Country': The Political Worlds of Midwestern German Democrats during the Civil War Era."

Mary Cay Sengstock contributed the two entries on Chaldeans. She is a professor of sociology at Wayne State University, in Detroit, Michigan, with a Ph.D. from Washington University. Her specialties are U.S. ethnic groups, family violence, and gerontology. She has written journal articles on a variety of topics, notably the use of sociology in applied settings, and the second edition of her book on Chaldeans in Detroit was recently published.

John M. Shaw, a graduate student in the History Department of the University of Arizona, Tucson, wrote some of the pieces on Native Americans. His primary field is American Indian history and U.S. history. He received an M.A. in American Indian studies from the University of Arizona in 1997.

Jeffrey P. Shepherd, a graduate student in the Department of History, Arizona State University, Tempe, wrote some of the biographies of Native Americans. His focus is on race, political activism, labor, and class in the South and West as well as indigenous issues in modern Latin America. His research focuses on American Indian history since the mid–nineteenth century.

David W. Shideler is responsible for the Hawaiian biographies. He has lectured on Hawaiian history and religion at the University of Hawaii, in Honolulu, and has worked as an archaeologist in Hawaii for twenty years.

Kristine Smets wrote the Belgian entries. She is the monograph copy cataloging coordinator for the Milton S. Eisenhower Library, Johns Hopkins University, Baltimore, Maryland. She studied history at the Catholic University of Louvain and Kent State University (M.A., 1994). Her master's thesis focused on the *Gazette van Moline* and its role in the Belgian-American community between 1907 and 1921. She also earned a master's of library science at Kent State University.

Gerald Sorin wrote half of the entries on Jews. Since 1983 he has been Distinguished Teaching Professor in the Jewish Studies Program and in the History Department at the State University of New York in New Paltz. He has published more than 100 articles, essays, and reviews centering on questions of ethnic identity and acculturation. His four major books deal with different phases of the American Jewish experience, principally during the past 120 years.

Eileen A. Sullivan contributed to the Irish biographies. She is a registered nurse with a Ph.D. who has held administrative positions in the State of Florida while being active in various community and political organizations and especially a variety of Irish associations in the United States and Ireland. She is executive director of the Irish Educational Association, which is particularly interested in Sullivans who have settled in America.

Emory Tolbert contributed to the African American biographies. He is professor and chair of the Department of History at Howard University, in Washington, D.C. His initial research focused on Marcus Garvey and the Universal Negro Improvement Association in Los Angeles and the West.

Benson Tong was responsible for the Chinese biographies. He is an assistant professor of history at Wichita State University, Wichita, Kansas, having previously taught at Oberlin and the University of Toledo. He is a specialist in Asian-American and Native American history and has published books in both fields, including one on Chinese Americans, as well as a volume of biographical sketches of people in the American West.

Silvio Torres-Saillant contributed several of the Dominican pieces. He is an associate professor of English and director of the Latino–Latin American Studies Program at Syracuse University, Syracuse, New York, and the founder of the CUNY Dominican Studies Institute at City College (New York). A codirector of the Inter-University Program for Latino Research, he is the author of *Caribbean Poetics* (1997) and coauthor of *The Dominican Americans* (1998), among other works.

William E. Van Vugt wrote two dozen biographies on people from England, Scotland, and Northern Ireland. He is a professor of history at Calvin College, Grand Rapids, Michigan, where he teaches English, American, and economic history, his specialties. His study of British emigration to the United States in the mid–nineteenth century was recently published. He also recently coedited a volume on race, ethnicity, and reconciliation in contemporary South Africa.

Ana M. Varela-Lago wrote the Spanish biographies. A native of Spain, she is a graduate student in the Department of History, University of California, San Diego, in La Jolla. Her M.A. thesis was on the response of Tampa's Latin immigrant community to the Spanish Civil War. She continues to do research on Spanish immigrant communities in the United States.

Zaragosa Vargas, who wrote most of the entries on Mexicans, is an associate professor in the Department of History, University of California, Santa Barbara, where he teaches U.S. labor history, Chicano history, and ethnic studies. His major study was on Mexican industrial workers in the Midwest and a new work will be on Mexican labor organizers and union struggles during the depression.

Diane C. Vecchio wrote most of the Italian biographies. She is an associate professor of history at Furman University, Greenville, South Carolina, where she teaches courses on, among other subjects, U.S. immigration history. Her forthcoming works deal with immigrant Italian working women in Milwaukee and Southern Baptists' missionary work among Italian immigrants. Her current research is a larger study of Italian immigrant women in the United States.

Juliet E. K. Walker wrote many of the entries on African Americans. She is a professor of history at the University of Illinois, Urbana. Her many publications include a study of peace activism and African Americans, a history of black business in the United States, and the editorship of the *Encyclopedia of African American Business* (1999). She has received numerous awards for her work, especially for top articles in *Business History Review* and the *Journal of Negro History.*

Tekle Woldemikael contributed the entries on an Ethiopian and an Eritrean. He is an associate professor of sociology at the University of Redlands, Redlands, California, having previously taught in the Sudan. He has published articles on Eritrea, ethnic relations in the Sudan, and Eritrean, Ethiopian, and Haitian immigrant experiences in the United States and a book on Haitians and American institutions.

William Wolkovich-Valkavičius wrote the Lithuanian biographies. Son of Lithuanian immigrants, he was born in Massachusetts and became an ordained Catholic priest in 1953. His personal research interests have been concerned with U.S. ethnic and immigrant history, notably focusing on Lithuanians, Poles, Albanians, Finns, and U.S. Roman Catholic history. His publications include thirteen books and fifty-five articles, especially a trilogy on Lithuanian religious life in America.

Kou Yang, who wrote the Hmong pieces, is an assistant professor of Asian American studies in the Ethnic and Women's Studies Department, California State University, Stanislaus, in Turlock. Yang has published studies of Hmong adjustment to life in the United States, particularly in the Central Valley of California.

David Yoo provided the entries on Koreans. He is an associate professor of history at Claremont McKenna College, Claremont, California, and chair of the Intercollegiate Department of Asian American Studies. His new book on the Nisei generation growing up between 1929 and 1949 was published in 2000 and he is editor of a recent volume on religion and Asian Americans.